MARKETING:
AN INTRODUCTORY TEXT

2

Other books by Michael J. Baker include

MARKETING: THEORY AND PRACTICE (ed.) (3rd edn)
MARKETING STRATEGY AND MANAGEMENT (2nd edn)
RESEARCH FOR MARKETING
MACMILLAN DICTIONARY OF MARKETING
AND ADVERTISING (2nd edn)

Also published by Macmillan

MARKETING IN EVOLUTION: Essays in Honour of Michael J. Baker
(edited by Susan A. Shaw and Neil Hood)

MARKETING: AN INTRODUCTORY TEXT

Sixth Edition

Michael J. Baker

MACMILLAN
Business

First edition 1971
Reprinted 1972, 1973
Second edition 1974
Reprinted 1976, 1977, 1978
Third edition 1979
Reprinted 1980, 1981 (twice), 1982, 1983
Fourth edition 1985
Reprinted 1986, 1987, 1988, 1990
Fifth edition 1991
Reprinted 1993, 1994
Sixth edition 1996

Published by
MACMILLAN PRESS LTD
Houndmills, Basingstoke, Hampshire RG21 6XS
and London
Companies and representatives
throughout the world

ISBN 0–333–66322–5 hardcover
ISBN 0–333–66323–3 paperback

A catalogue record for this book is available from the British Library.

10   9   8   7   6   5   4   3   2   1
05   04   03   02   01   00   99   98   97   96

Typeset by
Aarontype Limited, Easton, Bristol, UK

Printed in Great Britain by
The Bath Press, Bath

Contents

List of Figures

List of Tables

Preface to the Sixth Edition

Marketing: An Introductory Text first appeared in 1971 and has been continuously in print ever since. In that time it has appeared in five separate editions and also under the imprint of the English Language Book Society (ELBS). Clearly, the 'formula' appeals to a substantial number of teachers and students and has stood the test of time. Over the past 25 years there has been an enormous growth in the teaching of marketing with the number of students increasing from a few hundred in the late 1960s to tens of thousands in the mid-1990s. Indeed 'business studies' with marketing as a major element has become the largest subject grouping in the British university system.

Allied to this expansion there has been continued growth in the subject matter and some radical changes in emphasis. These are reflected in the content of this new, extensively revised 6th edition. That said, the perspective remains the same, marketing is an applied social science. Like many other professionally orientated subjects – medicine, engineering, architecture – marketing is a *synthetic* discipline which seeks to pull together theories and ideas from a variety of more theoretically based 'single' disciplines and integrate them into a holistic approach capable of implementation through practice. Its foundations are to be found in three major disciplines – economics (and particularly microeconomics which deals with the behaviour of individuals and firms in the market place), psychology – which is concerned with individual behaviour, and sociology – which is concerned with the behaviour of people in social groupings and organisations, both formal and informal.

The discipline of marketing is concerned essentially with the process of exchange, of the context within which it occurs, which is bounded and constrained by the environment and the infrastructure resulting from it, together with the managerial activities involved in shaping supply to match and satisfy demand. To this end the book is divided into four main parts. The first of these deals with the context of marketing, the second with the theoretical underpinnings, the third with the management of the major marketing functions – usually termed the marketing mix – and concludes with a discussion of the application of marketing in practice.

In the preface to the previous edition we commented on the enormous changes which had occurred during the 1980s which will undoubtedly come to be regarded as the era when belief in the power of market forces finally prevailed, symbolised indelibly in our consciousness by the tearing down of the Berlin Wall and the reunification of the two Germanies. In addition, the 1980s will also be remembered as symbolising the onset of a transition from conspicuous to caring consumption with the growing recognition of our responsibility to preserve and improve the fragile eco-system which is the world in which we live. The impact of these changes is still reverberating through the economies of the world and is both emphasised and reinforced by the growth of the Asian Tigers.

For teachers and students of marketing in Europe an equally significant change has been the conversion of American marketing educators to an interpretation of the subject more in sympathy with that reflected in the difference between the so-called Anglo-Saxon and Germanic-Alpine interpretations of capitalism. Prior to the collapse of the Communist Command Economy of the USSR this kind of economic organisation was generally contrasted with a simple but monolithic view of capitalism based largely on the free market economy of the USA and, to a lesser extent, the UK – the Anglo-Saxon version of capitalism! In turn, this interpretation of capitalism became translated into the marketing management school of thought which emphasises what organisations needed to do *to* customers (not *for* customers) if they were to be commercially successful. Such an orientation dominated marketing thinking, teaching and practice in most Western economies for 30 years despite the fact that it did not accurately reflect marketing practice in many other free market economies. Nor did it represent an appropriate interpretation of the marketing concept. These latter are more accurately reflected in what has come to be known as the Germanic-Alpine interp-retation of capitalism. This, in turn, is represented by what is characterised as 'relationship marketing'. We return to this issue in some detail in Chapter 1 and elsewhere in this extensively revised volume where this reorientation has resulted in several important modifications which permeate the treatment of earlier editions.

In addition to changes in content the opportunity has also been taken to publish the book in a revised format, to reorganise the references into a bibliography and to include review questions and suggestions for further readings at the end of each chapter. The review questions have been compiled from a variety of sources: Certificate and Diploma Examinations of the Chartered Institute of Marketing, degree examinations of the Univeristy of Strathclyde, the CAM Foundation, SCOTVEC and so forth. They are intended to provide the opportunity to test your knowledge and understanding of each chapter. Most, if not all, of the information required for a satisfactory answer is contained in the text. For revision purposes you should sketch out the points you would include in your answer and then refer back to the content of the relevant section or chapter to see you have covered all the major issues discussed there.

As noted in earlier editions, this text is one of a series which are intended to provide a firm foundation in the subject of marketing. Companion volumes are *Research for Marketing* (1991), *Marketing Strategy and Management* (2nd Edition, 1992), *Marketing: Theory and Practice** (3rd Edition, 1995), *The Marketing Book** (published by Butterworth-Heinemann, 2nd Edition, 1994) and the *Companion Encyclopedia of Marketing** (published by Routledge, 1995). In addition, the *Macmillan Dictionary of Marketing and Advertising* (2nd Edition, 1990) provides a valuable work of reference too. (*These three books, edited by the author, contain invited contributions from international experts on all the major topics discussed in this book. They should be your first source of reference.)

▌ Supplementary reading lists

It is clear that an introductory text can do no more than outline basic principles and provide an overview of the subject matter as a whole. Suggestions for additional reading are listed below which the author believes will prove useful in supplementing the material covered in this book. In addition, a supplementary reading list follows each chapter. Many of the references contain bibliographies, or cite other sources, which should prove useful in pursuing an indepth study of a particular topic. Many of the sources cited have been 'carried over' from earlier editions and now appear to be dated, but this is not believed to be the case – relatively few new books have been introduced which offer new perspectives or insights beyond those contained in what have come to be regarded as basic texts. However, the supplementary reading lists are by no means exhaustive and students should consult the lists published by the various examining bodies as well as those issued by their own tutors.

☐ *Magazines, periodicals, etc.*

To keep abreast of current developments, and update factual data, as least some of the following publications should be consulted on a regular basis:

Admap
Advertiser's Weekly
European Business
European Journal of Marketing
Financial Times
Harvard Business Review
International Journal of Advertising
Journal of Marketing (USA)
Journal of Marketing Management
Journal of Marketing Research (USA)
Journal of the Market Research Society
Management Decision
Management Today
Marketing Business
Sunday Times Business News
The Economist

☐ *General texts*

Many general texts have appeared in several editions and students should seek to obtain the most recent.

Cannon, T. (1995) *Basic Marketing*, 3rd edn (London: Cassell).

Davidson, J. H. (1975) *Offensive Marketing: or How to Make your Competitors Followers*, 2nd edn (Harmondsworth: Penguin).

Enis, B., Cox, K. K. and Mokwa, M. P. (1994) *Marketing Classics*, 8th edn (London: Prentice-Hall).

Kotler, Philip (1994) *Marketing Management*, 8th edn (Englewood Cliffs, N.J.: Prentice-Hall).

Kotler, Philip and Armstrong, Gary (1991) *Principles of Marketing*, 5th edn (Englewood Cliffs, N.J.: Prentice-Hall).

Levitt, T. (1962) *Innovation in Marketing* (New York: McGraw-Hill).

Levitt, T. (1983) *The Marketing Imagination* (New York: Free Press).

McCarthy, E. J. and Perreault, William D. Jr (1984) *Basic Marketing*, 8th edn (Homewood, Ill.: Irwin).

Packard, Vance (1957) *The Hidden Persuaders* (London: Penguin).

Ries, A. and Trout, J. (1986) *Marketing Warfare: Winning the Marketing War* (New York: McGraw-Hill).

Simmonds, K. (1987) *Short Marketing Cases* (Oxford: Philip Allen).

University of Strathclyde   MICHAEL J. BAKER

Acknowledgements

The author and publishers wish to thank the following for permission to use copyright material:

Audit Bureau of Circulations Ltd, for Table 16.13, using ABC data.

The Cinema Advertising Association, for Table 16.15, using CAA data.

A. C. Nielsen, for Table 5.3, using their own data.

Office for National Statistics, for Table 9.3, using data from *Business Monitor* SDA25. © Crown Copyright 1991.

Verdict Research Ltd, for data in 'Convenience Stores'.

Every effort has been made to trace all the copyright-holders, but if any have been inadvertently overlooked the publishers will be pleased to make the necessary arrangement at the first opportunity.

Part I
INTRODUCTION: THE CONTEXT OF MARKETING

■ *Chapter 1* ■

The Marketing Concept

Contents

Learning goals

The issues to be addressed in this chapter include:

1. What is marketing?
2. How has the marketing concept evolved?
3. How modern is modern marketing?
4. The emergence of 'relationship' marketing.
5. Is marketing a science or an art?
6. The transferability of marketing thinking.
7. Why study marketing?
8. What is the role of marketing and what are its basic functions?

After reading this chapter you will be able to:

1. State the basic principles underlying the concept and practice of marketing.

2. Trace the development of the marketing concept to its present stage of development and explain why marketing was 're-discovered' in the second half of the twentieth century.

3. Review the theoretical foundations on which the practice is based and determine the extent to which the subject may be considered a synthetic discipline.

4. Offer an opinion on the existence of a genuine theory of marketing in its own right.

5. Assess the relevance and extent to which marketing theory may be usefully applied to practical problems.

6. Justify the value of studying marketing in a formal way.

■ Introduction

In the 25 years which have elapsed since the first publication of this book 'marketing' has been transformed from a little known, and somewhat suspect, practice into a major academic discipline widely studied at both the undergraduate and postgraduate level. Even more important, marketing has come to be seen as an approach to exchange relationships which drives and informs the strategies of every conceivable kind of organisation – profit-making business and not-for-profit organisations such as universities, hospitals and charities.

But, despite the widespread interest in the subject of marketing, and frequent reference to it in everyday speech, there is still considerable confusion and not a little scepticism as to the exact nature and scope of the topic. The objective of this book is to make clear what marketing is and, in the process, eliminate any confusion and/or scepticism as to its importance to and value for society.

As a first step in the process this chapter traces the origins and development of the modern marketing concept from which it will become clear that the practice of marketing dates back to prehistoric times. In turn this raises the question 'How modern is modern marketing?' and the answer will demonstrate that it is not an American invention of the second half of this century as many mistakenly believe. Our review will also make it clear that marketing is both a concept and a practice and this has important implications for the adoption and implementation of marketing thinking.

To conclude this introductory chapter we look briefly at the theoretical basis of marketing and the frequently posed question 'Is marketing an art or a science?' Finally, we review the role of marketing and its various functions which underpin the structure and development of the rest of this introductory text.

■ What is 'marketing'?

As a student of marketing sooner or later someone is bound to ask you 'What is marketing?' As we shall see the answer is both simple and complex. The problem is that most people believe they know what marketing is when they don't. One reason for this is that we are all involved in marketing. This prompted me to make the following comment on the first publication (1976) of *Marketing: Theory and Practice* (Baker, 1995). 'The engima of marketing is that it is one of man's oldest activities and yet it is regarded as the most recent of the business disciplines'.

Marketing came into existence with the first barter exchange when someone realised that exchanges add value for both parties. It was this recognition which was to lead to the development of task specialisation which, as we shall see, was the first real step forward in economic development. Nowadays, many of the problems associated with marketing's definition arise because it is what we might call a 'synthetic' discipline.

In some senses people regard the word 'synthetic' as meaning 'artificial' or a substitute for the real thing. This is not its meaning here where synthetic means integrated into a complete whole. In other words, marketing like the disciplines of Architecture, Engineering and Medicine is based upon a foundation of knowledge developed by other disciplines which it then synthesises into a new body of knowledge which supports a professional *PRACTICE*. Thus marketing has strong foundations in Economics, Sociology and Psychology and borrows extensively from Statistics and the Management Sciences as well as from subjects like Anthropology. Above all else, however, marketing is something you do – a practice. So how shall we define marketing?

□ *Problems of definition*

On first acquaintance with a new subject most of us like to be given a definition which summarises its subject matter as succinctly as possible. Further, we expect this definition to be generally agreed upon by those who profess knowledge of the subject so that whatever personal idiosyncrasies may be demonstrated in the subsequent exposition there will be a common starting-point to which the student can return, and against which he may measure the expositor's interpretation. Herein lies the would-be student of marketing's predicament – virtually every text on marketing starts with a different definition. A selection of the better-known ones in circulation quickly demonstrates this point.

☐ *Marketing definitions*

1. The function of marketing is the establishment of contact (Cherington, 1920).
2. Marketing is the process of determining consumer demand for a product or service, motivating its sale and distributing it into ultimate consumption at a profit (Brech, 1953).
3. Marketing is not only much broader than selling, it is not a specialised activity at all. It encompasses the entire business. It is the whole business seen from the point of view of its final result, that is, from the customer's point of view. Concern and responsibility for marketing must therefore permeate all areas of the enterprise.
4. Marketing is the distinguishing, the unique function of the business (Drucker, 1954, items (3) and (4)).
5. Marketing is the performance of business activities that direct the flow of goods and services from producer to consumer or user.

   - Marketing is the creation of time, place and possession utilities.
   - Marketing moves goods from place to place, stores them, and effects changes in ownership by buying and selling them.
   - Marketing consists of the activities of buying, selling, transporting and storing goods.
   - Marketing includes those business activities involved in the flow of goods and services between producers and consumers. (Converse, Huegy and Mitchell, 1965.)

6. Marketing is the process whereby society, to supply its consumption needs, evolves distributive systems composed of participants, who, interacting under constraints – technical (economic) and ethical (social) – create the transactions or flows which resolve market separations and result in exchange and consumption (Bartels, 1968, pp. 29–33).
7. Marketing is the set of human activities directed at facilitating and consummating exchanges (Kotler, 1972).
8. Marketing is concerned with the creation and maintenance of mutually satisfying exchange relationships (Baker, 1976).
9. The purpose of a business is to create and keep a customer (Levitt, 1983a).
10. Marketing is the business function that identifies current unfilled needs and wants, defines and measures their magnitude, determines which target markets the organisation can best serve, and decides on appropriate products, services, and programmes to serve these markets. Thus marketing serves as the link between a society's needs and its pattern of industrial response (Kotler, 1988).
11. Marketing is both a set of activities performed by organisations and a social process. In other words, marketing exists at both the micro and macro levels. Micro marketing is the performance of activities which seek to accomplish an organisation's objectives by anticipating customer or client needs and directing a flow of need-satisfying goods and services from producer to customer or client.

    Macro marketing is a social process which directs an economy's flow of goods and services from producers to consumers in a way which effectively matches supply and demand and accomplishes the objectives of society (McCarthy and Perreault, 1994).
12. Marketing is the process of planning and executing the conception, pricing, promotion and distribution of ideas, goods and services to create exchanges that satisfy individual and organisational goals (American Marketing Association).
13. Marketing is the management process responsible for identifying, anticipating and satisfying consumer's requirements profitably (Chartered Institute of Marketing).

14. Activities that facilitate and expedite satisfying exchange relationships through the creation, distribution, promotion and pricing of products (goods, services and ideas) (Marketing Association of Australia and New Zealand, MAANZ).
15. Marketing is selling goods that don't come back to people who do.
16. The delivery of a standard of living.

The proliferation of definitions was the subject of an article entitled 'What Exactly is Marketing?' (Crosier, 1975), in which Keith Crosier reviewed over fifty definitions and which he classified into three major groups:

1. Definitions which conceive of marketing as a *process* 'enacted via the marketing channel connecting the producing company with its market', e.g. 'The primary management function which organises and directs the aggregate of business activities involved in converting customer purchasing power into effective demand for a specific product or service and in moving the product or service to the final customer or user, so as to achieve company-set profit or other objectives' (Rodger, 1971).
2. Definitions which see marketing as a *concept* or *philosophy of business* – 'the idea that marketing is a social exchange process involving willing consumers and producers', e.g. 'Selling is preoccupied with the seller's need to convert his product into cash; marketing with the idea of satisfying the needs of the customer by means of the product and the whole cluster of things associated with creating, delivering and finally consuming it' (Levitt, 1960).
3. Definitions which emphasise marketing as an *orientation* – 'present to some degree in both consumers and producer: the phenomenon which makes the concept and the process possible'. Only one example is cited by Crosier (from the philosopher Erich Fromm) and is felt to be an unconvincing argument in favour of a third category beyond the view of marketing as a function or as a concept.

Our own listing of definitions is essentially in chronological order and so reflects the changing emphasis as the discipline has evolved since the first Professor of Marketing was appointed at the Wharton Business School in the 1880s. Thus Cherington's 1920 definition, while not the first, expresses the view at the end of the nineteenth and beginning of the twentieth century that marketing was all about putting sellers and potential buyers in touch with one another. Brech's (1954) was one of the many formal definitions which emerged in the period of economic restructuring following the end of the Second World War which sees marketing as a commercial/business function motivated by profit. As we shall see, the domain of marketing has been transferred to and diffused through all sectors of the economy, profit and not-for-profit alike.

Drucker's definitions are probably the first to anticipate the emergence of marketing as the *key* business discipline. They take a managerial perspective underlying which is the recognition that marketing is the only business function which generates revenue – all other business functions create costs.

By the 1960s marketing and the marketing management school had become firmly established and saw the publication of numerous text books from which most of the remaining definitions are derived (4–11). The scope of these definitions indicates increasing refinement in the perception of marketing's role with the author's own definition (7) anticipating what has become the dominant view in the 1990s (relationships). Definitions 12, 13 and 14 are the current ones of three of the largest English-speaking professional marketing bodies. It is worth noting that neither the American or British definition mention relationships but the MAANZ does. We return to this later in the chapter.

Finally, we have two anonymous definitions (15 and 16). 'Selling goods that don't come back to people who do' captures, in my opinion, the very essence of mutually satisfying exchange relationships in a somewhat less pretentious and more memorable phrase. 'The delivery of a standard of living' is what it is all about – the provision of choice and the absence of coercion.

However, one cannot argue with Crosier's final group of definitions, which seem agreed only on the point that marketing is a complex and confusing phenomenon that combines both the philosophy of business and its practice.

There is a general consensus in these definitions but there is no single definition. An explanation of this is to be found in *The Meaning and Sources of Marketing Theory* (Halbert, 1965): 'Marketing, however, has no recognised central theoretical basis such as exists for many other disciplines, notably the physical sciences and, in some cases, the behavioural sciences' (p. 9). (Chapter 23 comments further on the development of theory in marketing in recent years.) We will return to this after considering evolution of the exchange process.

Fundamental problems of an economy

Essentially an economy is a system by which people earn a living and their standard of living is generally accepted as a reliable indication of the efficiency of the economy. Paul Samuelson (1989) states succinctly the three fundamental problems which an economy must grapple with in his standard text, *Economics – an Introductory Analysis*, namely:

1. *What* commodities shall be produced and in what quantities? That is, how much and which of alternative goods and services shall be produced?
2. *How* shall goods be produced? That is, by whom and with what resources and in what technological manner are they to be produced?
3. *For whom* are goods to be produced? That is, who is to enjoy and get the benefit of the goods and services provided? Or, to put it another way, how is the total of the national product to be distributed among different individuals and families?

Many solutions have been proposed and some at least have proved in part successful; others have merely aggravated this situation. At the same time no commonly agreed on solution has been achieved and there is an apocryphal story of a business tycoon who instructed his personnel director to find and employ a one-armed economist. When asked why he replied: 'I'm fed up of on the one hand this, on the other hand that!' In reality most economists agree that maximising satisfaction is the problem, but differ only in how this is to be achieved. Those who have accepted the marketing concept believe the real solution may be expressed something like this: 'If economies are comprised of people, and we are endeavouring to allocate scarce resources in order to maximise satisfaction, then it is the satisfaction of people which we are aiming at. This being so it is essential that we determine first what people want and then allocate our resources accordingly.' In other words, we must determine the nature and strength of demand and create supplies of goods and services to satisfy these demands.

In studying how this concept may be related to the solution of the problem two approaches are possible. Firstly, there is the macro approach which treats national economies as the basic unit and then investigates marketing as a part of a bigger whole. Secondly, there is the micro approach which looks at marketing from the point of view of the business organisation and its functioning within the economy. The latter viewpoint is the one adopted for the purpose of this book in the belief that although all of us are members of large groupings, be they national, ethnic or religious, we are more at home in dealing with smaller sub-groups the operation of which is easier to evaluate and comprehend. If the role and nature of marketing can be understood in these terms its functions in the economy as a whole will be more easily understood.

If the marketing concept is so simple, how is it that only in this century it has gained any credence and support? The answer is to be found in economic history, in which the evolution of economics may be studied, and no apologies are offered for the summary which follows. The objective underlying the inclusion of this summary is the need to put marketing in perspective – to try and explain why it is only in this century that marketing has emerged as a significant concept which is quickly converting many to its tenets.

Economic development and the evolution of a theory of consumption

If one examines the development of an advanced industrial economy such as our own, one can clearly distinguish a number of stages through which it has passed, each of which represents a step forward as compared with the preceding stage.

Perhaps the best known, and some would argue most important, discussion of the stages in economic development is to be found in W. W. Rostow's *The Process of Economic Growth* (1962). In his preface to the second edition, Rostow states 'The objective here is to provide a framework of theoretical concepts within which the variety of growth experiences can be systematically arranged, similiarities and differences systematically isolated.' The outcome is summarised in the penultimate chapter, 'The Stages of Economic Growth', in which he distinguishes the following:

1. The traditional society.
2. The preconditions for take-off.
3. The take-off.
4. The drive to maturity.
5. The age of high mass consumption.
6. Beyond the age of high mass consumption (subsequently Rostow designated this stage 'The search for quality').

The arguments underlying Rostow's thesis are not amenable to the kind of simplification which is necessary when addressing a sub-issue in an introductory text book and merit consideration in full. However, his 'stages' have proved to be a very robust concept and provide a useful framework for distinguishing between economies at different stages of development and, thereby, for discussing the relevance and application of various marketing principles and practices. It will be useful, therefore, to identify the salient characteristics of each stage.

*   *Traditional societies* are characterised by a lack of systematic understanding of their physical environment and 'the technology and tools necessary to achieve any significant improvement in productivity.' In such societies 75 per cent or more of all activity is focused in the food production necessary to sustain the society and any surplus tends to be controlled by rich land owners who dissipate it rather than invest in new technology.
*   The initial *preconditions for take-off* were created in Western Europe out of two characteristics of the post-medieval world which interacted and reinforced each other: the gradual evolution of modern science and the modern scientific attitude; and the lateral innovation that came with the discovery of new lands and the rediscovery of old, converging with the impulse to create new technology at certain strategic points. *The widening of the market* – both within Europe and overseas – brought not only trade but increased specialisation of production, increased inter-regional and inter-national dependence, enlarged institutions of finance, and *increased market incentives* to create new production functions (Rostow, *Process of Economic Growth*, my emphasis).
*   The *take-off* consists, in essence, of the achievement of rapid growth in a limited group of sectors, where modern industrial techniques are applied. Technically, take-off is distinguished as occurring when society is able to sustain an annual rate of net investment, of around 10 per cent, and 'usually witnesses a definitive social, political and cultural victory of those who would modernise the economy over those who would either cling to the traditional society or seek other goals'. To achieve this, the 'corps of entrepreneurs and

technicians must be enlarged, and sources of capital must be institutionalised' so that it can be deployed into the most promising growth opportunities.

- The *drive to maturity* is defined by Rostow as 'the period when a society has effectively applied the range of [then] modern technology to the bulk of its resources', and he offers the following symbolic dates:

Great Britain	1850
United States	1900
Germany	1910
France	1910
Sweden	1930
Japan	1940
Russia	1950
Canada	1950

Of maturity, Rostow makes the following trenchant observation:

> At maturity, however, the professional managers become more important – the nameless, comfortable, cautious committee men who inherit and manage large sectors of the economy, while the society begins to seek objectives which include but transcend the application of modern technology to resources.

- The *age of high mass consumption* is only one of three such objectives which Rostow distinguishes – the other two being increased security, welfare, and, perhaps, leisure to the working force; and enlarged power for the mature nation on the world scene. As he notes, 'A good deal of the history of the first half of the twentieth century can be told in terms of the pattern and succession of choices made by various mature societies' as among those three alternatives.

While commentators like Galbraith (*The New Industrial State*) would seem to agree that there is another stage *beyond high mass consumption* the nature of this has yet to be determined, and, like the highest stage in Maslow's need hierarchy 'self actualisation', may even consist of a recycling to the values of the traditional society. In *The*

Marketing Book (Baker, 1994) I suggested in the final chapter that Rostow's 'search for quality' has become the dominant theme in the advanced industrialised economies and seems likely to remain so for the foreseeable future.

The application of Rostow's stages model is clearly visible in the development of the British economy as a potted review of our economic history reveals.

Task specialisation and the development of craft industry

From the Norman Conquest to the mid-fourteenth century England's economy was organised on a feudal basis in which the Manor represented the major economic unit of production and consumption. The Manorial system was based on an ideal of self-sufficiency under which each self-contained community endeavoured to meet all its own requirements with regard to both production and consumption. Under such a system the variety of goods available for consumption depended directly on the factors of production possessed by the community, and the skill of the individuals comprising it. The limitations imposed by the size of the unit, coupled with similar limitations with regard to the skill and knowledge of its members, effectively reduced it to a subsistence economy concerned primarily with satisfying the essential requirements of life – food, shelter and clothing.

For a variety of reasons the feudal system broke down far earlier in England than was the case in Europe generally. Among the more important reasons may be distinguished the shortage of labour following the Black Death, and the demand for English wool to trade with Europe to secure supplies of commodities not readily available within the economy. This demand encouraged the Manorial lords to free the serfs from their feudal duties in order that the lords might repossess the land they occupied and rear sheep on it. This dispossession of the serfs in turn led to a migration of population from the country to the urban centres in search of employment in the developing craft industries.

Craft industry leads to specialisation in the production of particular goods, units of which can then be sold, enabling the craftsman to satisfy his needs by purchasing the output of other specialist producers. As a result there is an increase in individual skill which leads to greater productivity and output. At this stage of economic development, however, the volume of production is small, the average income is small, and the market is distinctly local with the exception of a very limited range of goods imported and exported to meet the demand of a gentry with sufficient income to afford them.

☐ *The division of labour*

The next stage of economic development is usually exemplified by Adam Smith's account of the pin-making industry, where an enormous increase in output followed job simplification with the same input of factors of production, excluding raw materials. Smith noted that where men were engaged in all processes involved in the manufacture of pins their average output was twenty pins per day; when the manufacture of pins was broken down into separate processes, output for the group rose to nearly five thousand pins per man per day.

Smith's description of this primitive production line identified at least ten separate tasks:

> One man draws out the wire, another straightens it, a third cuts it, a fourth points it, a fifth grinds it at the top for receiving the head; to make the head requires two or three distinct operations; to put it on is a peculiar business, to whiten the pins is another; it is even a trade by itself to put them into the paper.

Two points are of particular significance in this step forward. First, organisation is required to bring together the men, provide a place of work and supply raw materials. Second, the enormous increase in output reduces the price of the commodity, necessitates the development of channels of distribution to make the article available to those with a demand for it, and leads to the exploitation of a much larger market.

☐ *The industrial revolution*

The period when this change occurred coincided with the early stages of the industrial revolution, which was to give impetus to the growth of a factory economy, job specialisation and mass-production techniques. The nature of the steam engine as a power unit – large, inefficient and expensive – meant that the installation of such a plant was only justified if its power output was fully utilised in driving several smaller machines as, for example, looms. This in turn required the construction of factories in which a number of machines and operatives could be assembled, while the simplification of process meant that unskilled labour could be readily trained to perform simple operations.

Concurrent with the increase in output of both capital and consumer goods, lines of communication were developed (canals, and later railways), as were distributive channels, to cope with the movement and sale of this output. By 1800 we had already become a 'nation of shopkeepers', a derisory epithet used by Napoleon, who later learned to his cost that only a rich and strong nation can support extensive service industries. It is important to remember that at this stage of development the range of consumer goods offered for sale was limited, and that Britain constituted virtually the sole source of supply for a world market hungry for such manufactures. The disposable income of the home consumer was small, but a rapid expansion of population due to advances in medicine and public health created a continually expanding demand. The increase in knowledge of the nature and causes of disease in itself would have been of marginal value had not methods of large-scale production permitted the manufacture of the physical goods required in the creation of adequate sewerage and drainage schemes, and created the wealth with which to pay for them.

International trade and industrialisation

Throughout the nineteenth century home industry expanded enormously, as did world demand for our products. In 1850 Britain's exports amounted to nearly 40 per cent of all international trade, which, when it is realised that, by definition, the maximum any single nation could achieve is 50 per cent, is an extremely impressive performance and one which has never been surpassed since. This date marks a watershed, however, for it was to see the birth of the United States of America, and later other Western European countries, as competing industrial powers. At first the trend characteristic of the first half of the century continued; namely, the export of Capital goods to help establish basic industry in overseas countries in exchange for raw materials and food (coupled with a nearly insatiable demand for consumer goods). The development of industry in other countries resulted in a considerable increase in total output so that although our share of world trade declined, its value and volume continued to increase rapidly as the increase in income in other countries created an evergrowing demand for our products.

Initially, the newly emergent industrial nation must pass through the stages noted in respect of the British economy – namely, the development of basic industries such as iron and steel, which provide the raw materials of manufacturing industry, followed by the development of the latter along with lines of communication, and channels of distribution. However, the process is considerably speeded up for the newcomer as it is able to make use of existing knowledge and skill, and unite all the latest design in plant and equipment pioneered by someone else. As a result the new industrial nations are able to achieve rapid economic growth, e.g. the United States 1870–1900, Japan 1900–13 or 1945–65, creating a growing demand for basic consumer goods which can largely be met by the economy itself. In the meantime, however, the original industrial nations are not standing still but are channelling their skill and knowledge into the production of more sophisticated products which the newer industrial nations are eager, and able, to buy. A good current example of this is the demand for electronic equipment, machine tools and transportation equipment by the developing nations like India, replacing their former demand for basic products like steel or textiles in which they are now largely self-sufficient.

As a result of this economic development an increasing number of people are earning incomes which enable them to translate their latent demand for consumption goods into an effective demand.

The creation of 'excess' supply

However, the market, both nationally and internationally, has changed radically for, despite this growth in demand, increased productivity has resulted in a level of supply which is more than sufficient to cater for effective demand in any specific area. No longer is demand for a product chasing a limited supply of that good so that selling is an automatic result of production. Under present conditions large numbers of producers are competing for the privilege of supplying the consumer with their own output while trying to combat the claims of alternative or substitute goods. It is under these conditions that supply becomes directly controlled by demand, as opposed to demand accepting that which is supplied. Marketing must replace the narrower concept of selling in the sense of merely distributing one's output.

The situation with which we are faced, therefore, is one in which consumer demand dictates that which will be produced. In a sense this has always been the case, in that man has concentrated on producing those items in greatest demand. When the consumer has a limited income the majority of this is expended on essential requirements necessary for the maintenance of life, leaving very little for expenditure

Table 1.1 *Population and per capita GNP of some countries*, 1993*

Country	Population (millions)	GNP per capita US$	World rank	Country	Population (millions)	GNP per capita US$	World rank
Switzerland	7.0	36,410	1	Ireland	3.6	12,580	26
Luxembourg[1]	0.4	35,800	2	Portugal	9.8	7,890	29
Japan	124.8	31,450	3	Korea, Republic of	44.1	7,670	30
Denmark	5.2	26,510	4	Saudi Arabia	17.4	7,640	31
Norway	4.3	26,340	5	Greece	10.4	7,390	32
Sweden	8.7	24,830	6	Argentina	33.5	7,290	33
United States	258.1	24,750	7	Puerto Rico	3.6	7,020	34
Germany	80.8	23,630	8	Uruguay	3.1	3,910	42
Iceland	0.3	26,620	9	Mexico	86.7	3,750	43
Austria	7.9	23,120	10	Hungary	10.3	3,400	45
United Arab Emirates	1.7	22,470	11	Malaysia	19.0	3,160	46
France	57.7	22,360	12	Chile	13.8	3,070	47
Belgium[1]	10.1	21,360	13	Brazil	156.3	3,010	50
Netherlands	15.3	20,710	14	South Africa	40.7	2,900	52
Canada	27.8	20,670	15	Venezuela	20.8	2,840	53
Italy	57.8	19,620	16	Belarus	10.3	2,840	54
Singapore	2.9	19,310	17	Czech Republic	10.3	2,730	55
Finland	5.1	18,970	18	Panama	2.6	2,580	58
United Kingdom	58.0	17,970	19	Russian Federation	148.5	2,350	61
Hong Kong	5.9	17,860	20	Poland	38.4	2,270	62
Australia	17.7	17,510	21	Turkey	59.5	2,130	67
Qatar[1]	0.5	16,750	22	Indonesia	187.2	730	107
Israel	5.3	13,760	23	China	1,175.4	490	124
Spain	39.1	13,650	24	India	900.5	290	142
New Zealand	3.5	12,900	25	Mozambique	16.9	80	160

Notes: * GNP is calculated at market prices.
[1] GNP data for 1992.

All countries (outside the top 25) with less than 2 million people and, of necessity, those countries for which GNP data are not available have been excluded. The above table shows most industrial countries and selected other countries.

on desirable, but less essential, goods and services. This situation is to be found in the underdeveloped countries at the present time. For example in India 85–90 per cent of income is expended on basic essentials, leaving only 10–15 per cent for the purchase of medical services, non-essential foodstuffs, and so on. The comparative wealth of some national economies is shown in Table 1.1 and graphically in Figure 1.1.

In the eighteenth and nineteenth centuries poverty was prevalent throughout the world for the majority of the population. Production was concentrated in satisfying basic demands, with a limited output of luxury goods for a small market comprising the upper classes.

With the rise in real income which accompanied increased productivity and economic growth the proportion of expenditure absorbed by essential purchases is considerably reduced, despite changes in the nature of the demand for these essentials, for example, less bread and potatoes, more meat and butter, better houses, clothes, and so on, so that in an advanced economy only 50 per cent of disposable income is spent on these items, leaving an equal proportion for the purchase of non-essential goods, services and saving.

Within the realm of essential purchases the nature and volume of demand are relatively simple to predict, and patterns of group behaviour are notably marked. With regard to the balance of expenditure on other products determination of demand for a particular item is far more complex.

Figure 1.1 *Distribution of world GNP*

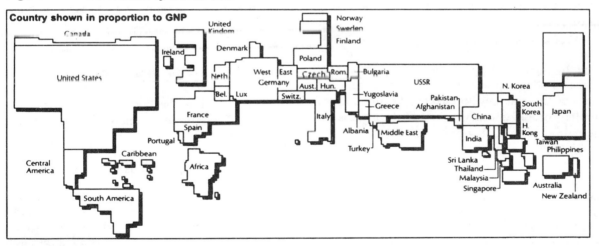

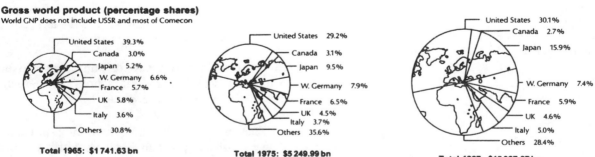

Source: *Financial Times*, 26 September 1989.

The marketing concept in an era of accelerating change

The 'potted history' of the stages through which an advanced economy passes does scant justice to the subject, and further reading is essential to a proper and objective understanding of it. As stated initially, the intention underlying its inclusion was to give some perspective to the development of economies to the point at which a need for a new economic concept emerged. A study of economic history develops, above all else, a sense of accelerating change. At the turn of the nineteenth century there were no steam engines or steam ships, large-scale steel production had still to be developed, as had the telephone, electricity, the internal combustion engine and innumerable others that were familiar, though not commonplace, by the end of the century. In this century the tempo has quickened and within fifty years of the first manned flight, man had a satellite in space orbiting the earth. By 1969 he had landed on the moon. Table 1.2 indicates the elapsed time between 'invention' and commercial development of a number of familiar 'products' and emphasises the increase in the tempo of technological advance.

Table 1.2 *Elapsed time, invention to commercial development, of a number of familiar products*

Product	Time from invention to commercial exploitation
Electric motor	65 years
TV	52 years
Vacuum tube	33 years
Zip-fastener	30 years
X-ray tube	18 years
Frozen foods	15 years
Nuclear reactors	10 years
Radar	5 years
Solar batteries	3 years

Two points need stressing in this context. First, each new development adds momentum to the process, in that it increases our ability to produce. This may be immediately discernible, as in the case when automation is introduced, or less directly so, when a computer is installed to permit the solution of complex problems hitherto considered insoluble. These in turn may provide the key to further technological advance. The second point is that increased wealth results in an overall improvement in the standard of living and, consequently, an increase in population.

Before examining the challenge of the population explosion it should be noted that the foregoing description of the economic evolution on an economy has been criticised as an explanation of the origins of the current marketing era. In an article entitled 'The Development of Marketing – A Compendium of Historical Approaches' David Gilbert and Nick Barley (1990) cite this description as 'The Traditional View' of the development of marketing which takes the 'view that modern business practice developed in three stages:

1. The Production Era – increasing supply/reducing costs
2. The Sales Era – selling what we can make
3. The Marketing Era – making what we can sell.

The authors continue to observe:

> Such a view infers that a sales orientation did not exist during (or before) the production era but came into being as a result of supply exceeding demand.
>
> Similarly, it suggests that marketing practices were not developed until it became apparent that pushing goods on to the market was not as effective as focusing on the provision of satisfaction.

In order for the two suppositions above to be true, the 'Marketing Era' school of thought makes the following inferences:

- That neither sales nor marketing practices were fully applied in business until towards the end of the production era which lasted from 1870 until the 1930s.

- That sophisticated marketing practices were not incorporated into business operations until the 1950s.
- There was little or no competition in the market place during the production era – and demand exceeded supply.
- Firms gave little thought to marketing before and during the production era.

These views are then contrasted with those of a number of other writers who claim that the production era never existed and that the importance of sales and marketing orientations were realised and the practice applied at a time when this supposed era would still have been in its infancy. Gilbert and Bailey then develop a series of arguments to support this view and conclude by offering a dynamic model of change.

How modern is modern marketing?

Gilbert and Bailey were no doubt influenced by a major article in the *Journal of Marketing* (Fullerton, 1988) in which the author posed the rhetorical question 'How modern is modern marketing?' In answering his own question Fullarton provides a number of arguments to dispute the existence of a production era. These may be summarised as follows:

1. It ignores well-established historical facts about business conditions – competition was intense in most businesses, over-production common, and demand frequently uncertain.
2. It totally misses the presence and vital importance of conscious demand stimulation in developing the advanced modern economies. Without such stimulation the revolution in production would have been stillborn.
3. It does not account for the varied and vigorous marketing efforts made by numerous manufacturers and other producers.
4. It ignores the dynamic growth of new marketing institutions outside the manufacturing firm.

Essentially, Fullerton is challenging the traditional production-era concept conceived of as one of technology 'push' rather than market 'pull' or, at least, a combination of the two. Richard Tedlow (Tedlow and Jones, 1993), in Chapter 2 of 'The Fourth Phase of Marketing' in *The Rise and Fall of Mass Marketing*, adopts a similar line of argument.

Tedlow opens by arguing that while occasionally some product innovations will succeed without aggressive marketing, the great majority will not and without such support they will fail. Indeed on first introduction many radical innovations, such as radial tyres or combined shampoo-hair conditioners, will not take-off and it may be many years before the market will accept them. To understand this phenomenon Tedlow believes one must understand the history of consumer product marketing and proposes that in the USA this may be divided into three or possibly four phases.

Phase I is seen as a period of *fragmentation* and characterised markets from the founding of the country until the 1880s. Because of its size, diversity and the distribution of its population the USA had fragmented into a number of geographical markets whose existence 'were usually dictated not by considerations of marketing strategy but rather by the brute facts of logistics' (p. 10). Only products with a very favourable ratio of weight and bulk to value could hope to achieve national distribution, and there are comparatively few products in distribution today that can trace their origins back before 1880.

Phase II – entitled *unification* – is dated to the 1880s when a fundamental change in consumer marketing took place. Three factors appear to account for this change – the creation of transportation and information infrastructures and innovation in manufacturing technology. By far the most important was the railroad. In 1840 there were about 3300 miles of track, by 1860 about 30,000 miles and by 1890 166,703 miles of which 40 per cent had been laid in the 1880s. It was the most important industry in the 19th century and it was its near demise which prompted Ted Levitt to write 'Marketing Myopia'.

In Tedlow's words:

The telegraph was also critical. It was the vehicle for the commercial information which business people demanded. It enabled them to direct a sales force whose members worked thousands of miles from the home office. It helped them learn from that sales force about market conditions in myriad localities. Thus, a far flung commercial enterprise could be intelligently managed from a central office.

(1993, p. 12).

The third major factor was 'a series of advances in machinery and manufacturing processes . . . [which] made it possible to produce a standardised product in large volume and, just as importantly, in small packages' (*op. cit.*, p. 12). Tedlow continues:

What could be packaged at the plant could be named at the plant. When the manufacturer could put his own name on millions of small packages thanks to this new machinery and distribute those packages nationally thanks to the railroad and telegraph, he could advertise nationally. The result was that he could transform the name of his product into a kind of supername – a brand.

It was as a result of these innovations that the 1880s marked the end of an era of commodities and heralded the advent of brand marketing and management. In the USA it saw the establishment of many famous American brands including the American Tobacco Company, Coca Cola, Johnson & Johnson, Campbell Soup, Pillsbury, Quaker Oats, Heinz and Kodak to name but a few. But, while manufacturers of advertised brands and, in some cases, retailers like Marshall Field assumed control of the channel they still tended to project themselves as appealing to all potential customers rather than any specific class or segment. The classic example throughout this phase was undoubtedly Coca Cola which resolutely avoided any modification of its product or packaging between 1886 and 1955.

Just as a series of external innovations created the opportunity for mass marketing so too did a number of external developments create the climate which was to see the transition to Phase III or *segmentation*. Tedlow cites radio and television advertising as amongst the most important accompanied by 'broad changes in American culture which exercised a profound influence on the nature of consumer demand' (Tedlow and Jones, 1993, p. 15).

As broadcast media, radio and television overcame the barriers of literacy which restricted print advertising and packaging to those who could read, they gave birth to the easily memorised jingle and, in the case of TV, provided unparalleled opportunities for demonstration. Analysis of audiences also revealed that different programmes appealed to different groups of people and so created the opportunity for segmentation.

This opportunity for segmentation had been recognised at least three decades earlier when General Motors attacked Ford's dominance of the automobile market with its policy of 'a car for every purse and purpose.' (*Fortune* described this as 'Chevrolet for *hoi pollio* . . . Pontiac . . . for the poor but proud, Oldsmobile for the comfortable but discreet, Buick for the striving, Cadillac for the rich' (Tedlow, 1992, p. 19).) However, it was the enormous economic change from the difficult years of the pre-World War II depression to the comparative affluence of the postwar generation of baby boomers which really created the opportunities for psychographic or lifestyle segmentation in addition to that based on demographics and income which underlay General Motors' strategy of product differentiation – a different strategy from market segmentation. As Tedlow (*op. cit.*) observes (p. 20) 'Unlike geographic market fragments of old, modern market segments are virtually created by clever marketers who figure out how to reconfigure and exploit latent consmer interests.'

To explain how and why consumer marketing in the USA was transformed over a period of some 125 years, Tedlow and Jones (1993) advance six propositions, namely:

1. The strategy of profit through volume was a breakthrough concept in the development of the mass market.

2. The drive and vision of individual business people played a vital role. People have mattered. Nothing was inevitable.
3. Mass production could not have existed without mass marketing. The entrepreneur organised the vertical system, and the manager ran the system and helped it evolve.
4. First-mover advantages have been real. They have led to high profits, not despite but because of low prices. These advantages have acted as barriers to the entry of new competition.
5. New entrants into a market faced a basic choice. They could either copy the first-mover's strategy or try somehow to turn the market against the first mover by attempting a new strategy.
6. Change has been the law of business. Over the long term, those forms which have best managed internal and external change over time have been winners.

While some of these propositions are near tautologous (especially 6), they summarise succinctly Tedlow's extended analysis. Tedlow acknowledges that not everyone who has studied the history of marketing sees it in precisely the same terms as himself. Specifically, he refers to work by Hollander and Germain (1991) and Strasser (1989) which identifies the existence of segmentation strategies in the late nineteenth and early twentieth centuries, and which suggests there was not a distinct break between Phases II and III as proposed by him. Tedlow rejects this suggestion on the grounds that the increase in the number of products offered to the consumer between Phases II and III represented a difference not only in degree but in kind. Further, while some segmentation on price (good, better, best) had existed for many years, in the post-World War II era segments were defined increasingly in terms of customers – their wants and beliefs. Thus Pepsi wished to become a 'necktie product' by telling the customer what kind of person would buy the product in question. Tedlow sees variety as the most important factor differentiating Phase II from Phase III.

With the developments in information technology of recent years Tedlow speculates that we may now be moving towards a fourth phase of marketing:

Information technology permits just-in-time systems which in turn facilitate the manufacture of a wide variety of products in short runs in situations where scale economies can still be captured. All through the distribution system, information allows this greater variety to be managed without overstocks or stock-outs and the end result is that the consumer has a greater variety of product from which to choose. (Tedlow and Jones, 1993, p. 27)

New technologies have enabled the development of 'micro marketing' or hyper-segmentation. As noted elsewhere (Baker, 1980), the act of consumption changes the consumer with the inevitable consequence that by offering greater variety and choice the producer stimulates the consumer to expect more. Tedlow sounds a cautionary note, however. At least two forces might inhibit micro marketing – consumer confusion and saturation of the distribution channels. Using Revlon's 157 shades of lipstick as an example, the question is 'is there too much choice' Even if this is not so now (Revlon argue there is someone who wants each shade or they wouldn't produce them), in the future lack of display space must surely restrict even greater product proliferation. As Tedlow and Jones (1993, p. 31) comment 'The distribution system has become the neck in the hour-glass through which manufacturer must reach consumer.' As retailers become channel captains and shelf allotment programmes the order of the day, 'What next?' still remains a difficult question to answer. Will combined shampoo-hair conditioners help consumers simplify the bewildering variety which assails them or will micro marketing gather still more momentum? Tedlow, like the rest of us, can only speculate but he concludes by offering the telling point that one thing marketing history does show – backing trends can pay handsome dividends.

Many of these issues will be addressed later in this book. At this juncture, however, it is important to recognise that our own brief history of economic development was not intended to endorse the 'three eras' model of the development. Our purpose in presenting an economic view of the evolution of marketing as a theory of consumption is simply to emphasise the *dominant* or prevailing theme at varying stages of economic development in Europe and later the USA. Of course, there has always been competition and the most successful suppliers have always been those who have best understood and served their customers using what we would now term marketing and sales practices. Our point simply is that it is only in the nineteenth and twentieth centuries that a fundamental shift in the balance between supply and demand has led to marketing becoming the dominant and prevailing orientation, although firms still survive which could be characterised as 'sales' or 'production' orientated. It is important to recognise, however, that the 1990s have seen a radical re-appraisal of the marketing discipline and we discuss this in the next section.

The emergence of 'relationship marketing'

As noted above the 'three eras' – production, sales, marketing – approach to marketing's rediscovery is too simplistic to reflect a complex reality. It did lead, though, to the development of a school of thought which dominated the teaching and practice of marketing for around 30 years from 1960 to 1990. This school is generally known as the 'marketing management' school and is epitomised by Eugene McCarthy's (1960) *Basic Marketing* (now in its 8th edition) and Philip Kotler's (eponymous) *Marketing Management* (also now in its 8th edition (1994)). It was McCarthy who introduced the 4 Ps of marketing – Product, Price, Place and Promotion – which provided structure to most books and formal courses during this period; while Kotler's subtitle 'Analysis Planning & Control' firmly positioned marketing as a managerial function.

While the marketing management model was undoubtedly dominant it was not the only

interpretation. Indeed, and as we shall see, an alternative model of the market economy had existed for well over a century and was widely practised in many countries. This practice emphasised relationships rather than transactions as the essence of the exchange process and so gave rise to what is now widely recognised as 'relationship marketing'.

The relationship marketing model can trace its lineage directly to the work of European economists from the 1930s onwards (the Copenhagen's School's 'parameter theory'). In turn this theory evolved as an explanation of the working of several free market economies in Europe which seemed quite different from the then dominant UK and USA economies. The existence of two different interpretations of capitalism – Anglo-Saxon which prevailed in the UK and USA, and Germanic-Alpine which existed in many European and other economies – was marked by the Cold War between the major capitalistic and communist countries of the world. As a result of this confrontation between different views on economic (and political) organisation, interpretations of the two states – capitalism and communism – tended to polarise into extreme versions. In the case of capitalism it was the model operating in the USA and, to a lesser extent, the UK, rather than that to be found in many other democratic, free market economies.

The collapse of communism in Eastern Europe, prompted a Frenchman, Michel Albert, to write a book entitled *Capitalisme contre capitalisme* in which he pointed out that the elimination of communism had thrown into relief that, in fact, there is not a single, monolithic model of capitalism but several. Further, it appears that the Germanic-Alpine model leads to superior economic performance than the alternative Anglo-Saxon model. Christian Dussart (1994) in *Perspectives on Marketing Management*, summarised the essential differences between the two models as shown in Table 1.3.

It must be appreciated that the idea of relationship marketing had been around for much longer than this. Indeed our own definition (p. 4) dating from 1976 explicitly recognised this and would certainly not claim to be original.

Table 1.3 *Major differences between the two models*

	Anglo-Saxon	*Germanic-Alpine*
Basic Principle	Free Competition	Controlled competition
Power Centres	The Stock Exchange	The Bank
	Customer (as consumer)	Company over Customer
		Management over Shareholder
Time Perspective	Short-term	Long-term
	The tyranny of the Quarterly Report	*Development* as opposed to *profit*
Types of Business Relationship	Ad hoc *transaction*	Long-term *Relationship*
Social Involvement	Weak	Strong

Source: Based on Dussart (1994) *Perspectives on Marketing Management.*

However, it was not until Fred Webster published a major article in 1992 entitled 'The Changing Role of Marketing in the Corporation' that there was any serious recognition that the marketing management model might be seriously flawed and explain why other countries' economies were performing more successfully.

Basically, the marketing management model is founded on the idea of manipulating the so-called 'marketing mix' first conceptualised by Borden (see p. 88) and summarised by McCarthy as the 4 Ps. In our view this model is flawed in that, like the production orientation which it purports to replace, it emphasises what producers or sellers do *to* customers not *for* them. Not only that but marketing mix management and the marketing department become synonomous with the marketing function, which tends to separate them from other functions and alienate them too. A far cry from the intention of marketing as a 'philosophy of business'!

During the 1990s relationship marketing has emerged as a conceptualisation which does capture the spirit or substance of marketing and a recognition that marketing is everybody's business. In a recent, unpublished, review of the literature Abbas (1995) has summarised the important aspects of the two paradigms of marketing thought (see Table 1.4).

In *Marketing: Theory and Practice* (1995) Chan and McDermott offer a comprehensive review of the application of relationship marketing in a new model they call FIRMS (Flexible and Intelligent

Relationship Management Strategy). As part of their review they cite Pathmarajah's contrast between Transactional and Relationship Marketing reproduced here as Table 1.5.

Space precludes further discussion of relationship marketing here but readers are strongly recommended to consult the sources cited in this section – particularly the work of Gronroos, Gummesson, and Webster. We must now return to the point made earlier (p. 4) that one of the major challenges still facing the implementation of marketing is that of population growth.

The challenge of the population explosion

This increase in population is largely attributable to an extension of the expectation of life, due to medical advance, rather than an increase in the crude birth rate, which, on the contrary, has tended to fall with the increase in affluence. More people represents a greater aggregate demand for goods and services. At the same time it represents an increase in a basic factor of production, labour, and thus provides one resource essential to the increase in supply necessary to satisfy this increase in demand.

Many economists have expressed concern over the population explosion pointing out that

Table 1.4 *The important aspects of the two paradigms of marketing thought*

	Relationship marketing paradigm	Marketing mix management paradigm
The evolution	Developed in the 1960s and 1970s in Europe and recently in the USA within the areas of industrial marketing and services marketing as well as customer relationship economics which can be rooted in the Copenhagen school's parameter theory[1][2][3][4]	Developed in the 1950s and 1960s in North America using empirical data concerned mainly with customer packaged goods and durables[5][6] The underlying philosophy behind this paradigm is the basic microeconomic paradigm with its emphasis on profit maximisation[6]
The definition of marketing	'Marketing is to establish, maintain and enhance relationships with customers and other partners, at a profit, so that the objectives of the parties are met. This is achieved by a mutual exchange and fulfilment of promises' (Gronroos, 1993, pp. 11–12)	'Marketing is the process of planning and executing the conception, pricing, promotion and distribution of ideas, goods and services to create, exchange and satisfy individual and organisational objectives'. 'AMA Board Approaches New Marketing Definition' (*Marketing News*, No. 5, March 1985)
The marketing philosophy	Marketing is both a managerial orientation and a business function[1] It has 3 distinct levels of strategy, the corporate, business or SBU, and functional or operating levels. In each of them there are 3 distinct dimensions of marketing – marketing as culture, marketing as strategy and marketing as tactics[6] The distinction between the firm and its market environment will disappear[6]	Marketing is a specialist function illustrated by the boundaries determined by the P's of the marketing function. The firm and its external environment are separated. Transactions are the link betweem them[6]
	The general focus is on building long-term relationships with customers and other parties as well[3] The units of analysis are people, processes and organisation[6]	The general focus is on transaction at a time as a central construct for the marketing discipline[3] The units of analysis are products, prices, firms and transactions[6]
The central concepts	Beside the concepts of the marketing mix management paradigm, 3 key concepts are central in relationship marketing (RM)* • The promise concept;[3] • The trust concept;[2] • The interactive marketing function[3]	The marketing mix, the product life cycle, and segmentation are distinguished concepts within the marketing mix paradigm as a marketing school of thought[10]

continued on following page

Table 1.4 *(continued)*

	Relationship marketing paradigm	*Marketing mix management paradigm*
The scope of marketing within the organisation	Depending upon the customer relations, marketing activities are spread over a large part of the organisation outside the realm of the marketing department[2] Consequently, the marketing function would be achieved by 2 groups:[7] • Specialists or full-time marketers (FTMs); • Part-time marketers (PTMs)	Marketing activities can usually be grouped in an organisational unit: marketing or sales department, and can be separated from other activities of the firm Specialists often take the responsibilities for marketing activities
Prospects and criticisms	Marketing theorists have argued for relationship marketing as the heart of marketing[6][7][8][9][10] because of the desire of customers and organisations, in many situations to create ongoing relationships[8], for the desired outcomes[9] and to avoid the difficulties which would face both if a transactional approach were followed. Thus it was advocated that marketing mix manipulation becomes relationship marketing and marketing management is replaced by marketing orientation company management[4][7]. Below, the figure illustrates the gradual shift of the marketing paradigm	Marketing theorists view that marketing mix management paradigm with its P's should be replaced for the following reasons:[1][2][3][6][7][10] • It is a production-oriented paradigm because its focus is on the firm and not in the market, it starts from the competitive situation and the competence of the firm and does not start from the customer • It has been criticised for being incomplete to be applied to other environments or other contexts. It disregards services and industrial marketing

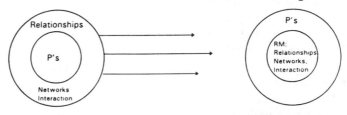

The Shift in Marketing Paradigm and the Expected International Breakthrough for Relationship Marketing in the mid 1990s

Based on Gummesson, 1994

• The P's and the whole marketing mix management paradigm are based on a loose foundation: the characteristics that are the basis for classification have not been identified, the categories are not mutually exclusive

continued on following page

Table 1.4   *(continued)*

	Relationship marketing paradigm	Marketing mix management paradigm
Prospects and criticisms *(continued)*	Relationship marketing will be appropriate from the customers point of view where they perceive high levels of risk relating to the product being purchased, where purchasing processes should be followed by a stream of services that are produced and consumed over a period of time and where the relationship can bring preferential treatment or semi-automatic responses to requests for services.[8] Relationship marketing will also be appropriate to sellers where the relationship will lead to continued exchanges at a profit[2], and where strong relationships help to facilitate loyalty from customers whose loyalty is challenged by other competitors and where such relationships can facilitate suppliers' task of collecting feedback from their customers[8]	Transaction marketing is more appropriate than relationship marketing for customers who have short time horizons and who can switch from one supplier to another with little effort or investment[11]

Sources: (1) Baker, 1994; (2) Gronroos, 1989; (3) Gronroos, 1993; (4) Gummesson, 1994; (5) Borden, 1964; (6) Webster, 1992; (7) Gummesson, 1991; (8) Palmer, 1994; (9) Morgan & Hunt, 1994; (10) Marion, 1993; (11) Kotler & Armstrong, 1991.

whereas population increases in a geometrical progression, increases in output, particularly of foodstuffs, tend to follow an arithmetical scale that will soon reach a point where demand will once again outstrip supply, at least in the areas of basic necessities. It would be foolish to deny that there is an element of truth in this contention, just as it would be foolish to adopt a fatalistic approach and accept the situation as inevitable. A superficial examination of the yield of Dutch farms as compared with those in the American Middle West will soon reveal a disparity of 5:1 in favour of the former in terms of yield. In the present situation there is no point in increasing the yield of the wheat farms of the United States as the present supply/demand situation is such that the increased investment necessary to increase yield would not be recoverable in profits owing to low market prices. On the other hand, if demand increases while supply remains static, prices will rise thus making further investments,

necessary to increase yield, a profitable exercise. It is realistic to assume that this increased output will be forthcoming. (For an extended discussion of these issues the reader should consult D. Meadows *et al.* (1972) *Limits to Growth*, and the critique of it in H. S. D. Cole *et al.* (1973) *Thinking about the Future*).

Over a longer time-scale it is possible to envisage a situation where supply created by conventional farming methods, as we know them today, will be insufficient to meet projected demand based on current world population trends. Marketing has no need for Jeremiahs, still less for fatalists! Recognising that a need exists or is likely to exist, the role of the marketer is to deploy resources to maximise satisfaction by meeting these needs. If we are to predict the nature of demand in the future it also behoves us to undertake courses of action which will enable us to satisfy this demand. To argue that present methods are insufficient to satisfy a predictable

Table 1.5 *Contrasting transactional and relationship marketing*

Transactional marketing	*Relationship marketing*
• Do the deal and disappear	• Negotiate a win-win sale situation and stay around, being a resource for better results
• Push price	• Promote value
• Short-term thinking and acting	• Long-term thinking and acting
• Build the business on deals	• Build the business on relationships
• Getting new customers	• Keeping all customers and clients
• No structure for on-going business	• Structure created to support relationship; special club and memberships for frequent users–buyers
• Selling focused	• Relationship focused for results
• Short-term empathy	• Long-term empathy and rapport
• Incentive for doing the deal	• Incentive for long-term relationships and revenue
• Foundation of sale telling and selling	• Foundation of revenue trust
• Race for a sale result	• Swift, strong, safe and enduring in results through relationship building
• After-sales support and service poor – seen as cost	• After-sales support and service strong – seen as an investment in the relationship
• Product-service focused	• People expectations and perception focused
• Rewards-incentive for 'doing deals'	• Rewards-incentive for maintaining and growing relationship and revenue
• 'The deal is the end'. Pursuit of deal	• The sale – just the beginning. Pursuit of long-term relationship and results

Source: Pathmarajah Allen (1993), in M. J. Baker (ed.) (1995), *Marketing: Theory and Practice* p. 393.

future demand ignores the facts. Icarus failed to master the secret of flight because he lacked a high melting point wax: this is a factor which is virtually irrelevant in terms of aerospace research today. Failures, more often than not, result from the narrow inflexible approach which presumes that no further improvement or advance is possible; that the status quo is immutable. The few examples quoted should suffice to show that each breakthrough opens up whole new territories for exploration. During the 1980s, the birth of a baby from a frozen embryo and successful heart-lung transplants were front-page news. When did you last read a front-page newspaper story about an operation for appendicitis? Other than those performed on notable personalities, or under unusual conditions, no reference is made to the thousands of such operations performed annually. Once they were newsworthy, now they are commonplace. This undoubtedly will be the case with test-tube babies, organ transplantation, bionic men and the like in the years to come – always providing that economies continue to grow and increase wealth so that the physical and human resources are available.

Much of the preceding discussion has examined the contribution of 'marketing' to economic progress and development. Inevitably this has raised questions as to the status of marketing. Is it an art or a science? We look at this question briefly in the following section.

■ Marketing: art or science?

The aim of Halbert's book quoted earlier is 'to explore the possibilities of having a science of marketing. How to put scientific concepts and marketing context together is the subject matter of this report' (Preface, p. XX). Tacitly, the rationale behind the publication of this book is an admission that marketing is *not* a science; it also demonstrates the belief that it *ought to be*.

In examining possible sources of marketing theory Halbert notes that marketing has borrowed heavily from the business disciplines (economics, law, etc.), the social and behavioural sciences and the methodological sciences (mathematics, etc.) and that these borrowings have included content, or data, techniques and concepts. As yet this material has not been synthesised into a generally accepted theory and so results in the apparent conflict inherent in the plethora of definitions. However, a closer examination of the definitions reviewed earlier does indicate that in addition to the classification proposed by Crosier one can also detect a clear chronological evolution in the development of marketing thinking. According to Professor Johan Arndt, who was one of the early marketing theorists, marketing thought is developing in precisely the same way as other disciplines, from simple imperatives, 'satisfy your customers', to more complicated notions such as consumer behaviour analysis, to even more complex, ambiguous and sometimes contradictory formulations. In a paper given in 1984 he argues that since the Second World War, marketing thought may be classified into three main periods – the Marketing Concept, the Broadened Marketing Concept and the New Institutional Concept.

As Arndt points out, 'the so-called Marketing Concept advocated focus on customers and customer needs and argued for integrated analysis, planning, and control of all elements of the marketing mix, popularised as the 4 P's (Product, Price, Promotion, and Place) by McCarthy (1966). Hence the main avenue to profits went through developing, producing and distributing products satisfying customer wants.' However, by the mid-1960s observers began to inquire about the potential for transferring marketing ideas and thinking into contexts other than regular economic exchanges in the market place, and in 1969 Philip Kotler and Sidney Levy published an article 'Broadening the Concept of Marketing' which argued that marketing techniques 'were used and *should* be used by all organisations needing favourable responses from internal interest groups' (Arndt).

As Arndt observes, 'This development is less a change than may be apparent at first look. As pointed out by Stidsen, this broadening is mostly a widening of *application* rather than theory, transplanting existing theory (mainly relating to promotional activities) into new settings. Another limitation is that the Broadened Marketing Concept, like its predecessors, is mainly a stimulus–response formulation using what Johnston and Bonoma (1977) term the "unit paradigm" focusing on the individual social unit, the firm or the consumer.'

Despite these criticisms the Broadened Marketing Concept is still the prevailing model among practitioners, and description and analysis of it will provide the perspective for this introductory text. However, the reader should be aware that marketing thinking and research is moving towards Arndt's third stage of development characterised by 'more complex ambiguous and sometimes contradictory formulations'. This third phase, which Arndt calls 'New Institutionalism', is seen as containing three distinct strands – the notion of marketing as exchange, the transaction cost economics approach, and the political economy approach. While elements of all these approaches will be referred to, detailed consideration and analysis is more appropriate to an advanced text-course in marketing. It is also the case that until a general theory is evolved the practitioners' and academics' view of the subject tends to be coloured by an emphasis of the discipline from which they came to marketing. This is certainly true of this book which is biased towards economics but, it is hoped, for reasons other than that the author was trained as an economist.

As indicated by the title, and in the Preface, this book is intended as an introduction to the subject. In view of the fact that many students have studied some economics it seemed logical to build upon this knowledge rather than give a behavioural or quantitative emphasis. Psychology, Sociology and Mathematics are less often found in the curriculum of 'business' courses at the undergraduate level and a 'Primer of Marketing' is an inappropriate place for an introduction of these disciplines. However, some discussion of concepts from the behavioural sciences is contained in the chapters on Consumer Behaviour (Chapter 6) and Marketing Communications (Chapter 15) and will be sufficient to indicate the relevance of these disciplines to the newcomer to marketing. The student who intends to progress beyond the elementary and descriptive aspects of marketing contained in this book will find sufficient references in the bibliography and recommended readings from which to launch into an investigation of other disciplines and their relevance to marketing.

From a negative point of view, then, marketing is just a hotchpotch of ideas 'borrowed' from other disciplines. More positively it rests on the simple principle that supply must be a function of demand. In the opinion of marketing people this offers the best approach to the solution of the central economic problem – the allocation of scarce resources so as to maximise satisfaction. However, to say that supply must be a function of demand is an over-simplification. Many economists would add that it is a truism which has been in currency since Adam Smith wrote his *Wealth of Nations* in 1776, in which he states that: 'Consumption is the sole end and purpose of production....'

The debate as to marketing's status will inevitably continue to rumble on. Whatever the final conclusion there appears to be little doubt that the subject has a major contribution to make which raises two further considerations which deserve brief discussion. Why study marketing? and How transferable is the marketing concept?

Transferability of the marketing concept

To this point the discussion of marketing, both as concept and function, has focused on its application in a business context. More than that, most references have been to consumer goods, and Fullerton and Tedlow's analysis of the evolution of modern marketing largely refer to consumer markets and consumer goods. Inevitably, this raises the question as to how transferable are the concepts and techniques to other areas of marketing? In this section we look briefly at this question.

During the 1950s and 1960s it appeared that firms manufacturing and selling consumer goods were generally performing better in terms of financial performance indicators such as Profits, Return on Investment, and so forth, than were their counterparts making industrial goods. An examination of practice in the two kinds of firms indicated that by and large they were very similar with the exception that consumer goods manufacturers seemed to have something called 'marketing', whereas industrial goods manufacturers did not. Accordingly, industrial goods firms set about establishing a marketing function but, apparently, with little noticeable effect, which prompted them to claim that 'marketing' didn't work. It was this criticism which led to the publication of a famous article in the *Harvard Business Review* (1970) the title of which has entered the vocabulary of marketing practice 'Trappings versus Substance' (in Industrial Marketing).

In his article, McKinsey consultant B. Charles Ames argued that it was not marketing that had failed but the firms which had misinterpreted and misapplied it. To a large degree it seemed that industrial companies had seen marketing as some kind of cosmetic exercise which involved re-titling the sales function 'marketing' and adding on some advertising to publicise the fact. In Ames' view such actions were merely 'trappings' and could not be expected to have any material effect on performance. What was called for was a radical revision of the way a firm conducted its business to make it market oriented and customer driven – the 'substance' of marketing.

Ames' diagnosis of the so-called 'failure' of marketing in industrial firms appeared shortly after the publication of a seminal article by Philip Kotler and Sidney Levy (1969) concerning the need to re-examine the scope of marketing. In the opening paragraphs the authors review briefly the traditional emphasis on the marketing of products in a business context and go on to assert: 'It is the authors' contention that marketing is a pervasive societal activity that goes considerably beyond the selling of toothpaste, soap and steel.'

In essence the argument that marketing is a pervasive societal activity is predicated on the observation that as man's productive capability has grown so he has been able to devote more of his energies to social activities, and that in order to do so he has had to develop organisations other than business firms. In reality, many non-business organisations have a longer history than the now dominant business firms; for example the Church, universities, government departments, hospitals, and so forth. However, the very forces which were to lead to an emphasis on marketing, namely the ability to create supplies in excess of basic consumption needs, were also necessary to permit such non-business organisations to realise their potential. Thus, only when we can release human and physical resources from the treadmill of satisfying the basic needs of food and shelter can we turn our attention to the satisfaction of higher needs such as education, the Arts, health, and social welfare. Further we require new forms of social organisation to cope with enfranchisement of the whole population, that is political societies; the need for organised labour to be able to express its view, that is the trade unions; and so on.

As Kotler and Levy point out, all these social organisations perform the classic business functions. Finance is necessary to pay for the organisation's operations and a personnel function is necessary to ensure that people are available to discharge such operations. A production function is necessary to organise the most economic use of inputs to achieve the desired level of outputs. Purchasing is necessary to acquire these inputs and presumably marketing is required to dispose of them. If the marketing function has not been particularly conspicuous, however, we should not be surprised for, as we have seen, the need for such a function has only just become apparent in the case of physical goods.

But, given the exponential acceleration which has characterised all spheres of human endeavour throughout history we may anticipate a rapid diffusion of the marketing concept through non-business organisations within the next few years. To determine *how* the marketing concept may be applied we must first identify those ideas which have appeared generally useful in marketing other goods and services. In our opinion in marketing industrial goods there is no fundamental difference in principle as compared with the marketing of consumer goods. This I believe is equally true of the marketing of services whether they emanate from profit or non-profit organisations.

In the same spirit Kotler and Levy suggest that a useful basic approach is to think in terms of three fundamental constructs or ideas – products, consumers, and tools.

First, products. All organisations produce a product although in the interests of definitional clarity we frequently prefer to differentiate between categories of products. Thus in Chapter 5 we offer specific definitions for categories of consumer and industrial goods. To these may be added services which are intangible, such as insurance and banking, although they may confer a tangible benefit such as health and welfare services. Such services may be offered by private or public organisations which may or may not have a profit motive. Evidence of the marketing of such services is most marked in the case of those private firms such as banks which are profit-orientated and least evident in the case of public-sector welfare services. To these easily recognised categories Kotler and Levy add persons, organisations and ideas, while in a more elaborate statement ('Beyond Marketing: The Furthering Concept', 1969) they add 'places'. In the case of these latter categories a limited marketing activity may be noted in the past but it has largely concentrated on public relations type activity supported by a limited amount of paid promotion. Clearly, there is considerable scope for the use of other elements of the marketing mix, especially in the field of marketing research, to better define consumer needs. This observation leads naturally to consideration of the second basic construct.

In a limited sense consumers are viewed solely as those persons or organisations which consume the output of another organisation. In the wider concept 'consumers' include at least three other groups with a *direct* interest in any given organisation. First, there are persons responsible for the control of the organisation. These may be shareholders in a company or those nominated by them (directors), they may be the trustees of a private foundation, or the elected ministers who control our government departments and so on. The second category is comprised of persons/ organisations which take a direct interest, and the third of those with a passive of *indirect* interest. Examples of the former are, say, consumer organisations or government departments in the case of business firms, former students and local and central government in the case of a university; while the latter category conveniently encompasses all those who might be influenced by or wish to influence the organisation at some future time.

The third construct is that of the tools of marketing. Among these we may distinguish the four 'P's of product, price, place (distribution) and promotional policy, each of which has an important role in marketing the output of any type of organisation. We have already stressed that change is symptomatic of the world in which we live – accordingly all organisations must continually reappraise and update their 'product' in order to best satisfy changing needs. Pricing has an important role to play although it frequently seems to be ignored in the provision of many public services. It is difficult for the individual citizen to decide whether the collective taxes we pay are being allocated to the ends we most desire except in a very gross way. Certainly it is impossible in the particular to determine whether we are getting value for money and the suppliers often seem insensitive to the concept of cost-benefit. Indications of changing attitudes in the latter area are to be seen in the concept of contract research in which the researcher is required to produce results in line with a prearranged budget and the suggestion that individuals be given 'tickets' which they can exchange for, say, education. In the present social climate it seems unlikely that the latter idea will gain support but its currency does imply that the

consumers of such services would like a more effective way of demonstrating their wishes other than at general elections. Equally some of the dangers of monopoly power which we monitor so closely in the private sector merit more attention for they appear to exist in the pricing and quality decisions of many public services. The publication of the Citizens' Charter and the intervention of Regulators in industries like electricity and water in the mid 1990s indicate that Government is aware of these concerns.

In the case of distribution and promotion there is also scope for the application of marketing techniques, although perhaps somewhat less than in the product and price areas. Distribution still merits attention, however, in that in many cases it appears to be dictated by the convenience of the supplier rather than the consumer. Similarly, some of the promotional techniques already in use would no doubt benefit from comparison with the sophistication typical of the promotion of consumer goods.

Essentially, therefore, we are arguing that the philosophy and techniques which have apparently worked so much to the advantage of private profit-oriented organisations are equally relevant and meaningful to all other forms of organisation. Three things must be appreciated, however. First, one must not strain the analogy between business and non-business organisations too far and so try to force the latter to fit patterns which have proved successful in the former context but which may be wholly inappropriate to non-business organisations. Second, success in marketing depends upon commitment – mere lip-service to the concept and changing the sales function's title is insufficient. (See, for example, B. Charles Ames, 'Trappings vs. Substance in Industrial Marketing', 1970.) Finally, success depends upon matching skills with opportunities.

Collectively, these three caveats indicate that the greatest benefit is likely to accrue where one attempts a transfer of basic ideas from the traditional content of marketing physical products rather than promote the wholesale adoption of particular marketing techniques. This is particularly apparent in the case of marketing for non-profit organisations.

Marketing as an academic discipline

In considering possible revisions for the sixth edition of this text book, several reviewers suggested that some reference should be made concerning the formal study of marketing, particularly as such reference is to be found in other leading text books. The omission of any discussion of marketing as a subject of study in earlier editions was based on the assumption that anyone reading a text book on marketing was presumably doing it for a purpose, and knew precisely what that was.

While this assumption may still hold true there are at least two reasons why some specific comment may be called for. First, the number of courses containing a marketing module of some kind has grown enormously. This is true not only of the ubiquitous undergraduate degree in Business Studies, or the MBA course, but of many other formal courses. Many engineering degrees contain a marketing module, with particular emphasis on the marketing/production interface and new product development. Pharmacy students who intend to enter the retail dispensing business are keen to get some insight into the role of marketing in such a business, as are scientists who intend to follow a career in industry. Added to this many other professional practices such as law, banking, medicine, public administration, etc. have been opened up to competition and the creation of 'market' economies which call for at least some understanding of the nature and practice of marketing. For many of these people it may come as a considerable surprise that there is a formal body of knowledge concerning marketing equal to that to be found in better known, and longer-established disciplines.

The second reason why some comment may be called for is that many people still believe that marketing is a craft or skill which can only be mastered through experiental learning 'on the job'. Such persons question the value of formal marketing education and may need to be persuaded of the value of marketing study and qualification. Equally, many other professional practices are sceptical of the claim that marketing is also a profession with a standing equivalent to that of architecture, engineering, accountancy, law, and so forth. So, for persons embarking on their first formal study of the subject it may be helpful to suggest some arguments which justify this.

As the preceding discussion of the historical evolution of marketing should have made clear, exchange is the main driver of economic growth and development, and the attainment of an acceptable standard of living. It was recognition of the benefits of task specialisation, and the division of labour, which encouraged the development of stable communities and the social institutions necessary to sustain them. In this sense the practice of marketing is an integral part of our everyday life and, as such, can get taken for granted. However, as our historical review has also made clear, the impact of technological innovation and change, accompanied by a slowing down of population growth in most developed economies, has resulted in a significant change in the balance between demand and supply.

For virtually all of recorded history demand far exceeded supply leading to the pre-occupation with production and productivity that gave rise to mass production and mass consumption. Because of this imbalance, the role of intermediaries linking producer and consumer was often seen as adding costs, but little value, and accounts for the low regard accorded to merchants, hucksters and salesmen from whom modern marketers are descended! But, as we have seen, our supply capability has now caught up with and overtaken demand with the result that decisions on how to deploy factors of production to create an output have become exceedingly complex and difficult. To diagnose such complex problems, and propose appropriate courses of action, calls for a much more sophisticated practice than was necessary hitherto.

This challenge is similar to that faced and overcome by practitioners in most, if not all, of what are now regarded as professions. As a noun the word 'profession' embraces a host of meanings including 'trade, art, a vocation, business, calling, career, discipline, work', to mention but a few. However, 'profession' is usually used in a more restricted sense to describe a practice which is regulated by its practitioners, admission to which requires formal qualification to confirm mastery of a body of knowledge which embraces the philosophy, laws, principles, wisdom and so on, considered necessary for effective practice. The professions of architecture, engineering, medicine, and others, have all gone through the process of defining and redefining what constitutes the appropriate body of knowledge and what one needs to achieve to be considered qualified in it.

Marketing, and its sister discipline Procurement, are now firmly established as professional practices as evidenced by their Chartered status. Such status is only granted when a body of practitioners can satisfy the Privy Council that there is a formal body of knowledge which can be examined, and that admission to the practitioner body is restricted to those who have successfully passed examinations in the subject at an appropriate level. As yet, members of the Chartered Institute of Marketing are not entitled to designate themselves as 'Chartered Marketers' in the same way as Chartered Engineers, but with the growth of the academic discipline and body of knowledge represented by it, it can only be a matter of time before such recognition is earned.

In common with other professions the body of knowledge which underpins the practice of marketing is derived from many sources. The core disciplines on which marketing is founded are economics, psychology and sociology; just as mathematics and physics underpin engineering, and anatomy, physiology, biology, chemistry, etc. underpin medicine. One thing which tends to distinguish the single or core disciplines from multi-disciplinary subjects like marketing is their level of abstraction. In economics, for example, it is necessary to specify a number of assumptions in order to develop a theory of competition as an abstract concept against which various real world competitive states can be compared and analysed. Professional practices, like marketing, tend largely to eschew this kind of formal theorisation and concentrate more of their efforts on seeking to synthesise or integrate the insights and findings from the core discipline to solve real rather than abstract problems. The difficulty with

the latter was summarised succinctly in an article entitled 'Decay of the Dismal Science' by Robert Chote (1995). He wrote:

> The obsession with algebraic elegance has led economists increasingly to interpret real world behaviour in ways that are theoretically defensible but palpably absurd. Some real business cycle theorists argue with straight faces, for example, that unemployment topped 3 million in the UK during the 1980s because the jobless were voluntarily taking more leisure time in the belief that work would be better paid a couple of years later.

There is, however, a significant difference between the more theoretically based social sciences such as economics, psychology and sociology and those based upon them like marketing. Comparatively few people who study the former subjects actually go into jobs as economists, psychologists or sociologists while the great majority of persons who study marketing intend to practice the discipline. It is for this reason that formal studies of marketing tend to place greater emphasis on application and less upon abstraction and theorising. This is not to say that marketing lacks theoretical foundations. We have already established that it does and these more theoretical foundations are the subject of Chapters 5 to 9 which comprise Part II of this book. But, as later chapters will make clear, the main emphasis is upon marketing as a practice.

■ The role of marketing

Marketing's role is to ensure the continuance in growth of economies, and the individuals' standard of living. In Chapter 5 the nature of demand will he considered in greater detail; at this point it is sufficient to point out that the determination of needs and wants, backed up by purchasing power, must indicate how management is to deploy the resources entrusted to it so as to maximise satisfaction in the total sense. If management succeeds in this, then human welfare will be optimised within the limitations imposed by the then available resources. Not only that; by thinking ahead and predicting the future needs and wants of people, action may be implemented now which will ensure their future satisfaction. (Aspects of welfare economics are largely ignored in this treatment on the basis that if private enterprise concentrates on profit maximisation the State will be able to implement the people's demand for welfare and social services from the taxes levied on these profits; that is, the bigger the profits the greater the potential revenue from taxation. It is recognised that corporate management frequently abstains from profit maximisation for social and ethical reasons, *inter alia*, but it will be simpler for our purpose here to assume that entrepreneurs seek to maximise consumer satisfaction as a means to maximising profits.)

To conclude this introductory review some reference must be made to the functional aspects of marketing with which the majority of this book is concerned.

■ Marketing functions

If we accept the marketing concept, essentially we are agreeing to a simple proposition that supply is a function of demand and, therefore subservient to it. Demand is the controlling factor, and an analysis and understanding of it must underlie all marketing functions. In their excellent book *Business Economics*, Bates and Parkinson distinguish four managerial aspects of demand which for brevity and lucidity would be difficult to better, namely:

1. Analysis and forecasting; that is, market research.
2. Product development and design.
3. Influencing of demand – design, advertising, and so forth.
4. Service – distribution, after-sales service, and so forth.

Much that follows is an examination, in greater depth, of these functions in isolation, but before proceeding to such a consideration, it is necessary

to understand that marketing depends on co-ordination of these separate ingredients to achieve a 'mix' suitable to the particular situation in hand.

The idea of a 'mix' of marketing functions was conceived by Professor Neil Borden of the Harvard Business School as:

a schematic plan to guide analysis of marketing problems through utilisation of

(a) a list of the important forces emanating from the market which bear upon the marketing operations of an enterprise;
(b) a list of the elements (procedures and policies) of marketing programs.

The marketing mix refers to the apportionment of effort, the combination, the designing, and the integration of the elements of marketing into a program or 'mix' which on the basis of appraisal of the market forces, will best achieve the objectives of an enterprise at a given time.   (1964, pp. 2–7)

Each function is a specialisation in its own right and it is unlikely that any single person could acquire full mastery of them all. Even if one could, it is doubtful whether one would then be able to make an objective assessment of the true relative value of each in any given marketing situation. Similarly, although many very successful marketing men have started life as a specialist in a single function, too high a degree of involvement is bound to bias decisions, albeit subconsciously. At such, the marketer, as a strategist and administrator, should aim at an understanding of the specialisations so that they may select the appropriate tactics to achieve their overall objective.

There is no need for a successful general to be a marksman, a ballistic expert, or expert at any other military skill for that matter. On the other hand, if he is not aware of the possibilities and limitations of the resources at his disposal it is unlikely that he will be able to combine them to achieve the maximum effect. As with the general so with the marketer. It is not necessary to be a clinical psychologist to appreciate the value of motivation research, or a statistician to understand the meaning of significance in relation to sampling results.

At the same time it is essential that the various marketing functions be isolated and examined before returning to the question of their co-ordination into an overall managerial concept. In general terms, the chapters which comprise Part III concern functional areas within marketing which are specialisations in their own right. At some time or other the aspiring general manager will come into contact with some, or all of them, just as they will endeavour to acquire knowledge and experience of production and financial management. All of us cannot become chief executive and, for most, a particular functional area such as market research may become a job for life from which great satisfaction can be derived. Whatever our ambitions, or our present occupation, it is of paramount importance that one recognises that the mix variables are interdependent and interacting. To view them as if they existed in isolation and in separate watertight compartments is to ignore the true import of the marketing concept. Everyone in a firm or an economy is making a contribution which in the aggregate will determine the material welfare of us all. Coordination of individual effort is critical to the overall standard of performance but this cannot be achieved by direction alone. Cooperation is an essential prerequisite, and this can only come from understanding how the separate parts together make a whole greater than the sum of those parts ('Synergy', q.v., H. Igor Ansoff (1968), *Corporate Strategy*).

Before proceeding to an examination of the mix variables:

- Marketing research
- Product development
- Pricing
- Packaging
- Distribution
- Advertising and sales promotion
- Selling and merchandising
- After-sales service

Some consideration has been given to a review of the basic elements – demand, supply, companies – to provide a broad background against which to relate these more specific areas.

Similarly an extended chapter is devoted to a description of patterns of distribution as they exist; partly to provide background information and partly to contrast the difference, often more real than imagined, in the markets for raw materials, industrial and consumer goods.

First, however, one should consider the environmental context within which all exchange processes occur and which creates the threats and opportunities that face all organisations in a competitive marketplace. It is this that we turn to in the next chapter.

Summary

In this chapter we have addressed 8 basic questions, namely:

1. What is marketing?
2. What contribution has marketing made, and what role has it played, in the evolution and development of the modern, advanced economies as we know them today?
3. How modern is modern marketing?
4. What factors have precipitated a revision of the dominant 'marketing management' model and its replacement by the new, extended model of relationship marketing?
5. Is marketing an art or a science?
6. How transferable is marketing thinking to other spheres of human activity?
7. Why study marketing? (Marketing as an academic discipline)
8. What is the role of marketing and what are its basic functions?

In attempting to provide answers to these questions we have established a foundation for a review of the content of marketing (Part I), of its theoretical underpinnings (Part II), of the discrete functions which make up the marketing mix (Part III) and their application in practice.

Review questions and problems

1. Why is there no single, generally accepted definition of marketing? Should there be such a definition? If so, what developments are necessary to permit its statement?

2. What is the 'marketing concept'? Is it solely applicable to firms selling goods and services, or is it a 'philosophy' which can be usefully adopted by all formal organisations?

3. Why is it that marketing has only recently become an issue of central concern to producers/sellers of goods and services?

4. What do you understand by the phrase 'accelerating change'? What factors underlie this phenomenon? Will they continue to apply in the future?

5. What is the 'marketing mix'? How useful is the concept to practitioners? In what respects?

6. Marketing: art or science? Discuss.

7. 'The marketing concept is applicable to all business organisations irrespective of their size or the nature of the goods or services marketed.' Give reasons for agreeing, or disagreeing, with this view.

8. How would you counter the view that marketing exists only as a loose collection of techniques practised by specialists?

9. Since we cannot observe demand curves, there is little need for the marketing manager to be acquainted with economic concepts. Critically appraise this statement.

10. Henry Ford is often quoted as having said 'You can have any colour you like so long as it is black.' Contrast this approach with a modern marketing approach and include in your answer an explanation of the limitations to adopting a total freedom of choice.

11. Many companies are still confused about the distinction between marketing and selling. As a newly appointed marketing manager how would you explain to your managing director the differences between the two?

12. What do you understand by the marketing concept? Explain why a company utilising the marketing concept is more likely to have longer-term success.

13. It has been argued that failures in marketing management can be attributed largely to failures in personal relationships. Discuss the significance of relationship management to the successful handling of distribution channels, paying attention to the desires of all parties concerned.

14. Define relationships marketing and indicate why it is of particular importance to service organisations in general and to management consulting firms in particular.

15. Explain how identifying the differences between transaction-based marketing and relationship-based marketing might determine the appropriate strategies for a firm in managing its relationships with its customers.

16. Clearly define what you consider to be the 'Marketing Concept'. Give your reasons for or against the argument that companies should be more marketing oriented.

■ Supplementary reading list

Baker, Michael J. (ed.) (1995) *Marketing Theory and Practice*, 3rd edn (Basingstoke: Macmillan).

Bartels, Robert (1965) 'Development of Marketing Thought', in G. Schwartz (ed.), *Science in Marketing* (New York: Wiley).

Borden, Neil H. (1965) 'The Concept of the Marketing Mix', in G. Schwartz (ed.), *Science in Marketing* (New York: Wiley).

Halbert, Michael (1965) *The Meaning and Sources of Marketing Theory* (New York: McGraw-Hill).

Howard, John A. (1963) *Marketing: Executive and Buyer Behaviour* (New York: Columbia University Press).

Hunt, Shelby D. (1983) *Marketing Theory* (Homewood, Ill.: Irwin).

King, R. L. (1965) 'The Marketing Concept', in G. Schwartz (ed.), *Science in Marketing* (New York: Wiley).

Laczniack, G. R. and Murphy, P. E. (1975) *Marketing Ethics Guidelines for Managers* (Lexington, MA: Lexington Books).

Meadows, D. *et al.* (1972) *The Limits to Growth* (London: Earth Island).

Robinson, P. J. and Luck, D. J. (1964) *Promotional Decision-Making, Practice and Theory* (New York: McGraw-Hill).

☐ *Articles*

Kotler, P. and Levy, S. J. (1969) 'Broadening the Concept of Marketing', *Journal of Marketing*, vol. 33, January.

Lipson, Harry A. and Reynolds, F. D. (1970) 'The Concept of the Marketing Mix: Its Development, Uses and Applications', *MSU Business Topics*, Winter.

■ *Chapter 2* ■

Environmental Analysis

Contents

Learning goals

The issues to he addressed in this chapter include:

1. The sources of major environmental change.
2 The need for the firm to take formal steps to monitor its changing environment.
3. Three broad approaches to environmental analysis – weak signal management, QUEST (Quick Environmental Scanning Technique) and formal environmental scanning systems.
4. The application of environmental analysis.

After reading this chapter you will:

1. Know why an understanding of the environment of marketing is an essential prerequisite for competitive success.
2. Be able to identify some of the long-run secular changes which are shaping the future environment.

3. Appreciate why organisations need to plan for uncertainty in order to maximise the opportunities open to them while avoiding potential threats to their continuing success.
4. Recognise the importance of formulating assumptions and developing contingency plans based upon them.
5. Comprehend the importance of environmental analysis and be able to distinguish various methods for monitoring change in the environment.
6. Understand the concept of weak signal management.
7. Be able to define and execute a QUEST (quick environmental scanning technique) analysis.
8. Be aware of the need to establish a formal routine for regular environmental analysis as a key input into the organisation's marketing information system.
9. Appreciate the importance of environmental analysis at both the macro (national) and micro (organisational) levels.

■ Introduction

In the preceding chapter it was proposed that marketing is concerned essentially with mutually satisfying exchange relationships. It was further proposed that as our ability to increase the supply of goods and services has grown so it has become possible to pay closer attention to the specific needs of more clearly defined sub-groups of consumers and to cater for these market segments through the provision of differentiated products. In the affluent industrialised economies such as the United States this potential to create an excess supply of any particular good or service led to greatly increased competition between the suppliers of such goods and services and led to what we have termed the rediscovery of marketing. No longer can suppliers be sure that their assumptions about the nature of demand are correct and are unlikely to change. In Table 2.1 are listed a number of cherished assumptions which are now thought to be obsolete. To readers brought up in the 1980s it probably seems incredible that anyone could have ever held such assumptions in the first place, but for many years it was assumptions such as these that underpinned most of the strategic thinking and planning of many of the world's most successful organisations.

In this chapter we shall examine some of the factors which have resulted in the need not only to revise our former cherished assumptions but to continuously monitor and review those which enjoy currency today. While it has become a cliché to talk of the pace of accelerating change, all the evidence points to the fact that this reflects reality and that, since it is competition which fuels the pace of change, we can look forward to even greater change in the 1990s as international competition intensifies. Accordingly, in this chapter we shall seek to identify some of the major changes which offer both threats and opportunities to the continued existence of an organisation. In order to cope with this change it will be suggested that an organisation must take formal steps to monitor the environment in which it is operating and intends to operate in the future. Three broad approaches will be proposed, namely: weak signal management as developed by Ansoff; QUEST (Quick Environmental Scanning Technique) the methodology first proposed by Burt Nanus; and, thirdly, a formal environmental scanning activity as an element in the marketing information system.

■ Plotting the future

In recent years it has been frequently suggested that one of the major factors which distinguishes the Japanese approach to business compared with that of the United States or Great Britain, is its willingness to take a long-term view of investment. By contrast it is argued that many British and American companies take a very short-term view on future investment and are unlikely to take on projects where the payback is more than three or at most five years. This reluctance to take decisions which will influence the fortunes of an organisation 10 to 15 years into the future is quite understandable given that the further one

Table 2.1 *Cherished assumptions now thought obsolete*

- Inflation will never exceed 5 per cent per annum
- Energy will always be cheap and abundant
- The price of oil will never exceed $2 a barrel
- Import penetration of home markets will never exceed 15 per cent
- The primary aim of business is to make money
- Strict financial control is the key to good administration
- Market growth of 10 per cent per annum
- Workers do not have an important impact on productivity or product quality
- The consumerist movement does not represent the concerns of a significant portion of the buying public
- Success comes from having the resources to quickly adopt innovations successfully introduced by others
- Frequent styling changes are more important to customers than product quality

Source: D. Brownlie (1994) *The Marketing Book*, 3rd edn. Ed. Michael J. Baker, Oxford: Butterworth-Heinemann, p. 154.

attempts to plan for the future the greater the uncertainty one is faced with, the less structured and more complex is the information with which one has to deal, the greater the judgement which has to be exercised and the higher the consequences if one commits an organisation to a course of action which cannot easily be changed once it has been embarked upon. Thus, long-term strategic planning is more like the navigation of a supertanker than a sailing dinghy where decisions to change the course of the former may have to be taken up to an hour ahead of any action, whereas one can change the direction of a sailing dinghy instantaneously. It is because environmental analysis possesses these characteristics that it is generally the preserve of senior managers. A survey of top European chief executive officers undertaken in the 1980s identified eight factors which characterise the environment which they felt faced management up to the millennium. These eight factors were:

1.   A demand for quality and advice;
2.   A move towards a service culture;
3.   An emphasis upon the specialist;
4.   Shortening strategic time horizons;
5.   Scenario planning replacing forecasting;
6.   A reduction in head office functions;
7.   A wider international outlook;
8.   Tighter legislation.

As we move into the next century it is clear these trends continue alongside those identified by Naisbitt as 'megatrends' referred to later.

The demand for quality and advice is everywhere apparent and closely related towards the move towards a service culture. In advanced industrialised economies service activities now count for almost two thirds of the gross domestic product of countries like the United States and members of the European Union. To a large degree this shift from manufacturing to service industries reflects the application of technology to manufacturing resulting in a greatly increased output of more sophisticated products with a much lesser labour content than previously. Advances in technology have also meant that any new ideas can quickly be imitated or copied by other suppliers. Indeed, it has been estimated that any new technological innovation will be fully diffused through the world within 18 months of its first appearance. Against such a background producers have found it necessary to add value to their core products by providing additional advice and services.

These two trends give rise to the emphasis upon specialisation as suppliers seek to define particular market segments with greater and greater precision in an attempt to exercise monopoly power over a particular market niche rather than compete head on with other suppliers of undifferentiated products in mass markets. However, increased competition and technological change put considerable pressure upon management to plan to recover their investment within a shorter and shorter strategic time horizon. It follows that in seeking to chart the long-term future of an organisation less reliance can be placed upon traditional forecasting methods most of which depend upon an extrapolation of current trends into the long-term future. However, experience shows that technological innovations have resulted in a steep change in activity rather than a smooth transition from the current solution to a problem to a new solution. In recognition of this management now has to plan by developing scenarios which represent their best expectations of what the future or futures facing the organisation may be like. The sixth factor identified in the survey, namely the reduction in head office functions recognises that with increased competition organisations need to remain flexible and responsive to changes in the market place. To do this, authority and responsibility need to be decentralised and located in the operating divisions which are close to the customers.

The two remaining trends referred to – a wider international outlook and tighter legislation – reflect the enormous increase in world trade which has taken place in recent years and the efforts of sovereign governments both to ensure that the quality of products and services traded meet the needs of their citizens, whilst also seeking to protect domestic producers from unfair competitive practices by third parties wishing to sell into their markets.

Table 2.2 contains a longer listing of what has been termed the 'new international business realities' which are perceived to be facing companies in the last decade of the twentieth century. These mirror the megatrends identified by John Naisbitt in his book of that name, first published in 1982. In an effort to determine the major trends which were taking place in American society Naisbitt hypothesised that as the relationship between news and advertising in print media remained approximately constant then new news would continuously displace old news. Accordingly, if one undertook a content analysis of the news contained in print media through the United States it should define the issues of most interest and concern to the American public. As a result of his analysis Naisbitt concluded that the United States was in a state of transition from an industrial society to an information based society. This megatrend has been confirmed in Western Europe and is a trend which may be anticipated to spread to more and more of the advanced industrial economies. The second major trend which he identified was that innovations pursue the path of least resistance. Essentially, this suggests that end users or consumers are more willing to take up major technological innovations than are business or industrial organisations. One explanation of this may be that ultimate customers are concerned with the benefits delivered by high technology and are less concerned how those benefits are delivered. By contrast, people in organisations feel obliged to try and understand the technology before exposing their organisations to the risk which its adoption might expose them to. Given

Table 2.2 *New international business realities*

- Continued structural unemployment in the OECD countries
- The end of the age of bureaucratic centralism
- Constant struggles with public spending
- Major shift in demographics
- Politics in democratic countries will increasingly become a matter of choice between hard and soft options
- Debt problems in developing countries will become institutionalised and there will be growth in aid dependency
- Gulf separating world's industrial nations from developing countries will remain wide
- Terrorism will continue as a disruptive force
- Investment will be oriented towards the short term
- Proliferation of small businesses
- Disappearance of 'automatic' growth in all major economies
- Heightened competition (Including the NICs)
- Common product values
- Erosion of patent protection
- The change in financial services
- Postal services will continue to deteriorate
- Trend towards dichotomy in many areas of business operation – global or national niche
- Continued shortening of product life cycles
- Decline in manufacturing will continue *vis-à-vis* services
- Economies of scale are disappearing in some industries
- Transportation will increasingly give way to communication
- Changes in technology have made obsolete some human and corporate assets and created new ones
- Extreme and unpredictable currency variations – inhibiting rational decision making in manufacturing, sourcing, pricing
- Volatility of basic commodity prices – leading to large changes in national purchasing power
- Merger mania
- Privatisation

that any new technology must represent significant potential risks it is unsurprising that organisations take longer to make such decisions than do consumers. However, while consumers embrace high technology gladly they have also exhibited a strong wish for greater social involvement with one another and this has created a burgeoning demand for new forms of leisure and recreational activity.

Improvements in information and communication have resulted in a much greater awareness of global issues, and recognition that national economies are part of a larger, interdependent world economy. Recognition of this global interdependence has pointed to the need for long-term thinking on development by contrast to short-term exploitation, such as the destruction of the Amazon rain forests, which has characterised much past decision-making. Four closely related megatrends are the move to decentralisation and diversity as opposed to centralisation and homogeneity, from institutional help to self-help, from representative to participative democracy, and to networks in place of hierarchies. All of these trends indicate the wish of individuals to be involved in planning and organising their own lives. In summary, we can see that we are moving towards a post-industrial information era with shifts from standardisation to customisation, from centralisation to decentralisation, from dependence to self-help, from transportation to communication, from autocracy to participation, from hierarchies to networks, and from a state of information scarcity to one of information overload.

Numerous other studies confirm the findings reported above and allow us to state a number of basic propositions which most authorities would agree with. First, without any doubt, the pace of change is accelerating. Second, as a consequence, most aspects of the future are characterised by high levels of risk or uncertainty. Thirdly, while some aspects of their future may be extrapolated from current trends most aspects of it are likely to be both dynamic and discontinuous. Confronted with uncertainty the reaction of many organisations is to seek more and better information. However, because of the pace of change, delays in

decision-making in the quest for more and better information is more likely to lead to a loss of competitive leadership than an improvement in competitive performance.

Faced with such a scenario it is clear that management must seek to organise its thinking about possible futures in a structured and systematic way. In an analysis undertaken in the 1960s, Francis Aguilar identified four main modes of what he termed environmental scanning. These modes are summarised in Figure 2.1 and represent a series of steps which might be termed successive focusing. Thus, undirected viewing is a part of the manager's everyday activity through which he seeks to ensure that he remains aware of information relevant to his responsibilities. As a result of this general awareness, he is likely to identify particular pieces of information which deserve to be

Figure 2.1 *Successive focusing*

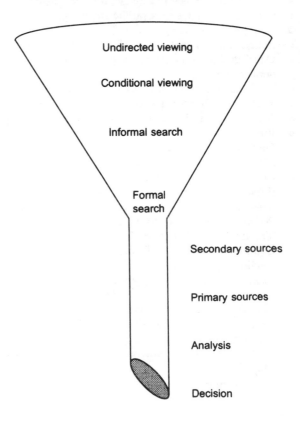

followed up. Initially, this follow up will be of a fairly informal kind which is summarised by the phrase 'keeping an eye on things'. If this informal search throws up events or information which could have a direct influence on the firm's actions, then a formal and deliberate search needs to be initiated. To assist management in organising its thinking three complementary approaches may be recommended – weak signal management, QUEST and environmental analysis. However, before reviewing these in more detail it will be helpful to look at the nature of uncertainty and the role of assumptions in helping cope with it.

Uncertainty and assumptions

In an article entitled 'Planning in a Changing Environment', Dale D. McConkey (1988) offered the following observation:

> Effective planning requires managers to plan for *uncertainty* – not for certainty. In the past planning for certainty made sense. Domestic and world economies were more stable. Change occurred less rapidly. The future could be predicted with a greater degree of accuracy. There were fewer uncontrollable variables. Product life cycles were longer; product development cycles were shorter. Planning was easier.
>
> But it is now more and more difficult to predict the future with any degree of accuracy. Thus planning must concentrate on uncertainty – in fact on multiple uncertainties.

In order to cope with such uncertainty McConkey argues that managers will have to subscribe to several practices that may represent dramatic departures from the way they previously planned. Specifically, firms will need to:

1. Place more emphasis on planning for uncertainty.
2. Integrate all planning – strategic, long- and short-range – more effectively.

3. Review product performance more rigorously and be prepared to redeploy resources more frequently to optimise total performance.
4. Acquire more and better information.
5. Improve their environmental scanning abilities.
6. Determine their strategy based primarily on external market opportunities rather than internally perceived strengths.
7. Emphasise marketing rather than selling.
8. Review their plans more frequently.
9. Provide better staff support for operating managers.

Faced with uncertainty it is necessary to try and predict or forecast the nature and direction of future events and articulate these as assumptions around which one can construct the strategic plan. McConkey (above) offers a useful definition of assumptions as follows:

> Assumptions are generally defined as best present estimates of the impact of major external factors, over which the manager has little if any control but which may exert a significant impact on performance or the ability to achieve desired results.

In the opening paragraph of this chapter, reference was made to assumptions and, in Table 2.1, we listed a number of cherished assumptions which had underpinned much of the strategic thinking and planning of firms in the 1950s and 1960s. While these particular assumptions are obsolete and not held by anyone any longer one should not underestimate the need for relevant assumptions as an essential element in the strategic planning process. The question is 'What are appropriate and relevant assumptions?' Most of the answers are to be found in environmental analysis of the kind discussed in this chapter.

Several clues as to the assumptions which should be built into strategic planning have already been reviewed in the first section of the chapter 'Plotting the future'. To develop formal assumptions, however, one must devise highly specific statements which are much more focused than the broad generalisation of the kind proposed by Naisbitt in *Megatrends*, or derived from surveys of senior executives and the like. For example, one needs to be specific about factors such as interest rates and the rate of inflation and cannot avoid the issue by making vague statements about increases or decreases. However, it is also important to recognise that one does not have to make assumptions about anything or everything which may occur in the future – only those events or issues which are significant and of direct relevance to the organisation developing the plan.

McConkey argues that the formulation of assumptions should proceed in orderly steps and proposes the following sequence:

1. Isolate those future events that are most likely to have a significant effect on the company's business;
2. Evaluate as accurately as possible the probable effects of these events;
3. Determine whether an assumption is necessary; if so, formulate the assumption;
4. Record all assumptions;
5. Continuously track the validity of all assumptions;
6. Revise the assumptions and plans and take corrective action when assumptions prove to be incorrect.

From this it is clear that assumptions represent our best guess as to the future state of affairs at the time we are drawing up or revising our strategic plan. With the passage of time these future events become nearer and the information available to us becomes more certain. It follows, therefore, that we should monitor the accuracy of our assumptions and be prepared to adjust our plans to reflect changes in our original assumptions.

When formulating assumptions it will also be helpful to try and quantify how likely or probable it is that a given assumption will materialise. Initially most people are more willing to express the likelihood of an outcome in qualitative or verbal terms such as 'Very likely', 'Likely', 'Unlikely', or 'Very unlikely'. When pressed, however, it is surprising how wide a discrepancy

may exist between two different people's expectations of a given outcome when required to quantify this. Thus one person may consider an event 'likely' when it is just better than an evens (50/50) chance, whereas another would only consider it 'likely' if the odds were 3 to 2 on (0.75 or 75 per cent probability). For planning purposes it is vital that all the decision makers share the same scale of values albeit that these values will be subjective, that is particular to each individual decision-maker, rather than objective in which case there would be a known or certain outcome for a given event.

In addition to formulating probability estimates McConkey also recommends that one should assign a confidence factor especially when dealing with highly critical assumptions upon which major investment decisions may be made. In this context 'Confidence' refers to the amount of confidence the manager has in the data on which his probability estimate was based, so that even though a manager might consider that a given event was very likely (90 per cent chance of occurrence) if he had no facts on which to base this assumption then it would have a low confidence value. Under such circumstances – a strong 'hunch' such and such would happen – the manager would be likely to increase his efforts to secure more and better information to test his belief. As noted earlier, there are several complementary approaches which will help the manager do this and these will be reviewed in the sections which follow.

■ Weak signal management

According to Ansoff most companies depend heavily upon extrapolative techniques in order to forecast sales, the economy and the much wider environmental issues which are of concern to them. In his view, such techniques do not have the ability to capture surprises and discontinuities which, as our earlier analysis has indicated, are more likely to be the norm rather than the exception. Accordingly, he suggests that other types of environmental appraisals are called for and proposes that managers should seek to structure their conditional viewing in such a way that they are more likely to pick up the weak signals which may herald future changes in the environment.

In examining why signals related to future change may appear weak to an organisation, Ansoff suggests that this may be due to at least one or other of four reasons. First, while the signal may have originally been strong, it may have become attenuated because the organisation is not tuned in to the right wavelength. The second explanation is that the original signal strength may have been reduced because of the existence of some filter between the organisation and the source of the signal or, possibly, because of 'jamming' between the receiver and the source of the signal. A third explanation is that the discontinuity or trend which is the source of the signal is a long way off and by the inverse square law the greater the distance between source and receiver the weaker the signal. Finally, it may be that at the very start of the discontinuity a signal is inherently very weak and so only likely to be recognised by those with specialist knowledge and/or paying particular attention to it.

Given that all firms face the same external environment it is obvious that the sooner any given organisation can pick up weak signals that herald future change the more likely it will be able to position itself, either to take advantage of the opportunity which they offer or to avoid any potential threat contained within them. In order to maximise the likelihood that the organisation will be able to do this, it needs to encourage persons who will act as gatekeepers, amplifiers and filters for weak signals in the environment. Gatekeepers, amplifiers and filters (GAFs) are people who are expert in the sector of the environment in which the organisation is scanning for information. In order to accomplish their task they must be positioned on the boundary between the organisation and its circumscribing environment. GAFs are at the forefront of expertise and are defined as gatekeepers because it is through them that the organisation is able to look out into the surrounding environment. They are amplifiers because they are closest to the

source of weak signals, and filters because it is through their expertise that they are able to distinguish the signal and screen out the 'noise' surrounding it.

While the concept of weak signal management is clear, and may be likened to the work of an astronomer or radio enthusiast scanning the heavens or airwaves in search of hitherto undetected signals, the operationalisation of the concept is not without difficulty. One approach which offers a means for reviewing and evaluating the weak signals that may be picked up by the firm's management, is the QUEST methodology proposed by Burt Nanus (1982).

■ QUEST

QUEST is an acronym for 'quick environmental scanning technique' and offers a broad and comprehensive first approximation to environmental trends and events that are critical to strategic decisions.

Nanus defines QUEST as:

> a future research process designed to permit executives and planners in an organisation to share their views about trends and events in future external environments that have critical implications for the organisation's strategies and policies. It is a systematic, intensive, and relatively inexpensive way to develop a shared understanding of high priority issues and to focus management's attention quickly on strategic areas for which more detailed planning and analysis would be beneficial.

Certain key assumptions underline the QUEST technique. First, it is assumed that the individual executives in a firm have a view of the dynamics of the changing environments which face them. It is further assumed that in the aggregate these views represent the organisation's understanding of its environment. However, in the absence of a technique such as QUEST it is unlikely that these separate views (assumptions) are articulated and shared. Thus, while individual executives may programme their future expectations into their decision-making, there is no guarantee that their perceptions and interpretations of the same facts are known to and/or shared by their managerial colleagues. Only if there is a formal mechanism for enabling the firm's executives to share their different perceptions and interpretations will it be possible to identify any mismatch or disagreement between them. However, if any disagreement or mismatch is made explicit it will then become possible for management to negotiate a consensus on the interpretation of the information available to it and on the desired future towards which the organisation is working.

As with most aspects of decision-making, a systematic approach within an agreed framework is likely to yield better results more quickly than would an unstructured approach. Further, given that the outcome is to be achieved through a negotiated consensus between the key managers, then such a process is more likely to instil a sense of ownership in the outcome than would separate independent evaluations. Table 2.3 summarises the steps involved in implementing a QUEST analysis. The purpose of step 1 is to achieve an agreed start point for the scanning exercise. As noted above, the purpose is to help bring out into the open and share the collective wisdom and experience of the participants in terms of their future expectations. The actual methodology for executing a QUEST analysis, is contained in steps 3 to 9 in Table 2.3.

Experience shows that the benefit of a QUEST analysis will be greatly enhanced by a review of other scenarios or projections of likely futures

Table 2.3   *QUEST: implementation*

1. Review current environmental conditions
2. Explain purpose and methodology
3. Review 'futures' literature to stimulate thinking
4. Define scope and boundaries for discussion including stakeholders and performance indicators
5. Identify key issues
6. Select agreed list
7. Assess probability of occurrence
8. Develop a Cross Impact Matrix (CIM)
9. Analyse CIM and develop scenarios

such as those contained in books like (Toffler, 1971) *Future Shock*, (Meadows *et al.*, 1972) *Limits to Growth* or the publications of the Brookings Institution or Hudson Institute. Such speculations by other futurists are both a source of useful ideas to stimulate thinking and an indication of the scope of the exercise. However, as step 4 in the sequence indicates, for a given organisation operating in a particular industry and markets it is important that some limitations be placed upon the exercise so that its scope and boundaries need to be defined as do statements as to the perspective from which the analysis is to be undertaken and what criteria or performance indicators are to be used in assessing the importance and/or relevance of any identified issue.

Step 5 is perhaps the most important step in the sequence as it is the one in which the participants are invited to define what they see as the strategic or key issues facing their organisation. Key issues may be defined as forthcoming developments, either inside or outside the organisation, which are likely to have an important impact on the ability of the organisation to meet its objectives. More simply put, key issues are those which could either make or break the organisation. Issues which, if well handled, will produce disproportionate benefit but which, if badly handled, could prove to be disastrous for the company. Key issues are often characterised by high opportunity costs for an organisation in that they are likely to foreclose other options. Clearly, there needs to be a limit to the number of key issues and the best way to proceed is to invite each of the participants to construct their own list of say five and then circulate these so that the group may proceed to stage 6, which is the agreement of a select list. Once the agreed list has been prepared the participants should then assess the likelihood or probability of occurrence of each of the events contained in the key-issue analysis. This, in turn, should be summarised in a cross-impact matrix of the kind illustrated in Figure 2.2 in which the impact of each of the key issues is examined in the context of the other key-issues. Finally, analysis of the cross-impact matrix should enable the group to develop scenarios

Figure 2.2 *Cross-impact matrix*

Event	Probability	1	2	3	4	5
1.		▓				
2.			▓			
3.				▓		
4.					▓	
5.						▓

which represent their own best expectation and understanding of the futures which face their own organisation.

From the foregoing description it is clear that QUEST is a broad brush and subjective approach. While its value cannot be over-estimated, it will be greatly enhanced if it is undertaken within the context of a formal environmental analysis activity. Indeed, it is such a formal environmental analysis activity which should provide the information input for both stages 1 and 3 of the QUEST methodology. However, while QUEST provides a means for structuring the knowledge and ideas of the senior managers responsible for strategic direction, environmental analysis is an integral part of the firm's marketing intelligence and information system and, as such, is a staff function which should be manned by professional researchers.

■ Environmental analysis

According to Aguilar, environmental analysis seeks to provide 'information about events and relationships in a company's future environment . . . which would assist top management in its tasks of charting the company's future course of actions'. Environmental analysis or scanning is responsible for three major activities. First, it is responsible for generating an up-to-date database of information on the changing business scene. Second, it is responsible for alerting management to what is happening in the market place, the industry and beyond. And, third, it is responsible for disseminating important information and analyses to key strategic decision-makers and influencers within the organisation.

In establishing a formal environmental analysis function certain key criteria must be satisfied. First, environmental trends, events and issues must be reviewed on a regular and systematic basis. In order to do this it is important that explicit criteria are established with which one may evaluate the likely impact of the monitored environmental trends. Because it is a formal activity then it should be guided by written procedures and responsibility for the implementation of these procedures must be clearly assigned. Experience indicates that scanning reports, updates, forecasts and analyses have greater impact when documented in a standardised format and when such documentation is generated on a regular basis and disseminated to predetermined personnel according to a timetable. Finally, successful environmental analysis and scanning systems depend upon the application of formal techniques such as Delphi studies and writing of multiple scenarios.

A survey undertaken in the 1980s of American corporations indicated that formal environmental analysis resulted in:

1. Increased general awareness by management of environmental change;

2. Better strategic planning and decision-making;
3. Greater effectiveness in government matters;
4. Better industry and market analysis;
5. Better results in foreign businesses;
6. Improvement in diversifications, acquisitions and resource allocation;
7. Better energy planning.

In other words an all-round improvement in performance.

Tables 2.4 and 2.5 summarise major sources of information on the business environment and their relative importance.

Environmental analysis at the national level

In 1995 a major report *Progress through Partnership* was published in the UK which summarised the findings of the Technology Foresight Programme set up by the Office of

Table 2.4   *Sources of information on the business environment*

Location	*Types*	*Sources of information on business environment*
Inside the company	Written	Internal reports and memos, planning documents, market research, MIS
	Verbal	Researchers, sales force, marketing, purchasing, advisors, planners, board
	Combination	Formal and informal meetings (e.g. working parties, advisory committees)
Outside the company	Written	Annual reports, investment reports, trade association publications, institute yearbooks, textbooks, scientific journals, professional journals, technical magazines, unpublished reports, government reports, unpublished papers, abstracts, newspapers, espionage
	Verbal	Consultants, librarians, government officials, consumers, suppliers, distributors, competitors, academics, market researchers, industry bodies, journalists, spies, bankers, stockbrokers
	Combination	Formal and informal meetings, membership of government working parties and advisory boards, industry bodies, trade associations

Source: Companion Encyclopedia of Marketing, Baker (1995), p. 325.

Table 2.5 *The relative importance of sources of environmental information*

1. Verbal sources of information are much more important than written sources; 75 per cent of information cited by executives was in verbal form
2. The higher the executive in the organization, the more important verbal sources became
3. Of the written sources used, the most important were newspapers (two-thirds), then trade publications, then internal company reports
4. The major sources of verbal information are subordinates, then friends in the industry, and very infrequently superiors
5. Information received from outside an organization is usually unsolicited
6. Information received from inside the organization is usually solicited by the executive
7. Information received from outside tends to have a greater impact on the decision-maker than inside information
8. The outside sources used varied according to the job of the manager. Thus, marketing managers talked more to customers
9. The larger the company, the greater the reliance on inside sources of verbal information

Source: *Companion Encyclopedia of Marketing*, Baker (1995), p. 326.

Figure 2.3 *Sectoral drivers*

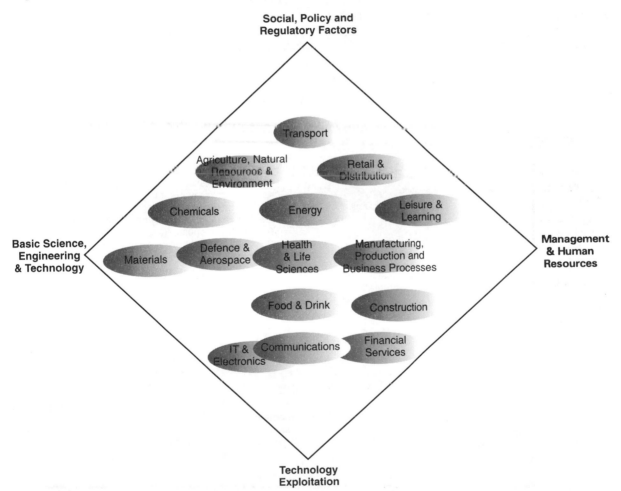

The four corners of the diamond represent the main sectoral drivers, all of which impact on each sector. The relative position of a Foresight sector indicates the relative balance of factors influencing that sector.

Source: *Progress through Partnership* (1995), Technology Foresight Programme (London: Office of Science and Technology).

Science and Technology. The Report identified four main sectoral drivers which influence and impact on the 15 major sectors identified for detailed study, and these are summarised in Figure 2.3. As the footnote to Figure 2.3 makes clear, the relative position of each sector *vis-à-vis* the 4 drivers is reflected by its position in the diamond. Each of the sectors is the subject of a separate report with the key findings and recommendations summarised in *Progress through Partnership*. For example, the sectoral findings for 'Manufacturing Production Processes' came up with the following key recommendations:

- Increased emphasis on business processes: research on best practices, and diffusion throughout industry.

- Technology priorities: improved process plant technology; new sensors and controls; modelling, simulation and visualisation; materials processing; IT and communications.
- Programmes in education and training: for business process/teamwork skills and continuing education.
- Encourage extended vision: improved market knowledge, 'foresight' and innovation.
- Sustain communications and support networks: customer, partner and supplier networks; and network services for manufacturers.
- Improve national infrastructure for competitiveness: action on education, transportation, deregulation and finance.

In addition, four long-term issues were identified, namely:

Figure 2.4   *Generic priorities in science and technology – relative assessment of attractiveness and feasibility*

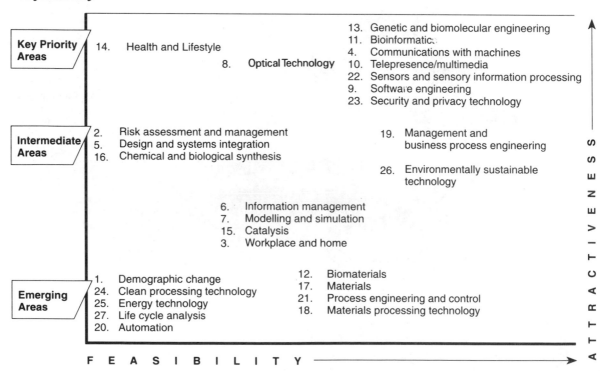

Source: *Progress through Partnership* (1995), Technology Foresight Programme (London: Office of Science and Technology).

- Continuing internationalisation of business;
- Increasing rate of improvement to catch up with foreign competition;
- Increasing influence of regulation and legislation;
- Industrial relevance of education and training.

From the overall analysis the Steering Group derived 27 Generic Priorities which it prioritised into three broad groups – Key Topic Areas, Intermediate Areas, and Emerging Areas. These were then plotted in a matrix structure in terms of the *feasibility* and *attractiveness* of achievement as shown in Figure 2.4.

The Steering Group then recommended 11 topics which it felt merited particularly urgent attention by organisations in the public and private sector, and so has established an agenda for future innovation and development to enhance and sustain the UK's competitiveness and international performance. For example, generic priority 10 'Telepresence/multimedia' is summarised as:

> ...the prospect of a great variety of on-line, interactive services in both traditional and new markets. Abundance of band width will facilitate the creation of new products in health, education, adult learning, skills training and leisure. The UK can play a major role in the generation of both the technologies and the product development they will support, both in its own right and in collaboration with European or other partners. (pp. 86–7)

☐ *Environmental analysis at the organisational level*

Environmental analysis of the kind described above clearly provides a major input into strategic analysis and planning at the level of the individual organisation. At the micro-level this macro-analysis will usually be supported by what is commonly referred to as a marketing audit. We return to the *marketing audit* in Chapter 3 (Marketing Strategy and Management) and also Chapter 20 (Planning for Marketing), but a short preview is merited here.

A basic objective of marketing is the identification of marketing opportunities and their exploitation by matching these with the organisation's objectives and capabilities. This requires the firm to evaluate or audit both itself (the internal audit) as well as its customers, competitors, suppliers and other intermediaries (the external audit). This external audit may also include other 'publics' which the macro-environmental analysis has indicated are of particular relevance and/or importance to the firm.

One of the first extended discussions of the marketing audit was written in 1959 for the American Management Association ('The Marketing Audit: its nature, purposes and problems'). In this, Abe Schuchman defines a marketing audit as:

> a systematic, critical and impartial review and appraisal of the total marketing operation: of the basic objectives and policies and the assumptions which underlie them as well as the methods, procedures, personnel, and organisation employed to implement the policies and achieve the objectives. (p. 13)

This definition focuses mainly on the internal operations of the organisation. More recent definitions would extend this to include all elements of the task environment including markets, customers, competitors, marketing intermediaries (distribution channels and dealers), suppliers and what may be called 'facilitators', that is other organisations or agencies which facilitate the marketing process. This latter category would include the provision of financial, communication, information, and transportation services, as well as consultancy, marketing research, advertising, and so on.

Much of the remainder of this book is devoted to describing and analysing the task environment as well as functional activities like marketing research and advertising which are often subcontracted to specialist agencies. Some discussion is also included in the next chapter and, is mentioned, in Chapter 20 which describes how the information collected through a marketing audit may be synthesised and used to inform the development of operational marketing plans. The reader may also wish to consult Chapter 10, 'Situation Analysis: The Marketing Audit' in Baker (1992), *Marketing Strategy and Management*, which is the more advanced companion volume to this book.

Summary

In this chapter it has been argued that competition takes place within an environment which is common to all the competing firms. This environment is becoming more complex and changing more rapidly due to *accelerating technological change* and *increased international competition*. Given this setting it is top management's responsibility to monitor the environment so that it may both anticipate and plan for the future. Such monitoring should be continuous and comprise both *formal environmental analysis* as an input into the marketing information system and informal through *weak signal management* and *environmental scanning* of the kind proposed by the *QUEST* technique. Formal environmental analysis needs to be structured to satisfy the needs of the decision-makers who will use this as an input to their strategic thinking and planning and has become a specialist function with many professional tools and techniques available.

Finally, we have looked briefly at the application of environmental analysis at the macro or national level and at the micro, organisational or 'task' level. The latter is often referred to as a marketing 'audit' and is returned to later.

Review questions and problems

1. Do most firms have a choice between adapting to or controlling their environment?

2. Using an industry of your choice as an example, explain the role of an environmental analysis, and how it might help a firm within the industry.

3. What is the significance of separating the 'task environment' from the 'wider environment' in an enviornmental appraisal of the firm? Give practical examples to illustrate your main points.

4. Since the mid-1980s the industrial, political, legal and social environment under which firms and consumers operate has undergone fundamental changes. Identify some of these major changes, and explain how they have affected a marketer's response to the market-place.

5. Describe the means at your disposal to evaluate the possible effects of changes in uncontrollable variables on the consumer market-place.

6. The commercial structure of any country develops, some argue, in stages, and is related to the stages of economic development. Describe these stages, and any action that governments can take to influence the progress of development.

7. How does 'going international' affect the environmental perspective of a firm?

8. Examine the importance of environmental scanning in the development of an international marketing strategy. In your answer, clearly identify the key components of the environment of concern to the international marketer, and their marketing implications.

9. How might the study of macromarketing influence the thinking of an industrialist in developing a marketing strategy and a government minister in considering competition policy?

10. Identify the main players in a company's external environment. Explain why marketers must monitor the environmental forces outside the firm.

11. Identify the main areas to be considered in a company's macro-environment. Explain why it is important for a company to take these forces into consideration when developing their marketing strategy.

12. Identify the main players in the company's micro-environment. Detail the effect each one has on the firm's effectiveness in serving its target market.

Supplementary reading list

See general texts and the notes following the Preface.

■ *Chapter 3* ■

Marketing Strategy and Management

Contents

Learning goals

The issues to be addressed in this chapter include:

1. The nature and definition of strategy and strategic planning.
2. The concept of organisational culture.
3. The concept of the product life-cycle.
4. The nature of marketing opportunity and competitive advantage.
5. The fundamental characteristics of the marketing audit and the marketing mix.
6. The idea that there is only a small set of strategic alternatives available to the firm.

After reading this chapter you will:

1. Be able to define strategy and understand the contribution which marketing has to make to the overall strategy of an organisation.
2. Be familiar with the concepts of organisational culture and the product life cycle.
3. Understand the concepts of market opportunity and competitive advantage.
4. Grasp the nature of the marketing audit.
5. Appreciate the need to set out clear objectives.
6. Be able to define the marketing mix.
7. Recognise the basic strategic alternatives open to an organisation.
8. Understand the concept of positioning and its central role in selecting a marketing strategy.

■ Introduction

In the first chapter we examined the substance of the marketing concept and observed how the process of economic development had tended to 'dehumanise' the nature of the exchange process.

This dehumanisation through the adoption of task specialisation, the division of labour and the application of technology to the production or supply side of consumption was essential to improve productivity and enhance the standard of living. However, as we have seen, a natural consequence of improved standards of living is an increase in the population – more infants survive, people live longer – which results in a concomitant increase in demand. In other words, the size of the market increases and the supply side has to work even harder to keep up.

One consequence of this struggle to keep pace with an ever growing demand was still further specialisation in production and the emphasis upon what Ricardo was to term 'comparative advantage'. While Ricardo was seeking to explain the benefits of international trade, precisely the same benefits existed within nation states and led to the concentration of particular industries in particular localities. Glass manufacturing at St Helens and St Gobain, iron smelting in South Wales and the Saar, textiles in Lancashire and Lille, ceramics in Staffordshire and Sèvres and so on. Because of the economies of scale and mass production such favoured locations were able to serve ever more distant markets more cost-effectively than smaller less well endowed local producers, resulting in a significant physical separation between producer and consumer.

In time this separation was to become psychological too, with producers assuming they knew what consumers wanted and justifying their assumptions by observing that the market was absorbing all their output and was clamouring for more.

So long as the market continued to expand exponentially through population growth there can be little doubt that the emphasis upon the mass production of undifferentiated products resulted in the maximum overall satisfaction. However, with a slowing down in population growth, and a continued acceleration in supply through technological innovation and change, the potential arose for the creation of an excess supply in certain markets. As soon as this occurs the nature of competition changes from so-called perfect competition, under which the product is assumed to be homogeneous, to imperfect competition under which suppliers recognise that if their output is indistinguishable from other suppliers then consumers will have no reason to prefer them to any other supplier with the possible result that they will be left with unsold goods. Given this possibility individual suppliers need to devise specific plans in order to compete with and succeed against other suppliers in the same line of business. In other words they need a strategy, which may be defined broadly as a statement of purpose and the means of achieving it. Why do we need a strategy? Because strategy is concerned with future action and it is a cliché but true that the rest of our lives will be spent in the future.

There are numerous books (including the companion volume to this – *Marketing Strategy and Management*) which are devoted solely to the subject of strategy – its definition, formulation and execution. In this chapter we can only touch on some of the bare essentials but it is felt to be important to introduce them early on as the whole purpose of marketing – both concept and function – is to help structure and improve both the efficiency and effectiveness of exchange relationships with the ultimate goal of maximising satisfaction from the consumption of scarce resources. Accordingly, in this chapter we shall seek to define the nature of strategy and strategic planning as well as the concepts of *organisational culture* and the *product life cycle* for the latter defines the inevitable pattern of change within which the firm must exist and the former the way the organisation chooses to approach and deal with its survival and growth. This consideration leads naturally to the concepts of *market opportunity* and *competitive advantage* which underlie all successful strategies.

In order to formulate a strategy it will be argued that one must carry out a *marketing audit* which will take in both the external threats and opportunities which exist in the competitive environment as well as the firm's own strengths and weaknesses. Based upon such an analysis the firm will wish to articulate clear *objectives* both to provide direction for the firm's efforts as well as milestones to record progress and achievement. In developing such objectives it will be shown that the firm has only a small number of strategic alternatives available to it and techniques for identifying and selecting these will be proposed.

Once a core strategy has been defined its effective execution will depend upon the optimal selection of the elements of the *marketing mix* – the combination of product, price, place and promotion – and this notion will be introduced for extended development in Part III of the book. In selecting the optimal marketing mix it is vital that the firm have a clear view of how it wishes to position itself against its rivals and the idea of 'positioning' will be introduced and described.

Strategy and strategic planning

All successful businesses owe their existence to the recognition and existence of a market opportunity. This statement is as true of the technologically driven inventor such as Clive Sinclair or the production orientated Henry Ford as it is of the marketing orientated Anita Roddick. Each of these entrepreneurs succeeded because they brought to the market place a new product which consumers instantly recognised as fulfilling a felt need. Subsequently, one (Sinclair) was to fail badly and another (Ford) was to falter because their initial intuitive success was not supported by a clearly defined strategy for building upon this. In the case of Sinclair the prospect of low-cost calculators, personal computers and miniature televisions, were enormously attractive to consumers captivated with the marvels of microelectronics. His products proved the markets existed but poor delivery and, even worse, poor product performance made him an easy victim for those second to the market with more reliable products, guaranteed delivery and after-sales service. Similarly, Henry Ford created the mass automobile market with his Model T but lost out to General Motors because he failed to develop a second generation motor-car to satisfy the increased needs of more sophisticated and demanding buyers.

It was failures of these kinds, but of industries rather than firms, which prompted Ted Levitt (1960) to write his seminal article, 'Marketing Myopia'. Using the American railroad system as his examplar, Levitt pointed out how the invention of the steam engine revolutionised overland transportation, opened up continents and created an industry which, by 1900, was amongst the richest and most successful in the land. By 1950 this once, all-powerful industry was in ruins surviving only with Federal aid and on a greatly reduced basis. What went wrong? Basically the railroad management lacked a strategy based upon clear understanding of the business they were in defined in terms of the needs served. What the railroad moguls failed to appreciate was that the steam locomotive and the railroad were but one step in the evolution of the transportation business. Railways offered significant benefits in speed, comfort and carrying capacity over the stage-coach, ox-train and river/canal barges they largely displaced. Their downfall lay in not appreciating that further technological progress would result in even more convenient, speedy and comfortable means of transportation with the invention of the internal combustion and jet engines. Consumers owe no loyalty to suppliers, only to themselves. If a superior product or service is made available to meet their needs they will have no hesitation in switching to it. Thus, as inner city congestion increases we are seeing an increased demand for improved public transportation systems and growing investment in mass transit/light railways. The question is, if you are a motor-car manufacturer or a director of National Car Parks what plans have you for coping with the implications of this change?

To answer this question effectively it is widely agreed that one should undertake a formal and structured analysis along the lines proposed by Kotler and others, namely:

- Diagnosis: where is the company now and why?
- Prognosis: where is the company headed?
- Objectives: where should the company be headed?
- Strategy: what is the best way to get there?
- Tactics: what specific actions should be undertaken, by whom, and when?
- Control: what measures should be watched to indicate whether the company is succeeding?

The first question 'where is the company now?' is frequently couched as 'what business are we in?' Following Levitt's analysis in 'Marketing Myopia' touched on above, it is now accepted that the answer to this question must be in terms of the need served rather than the specific means of serving it. Thus Levitt argued that if the railroad managers had perceived of themselves as being in the transportation business rather than the railroad business then they would have regarded the invention of the internal combustion engine as opening up a whole new range of transportation opportunities. As it was they ignored it initially as unsophisticated and undeveloped (just as steam engines had been 60 years previously) and then sought to compete with it in markets where railroads had little or no competitive advantage. Of course 'the transportation business' is far too broad a definition for operational strategic planning but it is the kind of fundamental assessment necessary to initiate such operational strategic planning.

If one considers an archetypal 'marketing' product such as detergents then we might wish to consider the manufacturers as being in the cleanliness business. If this is the case then there are at least three developments which could seriously threaten the industry out of which Procter & Gamble and Unilever make millions of pounds' profit every year. First, textile manufacturers have developed and are improving soil-resistant treatments which prevent fabrics from becoming dirty so easily, and so reduce the incidence of cleaning. Second, there is the potential of disposables – napkins, plates, cups, tablecloths and, above all else so far, babies' diapers. (Procter & Gamble saw this coming and market the leading Pampers brand!) Third, there is an ecologically benign technology known as ultrasonics which literally shakes dirt out of fabrics without any need for chemicals which pollute the environment. If you are Electrolux or Hoover making cleaning boxes (rather than washing machines) the change in technology is only a limited threat – if you are Procter & Gamble or Unilever it could be fatal. Perhaps Levitt summed it up best of all when he observed 'When a man goes into a hardware store to buy a

1/4″ twist drill he needs a 1/4″ hole'. As soon as someone like Black & Decker develop a hand-held laser gun which can drill holes with infinite accuracy in any material, then the twist-drill business will be dead but the hole-making business will continue to flourish.

This continuous cycle of innovation and change is described and analysed in one of marketing's central concepts – the product life cycle.

The product life-cycle concept

In *Market Development* (Baker, 1983) we described the product life-cycle concept as follows:

> The paradox of the product life cycle (PLC) concept is that it is one of a very small number of original marketing ideas to enjoy a wide currency and yet is largely discredited in terms of practical application and relevance. That it should be discredited reflects a failing on the part of practitioners to understand the role and potential contribution of theory and concepts rather than any intrinsic deficiency in the concept itself – an assertion we will now seek to substantiate.

The analogy of a product life-cycle is firmly founded in the biological sciences and the observation that living organisms pass through an inevitable cycle from conception through gestation to growth leading to maturity. In turn, the mature organism begins to decay progressively until its life is terminated in death. This progression is as familiar to us as life itself, and none would deny the inescapable sequence through which the normal organism will pass. That said, it would be a foolhardy bioscientist who would attempt to generalise about the expectations of a particular organism without first establishing its genus, species and sub-species, and even then they would only speculate about any distinct organism in terms of some form of probabilistic statement concerning expected future outcomes.

The validity of this assertion is easily demonstrated by reference to ourselves – human beings. An inspection of life expectancies quickly reveals major disparities between the inhabitants of advanced, affluent economies and their unfortunate brothers and sisters in the developing countries. Thus, while the average British male can look forward to a life-span of 72 years, an Indian has a life expectancy of only 53 years. However, if we were to compare a Briton and an Indian aged 30 years, the discrepancy in their respective life expectancies would be relatively small. The problem is a familiar one in the field of descriptive statistics; means or averages are largely meaningless unless we also possess some measure of dispersion about the mean. In the case of Indians, infant mortality is very high and the age distribution at death is heavily skewed towards young persons. On the other hand, if you survive the dangers of childhood, the probability of a reasonably long life is quite high. A broadly similar pattern also applies to Britons, in that infants and young children are more susceptible to disease and death by accident or genetic defect than are teenagers and adults. On the other hand, by enabling weak specimens to survive childhood one increases the probability of death in middle life, with the result that life expectancies for mature adults are very similar in advanced as well as in developing countries.

Actuaries understand this perfectly and base life insurance premiums upon average probabilities. The impression that your policy is written specifically for you is illusory, for no actuary would presume to predict your personal life expectancy. The irony is that while all of this is entirely commonplace and acceptable to us as insurance risks, as managers we expect analogous models to possess a level of predictive ability which cannot be achieved with very large populations of essentially homogeneous units.

The level of information which we are likely to possess about a product group such as detergents or industrial fasteners is minuscule by comparison with the demographic data available upon people in general or nationalities in particular. But, despite this, we try to make a generalised statement about the sales history of a successful (unspecified) product into a highly specific predictive device. In fact, PLCs can be used as forecasting tools, but only when one has a considerable amount of information about the product, or one analogous to it, and the market into which the product is to be introduced. In the present context, however, the relevance of the PLC is that it is a constant reminder of the inevitability of change and does mirror the stages through which all successful products pass. These stages and the titles given to them are represented in Figure 3.1. As can be observed, the conventional PLC is seen as comprising four basic stages when sales are plotted against elapsed time from introduction. First, there is a period of very slow growth when the new product or idea is introduced to prospective users. This phase is terminated by a transition to a period of very rapid growth which eventually levels off into a period of maturity followed by a decline culminating in termination of the life cycle.

As noted, this is a conventional representation of a life cycle and must not be taken too literally, for depending upon the product type, the length of the various phases may vary considerably in just the same way as the average length of the mature phase of human beings has a strong correlation with socio-economic status. Similarly, overall life spans will vary enormously, so that fashion goods, like mayflies, are here today and gone tomorrow, while basic materials such as steel have very extended lives analogous to, say, elephants. But, given these caveats, the PLC does contain a number of important messages for us at both a strategic and a tactical level, and we shall return to these frequently in later chapters. At this juncture we merely wish to emphasise the message expressed so eloquently by Ted Levitt (1960) in his seminal article, 'Marketing Myopia', which opens with a sentence which, while tautological, is a requiem for much of UK (and US) industry today: 'Every declining industry was once a growth industry.'

As we have seen earlier, Levitt's thesis is simplicity itself: too many companies and industries are product orientated and so become preoccupied with the manufacture and distribution of a

Figure 3.1 *The product life cycle*

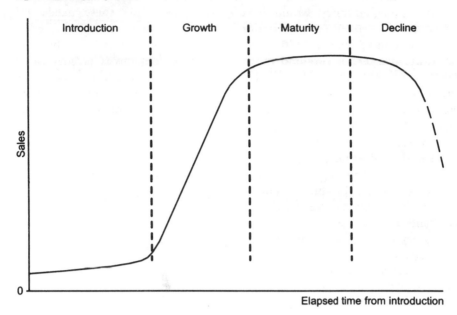

product to the extent that they lose sight of the basic need which the product satisfies. In consequence, such producers become vulnerable to attack by competitors with improved or substitute products, but their myopia usually prevents them from distinguishing this until it is too late to do anything about it. Myopia or complacency is always well to the fore in preventing the managers of declining industries from remembering the inevitable logic of the PLC: none of us is immortal. Furthermore, many entrepreneurs who rise to fame and riches through an intuitive ability to spot a market opportunity and to develop a product able to satisfy that opportunity overlooked what we have claimed is a marketing maxim: 'the act of consumption changes the consumer'. Railways opened up whole new possibilities for cheap, long-distance travel in comfort and at speed, but cars enabled travellers to plan their journeys to suit their own convenience and not be bound by the tyranny of the timetable while aeroplanes offered such enormous benefits in terms of speed that many services still largely ignore the total satisfaction of their customers.

But the seeds of self-destruction are built into every innovation. General Motors saw that once consumers had become accustomed to the basic benefits of a Model T, many of them aspired to something different and better, just as the Germans saw that economy and reliability would win a significant share of the market, only to be outperformed by the Japanese who added a high level of 'extras' as standard equipment to their own compact cars. Similarly, excess capacity in air transportation has resulted in significant changes in the competitive posture of many airlines.

Levitt's prescription for myopia is that firms think of their business in terms of the basic needs they satisfy, so that railroads, car manufacturers and airlines are all part of the 'transportation business' and thus are concerned with features such as accessibility, convenience, comfort, reliability, speed, frequency and relative cost. Of course, the railways do recognise this, and do attempt to maximise the attractiveness of their product offering within the limitations imposed by technology and their ability to generate finance for investment. It is conceivable that if they had recognised the incipient threat of the internal combustion engine, they would have diversified into an integrated transportation system and so could have shared in the part new, part substitute market for cars and buses. However, it is by no means certain that such a diversification would have proved successful. What is certain is that there is a finite demand for transportation of all kinds and that with the evolution of new forms, so the railroads were bound to mature then decline in the manner predicted by the PLC concept. Furthermore, within the industry, some products (models, brands) and the firms that make them will grow, prosper and decline so that they, too, exhibit the characteristic phases of the life cycle.

In defining product–market structures the key factor to be taken into account is the degree of differentiation recognised by suppliers in seeking to satisfy a market. At the most basic level there is the generic need of the kind described by Levitt in 'Marketing Myopia' such that 'transportation needs' could be satisfied by a myriad of different means ranging from bicycles to supersonic aeroplanes. Next, there is the industry level need in which suppliers of essentially similar products such as motor-car manufacturers or airlines are seen as competing directly with one another. However, experience shows that as soon as the industry's capacity matches or exceeds the demand for its undifferentiated output so individual firms will seek to protect their own market share by catering for a specific segment of demand and developing differentiated products which satisfy that *segment* of demand better than the undifferentiated product. (The concept of segmentation is a particularly important one in marketing and the subject of Chapter 8.)

In addition to product differentiation markets have traditionally been defined also in terms of geography. But, as we shall see in the discussion of globalisation in Chapter 22, the definition of markets on a local area basis is being rapidly eroded by advances in transportation and communication.

The discussion this far has emphasised the fundamental truth that business activity and exchange is based upon the existence of needs, and that while these needs are enduring the means of satisfying them are subject to continuous change. While the most basic of all business objectives is survival, some organisations succeed while others fail. To a large degree the explanation of this is to be found in another key concept – that of organisational culture.

■ Organisational culture

Irrespective of its stage in the firm's life cycle a major influence, if not *the* major influence upon an organisation's situation, is its culture. Two of the leading authorities on the concept of organisational culture (Deal and Kennedy, 1982) have the following to say:

> Every business – in fact every organisation – has a culture. Sometimes it is fragmented and difficult to read from the outside – some people are loyal to their bosses, others are loyal to the unions, still others care only about their colleagues who work in the sales territories of the Northeast. If you ask employees why they work, they will answer 'because we need the money'. On the other hand, sometimes the culture of an organisation is very strong and cohesive; everyone knows the goals of the corporation, and they are working for them. Whether weak or strong, culture has a powerful influence throughout an organisation; it affects practically everything, from who gets promoted and what decisions are made, to how employees dress and what sports they play. Because of this impact, we think that culture also has a major effect on the success of the business.

Deal and Kennedy's belief received strong support from research by the present author and Prof Susan Hart (1989) in *Marketing and Competitive Success*. During the 1980s there was an upsurge of interest in the nature of critical success factors following the publication of Peters and Waterman's (1982) path-breaking *In Search of Excellence: lessons from America's best run companies*. Based upon a detailed review of practices and performance in a cross-section of eminently successful American companies, the two McKinsey consultants identified eight critical success factors as follows:

1. A bias for action.
2. Close to the customer.
3. Autonomy and entrepreneurship.
4. Productivity through people.
5. Hands-on, value-driven.
6. Stick to the knitting.
7. Simple form, lean staff.
8. Simultaneous loose–tight properties.

Despite the enthusiastic reception and recognition given to Peters and Waterman's analysis and findings, many were critical of the methodology – especially its anecdotal approach, its emphasis solely upon obviously successful companies (although many were experiencing difficulties in the years immediately following the book's publication) without any reference to less-successful companies, many of which claimed to possess at least some of the desired attributes, and the absence of specific advice on how one could operationalise the recommendations for action.

To address these criticisms Baker and Hart (1989) undertook an analysis of a matched sample of both successful and less-successful firms within a cross-section of growth (sunrise) industries and declining (sunset) industries. The findings confirmed that many of the attributes of successful firms were also present in less-successful firms and so could not be used to differentiate between them. Indeed, one initially surprising result was that managers in sunset industries appeared generally to be more able than most of their counterparts in sunrise industries. On reflection it is clear that when the market is growing rapidly managerial mistakes are compensated for by buoyant demand and generous margins. Conversely in a declining market, mistakes or lack of attention to detail lead to loss of market share, pressure on margins and loss of competitive edge.

In the final analysis very few managerial practices emerged which were present in successful firms but absent in less successful firms such that one could recommend the latter to follow the example of the former (for example to invest in more marketing research). Consequently, we were driven to the conclusion that success is not so much a matter of what you do *but of how well you do it.*

In other words, culture and commitment are vital to organisational performance. However, this is not to say that professional managerial practices and procedures are unimportant, and the first step in developing successful competitive strategies must be to play to and exploit the firm's strengths while avoiding and/or improving upon its weaknesses.

The identification and listing of a firm's strengths and weaknesses comprises the internal element of the marketing audit or SWOT analysis (strengths, weaknesses (internal), opportunities and threats (external)). David W. Cravens (1988) suggests that the following information should be used to summarise the firm's strengths and weaknesses in each target market:

- Business scope and objectives; Market position;
- Market target(s) and customer base;
- Marketing programme positioning strategy;
- Financial, technical, and operating capabilities;
- Management experience and capabilities; and
- Special capabilities (for example, access to resources, patents).

Once identified and listed, the firm's strengths and weaknesses need to be related to the external environment which, as noted above, comprises the product-market, competitive and environmental situations. As we saw in the preceding chapter the external environment represents both the ultimate constraint and opportunity for the organisation's freedom of action. Further, because it is common to all competitors, those who understand it best will be able to use this knowledge as a source of competitive advantage.

Determining competitive advantage

In a major article, 'Assessing Advantage: A Framework for Diagnosing Competitive Superiority', April 1988) George S. Day and Robin Wensley (1988) observe:

> The notion that superior performance requires a business to gain and hold an advantage over competitors is central to contemporary strategic thinking. Businesses seeking advantage are exhorted to develop distinctive competences and manage for lowered delivered cost or differentiation through superior customer value.
>
> The promised pay-off is market share dominance and profitability above average for the industry.
>
> The advice is sound, but usually difficult to follow.

In the authors' view the main difficulty arises from deficiencies in available approaches to diagnosing competitive advantage which they analyse with a view to proposing a process which will ensure 'a thorough and balanced assessment of the reasons for the competitive position of a business'.

Two broad approaches to determining competitive advantage may be discerned, one based on customers and the other on competitors. Customer focused assessments best satisfy the marketing concept in that the firm seeks to define precisely the needs of specific market segments and then organise itself to satisfy a segment's needs better than any other supplier. By contrast, competitor assessment emphasises an analysis of the strategy and tactics of those firm(s) which are considered to be the major competitors for the segment or segments which the firm is seeking to dominate. Firms which emphasise competitor assessment '... watch costs closely, quickly match the marketing initiatives of competitors, and look to their sustainable edge in technology. Managers keep a close watch on market share and contracts won or lost to detect changes in competitive position'. By contrast, customer-focused firms pay relatively little attention to these criteria and emphasise the quality of customer relationships.

Experience and the available evidence indicates that firms tend to one or other of these two perspectives when what is required is a balance between them. However, as Day and Wensley point out such a balance is difficult to achieve because of the lack of any clear agreement as to just what constitutes competitive advantage. In essence Day and Wensley see competitive advantage (or distinctive competence) arising from either superior skills or superior resources which give rise to positional

Figure 3.2 *The creation and sustenance of competitive advantage*

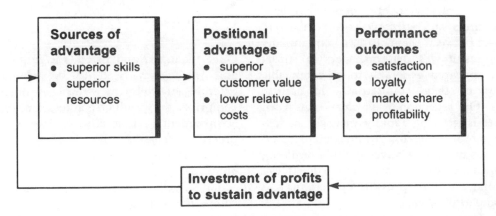

Source: G. S. Day and R. Wensley (1988), 'Assessing Advantage: A Framework for Diagnosing Competitive Superiority', *Journal of Marketing* (April).

advantages in terms of either superior customer value or lower relative costs with performance outcomes in terms of satisfaction, loyalty, market share and profitability which is then reinvested to sustain and improve the original source of advantage. These elements are summarised in Figure 3.2.

As Day and Wensley point out, analysing competitive advantage is but a means to an end – how to improve on one's performance and success. Such analysis frequently leads to the listing of so-called critical success factors – the Peters and Waterman listing of eight attributes of successful firms being a classic example (see p. 57). However, as the analysis by Baker and Hart (1989) referred to earlier revealed, critical success factors tend to be highly situation specific; that is, what works in one industry under one set of circumstances may be entirely inappropriate in another industry or under other circumstances. At best, critical success factors (CSF) of the kind listed in Table 3.1 tend to be necessary but hardly ever sufficient reasons for success and little, if anything, is usually said as to how CSF may be converted into actual advantage.

Indeed the rank ordering given in Table 3.1 really applies only to the views of the managers participating in the Baker and Hart study. Managers in other industries may have quite different views. For example, in markets such as clothing, household textiles, floor coverings and so on, most managers rank 'Design' first rather than last.

In the opening quotation from Day and Wensley, reference was made to lower delivered cost or differentiation which are two of the three core 'generic' strategies identified by Michael Porter (1980) in his seminal work *Competitive Strategy*. The third core strategy 'focus' has been rejected by critics of Porter such as Shiv Mathur of the City Business School on the grounds that 'focus' is concerned with the market scope of differentiation and cost leadership. (In passing it should be noted that Porter's analysis follows closely the much earlier distinction of core marketing strategies into undifferentiated (cost leadership), differentiated and

Table 3.1 *Critical success factors – product factors influencing competitiveness (in rank order)*

1. Performance in operation
2. Reliability
3. Sale price
4. Efficient delivery
5. Technical sophistication
6. Quality of after-sales service
7. Durability
8. Ease of use
9. Safety in use
10. Ease of maintenance
11. Parts availability and cost
12. Attractive appearance/shape
13. Flexibility and adaptability in use
14. Advertising and promotion
15. Operator comfort
16. Design

Source: M. J. Baker and S. Hart (1989), *Marketing and Competitive Success* (Philip Allan).

concentrated (focus).) Implicitly, Day and Wensley follow this view (although they appear to be singularly unaware of the UK and European literature on marketing strategy) when they stress the importance of the 'drivers' or structural determinants which convert superior skills or resources into positional advantages. Day and Wensley's analysis is more suited to an advanced rather than introductory textbook but, essentially, the point they make is that superior skills and resources are not automatically converted into competitive advantage. This transformation is accomplished by management taking strategic choices and implementing these tactically in accordance with a predetermined timetable. Success will accrue to those organisations most in tune with prevailing customer needs and the determination of these will be best achieved through a combined analysis of consumers themselves and of competitive offerings. Eleven methods of assessing advantage are discussed in detail by Day and Wensley and are summarised in Table 3.2.

Table 3.2 *Methods of assessing advantage*

Competitor-centred	*Customer-focused*

A. Assessing sources (distinctive competences)
   1. Management judgements of strengths and weaknesses
   2. Comparison of resource commitments and capabilities
   3. Marketing skills audit	

B. Indicators of positional advantage
   4. Competitive cost and activity comparisons
      (a) Value chain comparisons of relative costs
      (b) Cross-section experience curves
	5. Customer comparisons of attributes of firm versus competitors
	      (a) Choice mode
	      (b) Conjoint analysis
	      (c) Market maps

C. Identifying key success factors
   6. Comparison of winning versus losing competitors
   7. Identifying high leverage phenomena
      (a) Management estimates of market share elasticities
      (b) Drivers of activities in the value chain	

D. Measure of performance	
	8. Customer satisfaction surveys 9. Loyalty (customer franchise)
10a. Market share	
	10b. Relative share of end-user segments
11. Relative profitability (return on assets)	

Source: G. S. Day and R. Wensley (1988), 'Assessing Advantage: A Framework for Diagnosing Competitive Superiority', *Journal of Marketing* (April).

■ The marketing audit

The process of assessing advantage plays a central role in strategic marketing planning and is frequently described as a marketing audit or, particularly in texts dealing with corporate strategy as opposed to marketing strategy (the maintenance of this distinction is becoming increasingly difficult as more and more organisations adopt the marketing concept and accept that they should be market led and customer driven), a SWOT analysis. SWOT is an acronym for Strengths and Weaknesses (that is, the firm's internal status), and Opportunities and Threats which define the external environment.

Probably the most definitive statement of the nature of the marketing audit is to be found in an article by Philip Kotler, William Gregor and William Rogers (1977). According to Kotler *et al.*, 'The marketing audit as an idea dates back to the early fifties. Rupert Dallmeyer, a former executive of Booz–Allen–Hamilton, remembers conducting marketing audits as early as 1952.' As the term suggests, the practice in seen as similar in intention to the accounting audit and Kotler *et al.* offer the following definition:

A marketing audit is a *comprehensive, systematic, independent*, and *periodic* examination of a company's – or business unit's – marketing environment, objectives, strategies and activities with a view of determining problem areas and opportunities and recommending a plan of action to improve the company's marketing performance.

The author's own view is that the marketing audit should not go so far as recommending a plan of action, and prefers to regard it as an activity which will inform and guide the planning process. Indeed, a great deal of a marketing audit can be undertaken by specialist staff (just as an accounting audit is) with the final evaluation and interpretation being left to the company's operating management. The latter is an important part of successful planning.

During the 1960s and 1970s a great deal of planning activity was delegated to specially formed strategic planning departments. Despite the detail and sophistication of the plans developed by such planning units many formerly successful organisations which could afford them got into serious trouble in the late 1970s and early 1980s. In seeking to determine the reasons for their changed fortunes many of these organisations recognised that strategic planning is *the* senior management function and could not be delegated to staff specialists. Where this was done firms were ignoring the wisdom and experience of the senior management who, consequently, felt no ownership of the resulting plans and so were less committed to their implementation.

In the late 1980s and early 1990s a very similar reaction to formalised marketing departments also became apparent. As more organisations and managers accepted Drucker's (1954) definition of marketing as '...the distinguishing, the unique function of the business' and as relationship marketing displaced transactional marketing, so senior managers assumed direct responsibility for marketing and encouraged all employees to become involved with and responsible for marketing practice. The result has been a marked decline in the importance of formal marketing departments.

As stated above, a marketing audit should comprise a comprehensive, systematic and periodic review of all aspects of the organisation's internal operations and external environment. (The other criterion 'independent' is, naturally, one consultants would recommend but its value is regarded as limited unless a firm has seriously lost its way for the reasons touched on in the preceding paragraph.) The importance of the evaluation of the external environment was the subject of Chapter 2, but aspects of reviewing key elements of the firms' internal operations will be dealt with when discussing the elements of the marketing mix in greater detail in Part III.

■ The marketing mix

The concept of the marketing mix and its component elements comprises the content of Part III but, at this juncture, it will be helpful to provide a brief introduction to one of the longest established and most useful concepts in the marketing repertoire.

While the idea of a marketing mix is generally attributed to Neil Borden of the Harvard Business School he freely acknowledges that he picked up the idea from another HBS professor – James Cullinton. Like most ideas that withstand the test of time, the concept of the marketing mix is elegant in its simplicity and merely observes that the marketing manager has a limited number of ingredients at his disposal but, like a master chef, he can combine these into an almost limitless number of recipes.

Identification and listing of the ingredients of the marketing mix ranges from the very simple to the very complex. At one end of the spectrum there is Eugene McCarthy's 4 P's of Product, Price, Place and Promotion while at the other there is the much longer listing of Borden himself which is reproduced as Table 3.3.

While McCarthy's 4 P's still enjoy considerable currency most observers would agree that at the very least they need to be extended to include consideration of People, that is the most basic but probably most complex of the mix ingredients,

Table 3.3 *Elements of the marketing mix*

1. Merchandising – product planning:
    (a) Determination of product (or service to be sold – qualities, design, etc.)
         To whom, when, where and in what quantities?
    (b) Determination of new product programme – research and development, merger
    (c) Determination of marketing research programme

2. Pricing:
    (a) Determination of level of prices
    (b) Determination of psychological aspects of price, e.g. odd or even
    (c) Determination of pricing policy; e.g. one price or varying price, use of price maintenance, etc.
    (d) Determination of margins: freedom in setting?

3. Branding:
    (a) Determination of brand policy, e.g. individual brand or family brand

4. Channels of distribution:
    (a) Determination of channels to use, direct sale to user, direct sale to retailers or users' sources of purchase,
         e.g. supply houses
         Sale through wholesalers
    (b) Determination of degree of selectivity among dealers
    (c) Devising of programmes to secure channel cooperation

5. Personal selling:
    (a) Determination of burden to be placed on personal selling and methods to be employed
         (1) For manufacturer's organisation
         (2) For wholesalers
         (3) For retailers
    (b) Organisation, selection, training and guidance of sales force at various levels of distribution

6. Advertising:
    (a) Determination of appropriate burden to be placed on advertising
    (b) Determination of copy policy
    (c) Determination of mix of advertising:
             to trade
             to consumers
    (d) Determination of media

7. Promotions:
    (a) Determination of burden to place on special selling plans or devices and formulation of promotions:
         (1) to trade
         (2) to consumers

8. Packaging:
    (a) Determination of importance of packaging and formulation of packages

9. Display:
    (a) Determination of importance and devising of procedures

10. Servicing:
    (a) Determination of importance of service and devising of procedures to meet consumer needs and desires

11. Physical handling – warehousing – transportation – stock policy

12. Fact-finding and analysis – marketing research

and to acknowledge the importance of research in determining both the nature of the ingredients to be used and the most appropriate recipe.

Limited strategic alternatives

Many years before it became fashionable to draw analogies between military and business strategy the author proposed (Baker, 1975) the view that an organisation has only a limited number of basic strategies available to it. In simple terms these may be listed as:

- Peaceful co-existence or 'do nothing'.
- Direct assault or price competition.
- Indirect or flanking attack using product, place and/or promotion.
- By-pass or avoidance of competition through innovation.
- Withdrawal – a deliberate and planned decision to disengage.

(A very similar approach was popularised several years later (1981) by Kotler and Singh.) An even

simpler notion of competitive alternatives is contained in Igor Ansoff's (1968) 'Growth Vector Matrix' which is reproduced as Figure 3.3. In Ansoff's model only two dimensions are considered. 'Mission', which is equivalent to target market, and 'Technology'. Further, in the interests of simplicity, Ansoff only recognises two states – present and new – giving four basic alternatives which he describes as market penetration, market development, product development and diversification.

Given the present market and present product the organisation will only be able to grow if it can encourage its existing customers to consume more or attract customers away from other current suppliers (market penetration). As we have already seen if the firm is to win new customers then it must offer some advantage *as perceived by potential customers* which, if there is no change in the product, must be based upon price (a cost leadership strategy) or place and/or promotion (which offers differentiation). For reasons which will become clearer in later chapters most organisations avoid price competition (it reduces margins, is highly visible and may be seen as predatory by regulatory agencies) and prefer to use any cost advantage to differentiate

Figure 3.3 *Ansoff's growth vector matrix*

Product Mission	Present	New
Present	Market pentration	Product development
New	Market development	Diversification

Source: H. Igor Ansoff (1968), *Corporate Strategy* (Penguin), p. 99.

their product through other less obvious and less objective advantages such as reputation, availability, after-sales service, and so forth.

But, given that all consumers may have objective differences drawn to their notice while other, less tangible benefits of the kind listed in the previous sentence often exist largely in the subjective viewpoint of the potential purchasers and vary widely in nature (that is, the seller cannot control them in the same way as his product specification), most sellers' preferred growth strategy is product development. In the case of a product development strategy it is assumed that one already has detailed knowledge of one's customer base, and so is able to utilise this knowledge continuously to update and improve the product (or service) in order to match the increased expectation of one's own customers and offset the claims of one's competitors. (As a working rule of thumb it has been estimated that it costs five times as much to create or win a new customer as to retain an existing one.) Concentration on product development as the preferred strategy (differentiation) has resulted in an acceleration of technological change and shorter and shorter product life cycles. Despite this it is likely to remain a preferred strategy as it enables the seller to exploit his knowledge of particular customer groupings or market segments to the full.

The third strategy suggested by Ansoff's matrix is market development which assumes that the firm retains the same technology but finds new customers for it. Basically, it can do this in one of two ways. First, the firm can move into geographically new markets, that is it extends the place dimension; or, second, it can find new uses for the existing product. For example, Dow Chemicals developed what we now call shrink wrap as a packing material to protect weapons during the Second World War. With the end of the war this market was greatly reduced but Dow saw that the material had considerable potential in the domestic market and, after one or two setbacks, successfully launched it in this new market.

While new uses for existing products offer an opportunity for market development, the greater opportunity is undoubtedly that offered by extending the scope of the physical market by expanding into new areas. For the small or start-up company this may simply entail expansion into an adjacent region with no need to modify any of the elements of the marketing mix; that is, the potential customers in the new region are the same in terms of language, culture, social and economic characteristics, etc. as those in the original market. For the large or highly specialised company, however, extension of the physical market may well require it to cross national boundaries and sell to customers with different languages, customs, and so on. Such 'international marketing' is dealt with in greater detail in Chapter 21.

The final option offered by the Ansoff matrix is that of diversification, which is closely analogous to the by-pass or innovation strategy mentioned earlier. Clearly, this option carries the greatest risk for, by definition, the firm has no prior experience of either the market or the technology as is the case with all the preceding options. In many cases, indeed the great majority, innovation is introduced to the market by a new entrant as opposed to an existing player as the latter has a vested interest in protecting their current investment in the known and proven technology. That said, a characteristic of the long-established multinational corporation is its ability to recognise the inevitable implications of the product life cycle and to switch from old to new technology as the latter begins to take off in the rapidly expanding growth phase of the life cycle. (This is sometimes called 'the strategy of the fast-second' or 'imitative innovation'.)

Clearly, Ansoff's model is about as simple as one can get and, in fact, a more complex 3×3 matrix was proposed at virtually the same time, as shown in Figure 3.4. However, this simplicity is seen as a great virtue as the emphasis in this section has been upon reducing the nature of strategy formulation to the bare essentials. Once this has been done the key strategic variable(s) will be easier to identify and, as the later discussion of the mix elements will make obvious, the decision-maker will still be faced with a very wide ranging selection of tactical

Figure 3.4   *A product development matrix*

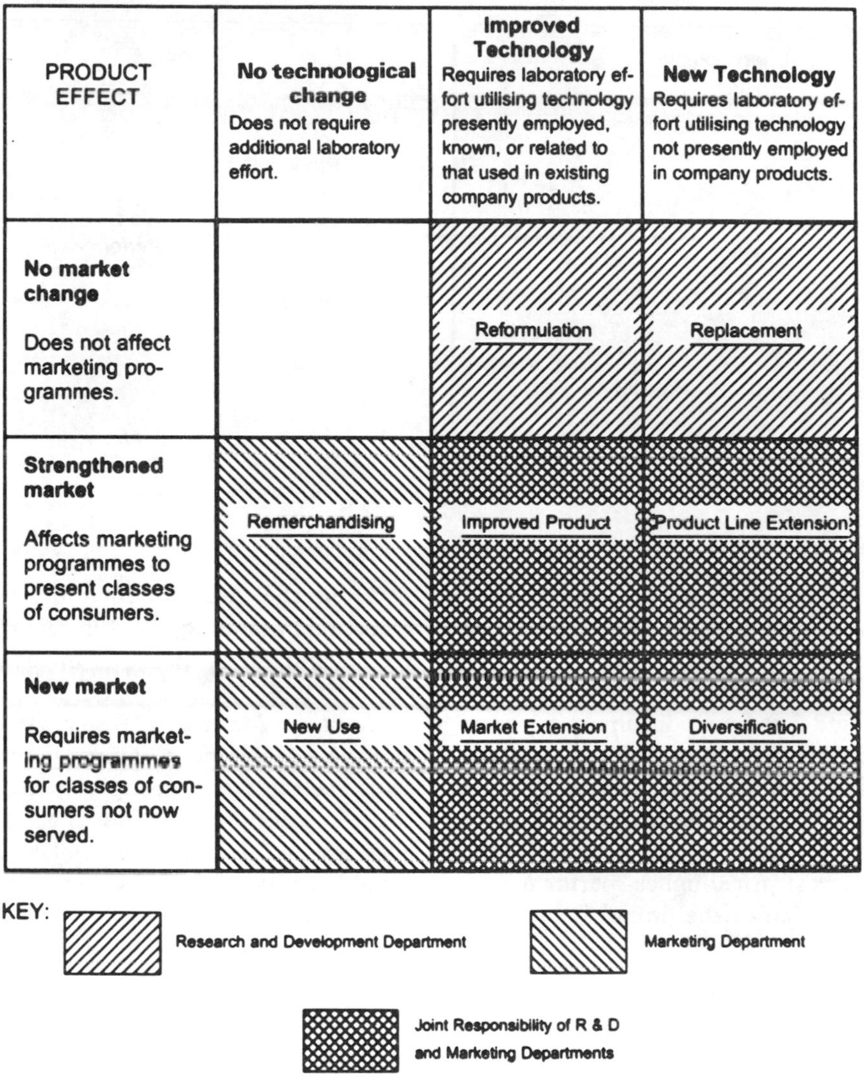

PRODUCT EFFECT	No technological change Does not require additional laboratory effort.	Improved Technology Requires laboratory effort utilising technology presently employed, known, or related to that used in existing company products.	New Technology Requires laboratory effort utilising technology not presently employed in company products.
No market change Does not affect marketing programmes.		Reformulation	Replacement
Strengthened market Affects marketing programmes to present classes of consumers.	Remerchandising	Improved Product	Product Line Extension
New market Requires marketing programmes for classes of consumers not now served.	New Use	Market Extension	Diversification

KEY:

▨ Research and Development Department   ▧ Marketing Department

▩ Joint Responsibility of R & D and Marketing Departments

Source: Samuel C. Johnson and C. Jones (1957), 'How to Organise for New Products', *Harvard Business Review*, vol. 35 (May-June).

alternatives. We will touch on this briefly in the final section on Positioning.

■ Positioning

In common with most of the other basic ideas introduced in this chapter the concept of positioning is both a simple and intuitively appealing one. In essence positioning means the achievement of a unique place in a competitive market for a particular product such that some worthwhile sub-group of consumers perceive you to be different in some meaningful and important respect from all other competitors. In order to determine the position of a product – whether one's own or a competitor's – the first step must be to establish what are the key criteria or

Figure 3.5 *Product positions in a competitive market*

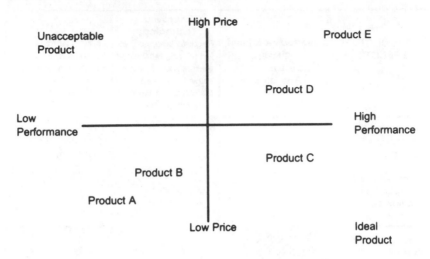

attributes which consumers use to judge performance and distinguish between the competitive offerings available to them. Once these key attributes have been defined a survey may be undertaken to find out how consumers perceive each of the different brands in terms of the relevant criteria. This information may then be plotted using pairs of dimensions such as price and performance to determine the position of the ideal product (lowest price/highest performance) and the actual position of the products surveyed as shown in Figure 3.5.

While the techniques (cluster analysis and perceptual mapping) used in this type of analysis are beyond the scope of an introductory text – a more extended description is to be found in *Research for Marketing* (Baker, 1991). Positioning and the development of brands targeted directly at pre-selected sub-groups, or market segments, is the subject of a separate chapter in *Marketing Strategy and Management* (Baker, 1992) and this should be consulted by readers interested in taking this topic further.

Summary

In this chapter we have explored some of the strategic dimensions of marketing in order to provide a framework and perspective for examining the key areas of marketing in greater detail throughout the rest of the book.

It has been argued that marketing is very much about change on the grounds that consumers in the pursuit of their self-interest will always prefer that product or service which offers them the greatest satisfaction. As producers strive to distinguish themselves one from another they will seek to capitalise on this pursuit of self-interest by defining the

particular needs of specific customer groups and seeking to satisfy them better than any of their rivals. In doing so they will tend to prefer the creation of objective differences in the physical product or service as these are more readily communicated and evaluated than are more subjective values which relate to aspects such as reputation or aesthetic qualities. Thus, every product has a *life cycle* in which new and better ways of serving basic needs continuously displace older and less satisfactory means of serving the same needs.

In order to succeed in a competitive environment great attention and effort is now given to determining what factors are critical to success. However, as our analysis shows, such *critical success factors* (CSFs) are necessary but not sufficient conditions for competitive success. In the real world what distinguishes between more and less successful firms is the quality of management and its implementation of the CSFs – something which may be seen in the *organisational culture* of a firm. It would also seem that successful firms are those which are skilled in identifying the existence of *market opportunities* and developing or exploiting those in which they enjoy a *comparative advantage vis-à-vis* their competitors. This ability to match strengths with opportunities while avoiding threats and making good weaknesses in the firm's performance is greatly enhanced by the conduct of formalised *marketing audits* or *SWOT analyses* and the articulation of clear objective.

In particular, competitive advantage arises from the manipulation of the ingredients of the *marketing mix* (product, price, place, promotion and people). Such manipulation requires first the selection of one of a very small number of *limited strategic alternatives*, most of which may be distinguished in terms of the two dimensions of *Ansoff's growth vector matrix* – mission or markets (people or demand) and technology or product (firms or supply). By definition, for competition to exist two or more suppliers will seek to serve the same market. Their success in doing so will depend very much upon the last concept introduced in this chapter – *positioning*. Positioning requires the supplier to determine the nature of the attributes which consumers use to judge the performance and satisfaction offered by different product offerings and seek to develop a unique combination which will appeal to a sufficiently large subgroup (or *segment*) of users to make the differentiation profitable to the supplier.

In sum, the selection of a successful marketing strategy depends very much upon the firm's ability to interpret the environment in which it is competing and to organise itself in such a way as to exploit those opportunities most in keeping with its own strengths and competences.

Review questions and problems

1. 'The product life cycle (PLC) concept is seriously deficient as a management tool, but continues to receive a great deal of management attention.' Why do you think this is, and how far do you consider that the PLC can play a useful part in shaping companies' new product development and launch strategies?

2. Critically evaluate the use of the Boston Consulting Group Matrix and the Ansoff Matrix in portfolio analysis.

3. What are the major headings that you would include in a situation analysis? What are their relevance to future decisions on strategy?

4. Discuss the ways in which Portfolio Planning Matrices can be of value to multi-product multi-market firms in formulating marketing strategy.

5. Assess the implications of the product life cycle (PLC) concept for strategic marketing planning.

6. Explain how knowledge of either: (a) the Boston Consulting Group Matrix or (b) the product life cycle concept might influence a firm's choice of marketing strategy.

7. 'Constraints and responsibilities severely limit the freedom of strategic action' (Ansoff, 1965). Discuss this statement in terms of the selection of marketing options open to a company seeking to grow.

8. In *Marketing Strategy and Management* it is suggested that a major implication of the product life cycle is that a firm should seek to develop more than one product so that as some lines mature and decline others are being developed to replace them. It is also suggested that as soon as a company has more than one product it becomes necessary to allocate resources between them, and an important tool for achieving this is provided in the Growth Share Matrix developed by the Boston Consulting Group. Explain, giving some typical examples, how both these concepts are important in the process of developing a firm's marketing strategy.

9. Explain the nature and importance of situation analysis as a first stage in marketing strategy.

10. The 'bottom line' of an internal appraisal of a firm's marketing system is to identify strengths and weaknesses; the environmental appraisal yields opportunities and threats.

   (a) How are strengths and weaknesses related to opportunities and threats in devising the marketing strategy for a firm.

   (b) How could you systematically search for strengths and weaknesses in a marketing strategy?

11. Discuss the ways in which a marketing manager might assess the position of a product in its life cycle.

12. Identify the components of the marketing mix and explain the importance of each in strategic planning.

13. Examine the view that the marketing planning function is central to the profitability of the organisation.

■ Supplementary reading list

Aaker, D. A. (1995) *Strategic Market Management*, 4th edn (New York: John Wiley & Sons).

Baker, Michael J. (1992) *Marketing Strategy and Management*, 2nd edn (Basingstoke: Macmillan).

Day, George S. (1984) *Strategic Market Planning: The Pursuit of Competitive Advantage* (St. Paul: West Publishing).

Day, George S. (1986) *Analysis for Strategic Market Decisions* (St. Paul: West Publishing).

Weitz, B. A. (1984) *Strategic Marketing: Planning, Implementation and Control* (New York: Kent Publishing).

□ *Articles*

Boxer, P. J. and Wensley, R. (1986) 'The Need for Middle Out Development of Marketing Strategy', *Journal of Management Studies*, vol. 23, no. 2, March, pp. 189–204.

Day, George S. and Wensley, Robin (1983) 'Marketing Theory with a Strategic Orientation', *Journal of Marketing*, vol. 47, Fall, pp. 79–89.

Jacobson, Robert and Asker, David A. (1985) 'Is Market Share All That It's Cracked Up to Be?', *Journal of Marketing*, vol. 49, Fall, pp. 11–22.

Oliver, Gordon (1986) 'Developing Marketing Strategy', in *Marketing Today* (Englewood Cliffs, N.J.: Prentice-Hall), Chapter 9.

Chapter 4

Market Structure, Conduct and Performance

Contents

Learning goals

The issues to be addressed in this chapter include:

1. The nature and definition of an industry.
2. An analysis of the factors which underlie the transformation from an agrarian to an industrial to a post-industrial society and their implications for employment and wealth creation.
3. The sources of structural change within industries.
4. The origins, nature and consequence of industrial concentration.
5. Alternative theories of competition and their implications for conduct and performance in the market place.

After reading this chapter you will be able to:

1. Explain what is meant by an 'industry'.
2. Define the terms primary, secondary and tertiary.
3. Describe the changes that have taken place in twentieth-century industrial structure.
4. Identify the causes of structural change.
5. Clarify the concept of industrial concentration.
6. Define the terms supply and demand.
7. Analyse the nature of competition and explain the effect this will have upon interactions between competitors in the market.

Introduction

A review of other major marketing text books, undertaken in preparing revisions for this edition, revealed that only one (*Mastering Marketing* by Foster and Davis), contained any significant discussion of the economic foundations on which the marketing discipline rests. Most other texts summarise the influence of economic factors within a chapter dealing with the External Environment under headings such as 'Economic and Competitive Forces'. Similarly, discussions of competition, demand and supply are generally confined to chapters dealing with pricing or, occasionally, general issues of strategy and competition.

Against this background some may question the continued inclusion of a chapter which looks at the structure of industry, theories of competition and the interaction of demand and supply at the macro level. While some of the detail contained in earlier editions has been removed, the author is firmly convinced of the importance of a chapter of this kind which provides a sound theoretical foundation for the development of our new synthetic discipline of marketing. One of the major problems which besets the social sciences is its proclivity to overlook past research and findings with the inevitable result that later generations continuously re-invent the wisdom of their forefathers. This is quite different from the physical sciences where students are grounded in the agreed knowledge base of their subject or discipline and invited to look forward to see how they may advance from this established base line. But, while students of the physical sciences only need to observe a horizon of 180° from their base line, social scientists, including business studies students, persist in ignoring the existence of a base line and so have to scrutinise a horizon of 360° – a much more difficult and time-consuming task.

While both sets of scientists inevitably criticise the other's approach and methodology, it is important to recognise that the physical scientist's establishment of an agreed base line is not the same as agreeing that the wisdom of the past is not subject to revision or even replacement. Indeed, the whole history of science is one of discovery leading to revision or rejection of previously accepted 'facts'. The point is, if you don't have a point of departure it is difficult to measure your progress – a principle which underlies all strategic planning. Similarly, it is important to recognise that in every field of inquiry we need at least a null hypothesis about the existing state of affairs as a basis for comparisons with reality established through inquiry and research.

Whether marketers like it or not their discipline is centrally concerned with the solution of economic problems in a social and behavioural context. As Chung and Heeler (1995) in the *Companion Encyclopedia* observe:

> The German Historical School of Economics provides much of the philosophical foundation of the discipline of Marketing. Both Harvard and the University of Wisconsin, considered two of the original centres of influence in the development of marketing thought in the USA, built their marketing departments around German trained economists (Jones and Monieson, 1990). This so-called Historical School was concerned with solving real economic problems and its 'practitioner' perspective still exerts major influence on Marketing scholarship today.   (Chung and Heeler, in Baker, 1995, p. 47)

It has also been claimed (Bartels, 1988) that 'economic theory has provided more concepts for the development of marketing thought than has any other social discipline.' It follows that one should give at least some consideration to the discipline of economics in establishing a base line for marketing.

In the first chapter we looked briefly at the stages of economic development which led to the emergence of advanced economies with the potential of creating an excess supply of goods and services. To cope with this change in the traditional balance between supply and demand a new approach to resource allocation became necessary and we termed this the marketing concept because of its emphasis upon the market (demand) as the primary basis for investment and production (supply) decisions.

Of course the marketing concept is not new, for producers have always sought to identify those goods in strongest demand and then set out to supply them. However, under conditions of chronic supply deficiency it requires little expertise or sophistication to identify beforehand the most salient demands. Successful entrepreneurs have always been those who have intuitively identified such unsatisfied demands. But in complex, modern markets this is rarely possible without a sound understanding of market structure and market forces and it is these factors which comprise the subject-matter of Part II.

In this chapter we look first at the structure of industry before examining the phenomenon of concentration in some detail. Attention is then turned to theories of competition and the interaction of supply and demand at the macro level, and this is followed by a discussion of competition and market structure. Chapter 5 then explores micro aspects of supply and demand in more detail.

Students of economics may well be familiar with the content of this chapter while others may consider it peripheral to a marketing textbook (a view that has been put to me often!). My own view, and the reason for the chapter's inclusion, is that marketing is all about securing competitive advantage and that competition occurs within markets served by firms which belong to particular industries. As has been argued in the previous two chapters, it follows that the practice of marketing at the level of the individual firm is determined largely by external factors within which the firm has to operate. A knowledge of the structure of markets and competitive behaviour is thus essential to the identification of market opportunity, the development of effective marketing strategies and their efficient and profitable execution. This view has prevailed since the third edition appeared in 1979, and has been greatly reinforced by the fact that industry analysis of the kind advocated here has been central to the highly influential writings of Michael Porter of the Harvard Business School (*Competitive Strategy: Techniques for Analysing Industries and Competitors*, 1989; *Competitive Advantage*, 1985; and *The Comparative Advantage of Nations*, 1990).

Without in any way wishing to detract from Michael Porter's seminal contribution to competitive analysis and strategic planning at both the national and firm level, he would be the first to acknowledge that his insights developed from his study of the field known as Industrial Economics at Harvard College. It is against this background that this chapter has been developed.

■ The structure of industry

Any discussion of the role of industry should start with some definition of what we understand by the term. In everyday usage we are accustomed to refer to industries such as the textile industry, the motor industry or the chemical industry without specifying the basis on which a given firm may be judged to be a member of a particular industry. Essentially, individual firms are categorised as belonging to particular industries by virtue of the nature of their output. Thus most definitions of an industry tend to rest upon the existence of competition between sellers of similar products. However, as we shall see, changes in the nature of industrial organisation have resulted in many firms becoming members of more than one industry. Similarly, changes in a firm's product mix may well lead to a change in its basic industrial classification. We return to some of these distinctions below but first we must consider a more fundamental distinction between types of industry.

Conventionally all industry is divided into three major groupings, which are frequently referred to as the primary, secondary and tertiary sectors. Primary industry is concerned with the production of raw materials and includes agriculture, forestry and fishing. Secondary industry includes mining and quarrying and incorporates all those firms concerned with changing the nature and form of raw materials through some form of manufacturing process to the point where they are suitable for consumption either by other industrial users or by ultimate consumers. Finally, the tertiary sector embodies all those organisations which provide services, such as wholesaling, retailing, transportation, banking, entertainment, tourism, and so on.

In the twentieth century, considerable changes have taken place in the relative importance and size of these three sectors. As can be seen from Table 4.1 employment in the primary sector fell from 8.14 per cent in 1911 to 1.41 per cent in 1988. In fact this downward trend has persisted since the industrial revolution and was apparent even before that. At the time of the industrial revolution alternative employment opportunities in manufacturing industry encouraged a migration from the rural areas to the new factory towns and allowed farmers to substitute capital for labour through the employment of more efficient

Table 4.1 *Industrial analysis of occupied population of the United Kingdom, 1911–88 (per 10000 occupied persons)*

Industry	1911	1951	1973	1982	1988
Service industries	4541	4556	5433	6299	15168
Agriculture, forestry and fishing	814	507	191	168	313
Energy and water supply	64	106	152	162	487
Other mineral and ore extraction	712	382	160	154	687
Manufacturing	3351	3760	3455	2727	4528
Construction	518	635	609	492	1043
Total occupied population	18351	22610	22662	21090	22226

Source: *Annual Abstract of Statistics*, various dates.

farming methods. This trend has continued to the present day with the result that mechanisation, advances in plant and animal breeding, and the development of chemical aids have enabled the primary sector to register a significant improvement in output despite a continually declining workforce.

As can be seen from Table 4.1, there has been a decline in numbers employed in the primary and secondary sectors. This has been balanced to some extent by the significant increase in numbers in the tertiary sector.

However, the numbers employed in an industry are only one measure of the level of activity. An equally, if not more significant measure is output, and comparative statistics are given in Table 4.2.

Data such as those presented in Tables 4.1 and 4.2 clearly indicate the marked changes which have taken place in industrial structure within a decade. Before examining some of the causes which would seem to account for this change it is important to stress that precise comparisons are difficult due to changes in the definition of industries and in the manner in which data have been collected. It is also important to emphasise that broad categories such as those in the two tables disguise marked changes within the categories themselves. Thus in the engineering industry motor-cars and aircraft have come into existence and exhibited marked growth while more traditional industries such as railway locomotives and shipbuilding have exhibited a

decline. Similarly, in the textile industry a chemical revolution has led to the substitution of synthetic fibres for their natural counterparts.

More than anything else, change in industrial structure in the twentieth century reflects the application of technology which has led to extensive modification of the traditional craft industries and the birth of completely new industries such as electronics and aviation. The impact of this technological revolution is implicit in the disproportionate increase in productivity *vis-à-vis* employment and other factor inputs. However, technological discovery and advance are only a partial explanation of the radical changes which have taken place during this century.

 Causes of structural change

As noted in the preceding section, changes in industrial structure are not an invention of the twentieth century and are to be discerned from the industrial revolution onwards. As a very broad generalisation it would seem that the catalyst for change has been on the supply side, but that ultimately the nature and extent of change has been determined by demand. In simple terms the industrial revolution was the joint outcome of a mechanical and an organisational revolution. The mechanical revolution is

Table 4.2 *Industrial and sector analysis. Gross domestic product by industry 1979–89 (£m)*

	1979	1980	1981	1982	1983	1984	1985	1986	1987	1988	1989
Agriculture, forestry and fishing	3 690	4 197	4 767	5 406	5 214	6 265	5 553	6 026	6 123	5 984	6 561
Energy and water supply	13 864	19 390	23 496	26 104	30 085	29 750	32 659	23 945	24 415	22 394	22 619
Manufacturing	48 835	53 095	54 212	58 729	61 401	66 446	72 615	77 831	82 579	91 196	97 380
Construction	10 637	12 225	13 009	14 076	15 711	16 928	17 748	20 127	23 051	26 953	30 274
Distribution, hotel and catering; repairs	22 855	25 779	27 274	30 135	33 230	36 188	40 497	44 827	48 937	56 561	62 133
Transport and communication	13 210	14 344	15 908	17 201	18 285	19 846	21 243	23 025	24 830	27 614	30 074
Banking, finance, insurance, business services and leasing	20 001	24 355	26 038	29 623	35 553	39 080	46 518	54 209	62 239	74 378	86 628
Ownership of dwellings	10 306	12 147	13 895	15 044	15 945	16 732	17 960	19 583	21 104	23 331	25 482
Public administration, national defence and compulsory social security	11 439	14 518	16 249	17 371	18 821	20 167	21 409	23 019	24 934	27 504	29 571
Education and health service	14 146	18 022	20 616	21 235	23 380	24 649	26 570	29 996	33 237	37 606	42 547
Other services	9 227	10 682	12 004	13 332	15 107	16 557	18 401	20 748	23 250	26 226	29 715

Source: CSO, *UK National Accounts, 1990.*

generally attributed to the harnessing of steam-power, which led to an organisational revolution in the setting up of a factory system to replace the cottage industry which had preceded it. The enormous increase in output which accompanied these changes led to a marked improvement in living standards and set in train widespread changes in demand.

It is difficult to generalise about changes in demand as these arise from a number of different yet inter-related causes. The trend towards greater social equality has led to enormous improvements in education as well as to a redistribution of income and it is clear that both education and income have marked effects upon consumption patterns. In turn the move to greater social equality has had a major impact on the supply side of the economy. In the UK since the end of the Second World War in 1945 we have seen the State take control of many industries and the provision of services such as Healthcare, Gas, Electricity, Water, etc. etc. During the 1980s, under Margaret Thatcher, a Conservative government set about returning many of these industries to private ownershuip. In 1995, the Labour Party under Tony Blair revised Clause 4 in its Constitution concerning public ownership of industry in recognition that public opinion tended to prefer private to public ownership.

At the same time industry has not been slow to realise the opportunity which is implicit in increased personal disposable incomes. As personal incomes increase the proportion expended upon purchases essential to life diminishes, and even allowing for increased saving the individual is able to increase his consumption. The latent demand represented by unexpended personal incomes is one of the major spurs to new-product development whereby manufacturers compete to translate this latent demand into an effective demand for their own output. In their efforts to communicate the availability of their new and improved products the manufacturer is aided by the evolution and growth of new channels of communication.

Demographic changes, too, have their impact upon demand. With an increased life expectation Britain now has an ageing population with a concomitant increase in the demand for products suited to the older age groups, for increased medical services, and so on.

Further changes in the structure of industry can be attributed to the impact of foreign competition. Until the middle of the nineteenth century Britain had few competitors for manufactured goods. However, since that time many other nations have industrialised and our dependency on imported food and raw materials has required that we open our markets to these foreign manufacturers. Certainly the decline of the traditional textile industries owes much to highly competitive imported textiles from countries with lower labour costs than our own.

Collectively all these changes in demand have resulted in a corresponding change in industrial structure. Some firms will decline and disappear while others will adjust to the changed environment within which they operate and continue their existence. Similarly, new technology will spawn new firms and new industries.

In his book *The Structure of Industry in Britain*, G. C. Allen (1970) advances six reasons to explain how firms are persuaded to take up new lines of manufacture, namely:

> the movement may occur as a by-product of efforts to solve some problems of production and distribution, or as the result of growth which leads to plant imbalance, or as the consequence of some technical discovery which may have a wider application than the original context, or simply because firms see enlarged opportunities in pressing their existing marketing organisation into new uses. The spreading of risk may provide the motive, or the pressure of adversity may impel firms to try new fields as their only chance of survival as substantial producers.

The phraseology used by Allen tends to suggest, albeit unintentionally, that firms only embark upon some new form of activity by chance or because they are driven to it. As will become clearer later, in dealing with product policy firms tend to adopt a more purposive attitude than that implied in the above extract.

Without dwelling on the causes of industrial change, many of which are dealt with in greater detail hereafter, it is appropriate here to examine an apparent consequence of central interest to any discussion on industrial structure, namely the degree of industrial concentration.

■ Industrial concentration

In addition to the changes that have taken place between and within industries in terms of their overall size measured by numbers employed or value of their output, there have also been marked changes in the nature of the firms which comprise these industries. A frequently remarked trend has been what J. K. Galbraith (1974) in *The New Industrial State* has termed the rise of the 'super corporation'. In simple terms Galbraith's argument is that an increasing proportion of all output is being concentrated in the hands of a limited number of producers. By virtue of the control which these super corporations exercise over supplies of essential goods and services it is implied that the super corporation may exercise undue influence over the operation of the state. More explicitly it is maintained that supply dominance of this kind eliminates competition to the detriment of the average consumer.

Not all students of industry subscribe to the Galbraithian view, and maintain that the emergence of a limited number of very large firms does not necessarily imply the elimination of competition in the market place. Clearly, if one is to determine the relative merits of the opposing arguments, some form of measure is required which enables us to make a comparative industry analysis over time. A convenient and widely used measure is the *concentration ratio*.

In fact economists have two concepts of concentration. At the macro, or national level, the concept of concentration is used to define the proportion of total industry output accounted for by some predetermined percentage of all firms. At the micro or industry level the concentration ratio expresses the percentage share of total sales of that industry accounted for by a predetermined percentage of all firms in the industry. It will be noted that both descriptions of concentration

ratios state that they are computed by calculating the proportion of all output accounted for by a predetermined number of firms, and it should be noted that there is no universally agreed convention to state what this number should be. Accordingly, when one is interpreting concentration ratios it is most important to ascertain the basis of the computation. In the United Kingdom the most widely used concentration ratios are based on the proportion of all sales in a given product group accounted for by the five largest firms.

As indicated earlier, there is disagreement between economists as to the degree of concentration in UK manufacturing industry and to the extent of change in such concentration over time. Writing in 1969, Allen (in the book referred to earlier) took the view that while the available evidence was fragmentary, such calculations as had been attempted seemed to indicate a stabilisation and possibly a slight decline in the overall concentration in industry since 1930. Further, an examination of the identity of the largest companies shows marked changes in this period, reflecting the changing fortunes of the different industries, with the emergence of new areas of activity such as electronics.

The calculation of concentration ratios in the UK is made difficult by the quality of the data. For example, in 1974 David Elliot ('Concentration in UK Manufacturing Industry'), explained that his data was incomplete because:

(a) The Business Statistics Office is bound by disclosure rules and does not publish product groups where individual firms may be identified.
(b) Product groups where sales are less than £10 million were not generally shown.
(c) No product groups had been selected covering work-done activities.
(d) Products that could not be identified as being homogeneous were omitted.

Despite these deficiencies Elliot's analysis contradicted Allen's and showed an increase in concentration. This increase was attributable to two major causes. First, certain firms like IBM and Xerox grew disproportionately in the 1960s

Figure 4.1   *Trends in concentration in UK manufacturing, 1980–89*

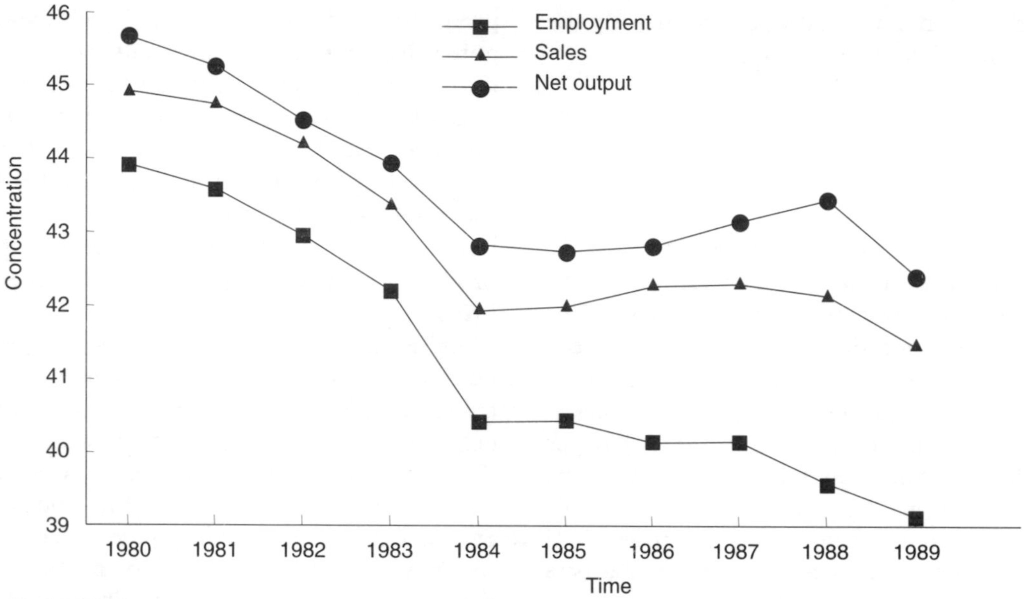

Source: Clarke (1993).

and early 1970s due to the superior nature of their products and management. Second, considerable growth was attributable to merger and acquisitions.

A more recent analysis by Roger Clarke (1993) shows that during the 1970s concentration was relatively stable or declining despite high levels of merger activity. During the 1980s, however, concentration fell markedly as can be seen from Figure 4.1 taken from Clarke.

Clarke also expresses reservations about his data but feels the general trend is clear. He observes: 'Part of the fall in concentration was due to the continuing growth in foreign trade and its effects were similar to those found in the 1970s. In addition to this, however, substantial falls in domestic concentration were also observed. These could reflect the effects of government "supply-side" policies in the 1980s or they may be associated with technological changes (for example, in electronic engineering) tending to favour smaller firms' (pp. 13–16). Other explanations are firms moving production offshore and downsizing their operations.

Historically, such changes in industry structure have been accompanied by significant changes in competition and performance but research is lacking to document this. This lack of research implies a lack of interest in the subject which is confirmed by Michael Waterson (1993) in 'Are Industrial Economists Still Interested in Concentration?' A major reason for this is the shift in emphasis from structure to conduct or behaviour. Waterson's view is that concentration is still a 'big question' in industrial economics and deserves more attention. We concur with this view. Firm size and market share are subject to close scrutiny and regulation in most countries, as indeed they are in the European Union as a whole, a fact reflected in mergers and acquisition policy.

Concentration and organisational structure

The development of the large business organisation is closely associated with the growth of

Improved communications, and in the case of the United States, where most research has been undertaken, with the development of the railroad in particular. Improvements in communications extend the firm's ability both to obtain supplies of factor inputs and especially raw materials while simultaneously expanding the market for its output. In the early stage of their evolution most large firms concentrated their efforts upon a single product line or functional activity. Similarly, in the early stages of their development the managers of the more successful firms, who are also usually the owners, focus their attention upon expanding though a process of horizontal integration by means of acquisition and merger with other organisations in direct competition with them. Once a firm has attained a certain degree of dominance over one phase in the productive/distributive process the benefits of vertical integration become increasingly attractive. Thus a firm which has become dominant in the extraction or production of a basic raw material may integrate forward into the processing of that raw material into a finished product. Conversely, a manufacturing concern may decide to integrate backwards into primary production in order to achieve control over essential factor inputs. Similarly, firms engaged in primary or secondary industries may perceive advantages through integrating forward into the tertiary sector and achieving control of the distributive function. Clearly, dominant retail and wholesaling organisations may see similar advantages to be gained through integrating backwards into manufacturing and primary production.

With increasing size there developed a need for a more specialised organisational structure and for the delegation of authority and responsibility to subordinates. In the early stages of their development most large corporations adopted a functional form of organisation with professional managers appointed to head each of the various functions, for example finance, production, sales, and so on.

With the transfer of control from owner-entrepreneurs to professional managers it is possible to discern a change in the primary goal of the firm. Thus, while owner-entrepreneurs tend to pursue a primary objective of profit maximisation, professional managers tend to emphasise survival and a satisfactory level of earnings, to be achieved through sales maximisation rather than profit maximisation.

However, as noted earlier when discussing the six causes of change cited by Allen, this view is essentially a negative one. While it is true that most firms adapt themselves to their environment and react to changes in their market, the really dominant firms in any industry appear to have adopted a more positive approach. In A. C. Chandler's (1966) classic study *Strategy and Structure*, two alternative strategies to integration were identified. In essence these two alternative strategies are growth through geographical expansion, and diversification. However, as firms pursued either or both of these alternatives it soon became apparent that the traditional functional form of organisation was inappropriate for multi-product firms operating in a number of different markets. Thus in the 1920s Dupont and General Motors began to develop a divisional structure which has now become the dominant form of organisation.

It is not proposed to dwell on such issues here but it is important to point out that since the 1920s there has been an increasing trend towards diversification. As a result of this diversification many of the larger firms operate in several different industries and one must not assume automatically that the very large firms are necessarily dominant in all markets in which they compete.

Interest in the degree of concentration in industry arises largely because of the light which it throws upon market structure and, as Richard Caves (1972) notes, 'market structure is important because the structure determines the behaviour of firms in the industry, and that behaviour in turn determines the quality of the industry's performance'. However, as Caves points out, concentration is but one element of market structure, other main elements of which are product differentiation, barriers to the entry of new firms, the growth rate of market demands, the elasticity of market demand, and the ratio of fixed to variable costs in the short run. Collectively all these determine the nature of competition in the market place and it is to this that we now turn our attention.

■ Theories of competition

Current thinking about competition, like many other economic concepts, owes much to the original contribution of Adam Smith, whose *Wealth of Nations* was first published in 1776. As J. M. Clark (1961) points out, Smith lays the foundation of this thought by defining two competition states – full and free competition, and complete monopoly – and, in a loose fashion, the contrasting outcomes to be expected of each of these states.

Clark offers a useful summary of the evolution of economic thinking about competition from Smith's original and sometimes rather vague specification through to the contributions of Ricardo, Cournot and Marshall, in the course of which he points out how theory has changed to reflect reality. At the time when Smith first proposed the two basic competitive states, monopoly was essentially a local phenomenon which was to be eroded during the nineteenth century with the development of more efficient lines of communication and transportation, while perfect competition mirrored the bargaining power of people engaged in cottage industries such as weaving. Similarly, as we have noted earlier, agriculture was a much more dominant form of economic activity in terms of employment and the markets in agricultural commodities have traditionally approached most nearly to the model of perfect competition.

Just as the impact of the industrial revolution was to lead to improvements in communication and transportation which diminished local monopolies, so the growth of manufacturing industry diminished the importance of agriculture and led to attention being focused upon intermediate competitive states distinguished as being 'imperfect'.

During the nineteenth century the major emphasis of economic activity was upon supply creation or output and its effect upon price. Together these were seen as the crucial competitive variables. In Clark's view it was the addition of the chemical revolution to the preceding mechanical and electrical revolutions which was to give rise to product proliferation and lead to a situation in which 'automatically, the differentiated product has become an economic variable at least as important as price, along with the methods of selling efforts and demand creation that necessarily go with product differentiation'.

The addition of product and selling efforts as variables alongside the traditional inputs of price and output demanded a radical restructuring of the economist's original model, and gave rise to the theories of imperfect competition formulated by Edward Chamberlin (1933) and Joan Robinson (1933).

Thus we now recognise that between the polar extremes of monopoly and perfect competition there exists an almost infinite variety of states of imperfect competition. For purposes of analysis, understanding and prediction it is important that one should be able to distinguish how certain basic elements influence the development of a particular competitive state. It is also important that one should be able to identify the salient facets of each of these states. To this end we are here concerned primarily with the three basic elements of an economic system – supply, demand, and the market – and their interaction, that is the state of competition.

Our discussion of supply will concentrate first upon those organisations responsible for its creation, and will then examine the nature of their output. This consideration will be followed by a summary of some of the more salient factors which go together to make up and influence demand. Next we examine the nature of the mechanism through which supply and demand are brought together – the market – and finally we review the basic competitive states to establish the emergence of product differentiation as a major competitive strategy.

■ Supply: firm and product

Although we deliberately referred to 'organisations' in the previous paragraph, thereby implicitly recognising that there are several distinct types of formal association which might be responsible for supply creation, our main concern here is with the form of business organisation which we call the firm.

In economic theory certain simplifying assumptions are made about the firm. It is assumed that a single person, the entrepreneur, is the owner of the individual firm and that he behaves rationally in that his prime objective is to maximise money profits. Further, it is assumed that entrepreneurs will always minimise costs and that the price of all factor inputs are known and fixed and that each firm produces only one product. Now, no sane economist really believes in these assumptions. He merely adopts them in order to simplify his analysis in order to develop explanations of the ways firms will behave given these conditions. In other words the economist is attempting to develop a benchmark model so that he can then determine how relaxation of the simplifying assumptions might affect real-world behaviour. Unfortunately many students who have only taken an introductory course in economics never proceed to the stage when real-world considerations are introduced into the model. Accordingly such students find it very difficult to relate observed reality, implicit in the earlier discussion concerning changes in firm structure and organisation, and the simplistic descriptions contained in introductory economic texts.

We have already noted that few, if any, firms regard profit maximisation as their primary goal. The reasons why the unbridled pursuit of profit should not be the sole objective of management is apparent in the role of profit itself. Profit is generally regarded as the reward for the assumption of risk and on the whole it is accepted that the greater the risk, the greater should be the reward. It is also accepted that risk is usually measured in terms of the likelihood of loss. Accordingly professional management tends to try and balance its activities in such a manner so as not to put the whole corporation at risk. Clearly by doing so it forgoes the possibility of maximising profits. It also avoids the possibility of maximising losses!

One area where the firm does make a conscious decision is in terms of its product mix. Fundamentally there is a basic conflict between the relative merits of specialisation and the attractions of diversification. If one pursues a policy of specialisation, one should be able to benefit from the economies of scale in purchasing and production and so reduce costs to the minimum. At the same time it is clear that any diminution of demand for the single-product firm will result in an immediate loss in earnings and, if continued, this could result in the firm operating at a loss.

Diversification offers a firm the opportunity to spread the risk associated with fluctuation in demand for a particular product. At the same time diversification usually requires a firm to duplicate many of the basic business functions, especially in production and marketing, and so increases its cost base. It is clear that if the firm is not operating on a basis of minimum cost, then it will be able to earn less profits than firms which have chosen to specialise in the production of a single product – at least in the short term.

Just as economists make simplifying assumptions about the firm, so too they make simplifying assumptions about the firm's output – its product. The basic assumption which is made is that the output of different firms competing in the same market are viewed as homogeneous by potential consumers. Given this assumption, together with that of a single price, it is clear that users have no rational basis for differentiating between different suppliers of the same product. Accordingly decisions by a consumer to buy a product are perceived as decisions between different categories of products rather than choices between similar products produced by different firms. Thus elementary economic theory proposes that, given a finite disposable income, the consumer will adjust his purchases of different product categories in order to maximise his overall satisfaction. In the sense that all products which the consumer might consider purchasing are competing with one another, they are to some degree substitutes for one another.

However, this concept of substitution is too crude to explain the nature of competition between companies like Lever Brothers and Procter & Gamble in the detergent market, Ford and General Motors in the motor-car market, Hoover, Electrolux and Goblin in the vacuum-cleaner market, and so on. For this purpose we need a clearer definition of possible degrees of difference between products. That proposed by J. M. Clark (1961) provides a useful basic distinction.

Essentially Clark proposes three categories of products. 'First there are those which satisfy the same principal want, and in which the producer is free to imitate others as closely as he wishes, using techniques that are not radically different from theirs and differentiating his product only to the extent that it seems advantageous to him to do so, in order to appeal to some subsidiary want more effectively than other variants do, and thus fit into a gap in the array of variant products'. Clark terms this first category 'differentiated competition' and it is clear that different brands of detergent, motor-car and vacuum-cleaner fall into this category.

Clark's second category, which he terms 'substitution', is defined as including 'products that appeal to the same principal want but which are inherently and inescapably different, due either to different materials or basically different techniques'. Into this category, perhaps, we might put the use of a laundry service in place of the purchase of detergents for home washing; the use of public transport or perhaps bicycle or motor-bicycle in place of a motor-car; or a manual carpet-sweeper, or even a brush, in place of an electric vacuum-cleaner. Clearly in all these instances the substitute product is competing directly with that for which it is a substitute, and seeks to satisfy the same basic want.

In Clark's words 'the third category embraces products that serve independent wants and are substitutes only in the mathematic sense that spending more for one leaves less to spend on others'. We return to issues of product differentiation later in this book. Having briefly considered the supply side of the economic equation, it is now necessary to review some basic concepts of demand.

■ Demand

By and large, economists tend to be concerned only with what they term *effective* demand, which is defined as demand backed up by purchasing power. However, most managers are also interested in two other types of demand – which we may describe as 'potential' demand and 'latent' demand.

A latent demand may be thought of as one which the consumer is unable to satisfy, usually for lack of purchasing power. For example, many housewives may have a latent demand for automatic dishwashers, but, related to their available disposable income, this want is less strong than their demand for other products and so remains unsatisfied. In other words wants are ranked in order of preference and satisfied to the point where disposable income is exhausted. From the manufacturer's point of view, the problem is to translate latent demand into effective demand by increasing the consumer's preference for his particular product *vis-à-vis* all other product offerings.

Latent demand may also be thought of as a vague want in the sense that the consumer feels a need for a product, or service, to fill a particular function but is unable to locate anything suitable. It is clear that latent demand constitutes an important consideration in management planning. In the case of a demand which is latent due to lack of purchasing power a manufacturer may be able to change a consumer's preference through his marketing and promotional activities. Alternatively, if there is a trend towards increasing disposable income, then the producer may be able to project how such increases in purchasing power will enable consumers to translate their latent demand into an effective demand. Given such a forecast he will be able to plan increased production, distribution and sales to keep pace with rising disposable incomes.

In the case of a demand which is latent because the consumer is unaware of the existence of a product or service which would satisfy his ill-defined want, then clearly if the manufacturer produces a product which he feels should satisfy the need, he will wish to bring it to the attention of those with a latent demand for it. Alternatively, if a manufacturer does not produce a product which should satisfy a known latent demand but is able to specify what the characteristics of such a product would be, then the latent demand becomes a marketing opportunity which he may wish to exploit.

Potential demand may be said to exist where a consumer possesses purchasing power but is not currently buying. Thus, where a marketer has identified a latent demand and developed a new product to satisfy it, the potential demand consists of all those who can back up their latent want with purchasing power. In another context potential demand may be thought of as that part of the total market or effective demand for an existing product which a firm might anticipate securing through the introduction of a new competitive product.

Once again it must be stressed that while the economists' model serves a useful purpose as a basis for analysing the real world, the assumptions upon which it rests are clearly unrealistic. Thus elementary economic texts usually make assumptions about consumer demand as follows:

1. The consumer's wants remain unchanged throughout.
2. S/he has a fixed amount of money available.
3. S/he is one of many buyers.
4. S/he knows the price of all goods, each of which is homogeneous.
5. S/he can, if s/he wishes, spend their money in very small amounts.
6. S/he acts rationally.

Of these assumptions only 2 and 3 seem likely to be true with any frequency in the real world. For the rest, as managers are only too aware, consumer demand is fickle and changes frequently. Knowledge of the existence of all those goods which the consumer might buy, let alone their prices, seems unlikely. Further, goods are not infinitely divisible and consumers have to pay the price asked for a product, whether it be 10p for a box of matches or £250 for a colour television set. While these differences between the model and the real world are fairly obvious, this is not always true with respect to the correct interpretation of what constitutes rational behaviour.

While the economist talks about rationality in terms of consumers maximising their satisfaction,

satisfaction is usually defined in terms of solely objective criteria. Using such an interpretation the price–quantity relationship assumes a distorted level of importance and excludes any concept of subjective satisfaction. That consumers do gain subjective satisfaction is apparent from the existence of brand preference for largely undifferentiated physical products, such as flour, baked beans, detergents and so on. In fact the creation of subjective differentials in the mind of consumers may be just as important in differentiating a product as the development of real physical differences.

Because consumers take cognisance of subjective values this is not to say that they are behaving irrationally, for clearly it would be irrational to ignore such subjective preferences. It is just because consumers do have different preferences and perceptions that producers have found it necessary to develop differentiated products and sophisticated marketing techniques.

If one traces the development of management thought during this century, one can distinguish three main phases. First, there was a production orientation which mirrored a condition which dates back from before recorded history – namely an excess of demand over available supply. However, because of the technological revolution of the eighteenth, nineteenth and twentieth centuries a position was reached by the 1920s where the advanced economies of the Western world were producing more basic goods than they were able to consume or sell elsewhere.

Faced with a situation in which one is producing more than the market is absorbing the immediate reaction is to try and stimulate consumption further. Such efforts gave rise to the second major managerial orientation, which has been termed the 'sales management orientation'. While it is understandable that producers should increase their efforts to sell what they can currently make, it is also clear that this can be but a short-term remedy if there is a basic imbalance between supply and demand. This in fact was the case with the industrialised economies of the West, but the full implications of such a situation were deferred owing to the outbreak of the Second World War. On the conclusion of the war there was a backlog of unsatisfied consumer demand, with the result that most producers found themselves in a sellers' market until the early 1950s. At this time excess supply once again began to develop and producers began to look for a new managerial philosophy to enable them to earn a satisfactory return on the resources under their control.

The philosophy which emerged and which was to give rise to the third major 'managerial orientation' was that of marketing. As we have seen, in its simplest terms the marketing philosophy postulates that supply is a function of demand and therefore must be subservient to it. To this end producers set out to measure the nature of demand in terms of both objective and subjective influences on consumer buying behaviour.

Competition and market structure

In essence the nature of competition and of market structure is the outcome of the interaction between supply and demand. As indicated above, it is normal to define two limiting conditions – monopoly and pure competition – and to categorise intermediate forms of competition as 'imperfect'. What, then, are the salient characteristics of these states? Before addressing this issue it is necessary to introduce the concept of *demand elasticity*, for it is this factor which is usually used as the basic indicator of the nature of competition.

Under normal conditions most people anticipate that an increase in the price of a good will result in a decline in the amount demanded, while conversely any fall in price should be accompanied by an increase in the quantity demanded. In simple terms elasticity is a measure of the degree to which a change in price will result in a change in demand. Where a very small change in price is accompanied by a major change in demand, we say that that product has a high elasticity of demand.

Conversely, even where significant price changes have only a limited impact upon the quantity demanded, we say that that product has a low elasticity of demand. Thus in order to determine the elasticity of demand for the given good we need to measure the magnitude of changes in the quantity demanded in relation to changes in the unit price. Such information is termed a demand schedule, and is frequently represented graphically as in Figure 4.2, from which it can be seen that infinitely elastic demand is represented by a horizontal line, infinitely inelastic demand by a vertical line, while varying degrees of elasticity are represented by the angle assumed by the demand curve.

In terms of basic competitive states demand under pure competition is usually represented as

Figure 4.2   *Demand curve*

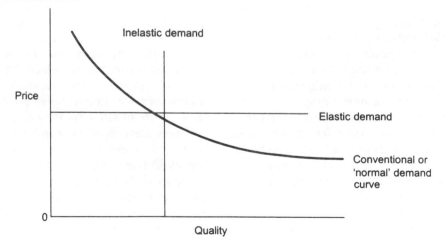

being highly, if not infinitely, elastic, while under monopoly conditions demand is considered highly inelastic. However, for a state of pure competition or monopoly to exist certain other conditions must be satisfied.

In the case of pure competition three basic conditions must be satisfied: namely, large numbers of producers, homogeneous output, and freedom of entry. In fact, when talking of a large number of firms it would be more accurate to speak of low levels of concentration, for the basic condition which we are seeking to define is one in which decisions by any single firm have little or no effect upon the output of the industry as a whole. As we have noted earlier, homogeneity in a product depends upon the perception of a prospective buyer. Only in the case of commodities and raw materials is it usual to find agreement that the output of two different producers which meets a given specification can in fact be treated as identical products. The third condition for the existence of pure competition is freedom of entry, by which we mean that there are no barriers or artificial restrictions to prevent any individual or firm from setting up in business to produce supplies of the product in question.

It should be noted that pure competition is not synonymous with perfect competition, for the former only describes the competitive state between suppliers, while the latter makes further assumptions about conditions in the market. Essentially these assumptions are that all buyers and sellers have perfect knowledge of the activities of one another, that there are no transportation costs and that there is perfect mobility of factors of production between industries. Under these conditions the market determines the price of a product and effectively the firm has no control over its destiny whatsoever.

The polar extreme to a situation of perfect competition is one of pure monopoly. By definition a monopolist is the sole supplier of a particular product or service, with the result that firm and industry are synonymous. In economic theory a pure monopolist has no competition at all. Clearly such a position cannot exist, for it presumes that the monopolist commands all of a consumer's income. For practical purposes we consider that a state of monopoly exists when there is no close substitute for the monopolist's output. Applying the concept of concentration a monopolist would have a concentration ratio of 100 per cent. Because the monopolist does not face direct competition from other suppliers, as is the case under conditions of perfect competition, it is frequently held that he has no incentive to maximise his efficiency.

Clearly under conditions of perfect competition the producer must maximise his efficiency, for if he does not his costs will rise above those of his rivals, but he will be unable to recoup these higher costs through increased prices. In the long run, therefore, the inefficient producer under conditions of perfect competition will be forced out of business.

From the foregoing descriptions it is clear that conditions of perfect competition and pure monopoly are exceptions rather than the rule. They are the limiting conditions. Under both sets of conditions the seller reacts solely to external environmental forces. However, in intermediate states between the two extremes the factor which really distinguishes imperfect competition is that the firm has to take account not only of the external environment within which it must operate, but also of the action of other suppliers in the market place. The need, under conditions of imperfect competition, for firms to take into account the actions of their immediate competitors makes for a much more complex situation, and one demanding a far higher level of managerial skill. Under conditions of imperfect competition sellers are mutually interdependent, and so must allow for each other's actions when formulating their plans.

As noted earlier when discussing different managerial orientations during this present century, the growth of imperfect competition is of relatively recent origin. In fact it was not until the early 1930s that Edward Chamberlin and Joan Robinson first put forward their theories of imperfect competition. In time, therefore, the proposal of a theory of imperfect competition coincided with a change from the production to the sales management orientation and the need for companies to compete with one another along dimensions other than cost and price.

Theories of imperfect competition frequently invite an analogy with games in which choices of courses of action are limited not only by the rules of the game but also by the actions of one's competitors. Thus we find that the study of competition places increasing emphasis upon the strategic choices made by participating firms and the impact which these have upon both the fortunes of their competitors and market structure.

In making such choices firms have to operate within the environmental constraints – political, legal and social – common to them all. Thus in order to develop a distinctive and, it is hoped, successful strategy they have found it beneficial to give much closer attention to microeconomic aspects of supply and demand – especially in the latter. It is these topics with form the subject-matter of the next chapter.

Summary

In this chapter we have looked at the Structure–Conduct–Performance (SCP) model which is central to the sub-field of economics known as Industrial Economics. Paul Ferguson (1988) cites Stigler as a distinguished economist who did not recognise industrial economics as a separate discipline. But, as Ferguson points out, to ignore or dismiss industrial economics and the SCP model is to miss the point. Industrial economics emphasises empirical work; that is, what's really going on out there, as opposed to theoretical speculation.

One of the major schools of industrial economics is the Harvard School based on the work of Mason in the 1930s and his student J. S. Bain in the 1950s and 1960s. While this school initially perceived a simple causal relationship Structure → Conduct → Performance, more recent work has recognised the complex relationships between these three factors and the existence of feedback loops of the kind suggested by Ferguson in Figure 4.3.

In this chapter we have focused on structure, and particularly the concept of concentration, theories of competition, and the basic nature of supply and demand; that is, Basic Conditions and Structural factors in Table 4.3. Much of the rest of this book deals with issues of conduct and performance and, specifically, the role and impact of marketing on these outcomes.

Finally, we would reiterate the point made in the introduction that the highly influential work of Michael Porter is directly derived from his studies in the Harvard School in the late 1960s as applied to the study of Business Policy at the Harvard Business School where he now teaches. With such a pedigree it would be foolish to underestimate the insights offered by SCP analysis.

Figure 4.3 *Basic conditions and structural factors*

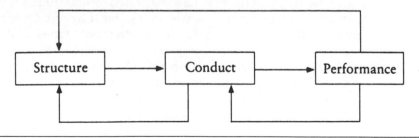

Review questions and problems

1. It is said that oligopolies could not be created except by means of heavy consumer advertising. The advertisers maintain that the security created by this relatively stable situation gives protection and time to embark on product development and improvement. Discuss this statement in relation to the detergent market.

2. What are the advantages and disadvantages of industries which are dominated by a few large-scale companies manufacturing similar, but differentiated, products?

3. What does the Government mean when it refers to its 'industrial strategy'? Say whether you think the strategy is viable and describe, using examples, the effect it has had on the structure of UK industry.

4. What relationship is there between oligopoly and the concept of product differentiation?

5. To what extent do you accept the statement that much so-called planned obsolescence is actually the working out of competitive and technological factors, both signifying a dynamic economy?

6. Under what circumstances might a fall in the price of a commodity lead to a decrease in the quantity demanded?

7. Define and distinguish between price elasticity of demand and income elasticity of demand.

8. In an oligopolistic market, why do prices tend to respond slowly to changes in market conditions?

■ Supplementary reading list

Porter, Michael E. (1980) *Competitive Strategy* (New York: Free Press).

Porter, Michael E. (1985) *Competitive Advantage* (New York: Free Press).

Porter, Michael E. (1990) *The Competitive Advantage of Nations* (London: Macmillan).

Scherer, F. M. and Ross, D. (1990) *Industrial Market Structure and Economic Performance*, 3rd edn (Boston: Houghton-Mifflin).

See also any introductory economics texts or introductory marketing texts.

Part II
THE THEORETICAL UNDERPINNINGS

■ *Chapter 5* ■
Demand and Supply

Contents

Learning goals

The issues to be addressed in this chapter include:

1. The nature of demand and the distinction between needs and wants and the nature of choice.
2. The major determinants of demand – socioeconomic and psychological.
3. The nature of supply and its adjustment to market needs.
4. The classification of goods and services.

After reading this chapter you will be able to:

1. Define and describe a demand schedule and a demand curve.

2. Distinguish between needs and wants.
3. List the determinants of demand and distinguish between potential, latent and effective demand.
4. Define a product and list its characteristics.
5. Define supply and explain the concept of diminishing returns.
6. Explain the nature and relevance of Maslow's Hierarchy of Needs.
7. Discuss the origins and importance of branding.
8. Define the various categories of industrial and consumer goods and the distinguishing characteristics of services.

■ Introduction

Most students of marketing have pursued an introductory course in economics and are familiar with the concept of demand as a function of price. According to this concept, the quantity of a good or service which will be purchased is dependent upon its price, such that the higher the price the less will be demanded, and vice versa. This relationship is frequently expressed in tabular form as a demand schedule, and depicted graphically as a demand curve, as shown in Figure 5.1.

In the real world it is clear that many factors other than price affect demand, and the exclusion of such factors is often seen as invalidating economic price theory. Such an attitude misses the point that the economist is seeking to define an essential functional relationship with which he

Figure 5.1 *Simple demand schedule and curve*

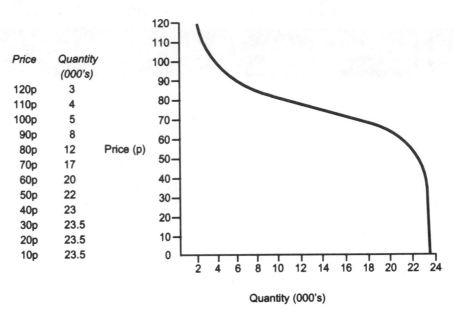

Price	Quantity (000's)
120p	3
110p	4
100p	5
90p	8
80p	12
70p	17
60p	20
50p	22
40p	23
30p	23.5
20p	23.5
10p	23.5

may then investigate the effect of other independent variables upon the dependent variable, demand. It is not proposed to investigate the sophisticated techniques developed by economists which validate the basic theory, however, and attention here will be concentrated on the nature of these other, independent variables.

In this chapter we look first at the distinction between needs and wants as determinants of choice. Next, we examine some of the major influences on demand with particular emphasis upon the socioeconomic and psychological factors. This leads to a consideration of how demand influences supply and the chapter concludes with a set of definitions of different kinds of products.

◼ Needs, wants and choices

Before proceeding to discuss demand variables it will be useful to distinguish between needs, wants and the function of choice.

A *need* is something fundamental to the maintenance of life, such as food, drink, shelter and clothing. Needs are largely physiological in the sense that they are basic and instinctive drives with which we are born. It is clear, however, that a need may be satisfied by any one of a large number of alternatives; for example thirst may be assuaged by water, tea, coffee, beer, wine and so forth. The availability of alternative means of satisfying a need constitutes *choice*, provision of which is central to the practice of marketing. In the absence of substitute, or alternative, goods there can be no choice, and needs and wants become synonymous.

Where there is more than one way of satisfying a basic need, physiological drives will be modified by economic, sociological and psychological factors. Variations in these factors will predispose individuals to prefer a specific alternative and this preference constitutes a *want*. As will become clear when considering economic and psychological factors in greater detail below, wants are not necessarily synonymous with the concept of demand implicit in a demand schedule. A demand schedule for a specific product may be thought of as expressing effective demand, by which is understood demand backed by the ability to pay a given price. From this it follows that there are two further types of demand – latent and potential.

As noted in the preceding chapter a latent demand may be thought of as a demand which the consumer is unable to satisfy, usually for lack of purchasing power. For example, many housewives may have a latent demand for automatic dishwashers but, related to their available disposable income, this want is less strong than their demand for other products and so remains unsatisfied. In other words, wants are ranked in order of preference and satisfied to the point where disposable income is exhausted. From the manufacturer's point of view the problem is to translate latent demand into effective demand by increasing the consumer's preference for his particular product *vis-à-vis* all other product offerings, As will be seen, marketing is largely concerned with solving this problem.

Latent demand may also be thought of as a vague want in the sense that the consumer feels a need for a product, or service, to fill a particular function but is unable to locate anything suitable. If such a product exists, marketing's role is to bring it to his attention; if it does not exist, then marketing should seek to identify the unfilled need and develop new products to satisfy it.

Potential demand exists where the consumer possesses the necessary purchasing power, but is not currently buying the product under consideration. Thus, where a marketer has identified a latent demand and developed a new product to satisfy it, the potential demand consists of all those who can back up their latent want with purchasing power. In another context, potential demand may be thought of as that part of the total market (effective demand) for an existing product which a firm might anticipate securing through the introduction of a new, competitive brand.

■ Determinants of demand

As implied earlier, basic economic theory is concerned largely with price–quantity relationships, and other demand determinants are invariably excluded for more sophisticated treatment. However, corporate success is very closely related to the manufacturer's ability to predict the strength and nature of demand as a basis for deploying the firm's resources. Consequently, management is deeply concerned with all those variables which condition demand. Broadly speaking, demand determinants may be grouped under two headings – socio-economic and psychological – and the next section will be concerned with identifying the more important factors within these groups.

□ *Socioeconomic factors*

Population

People constitute the basic raw material from which markets are made, for, ultimately, the demand for any given product or service depends upon the aggregate demand of individual consumers, and can never exceed the sum of their numbers. One of the major arguments behind our attempts to gain membership of the European Economic Community was that this would open the door to a market with a population five times as great as that of the United Kingdom. Clearly, this represents an enormous potential for increasing sales.

Absolute numbers are only one aspect of population, however, three other important aspects being age and sex distribution, geographical distribution and family size.

In the past decade the age distribution of the population of the UK and many other advanced industrial countries has attracted increasing attention. Essentially this attention has arisen from the realisation that, with declining birth rates and longer life expectancies, the population is 'ageing'. Thus, an increasing proportion of people are to be found in the older age groups and a lesser proportion in the younger and 'working' age groups. The implications of these changes in the composition of the population are profound. Consider, for example, the markets for education and health care.

In the case of education many of the readers of this book will be aware that as they grew up in the

1980s many primary and secondary schools were being closed down for lack of 'customers'. In their naivety planners in the Department of Education and Science extrapolated this trend and predicted a decline in the need for places in further and higher education and began to cut back on funding. Fortunately, the educationists were able to point out the difference between potential demand (all young people leaving secondary education) and effective demand (the proportion able and wanting to benefit from higher education). In addition to a growing interest in higher education a closer examination of the population statistics, also revealed that although the overall birth rate had declined, in fact it had increased in Social Classes I and II which traditionally have the highest participation rates in higher education. The lesson is clear; while absolute numbers are important in defining market potential it is usage or effective demand which determines market size. When the government recognised this fact in the early 1990s and proposed a significant increase in higher education, its projections of a 30 per cent participation rate were quickly exceeded by the demand for these additional places.

At the other end of the age spectrum the effect of an ageing or 'greying' population has also had a marked effect on consumption patterns. Nowhere is this more evident than in the demand for health care and the provision of sheltered housing, nursing homes and geriatric facilities in hospitals. Here again, careful analysis of trends in the population informed by knowledge of the likely incidence of particular diseases or disabilities such as arthritis can offer considerable insight into future demand and market opportunities. Table 5.1 is based on Government Actuaries projections and indicates how the proportion of those under and over age 30 is expected to change from 42.7% : 53.6% in 1985, to 38.1% : 61.9% by 2006.

As implied in the preceding paragraphs many products are associated with a particular stage of the human life cycle, as are many other products, and recognition of this has led to the adoption of the life-cycle concept as a useful means of distinguishing the effect of age on consumption patterns. Although it is increasingly recognised that young children influence purchasing decisions, their lack of purchasing power usually excludes them from life-cycle classificatory systems which concentrate on decision-making units (DMUs). A widely accepted system distinguishes the following eight stages:

1. Young, single.
2. Young, married, no children.
3. Young, married, youngest child under six.
4. Young, married, youngest child over six.

Table 5.1 *Projected population by age to 2030*

	000s					
	1992	*1995*	*2000*	*2010*	*2020*	*2030*
Total	57,998	58,576	59,613	61,138	62,080	62,285
Males	28,358	28,726	29,360	30,307	30,849	30,927
Females	29,640	29,849	30,253	30,831	31,231	31,358
0–14	11,198	11,408	11,641	11,082	10,657	10,626
15–29	12,773	12,050	11,241	11,680	11,499	10,686
30–44	12,213	12,677	13,475	12,146	11,232	11,680
45–59	9,813	10,430	11,032	12,368	12,977	10,982
60–74	7,970	7,905	7,765	9,090	10,335	11,685
75+	4,034	4,116	4,459	4,768	5,378	6,626

Sources: Government Actuaries Department, NTC.

5. Older, married, with children.
6. Older, married, no children under eighteen.
7. Older, single.
8. Other.

Although the distinction between Young and Older is not explicit, and category 8 is a meaningless 'catchall', the concept provides a useful basis for breaking down the total population into sub-groups for more detailed analysis. (A useful exercise is to visualise the variations that one would anticipate in consumption patterns as between the different categories in this system.) Life-style analysis is currently enjoying an enormous wave of popularity amongst marketers and numerous references to its application are to be found in the management literature. An extended review of the application of the family life-cycle concept is given by Rob. W. Lawson (1988), 'The Family Life Cycle: A Demographic Analysis'. Table 5.2 (p. 94) shows the classification of UK households according to alternative life-cycle structures.

The physical distribution of the population has a direct bearing upon the marketer's ability to make his product available to potential customers at an economic cost. The concentration of population in Britain, backed by extensive transportation facilities, make this factor less important than in many other parts of the world, for example the United States, Australia and Africa. In the case of bulky materials of low unit value, such as cement, or when considering entry into an export market, it will take on added significance in measuring potential demand. Physical location also has an important bearing upon the existence of regional wants and preferences; porridge, tripe and jellied eels immediately call to mind Scotland, Lancashire and London respectively. Similarly, woollens are in greater demand in the north, and cottons in the south. Overall, however, such differences are less marked than in many larger countries.

For planning and administrative purposes, the marketer will often find it convenient to subdivide the country into areas in some systematic way. An obvious approach is to use the Registrar-General's Standard Regions, namely:

North
Yorkshire and Humberside
North-west
East Midlands
West Midlands
East Anglia
South-east
South-west
Wales
Ireland:
Northern
Eastern
Southern
Western

Scotland and the planning sub-regions of Scotland:
Borders
Central
Dumfries and Galloway
Fife
Grampian
Highlands
Lothian
Strathclyde
Tayside

At the time of writing (1995) it is not known how local government reorganisation may affect these.

The great advantage of using this scheme is that the standard regions are widely used in the collection of Government statistics, and are capable of further subdivision into countries, conurbations, boroughs, and so on. On the other hand the standard regions listed above differ from those used prior to the 1971 Census and may be subject to change with Local Government reorganisation. With the ever-growing range of services offered by the independent television companies, many firms now use television areas as a basic unit, although some difficulties arise due to overlap. To some extent this is overcome by the ITV companies distinguishing between primary and secondary areas; that is, a primary area is unable to receive satisfactory transmissions from adjacent and competing stations, while a secondary area can.

Several other alternatives are available, including the Nielsen Areas, and 'Geographia's' marketing regions, each of which has its advantages and disadvantages. However, all are to be preferred to a purely arbitrary subdivision which precludes direct use of published data.

Family size has a direct bearing on housing, the size of appliances and cars, container size, etc., etc. In conjunction with income, it also has an important effect on household purchasing patterns for, despite certain economies present in large families, it is clear that for a given income such families will spend more on essentials than small families.

Table 5.2 *Classification of UK households according to alternative life-cycle structures*

Stage	Number of households	Percentage of households
(a) Murphy and Staples		
Young single	25 118	1.42
Young (aged under 35):		
(a) married without children	55 018	3.11
(b) divorced without children	—	—
(c) married with children	185 296	10.46
(d) divorced with children	22 271	1.26
Middle aged (aged 35–64):		
(a) married without children	21 017	1.19
(b) divorced without children	—	—
(c) married with children	322 970	18.42
(d) divorced with children	34 065	1.92
(e) married without dependent children	167 248	9.45
(f) divorced without dependent children	—	—
Older (aged over 65):		
(a) older married	168 308	9.51
(b) older unmarried (divorced and widowed)	250 891	14.14
Total	1 277 787	72.1
(b) Wells and Gubar		
Bachelor	25 118	1.42
Newly married couples	55 018	3.11
Full nest 1 (youngest child under 6)	210 888	11.91
Full nest 2 (youngest child over 6) ⎫		
Full nest 3 (older married with dependent children) ⎬	300 534	16.97
Empty nest 1 (in labour force, no children at home)	167 248	9.45
Empty nest 2 (retired, no children at home)	168 308	9.51
Solitary survivor in labour force	47 186	2.66
Solitary survivor retired	25 089	114.17
Total	1 225 191	69.19
(c) Rodgers		
Beginning families	55 018	3.11
Pre-school families (oldest child under 6) ⎫		
School age families (oldest child 6–13) ⎬	210 888	11.91
Teenage families (oldest child 13–20) ⎫		
Adult families (oldest over 20) ⎬	300 534	16.97
Launching families (with non-dependent children)	111 563	6.30
Middle years (all children launched until retirement)	167 248	9.45
Ageing couples (retired)	168 305	9.51
Widowhood	250 891	14.14
Total	1 264 450	71.41

Source: Household and Family Composition, 1981 Census, 10% sample.

Income

This variable is a major demand determinant and is widely used as a measure of potential demand. With the increase in the number of 'working wives', and recognising that the household is the most common decision-making and purchasing unit, it is more useful to think in terms of aggregate household income than to consider the major wage-earner's income alone.

Two concepts are particularly useful in analysing income levels – net disposable income, and discretionary purchasing power. The former consists of income from all sources including wages, interest on savings and investments, health and welfare benefits and so on, less taxes. It is a measure of the amount available for saving and expenditure. Discretionary purchasing power comprises that amount available after all 'essential' expenditures have been met – it is 'uncommitted' income which the consumer may spend, or save, as he or she pleases. As noted in Chapter 1, increasing income levels are invariably paralleled by an upgrading in what is considered essential but, overall, Engels's Laws seem to hold, namely: As real income increases the proportion spent on food tends to decline, expenditures on rent, heating, etc., remain constant while the proportion spent on clothing, education, recreation and travel, etc., tends to increase.

Most incomes are earned in payment for services rendered, and so depend upon the demand for the services in question (as modified by restrictive labour practices). In broad terms, occupation is determined by education, and there exists a strong correlation between the two and income so that, in the absence of income data, many researchers use education/occupation as a surrogate. Incomes vary considerably across occupational categories and the reader should consult the Department of Employment's *Employment Gazette* for detailed information on wage rates and earnings. One must be careful not to confuse the two, for wage rates do not necessarily bear any resemblance to the actual wages paid in a particular job or area. Further, the incidence of overtime has a marked effect on earnings, and it is the latter with which the demand analyst is primarily concerned.

Effective demand, as defined earlier, implies that consumption is a function of available income, and this relationship has been the subject of extensive research over a long period. Three separate theories have evolved out of this research in an attempt to explain variations in aggregate consumption functions and may be summarised as:

1. *The absolute income hypothesis*, which holds that expenditures/savings are a function of income.
2. *The relative income hypothesis*, which holds that expenditures/saving patterns depend upon the relative position of the spending unit on the income scale, and not on the absolute income earned. This hypothesis recognises the 'keeping up with the Joneses' phenomenon.
3. *The permanent income hypothesis*, which holds that expenditures are based on average income expectations over time. This hypothesis recognises that consumption patterns are relatively stable over time, which suggests that consumers average out their expenditures; that is, under inflation they anticipate that they will make good current dissaving, due to price increases, out of future wage increases.

An additional, and complicating, factor in recent years has been the increased availability of credit. Although the amount of credit an institution is prepared to extend to an individual is usually related to their income, there are now so many separate sources that the relationship between credit and income has become tenuous. Clearly, the ready availability of credit has done much to enable the consumer to translate latent demand into an effective demand, and has become an important demand determinant.

Collectively, the factors reviewed above are socio-economic variables, and form the basis of a broad but useful classificatory system. Within the United Kingdom, differences in ethnic origin and religion have usually been considered too slight to merit inclusion in such a system, although they may be relevant in foreign markets. (The upsurge of Welsh and Scottish 'nationalism' and the

Protestant–Catholic confrontation in Northern Ireland suggest that greater attention may have to be given to these factors in future as does the concentration of ethnic/religious groups in cities such as Bradford or Notting Hill.)

☐ *Psychological factors*

When discussing the distinction between needs and wants it was noted that needs are essentially physiological and instinctive, but that such generalised, basic drives are subject to modification by other factors, resulting in specific wants. To a large degree these 'other factors' are psychological. However, people live in social groups, membership of which modifies behavioural response to the extent that it would be more correct to identify these factors as psycho-sociological and/or socio-psychological. Collectively, the study of these influences has created a whole new field of marketing, usually referred to as 'consumer behaviour'. An extended discussion of the more important concepts follows in Chapter 6, but before turning to this it will be helpful to review the other half of the market equation – supply.

■ Supply: products and services

In the preceding section attention was focused on those factors which determine the precise character of demand for specific goods and services. Here, our objective will be to examine how these demand determinants are reflected in the supply of products designed to satisfy particular wants as identified by the marketer.

☐ The 'product' in theory and practice

As a subject, economics is largely concerned with maximising satisfaction through the optimum use of scarce resources. Inherent in this construct is tacit acceptance of the fact that available resources are insufficient to satisfy all conceivable demands of mankind, although it is recognised that conditions of over-supply are perfectly possible in the particular.

In theory, production, or the creation of supply, is a function which expresses the relationship between inputs and outputs. Inputs are referred to generically as 'factors of production', and broadly classified as land, labour, capital and management, while outputs are identified as products. (To avoid endless repetition the term 'products' will be taken to include both physical goods and services, unless stated to the contrary.)

Given that there is a finite limit to the availability of factors of production, whereas demand is infinite, it follows that we need a criterion which will enable us to determine priorities in the use of these factors in order to maximise satisfaction. Such a criterion is provided by the Law of Variable Proportions or, as it is more usually termed, the Law of Diminishing Returns. This law states that incremental units of a given factor of production, other factors being held constant, will yield increasing returns up to a certain point, beyond which diminishing returns will set in. This point is not fixed, and will vary with changes in technology and the other inputs. However, at any given point in time, it is theoretically possible to determine the optimum allocation of inputs which will maximise total output.

In reality, the multi-dimensional complexity of products precludes viable analysis, and economists have found it necessary to suppress such variables in developing theories of competition. Thus, although more sophisticated treatments recognise product differentiation as a competitive variable, in theory the product is usually viewed as a homogeneous entity. In practice, products may be differentiated by any one of a multiplicity of variables as indicated by the following definition:

Those aspects of the good or service exchanged whether arising from materials, or ingredients, mechanical construction, design durability, taste, peculiarity of package or container or service...all products beyond the raw material stage are highly variable, for the most part on a continuous scale.

(E. Chamberlin, 1957)

To further complicate the issue, product differences are determined by the perception of the individual consumer, from which it follows that Daz, Persil Automatic, Bold and Ariel Automatic are all different products, whereas 'detergent' is a generic name for a group of products possessing similar physical characteristics.

In an article entitled 'What is a Product?', C. P. Stephenson (1968) emphasised this point by defining a product as 'everything the purchaser gets in exchange for his money', and listed the following 'extras' associated with the physical product:

- Advisory services
- After-sales service
- Replacements
- Designing and planning services
- Deliveries
- Guarantees
- Credit terms
- Reputation
- Experience

The idea that the product is 'everything the purchaser gets for his money' has been developed considerably in recent years through the writings of marketing gurus like Ted Levitt and Philip Kotler and the emergence of the *augmented* product or service, as illustrated in Figure 5.2. (The growing interest in the marketing of services is reviewed in Chapter 23 but, at this point, it is worth drawing attention to the convergence in thinking which recognises that physical products possess intangible benefits while intangible services usually require physical inputs in their creation and consumption.)

The idea of the augmented product is probably a direct descendant of Levitt's 'Marketing Myopia' in which he argued that one must define market opportunities in terms of the core benefit desired by the potential consumer. Thus, the hungry man wants 'food' but, within the constraints of disposable income

and physical availability, will probably have access to literally hundreds of possible solutions to his need. In selecting a particular type of food he will have regard to a wide range of attributes which distinguish one food from another ranging from physical attributes such as animal or vegetable origin, taste and consistency through considerations such as its perceived quality, packaging or presentation and brand name or reputation of the supplier. Finally, the hungry man will have regard for any other benefits associated with different product offerings which will enable him to distinguish between them and select that which most closely meets his needs at the time at which the decision is to be made. For example, is the food prepared or not, can he consume it on the premises or will he have to consume it elsewhere, is it to be served or self-service, and so on? The use of increasingly specific criteria to discriminate between goods which pure economists would regard as largely homogeneous or 'generic' products like breakfast cereals, soap, detergent, bread, and so on, lies at the very heart of buyer decision making. As a consequence it also lies at the heart of successful product development and the execution of effective marketing strategies. We shall return to this theme many times, especially in the discussions of Consumer Behaviour (Chapter 6), Market Segmentation (Chapter 8) and Product Policy (Chapter 11).

Individually, and collectively, all these factors will lead consumers to distinguish between the product offerings of competing firms in order to best satisfy their particular wants.

Competition and the provision of choice

As noted, the ability to create excess supplies of basic goods is of relatively recent origin and is largely responsible for the current emphasis on marketing, as opposed to production. This change of emphasis recognises that the competi-

Figure 5.2   *What is a brand?*

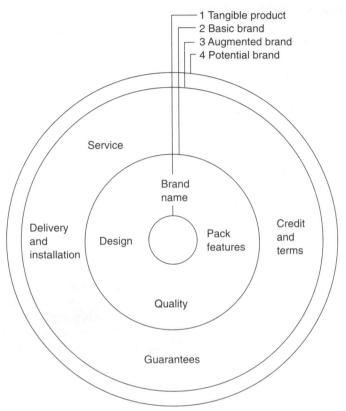

1 Tangible product
2 Basic brand
3 Augmented brand
4 Potential brand

Service

Brand name

Delivery and installation

Design

Pack features

Credit and terms

Quality

Guarantees

Source: Adapted by the author from T. Levitt (1983) *The Marketing Imagination* (London: Collier Macmillan).

tive 'ground rules' appropriate to conditions of excess demand must be modified under the threat of excess supply.

Maslow's concept of a need hierarchy (discussed at greater length in Chapter 6, pp. 113–14) is reflected in the nature of consumer demand. At the first level, the consumer's prime concern is to satisfy a basic need such as hunger, thirst or shelter, by whatever means are available. Under conditions where there is an insufficiency of supply to satisfy these basic needs, factor inputs are restricted to those alternatives which offer the maximum output consistent with certain minimum levels of satisfaction. In the last century this objective was achieved by product standardisation, which permitted the division of labour and the adoption of mass production techniques. Such conditions prevailed in the United States during

the second half of the nineteenth century and, to a lesser degree, in much of Western Europe. Today they are typical of the developing economy.

Once the basic needs have been satisfied, however, consumers advance to a higher and more sophisticated level of demand. Deficiencies in the 'standard' product become apparent, through possession and consumption, and are expressed in the market place by a preference for differentiated products which more nearly satisfy specific wants. Moreover, the economic growth associated with mass production, and its attendant economies of scale, increases discretionary purchasing power to the point where consumers can afford to pay more for improved, and differentiated, products.

Product homogeneity is fundamental to the existence of perfect competition, under which price is determined solely by market forces and so is beyond the producer's control. In these circumstances a firm's profitability is a direct consequence of its cost structure, and the natural emphasis is on production. The realisation that consumers are both willing and able to pay a premium for products with distinctive attributes offers the firm the opportunity to exercise a degree of control over the market, and escape direct competition with its rivals. Such a position is clearly to be preferred and has led to the present concentration on marketing with its emphasis on the provision of choice to meet varied consumer preferences.

■ Branding

Recognising that homogeneity of product offering precluded identification of a given producer's output at the point of sale, manufacturers 'revived' the practice of branding as a means of distinguishing their product from that of their competitors.

Craftsmen have long been accustomed to identifying their work, either by signature or by the use of a distinctive symbol particular to them. In fact this practice was mandatory under the gild system to protect customers and to ensure that shoddy workmanship could be traced back to its originator. An extant example of this is the 'hallmark' used on silver as a guarantee of purity and indicator of its origin. Over time, this practice has enabled consumers to form judgements as to the value of given names and symbols as indicators of the quality of the product, and as a guarantee of satisfactory performance.

Clearly, the identification of a product is two-edged in the sense that although it permits satisfied customers to repeat purchase, it also allows them to avoid repetition of an unsatisfactory purchase. None the less, branding is now standard practice for the majority of goods, although it is most frequently associated with products purchased for personal consumption.

From both the consumer's and producer's point of view the brand serves as a useful

shorthand expression for a whole collection of attributes and properties associated with a given product. In part these associations are built up by advertising; in part they are the result of the consumer's perception and past experience. Whatever their origin, the brand enables the purchaser to obtain products which satisfy highly specific wants, without having to resort to a detailed description of them.

Brand names may be given to individual products, for example Daz, Bold, Persil Automatic and Ariel Automatic, and so on; or a generic, or family, brand may be used for a firm's complete product line, for example Heinz, Black & Decker, St Michael. Individual brand names are expensive to establish, and usually require a large investment in advertising and sales promotion. Their use is usually restricted to situations where:

1. Potential sales of each product are sufficient to justify the necessary expenditures.
2. The products vary in price, quality, etc., and are designed to appeal to different market segments.
3. There is a radical innovation with a high risk of failure and the company does not wish to prejudice the success of existing brands.

The UK detergent and laundry aids market provides an excellent example of brand competition with developments regularly documented in reports published by companies such as the Economist Intelligence Unit (*Retail Business*), Nielsen and Mintel. The following comments are based on Mintel's Market Intelligence reports on 'Detergents and Laundry Aids'. The detergent sector is dominated by two major companies, Lever Brothers and Proctor & Gamble who have a combined market share of 86 per cent. The sector is a fairly mature one. Recent impetus in this sector has come from the advent of liquid detergent which has had a remarkable effect on the market. Concentrated liquid detergents are a recent growth area and have maintained the impetus that has resulted in the clothes washing sector being resilient despite recessionary pressures. In 1992 the growth rate in this sector was 8 per cent and a rate of 5 per cent was anticipated right through to 1996. In 1991 sales for detergents and laundry aids reached £1166m which was an 11 per cent increase over 1990.

In the detergent market, product launches are a vital component for each of the giants to maintain or increase market share. Because of this, brand shares within the market remain highly volatile. Currently the battle for supremacy is being waged between Proctor & Gamble's Ariel brands (27 per cent market share) and the Persil brands (26 per cent market share) of Lever Brothers. The introduction of Ariel Liquid in 1987 was a key product development and proved highly successful. It took Lever's a year to respond and introduce Persil Liquid. Own label brands continue to be a strong force in the market *vis-à-vis* the two giants and hold an 8 per cent share of the market by volume. To counteract this the majors have continued to launch more 'new' brands. In January 1995 Proctor & Gamble launched Ariel Future and Ariel Future Colour whilst Lever Brothers launched two brands in August 1994 – Surf Super Concentrated and Radion Micra Active. In such a volatile market with a proliferation of new brands market shares are difficult to pin down and exhibit all the characteristics of the rapid growth phase of the product mix and these can be seen in terms of new product launches, brand extensions and the packaging of products. (*Source*: *Mintel Market Intelligence Report*, January 1993 'Detergents and Laundry Aids'.)

In early 1995 Lever Brothers announced the decision to drop their newly launched Persil Power which contained a controversial manganese accelerator which critics claimed rotted clothes. There therefore followed a need to launch a new 'Persil' product called New Generation Persil to make up for lost competitive impetus. Problems also existed with other Lever detergents using the accelerator, namely Radion Micra Active and Super Concentrated Surf. (*Source*: *Marketing Week*, 20 January 1995.)

Family brands tend to be preferred in circumstances where physical differentiation between brands is difficult to establish, the potential market is small, and the firm has an established line of complementary products. Hence a firm like Heinz, Max Factor or Marks & Spencer will usually concentrate its effort on the development of an overall image/reputation and rely on this to introduce new products into the market.

Increased competition at the retail level has prompted many retailers and wholesalers to develop 'own', or 'private', brands which are sold in competition with the manufacturers' brands. (The latter are often termed 'national brands' as they are usually promoted on a national basis.) By avoiding the promotional expenditures necessary to maintain a national brand, private brands can be offered at a lower price, and are widely used in building store 'traffic'; that is, to induce price-conscious shoppers to come into the store in the hope that they will make other purchases.

In many instances private brands are identical with the better-known national brands and, in fact, are produced by the same manufacturers. The use of a second brand allows the manufacturer to sell off his excess production at a lower price than that asked for the major, promoted brand. Naturally, few manufacturers are willing to admit that they are practising this form of price discrimination, and the origin of such private label brands is usually a closely guarded secret. For the price-conscious shopper, private brands offer considerable savings, and are perceived as of equivalent quality to the better-known national brands. However, most consumers prefer the national brands with which they are familiar, and from which they derive additional satisfactions. Whether these arise out of associations built up by advertising, or represent real differences in quality, which is often the case (for example washing-up liquids), is largely irrelevant, for the final choice rests with the consumers who will optimise their own choice criterion.

However, the use of own label brands has become an increasingly important area within UK retailing. It has produced a dilemma for many branded manufacturers, who, by producing own label products for major retailers are often undercutting the success of their own products. Supermarkets are now packed with lookalike products that compete directly with the major brands – in terms of quality and packaging – and yet are often far cheaper. The use of own label goods by retailers has been in existence since the end of the nineteenth century. Retailers saw that by producing products to certain specifications and by using economies of scale they could produce lower priced goods to compete with the major manufacturers and increase their own profit margins. This developed a cheap alternative for consumers. Initially, retailers accepted that the quality levels of their own label products would be lower than those on the top brands but that this was balanced by price savings for the consumer.

The own label brand has developed into a far more complex issue. Three quarters of all grocery sales occur in multiple retailers and now the multiples see 34 per cent of their sales coming from own label goods. Sainsbury's have 54 per cent of their sales from own label products whilst Tesco and Safeway have 41 per cent and 36 per cent respectively. The multiples now use the own label as a means to compete on quality and service as well as price. Own labels have rigorous quality controls and are often equivalent to, or better, than those of branded manufacturers and yet remain around 10 per cent cheaper.

Many of the key brand manufacturers in the grocery products sector refuse to make products for other brands, instead investing in the uniqueness of their own products – for example Coca-Cola, Kellogg, Lever Brothers and Heinz. More commonly it is the second and third-ranked brand manufacturers that see own label produc-

tion as an opportunity. Some manufacturers see the competition from own label brands as being inevitable and therefore it is better to be serving it than letting the competition do so.

The modern own label product is now regarded as a high quality product. Retailers like Marks & Spencer's have extremely detailed specifications and stringent quality controls. As a result consumers are becoming more aware that they are purchasing products from a high level manufacturer at a reduced cost. Major brand owners are becoming increasingly irritated and many supermarkets produce lookalike products that resemble the originals so closely that it is argued they are stealing part of the brand's personality. Distinctive packaging is now more closely protected by the new Trade Marks Act but still much attention has been given to the similarities that exist between products such as Sainsbury's Classic Coke and the brand leader Coca-Cola. The cola market is a huge one and is growing globally. In the UK own label brands are becoming a worry to the market leaders Coca-Cola and Pepsi who lost 6.7 per cent and 1.6 per cent market share over a 14 month period up to 1995. Most of this loss was to Sainsbury's Classic Coke and Virgin Cola. (*Sources*: L. de Chernatony and M. H. B. McDonald (1992) 'Creating Powerful Brands'; C. Murphy 'Own-Goal' *Marketing Week*, 19 August 1994, p. 28; *The Grocer* – News 'Gloves come off in look-a-like battle', 9 July 1994; *Marketing Week*, 27 January 1995.) The market share of private label brands is shown in Table 5.3 for 1993.

Table 5.3 *Private label shares by value, 1993*

	%		%
Fresh poultry	93.5	Tea bags	32.1
Kitchen towels & clothes	60.2	RTE cereals	22.7
Frozen vegetables	58.3	Dog food	14.0
Wrapped bread	54.1	Granulated white sugar	11.7
Ice cream	47.6	Toilet tissue	51.0
Baked beans	35.8	Toothbrushes	21.8
Canned fish	33.2	Deodorant	10.4

Source: *Marketing Pocket Book*, Advertising Association (London), 1995.

More recently supermarkets have upgraded the quality of their own brands and have used them as a means of enhancing their store image. This left a gap in the market which has been filled by the introduction of 'generic' brands – virtually the 'own label' version of supermarkets' own label goods. They have been introduced into the basic food and grocery items market and encompass products such as washing-up liquids, tinned dog meats, flour, sugar and instant coffee. These goods are stripped of expensive packaging and promotion costs and may be of lower quality than branded goods. Their prices can be substantially lower than branded goods. Generic brands are proving to have a widespread appeal to the consumer and already appear to have a significant share of the grocery market.

However, there has been a mixed reaction from both manufacturers and retailers alike. The major manufacturers with strong brands have so far refused to make own label or generic products (for example Heinz, Kellogg's and Nescafé, who are even going so far as to advertise the fact). However, manufacturers with weaker brands do produce own label and generic products. The reaction of the supermarkets has also been varied, with Tesco, Presto, Safeway, Gateway and Carrefour all stocking generic goods. Marks & Spencer and Sainsbury's, however, have not yet accepted the concept; this is because both companies have built their reputation on their own label products, Sainsbury's own label goods accounting for over half of its business and Marks & Spencer's 100 per cent.

The idea of simple packaging was originated by Carrefour Supermarkets in France into the mid 1970s, the idea then spread to America in 1977 and into Britain in 1979. The grocery trade has accepted this concept in its efforts to boost the volume of sales at a time when the rate of food price increases has fallen, leading to a problem for supermarkets, which as a rule have high fixed costs. Although at first they were thought to be a reaction to the world-wide recession, generic brands appear not to be solely a recession concept, as a Fine Fare (now Gateway) spokesman pointed out: 'it appears in the UK as well as the US to have high appeal to relatively high income, affluent and well-educated young shoppers'.

We can conclude by noting that generic products do appear to have gained a foothold in the market and seem likely to be here to stay. However, because of the higher profit margins on own label products, it is predicted that retailers will concentrate more on their development in the future.

■ Classification of products

Given that products may be differentiated in a multiplicity of ways, some form of classification is desirable to simplify discussion and permit the formulation of general principles. Although several bases for classification have been proposed, the most widely adopted system distinguishes two major categories – industrial goods and consumer goods – and is based on the purpose for which the goods are purchased. In the case of industrial goods this same criterion is used to further subdivide the category, but in the case of consumer goods a second criterion, method of purchase, has been found more useful.

It is the author's opinion that little useful purpose can be served by following the example of many writers who attempt to develop their own definitions. Verbal dexterity is rarely mistaken for originality and, in the case of definitions, usually only serves to confuse what it is intended to clarify. Accordingly the definitions used here are those adopted by the American Marketing Association.

Consumer goods

Goods destined for use by the ultimate household consumer and in such form that they can be used by him without further commercial processing.

Consumer goods are generally divided into three sub-categories according to the method in which they are purchased following the terminology first proposed by Melvin T. Copeland – convenience goods, shopping goods and specialty goods (Copeland, 1923, 'Relation of Consumers' Buying Habits to Marketing Methods').

Convenience goods

Those consumer goods which the customer usually purchases frequently, immediately and with the minimum of effort.

This category encompasses a wide range of household products of low unit value. It is implicit that products in this category have low brand loyalty, as the user is not prepared to go to any effort to secure a supply and will accept a substitute. From this it follows that the producer must secure the widest possible availability if he is to maximise sales.

Shopping goods

Those consumer goods which the customer in the process of selection and purchase characteristically compare on such bases as suitability, quality, price and style.

Products in this group are more complex than convenience goods and exhibit a higher degree of differentiation. Usually they are purchased less frequently and are of higher unit value. Many consumer durables fall into this category.

Specialty goods

Those consumer goods on which a significant group of buyers characteristically insists and for which they are willing to make a special purchasing effort.

Some critics argue that this is a meaningless category as the 'special purchasing effort' required is due to limited availability and that otherwise such goods would fall into one of the other groups. This argument is rejected on the grounds that brand insistence has a very real bearing on the consumer's patronage of different outlets and therefore on the retailer's stock policy. Thus, although the housewife may be indifferent to the brand of canned peas she buys and will take what is available, she may well change to another store altogether if she cannot find her preferred brand of baby food, cigarette or headache remedy.

Industrial goods

Goods which are destined for use in producing other goods or rendering services, as contrasted with goods destined to be sold to ultimate consumers.

Certain goods which fall into this category may also be classified as consumer goods; for example paper, typewriters, chairs, fuel oil, and so on. Where such an overlap exists, the purpose for which the product is bought determines its classification.

Industrial goods fall into four main categories:

- Raw materials

  Those industrial materials which in part or in whole become a portion of the physical product but which have undergone no more processing than is required for convenience, protection, economy in storage, transportation or handling.

  Threshed grain, natural rubber and crushed ore fall into this category.

- Equipment

  Those industrial goods which do not become part of the physical product and which are exhausted only after repeated use, such as major installations or installations equipment, and auxiliary accessories or auxiliary equipment.

  Installations equipment includes such items as boilers, presses, power lathes, bank vaults, and so on, while auxiliary equipment includes trucks, office furniture, hand tools and the like.

- Fabricated materials

  Those industrial goods which become a part of the finished product and which have undergone processing beyond that required for raw materials but not so much as finished parts.

  Steel, plastic moulding powders, cement and flour fit this description.

● Supplies

> *Those industrial goods which do not become a part of the physical product or which are continually exhausted in facilitating the operation of an enterprise.*

Examples of supplies include fuel, stationery and cleaning materials.

Although few producers give much thought to actually classifying their output along the above lines, this is probably due to the fact that their product line falls within a single category, and not because there is no value in developing such a classification. In fact the product category has a fundamental effect on the firm's marketing strategy as a whole, as well as having far-reaching implications for its internal organisation and operation. This point will be examined in greater detail in Chapter 19.

☐ *Services*

As acknowledged at several points in this chapter it is commonplace to speak and write of products – both consumer and industrial – as if the term automatically embraces services. In reality, as the burgeoning literature of services marketing testifies, there are many important differences which demand separate recognition and treatment. Chapter 23 attempts to review the most significant of these differences but, at this juncture, it will be helpful to recognise that services are generally distinguished from physical products in terms of their *intangibility*; the difficulty of separating the service from the supplier of the service and its consumption (*inseparability*); their *heterogeneity* or lack of standardisation, and the problems of matching highly *perishable* outputs with *fluctuating demands*.

─ Summary ──

This chapter has introduced and defined some of the basic factors which underpin marketing practice with a particular emphasis on the nature of demand and supply. Many of these ideas and concepts will be developed in greater detail in subsequent chapters starting with consumer behaviour as a determinant of demand.

─ Review questions and problems ──

1. Complete the following 'shopping list' of needs and wants:

Need	Want
Bread	...
...	P.G. Tips
Meat	...
...	Radion
Cooking fat	...
...	Blue Band
Floor cleaner	...
...	Birds Eye Frozen Peas
Heat	...

2. What factors would you consider most important in forecasting the demand for:

   ● Automatic washing machines
   ● Classical records
   ● Colour television
   ● Cold water detergents
   ● Fluoride toothpaste
   ● Frozen dinners
   ● Package tours?

3. Which 'personality theory' do you subscribe to? Why?

4. What utility has reference group theory for the practising marketer?

5. How is Maslow's 'hierarchy of needs' reflected in the nature of consumer demand?

6. One of the most difficult decisions any marketing executive has to take concerns the determination of those consumer characteristics which can be used to segment a market in the best possible way. What are the particular difficulties he has to face?

7. Discuss the advantages/disadvantages of:

   (a) Individual brands
   (b) Family brands

8. Account for the widespread development of private branding in recent years.

9. How useful is the classification of goods described in the text? Suggest an alternative classificatory system.

10. How, and on what grounds, would you classify the following products:

    (a) Branded pain remedies, butter, detergents, frozen peas, matches, petrol, shirts, stockings?

    (b) Cement, lathes, lubricants, sulphuric acid, transistors, wood pulp?

11. Describe the problems confronting the marketing executive when they set out to discover what the consumer wants.

12. Clearly explain what you understand by the term 'demand'. In what sense can a knowledge of this economic concept have practical application?

13. Demand is made up of two elements, the ability to buy and the willingness to buy. Discuss the advantages to be gained from studying the effects of both elements separately.

14. Explain what is meant by family and individual branding, and under what circumstances it would be advantageous to use either of these methods of branding.

15. Identify some of the effects that the current recession and high levels of unemployment will have on spending patterns, decision patterns and family roles.

16. Examine why corporate brand management is a more complicated affair than classic brand management. Use case examples to support your line of argument.

▌ Supplementary reading list

Porter, Michael (1980) *Competitive Strategy* (New York: Free Press).

Spencer, Milton H. (1975) *Managerial Economics*, 4th edn (Homewood, Ill.: Irwin).

■ *Chapter 6* ■

Consumer Behaviour

Contents

Learning goals

The issues to be addressed in this chapter include:

1. A review of the multiplicity of factors – social, psychological and economic – which form and influence consumer behaviour.
2. The nature of the buyer decision process.
3. The role of perception in determining behaviour.
4. The nature of learning, motivation, personality and attitude and their influence on behaviour.
5. The concepts of culture, social class, reference groups, personal influence and life style as social influences on behaviour.
6. The relevance and explanatory power of composite models of consumer behaviour.

After reading this chapter you will be able to:

1. Explain and justify a simple, generalised model of the buying decision process.
2. Describe the phenomenon of perception and clarify its role in determining how individuals interpret the world around them.
3. Distinguish the salient characteristics and differences between the stimulus–response and cognitive explanations of learning.
4. Elaborate Maslow's theory of motivation.
5. Understand why personality is only one of several major influences on consumer decision-making.
6. Explain the essential differences between the CAC and expectancy-value models of attitude and the nature of hierarchy of effects models of decision-making.
7. Spell out the influence of culture on buyer behaviour.
8. Describe the concepts of social class, reference groups, personal influence and life style and show how they can be used to help sellers devise effective marketing strategies.
9. Summarise the key features of the best known models of consumer buyer behaviour and their respective strengths and weaknesses.

■ Introduction

In *Consumer Behaviour*, Engel, Blackwell and Miniard (1986) define consumer behaviour as 'those acts of individuals directly involved in obtaining and using economic goods and services, including the decision processes that precede and determine these acts'. This definition enjoys a very wide measure of support in the majority of texts concerned primarily with consumer behaviour as a field of study in its own right but, in my opinion, it is important to stress that such an emphasis upon *individuals* tends to ignore largely an equally important area of consumption behaviour – that of organisations.

Since the first publication of this book in 1971 there has developed a major interest in organisational buying behaviour as a major sub-field of marketing. This interest was reflected by the inclusion of a separate chapter on the topic in the fourth edition which is continued in this edition.

In the last ten years or so the field of organisational buying behaviour has tended to become known as 'business to business' marketing (see Bernard, 1995, *Marketing: Theory and Practice*, Chapter 15). This trend is particularly noticeable in the USA. In our view the terms organisational buying behaviour (OBB) and business to business marketing largely deal with the same subject matter. That said, we prefer OBB because it includes exchanges between all kinds of organisations and not just profit oriented businesses. If we were to limit discussion to the latter kind of organisation then we would exclude many not for profit organisations which purchase significant volumes of goods and services such as government departments, local authorities, NHS Trust Hospitals and so on. We regard the purchasing practices of all such organisations as falling within the scope of OBB and so retain this term.

However, the existence of separate texts dealing with consumer and organisational buying behaviour is symptomatic of a much larger division within marketing, of which new students of the subject should be especially sensitive – namely, the dichotomisation of the subject into 'industrial' marketing and consumer marketing. Ever since the first edition of this book appeared in 1971 I have argued that while there are differences between these two branches of marketing they are a matter of degree only and in essence both rest upon the same foundations, as do new branches such as the marketing of services or marketing by non-profit-making organisations. Accordingly it might be more realistic to classify consumption behaviour as 'individual' or 'collective' depending upon whether such behaviour is undertaken solely in pursuit of one's own satisfaction or is engaged on in conjunction with and/or on the behalf of others. Such a classification would require one to include households in the 'collective' category and it is probably preferable to maintain the generally recognised distinction between consumer and industrial or organisational (business) behaviour which exists in the marketing literature.

In this chapter we will accept the traditional approach in which discussions of consumer behaviour are focused upon individuals or ultimate consumers and their consumption behaviour; that is, what they consume, how they buy, and why. In doing so it will be necessary to review a number of key concepts and ideas which have been borrowed from other behavioural sciences – notably psychology and sociology – before considering how these ideas have become incorporated in composite models of consumer behaviour. To this end we look first at contributions from psychology: namely, perception, learning, personality, motivation and attitude. Attention is then directed to social influences on consumer behaviour with specific reference to culture, social class, reference groups, role and family influence, with that section concluding with a discussion of life-style as an explanation of how and why people consume, which illustrates how the psychological and sociological foundations have been built upon by marketers. This theme is further developed by a survey of some of the major models of consumer behaviour which illustrate the main schools of thought, concluding with my own composite model of buying behaviour in which I seek to justify my earlier claim that differences between different branches of marketing are a matter of degree and not of principle.

 The buying decision process

Before looking at some of the factors which influence buying decisions it will be helpful first to consider a simple and generalised model of buying as a decision process. In broad terms this may be represented by a flow diagram containing five elements as follows:

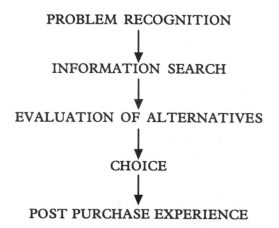

PROBLEM RECOGNITION

↓

INFORMATION SEARCH

↓

EVALUATION OF ALTERNATIVES

↓

CHOICE

↓

POST PURCHASE EXPERIENCE

As will become clear later in this chapter the reality is far more complex than implied by this model. As we accumulate experience and learn from past behaviour so this knowledge and the attitudes associated with it will generate feedback loops in the sequence and may short circuit the process so that one moves almost instantaneously from problem recognition to choice. For example, people shopping in a supermarket depend heavily upon the display to stimulate problem recognition – 'I'm short of instant coffee' – and immediately select a preferred brand and size which their past experience has shown to give satisfaction. (Or at least sufficient satisfaction that the opportunity cost in their time and effort to collect new information and evaluate it is not considered worthwhile.) Such behaviour does not invalidate the basic model which emphasises that the consumer purchase decision is sequential and combines both mental and physical activities. As my former colleague Jenny Drayton has explained:

The sequence can be divided into three basic stages:

(i)   a decision process
(ii) an act of purchase
(iii) a period of usage

This sequence of events shows a consumer to be actively involved in the market-place long before the actual buying of goods and to retain such involvement for some time after the purchase has been completed.

(i)   The recognition of a decision process acknowledges the purposive nature of making a purchase, introducing the ideas of pre-purchase deliberation, the willingness to seek information, and the existence of an internal evaluation system to provide the criteria which will guide the choice decision.

The decision process emphasises that, a consumer prior to buying is *purposive, deliberate* and *evaluative*.

(ii) The subsequent act of purchase is inevitably shaped by this preceding decision-making activity. Going out to buy goods is to implement the decision: the buyer is taking a specific course of action bearing upon acquiring a predetermined choice of goods. For example, where household income may be used for *either* domestic appliances *or* for home entertainment equipment, both in themselves deemed desirable, the decision between the two product classes will be made prior to, not at the time of, buying the goods. Equally, when arriving at a choice within a range, pre-purchase thought and evaluation will affect the buying activity by reducing the total number of brands available to a smaller number of brands which the buyer will consider at the time of purchase. Thus the act of purchase becomes simplified, an extension of the pre-purchase consumer activity.

(iii) At the third stage is the gaining of experience through using the goods. Here the consumer can assess all his previous actions in acquiring the goods, to store in the memory to act as reinforcement, or to initiate change. The consumer may consider such things as whether the goods live up to expectation, whether information was readily available and accurate, the nature and surroundings of the shopping situation, and so on. Whatever the answers, this assessment becomes an integral part of the consumer's internal evaluation system, to influence future behaviour in the acquisition of economic goods and services. Thus the consumer learns through experience patterns of behaviour which develop and strengthen.

The 'consumer' then, rather than the 'buyer', implies an active and demanding partner in the economic transaction. In response, the marketer needs to be equally active and aware, employing the tools of marketing in concert with the consumer behaviour sequence to bring together the potential buyer and the company's product.

As we shall see (for example the Hierarchy-of-effects models in Table 6.2), simple flow diagrams of the type on the previous page are capable of considerable elaboration to reflect the real complexity of most marketing problems. For example, in *The Marketing Book*, M. J. Baker (1994) offers the expanded model shown in Figure 6.1.

Figure 6.1 *The consumer choice process*

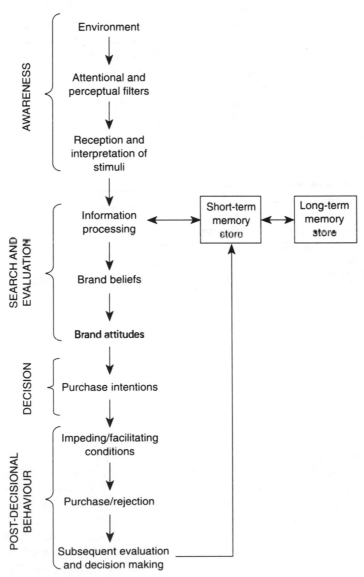

Source: Baker (1994) *The Marketing Book*.

For the purposes of an introductory text the shorter and simpler diagrams are to be preferred.

■ Psychological influences

□ *Perception*

In psychology an important and fine discrimination is made between the concepts of sensation and perception. Sensation occurs when a sense organ receives a stimulus, while perception is the interpretation of that stimulus. The distinction is particularly important for marketers, for in order to initiate an exchange process we must first establish contact through the generation of a stimulus capable of sensation by the intended recipient. For practical purposes there are five senses – seeing, hearing, touching, smelling and tasting, though experimentation has established eleven sensory mechanisms in all – and it is to one or more of the five basic senses that marketing communications stimuli are directed. However, perception is the critical factor, for this is the interpretation placed upon the stimulus and can vary widely between individuals and even within individuals over time. A frequently used example which makes this point is to compare a photograph – what the eye and the camera physically see – with a painting, which is the receiver's interpretation of that sensation. Clearly Rembrandt and Picasso perceived things rather differently and the critical question must be: 'What factors influence perception?'

In essence, if perception consists of the interpretation of a received stimulus, then, as Sperling (1967) points out, 'What we perceive at any given time, therefore, will depend not only on the nature of the actual stimulus, but also on the background or setting in which it exists – our own previous sensory experiences, our feelings of the moment, our general prejudices, desires, attitudes and goals.' Given that so many forces influence perception it is not surprising that there should frequently occur a mismatch between the interpretation intended by the originator of a stimulus (usually the seller in a marketing context)

and the receiver (intended customer). It follows that those responsible for marketing stimuli should pay very careful attention to psychological findings concerning how people perceive things.

A fundamental aspect of perception is that it represents the receiver's effort to organise received stimuli into a meaningful structure. In doing so two major groups of factors are involved – stimulus factors and functional factors. Stimulus factors are neutral in the sense that they are intrinsic to the stimulus and so will be received in exactly the same way by all receivers with normal sensory capabilities. On receipt the brain organises the incoming stimuli into patterns following four basic tendencies: similarity, proximity, continuity and context.

By similarity we understand the tendency of the receiver to group similar things together, while proximity results in the perception that things which are close to one another belong together. In marketing practice similarity is to be seen in the concept of segmentation, while proximity is employed in the use of prominent people to endorse particular products, in the use of generic brands like St Michael's, and so on. The need to impose a meaningful structure on stimuli is particularly noticeable in the case of continuity, which is closely associated with closure. The phenomenon of continuity is well illustrated by Sperling with the use of a simple diagram like that below:

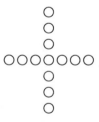

In this one sees the dots as straight lines rather than as separate dots, and as two continuous lines rather than three or four short ones. Closure occurs when one completes an otherwise incomplete diagram, picture, sentence, and so on. For example, we all know what 'Beans means'.

Finally, context, or the setting in which a stimulus is received, will have a marked effect upon perception (see any basic book for illustrations of the context influencing perception). In this sense context can have a similar 'halo' influence to proximity and is frequently used by marketers when seeking to develop an image of a product by using media or a setting which conveys the overall impression they wish to create; for example use of the Sunday colour supplements to convey a feeling of quality allied to value for money, or young people in leisure situations for Coca Cola.

As noted, stimulus factors are neutral and create sensations which are then interpreted in the light of what are generically termed functional factors. Thus individuals have an ability to screen out stimuli which they do not understand or do not wish to recognise, just as they also have an ability to modify stimuli to make them acceptable to us – a phenomenon sometimes termed 'selective perception'.

The classic example of selective perception is that reported by Hastorf and Cantril (1954), in 'They Saw a Game: A Case History', of supporters of two American football teams - Dartmouth and Princeton. The match contained a number of incidents which led to players being injured and penalties being imposed. While most uninvolved viewers felt these were the joint responsibility of both teams, supporters of the two sides were almost unanimous in their view that all the trouble was the fault of the other team.

This tendency to perceive what one wants to 'see' can be traced to several factors. First, there is our ability to screen out or ignore a very large number of stimuli and so enable us to give our full attention to those which have some particular relevance or which strike a discordant note because of the contrast they make with other stimuli. Research has shown that we screen out the vast majority of advertisements to which we are exposed and, in fact, perceive less than 1 per cent of all those we come into contact with. Thus in order to secure our attention advertisers must use contrast, for example a colour advertisement in a black-and-white medium; loud noise (or silence) in broadcast media; luxury yacht advertisements in *The Economist*, and so forth. By the same token we possess perceptual defences which

block out stimuli which are offensive, or are otherwise in conflict with our values or attitudes.

The issue of relevance is also important, for clearly we will be more likely to perceive stimuli which cater to our needs, both physiological and emotional, than those which do not. On occasion physical and emotional needs may generate a conflict (termed 'cognitive dissonance') such that acquisition of a physical object to satisfy a need (a car for transportation) may generate uncertainty as to the wisdom of that choice. Under these circumstances it has been shown that purchasers of objects pay more attention to advertising or other stimuli relating to the object than do intending purchasers.

Another perceptual phenomenon of importance to the marketer is that of preparatory set, which, put simply, means that people tend to perceive objects in terms of their expectations (cf. closure, discussed above). A well-known marketing manifestation of the influence of preparatory set is the use of branding and price labelling. Hence, while consumers are unable to distinguish between unbranded products they have no such difficulty when brand names are given. Similarly, Gabor and Granger, Shapiro and others have clearly demonstrated that we use price as an indicator of quality and will select products with a higher price as 'better' when no differences exist with those carrying a lower price and even when the higher-priced items are objectively inferior.

In recent years marketers have made considerable use of psychological explanations of perception in developing their communications strategies and have developed a number of specific applications of their own. Perhaps the most sophisticated of these applications is known as *perceptual mapping*, which is founded on the premise that individuals will seek to relate to new things in terms of their relationship with or similarity to things with which they are already familiar. By collecting information from consumers of their perceptions of existing brands in a product category one can develop a two-dimensional map (usually by making use of a powerful computer program) which shows the relationships between the various brands in terms of the variables used. In Figure 6.2 it can be seen that

Figure 6.2 *Perception of different brands of whisky in US market*

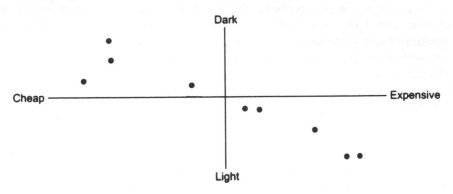

the various brands are clustered in groups, suggesting that they are perceived as very similar. If one were to develop a new brand in this category, then this knowledge would be very valuable – either one has a product with certain characteristics and can identify the immediate opposition, or one can identify 'gaps' which it may be worth filling with a different type of product (cheap and light?). (The example shown is fictitious but it should be stressed that while Americans prefer lighter whiskies and pay a premium for them, the opposite is largely true in Britain.)

☐ *Learning*

Our discussion of perception has made it clear that in every circumstance our perception is conditioned by our prior experience, for it is this which constitutes our preparatory set or expectations and the framework into which we seek to place and organise new stimuli. In other words we have learned from our earlier experience and seek to maintain balance or consistency by relating to and interpreting new stimuli in terms of past or learned stimuli.

Learning may have a number of meanings, depending upon the context in which it is used, and Sperling (1967) comments that 'the process of learning can consist of all, or some, or one of three steps: INVENTING an original solution to a problem, or THINKING: COMMITTING a solution to memory, or MEMORISING: BECOMING EFFICIENT at applying the solution to a problem, or FORMING A HABIT'.

In essence there are two schools of thought concerning what is learned – the stimulus–response (S–R) school, and the cognitive school. Although there are some divisions within the S–R camp, the basic theory is that we learn to associate given responses to specific stimuli and these become habitual. One group of S–R theorists subscribe to the view that learning occurs only when there are rewards or punishments to reinforce the correct response, while others believe that learning is the result of an association between a stimulus and response occurring together, that is they are contiguous, and that reinforcement is not necessary.

In contrast to the S–R theorists the cognitive school argue that we learn cognitive structures; that is, more broadly based interpretations of the association between stimuli and alternative courses of action.

In a marketing context there would seem to be support for both theories, in that some consumption behaviour is routinised and habitual (S–R school), while other purchasing decisions are subject to extensive problem-solving generalising from past experience (cognitive school).

The division of opinion about what we learn also exists in the case of how we learn. S–R theorists maintain that learning occurs through a process of trial and error – a view based on extensive experimental evidence using animals.

However, some leading members of the cognitive school (notably Wolfgang Kohler, 1925) developed what is termed the *Gestalt* explanation of learning as being based on insight.

While it seems likely that the truth is a combination of both schools of thought, in which some actions are learned through direct personal experience based upon trial and error, while others are the product of reasoning, that is seeking solutions through symbolic thinking, the S–R explanations tend to dominate in consumer-behaviour research in marketing. In turn the most sophisticated statement of S–R theory which underlies much of this consumer-behaviour research is that developed by Clark Hull (1943) in *Principles of Behavior: An Introduction to Behavior Theory*, whose basic model is

$$E = D \times K \times H \times V$$

where E = behaviour and is a multiplicative function of D = drive, K = incentive potential, H = habit strength, and where V = intensity of the cue.

Drives are discussed at greater length in the section on motivation research which follows, where a distinction is made between a drive which is viewed as the initial stimulus and a motive which is a tendency to activity. It is not felt that this distinction is important in the context of Hull's model. The remaining terms are essentially self-explanatory, and it is clear that in a marketing situation two of the variables – the incentive potential, or satisfaction offered by the product, and the intensity of the cue – are controllable to a considerable degree by the seller. It should also be noted that as the equation is multiplicative no reaction will occur if any of the variables has a zero value. At first sight this would seem to suggest that consumers would never try new products, for if they have not consumed them before, then H (or habit) would be expected to have a zero value. However, this possibility is negated by the principle of generalisation, whereby we extrapolate from past experience to a new situation. This potentiality is exploited by companies with generic brand names, where satisfactory experiences

with one product group creates a favourable predisposition towards new product groups; for example buyers of clothes from Marks & Spencer towards M & S foodstuffs. Of course, generalisation is only potential, and past experience soon teaches us that it is not always true that all the products introduced by a company will automatically yield the same level of satisfaction as the one which we originally approved of. In other words we learn to *discriminate* between very similar cues or stimuli.

Before leaving this brief overview of some learning-theory concepts which have been incorporated into studies of consumer behaviour it should be noted that Howard and Sheth's (1969) *Theory of Buyer Behaviour* is essentially a learning model. It should also be noted that two important areas of research in marketing draw heavily upon learning theory for their conceptual framework – namely, the study of advertising effectiveness and of brand loyalty.

☐ *Motivation*

Reference was made in the last section to the distinction between a drive as an initial stimulus, and motive as a tendency to act, though the terms tend to be used interchangeably in everyday speech. However, perhaps a clearer distinction is apparent if one defines drives as physiological stimuli to action, while motives constitute the intervening variable between the stimulus and response. For example, I have a strong drive to smoke a cigarette but my doctor has told me it is bad for my health and will shorten my life. I wish to live to a ripe old age and am strongly motivated to avoid anything which prejudices that goal – result, I stop smoking and resist drive.

Drives and motives are also often called 'needs' and one of the most enduring and widely used classification of needs is that proposed by Abraham Maslow (1943) in 'A Theory of Human Motivation'. According to Maslow's basic theory we possess five basic needs which can be placed in a hierarchy such that as lower-order needs are satisfied we lose interest in them and concentrate upon satisfying needs at the next higher level which have become the most pressing. The five steps in the hierarchy in ascending order are:

1. Physiological needs;
2. Safety needs;
3. Love needs;
4. Esteem needs;
5. Self-actualisation needs.

Physiological needs or basic drives arise mainly from internal stimuli such as hunger or thirst, though some arise from external sources which threaten the individual with pain, injury or death. It is generally believed that satisfaction of these needs is dominant and overrides all other considerations. It is significant that a marketing function as it has developed in advanced economies in the past fifty to sixty years is irrelevant in countries where basic needs are not satisfied.

Safety needs come next in importance and can themselves be ranked into a rough hierarchy – physical security; stable and routine pattern of living, that is avoid the risk of the unknown; acquisition of protection against an uncertain future (religion, insurance).

Love needs include the need for affection and the feeling of belonging to a group – family, social group, work group, and so on. Much marketing activity seeks to cater for these needs and includes some approaches most criticised by anti-marketers, for example advertising which suggests that failure to use a product (toothpaste, shampoo, etc.) will lead to ostracism or exclusion from a group which you aspire to join.

Esteem needs include such things as recognition, status, prestige, reputation, and so forth. In affluent societies achievement of these needs is often reinforced and made public through the acquisition of physical objects which are felt to be appropriate to a person's position in life. (Consider the Sunday colour supplements for a sample of such objects.)

Self-actualisation represents the highest level of need to 'do one's own thing'. Relatively few people would seem to achieve this level and when they do they are unlikely to be much influenced by or interested in the market-place!

Maslow's hierarchy of motives constitutes a general statement of behaviour at the macro level – to understand the behaviour of the individual we need a more comprehensive classificatory scheme such as that provided by the concept of personality.

☐ *Personality*

In his *Introduction to Psychology*, Ernest Hilgard (1967) defines personality as 'The configuration of individual characteristics and ways of behaving which determine an individual's unique adjustment to his environment.' While Hilgard is atypical in offering a definition, as most psychologists fail to do so, his definition reflects the consensus concept of personality as a consistent pattern of response. Because of this overall consistency in an individual's pattern of behaviour it is possible to categorise dominant traits and develop a classification of personality 'types'. In turn such classification provides a valuable working construct for marketers, as it enables them to use personality as a factor in developing marketing strategies and marketing mixes to suit them.

However, if we are to make use of personality as a basis for trying to predict human behaviour, then it follows that we must be able to agree upon what variables we need to measure, and how to measure them, as a basis for classifying individuals. Sperling (in *Psychology*) records that Gordon Allport found 4500 words which designate distinct personal forms of behaviour in the 1925 edition of the unabridged *Webster's New International Dictionary*, and while many of these are no doubt synonyms it underlines the problem of what traits one is to measure to arrive at a personality 'type'. As a result of this extensive range of possibilities, psychologists have devised a battery of personality tests (Allport's being one of the best known and widely used) which reflect different personality theories (Freudian, neo-Freudian, S–R learning theories) and/or the purpose for which the test has been devised. For example, if an employer is looking for persons with a particular and strongly developed personality trait, then they will prefer a test which emphasises identification and measurement of that trait.

Further, although it was stated earlier that personality is a valuable working construct for marketing practitioners, it must be recognised that the research evidence on the relationship between personality variables and consumer behaviour is conflicting. The most widely cited study is that of Franklin B. Evans (1959) 'Psychological and Objective Factors in the Prediction of Brand Choice: Ford versus Chevrolet', in which he used the Edwards Personal Preference Schedule to test for personality differences between owners of the two different makes of car, but concluded that personality is 'of little value in predicting whether an individual owns a Ford or a Chevrolet'. A number of subsequent studies would seem to confirm this conclusion, but at least as many maintain the opposite. Indeed, many writers have criticised Evans's whole approach, but Thomas S. Robertson (1970) in *Consumer Behavior*, probably makes the most useful observation when he points out that while personality data only classified correctly 63 per cent of Evans's sample, this is 'some improvement over chance'. For many marketing problems this is all we can expect, and any approach which can reduce uncertainty is to be welcomed.

However, over 40 years after Evans's study we are able to take a more balanced view of the value of personality variables as predictors of specific behaviour such as brand choice, and recognise that it is only one of several major influences upon consumer decision-making. Engel, Blackwell and Miniard (*Consumer Behavior*, 1995) are of the opinion that personality is unlikely to prove a useful segmentation variable, not least because a homogeneous personality profile does not necessarily imply homogeneity in other respects, and most marketing media and channels of distribution tend to be designed to match other forms of homogeneity. None the less Engel *et al.* indicate several ways in which personality theory has considerable promise for marketing applications, particularly in its role as a moderating variable (that is where a personality trait can help explain differences in the behaviour of groups which are homogeneous in other respects), or as an intervening variable where primary segmentation is based upon objective factors such as demographics, but intra-group differences can be best explained in terms of motivational attributes. However, Engel *et al.* also point out that research on personality 'has stimulated the development of broader, more behavioural concepts that are likely to be better targets for market segmentation – namely life-styles'.

In some situations individual attributes or traits may prove sufficient, but in others a more generalised statement of personality may be useful. Sperling (1967) gives a list of twelve primary dimensions of personality which is based upon extensive measurement of traits which have a very low correlation with one another but whose defining traits have a very high correlation with one another (see Table 6.1).

Table 6.1 *Primary dimensions of personality*

1. Easy-going, generous, genial, warm versus cold, inflexible
2. Independent, intelligent, reliable versus foolish, frivolous, unreflective
3. Emotionally stable, realistic, steadfast versus emotionally changeable, evasive, neurotic
4. Ascendant, dominant, self-assertive versus self-effacing, submissive
5. Cheerful, placid, sociable, talkative versus agitated, depressed, seclusive, sorrowful
6. Sensitive, sympathetic, tender-hearted versus frank and hard-boiled, poised, unemotional
7. Cultured, aesthetic versus boorish, uncultured
8. Conscientious, painstaking, responsible versus emotionally dependent, impulsive, irresponsible
9. Adventurous, carefree, kind versus cautious, inhibited, reserved, withdrawn
10. Energetic, persistent, quick, vigorous versus day-dreaming, languid, slack, tired
11. Calm, tolerant versus excitable, high-strung, irritable
12. Friendly, trustful versus suspicious, hostile

Source: A. D. Sperling (1967) *Psychology Made Simple* (W. H. Allen) p. 174.

A more condensed statement of psychographic variables is offered by Kotler (1988) and contains the following seven items:

- Compulsiveness: compulsive; non-compulsive
- Gregariousness: extrovert; introvert
- Autonomy: dependent; independent
- Conservatism: conservative; liberal; radical
- Authoritarianism: authoritarian, democratic
- Leadership: leader; follower
- Ambitiousness: high achiever; low achiever

In common with most other aspects of consumer behaviour, personality has been the subject of extensive research. For example, William Wilkie reports that over 300 studies of personality and consumer behaviour have now been reported in marketing literature. (William K. Wilkie is the author of one of the many specialised texts available on the topic. His *Consumer Behavior* (1994) extended to 614 pages, contains 78 pages of notes and references, a 23-page glossary and 31 pages of index. A book such as this is essential reading for the serious student). However, Wilkie reports that the findings of these numerous studies are, to quote Harold Kassarjian, 'equivocal'. The main reason for this is that while individuals may share personality traits their behaviour is influenced by a host of other factors. It is for this reason that personality, like many other dimensions of consumer behaviour, can contribute to our understanding of why people behave the way they do but rarely provide a complete explanation.

Wilkie (*op. cit.*) suggests that personality research currently exhibits four distinctive trends:

1. A more holistic approach to studying patterns of behaviour rather than single decisions.
2. Focusing on consumption rather than general needs – the domain of consumer psychographics.
3. Shifting attention to related areas, for example physiological influences; the idea of a self-concept.
4. Studying how personality affects responses to advertising.

Overall these trends have shifted attention and interest more towards the subject of consumer values and away from personality *per se*.

☐ *Attitude*

Attitude is one of the most frequently invoked behavioural-science concepts in marketing. While its relationship to behaviour is not entirely clear, the frequent association between attitude and likely future action has resulted in extensive use of attitude surveys in the area of new-product development and in the design and execution of many promotional campaigns. Similarly, public opinion (belief or attitudes) is playing an increasing role in shaping and modifying corporate policy in areas such as consumer protection. It follows that a basic understanding of the current state of knowledge of attitude theory is vital to the student of marketing.

Just as there is no single agreed definition of marketing, so there is a multiplicity of definitions of 'attitude'. In broad terms most of these definitions fall into one of two categories which reflect two basic models in current use, which may be defined as the cognitive–affective–conative (CAC) and expectancy–value (EV) models. The cognitive–affective–conative model has been traced back to Plato's elements of the human soul – reasonable, spirited, appetitive – which in more modern terms may be defined as the realms of thought, emotions and motives, or knowing, feeling and acting. Marketers have developed a number of variants of their own of the CAC model, some of the better known of which are contained in Table 6.2 under the general heading of hierarchy-of-effects models. In all of the marketing versions, starting with Strong's AIDA (1924) and progressing through Lavidge and Steiner (1961), Rogers (1962) to Engel, Kollat and Blackwell (1978), it is assumed that one proceeds from awareness (cognitive) to preference (affective) to action (conative) – an assumption of the direction of cause and effect for which there is little empirical support. In fact

Table 6.2 *Hierarchical models of advertising effect*

Model	Characteristic
Starch, 1923:	*To be effective, an advertisement must be …* seen → read → believed → remembered → acted upon
Strong, 1925:	*AIDA[a,b]* attention → interest → desire → action
Sandage and Fryburger, 1935:	*Interaction Model* exposure → perception → integration → action
Lavidge and Steiner, 1961:	*Hierachy of Effects* awareness → knowledge → liking → preference → conviction → purchase
Colley, 1961:	*DAGMAR[c]* unawareness → awareness → comprehension → conviction → action
McGuire, 1969:	*Information Processing Model* presentation → attention → comprehension → yielding → retention → behaviour
DeLozier, 1976:	*Psychological Responses to Advertising* attention → perception → retention → conviction → action[d]
Peston and Thorston, 1984:	*Expanded Association Model[e]* Exposure → awareness → perception → evaluation → stimulation → search → trial → adoption

Notes:
(a) The initials of the four steps
(b) It is an interesting comment upon the intellectual condition of marketing communications practice that this model was found to be the most widely quoted of the seven in a range of current British, American and French textbooks, despite being today well past normal retirement age
(c) Colley's model is always called 'Dagmar', actually the initials of the monograph in which it was first proposed: Defining Advertising Goals for Measured Advertising Results
(d) DeLozier's model includes a final step, 'post-purchase behaviour', which is omitted here – partly for purposes of comparison and partly because it is not actually a response to advertising but a consequence of action.
(e) The Preston & Thorston model appears very different from the rest because of its many incorporated ramifications – for example, separating awareness of the advertisement from awareness of its elements from awareness of the advertised product
Source: Crosier, K. (1995) *Marketing: Theory & Practice*, 3rd edn., p. 226.

it is widely recognised that frequently one or more stages occur simultaneously, for example awareness and evaluation, while impulse purchases suggest that the cognitive and affective may occur together, while the conative may, or may not, follow. Despite these deficiencies the CAC model enjoys wide support, and the effectiveness of marketing strategy is often measured in terms of its ability to move consumers up the hierarchy of effects; that is, from unawareness to awareness, from desire to action – in other words attitude is seen as a predisposition to act.

The expectancy–value model views attitude as comprising two components – beliefs and values – which are broadly equivalent to the cognitive and affective dimensions of the CAC model. It follows that the EV model is lacking a behavioural or action element and so is much more limited in its application.

The EV model is particularly associated with the work of Martin Fishbein (1975), who built upon the work of Rosenberg, which in turn was developed from Fritz Heider's consistency model. In essence Fishbein argues that an attitude comprises two components – beliefs about the attributes of an object and the values ascribed to these beliefs. In order to maintain consistency (or balance, or congruity as it is sometimes called) consumers need to act in accordance with their beliefs and the *values* associated with them. Thus, while EV models do not seek to establish a link between attitude and behaviour, the association between expressed beliefs and action is strong where action occurs; that is, beliefs experienced about different brands have been found to be good predictors of actual brand preference, where the person expressing a belief about a brand actually consumes an item from that product category. However, there is a world of difference between holding a neutral or positive belief about a product and a willingness to buy it; for example, 'I believe Romeo and Juliet cigars are of the highest quality, but I would never buy them, because I do not smoke.'

This latter caveat is particularly important and explains why the EV model is theoretically more acceptable than the CAC model, which extends the link between an attitude as a *predisposition to act* into *behaviour* without specifying the catalyst which makes action necessary. From a practical point of view it is this missing link which is of crucial importance in converting the results of attitude surveys into realistic sales forecasts. In my own model of buying behaviour I term this motivation to act 'precipitating circumstances', and suggest that the precise nature of these will depend very much upon specific circumstances. Clearly the implication of this is that one must seek to develop one's own check-list of causal factors in the context of one's own marketing problem. In doing so there are a number of other behavioural-science concepts which will prove helpful, including those of change agents, opinion leadership and source credibility. A review of these follows.

While we cannot prove a causal relationship between attitude and behaviour, it is clear that a favourable attitude is more likely to lead to desired action than is an unfavourable attitude. Consequently much marketing activity is devoted to creating a favourable attitude, or climate of opinion, towards an object, or to reinforcing such favourable attitudes if they already exist.

It is generally agreed that attitudes are learned initially from one's family and then from the groups to which one belongs or wishes to belong. From a marketing point of view favourable attitudes to the consumption of particular products and/or services are usually a by-product of more basic group affiliations/aspirations. For example, I wish to be accepted as a student, students wear scarves and jeans, therefore I wear a scarf and jeans. The question is, who sets the group norm which specifies scarf and jeans as the accepted dress of the group?

As in most marketing/behavioural-science issues, there is no single universally accepted answer, but the balance of evidence is that certain individuals take it upon themselves to mould and change attitudes and behaviour by setting themselves up as *opinion leaders*.

Opinion leaders achieve their satisfaction through their status as the expert adviser on some aspect of importance to a group of which he or she is a member. This status is often highly specific, for example the group expert on hi-fi systems, bargain travel, cheap places to eat, and so on, and it is unusual to find an individual who is the opinion leader on all topics of interest to a group. In other words while the existence and role of opinion leaders in influencing attitudes/behaviour is widely accepted, using this idea operationally is restricted, due to the absence, and possibly non-existence, of a profile enabling one to identify the opinion leader.

However, to the extent that opinion leaders act as filters and amplifiers in the communication channel (see Chapter 15, pp. 350–1), their potential role as change agents is particularly significant, as is the concept of source credibility.

Source credibility refers to the confidence we place in the source of information, and has been shown to have an important influence upon the acceptability of new information as a basis for attitude change (as does the presentation of the message itself). Broadly speaking sources may be divided into two categories – personal and impersonal – and may be 'objective' or marketer-dominated ('objective' only in the sense that the source is not paid for by the marketer in the same way as advertisements and salesmen are). The effectiveness of the different sources in the stages of the consumer decision process, which coincide with the stages in the CAC or EV models, has been the subject of a great deal of research, and an excellent summary table is to be found on pages 248 and 249 in Engel, Kollat and Blackwell's (1978) *Consumer Behavior*.

For an extended and rigorous discussion of the issues touched upon in this section on *Attitude* the reader is strongly recommended to consult a companion volume by Gordon R. Foxall (1983) entitled *Consumer Choice*. In this book Foxall argues that researchers have been too ready to conceive of buyer behaviour as a function of 'the black box of the consumer's psyche', and proposes that more attention should be given to situational, especially social, influences on consumer choice. As Wilkie (*op. cit.*) notes (pp. 178–9) the traditional black-box model has now conceded ground to the Consumer Information Processing or CIP approach which focuses more on the ways consumers handle information rather than the inputs/outputs of the process.

In a comprehensive review of the extant research Foxall cites the findings of Ajzen and Fishbein whose analysis of 142 studies of attitudes and behaviour indicated that in 107 of these only 16 per cent or less of the observed variance in behaviour could be explained in terms of attitude. Hardly a convincing argument in favour of this model! Because of this weakness Foxall argues cogently that we should pay much closer attention to the 'behaviour modification perspective' according to which:

> the proposed sequence is now (i) brand trial, stimulated by the reception and acceptance of some modicum of information but, of necessity, an experiment which occurs in a state of great uncertainty, followed by (ii) the reinforcement of the

purchase, partly through advertising and social communication but primarily as a consequence of the user's evaluation of the merits of purchase and consumption outcomes.   (p. 27)

This model corresponds quite closely to that developed by Ehrenberg and Goodhardt (1980) which proposes a three-stage buying sequence – awareness – trial – reinforcement, or ATR, that 'is consistent with a "weak theory of advertising" in which marketing communications work primarily through suggestion and reinforcement' (p. 26).

While Ehrenberg and Goodhardt (and Foxall) present some compelling evidence, this is also open to objection on the grounds that while it may be a good predictor in low-involvement and low-risk situations where trial is possible and the most economic and cost effective way of determining what one's attitude is or should be is to try it out for oneself, it is much less accurate as a description of behaviour and attitude formation for high-involvement, high risk decisions where trial is impractical if not impossible.

Clearly the matter is not closed and the present state of knowledge would seem to suggest that both CAC and ATR or behaviour-istic models are correct under certain specific conditions. This situation-specific aspect of marketing was well exemplified in a report by Hugh Davidson (1981), 'How and Why Shoppers Buy'. While somewhat dated this account is still considered a useful analysis of the consumer buying process.

☐ *How and why do shoppers buy*

The manner in which housewives shop for frequently purchased consumer goods and the attitudes and motivations which underlie this behaviour are clearly questions of major concern to manufacturers and retailers alike. In consequence the topic is one which has been the subject of considerable research. One study which adopted a novel approach, and which largely confirmed the findings of alternative research designs, was that commissioned by *Marketing* magazine and executed by the Schlackman Group (Davidson, 1981).

The method used by Schlackman followed the classic pattern of qualitative research to establish the major dimensions of the research problem followed by a sample survey using a formalised questionnaire in order to quantify the frequency and importance of the behaviour noted in the qualitative phase. Specifically the research technique was summarised as follows:

1. Researchers selected 30 representative housewives who normally did one main shop weekly at a supermarket.
2. Interviewer met housewife at home, accompanied her to the supermarket, and observed a few feet behind.
3. In most cases, the housewife soon became unaware of being observed.
4. Interviewer accompanied housewife home and watched unpacking.
5. In-depth interview, lasting about 45 minutes.
6. Self-completion questionnaire, mailed to 450 housewives on home testing panel.
7. 325 questionnaires returned and analysed. Sample representative by age, class, north/south and family structure.

Of particular note is the combination of both observational techniques and in-depth interviewing in the qualitative stage of the research.

The qualitative research suggested three different 'shopping types' and these were confirmed in the quantitative survey which followed – namely *relaxed*, *controlled*, and *rigid*. Classification was based on several criteria, including:

- Degree of pre-planning;
- Willingness to experiment and try new products;
- Attitude to price and budgeting;
- Flexibility in accommodating to different tastes of individual family members.

Based on these and similar criteria Davidson caricatures the three types as:

1. *The Relaxed Shopper* – prepared to experiment with new products, looks carefully at displays, and not especially budget conscious.
2. *The Controlled Shopper* – the majority fall into this category. While not prone to experiment she seeks variety and often buys and cooks for individual family members. Uses a shopping list for basic requirements but most decisions are made in-store using the display as a prompt.
3. *The Rigid Shopper* – is very controlled and her behaviour is highly planned and controlled. Shopping is planned in advance, a list is prepared and seldom departed from. Little or no allowance is made for individual family preferences and shopping is performed very quickly. Persons in this category fall in two distinct sub-groups – those who are rigid by personality and those who have to be rigid for reasons of economy.

Based on the survey Davidson proposes a typical shopping sequence. While he depicts this as an orthodox ladder or hierarchy it is felt that the process is more circular in nature and so has been recast in this format (see Figure 6.3).

Davidson comments:

The key is that housewives buy meals, not products. Meals, including snack meals, are always the starting point for the shop. The housewife roughly works out the number of meals she has to do before the next main shop, how many people will be present at each, how many will contain 'real meat' and so on. Meal planning is then translated into product needs.

In terms of the amount of preplanning the following emerged:

- Usually make a list of everything to avoid forgetting   23%
- Usually make a list and buy nothing else   3%
- Usually make a partial list, decide on rest in shop   36%

Figure 6.3   *Typical shopping sequence*

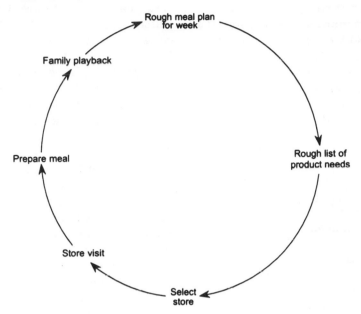

Source: Adapted from 'How and Why Shoppers Buy', Hugh Davison, *Marketing*, 28 October 1981.

- Don't make list – know exactly what
  is wanted   26%
- Don't make list – decide in shop   12%

Among the other main findings the most striking
were:

1. Only 22 per cent enjoyed shopping, 46 per
   cent disliked it, and the remaining 32 per cent
   tolerated it.
2. 77 per cent of housewives shop regularly at
   the same store.
3. 'Value' is more important than price and low
   prices/value for money was the outstanding
   reason for choice of store.
4. Shoppers don't distinguish manufacturers'
   from 'own' brands – they are all 'brands' to
   shoppers and selected on the basis of price
   and perceived quality.

In sum, the findings accord well with generalised models of buyer behaviour whilst also
demonstrating the significant variations which
may occur within the general model.

■ Social influences

The preceding discussion of psychological influences has concentrated largely upon individual
characteristics. In this section we are concerned
primarily with people as members of groups, for,
as will become clear, group membership has a
profound influence upon individual behaviour.
The approach followed is to start with macro
concepts of culture and social class, and then
refine the analysis to look at reference groups,
role and family influences, and, finally, the
concept of life-style.

□ *Culture*

Bennett and Kassarjian (1972), in *Consumer
Behaviour*, define culture as 'a set of *learned*
beliefs, values, attitudes, habits, and forms of
behaviour that are *shared* by a society and are
transmitted from generation to generation within
that society'.

Bennett and Kassarjian's definition has been expanded by many more recent authors but it is still current. In the summary to his chapter on cultural influences, Wilkie (*op. cit.*) observes:

Culture refers to the way of life of a society. It is a very powerful force in shaping people's lives. Two major components of culture are *external, material culture* and *internal, mental culture. Cultural norms* range from fads and fashions (that may come and go very quickly), to folkways (everyday practices), to mores (moral or religous values), to laws (strict codes of behaviour). (p. 340)

The emphasis upon learned, shared and transmitted in the Bennett and Kassarjian definition is important, for it reflects attributes common to a vast multiplicity of definitions of culture. Values and beliefs are *learned*; they are not innate or instinctive in the way in which physiological drives are. Because they are *shared* they become a yardstick for behaviour, departure from which is regarded as deviancy and may be punished with considerable severity. Third, while a culture will evolve over time it possesses an enduring quality which enables it to be *transmitted* from generation to generation.

There are many different cultures, and Robertson suggests that a structural framework for classifying these may be developed, using three dimensions – distributive, organisational and normative. In his words:

The *distributive* dimension summarises demographic characteristics, such as income and education levels, and the distribution of the population ecologically (for example, urban, suburban, or rural) and occupationally. The *organisational* dimension summarises participation patterns within the culture, and the structure of cultural institutions. Social class structure and the rigidity or flexibility of this structure, as well as the nature of family relationships, are organisational topics. The *normative* element treats values and norms, including economic or religious philosophy.

While these three dimensions are very useful in drawing broad distinctions between, say, Eastern and Western cultures, it is obvious that they must be used with caution and as a first broad-brush basis for distinguishing between behavioural patterns. Indeed, for most marketers it is sub-cultures which are of more direct and immediate interest because they provide a meaningful way of segmenting a society. *Sub-cultures* usually develop from a basic dimension of race, religion or nationality, and it is these which tend to have most influence upon consumer behaviour. However, age and ecological sub-cultures are also distinguishable and important.

Bennett and Kassarjian (in *Consumer Behavior*) suggest that culture exerts this influence mainly upon consumption *per se* and media image and has greatest relevance in the sphere of international marketing. In the case of consumption differences food preferences are probably the most obvious case in point, followed by clothing and beverages (for example Muslim attitudes to alcohol). Sub-cultures have an important influence upon the acceptability of message content, particularly in terms of the cultural expectancies of the audience, e.g. technical information for men, style information for women for consumer durables, and demands careful attention by advertising strategists. (Robertson gives a number of interesting examples of 'cultural implications for marketing'.)

While it may seem obvious that culture is of most relevance to the international marketer, there is a tendency to exaggerate this. Specifically, the generalisations which are usually cited as dire warnings of the perils of ignoring the cultural differences between different international markets often serve to disguise the fact that there are probably as many different and diverse segments within an overseas market as in the domestic one. Further, given modern communications systems, it is highly likely that very similar segments for particular products may be found in most countries, despite the fact that the commonplace in the United States may be a luxury in Africa or India (or the commonplace in Saudi Arabia a luxury in the United States!). Perhaps the safest policy is to be sensitive to cultural differences but act upon the existence of common sub-cultures. It is for this reason that although the EEC became a single market in 1992 in economic terms it still comprises a large number of distinct markets based upon cultural and other regional differences.

☐ *Social class*

A particularly strong and pervasive, indeed universal, sub-cultural division is that of social class, whereby members of a society are stratified into a number of subdivisions. These subdivisions or classes are based upon many common characteristics, which usually include income, education, occupation and social status or prestige. These characteristics give rise to similar behavioural patterns and activities which can be differentiated from those of other social classes. This latter point is of particular importance to marketers, for the value of such a classification lies in the ability to discriminate between groupings of people and, it is hoped, to predict their behaviour under given conditions.

Many people find the concept of class offensive, because of the intrinsic implication that people can be ordered according to their worth, and argue that all people are equal. Such an argument would appear to be based largely upon an economic interpretation of equality and leads to attempts to distribute wealth more evenly through society. However, it is clear that the redistribution of wealth has relatively little to do with the value attached to the various roles filled by individuals and it is this which is the essence of social stratification. Thus in most societies teachers and priests are accorded relatively high status and prestige but earn incomes more in keeping with members of a lower class; similarly, pop singers earn more than opera singers but their earnings are probably inversely related to their prestige. So, while it is true that the status associated with given roles may change over time, it seems highly improbable that there will ever be a truly classless society.

It follows that if we wish to make use of this universal tendency for societies to 'classify' themselves, then we must identify and measure those factors or criteria upon which such a classification rests. In doing so one must not be

surprised if different sets of criteria result in a different number of classes. However, most systems used in Western cultures have a close allegiance to the six-class model proposed by W. Lloyd Warner (1960) in his celebrated study of a small New England Town, *Social Class in America*:

Social class	*Membership*
Upper-upper	Aristocracy
Lower-upper	New rich
Upper-middle	Successful business and professional
Lower-middle	White-collar worker
Upper-lower	Blue-collar worker
Lower-lower	Unskilled

While this scheme recognises two more classes than did Centers's 1949 division into upper, middle, working and lower classes, Warner himself saw the issue as a false one in that the number of divisions is relatively arbitrary and dependent upon whose opinion you are seeking. It should also be noted that in many instances one is as much concerned with differences within classes as between them.

The most widely used system in the United Kingdom is that developed for use in the *National Readership Survey* (see Table 6.3).

Just as the concept of culture is useful for classifying people into broadly similar groupings, so social-class concepts help refine the classification into smaller and more specific segments with greater operational potential for practitioners. Engel *et al.* (1995) cite a large number of studies which illustrate the application of social class in helping to interpret and predict consumer behaviour – social class has been found to be especially useful in predicting preferences for kind, quality and style of clothing, home furnishings, leisure activities, cars, consumer durables, and use of credit cards. Social class has also been shown to be associated with patterns of media usage, language patterns, source credibility and shopping behaviour. This predictive power is considerably enhanced if one is able to add to it knowledge concerning reference groups, role and family influence.

Table 6.3   *NRS social grade definitions**

Social grade	Social status	Occupation
A	Upper middle class	Higher managerial, administrative or professional
B	Middle class	Intermediate managerial, administrative or professional
C₁	Lower middle class	Supervisory or clerical and junior managerial, administrative or professional
C₂	Skilled working class	Skilled manual workers
D	Working class	Semi and unskilled manual workers
E	Those at the lowest level of subsistence	State pensioners or widows (no other earner) casual or lowest-grade workers

* These are the standard social grade classifications using definitions agreed between Research Services Ltd., and NRS.

Source: National Readership Survey.

Reference groups, role and family influence

When discussing psychological influences upon behaviour the emphasis was upon the individual. But 'No man is an island', and all of us are subjected to the influence of others with whom we come into contact. This influence is particularly strong in the case of what are termed *reference groups*.

Social psychologists reserve the description 'group' for collections of two or more persons who interact with one another over time. In other words there must be some relationship between the group members which goes beyond collections of persons with common interests such as a theatre audience or passengers in an aeroplane. Bennett and Kassarjian (1972) in *Consumer Behavior* cite Krech, Crutchfield and Ballachey's (1962) definition from *Individual in Society*, namely: 'a group is (1) persons who are interdependent upon each other, such that each member's behaviour potentially influences the behaviour of each of the others, and (2) the sharing of an ideology – a set of beliefs, values, and norms – which regulate their mutual conduct'.

Several different types of reference groups may be distinguished, the most basic distinction being between primary and secondary groups. A primary group is one which is small enough for all of the members to communicate with each other face to face (the family, a seminar group, the area sales team), while a secondary group is one where less continuous interaction takes place (professional societies, trade unions, companies, and so on).

When a group possesses a specified structure and specified functions then it is termed a *formal* group, but where the structure and function are unspecified, as in a circle of friends, we have an *informal* group. Both formal and informal groups have norms which prescribe the pattern of behaviour expected of members and the transmission of these norms to new members is known as *socialisation*. In formal groups the norms are usually much more explicit and readily identified than in informal groups, but the norms of the latter are no less demanding if one wishes to remain in membership of the group. In all cases the influence of the group is towards conformity, and the strength of this tendency will depend upon the pressure the group can bring to bear upon the individual, the importance of the group to the individual and the number of groups to which the individual belongs.

In a marketing context perhaps the most important group of all is the family – specifically the *nuclear family* of husband, wife and children (the extended family includes grandparents, aunts, uncles, cousins, and so on). The nuclear family is frequently referred to as 'the household' in consumer studies but such usage is often looser and may include any group of persons occupying

Table 6.4 *Characteristics of household population[1]*

(a) Number of households in Great Britain: 22 675 000 (March 1995)

(b) **Size of households, 1993**

	%
1 person	27
2 persons	35
3 persons	16
4 persons	15
5 persons	5
6 persons	2
	100

Average (mean) h/h size:	1993	2.44
	1971	2.91

(c) **Sex of head of household, 1993**

	%
Male	73
Female	27
	100

46% of the female heads of household are over 60 and living alone.

(d) **Marital status by sex, 1993**

16 and over	Men %	Women %
Married	62	56
Cohabiting	6	5
Single	24	18
Widowed/divorced etc.	8	21
	100	100

(e) **Female housewives with/without children under 15, 1994–95**

	%	%
With children, (total)		51.0
0–23 months	6.3	
0–4 years	14.1	
0–15 years	30.6	
Without children		48.9
		100.0

(f) **Working status of housewives (female)[2], 1994–95**

	%	%
Working full-time		
30+ hours per week	25.6	
Working part-time		
8–29 hours per week	19.0	
Working full- or part-time		44.6
Not working; and part-time		
under 8 hours per week		55.4
		100.0

(g) **Number of economically active persons in household, 1994–95**

	%
No person	33.2
1 person	28.8
2 persons	29.9
3 or more persons	8.1
	100.0

(h) **Retired/non-retired h'holds[3], 1994–95**

	%
Retired, (total)	39.1
Dependent on state pensions	26.1
Other	13.0
Non-retired	60.9
	100.0

(i) **Static/non-static households, 1995/Q1**

	%	%
Static		98
Non-static, (total)		
Newly weds' h'holds	0.2	
Movers into:		
– new homes	0.2	
– other movers	1.5	
		100

Notes: [1] (g), (h) refer to the UK; (b), (c), (d), (e), (f), (i) to Great Britain
[2] According to the Family Expenditure Survey 1994–95, 15% of households have working married women with dependent children
[3] Households consisting of one adult or one man and one woman only

Source: (a), (i):   GfK Marketing Services Ltd
(b), (c), (d): General Household Survey
(e), (f):   National Readership Survey (NRS Ltd.) July 1994–June 1995
(g), (h):   Family Expenditure Survey 1994–95

the same housing unit, as does the official US Census Bureau definition.

In the 1990s there has been a continuing trend away from the traditional nuclear family or household. The characteristics of the UK Household Population are set out in Table 6.4.

From this table it is clear that the number of single-person households is considerable (27 per cent) and, with an aging population, is set to increase. It is also clear that there is a significant number of single-parent households, of working 'housewives', economically inactive persons (retired and unemployed) and so on. All of these changes are having, and will continue to have, an important impact on consumption behaviour.

Nonetheless, as a primary group the family has great influence upon motives, personality and attitudes and acts as a mediating influence upon external influences which impinge upon it from culture, sub-culture, social class and other reference groups. Because of this mediating influence, and due to the economic inter-dependence of its members, family (household) decision-making has a profound influence upon purchasing and consumption behaviour. All of the basic disciplines upon which marketing is founded have advanced their own explanation of household decision-making and there is no shortage of theories for the marketer to consider. J. L. Drayton (University of Strathclyde Student Notes) has traced the basic themes from these disciplines as follows:

Economics: the household has tended to be viewed as an efficiency unit, using an input/output analysis in which input = time and labour (income) and output = goods and services (wealth). This approach uses a unified demand and preference schedule, i.e. each member of the household views each purchase in the same light in terms of utility gains, maximisation of family satisfaction.

One attempt has been made to derive a household preference theory from Hicks' individual preference schedule (drawn from a marginal rate of substitution of one product for another). Empirical testing of this theory caused it to be abandoned – since no apparent relationship existed between the individually stated preference and actual family choice of products.

Psychology: individuals seeking to meet their own needs; finding a balance between power and harmony; suggests a host of separate utility patterns – but little direct contribution to how these combine (given a limited income).

Sociology: with the sophistication of techniques and theory provided by the study of small groups, family sociologists have been the major researchers in the field of how families actually reach a decision. As one would expect, starting from the basis of small group studies, the emphasis has been upon establishing patterns of leadership roles – a dominant partner typology, which might suggest for instance that the UK is basically patriarchal in outlook (therefore husbands will dominate decision making); or that the US is matriarchal! Neither typology has been empirically proven. The idea of producing a typology is that this then becomes the 'Family norm' – anything differing from this norm can be analysed to discover why.

Anthropology: concentrates upon the transfer of cultural values from generation to generation; thus decision making here becomes a factor in the socialisation process, with the roles (or status) within a family (and within a society) determined at birth and learned in childhood.

Thus when marketers require information about household consumption there is no shortage of theories to turn to. The problem confronting us is rather 'which one is the most useful in its application to the marketing of goods and services to families?' As we have noted elsewhere marketing is, by its very nature, a synthesising discipline, as are most professional practices, and the challenge for the marketing manager is to choose the explanation which appears most useful in any given context.

The question may well be raised as to how a greater knowledge of the decision-making processes can assist the marketing practitioner. Three obvious areas spring to mind:

1. Product planning and design;
2. Distribution channels;
3. Communication strategies.

In terms of design factors of household products (e.g. consumer durables) there may be a conflict between the technical perfection the design engineers and production techniques are capable of and the needs of the eventual user. In the trade-off between efficiency and ease of use the marketer needs to know what are the important characteristics of the product as perceived by the product-user/decision-influencer. A good example of this was the heating and ventilation company which was seeking to develop a 23-function controller to out-perform the 21-function product of their nearest rival. It was accepted that the increased complexity would add to both the purchase price and servicing cost but it was felt this was justified in regaining their technical lead. The engineers were asked how many functions the owners of existing room controllers used. They didn't know! A small survey of consumers established that many people used the controller solely as an on-off switch (2 functions) and many more just to programme their heating to come on and off for 2 different time periods every day (4 functions). In other words, the design engineers had completely lost touch with the market reality.

A review of empirical studies of family decision-making reveals two major underlying currents:

1. Ideological role theory;
2. The resource theory of power.

The primary hypothesis in the ideological theory of roles is that household decision-making and activity patterns can be explained in terms of role expectations developed through the pervading culture. Each member of the family has a meaningful set of chores to perform – meaningful in the sense that such chores contribute to family survival and well-being.

The traditional and best-known exposition of family roles is the goal-orientated husband who 'gets things done', complemented by a supportive wife playing a social emotive role of 'keeping the family together'. Division of roles in this way generalises that husbands are responsible for decisions which are essentially concerned with the interface between the household and the external world, while wives take responsibility for activities within the family.

Although role theory has been useful to sociologists in understanding family survival in periods of social change, research into product decisions utilising role theory has been ambiguous and conflicting.

The alternative explanation of household power structure is resource theory. The main thesis is that authority and activity patterns within the family can be analysed in terms of such variables as income, education and social status. The right to make decisions influencing family welfare is related to the comparative resources brought to the marriage.

A resource in this context is defined as 'any special characteristic, skill or competence of one partner that contributes to family goal attainment' and embraces the following:

- Earning capacity (present and potential);
- Occupation (both partners);
- Education level;
- Religion;
- Life-style;
- Age.

From a practical point of view it is useful to try and classify the extent and nature of influence in the household decision-making unit and four basic role-structure categories may be distinguished:

1. Husband dominant;
2. Wife dominant;
3. Autonomic (an equal number of decisions is made by each partner but without consultation);
4. Syncratic (most decisions made jointly).

As suggested earlier, an ability to relate role-structure category and purchase of specific products will be of great value in developing new products and the most effective marketing mix to promote and sell them. A very useful review of research in this area is to be found in Engel *et al.* (1987), pp. 269–304.

The physical or demographic composition of the family will also have a significant influence upon its consumption behaviour and the concept

Table 6.5 *Family life-cycles*

Age	Developmental level		Stage in the family life-cycle
18–34	Early adulthood	1	The bachelor stage: young, single people
		2	Newly married couples: young, no children
		3	The Full Nest I: young married couples with dependent children: (a) Youngest child under six (b) Youngest child over six
35–54	Middle adulthood	4	The Full Nest II: older married couples with dependent children
55 and older	Later adulthood	5	The Empty Nest: older married couples with no children living with them: (a) Head in labour force (b) Head retired
		6	The Solitary Survivors: the older single people (a) In labour force (b) Retired

Source: Fred D. Reynolds and William D. Wells (1977) *Consumer Behavior* (McGraw-Hill).

of the family life-cycle is a particularly useful framework for analysis. The most extensive model contains six stages (as shown in Table 6.5).

For a very extensive analysis of the relationship between these stages and consumption behaviour the book by Reynolds and Wells contains five chapters dealing specifically with this topic. All major text books devote a chapter, or major part of one, to household/life cycle analysis although some now refer to the *consumer life cycle* (for example Wilkie, 1994, Chapter 14) recognising that the traditional family is less typical than it used to be. Many research organisations have developed distinctive approaches to life cycle analysis and examples are to be found in *The Marketing Pocket Book* (1995) and the companion *Lifestyle Pocket Book* (1996). (See Life-style in the next section.)

☐ *Life-style*

So far the discussion has focused upon major sociological concepts which have been borrowed and adapted by marketers in seeking to explain and predict consumer behaviour. We now con-

sider a composite concept which has been developed extensively by consumer-behaviour researchers during the 1970s and early 1980s that seeks to synthesise the economic, psychological and sociological influences, namely 'life-style'.

In essence life-style summarises the way in which we live and is founded upon the observation that people seek consistency or balance in their lives – the old concept of homoeostasis – and so organise their behaviour to try and achieve this state. We have already noticed this tendency in discussing the concepts of perception, personality and motivation and observed how it becomes socialised in cultural traits, norms and values. Given this tendency towards consistency in behavioural response it follows that if we can identify a consumer life-style in one context, then we should be able to extrapolate from that situation and predict how he will behave in different sets of circumstances.

The measurement of life-style in the subject of an area of research known as *psychographics* is discussed at length in Engel *et al.* (1987). An excellent overview of the subject is also to be found in an article by William D. Wells (1975), 'Psychographics: A Critical Review'. In this article Wells proposes an operational definition of psychographic research as 'quantitative research intended to place consumers on psychological – as distinguished from demographic – dimensions', a definition which emphasises the distinctive features of the area – it has a quantitative rather than a qualitative orientation and goes beyond demographics. (Engel *et al.* point out that 'psychographics' is often used interchangeably with the mnemonic AIO standing for Activities, Interests and Opinions as a research area.) The use of life-style for segmenting consumer markets is discussed in more detail in Chapter 8.

Composite models of consumer behaviour

For many years prominent researchers in the consumer-behaviour field have attempted to develop comprehensive theories of consumer behaviour. In *Marketing: Theory and Practice* (1983), my colleague Jennifer Drayton summarised a number of the more important models – those of Nicosia, Andreasen, Engel, Kollat and Blackwell, Clawson, and Howard and Sheth – as follows:

> These models differ in respect to their complexity and orientation but are nevertheless based upon the same strands of thought. Thus similarities are to be found in the isolation and identification of the relevant variables, and in the perspective of a dynamic decision process, with the actions of the consumer viewed as a movement towards some decision point. Although little or no attempt has been made to modify or update these models they still represent an important step in the development of our understanding of consumer behaviour.

We still subscribe to this view and so retain the short descriptions of some of the major models in this 6th edition. Many text books, for example Wilkie (1994), make no explicit reference to them; while others, for example Leon Schiffman

and Leslie Kanuk's *Consumer Behavior*, have consigned them to an Appendix.

Nicosia

Nicosia (1966) uses as a base for his model a computer flow-chart technique, divided into four distinct areas, or 'fields'. The output from each field becomes the input to the succeeding field.

The model depicts a message (for example, an advertisement for a new product) flowing from its source (in this case the business firm) in the direction of an eventual decision outcome by the consumer. In Field 1 the consumer is exposed to and receives the message, with an outcome of the development of some predisposition, or attitude, towards the product; Field 2 is concerned with the search and evaluation process, which has as its output the arousal of the individual's motivation, leading to Field 3, which is defined as 'possible transformation of the motivation into an act of purchase'. If purchase occurs, Field 4 becomes the area of storage and use of the product, with a related output of experience.

In each of the fields the relevant influences upon the eventual outcome are delineated. As the message flows from the business firm to the formation of a consumer attitude, it will be modified or distorted by internal subjective perceptual elements. During the period of 'search and evaluation' (Field 2) the internal and external forces are differentiated in terms of additional information input. Internally initiated data are concerned with the associations, conscious or unconscious, with the firm, the brand or the product, while external data are culled from the environment in the form of word-of-mouth communication, or an increased receptivity to advertising in the product area.

Andreasen

Andreasen (1965) has developed the concepts of 'attitude formation' and 'attitude change' contributed by social psychologists to construct a consumer-decision model as an information-processing cycle. This model indicates that attitude change can be achieved via exposure to information. Change of attitude is assumed to be a logical preliminary to a change in behaviour, an assumption which is lacking in verification since the complexity of the attitude – behaviour relationship remains a controversial area in social-psychology studies. It is as yet far from certain that influence in this area is a one-way flow from attitude to behaviour as the model suggests.

Andreasen's model centres upon the individual utilising a message input to reach a decision outcome, with attitude formation and change as the central concepts. The predispositional nature of attitudes (that is, not based on actual experience) is shown to impinge upon the individual's perceptions, which operate as a filter through which the information must pass to reach the cognitive system. Thus attitudes to message source or 'channel' may effectively alter the character of the original communication.

Engel, Kollat and Blackwell

These researchers (1968) have produced a sequential approach to the purchase decision which has been described as a complete model of buying behaviour. It is a general model which gives a framework for examining the diverse range of influences to which the buyer is subject as the decision process moves from its initial stage of the beginnings of need awareness through its subsequent steps up to the terminal stage of after-the-event evaluation and rationalisation. The contributions of the three basic internal processes – perception, learning and motivation – represent major steps in the model, while personality and attitudes are seen to exert pressure upon the process. The social and cultural aspects of the possible purchase decision are also shown as influencing the individual's movement through the decision stages.

Clawson

Clawson (1950) has extended the views propounded by Lewin in his behavioural studies, with the contribution of *Gestalt* theories clearly in evidence.

The analysis is concentrated in some depth upon the tension element in a purchase decision as the individual assesses the positive and the negative aspects attached to the decision outcome, producing a situation of psychic conflict. The fact that both the positive and the negative features are perceived subjectively by the consumer is also stressed, indicating that the conflict cannot be resolved on the grounds of objective product characteristics or information. These objective criteria may not penetrate the net of selective perception, or may be distorted on the way.

Howard and Sheth

Howard and Sheth (1969) have based their approach to the formulation of a general consumer model on the standpoint of the consumer playing an active role in the business transaction. S/he is not merely exposed to communications but is portrayed as vigorously collecting and processing information.

Fundamentally the model is constructed around a series of stimulus variables passing into the individual's processing system and being acted upon by the internal factors of perception and learning, termed by the researchers 'the hypothetical constructs'. A response variable terminates the process, with the whole being surrounded by the exogenous variables of social class, culture and personality, plus such constraints as time and income availability.

Inputs are separated out into three groups which distinguish source differences. The first group relates to the actual product communications of price, quality, availability, distinctiveness and service. The second group derives from indirect and impersonal sources, such as salesmen or the mass media. The third group of stimulus variables identifies the activity of the consumer collecting data from his social environment via the personal influence of word-of-mouth communication. Thus the interaction between the consumer and his social environment is distinguished and extended, showing the external forces in the decision process not only as a constraint upon behaviour but also as a reference point for the gathering of credible information. Interaction between the individual and their environment is seen to be a two-way function.

The hypothetical constructs of perception and learning detail the manipulation of the information gathered from the various sources, affecting the amount and quality of objective information which reaches the system.

Howard and Sheth have acknowledged that these hypothetical constructs and their interrelationships are a consequence of the integration of a number of well-known theories – Hull's learning theory, Osgood's cognitive theory and Berlyne's theory of exploratory behaviour.

Paradigms of consumer behaviour

Based upon the above review it is possible to identify two broad paradigms or models of consumer behaviour which may be distinguished respectively as the *cognitive* and *behavioural* explanations.

In essence the cognitive explanation sees consumer behaviour as the consequence of an interpersonal, cognitive, information processing activity which results in choice as the outcome of deliberation and decision-making. By contrast the behavioural paradigm regards choice behaviour as the consequence of prior behaviour and sees choice decisions as the consequence of determined responses to environmental stimuli (G. R. Foxall, 1983).

Most major models such as those of Nicosia, Engel, Kollat and Blackwell, Howard and Sheth fall into the cognitive category and 'depict the consumer advancing along a problem-solving and decision-making sequence, the outcome of which is determined by the buyer's intellectual functioning and rational processing of information. Consumers are credited with the capacity to receive and handle quantities of information as they engage in extensive pre-purchase searches and evaluations. Further, the consumer is viewed as perceiving information critically, using decision rules and evaluative criteria to establish its

personal relevance to his goals and purposes, while generally employing mental processes to reach a decision' (Shams, 1989). Subscribers to cognitive explanations of consumer behaviour regard marketer initiated communications as vital cues or stimuli which make consumers aware of needs and wants and of possible solutions to these felt needs.

Thus, as Foxall (1987) has pointed out 'choice is essentially the resolution of conflict, brought about by awareness of a number of options, through cognitive evaluation of the possibilities available and a reasoned consideration of the costs and benefits which each entails'.

In her review of cognitive explanations, Shams (1989) points out that numerous authors have criticised his approach and quotes Markin and Narayana (1976) who concluded that most empirical research points to an opposite conclusion; namely, that consumers:

1. Do not seek extensive amounts of information in relation to purchase and consumption problems;
2. Do not process large amounts of information when confronted with purchase and consumption problems; and
3. Do not appear to engage in extensive problem-solving behaviour even in relation to high expenditure purchases.

– all conclusions reached by my colleague Keith Fletcher (1986) in his doctoral research 'Social Behaviour: an analysis of information and usage during the decision process'.

As a result of the criticisms of the cognitive school there has developed a renewed interest in behavioural explanations. Two main schools may be distinguished – *classical* conditioning and *operant* conditioning. Classical conditioning was referred to in the section on Learning earlier in the chapter and is usually associated with Ivan Pavlov's experiments with dogs in which he showed that a physiological response – salivation on the presentation of food – could be conditioned by the simultaneous presentation of a second stimulus – the ringing of a bell – such that a dog could be conditioned to salivate on the ringing of the bell alone. Operant conditioning is associated with the work of B. F. Skinner who argued that 'behaviour is shaped by its consequences' and so emphasises actions under the conscious control of the individual by contrast with involuntary responses of the kind studied by Pavlov. Further, operant conditioning is focused on consequences which follow behaviour while classical conditioning emphasises stimuli which precede behaviour. As noted earlier in the chapter, we learn patterns of behaviour based upon the level of satisfaction we derive. Thus satisfactory outcomes reinforce a pattern of behaviour while unsatisfactory outcomes (punishers) dissuade us from repeating such behaviour in future.

It follows that once a consumer has determined a satisfactory pattern of behaviour then he will continue to repeat that behaviour until it either causes dissatisfaction ('familiarity breeds contempt') or he becomes aware of a stimulus which suggests that a modified form of behaviour could lead to even greater satisfaction. In an attempt to accommodate both the cognitive/rational and behavioural explanations of consumer choice – both of which have clear merits and weaknesses – a composite model of buying behaviour is proposed.

A composite model of buying behaviour

As noted in the introduction to this chapter there is a tendency to distinguish between individual and organisational buying behaviour by emphasising the qualitative/behavioural nature of the former and the quantitative/rational/economic nature of the latter. In my view this distinction is largely spurious as I believe that all buying decisions are subject to the same economic and behavioural influences and in the majority of cases follow the same basic process. This process is best observed by analysing the purchase of a product of which the user has no prior experience, for otherwise several stages may be omitted,

that is the purchase of a familiar brand or the automatic re-ordering of an industrial supply.

For a number of years now I have been developing a composite model of buying behaviour which attempts to combine both economic and behavioural factors as well as capturing the essentially sequential nature of buying decisions. The current version of the model may be expressed notationally as follows:

$$P = f[SP(PC, EC, IS, PF, CB)BR]$$

P = purchase
f = a function (unspecified) of
SP = selective perception
PC = precipitating circumstances
EC = enabling conditions
IS = information search
PF = performance factors
CB = cost–benefit
BR = behavioural response

The first point to be made is that this is a sequential process model very similar to the Buying Decision Process model introduced at p. 108. *PC* is equivalent to problem recognition, *EC* to *interest* (that is the problem is accepted as a real one deserving further consideration). *IS*, a new variable corresponds to information search and recognises that if a review of the enabling conditions confirms a continuing interest then one will have to gather additional information on which to make a decision. *PF* and *CB* summarise the objective data concerning performance or 'fitness for purpose' and the economic benefits of acquisition and comprise the 'rational' elements of evaluation. *BR* is a surrogate for the subjective and judgemental factors which will invariably be taken into account when a prospective buyer has more than a Buy–Don't Buy choice; that is, there are two or more objectively similar products or services which could solve the prospective buyers' consumption problem which initiated the process. Thus *BR* is a composite of one's prior experience and attitudes which may or may not include direct post-purchase experience of the object under consideration.

Second, the precise nature of the function is not specified for the simple reason that it is not known and that it is unlikely, to say the least, that any single functional form could capture the interaction between the other variables in the model.

SP, or selective perception, is a new variable in the model. In earlier versions, the influence of this factor was subsumed within *BR*, which occurs at the end of the process. By placing *SP* at the beginning as a factor mediating the other variables it is possible to communicate that this is a process model and that selective perception will determine whether or not one will even become aware of a purchase opportunity (*EC*), besides conditioning the information selected for evaluation and the interpretation placed upon it.

Finally, the behavioural response may be almost automatic, as, for example, when the preceding evaluation indicates that one option is clearly to be preferred. Alternatively, it may be an extremely difficult and protracted stage when the preceding analysis has failed to suggest one choice before all others – a common occurrence in many markets.

Having described the general model, some elaboration of the variables will indicate what sort of factors one would need to take into account to use the model.

In the Pavlovian learning model of buyer behaviour, reference is made to the need for some cue or stimulus to activate a drive and initiate action. In our model, this factor is termed a precipitating circumstance – what is it that would make a buyer consider a change in the status quo? Clearly, dissatisfaction with existing alternatives constitutes a marketing opportunity and is one type of precipitating factor. The need to replace or renew a piece of capital equipment or consumer durable is another opportunity, whether the need is caused by breakdown, loss, destruction or a planned replacement policy. Knowing which customers might be in this state would enable the firm to focus its marketing effort to much greater effect, both in terms of the information to be conveyed and the means of conveying it. Similarly, being able to satisfy a known need – to have a faster computer, a more

economical car, and so forth – is a claim likely to precipitate active consideration of a new purchase.

Enabling conditions embraces all those factors which make it possible for a prospective purchaser to benefit from the new product. A television is no use if you have no electricity, nor a gas oven if you have no gas. In the same way, many manufacturers try to avoid mixing materials such as steel, aluminium and plastics, since each requires different skills and techniques in use and increases the investment necessary in both plant and labour. In other words, a new product must be compatible with the user's current status and, in many cases, also with their self-image. In the absence of such enabling conditions, interest is likely to be short-lived and unlikely to proceed further to an evaluation.

Technology or performance and the economics or cost–benefit of a purchase are at the very heart of the Marshallian and 'rational' schools of buying behaviour's models – *PF* and *CB* in our model.

Finally, however, it must always be remembered that the majority of buying decisions turn on highly specific characteristics – another reason why a general model cannot possibly accommodate all conceivable sets of circumstances.

We have already stipulated that the importance of behavioural response will depend heavily upon the objective evaluation of the available facts (albeit that these are perceived subjectively), and 'build a better product at an equivalent price or an equivalent product at a lower price' is clearly the best advice to management. But, in most competitive markets, there is often little to choose objectively between alternative offerings, and the buyer will have to make deliberate recourse to subjective value judgements to assist in distinguishing between the various items available. Because housewives do this daily when preferring Bold to Persil, Sunblest to Mother's Pride and so on and so forth, they are often characterised as choosing irrationally. Nothing could be further from the truth. The important objective decisions about a shopping basket relate to its overall mix and composition *vis-à-vis* the available budget – the choice decision is which detergent, which bread, and so on. It would be a fatal mistake to imagine that the industrial buyer doesn't have just the same problems when deciding between Scania, Mercedes, or Leyland for his lorries or Cincinnati and/or Kearney and Trecker for his machine tools.

The red meat market: a consumer behaviour example

Many of the key variables that exist in the analysis of consumer behaviour can be examined using the example of the red meat industry. In 1992 the UK meat market was worth £9.9 bn and was therefore the most important food retail sector. Within this sector the red meat market has seen a substantial decline in consumption and some clear changes in the behaviour of its consumers. In the late eighties and early nineties the UK consumption of red meat fell from 36.77 to 34.11 ounces per person per week, whilst the percentage of household food expenditure on meat fell from 25 percent in 1985 to 22 percent in 1992. Household expenditure on alcohol is twice what it is on red meats. These trends obviously have serious ramifications for the UK red meat industry. The only areas that have experienced recent growth are exports (for example to Europe) and catering sales (for example fast food retailers).

Traditionally, the social influences on the British consumer have been conducive to the selection and consumption of red meat. The national dishes of the UK are often centred upon the use of red meat (for example roast beef and Yorkshire pudding, Aberdeen Angus steak) and this has derived and been reinforced by the farm production and climate of the UK. Cultural influences have generally been devoid of the taboos inherent in many other cultures that can prevent red meat eating. In the past one of the main social influences that affected the consumer's behaviour with regard to red meat consumption was income. However, this did not so much dictate whether or not you ate red meat but what sort of red meat you could afford to purchase. Now the Meat and Livestock Commission suggest that consumers lack a 'feel good' factor about buying meat and that this may relate to factors such as job fears or lowering personal disposable incomes.

The red meat market has seen a declining rate of consumption due to the changing lifestyles and attitudes of its consumers. People are increasingly health conscious and this has caused them to turn towards other food products like white meats and vegetables as a means of reducing cholesterol and improving the diet. Negative publicity has also been to the detriment of red meats with food scares like the BSE disease amongst cattle, the use of growth hormones and campaigns highlighting cruelty to animals in food production. Consumers have also been attracted by the new eye-catching alternatives that take up an increasing amount of shelf space, such as fresh pasta and pizza. In effect the consumer behaviour of the British red meat eater is changing dramatically and there is a need for marketing strategies to adapt to this; for example producing and promoting lean, low-fat cuts and concentrating on the benefits that can be gained by promoting healthy new recipe ideas. Meat producers are clearly aware of the need to redress the increasingly negative attitudes towards red meat and to counter the growth of vegetarianism amongst younger consumers and reference groups. In America where there has been a 33 per cent decline in per capita meat consumption, the American Beef Industry Council has been behind campaigns to promote red meat such as 'Real Food for Real People'. The UK Meat and Livestock Commission has backed similar campaigns such as 'Meat to Live'. The hope is that the attitudes and norms displayed by consumers will not continue to change to the detriment of red meat consumption. (*Source*: Keynotes (1992) 'Meats and Meat Products'.)

Summary

This chapter has ranged over a very wide area that is the subject of many substantial books in their own right. Its purpose has been to sensitise the reader to factors which influence behaviour in the market-place but a full appreciation must depend upon extensive study of the major sources cited.

The chapter opened with a simple and generalised model of the buying decision process as the basis for a brief review of some of the major factors which are involved in and influence the process. Thus we looked at perception, learning, motivation, personality and attitudes as psychological factors. Next, we examined social influences on behaviour, including culture, social class, reference groups, role and family influences and the concept of life-style. This was followed by an overview of some of the major composite models of buyer behaviour before introducing our own model designed to provide a simplified but synoptic explanation of the process.

In the next chapter we look at buying behaviour in an organisational setting.

Review questions and problems

1. Attitudes have a central role in the development of behavioural patterns. Consider the use of attitude studies as a guide to the marketing practitioner.

2. Consider the value of the life-style concept as an approach to market segmentation.

3. The main alternative to problem-solving behaviour is habitual behaviour. Discuss the application of these patterns of behaviour to the market-place.

4. Measures of social class have been both valuable and misleading as an aid to market segmentation. Discuss the use of social class, and the possibilities offered by the addition of complementary psychographic techniques.

5. Should the marketer assume that organisational buying decisions are always based upon rational/economic considerations?

6. What do you understand by the term 'Learning'? Briefly outline any one learning theory and discuss its relevance to an understanding of consumer behaviour.

7. Maslow's theory of motivation postulates five general types of needs. Define these needs and explain with examples how their economic importance can be exploited by advertising.

8. Culture has a pervasive influence on consumption patterns. Discuss the implications of cultural factors in new product diffusion.

9. Why do groups have such a considerable influence on individual consumer behaviour? What are the implications of this for product promotion and advertising?

10. Explain how an understanding of how consumers make decisions might aid the marketer in developing a strategy.

11. Discuss the relationship between social class membership and consumption patterns.

12. Examine the view that psychological explanations of consumer behaviour may be useful theories but they are of little practical value to the marketer.

13. What are attitudes? Can they be changed? What is the relevance of attitudes to communications, advertising and marketing?

14. 'The consumer is not the completely rational animal dreamed up by the classical economists and fondly termed "Economic Man"' (Shanks). To what extent do you agree, and give reasons for your viewpoint.

15. In what way can a knowledge of the Behavioural Sciences (Sociology, Psychology) help the marketing/advertising executive to have a better understanding of consumer choices and purchasing behaviour?

16. Homogeneous products are for homogeneous consumers. Discuss.

17. Define each stage of the consumer buying decision process, explaining why marketers need to understand each stage.

18. Explain what is meant by the consumer buying decision process. Why is it important for marketers to understand the influencing factors at each stage of the process?

19. Explain how the various stages of the consumer decision-making process vary according to whether the product being chosen is classified as high involvement or low involvement.

20. Define the concept of attitudes. Describe, using a real product, strategies marketers could use to change negative attitudes which consumers may hold about their products.

21. Discuss the significance of the family in consumer behaviour.

22. Detail the various stages included in the Consumer Buying Decision Process. Why is it important for marketers to understand this process?

▌ Supplementary reading list

Aaker, D. A. and Day, G. S. (eds) (1982) *Consumerism: Search for the Consumer Interest* (New York: Free Press).

Engel, J. F., Blackwell, R. D. and Miniard, P. W. (1995) *Consumer Behaviour*, 8th edn (London: Dryden Press).

Foxall, G. R. (1986) *Consumer Behaviour: A Practical Guide* (London: Routledge).

Foxall, G. R. (1996) *Consumers in Context* (London: Routledge).

Kassarjian, H. H. and Robertson, T. S. (1991) *Perspectives in Consumer Behaviour*, 4th edn (Prentice-Hall International).

Loudon, D. and Della Bitta, A. J. (1993) *Consumer Behaviour Concepts and Applications*, 4th edn (London: McGraw-Hill).

Mowen, J. C. (1992) *Consumer Behaviour*, 3rd edn (London: Macmillan).

Schiffman, J. G. and Kanuk, L. L. (1994) *Consumer Behaviour*, 5th edn (Englewood Cliffs, N.J.: Prentice-Hall).

Solomon, M. R. (1994) *Consumer Behaviour: Buying, Having and Being*, 2nd edn (New York: Allyn and Bacon).

Wilkie, W. L. (1990) *Consumer Behaviour* (New York: Wiley).

Worcester, R. M. and Downham, J. (1988) *The Consumer Market Research Handbook*, 3rd edn (London: McGraw-Hill).

■ Chapter 7 ■

Organisational Buying Behaviour

Contents

Learning goals

The issues to be discussed in this chapter include:

1. The similarities and differences between organisational and consumer buying behaviour.
2. The role and importance of organisational buying behaviour.
3. The nature, functions and practices of organisational buyers and the buying process.

After reading this chapter you will be familiar with:

1. The nature of organisational buying behaviour.
2. The similarities and differences between consumer buying behaviour and organisational buying behaviour.
3. Why organisational buying is important.
4. The key concepts in organisational buying behaviour.
5. The factors which influence organisational buying behaviour.
6. What is meant by 'an interaction approach' to organisational buying behaviour.

■ Introduction

In the preceding chapter the emphasis was on individual behaviour and the influence and consequences of this in terms of buying or consumption decisions. In this chapter our attention is focused upon the way the same individuals behave when faced with the responsibility of acting on behalf of an organisation and often as part of a decision making unit (DMU) or buying group.

At the outset it must be stressed that in exactly the same way that it was argued that while one can discern many differences between the marketing of consumer and industrial goods it is important not to overlook the similarities, so in the case of individual and organisational buying behaviour one must be careful not to overlook the fact that the *process* is the same. Thus the generalised model of buying behaviour presented at the end of Chapter 6 is believed to be just as applicable to both individual and group buying decisions, although it is immediately acknowledged that groups may undertake a much more formal and rigorous approach than do most individuals.

In our Introduction to the preceding chapter we explained that many researchers and authors now refer to business to business marketing to emphasise differences between organisational buying and individual buying behaviour. For the reasons given we prefer to stick with organisational buying behaviour (OBB) as this includes a wider spectrum of organisations than businesses – a view shared by Wilkie (1994) who includes OBB as a 'special topic' in his Chapter 21. The purpose of this chapter, therefore, is to identify and describe some of the more salient features of organisational buying behaviour and point out the similarities and differences between it and individual behaviour.

To this end we shall first review the better known models which seek to describe and analyse the nature of the organisational buying process.

Having established a broad framework which defines the general process we shall then look more closely at some of the more important constituent elements beginning with the composition and activities of the buying group, together with the influence of various factors – organisational, environmental and product-related upon these activities. Finally, we shall examine the stages of the purchasing process or 'buyphases' as they are frequently called.

Models of organisational buying behaviour

One of the first serious attempts to impose some structure upon the wealth of descriptive material about industrial buying behaviour was provided by Frederick Webster Jr (1965) in an article entitled 'Modelling the Industrial Buying Process'. In an effort to distinguish the important variables and the relationships between then, Webster proposed four key areas – *Problem Recognition*, the assignment of *Buying Responsibility*, the nature of the *Search Process* and the nature of the *Choice Process*, with the inference that these are sequential steps in the overall buying process.

According to Webster a buying situation is created by the recognition that there is a difference between an organisation's goals and its performance which may be remedied or solved through a purchase. In that both goal-setting and problem recognition are influenced by personal and impersonal factors, both internal and external to the organisation, it follows that these have to be identified and analysed if we are to understand organisational buying decisions. In terms of the personal factors it has to be remembered that ultimately the organisational decision will be delegated to individuals and the allocation of this responsibility will be influenced by individual, company, product, industry and market factors, so these too must be specified and understood. These same factors will also influence both the search and choice processes.

The next important contribution to the OBB literature was provided by the publication of *Industrial Buying and Creative Marketing* by P. J. Robinson, C. W. Faris and Yoram Wind (1967), which reported the results of a project sponsored by the Marketing Science Institute. Based upon in-depth studies of three companies in the United States over a two-year period, Robinson, Faris and Wind proposed that industrial buying may be conceived of as a process consisting of eight sequential steps or buyphases, namely:

1. The anticipation or recognition of a problem or need, including the realisation that a problem exists, and the awareness that a solution may be possible through a purchase of an industrial good.
2. The determination of the quality and characteristics of the needed item.
3. The specific description of the item needed.
4. The search for, and qualification of, potential sources.

5. The examination of the sources, leading to a decision concerning how the item is to be purchased.
6. The evaluation of proposals and the selection of suppliers.
7. Selection of an order routine.
8. Performance feedback and evaluation.

In addition, Robinson, Faris and Wind identified three distinct buyclasses, which may be defined as follows:

1. *New task* – the recognition of a purchasing problem which has not been encountered previously. The buyer will face considerable uncertainty and will seek to reduce this through the acquisition of as much information as he can obtain from both personal and impersonal sources. All the buyphases are likely to receive careful and explicit attention.
2. *Modified rebuy* – the buyer has prior experience of the purchase problem but has reason to re-evaluate this in light of some new information or precipitative circumstance, for example a lower bid from another supplier, a change in design or specification, and so forth. Some of the buyphases may be truncated or omitted.
3. *Straight rebuy* – the buyer is satisfied with an existing source of supply and sees no reason to change. Phases 4–7 are likely to be omitted altogether and only cursory attention given to the others; that is purchase has become habitual and routinised.

Figure 7.1 *The buygrid analytic framework for industrial buying situations*

		BUY CLASSES		
		New Task	Modified Rebuy	Straight Rebuy
B U Y P H A S E S	1. Anticipation or Recognition of a problem (Need) and a General Solution			
	2. Determination of Characteristics and Quantity of Needed Item			
	3. Description of Characteristics and Quantity of Needed Item			
	4. Search for and Qualification of Potential Sources			
	5. Acquisition and Analysis of Proposals			
	6. Evaluation of Proposals and Selection of Supplier(s)			
	7. Selection of an Order Routine			
	8. Performance Feedback and Evaluation			

Source: Robinson *et al.* (1967) *Industrial Buying and Creative Marketing* (Allyn & Bacon).

By combining Buyphases and Buyclasses we obtain the *Buygrid* as depicted in Figure 7.1.

This framework appears simplistic by comparison with the more complex and sophisticated models developed since. However, this is seen as its greatest strength, for it is relatively easy to recall, and by classifying the kind of buying decision and the stage in the process one can quickly focus attention on the key factors which apply to that location in the grid; for example, for most straight rebuys one can establish routines and procedures for automatic ordering from qualified suppliers provided that previous orders have met the predetermined requirements. In *Marketing: Theory and Practice*, Shan Rajagopal (1995) provides a useful comparison of buying classes which is reproduced below as Figure 7.2.

The next important contribution to modelling OBB was that of Frederick Webster Jr and Yoram Wind (1972) who joined forces to offer 'A General Model for Understanding Organisational Buying Behaviour'. Diagrammatically this model appears as in Figure 7.3 and may be explained as follows. Organisational buying is a decision-making process carried out by individuals, in interaction with other people, in the context of a formal organisation which is subject to a variety of environmental forces. Thus the factors which impinge on and influence OBB may be classified as individual, social, organisational and environmental. In turn each of these factors may be categorised as comprising task variables, which are directly related to the specific buying problem, and non-task variables which are not.

Figure 7.2   *Comparison of buying classes*

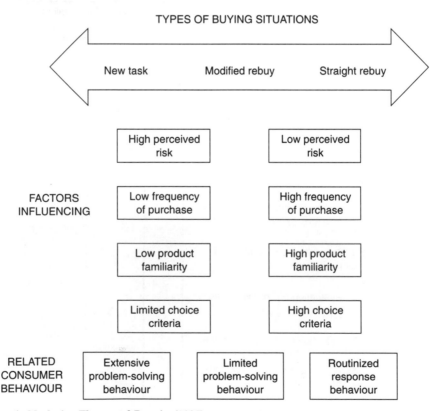

Source: S. Rajagopal, *Marketing Theory and Practice* (1995).

Figure 7.3 *The Webster and Wind model for understanding organisational buying behaviour*

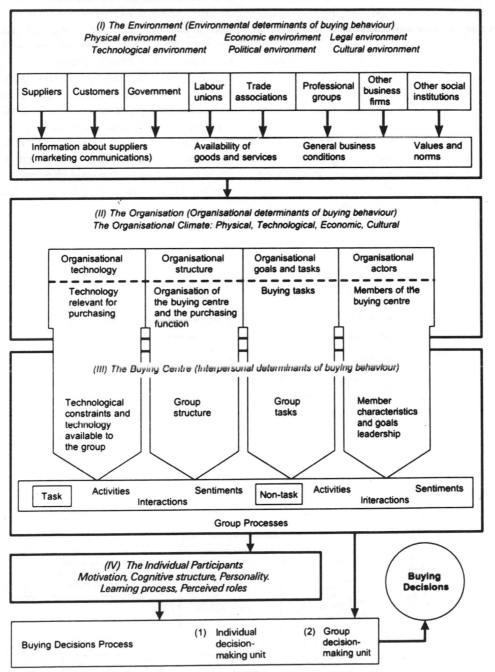

Source: Webster and Wind (1972), 'A General Model for Understanding Organisational Buying Behaviour', *Journal of Marketing* (April).

The earlier work of the authors is readily identified in their joint model which conceives of OBB as a complex process involving many persons, multiple goals and potentially conflicting decision criteria. The process may extend over a considerable period of time, demand large amounts of information from many diverse sources and require numerous inter-organisational relationships. At the heart of the process is the *buying centre* which includes all members of the organisation who may be involved in the various roles of user, influencer, decider, buyer and gatekeeper (the person or persons who control the flow of information into the buying centre).

Members of the buying centre are subject to both individual and organisational goals and so their relationships encompass all the complexity of interpersonal interaction which the organisation seeks to structure, influence and control through the subsystems of tasks, structures, technology, and people. Finally, the organisation has to operate within the constraints and opportunities of the environment and the economic, technological, physical, political, legal and cultural forces which comprise it.

As Hill and Hillier (1977) point out, the main deficiency of the actual model is that it conveys a static rather than a dynamic impression, although this is partly compensated for in their description

Figure 7.4   *The Sheth integrative model of industrial buying behaviour*

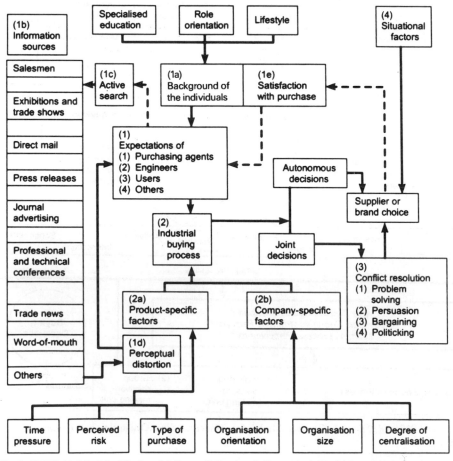

Source: J. N. Sheth (1983) 'A Model of Industrial Buyer Behaviour', *Journal of Marketing* (October).

of it. Hill and Hillier also criticise the model as 'a basic skeleton of organisational buying behaviour, without any muscles or nerves', but clearly it is more complex and comprehensive than the Robinson, Faris and Wind model discussed previously. This is even more true of 'A Model of Industrial Buyer Behaviour' proposed by Jagdish N. Sheth (1983), which is summarised in Figure 7.4.

According to Sheth, OBB comprises three distinct dimensions:

1. The psychological world of the decision-makers.
2. The conditions which determine joint decisions among and between these individuals.
3. The process of joint decision-making and conflict resolution among decision-makers.

In terms of the first dimension it is recognised that most industrial buying decisions are made by a number of people from different backgrounds and performing different roles – Purchasing agents, Engineers, Users and Others in Box (1) of the model. The differential expectations of these individuals is seen as the result of their background (1a), information sources (1b), their active search (1c), and perceptual distortion (1d)

of these sources and their satisfaction with past purchases (1e). These expectations are modified by product specific factors (2a) such as time pressure, perceived risk and the type of purchase, and company specific factors (2b) such as organisational orientation, organisational size and degree of centralisation in the course of the industrial buying process Box itself.

The third dimension and central concern of Sheth's model is how the different participants in the buying decision resolve potential conflicts between themselves arising from their different roles, expectations and perceptions. Box (3) suggests four different approaches to conflict resolution – problem solving, persuasion, bargaining, and politicking. However, in the course of arriving at their joint decision a number of *ad hoc* situational factors Box (4) such as temporary economic conditions, industrial relations problems, production bottlenecks and so on will play an important part. Recognition of these factors clearly injects the dynamism absent from the Webster and Wind model and so makes it more useful in an operational sense.

Since Sheth's and Webster and Wind's attempts to provide a comprehensive model of OBB the emphasis has shifted to a much more detailed analysis of how actual buying decisions

Figure 7.5 *The constituent elements of the anatomy of the purchase*

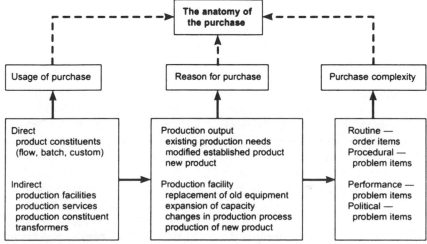

Source: Hill and Hillier (1977), *Organisational Buying Behaviour* (London: Macmillan), p. 25.

are made and the precise nature of the various forces and influences involved – what Hill and Hillier characterise as 'the anatomy of a purchase', although they use this description in a narrower way than implied here.

The Hill and Hillier model reproduced as Figure 7.5 is intended to analyse a purchase decision from the perspective of the buyer, and contains three major elements – usage of the purchased item, reasons for the purchase, and the purchase complexity. The intended use for the proposed purchase is seen as a vital piece of information to the seller, because it will indicate the technical content involved, the value and essentiality of the item, and therefore the degree of risk involved; the likely timing of the purchase; and whether the product is more likely to be buyer or supplier specified. Hill and Hillier then propose five main categories of use as follows:

1. For incorporation in production output which may be to order or to stock and in the latter case production may be either batch or continuous;
2. For utilisation during the production processes but not incorporated in the product;
3. To provide a production facility in either manufacture, service or resale;
4. For use in maintenance operations;
5. For use in development or engineering work.

Basic reasons for purchase are summarised in the diagram and will have a significant influence upon the criteria used in arriving at a decision. This is also true of the complexity of the purchase which builds upon distinctions made by Lehmann and O'Shaughnessy (1974) who argued that 'if products could be classified on the basis of problems inherent in their adoption, such a classification might be both predictive of weightings of the relative importance of product/supplier attributes, and predictive of buyer preferences with regard to suppliers'. Four categories are then proposed which Hill and Hillier summarise as:

1. Routine order products which are frequently ordered, and present no significant usage

problems because everybody is familiar with them, and it is known that they can 'do the job'.
2. Procedural-problem products, which are known 'to do the job', but problems may arise because personnel must he taught how to use them.
3. Performance-problem products, where the problem concerns the technical outcome of using the products.
4. Political-problem products, where there is likely to be difficulty in reaching agreement among those affected if the purchase is made. This kind of problem arises when large capital outlays are involved, and more frequently when the products are an input to several departments whose needs may not be compatible.

This classification goes beyond Robinson *et al.*'s novelty of purchase buyclasses and also differs in that the four categories are not seen as mutually exclusive but indeed may overlap with one another.

According to Daragh O'Reilly (1995), more recent research by Bunn (1993) has suggested that the number of basic buying situations could be increased to six.

Bunn's view was that organisational buying is affected by situational characteristics and buying activities. Situational characteristics were basically four in number:

- Purchase importance: the buyer's perception of the significance of the buying decision in terms of the size of the purchase and/or the potential impact of the purchase on the functioning of the firm;
- Task uncertainty: the buyer's perceived lack of information relevant to a decision situation;
- Extensiveness of choice set: the buyer's perception of the breadth of alternatives available as choices in the context of a particular decision situation;
- Perceived buyer power: the buyer's perception of the firm's negotiating strength in a particular buying decision situation.

Buying activities, what buyers actually do when making buying decisions, could be broken down into four principal categories:

- Search for information: the buyer's effort at scanning the internal and external business environment to identify and monitor information sources relevant to the focal buying decision;
- Use of analysis techniques: the extent to which the buyer makes use of formal and/or quantitative tools to objectively evaluate aspects of the buying decision;
- Proactive focusing: the extent to which decision-making related to the focal purchase is prospective and thus considers the strategic objectives and long-range needs of the firm;
- Procedural control: the extent to which the evaluation of a buying decision is guided by established policies, procedures or transaction precedents.

The research revealed six different categories of buying decision approach (situation), as follows:

- Casual: involves no search, no analysis, no strategic view and a lot of procedural control, low-value items – for example: an electricity supply firm buys a relay for repair purposes;
- Routine low priority: basically a repeat buy, checking to make sure nothing new is on the market;
- Simple modified rebuy: likely to involve essential items for which the buyer perceives a limited number of options available;
- Judgemental new task: first-time purchase of a special type of equipment;
- Complex modified rebuy: a structured and rational process, extensive quantitative analysis; for example a competitive bidding process;
- Strategic new task: focus on long-term planning, infrequent purchase, may involve different departments, can be a lengthy process.

The benefits of this research is the greater fine tuning of the buying decision approach – indeed, the use of the term 'buying decision approach' instead of 'buying situation' is an important clarifying point. So also is the definition of the key buying activities and situational characteristics separately from the situation.

Organisational buying behaviour as an interactive process

Thus far all the models of organisational buying behaviour we have discussed have been unidimensional in the sense that they have looked exclusively at behaviour and processes within the customer organisation. Over the past twenty years (since the mid-1970s) the deficiencies of such an approach have been increasingly recognised, and have led to the development of much more sophisticated models and analyses in which purchasing is seen as an interactive process taking place within a network of suppliers and users. Foremost among the exponents of this approach is the IMP Group, which initially comprised 14 researchers drawn from five European countries (France, Germany, Italy, Sweden and the UK) and later extended to include colleagues in the USA. The major findings of the Group are reported in two major publications: *International Marketing and Purchasing*, by P. Turnbull and M. Cunningham (1980), and *International Marketing and Purchasing of Industrial Goods*, ed. Håkan Håkansson (1982). More recently another member of the Group, David Ford (1990) has edited a collection of the Group's findings in a book entitled *Understanding Business Markets: Interaction of Relationships and Networks*. The key concepts and assumptions underlying the interaction approach are described at some length in Chapter 2 of the latter book and a synopsis of these is given below.

At the outset it is important to recognise that marketing is a synthetic discipline, in the sense that it seeks to combine insights and ideas from a wide range of other disciplines in the hope that by so doing it will be able to come up with a more powerful explanation of behaviour in the real world. Thus economics, psychology, sociology, anthropology, statistics, law and so on all provide important contributions to our new discipline of marketing whose own distinctive contribution is to combine and synthesise these in new ways. In the case of the interaction approach the models of OBB described earlier provide an important input, but this has been extended by drawing upon two major theoretical models from outside the marketing literature – Inter-organisational Theory and New Institutional Economic Theory. As Håkansson notes, 'Much of the work in Inter-organisational Theory involves attempts to apply theory and concepts from intra-organisational studies to problems where several organisational units are involved. Here the focus of attention is on relationships between those organisations (hence 'relationship marketing') rather than within each individual organisation.' Three distinct approaches may be distinguished which may be identified as:

1. *Organisation based studies* in which the organisation is studied in terms of the environment within which it has to operate and interact with. The models of OBB described above fit into this category which until now has been the predominant marketing perspective and contains 'two distinct and *separate* approaches to the study of what occurs in industrial markets. On the one hand, there is an analysis of the manipulation of marketing variables by the seller to achieve a desired market response. On the other hand, there is a separate analysis of a single buying process and the factors which affect that process, from which lessons can be drawn for marketing.'
2. *Studies based on several organisations* which are seen as part of a network. In a marketing context this conforms with the 'distribution system perspective' in which the market is seen as 'a system of interconnected institutions performing the economic functions required to bring about exchange of goods or services'.

3. *Studies of the organisation in a societal context* in which 'the organisation is seen as an integrated part in a larger social system'. This approach has been little developed by the IMP Group whose work is mainly focused on approach (2) with a limited recognition of (3).

With regard to the 'New Institutional Economic Theory' the main foundation is to be found in the seminal contribution of O. E. Williamson (1975), *Markets and Hierarchies: Analysis and Antitrust Implications*. Williamson's work constitutes a criticism of perceived deficiencies within traditional micro-economic theory, particularly the view that market exchanges will maximise efficiency.

According to Williamson one must distinguish between situations where exchange efficiency will be maximised through the existence of independent units operating in a market, and those where such efficiency will be achieved through vertical integration within a single unit. Only by examining carefully the factors which influence transaction costs will one be able to determine the most effective institutional structure (including intermediary structures) and such an examination focuses attention on those variables such as bargaining relationships, organisational characteristics, information handling behaviour, and so on which are central to the study of OBB.

In the IMP Group's model, 'the marketing and purchasing of industrial goods is seen as an interaction process between two parties within a certain environment', and comprises four basic elements:

1. The interaction process;
2. The participants in the interaction process;
3. The environment within which interactions take place;
4. The atmosphere affecting and affected by the interaction.

The model is conceptualised as in Figure 7.6 and a full description of the elements is to be found in Håkansson (1982, pp. 16–23). Clearly, the approach proposed above goes a long way

Figure 7.6 *An illustration of the interaction model*

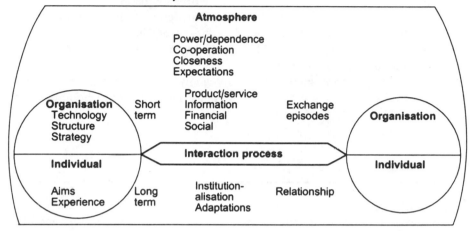

Source: IMP Group, *op. cit.*

towards capturing the dynamic complexity of organisational buying and selling behaviour. In light of this, and not forgetting the composite model proposed in the previous chapter, it will be helpful now to look more closely at some of the constituent elements.

The composition of the buying group

All of the models of OBB recognise that buying is a complex process in which purchasing decisions are made by a group or 'buying centre' rather than by an individual. It follows, therefore, that if one is to understand the process then one must be able to define the buying group or centre in terms of its possible composition *vis-à-vis* the various buying situations and phases in the buying process.

As Wind (1976) has pointed out, 'the basic concept of a buying centre suggests that it is a temporary organisation unit, which may change in components and functions from one purchase to another'. This view has been supported by numerous other studies which confirm that not only do buying groups vary from decision to decision but that their composition varies over the life of a particular purchasing decision.

With regard to who actually is involved, the *Financial Times*/IMR survey, 'How British Industry Buys' (1974), indicated a wide range of participation, including:

1. Collective decisions	Board Management Committee
2. Individual (non-departmental)	Managing Director Other Director General Manager Company Secretary
3. Department (collective and individual)	Department Manager Operating Manager Other Design and Engineering Production

Purchasing
Sales and Marketing
Research &
    Development
Finance/Accounts
Other

4.   External decision

Several studies which have analysed the composition of the buying group argue that it should be and often is a function of product-related variables. The most frequently cited such variables are:

1.   The technical complexity of the product;
2.   The value of the item to be purchased;
3.   The frequency of purchase;
4.   The product's essentiality to the production process;
5.   The potential consequences of making a wrong decision;
6.   The degree of inherent innovation or novelty in the product;
7.   The product's overall complexity.

By analysing and rating the product on these dimensions one should be able to conclude who

Table 7.1   *Buying centre roles defined*

Role	Description
User	As the role name implies, these are the personnel who will be using the product in question. Users may have anywhere from inconsequential to an extremely important influence on the purchase decision. In some cases, the users initiate the purchase action by requesting the product. They may even develop the product specification
Gatekeepers	Gatekeepers control information to be reviewed by other members of the buying centre. The control of information may be in terms of disseminating printed information or advertisements or through controlling which salesperson will speak to which individuals in the buying centre. To illustrate, the purchasing agent might perform this screening role by opening the gate to the buying centre for some sales personnel and closing it to others
Influencers	These individuals affect the purchasing decision by supplying information for the evaluation of alternatives or by setting buying specifications. Typically, technical personnel, such as engineers, quality control personnel and research and development personnel and individuals outside of the buying organisation can assume this role (for example an engineering consultant or an architect who writes very tight building specifications)
Deciders	Deciders are the individuals who actually make the buying decision, whether or not they have the formal authority to do so. The identity of the decider is the most difficult role to determine: buyers may have formal authority to buy, but the president of the firm may actually make the decision. A decider could be a design engineer who develops a set of specifications that only one vendor can meet
Buyers	The buyer has formal authority for selecting a supplier and implementing all procedures connected with securing the product. The power of the buyer is often usurped by more powerful members of the organisation. Often the buyer's role is assumed by the purchasing agent, who executes the clerical functions associated with a purchase order

Source: Adapted from Webster, F. E., and Wind, Y. (1972), *Organisational Buying Behaviour* (Englewood Cliffs, NJ: Prentice-Hall), pp. 77–80.

might be involved and the extent of their involvement in a purchasing decision.

An alternative approach to the study of the composition of buying groups has focused on the roles played by different members, which have been characterised as users, influencers, deciders and gatekeepers (Webster and Wind, see Table 7.1), or as contributors, participants, responsibles and directors (B. Klass 1961, 'What Factors Affect Industrial Buying Decisions'). Another schemata proposed by *Sales Management* in 1963 distinguished those who make major buying decisions, make recommendations, must approve purchases, affect the conditions of use, and conduct the buying negotiations. However, as Shan Rajagopal points out in Chapter 5 of *Marketing: Theory and Practice* (ed. M. J. Baker, 1995), 'Operationally, conceptualisation of the buying centre by role definition is of little use to a researcher wishing to study the purchasing decision-making process. Specifically, the notion of generalised role relationships within the buying centre does not accommodate a method for ascertaining the individual membership of the buying task group, nor its decision making potential.' (This chapter on 'Organisational Buyer Behaviour' is strongly recommended for further reading on the subject.)

On the other hand, if one has a model defining the possible roles which members of a buying group may perform, then one is more likely to recognise their existence in an actual buying decision and formulate tactics for overcoming possible resistance while reinforcing and supporting those who are favourably disposed to a sales offer.

Another important contribution of the concept of a buying group is that it reminds us that other people in the organisation are likely to be involved in the purchase decision in addition to the designated purchasing agent or buyer. Thus while most order inquiries are initiated by purchasing agents, and 'the buyer' is the obvious person to approach first with a selling proposition, it is important to recognise that this individual or department may have neither the discretion nor authority to make a decision. How then should one assess the purchasing function's role?

The role of the purchasing function

In her review of industrial buying behaviour, Kennedy (1983) in *Marketing: Theory and Practice*, suggests that purchasing's involvement in buying decisions is a function of four sets of factors:

1. The nature and status of purchasing within the organisation;
2. The purchasing agent's perception of his function;
3. Task versus non-task behaviour;
4. Environmental and extraneous market conditions.

With regard to the nature and status of purchasing within an organisation it has been shown that the existence of a separate purchasing function and its size depend very much upon the overall size of the organisation as a whole. However, the size of a purchasing department does not necessarily indicate that it occupies an important place in the organisational hierarchy as it may be charged merely with an order processing-function while all the key decisions are made by R&D or manufacturing. To some extent the status of the purchasing department may be inferred from the status of its senior manager – are they a main Board director, or do they report to the Board, if at all, through a hierachy of other more senior managers? According to Webster (1965), 'Modelling the Industrial Buying Process' the purchasing department's influence on a buying decision will tend to increase as:

- Market variables become more important in relation to product variables;
- The size of firm and spatial separation of activities increase;
- The organisation formally assigns specific responsibility to the purchasing department.

With regard to the purchasing agent's own perception of his role, most of the evidence suggests that buyers feel their contribution is undervalued. When one reflects on the contribution which efficient buying can make to the firm's overall profitability, there would seem to be some justification for this point of view. Consider, for example, a firm with the following sales and cost structure.

	Sales revenue	100
Less	Bought in materials	46
	Labour and overheads	20
	Cost of goods sold	68
		32
Less	Selling, general and administrative expense	20
	Profit before tax	12

It is clear that any increase or decrease in the price of bought in materials will have a greater effect than a proportionately equivalent change in efficiency of any of the other business functions either separately or together.

Of course, savings on bought in materials may have nothing directly to do with the buyer but result from changes in design or specification initiated by other members of the buying group. None the less, there is good reason to believe that the purchasing agent can play a critical part in the interface between an organisation and existing and potential suppliers, and so should be accorded equal status with senior managers in the other business functions. However, pending such explicit recognition, purchasing agents will no doubt continue to use the tactics described by Strauss (1962) in his frequently cited study, 'Tactics of Lateral Relationships: The Purchasing Agent', for handling conflicts with other functions:

1. Rule-oriented tactics – the buyer works to the book. In this case a written responsibility to purchase is required.
2. Rule-evading tactics – the buyer revises requisitions and follows a tactic of feigned acceptance.
3. Personal–political tactics – the buyer projects an aura of friendship and willingly exchanges favours.

4. Educational tactics – the buyer attempts to persuade others to think in purchasing terms.
5. Organisation-interaction tactics – the buyer exhibits the willingness to communicate with other organisational departments and to participate in decision-making.
6. Organisational change tactics – in this case, the buyer attempts gradually to evolve change in organisation procedures. One example of these tactics is the materials management idea.

The third factor which influences the purchasing agent's involvement in buying decisions is the emphasis upon task and non-task behaviour. In simple terms, the task elements of buying are those which may be defined and, usually, measured using objective criteria; for example supplier identification and qualification, value analysis, price, and so on. By contrast the non-task elements tend to be subjective and difficult to quantify – reputation, performance, reliability and so on. As a generalisation, it would seem that the greater the focus upon task elements and the greater the purchasing agent's perceived competence in handling these, then the greater will be the role played by the purchasing department.

The final element which seems likely to influence the importance given to purchasing is the environmental context within which the buying firm has to operate. When the external environment is dynamic and uncertain then the purchasing function is likely to assume more importance as it is called upon to help reduce the uncertainty which these conditions create. Similarly, under conditions of recession more attention is likely to be given to the cost incurring functions and purchasing will assume increased visibility and importance. It is under such conditions that other management functions are forced to consider the relevance of the task elements, with techniques like value analysis calling for close cooperation between purchasing and R&D and manufacturing and inventory control calling for involvement of the finance function.

Another environmental change which is tending to increase the role of the purchasing function is the increasing concentration in many industries which is resulting in the creation of very large and professional buying groups. Indeed, in some consumer goods markets the retail buying groups are much bigger than the manufacturers that supply them and in 1984 the Federation of Food Manufacturers persuaded the Office of Fair Trading to inquire into the impact this was having on profit margins. In its report (*Competition in Retailing*, June 1985) the OFT found that there had been no material change in the facts which led the MMC (Monopolies and Mergers Commission) to conclude in 1991 that the general effects of multiple buying power had not been harmful to the public interest.

■ Buy-phases

In the earlier review of composite models of OBB we looked at the model proposed by Robinson, Faris and Wind (1967) which conceived of buying as a process consisting of eight sequential steps or buy-phases. In evaluating this model it was argued that while it may appear simplistic by comparison with other, later models it possesses the particular strength that it is straightforward, robust and accords well with best practice. The model also draws attention to the sequential nature of buying decisions and invites us to consider whether the different phases are likely to involve different kinds of decisions and different members of the buying group. If so, then clearly one will need to modify one's selling tactics as the process unfolds.

As Kennedy (1983) reported, a number of empirical studies which have analysed industrial buying decisions confirm the existence of such a process which has been characterised by the various authors as follows.

In his doctoral study of over forty capital equipment purchases, T. J. Hillier (see Hill and Hillier, 1977, *Organisational Buying Behaviour*) suggested a 4-phase model:

1. The precipitation decision stage – when a definite course of action to solve a problem is confirmed.
2. The product specification stage – when broad solutions to a problem are translated into specific hardware and software requirements.
3. The supplier selection stage – when potential suppliers are identified and one or more selected.
4. The commitment decision stage – when a customer decides to what extent a supplier has fulfilled its expectation.

Such a sequence suggests that each purchase decision commenced *de novo* without prior experience on either side (as do the other buy-phase models). In reality, of course, buyers and sellers tend to interact and build up relationships with each other over time so that a more correct representation of the process is provided by the diagram of Figure 7.7.

Gordon T. Brand (1972) in *The Industrial Buying Decision*, proposes an 8-step model very similar to the original one of Robinson *et al.* (1967) namely:

Figure 7.7   *The cycle of industrial-buying decisions*

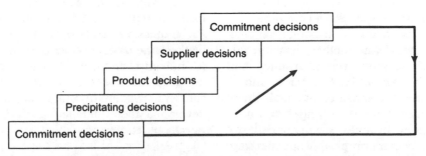

Source: R. W. Hill and T. J. Hillier (1977), *Organisational Buying Behaviour* (London: Macmillan), p. 45.

1. Problem recognition;
2. Determine characteristics of needed items;
3. Specific description;
4. Search for potential supplier;
5. Evaluate sources and products;
6. Select supplier;
7. Establish order routine;
8. Evaluate feedback.

With regard to the question of who might be involved in each of these stages, this provided the focus for the *Financial Times* survey mentioned earlier in which the following questions were asked:

1. Who originates the initial decision?
2. Who surveys alternatives and determines the basic characteristics of the product required?
3. Who makes the final decision?
4. Who identifies the potential suppliers?
5. Who collects tenders/information from suppliers?
6. Who evaluates products offered?
7. Who authorises the purchase?

8. Who finally chooses the supplier?
9. Who monitors and evaluates the performance of both the product and the supplier?
10. Who is most likely to initiate the decisions to change supplier?
11. Who finally decides on a change in supplier and selects the new supplier?

As noted earlier, this survey established that a wide range of participants are involved in a purchase decision. During the 1980s, an international group of researchers from six countries (including the author) undertook a series of in-depth case analyses of specific buying decisions in a variety of industries and settings in an attempt to determine more precisely the decision and behavioural routines in the organisational buying process. The findings of this research were published in 1986 (Parkinson and Baker, *Organisational Buying Behaviour*) and confirmed that processual interaction models best capture the organisational purchasing decision. The research also confirmed that the composite model presented in the previous chapter is equally applicable to both individual and group buying decisions.

Summary

In this chapter we have looked at some of the major dimensions of the rapidly growing field of study known as organisational buying behaviour. With increasing maturity it is both right and proper that such specialised sub-fields should develop, and clearly there are sufficient differences between the way in which organisations and individual consumers make buying decisions to justify such specialisation. However, it must also be remembered that the 'actors' who participate in organisational buying decisions are, in another capacity, the individuals whose motivations, attitudes and behaviour are looked at in Chapter 6, and it would be naive to dismiss or overlook these when analysing corporate buying behaviour. By the same token it would be equally naive to ignore the fact that if groups of people develop procedures, processes and stratagems for making buying decisions which satisfy them, then why should not individuals behave in a broadly similar manner? It is for this reason that I believe the composite model of buying behaviour proposed in the previous chapter is applicable in principle to all buying decisions. This is not to say that each of its elements will receive explicit and conscious attention every time a purchase is made nor that the weighting and emphasis given to the component parts will be the same from product to product, industry to industry or decision-maker to decision-maker. But it does offer a robust and workable conceptualisation or model around which to develop a more detailed analysis of specific purchase decisions.

Review questions and problems

1. 'The importance of conceptual knowledge (models) of buying behaviour in understanding and predicting the possible response of the relevant market segments is widely accepted when the buyers are individuals and households: it is largely ignored, unfortunately, when the buying unit is an organisation.' (Webster and Wind, 1972). What factors do you think may have contributed to the apparent neglect of organisational buying behaviour suggested by this quotation, and what factors explain the current higher level of interest in the subject?

2. Why is the post-purchase stage included in some models of the buying process?

3. Describe, preferably with the aid of a diagram, Sheth's or any other recognised model of industrial buyer behaviour.

4. Discuss the main behavioural influences affecting organisational buying behaviour.

5. Discuss the relevance of product classification schemes to the analysis of industrial buying decisions.

6. Cabinets, Calendars, Carburettors, Carpets, Chisels and Computers are a randomly selected group of products which could be marketed both to organisations and individuals. Is there any benefit for a company serving both markets to develop separate marketing strategies for consumer and industrial markets?

Supplementary reading list

Baily, P. J. and Farmer, D. H. (1990) *Purchasing Principles and Management*, 6th edn (London: Pitman).

Chisnall, P. M. (1995) *Stategic Business Marketing*, 3rd edn (Hemel Hempstead: Prentice-Hall).

Christopher, M., Payne, A. and Ballantyne, D. (1991) *Relationship Marketing* (London: Heinemann).

Davies, G. (1993) *Trade Marketing Strategy* (London: Chapman).

Hill, R. W. and Hillier, T. J. (1977) *Organisational Buying Behaviour* (London: Macmillan).

Hutt, M. D. and Speh, T. W. (1995) *Business Marketing Management*, 5th edn (Fort Worth: Dryden Press).

Parkinson, S. T. and Baker, M. J. (1986) *Organisational Buying Behaviour* (London: Macmillan).

See also the *Journal of Purchasing and Supply Management*.

■ *Chapter 8* ■

Market Segmentation

Contents

Learning goals

The issues to be addressed in this chapter include:

1. The concept of segmentation.
2. Bases for segmenting markets – geo-demographic, preference, benefit, social character, social grading, industrial and international.
3. Methods of segmenting markets.
4. The selection and use of segmentation techniques.

After reading this chapter you will be able to:

1. Distinguish between product differentia-tion and market segmentation as alternative marketing strategies.
2. Outline the benefits of using a segmenta-tion approach.

3. Summarise the basis for segmenting mar-kets and describe various approaches in some detail, including:

   ● geodemographic segmentation;
   ● preference segmentation;
   ● benefit segmentation;
   ● social character segmentation using life style and psychographics; social grading segmentation;
   ● industrial segmentation;
   ● international segmentation.

4. Describe *how* to segment a market.
5. Determine how to select a segmentation approach.
6. Specify when it is appropriate to use market segmentation.

■ Introduction

From reading Chapter 1 it should be clear that while there are many definitions of marketing there is only one marketing concept. However, it is also true that many criticisms of marketing are prompted by misunderstanding and/or misappli-cation of this concept. Usually, the 'mistaken marketing concept' is interpreted as 'give the customer what he wants', which, in many cases, is a sure road to commercial ruin. In reality the marketing concept advises that we should establish user needs and determine if, how, and to what extent it may he possible to satisfy these given one's existing and potential resources, to the mutual benefit (profit) of both parties to the exchange.

Clearly the 'real' marketing concept requires the marketer to steer a careful course between regarding every individual as a discrete marketing opportunity and considering all customers as being the same. From the preceding chapters on Consumer and Organisational Buying Behaviour it is apparent that one can either disaggregate a population into separate groups or sub-groups or else aggregate individuals into sub-groups, groups or populations through the use of a variety of distinctive features which must be possessed by those within the group but are absent from those excluded from it. In marketing this process is known as *market segmentation*.

In this chapter we shall look first at the concept of market segmentation and the benefits associated with the practice. Next we shall examine the basic approach to segmentation as a preliminary to a more detailed review of segmentation methods in consumer, industrial and international markets. Finally, we will consider how segmentation techniques may be applied and assess their role in marketing planning.

The concept of market segmentation

According to Engel *et al.*, (1972), the concept of segmentation is based upon three propositions:

1. That consumers are different;
2. That differences in consumers are related to differences in market demand;
3. That segments of consumers can be isolated within the overall market.

While these three propositions may seem eminently reasonable it has to be appreciated that according to classical economic theory supply and demand are homogeneous. Thus it was not until the 1930s when Chamberlin and Robinson proposed their theories of imperfect competition that explicit recognition was given to the observed reality that in the great majority of markets both supply and demand are heterogeneous. In turn it was not until the mid-1950s that a marketing writer, Wendell Smith, was to point out how recognition of diversity or heterogeneity in demand and supply suggested the existence of two quite different marketing strategies – product differentiation and market segmentation.

In his seminal article 'Product Differentiation and Market Segmentation as Alternative Marketing Strategies', Smith (1956) argued that both planned and uncontrollable differences exist in the products of an industry which result in sellers making quite different appeals in support of their marketing efforts. Among the reasons for this diversity Smith proposed the following:

1. Variations in the production equipment and methods or processes used by different manufacturers of products designed for the same or similar uses.
2. Specialised or superior resources enjoyed by favourably situated manufacturers.
3. Unequal progress among competitors in design, development and improvement of products.
4. The inability of manufacturers in some industries to eliminate product variations even through the application of quality control techniques.
5. Variations in producers' estimates of the nature of market demand with reference to such matters as price sensitivity, colour, material or package size.

Four decades later it is revealing to consider the essential production orientation of Smith's analysis with its emphasis upon variations or heterogeneity on the supply side. Even point 5 seems to imply that variations exist in the suppliers' perception of demand rather than in the demand itself. However, given that such differences exist, Smith argues that marketing managers could pursue one or other of two alternative strategies. Either they could seek to bring about the *convergence* of individual market demands for a variety of products upon a single or limited offering to the market, which is a strategy of *product differentiation* usually through advertising or promotions. Or, 'In some cases, however, the marketer may determine that is better to accept *divergent* demand as a market characteristic and to adjust product lines and marketing strategy accordingly,' which is a strategy of *marketing segmentation*.

Smith summarises the differences between these two strategies admirably when he writes:

> In its simplest terms *product differentiation* is concerned with the bending of demand to the will of supply. It is an attempt to shift or to change the slope of the demand curve for the market offering of an individual supplier ... *Segmentation* is based upon developments on the demand side of the market and represents a rational and more precise adjustment of product and marketing effort to consumer or user requirements.

From this definition it is clear that segmentation is a genuine marketing concept which is intermediate between the polar extremes of the perfectly homogeneous market, which is an underlying assumption of much economic theory, and the completely heterogeneous market perspective, which constitutes the perspective of the behavioural scientist. Enis (1980) illustrates these distinctions in Figure 8.1.

In the opinion of Engel *et al.* (1972), a segmentation approach offers the marketer the following benefits:

1. A segmentation perspective leads to a more precise definition of the market in terms of consumer needs. Segmentation thus improves management's understanding of the customer and, more importantly, why he buys.

2. Management, once it understands consumer needs, is in a much better position to direct marketing programmes that will satisfy these needs and hence parallel the demands of the market.

3. A continuous programme of market segmentation strengthens management capabilities in meeting changing market demands.

4. Management is better able to assess competitive strengths and weaknesses. Of greatest importance, it can identify those segments where competition is thoroughly entrenched. This will save company resources by forgoing a pitched battle of locked-in competition, where there is little real hope of market gain.

5. It is possible to assess a firm's strengths and weaknesses through identifying market segments. Systematic planning for future markets is thus encouraged.

6. Segmentation leads to a more efficient allocation of marketing resources. For example, product and advertising appeals can be more easily co-ordinated. Media plans can be developed to minimise waste through excess

Figure 8.1　*A model of market segmentation*

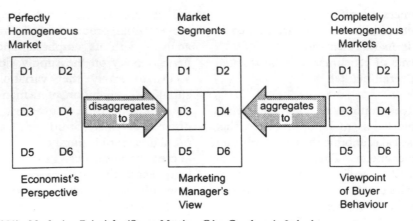

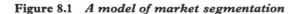

Source:　B. Enis (1980), *Marketing Principles* (Santa Monica, CA.: Goodyear), 3rd edn.

exposure. This can result in a sharper brand image, and target consumers will recognise and distinguish products and promotional appeals directed at them.

7. Segmentation leads to a more precise setting of market objectives. Targets are defined operationally, and performance can later be evaluated against these standards. Segmentation analysis generates such critical questions as these: Should we add another brand? Should we drop or modify existing products, or should we attempt to reposition a faded and obsolete brand image?

However, as Michael Thomas (1980) has pointed out, there are at least three situations when the concept of market segmentation cannot be used, namely:

1. Where the market is so small that marketing to a portion is not profitable;
2. Where heavy users make up such a portion of sales that they are the only relevant target;
3. Where the brand is a dominant brand in the market, there is no basis for segmenting.

But, apart from such situations which call for an undifferentiated marketing strategy, most academics and practitioners are agreed that some form of segmentation offers the best opportunity of securing a competitive advantage in the market place. This being so it will be useful to consider the various approaches to market segmentation in common use and the basis on which they have developed.

■ Bases for segmentation

According to Engel *et al.* (*Marketing Segmentation*), marketing managers usually divide consumers into three classes for the purpose of marketing strategy, namely:

1. *Similarity*. All consumers are basically similar. Although differences exist among consumers (for example, age, income, and so

forth), these differences are not thought to be important in affecting the purchase of their specific product class. A standard product will essentially satisfy the large majority of consumers.

2. *Unique*. All consumers are unique. The differences among consumers (for example, age, income, needs, preferences, and so forth), make a standardised product or service unacceptable. Market offerings must be tailored specifically to the needs of each individual consumer.

3. *Differences/Similarities*. Consumer differences and similarities exist and are important sources of influence in market demand. Such differences can be regarded as differences in consumer needs and wants. These differences and similarities facilitate the grouping of consumers into aggregates of *segments* according to their needs and wants and the degree to which they are present. Marketers using a segmentation approach adapt marketing programmes to match the peculiar need combinations of each of some market segment.

The obvious question is 'How do marketing managers arrive at these decisions?', to which the answer is 'By examining the variables which may be used to describe consumers and their behaviour'. According to Frank *et al.* (1972), these variables may be classified into two broad categories:

1. *General variables* where consumers are classified by broad characteristics such as demographics, personality traits or life styles.
2. *Situation-specific* variables where consumers are grouped according to consumption patterns such as frequency of usage, brand loyalty, product benefits or perceptual maps.

In Table 8.1 we provide a summary listing of the major segmentation variables.

Clearly, many of these variables are appropriate to individual consumers rather than to organisational buyers. That said, the preceding discussion of organisational buying behaviour

Table 8.1   *Major segmentation variables*

Demographics	Age, Sex, Education, Occupation, Income, Social Class, Family/Household status, Life-cycle stage, Religion, Nationality, Race
Location/Geography	Type of property, Urban, Suburban, Rural, Region, Country, Climatic Zone
Geodemographic	Combination of Demography and Geography
Psychographic	Personality, Perception, Motivation
Life-style	AIO (Attitudes, Interests, Opinions)
Behavioural	Benefits sought, Usage, Loyalty Preference, Perceptions, Readiness stage (unaware, aware, informed, interested, desirous, intending to buy), Marketing Factor Sensitivity (quality, price, service, advertising, sales promotion, etc.)
Organisational	Composition of DMU (decision-making unit) – Household, organisation; Loyalty, Reciprocity, etc.

should have made it clear that demographic, psychographic and behavioural factors will all have some influence on the way in which organisational buyers will perceive information and their reactions to it. This being so it will be both useful and relevant to examine some of the bases for consumer segmentation in more detail before moving on to the particular case of industrial and international market segmentation.

☐ *Demographic segmentation*

The first question to be answered in developing a marketing strategy is, invariably, 'Who?' That is, who is the intended customer? The most straightforward and simplest answer to this question when profiling individual customers is to use demographic factors such as Age, Sex, Marital Status, and so on. When profiling organisational customers then characteristics such as Standard Industrial Classification (SIC) code, turnover, number of employees will be used. The great advantage of demographic factors is that they are usually easy to establish/ identify and provide the basis for a great deal of

data collection by governments, public sector bodies and marketing research agencies.

Given that so much consumption is closely correlated with demography, and that so much data is available, it is surprising that greater use is not made of demographics both for analysing current behaviour and, even more importantly, for forecasting and predicting future behaviour. For example, the consumption of basic social services such as health and education is closely age-related, yet public-sector authorities seem to be singularly inept in projecting future demand. Given the number of live births in a given year one would think it would be a simple matter to forecast the demand for post-natal care, preventive care (innoculations, and so on), nursery education, primary schooling, secondary and tertiary education and so forth. Given this information, some of which gives a lead time of 17+ years, it is difficult to understand why the necessary infrastructure is not available to meet demand. Similarly, if we know that people are living longer, and that the proportion of the population over retirement age is increasing, then it should not be difficult to predict the likely demand for sheltered housing, age-related medical care, and so on.

Commercial organisations are much more adept at using Age as a predictor variable and developing specific products targeted directly at closely defined age groupings. For example, in the USA the 46 million people in the age group 18–29 have been defined as Generation X (sometimes called Xers or baby busters by contrast to their parents, many of whom were baby boomers and now comprise the new 'grey' market). With an effective demand in excess of $125 billion this age grouping represents a major market opportunity for the providers of goods and services.

Gender is another variable which is easy to establish and is closely associated with certain consumption behaviour. However, one needs to be careful not to fall into the trap of role stereotyping of yesteryear with males seen as the primary earner/breadwinner and females as household managers. Within such stereotypes products such as tyres, car batteries, power tools, home maintenance equipment and so on would be regarded as 'male' products, and clothing, food stuffs and household remedies/medicines as 'female' products. No longer! That said, one would anticipate that older men and women might still conform somewhat to these stereotypes whereas their children would not. The important point here is that in developing a marketing segment one will need to use more than one criterion to describe it precisely and accurately.

Other demographic variables which are frequently used in segmentation studies include education, occupation and income, and composite measures such as socioeconomic grouping or social class (see Chapter 5). Similarly, family/household status, life-cycle stage and so on provide a useful first set at segmenting a market and a great deal of detail on these factors is to be found in *The Marketing Pocket Book* (1995) and, especially, the *Lifestyle Pocket Book* (1996).

In recent years demographic factors have been combined with geographic/locational data to provide very powerful segmentation tools. This *geodemographic* segmentation is the subject of the next section.

☐ *Geodemographic segmentation*

In his editorial to a special edition of the *Journal of the Market Research Society* (1989) on 'Geodemographics', James Rothman traces the formal use of geodemographics (the classification of small areas according to the characteristics of their inhabitants) to 1889 and the publication of Charles Booth's *The Life and Labour of the People in London*. Based upon his survey into the economic and social circumstances of all the families in London, Booth prepared a series of maps which depicted clearly and graphically the distribution and exact location of the eight categories or classes derived from his analysis.

However the real development of geodemographics dates from the 1960s and the publication of Claus Moser's (1961) *British Towns: a Statistical Study of their Social and Economic Differences*. Although this 'received little practical application' (Rothman, 'Geodemographics') it preceded the seminal work of Richard Webber at the Centre for Environmental Studies which was to lay the foundation for the numerous proprietary systems such as ACORN, MOSAIC, SuperProfiles and CDMS.

As Rothman points out:

Geodemographics is based on two simple principles. The first is that two people who live in the same neighbourhood, such as a Census Enumeration District are more likely to have similar characteristics than are two people chosen at random. The second is that neighbourhoods can be categorised in terms of the population which they contain, and that two neighbourhoods can be placed in the same category, i.e. can contain similar types of people, even though they are widely separated. These two principles used in combination, mean that demographic information about the neighbourhood in which a person lives can be used to provide information about the probability of their having certain characteristics.

This ability clearly offers an attractive opportunity for market segmentation and the development of targeted marketing strategies.

Several aspects of the application of geodemographics to marketing are developed in considerable detail in the special issue of the *JMRS* and should be consulted by those interested in delving deeper into this topic (for example store location, designing market research surveys, sampling, targeting and so on). For the purposes of an introductory text we will confine our discussion to probably the best known of the 'off the peg' systems – ACORN (A Classification of Residential Neighbourhoods).

ACORN and the ACORN Family of consumer classification

ACORN is CACI's geodemographic consumer classification. ACORN is based on the premise that people living in similar areas are likely to have similar lifestyles. Using a range of data variables from the Census including age, family structure, occupation, ethnic group, dwelling type, car availability and lifestage, ACORN clusters Census geographies called Enumeration Districts (EDs) into distinct types.

The current version of ACORN, developed using information from the 1991 Census is a three level classification with 54 Types, 17 Groups and 6 Categories. These Categories are A – Thriving, B – Expanding, C – Rising, D – Settling, E – Aspiring and F – Striving.

The ACORN classification is used to help improve target marketing activities. This can include targeting of direct mail and leaflet drops, planning a media campaign, estimating market potential for a particular product within a store catchment evaluating branch performance, assessing locations for network expansion and many other activities.

To enhance the power of ACORN further, CACI has developed a family of classifications which provide high levels of discrimination for specific market applications.

The members of the ACORN Family include:

- Financial ACORN – which uses market research data from the Financial Research Survey (FRS) combined with Census data to supply profiles of consumers for the financial services market.

- Investor*ACORN – which uses data from the Investors Register Database to identify consumers likely to purchase goods of high net worth or invest in high value opportunities.

- Change*ACORN – which classifies the change that has occurred in different areas between the 1981 and 1991 censuses. Change*ACORN give an indication of how areas are developing or otherwise, and the likely impact these changes will have on consumer confidence and purchasing decisions.

- Scottish*ACORN – which uses additional data only collected in the Scottish Census areas to provide a profile of characteristics only relevant to the Scottish market.

- Northern Ireland*ACORN – which uses data collected by the Northern Ireland Census. The major difference between the GB Census and Northern Ireland Census is that the question on ethnicity is replaced by one on religion. Data on Northern Ireland has only ever been made available from the 1991 Census.

- Household*ACORN – which takes ACORN down from ED level to households level by factoring in information on household composition and age, building on CACI's MONICA classification, which estimates age by identifying first names within the household structure.

- Custom*ACORN – which takes a client's own customer and marketing data to build a segmentation system tailored to the specific requirements of that client.

InSite

InSite is CACI's PC-based Geographical Information System (GIS). This software is specifically designed for market analysis and targeting applications, by focusing on mapping capabilities. InSite is often used to compare and contrast different geographical areas; for example, store catchment areas or media geographies. Clients own customer and marketing data can be built into the system customising it for that company's specific applications. Data can be output as maps or tabular reports on screen or hard copy. InSite can also be used as a direct marketing tool – postal sector ranking can easily be carried out. Clients range from high street retailers to private health companies, building societies to market research companies.

Market*Master

Market*Master is a powerful marketing database system, designed as a tool for Direct Marketers. It provides the core functionality required for executing Direct Marketing campaigns across all business sectors. Again the system is customised for each client's requirements. Market*Master is a customer focused package which structures data for marketing purposes rather than operational and administrative purposes. It can be used for a number of applications including:

- Centralising customer information for improved targeting capabilities;
- Setting up a campaign for a mailshot;
- Producing mailing files in Mailsort order;
- Maintaining customer history and tracking response to each campaign;
- Cleaning and standardising name and address records;
- Coding records with ACORN.

ACORN*Profiler

ACORN*Profiler is CACI's profiling system for analysing geographical areas and customer databases by their demographic make-up. ACORN*-Profiler can incorporate the ACORN Family of classifications as well as CACI's Market Indicators (top line discriminators focusing on key market drivers – Lifestage, Housing, Ethnicity and Wealth) for the analysis process.

ACORN*Profiler holds all GB postcodes enabling any postcode imported from a client database to be analysed. Geographical areas can be created within the system enabling breakdown of the geodemographic profile of any specified area to be generated.

A by-product of importing data into ACORN*Profiler is the cleaning, reformatting and coding of customer records with CACI classification codes.

AreaData

AreaData is a set of standardised demographic reports including 5 Census-based reports including ACORN profiles and 20 market research reports covering consumer buying and spending. The reports can be delivered as hard copy or on diskette and will give an overall feel for any area down to neighbourhood levels. All figures are compared with a set of base statistics, usually that of GB as a whole. The AreaData reports are comparatively inexpensive and can be produced to very quick turnaround times.

ACORN List

The ACORN List is CACI's primary list source for targeting prospect names and addresses. It consists of an Electoral Roll database of over 44 million adults at over 22 million addresses. CACI use annually updated information which is verified and cleaned before being made available. It is also used as a base against which clients can clean their own database records. All records on the ACORN List are coded with MONICA and Household*ACORN codes. Additional information is added to enhance the individual records including:

- New Movers
- Length of Occupancy
- Young Persons
- Mailing Preference Services flag (MPS)
- Attainer flag

Lifestyle Plus Database

The Lifestyle Plus Database has been brought about by CACI's recent partnership agreement with lifestyle company ICD Marketing Services. The Database comprises over 5 million consumer names and addresses with up to 3000 pieces of information on each record. These details are gathered by questionnaire and so provide a variety of data direct from the consumer on such issues as brand loyalty, car purchasing, holiday plans and financial planning. CACI is now the only data supplier in the UK to hold substantial amounts of Census and Lifestyle data in-house.

National Mortgage Market Database

The National Mortgage Market Database is a subscription-based pooling of personal mortgage information by all the major mortgage lenders in the UK. The Members supply details on a quarterly basis (soon to be monthly), listing data on each mortgage granted. Deliverables consist of details of total accumulated market across the UK, then individually by company on number and value of mortgages as a portion of the whole, plus type and source of mortgage and many other options.

The Members use this data for local marketing, distribution planning, sales and performance targeting, product design and positioning and other evaluation and planning activities.

Table 8.2 summarises the CACI ACORN Profile of Great Britain. Another well-known system developed by Richard Webber is MOSAIC which profiles consumers according to 58 lifestyle categories and claims to differ from competitive systems in three major respects: it analyses the country in geographical units averaging 15 households, not 150; it does not rely on Census data but uses CCN's continually updating databases to track population movements; and, finally, it incorporates information on financial behaviour at postcode level by taking advantage of CCN's position as the UK's leading credit reference agency (CCN Systems Ltd is a subsidiary of Great Universal Stores PLC). In 1988 CCN launched MOSAIC Systems, a powerful PC-based product for identifying the unique characteristics of any given catchment area and designing the most effective marketing approach.

MOSAIC Systems is designed to bridge the gap between longer-term strategic decisions on matters such as product development, national advertising and pricing, and day-to-day tactical decisions on in-store promotion, distribution, coupon drops, branch location and other locally based activity. Being PC-based, users can test out any number of marketing tactics and have the results displayed instantly, without recourse to a bureau or to internal computing facilities. Results from the system can be either straightforward tabulation or full colour maps similar to that in Figure 8.2 which identifies areas where there are older couples in leafy suburbs within a 25-minute drive-time of central Plymouth.

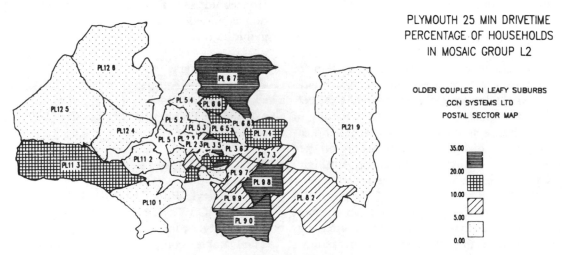

Figure 8.2 *This sample map, produced by MOSAIC Systems, identifies areas where there are older couples in leafy suburbs within a 25-minute drive-time of central Plymouth*

Table 8.2 *CACI ACORN profile of Great Britain*

CACI's ACORN classification profiles customers in a trading area or on a database into 6 Categories, 17 Groups and 54 Types (plus 1 unclassified), so that marketeers can understand more about their likely consumer characteristics. The table below shows the ACORN profile of CACI's 1995 population for Great Britain.

	ACORN Groups	ACORN Types	'000s	%
1	Waelthy Achievers, Suburban Areas	Wealthy suburbs, large detached houses	1,443	2.5
		Villages with wealthy commuters	1,798	3.2
		Mature affulent home owning areas	1,529	2.7
		Affluent suburbs, older families	2,097	3.7
		Mature, well-off suburbs	1,691	3.0
2	Affluent Greys Rural Communities	Agricultural villages, home based workers	914	1.6
		Holiday retreats, older people, home based workers	397	0.7
3	Prosperous Pensioners Retirement Areas	Home owning areas, well-off older residents	799	1.4
		Private flats, elderly people	538	0.9
4	Affluent Executives, Family Areas	Affluent working families with mortgages	1,209	2.1
		Affluent working couples with mortgages, new homes	728	1.3
		Transient workforces, living at their place of work	200	0.4
5	Well-Off Workers Family Areas	Home owning family areas	1,474	2.6
		Home owning family areas, older children	1,708	3.0
		Families with mortgages, younger children	1,266	2.2
6	Affluent Urbanites, Town & City Areas	Well-off town & city areas	615	1.1
		Flats & mortgages, singles & young working couples	426	0.7
		Furnished flats & bedsits, younger single people	253	0.4
7	Propserous Professionals, Metropolitan Areas	Apartments, young professional singles & couples	645	1.1
		Gentrified multi-ethnic areas	454	1.0
8	Better-Off Executives Inner City Areas	Prosperous enclaves, highly qualified executives	420	0.7
		Academic centres, students & young professionals	374	0.7
		Affluent city centre areas, tenements & flats	253	0.4
		Partially gentrified multi-ethnic areas	399	0.7
		Converted flats & bedsits, single people	499	0.9
9	Comfortable Middle Agers, Mature Home Owning Areas	Mature established home owning areas	1,874	3.3
		Rural areas, mixed occupations	1,963	3.4
		Established home owning areas	2,276	4.0
		Home owning areas, council tenants, retired people	1,504	2.6
10	Skilled Workers Home Owning Areas	Established home owning areas, skilled workers	2,569	4.5
		Home owners in older properties, younger workers	1,737	3.1
		Home owning areas with skilled workers	1,768	3.1
11	New Home Owners, Mature Communities	Council areas, some new home owners	2,161	3.8
		Mature home owning areas, skilled workers	1,753	3.1
		Low rise estates, older workers, new home owners	1,608	2.8
12	White Collar Workers, Better-Off Multi-Ethnic Areas	Home owning multi-ethnic areas, young families	634	1.1
		Multi-occupied town centres, mixed occupations	1,037	1.8
		Multi-ethnic areas, white collar workers	603	1.1
13	Older people, Less Prosperous Areas	Home owners, small council flats, single pensioners	1,083	1.9
		Council areas, older people, health problems	969	1.7
14	Council Estate Residents, Better-Off Homes	Better-off council areas, new home owners	1,368	2.4
		Council Areas, young families, some new home owners	1,711	3.0
		Council Areas, young families, many lone parents	894	1.6
		Multi-occupied terraces, multi-ethnic areas	484	0.9
		Low-rise council housing, less well-off families	1,003	1.8
		Council areas, residents with health problems	1,098	1.9
15	Council Estates, Residents, High Unemployment	Estates with high unemployment	631	1.1
		Council flats, elderly people, health problems	383	0.7
		Council flats, very high unemployment, singles	495	0.9
16	Council Estate Residents, Greatest Hardship	Council areas, high unemployment, lone parents	1,056	1.9
		Council flats, greatest hardship, many lone parents	516	0.9
17	People in Multi-Ethnic, Low-Income Areas	Multi-ethnic, large families, overcrowding	359	0.6
		Multi-ethnic, severe unemployment, lone parents	553	1.0
		Multi-ethnic, high unemployment, overcrowding	297	0.5
	Unclassified		280	0.5
	TOTAL		56,889	100

Notes: © CACI Limited, 1995. Tel 0171 602 6000/0131 557 0123.
    ACORN is a registered servicemark of CACI Limited.
Source: OPCS & GRO(S) © Crown Copyright 1991. All rights reserved.

On launching the system, which is supplied as an integrated software and data-learning package costing up to £20 000 per annum including updates, Richard Webber claimed:

MOSAIC Systems is going to bring a hitherto unobtainable level of accuracy to local area marketing. Any one of the questions that this product addresses would have taken many hours to research. Now marketers can test out their theories in moments – quite literally at the touch of a button. It has brought the business of marketing firmly into the computer age.

☐ *Segmentation by social grading*

The use of social class as a basis for distinguishing the consumption behaviour of groups of individuals was discussed in Chapter 6. However, the validity and effectiveness of this approach has been subject to criticism in recent years and led to the establishment by the Market Research Society (in 1979) of a working party to examine the issues. An article by Francis Quinlan (1981), 'The Use of Social Grading in Marketing', reflected some of its conclusions and findings. Thus he writes 'It is suggested that social-grading of almost any kind is becoming of only marginal practical interest to most marketers', and cites the fact that much consumer expenditure relates to family purchasing rather than individual purchasing, with the result that household or family income/expenditure is a much better indicator of market potential than information about the individual head of household or housewife. Similar criticism has also been levelled against life-style as a basis for market segmentation.

However, while Quinlan argues that 'teachers and textbooks of marketing should not continue to refer to social grading for segmentation purposes as if it were as simple as ABC', it has to be recognised that by combining socioeconomic factors with demographic and housing characteristics even more powerful and discriminating approaches to market segmentation have been developed. The most recent and sophisticated of

these approaches is the Consumer Location System, or CLS, developed by the Post Office by combining BMRB's Target Group Index and CACI Inc.'s A Classification of Residential Neighbourhoods (ACORN). The logic behind the technique is set out clearly in the PO's explanatory leaflet:

PRECISION ADVERTISING IN MASS MARKETS

The need for direct, tightly defined targeting of mass consumer markets is becoming increasingly evident. It is getting less and less feasible to write off the wastage inherent in the mass media as a marginal penalty incurred for the sake of 'cheap' media coverage – the penalties are no longer marginal.

The secret to success, however, is not simply in defining these markets more accurately, but in defining them in a way which helps maximise the advertising effort. Furthermore, by identifying the key consumer groups within a market in this way, the advertiser's options are automatically expanded to include highly targeted media such as direct mail.

Turning the theory into practice no longer presents a problem. It's now perfectly possible to:

1. Specify mass consumer markets in much tighter terms than in the past.
2. Establish a rational basis for inter-media comparisons, and consider direct mail as a consumer media option alongside TV, press, and radio – and direct mail comes out of the comparison very well in many product fields.
3. Access accurate lists of potential purchasers within the specified target market while integrating this with other media plans.

In other words, it is possible to reap the benefits of direct mail's precision and high impact in a mass market environment.

This revolutionary technique in targeting is called the Consumer Location System.

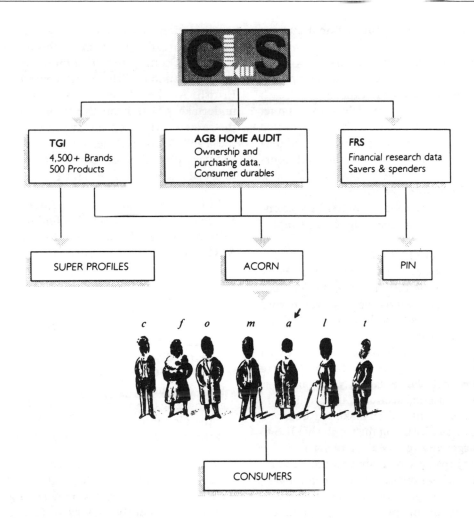

WHAT IS THE CONSUMER LOCATION SYSTEM?

CLS is a computerised system for analysing people's purchasing, reading and viewing habits, and relating these to the neighbourhoods in which they live. It will provide a refined consumer profile related to propensity to consume and will also produce media performance evaluations related to cost-effective reach of the specific target audience.

WHAT DOES IT DO?

CLS does three things. Firstly, it segments markets in a way which helps the user understand that market more fully. Secondly, it tells the user where the key consumers in that market live. It does this in a way which enables the user to reach those people through direct mail. Finally, it tells us how that market consumes different types of media – a useful gauge for those interested in the performance of different media groups in reaching their customers.

HOW DOES CLS DO IT?

It takes the data from major research sources such as Target Group Index, Financial Research Services and AGB Home Audit and it analysis markets defined by these sources using an area based classification system such as ACORN. With the use of a simple index it ranks the area types according to their level of consumption in that market. Therefore, if an area type has an index of 200 it has two times higher a level of consumption than the national average in that market – the national average always equals 100.

It also looks at the market in terms of its consumption of different media groups by taking the total level of exposure to each media group experienced by the target market, and comparing it with the expected level of exposure. For example, market 'X' may account for 10% of the total number of hours of ITV viewed in one week, but the market is only 5% of the total population. The target market is consuming twice as much ITV as one would expect (ten is twice as much as five).

HOW CAN YOU USE CLS?

You can use it as a descriptive tool which helps you to understand your market better. You can also use it to evaluate how you can reach your market most effectively with media advertising and thus reduce wastage.

The analysis will probably demonstrate that your market is heavily segmented and that a disproportionately large part of your market is situated within a small section of the population. If this is the case it may then make sense for you to exploit this fact by using the results of CLS to help you target a Direct Mail campaign.

Using the area classification and the electoral register (which is now on various computers), it is easy and inexpensive to select the names and addresses of people in your catchment areas who are the types identified by the Consumer Location System.

WHO CAN BENEFIT FROM CLS?

Anyone concerned with the task of planning the advertising of goods or services should seriously consider what the Consumer Location System has to offer. Similarly, anyone who has limited knowledge of their market's level of segmentation will find it a useful tool.

☐ *Social class and segmentation*

As noted earlier, during the 1980s many marketers in the UK came to question the relevance of the traditional social class approach to market segmentation in an increasingly more egalitarian society. In order to examine the usefulness and stability of some alternative methods of measurement Granada Television commissioned the British Market Research Bureau (BMRB) to undertake research on the topic. The results of the research received the award of Best Paper at the 1988 Market Research Society Conference and were published as 'Can we at last say goodbye to social class?' (O'Brien and Ford, 1988).

In their paper the authors, Sarah O'Brien and Rosemary Ford, report the findings of a joint working party of the IPA, ISBA, ITCA and MRS whose report published in January 1981 concluded that:

1. Social grade provided satisfactory discriminatory powers.
2. No alternative standard classification variables were found to provide consistently better discriminatory powers.
3. No classification variables worked best across all product fields or data types.
4. There was no evidence to show a decline in the discriminatory power of social grade over the previous ten years (preceding 1979).

However, these findings appear at variance with reports such as those published by the Henley Centre and others on changing life-styles and the frequently observed fact that single earner AB households with children in private education frequently have less disposable income than C2D households with multiple earners occupying low cost public housing. Further, research by BARN indicated (1987) that in one year 32 per cent of their TV audience panel had changed social class. Although this was seen as exceptional the fact that between 4 and 7 per cent of the panel change social class every year clearly points to a very mobile population in terms of the factors used to define social class.

Against this background O'Brien and Ford felt it would be opportune to compare the usefulness of social class with some of the newer non-occupation based techniques for classifying consumers which had emerged in the 1970s and 1980s. Based upon a 50-minute interview with

1380 adult respondents the researchers were able to build up a very detailed picture of people's lives, motivations and possessions capable of being analysed by a range of non-standard demographic classifications. In the event three different variables were used – social class, life-stage and lifestyle. Social class was employed using the categories described in Table 6.3, but collapsing A and B into a single category. Life-stage is a classification based upon a number of variables such as age, marital and working status, and presence of children. Six groups governing 83 per cent of the adult population were defined as 'power groups' reflecting their spending power in terms of disposable income, namely:

- *Granny power* (14 per cent) People aged 55–70, not in full-time employment and with no children or young dependent adults.
- *Grey power* (12 per cent) People aged 45–60 with one adult working full-time and no children or young dependent adults.
- *Older silver power* (18 per cent) Married people with older children (5–15 years) but no under fives.
- *Young silver power* (16 per cent) People who are married with children aged 0–4 years.
- *Platinum power* (7 per cent) Married people aged 40 or under but with no children.
- *Golden power* (15 per cent) Single people, with no children, aged 40 or under.

The remaining 18 per cent did not fall into any of these categories.

The Lifestyle variable was derived from a factor and cluster analysis of 54 attitudinal dimensions and yielded five clusters.

The paper by O'Brien and Ford comprises an extended and rigorous analysis of the discriminatory power of the three different classificatory systems and comes to the conclusion that social class is not dead. In fact their conclusions are very similar to those of the Working Party reported above, namely:

- Social class *does* discriminate;
- No alternative classification provides *consistently* better discriminatory powers;

- No *one* classification works best across all product fields.

However, the researchers also conclude that:

- Sometimes other classifications discriminate *more*, and frequently they are *just as powerful* as social class.

In other words, marketers should always consider other classifications when designing surveys and analysing data.

The second part of O'Brien and Ford's research looks at the stability and replicability of the three approaches and comes to the conclusion that life stage is superior to both lifestyle and social class on the following grounds:

- Unlike social class it can be applied consistently at an international and cross-cultural level;
- Unlike geodemographic classification it does not require a very large sample size;
- Also unlike geodemographics it is not *falsely* stable (that is, systems like ACORN are based on census data which can become out of date due to the period between censuses);
- Lifestyle data require only a minimal extension to standard demographic data and so can be collected quickly;
- In contrast to social class, lifestage data are less likely to be regarded as 'personal' which makes the interviewers' task easier.

These conclusions reinforce those relating to the discriminatory power of the different approaches (assuming the base data is valid and reliable), namely, social class may be an appropriate method for analysing markets but one should always consider alternative approaches which may be better given the particular context and the purposes to which the research is to be put.

☐ *Preference segmentation*

While demographic factors may provide a more than adequate description of a market segment and in some cases be a major influence on consumption

Figure 8.3 *Basic market-preference patterns*

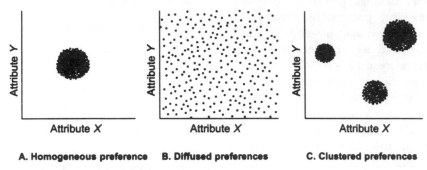

A. Homogeneous preference   B. Diffused preferences   C. Clustered preferences

Source: P. Kotler (1988), *Marketing Management*, 6th edn. (Prentice-Hall).

behaviour – for example baby products, health care products – a marketing orientation requires that we look beyond demographics to the nature of preferences, as these will permit a much better understanding of the reasons underlying differences and similarities in actual consumption behaviour. Kotler (1988) distinguishes three broad classes of preferences – homogeneous, diffused, and clustered – and illustrates how these may be plotted in terms of key attributes as shown in Figure 8.3 (creaminess and sweetness for ice cream).

In the case of homogeneous preference there are no apparent segments (at least in terms of the attributes selected), and one would expect all suppliers to pursue an *undifferentiated* strategy, with price and availability as key elements with advertising and promotion being used to try and develop a distinctive brand image.

Where preferences are diffused, 'A brand in the centre minimises the sum of total consumer dissatisfaction', but a more appropriate strategy might be to *concentrate* on one or other dimension and seek to develop a market segment and build up brand loyalty for the distinctive, brand.

Finally, where preferences are clustered, the segments are clearly identified and the producer can either concentrate on one or else develop a series of different products targeted at each of the distinct segments – a *differentiated* marketing strategy.

Examples of identifying new market opportunities through preference segmentation are regularly reported in the 'trade' press such as *Marketing Week* and *Campaign. Marketing Week* (23 Nov. 1990) carried a report of how tissue-maker Scott was relaunching Big Value Scotties Regular 200s Tissues as a high quality facial product made from 65 per cent recycled paper in a response to Tesco, Sainsbury's and Dixcel who had previously launched 100 per cent recycled paper brands to cater for those consumers concerned for the environment. In Scott's view 100 per cent recycled papers could not achieve the quality expectations associated with facial tissues and so saw an opportunity to plug a gap in the high-quality recycled sector.

Similarly, in a report 'Going Organic', Coopers and Lybrand Deloitte cite research by Mintel which indicated that roughly one in four adults would prefer processed foods to be organically grown. Although the strongest preference (best target markets) comes from those aged 25–44, the ABs and the South West, there was surprisingly little difference between sub-groups using geo-demographic segmentation variables underlining that in this case it was expressed preferences which provided the best basis for segmenting the market.

☐ *Benefit segmentation*

Another well-known approach to market segmentation is to subdivide the total market in

Table 8.3   *Toothpaste market segment description*

Segment name	The sensory segment	The sociables	The worriers	The independent segment
Principal benefit sought	Flavour, product appearance	Brightness of teeth	Decay prevention	Price
Demographic strengths	Children	Teens, young people	Large families	Men
Special behavioural characteristics	Users of spearmint flavoured toothpaste	Smokers	Heavy users	Heavy users
Brands disproportionately favoured	Colgate, Stripe	Macleans, Plus White, Ultra Brite	Crest	Brands on sale
Personality characteristics	High self-involvement	High sociability	High hypochondrias	High autonomy
Life style characteristics	Hedonistic	Active	Conservative	Value oriented

Source: Haley, R.I. (1968), 'Benefit Segmentation', *Journal of Marketing*, vol. 32, pp. 30–5.

terms of the specific benefits looked for by different consumers. This approach, pioneered by Haley, is illustrated by Table 8.3, which shows how the toothpaste market can be broken down into four distinct segments in terms of the principal benefit sought by users.

□ VALS

One approach to market segmentation seeks to combine psychographic measures of values with lifestyles. Probably the best known example of this approach is the VALS (Values and Life-styles) program developed by SRI International, a Californian consulting firm. The first version of VALS was developed in the late 1970s and has now been comprehensively revised as VALS 2. VALS 2 classifies the American population into three major groupings – Principle oriented, Status oriented and Action oriented – which are sub-divided into eight segments.

The VALS approach is derived from the basic ideas developed in Maslow's need hierarchy (p. 114). Thus Principle-oriented consumers are motivated by their beliefs (self-actualisation) rather than a desire for approval (esteem) and

comprise two segments – the *Fulfilled* (more resources) and the *Believers* (less resources). Status-oriented persons are strongly influenced by the attitudes and opinions of others. Their behaviour is also affected by their disposable income so that four segments emerge: *Actualisers* (can afford their aspirations) and, in descending order *Achievers*, *Strivers* and *Strugglers*. The Action oriented are motivated by a desire for social and physical activity, novelty and risk taking. The better off are classified as *Experiencers* and the less well off as *Makers*.

Each of these segments is seen as quite distinct and are defined as in Table 8.4. The distribution of the American population is summarised in Table 8.5. Approaches such as VALS, which combine life-styles and psychographics, have been challenged in terms of their validity and care should be taken when using such composite methods.

□ Segmentation by social character

Segmentation by social character depends heavily upon the measurement of life-style and the use of psychographics. In the article by Wells cited in

Table 8.4　*Summary descriptions of the eight VALS 2 segments*

Actualizers are successful, sophisticated, active, 'take-charge' people with high self-esteem and abundant resources. They are interested in growth and seek to develop, explore, and express themselves in a variety of ways – sometimes guided by principle, and sometimes by a desire to have an effect, to make a change. Image is important to *Actualizers*, not as evidence of status or power, but as an expression of taste, independence, and character. *Actualizers* are among the established and emerging leaders in business and government, yet they continue to seek challenges. They have a wide range of interests, are concerned with social issues, and are open to change. Their lives are characterized by richness and diversity. Their possessions and recreation reflect a cultivated taste for the finer things in life.

Fulfilleds are mature, satisfied, comfortable, reflective peoeple who value order, knowledge, and responsibility. Most are well educated, and in (or recently retired from) professional occupations. They are well-informed about world and national events and are alert to opportunities to broaden their knowledge. Content with their careers, families, and station in life, their leisure activities tend to centre on their homes. *Fulfilleds* have a moderate respect for the status quo, institutions of authority, and social decorum, but are open-minded about new ideas and social change. *Fulfilleds* tend to base their decisions on strongly held principles and consequently appear calm and self-assured. Although their incomes allow them many choices, *Fulfilleds* are conservative, practical consumers; they are concerned about functionality, value, and durability in the products.

Believers are conservative, conventional people with concrete beliefs and strong attachments to traditional institutions: family, church, community, and the nation. Many *Believers* possess moral codes that are deeply rooted and literally interpreted. They follow established routines, organized in large part around their homes, families, and the social or religious organizations to which they belong. As consumers, they are conservative and predictable, favouring American products and established brands. Their education, income, and energy are modest but sufficient to meet their needs.

Achievers are successful career and work-oriented people who like to – and generally do – feel in control of their lives. They value structure, predictability, and stability over risk, intimacy, and self-discovery. They are deeply committed to their work and their families. Work provides them with a sense of duty, material rewards, and prestige. Their social lives reflect this focus and are structured around family, church, and business. *Achievers* live conventional lives, are politically conservative, and respect authority and the status quo. Image is important to them. As consumers, they favour established products and services that demonstrate their success to their peers.

Strivers seek motivation, self-definition, and approval from the world around them. They are striving to find a secure place in life. Unsure of themselves and low on economic, social, and psychological resources, *Strivers* are deeply concerned about the opinions and approval of others. Money defines success for *Strivers*, who don't have enough of it, and often feel that life has given them a raw deal. *Strivers* are easily bored and impulsive. Many of them seek to be stylish. They emulate those who have more impressive possessions, but what they wish to obtain is generally beyond their reach.

Experiencers are young, vital, enthusiastic, impulsive, and rebellious. They seek variety and excitement, savouring the new, the offbeat, and the risky. Still in the process of formulating life values and patterns of behaviour, they quickly become enthusiastic about new possibilities but are equally quick to cool. At this stage in their lives, they are politically uncommitted, uninformed, and highly ambivalent about what they believe. *Experiencers* combine an abstract disdain for conformity and authority with an outsider's awe of others' wealth, prestige, and power. Their energy finds an outlet in exercise, sports, outdoor recreation, and social activities. *Experiencers* are avid consumers and spend much of their income on clothing, fast food, music, movies, and video.

Makers are practical people who have constructive skills and value self-sufficiency. They live in a traditional context of family, practical work, and physical recreation, and have little interest in what lies outside that context. *Makers* experience the work by working on it – building a house, raising children, fixing a car, or canning vegetables – and have sufficient skill, income, and energy to carry out their projects successfully. *Makers* are politically conservative, suspicious of new ideas, respectful of government authority and organized labour, but resentful of government intrusion on individual rights. They are unimpressed by material possessions other than those with a practical or functional purpose (e.g. tools, pickup trucks, or fishing equiment).

Strugglers' lives are constricted. Chronically poor, ill-educated, low-skilled, without strong social bonds, aging, and concerned about their health, they are often despairing and passive. Because they are so limited they show no evidence of a strong self-orientation, but are focused on meeting the urgent needs of the present moment. Their chief concerns are for security and safety. *Strugglers* are cautious consumers. They represent a very modest market for most products and services, but are loyal to favourite brands

Source: Reprinted with permission of SRI International.

Chapter 6 he provides a number of case histories to illustrate the applications of such research in profiling consumers as a basis for segmentation. The example is best illustrated by Tables 8.6 and 8.7 which comprise a demographic and psychographic profile of the heavy user of shotgun ammunition.

As Wells comments:

In spite of this lack of focus, the data [in Table 8.7] show some interesting patterns. First, it is obvious that hunting is not an isolated phenomenon but rather is associated with other rugged outdoor endeavours. Shotgun shell buyers not only like to hunt, they also like to fish and go camping. They even like to work outdoors. These relationships are interesting and useful because they suggest activities and settings, other than hunting scenes, that might be appropriate for shotgun ammunition advertising. They suggest products that might be especially appropriate for joint promotions or other cooperative marketing ventures, such as displaying shotgun ammunition near camping or fishing equipment in retail outlets. [Table 8.7] also shows that ammunition buyers are apt to be do-it-yourselfers, which suggests that hunters are apt to be buyers of hardware and tools.

Items in the third group [in Table 8.7] suggest some hypotheses about the psychological makeup of the shotgun ammunition buyer. Compared with the non-buyer he is definitely more attracted by violence, suggesting that detective, war, and violent Western TV programs ought to draw audiences with disproportionate numbers of shotgun users, and that action and adventure magazines ought to be considered when placing advertising associated with hunting. Relationships between product use and media exposure are always best documented by direct cross-tabulation, but when these data are not available (and they often are not) relationships suggested by life-style patterns can provide helpful direction.

Table 8.5 *A brief demographic/socioeconomic profile of the eight VALS 2 segments*

Segment	% of population	Sex (M)	Median Age	Median Income	Education (some college)	Occupation white collar	Married
Actualizer	8%	59%	43	$58 000	95%	68%	72%
Fulfilled	11	47	48	38 000	81	50	73
Believer	16	46	58	21 000	6	11	70
Achiever	13	39	36	50 000	77	43	73
Striver	13	41	34	25 000	23	19	60
Experiencer	12	53	26	19 000	41	21	34
Maker	13	61	30	23 000	24	19	65
Struggler	14	37	61	9 000	3	2	47

Source: Reprinted with permisson of SRI International.

Table 8.6 *Demographic profile of the heavy user of shotgun ammunition*

	Per cent who spend $11+ per year on shotgun ammunition (141)*	Per cent who do not buy (395)
Age		
Under 25	95	
25–34	33	15
35–44	27	22
45–54	18	22
55+	13	36
Occupation		
Professional	6	15
Managerial	23	23
Clerical/sales	9	17
Craftsman	50	35
Income		
Under $6000	26	19
$6000–$10 000	39	3
$10 000–$15 000	24	27
$15 000+	11	16
Population density		
Rural	34	12
2500–50 000	11	11
50 000–500 000	16	15
500 000–2 million	21	27
2 million+	13	19
Geographic division		
New England/Mid Atlantic	21	33
Central (N, W)	22	30
South Atlantic	23	12
E. South Central	10	3
W. South Central	10	5
Mountain	6	3
Pacific	9	13

* Number of respondents in the survey.
Source: W. D. Wells (1975), 'Psychographics: A Critical Review', *Journal of Marketing Research*, vol. XII (May).

The relatively high levels of agreement with the fourth section [of Table 8.7] suggest that the hunter is generally less risk-averse than is his nonhunting counter-part. To policy makers charged with keeping hunters from shooting themselves and each other, this willingness to accept risk would suggest that sober warnings about the dangers of firearms may well be ineffective. Lest this conclusion seem hopelessly naive, let it be noted that sober warnings about the dangers of firearms are exactly what some policy makers have attempted.

The relatively high levels of agreement with the fifth section suggest a combination of self-indulgence and lack of internal control that seems congruent with the attitude toward risk just noted. If the hunter is in fact self-indulgent and relatively conscienceless, it would seem unwise to rely on appeals to fair play and conservation to regulate his activities. Again, such appeals have been tried with less success than expected.

The level of agreement with 'I love to eat' and the hunter's professed willingness to spend money on himself suggest markets for premium foods designed

Table 8.7 *Psychographic profile of the heavy user of shotgun ammunition*

Base	Per cent who spend $11+ per year on shotgun ammunition (141)*	Per cent who do not buy (395)*
I like hunting	88	7
I like fishing	68	26
I like to go camping	57	21
I love the outdoors	90	65
A cabin by a quiet lake is a great place to spend the summer	49	34
I like to work outdoors	67	40
I am good at fixing mechanical things	47	27
I often do a lot of repair work on my own car	36	12
I like war stories	50	32
I would do better than average in a fist fight	38	16
I would like to be a professional football player	28	18
I would like to be a policeman	22	8
There is too much violence on television	35	45
There should be a gun in every home	56	10
I like danger	19	8
I would like to own my own air-plane	35	13
I like to play poker	50	26
I smoke too much	39	24
I love to eat	49	34
I spend money on myself that I should spend on the family	44	26
If given a chance, most men would cheat on their wives	33	14
I read the newspaper every day	51	72

*Number of respondents in the survey.
Source: W. D. Wells (1975), 'Psychographics: A Critical Review', *Journal of Marketing Research*, vol. XII (May).

to be taken along on hunting expeditions. These two findings also suggest the suitability of game-preparation recipes for hunting magazines, and they indicate that quantity and quality of food should get particular attention from proprietors of hunting lodges. Hunters don't mind roughing it, but they want it to be a well-fed roughness.

Finally, the relatively low level of agreement with 'I read the newspaper every day' should serve as a warning to shotgun ammunition advertisers. This is not to assert that media decisions, positive or negative, should ever be based on responses to a single survey item. Rather, it suggests that any shotgun ammunition advertiser who is spending his budget in newspapers should think twice about alternatives.

Psychographic profiles are usually developed from large-scale surveys (200–300 questions, 1000+ respondents) using self-administered questionnaires covering a wide range of attitudes, opinions, and interests and Likert scales (see Chapter 10, p. 246). Responses may be analysed by simple cross-classification techniques, but given the wealth of information it is more usual to make use of the powerful multivariate techniques available in packaged computer programs such as SPSS (Statistical Package for the Social Sciences). Using techniques such as *factor analysis* it becomes possible to reduce the mass of data into a series of principal components which distinguish

Table 8.8 *Eight male psychographic segments*

Group I 'The Quiet Family Man' (8 per cent of total males)

He is a self-sufficient man who wants to be left alone and is basically shy. Tries to be as little involved with community life as possible. His life revolves around the family, simple work and television viewing. Has a marked fantasy life. As a shopper he is practical, less drawn to consumer goods and pleasures than other men.

Group II 'The Traditionalist' (16 per cent of total males)

A man who feels secure, has self-esteem, follows conventional rules. He is proper and respectable, regards himself as altruistic and interested in the welfare of others. As a shopper he is conservative, likes popular brands and well-known manufacturers. (Low education and low or middle socio-economic status; the oldest age group.)

Group III 'The Discontented Man' (13 per cent of total males)

He is a man who is likely to be dissatisfied with his work. He feels bypassed by life, dreams of better jobs, more money and more security. He tends to be distrustful and socially aloof. As a buyer he is quite price conscious. (Lowest education and lowest socio-economic group, mostly older than average.)

Group IV 'The Ethical Highbrow' (14 per cent of total males)

This is a very concerned man, sensitive to people's needs. Basically a puritan, content with family life, friends and work. Interested in culture, religion and social reform. As a consumer he is interested in quality, which may at times justify greater expenditure. (Well-educated, middle or upper socio-economic status, mainly older.)

Group V 'The Pleasure-orientated Man' (9 per cent of total males)

He tends to emphasise his masculinity and rejects whatever appears to be soft or feminine. He views himself a leader among men. Self-centered, dislikes his work or job. Seeks immediate gratification for his needs. He is an impulsive buyer, likely to buy products with a masculine image. (Low education, lower socio-economic class, middle-aged or younger.)

Group VI 'The Achiever' (11 per cent of total males)

This is likely to be a hardworking man, dedicated to success and all that it implies – social prestige, power and money. Is in favour of diversity, is adventurous about leisure-time pursuits. Is stylish, likes good food, music, etc. As a consumer he is status conscious, a thoughtful and discriminating buyer. (Good education, high socio-economic status, young.)

Group VII 'The He-Man' (19 per cent of total males)

He is gregarious, likes action, seeks an exciting and dramatic life. Thinks of himself as capable and dominant. Tends to be more of a bachelor than a family man, even after marriage. Products he buys and brands preferred are likely to have 'Self-expressive value', especially a 'Man of Action' dimension. (Well-educated, mainly middle socio-economic status, the youngest of the male groups.)

Group VIII 'The Sophisticated Man' (10 per cent of total males)

He is likely to be an intellectual, concerned about social issues, admires men with artistic and intellectual achievements. Socially cosmopolitan, broad interests. Wants to be dominant, and a leader. As a consumer he is attracted to the unique and fashionable. (Best educated and highest economic status of all groups, younger than average.)

Source: W. D. Wells (1975), 'Psychographics: A Critical Review', *Journal of Marketing Research*, vol. XII (May).

major groupings within the data. The output of such an analysis is shown in Table 8.8 (again taken from Wells's article).

■ Industrial segmentation

While most segmentation studies are concerned with consumer markets the need is equally as great in many industrial markets, as was brought out by Richard Cardozo (1980) in his article 'Situational Segmentation of Industrial Markets'. Cardozo identifies four dimensions which may be used separately or in combination to classify organisational buying situations which may be regarded as 'market segments', namely:

1. Familiarity with the buying task; that is, Robinson *et al.*'s 'buyclasses'.

2. Product type. Here one may segment on the basis of product use in terms of components, materials and equipment (see Chapter 9 for a classification of industrial goods) which may be related to the 'degree of standardisation', namely:

Custom – unique design for a particular customer;

Modular – unique combination of standard available components or materials;

Standard – combination of ingredients that has been offered previously.

3. Importance of purchase to the buying organisation.

4. Type of uncertainty in the purchase situation.

Clearly, Cardozo's approach seeks to add a behavioural and situational dimension to the more traditional Standard Industrial Classification (SIC) which is based on the nature of the product and encompasses very broad distinctions at the industry level (2 digit codes) as well as very narrow distinctions between firms (4 digit codes).

Another important dimension in both industrial and consumer markets is geography, particularly where this is a surrogate for national boundaries with all the implications these have for cultural, legal and political differences between markets.

International segmentation

Yoram Wind and Susan Douglas (1972) provided a useful schemata for segmenting international markets in an article 'International Market Segmentation', and this is reproduced as Table 8.9.

Based upon these characteristics the authors then propose a 2-step process for segmenting international markets. First, one defines the macro segment, which may be one or more countries with similar market characteristics and then one sub-divides the macro segment on the basis of customer characteristics within it. This may be represented by a flow diagram as shown in Figure 8.4.

Table 8.9 *A classification scheme of various bases for international market segmentation*

	Enduring characteristics	Situation specific characteristics
Country characteristics	Geographic location Demographic and population characteristics	Economic and legal constraints Market conditions
	Socioeconomic Cultural patterns Political factors	Product bound Culture and lifestyle characteristics
Customer characteristics	Demographic characteristics: age, sex, life cycle Geographic location	Consumption patterns Loyalty patterns Buying situations Attitudes (perceptions and preferences)
	Socioeconomic Personality and life style characteristics	

Source: Wind and Douglas (1972) 'International Market Segmentation', *European Journal of Marketing*, vol. 5, no. 1.

Figure 8.4 *The hierarchy of segments approach to international market segmentation*

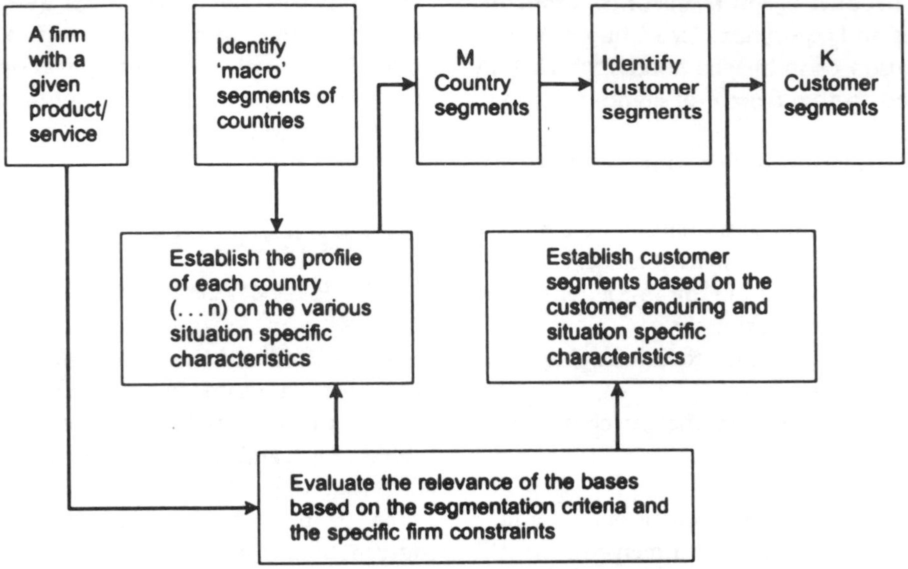

Source: Wind and Douglas (1972) 'International Market Segmentation', *European Journal of Marketing*, vol. 5, no. 1.

From the Wind and Douglas analysis it is clear that international segmentation, like industrial market segmentation, is a 'special case' of segmentation. By this we mean that the same factors or approaches described earlier are equally applicable to other contexts as they are to the consmer marketing environment in which they were originally developed. On the other hand, while the same *principles* will apply they will probably need modifying to take into account the special circumstances which enable us to identify industrial (or organisational) and international markets as being different from the general case described in most text books.

Not only will culture vary between countries, which will have a major bearing on attitudes and behaviour, but so will the institutions and infrastructure through which the marketer will seek to reach the prospective customer. Language and symbolism will also demand particular care in developing a communication strategy, all of which reinforces the point that successful segmentation is invariably based upon careful and effective marketing research. Given that marketing is a 'matching' process which seeks to ensure the seller deploys resources and skills to maximum effect in meeting customer needs market segmentation based on sound analysis has a major role to play. We return to this theme in the final section of this chapter on 'Targeting and Positioning'

■ Methods of segmentation

In the preceding section we have looked at a number of different bases for segmenting markets without addressing the question of *how* one should set about the task. As is apparent from the references already cited there is a wealth of information on the subject and the discussion here can only scratch the surface. However, for a concise but comprehensive discussion of the topic one cannot better the article 'Issues and Advances in Segmentation Research' by Yoram Wind (1978). The following discussion of methods draws heavily on this source.

As Wind points out, 'Four major types of models can be used in an effort to segment a market. They include the traditional *a priori* and *clustering-based* segmentation models, and the new models of flexible and componential segmentation which are based on different sets of assumptions.' He continues:

A priori segmentation models have had as the dependent variable (the basis for segmentation) either product-specific variables (e.g. product usage, loyalty) or general customer characteristics (e.g. demographic factors). The typical research design for an *a priori* segmentation model involves seven stages:

1. Selection of the (*a priori*) basis for segmentation.
2. Selection of a set of segment descriptions (including hypotheses on the possible link between these descriptors and the basis for segmentation).
3. Sample design – mostly stratified and occasionally a quota sample according to the various classes of the dependent variable.
4. Data collection.
5. Formation of the segments based on a sorting of respondents into categories.
6. Establishment of the (conditional) profile of the segments using multiple discriminant analysis, multiple regressional analysis, AID or some other appropriate analytical procedure.
7. Translation of the findings about the segments' estimated size and profile into specific marketing strategies, including the selection of target segments and the design or modification of specific marketing strategy.

Clustering-based methods are very similar to *a priori* methods with the essential difference that one does not specify in advance a dependent variable but rather looks for natural clusters occurring in a data base. Needs, benefits, attitudes, life-style and psychographic characteristics are the most commonly used factors in establishing the existence of a cluster. This approach is also known as the *post hoc* method of segmentation.

On occasion *a priori* and *post hoc* methods may be combined in a hybrid approach: for example, one might segment first on usage and seek to determine if there are clusters or sub-groups within these segments, using benefits, needs and so on as a basis for refining the discrimination.

As the name implies, flexible segmentation is a dynamic methodology which offers management 'the flexibility of "building up" segments (cell or cell combination with any specific brand-switching matrix) based on the consumers'

response to alternative product offerings (under various competitive and environmental conditions)' (Wind, 1978, 'Issues and Advances'). The technique depends heavily on conjoint analysis and computer simulations of choice behaviour and is particularly suited to concept and new product testing.

The fourth approach, which also depends upon sophisticated statistical analysis and extensive computing power, is componential analysis. The model, proposed by Green, differs from other segmentation models in that it seeks to predict which type of consumer will be most responsive to which product feature. The method has many similarities with flexible segmentation and is applicable to both industrial and consumer markets.

In Quinlan's opinion, flexible and componential segmentation 'has become highly academic and out of touch with real world practice', which is a view shared by Graham Hooley of the Aston Business School. In an article entitled 'Multivariate jungle – The Academic's Playground but the Manager's Minefield' (1980) he argues forcefully that the development of multivariate statistical techniques and the ready availability of massive computing power have resulted in academics presenting such methods as if they were the panacea for all ills. Such claims are regarded sceptically by practitioners and lead Hooley to propose seven commandments to govern their use, namely: 'do not be technique oriented; consider multivariate models as information for management; do not substitute multivariate methods for researcher skill and imagination; develop communication skill; avoid making statistical inferences about the parameters of multivariate models; guard against the danger of making inferences about market realities when such inferences may be due to the peculiarities of the method; exploit the complementary relationship between descriptive and predictive methods.'

☐ *Using segmentation techniques*

In order to justify market segmentation most writers agree that a market segment must possess four distinct characteristics:

1. It must be *measurable*;
2. It must be sufficiently *substantial* to warrant the effort invested in it;
3. It must be *accessible* in the sense that there are channels of distribution, media and so on which permit a focused approach to it;
4. It must respond *uniquely* to the efforts directed at it.

To these four conditions defining a viable market segment Thomas, 1980 ('Market Segmentation') adds a fifth – *stability* – by which he means that the segment's behaviour is such that its future response may he predicted.

However, authors are less agreed upon the role which segmentation has to play in marketing strategy. Some see its role as offensive, in the sense that segmentation should be used to identify opportunities and unfilled niches in the market place which can be exploited through an aggressive strategy. Conversely, other authors see market segmentation as a means of avoiding cannibalisation of one's existing products by defining distinct segments for new products and as a defensive strategy for deterring new entrants to the market.

Clearly these alternatives are not mutually exclusive for a firm with a portfolio of products, when defensive strategies will be more suited to products in the mature or decline phase of their life-cycle, while offensive strategies will be appropriate for guiding new product development and managing products in the launch phase of their life-cycle.

However, it is well to heed the warning given by Resnik, Turney and Mason (1979) in 'Marketers Turn to Counter-Segmentation', who state, 'Many markets today may be characterised as hypersegmented, a condition under which increasingly smaller market segments are identified and targeted.' This fragmentation may cause consumers to become confused, retail distribution difficult to maintain, and result in major diseconomies in both production and marketing. To avoid this, Resnik *et al.* propose that marketers will have to turn to 'counter-segmentation', involving:

1. The elimination of market segments by dropping products.

2. The *fusion* of segments by persuading customers to accept simpler and less-differentiated products.

On the other hand, G. Mueller-Heumann (1992, pp. 303–14) suggests that due to widespread changes, such as the shifts being experienced in demograpahic and psychographic population characteristics, markets will become increasingly fragmented and that 'mass customisation' of production will result. All this will have serious implications for future marketing strategies in the future, challenging the 'traditional marketing thinking'.

Mueller-Heumann points to the rapid increases in direct marketing as a signpost for future trends. Direct marketing has become more and more influential although most current strategies still work in conjunction with a 'mass marketing focus'. The growth of direct marketing is set to increase with the rapid improvements in the use of information technology, the greater flexibility of production technology and a fragmentation of consumer demand. Future segmentation approaches, therefore, will become closer to the consumer.

 # Selecting market segments

All of the preceding discussion has been concerned with the identification of market segments. To conclude this chapter it is important to recognise that having disaggregated a market into a set of distinctive characteristics which meet the five criteria set out in the preceding section, very few organisations will wish, or be able to service them all. It follows that one must establish criteria for selecting that segment or segments that offer the greatest opportunity for the firm. This activity is frequently referred to as *targetting* and *positioning*.

In order to target a market segment Wind (1995, p. 402) suggests one must answer the following questions:

- What is the likely response to the firm's offering, including response to the positioning of the firm's products and services?
- What is the size of the segment in terms of the revenues and profits it is likely to generate?
- Can the segment be reached? (via controlled media and distribution or via a self-selection strategy)?
- What are the current and likely competitive activities directed at the target segment?
- What are the likely costs of reaching effectively the target segment?
- What is the likely impact of changes in relevant environmental conditions (for example economic conditions, life-style, legal regulations, and so on) on the potential response of the target market segment?
- Do we have the required offerings and competencies effectively to develop, reach and serve the selected segments?
- How many segments can you manage effectively?

By answering questions such as these one should be able to decide which segment(s) represent the best opportunity. This is known as *targeting*. But, selecting a target segment is only part of the problem. Rarely will a viable market segment be unoccupied so the new entrant will have to *position* themselves in the minds of the potential customers as being different, and better, than other competitors.

Earlier (Chapter 5) we introduced the concept of Branding. Positioning is very much concerned with branding and vice-versa. In the *Macmillan Dictionary of Marketing and Advertising* we find that 'Product positioning defines the location of a product or service relative to others in the same market place and then promotes it in such a way as to reinforce or change its "position"'.

According to Ries and Trout 'positioning' got started in 1972 when they wrote a series of articles entitled 'The Positioning Era' for *Advertising Age*. These ideas are fully developed in their book *Positioning: The Battle for your Mind* (1986) which is highly recommended reading. In their book, Ries and Trout claim

that 'Positioning starts with a product, a piece of merchandise, a service, a company, an institution, or even a person, perhaps yourself. But positioning is what you do in the mind of a prospect. That is, you position the product in the mind of the prospect'.

To make good positioning decisions one needs to be able to answer four questions:

- What critical success factors do consumers use in choosing between competing offerings?
- How important are these relative to one another?
- How do we compare with the competition on these factors? (Competitor analysis)
- How do consumers use this information to make choices? (Buyer behaviour)

The answers to these questions may well be used to create a perceptual map as described in Chapter 6 so that one may determine how one's offering compares with the competition. Once this has been established the key issue is how does one reinforce people's perceptions if they are favourable to you, or modify them if they're not, to maintain or create a competitive advantage? Ries and Trout suggest that 'Positioning is an organised system for finding a window in the mind. It is based on the concept that communication can only take place at the right time and under the right circumstances.'

The problem faced by the marketer is that people are faced with an over-supply of information and so screen out the great majority of it. (Remember Selective Perception in the model of Buyer Behaviour in Chapter 6?). Thus, finding the window of opportunity requires a detailed understanding of the customer's needs. Ideally, one would like to find a niche which is unoccupied by anyone else. However, this is seldom possible and this makes it necessary to 'reposition the competition'. To do so one has to change consumers' existing perceptions, which is recognised as a difficult task. The most effective way is to provide 'proof' or evidence which people can readily verify for themselves. This is best achieved using objective factors which would be taken into account in a cost–benefit analysis. Alternatively, one can attempt to reduce the credibility or acceptability of competing products – usually by comparative advertising pointing out benefits your product has which the competition has not.

The identification and communication of intangible (service) and subjective benefits has assumed ever-increasing importance as it becomes more and more difficult to create, let alone sustain an objective competitive advantage. It is for this reason that Branding has assumed such importance in modern marketing practice. We return to this topic again in Chapter 11.

Summary

In this chapter we have looked at an analytical approach to the clear identification of consumer needs and wants as the basis for developing focused marketing strategies.

While it is true that producers have always sought to differentiate their products this strategy of product differentiation is quite different from one of market segmentation. The former tends to reflect a product orientation, in which the seller *assumes* that different people will have different tastes, while the latter reflects a market orientation whereby the seller finds out what people want and then sets out to create a supply of appropriate goods and services. Indeed, market segmentation is an original marketing concept and an important theoretical underpinning of the subject of central importance.

The chapter itself has first defined the concept of market segmentation before moving on to look at some of the bases or methods available. Particular attention has been given to Demographic, Geodemographic, Social, Psychographic and Behavioural factors. The application of these to the industrial and international context was touched on briefly before considering when and how to use segmentation techniques in order to target markets and position oneself in the chosen segment.

In the next chapter we consider Channels of Distribution as a critical element in the marketing infrastructure within which marketers have to operate.

Review questions and problems

1. 'Whenever a market for a product consists of two or more buyers then it is capable of division into meaningful buyer groups.' Discuss the validity of this statement.
2. 'Without market segmentation there can be no marketing strategy.' Briefly define these terms and discuss the extent to which the statement is true.
3. Discuss the concept of reference groups as a basis for market segmentation.
4. The same market can sometimes be segmented by a number of variables. What are some of the problems that might be encountered in segmenting a market under such conditions?
5. Market segmentation is a recognition of the classification of products by consumers. Discuss.
6. Explain the problems associated with market segmentation and whether it is desirable or feasible in all situations.
7. Recommend the ways most likely to improve your marketing efforts by using a segmentation approach in each of the following markets:

   (a)   women's magazines;
   (b)   toilet soaps;
   (c)   computers.

   Give reasons for your decision.

8. Using examples of your choice, explain how the element of social class can be used as a segmentation variable.
9. What segmentation approaches would be most appropriate for the following products: frozen vegetables, clothing, dog food, airline travel, televisions? Justify your answers.
10. Discuss how a position strategy might be employed in the marketing of a service such as packaged holidays.

Supplementary reading list

See general texts and the notes following the Preface.

Chapter 9

Channels of Distribution

Contents

Learning goals

The objective of this chapter is to introduce the student to the formal systems and structures which have developed over time to facilitate the physical transfer of goods from the raw material stage into ultimate consumption.

The issues to be addressed in this chapter include:

1. The role of distribution in the business system.
2. The functions of the distributive channel.
3. The nature of primary production, commodity markets and the channels of distribution which serve them.
4. The nature of business-to-business marketing.
5. Factors influencing the structure of business to business marketing channels.
6. The influence of industry concentration on channel structure.
7. The nature of retail distribution.
8. The evolution and structure of the retail trade.

9. Current trends and their impact upon competition.

On completion of this chapter you should be able to:

1. Define the nature of and role played by the distribution system.
2. List the five essential functions performed by a distribution channel.
3. Review the advantages and disadvantages of the three basic alternatives available when selecting a distribution policy:

   - direct sale;
   - sale through an intermediary;
   - a dual policy.

4. Define raw materials and the distinction between finite and renewable raw materials.
5. List some salient features of extractive industries.
6. Account for the development of producer–user agreements.

7. Discuss some key aspects of agricultural production and marketing.
8. Explain the features underlying the growth of processing.
9. Describe the channels used for fresh produce and the role of Marketing Boards.
10. Identify the distinguishing characteristics of business to business marketing.
11. List the main factors which influence the structure of industrial distribution channels.
12. Describe the effect of industry concentration on industrial channels and exemplify this by reference to the distribution of steel.
13. List the main functions performed by retailers and describe their key features.
14. Describe the structure of the retail trade and the main kinds of outlets.
15. Explain the concept of the Wheel of Retailing.
16. Summarise some of the main innovations which have taken place in the past forty years.
17. Identify the advantages and disadvantages of various patterns of retail distribution.
18. Review some current trends in retailing and their implications for the industry's future.

■ Introduction

In Chapter 1 we considered briefly some of the issues which define an economy. It will be recalled that the first of these stages was termed 'Traditional society' which is characterised by its lack of a systematic understanding of the environment and the technology and tools necessary to achieve any significant improvement in productivity. In such societies, and particularly the most primitive ones, the great majority of people's time is taken up with survival and the satisfaction of basic physiological needs. The first real step in the process of civilisation occurred when people began to establish settlements, rather than pursue a nomadic existence in which they moved from place to place seeking food and other essential materials. The point we are seeking to establish is that *place* and *location* has played a fundamental role in the evolution of exchange and the development of marketing.

Originally, the market was a physical location where people could exchange surpluses at first in kind (barter or countertrading) and subsequently through a medium of exchange such as money. The opportunity to exchange surpluses and thereby increase satisfaction encouraged task specialisation which, in turn, increased productivity and output. However, early settlements were severely limited in their production/consumption opportunities by virtue of the raw materials or factors of production available to them. Over time trade between settlements developed and further specialisation of function occurred based upon the exploitation of natural local advantages. It was observation of this phenomenon which prompted Ricardo to formulate his *theory of comparative advantage* in which he demonstrated that through specialisation and exchange two countries could both gain even though one country had a natural advantage (that is, was more cost-effective) in producing both the products which were to be exchanged. More recently, Michael Porter (1990) in his *Competitive Advantage of Nations* has argued that the classical theory based upon the concept of factor endowment 'is at best incomplete and at worst incorrect' as an explanation of the competitive performance of nations. Porter's thesis is that while a natural endowment is important it is the way such endowments are used which is important and he points to the fact that in many cases, such as Japan, factor deficiencies have acted as a spur to innovation and superior performance. However, one does not need to develop the argument further to appreciate that the potential to innovate and specialise will only add value and increase satisfaction if the goods produced can be made available to users and consumers who have a demand for them. To achieve this requires the existence of channels of distribution and of specialists and intermediaries to facilitate the flow of goods from producers to consumers. It is this topic which forms the subject of this chapter.

It should be noted that this chapter is concerned with the infrastructure of distribution and is largely descriptive. Its inclusion and the detail it contains are believed to be important as an understanding of existing channels of distribution and the factors which underlie or condition their structure and operation represent external factors over which the individual firm or supplier has limited control. This understanding is essential when making channel decisions and using 'place' as an element in the marketing mix. Channel Management is returned to in more detail in Chapter 14 but in this chapter we first consider the basic functions of distributive channels before looking at the distribution of raw materials as the first step in the so-called value chain. The value chain is the modern equivalent to McKinsey's conceptualisation of the 'business system' which was first introduced by the author in a teaching note at the Harvard Business School in 1970 when he taught the class in Creative Marketing Strategy. We return to this in a later chapter (The Written Analysis of Cases). The basic version may be represented as follows:

Raw → Production → Wholesale →
materials Distribution

    Retail → Consumer → After-sales
    Distribution or User Service

Next we look at the distribution of industrial goods; that is, those products and services sold by one producer to another for use in the creation of consumer goods and services. Traditionally this field of activity was known as industrial marketing although, as we shall see, many people now refer to this as business to business marketing. Following this the distribution of consumer goods is considered with a brief look at wholesaling and a more extended look at retailing.

Distribution: a neglected subject

It is generally agreed that the modern subject of marketing owes its origin to economists' inquiries into the nature of the distributive process at the end of the last century.

However, despite this early interest, it is only in recent years that the firm has turned its attention to the role which distribution has to play as an element of competitive strategy.

In a review of the status of distribution in the 1960s, Donald Bowersox (1969) advanced two reasons which he felt accounted for the delay in the development of this area of marketing: (a) the lack of computers and applied analytical tools sufficient to deal with the complexities of the problem; and (b) the absence of adequate motivation. Of these it was felt that the latter was the more important, and two main factors may be distinguished which were to provide the necessary motivation – technological innovation and increased competition.

Writing in the April 1962 issue of *Fortune*, Peter Drucker characterised distribution as the 'Economy's Dark Continent' and noted that whereas the cost of physical distribution accounted for as much as half of the total cost of finished goods, it had received relatively little attention by comparison with managements' cost reduction efforts in other directions. Since the publication of this article there has been an enormous expansion in the literature of physical distribution, but it is significant that little of the research represented by this literature has been concerned with the strategic implications of channel policy. As Bowersox notes, extant concepts assume vertical integration or, alternatively, take the viewpoint that physical distribution operations and responsibilities cease where a transfer of ownership occurs. The latter ignores the fact that many manufacturers sell at least part of their output through intermediaries, and implies that they take no further interest in the sales process once their output has passed into the wholesaler's inventory. Similarly, vertical integration is atypical of present distributive structures.

Given the competitive pressures attributable to escalating costs, increased industrial concentration as the result of acquisition and mergers, and the threat of product obsolescence inherent in accelerating technological innovation, it is clear that distribution policy has become a question of acute importance to the marketer.

The function of the distributive channel

In order to avoid misunderstanding, a channel of distribution is here defined as: 'The structure of intra-company organisation units and extra-company agents and dealers, wholesale and retail, through which a commodity, product or service is marketed.' This definition was designed to be broad enough to include: (a) both a firm's internal marketing organisation units and the outside business units it uses in its marketing work and (b) both the channel structure of the individual firm and the entire complex available to all firms (*Marketing Definitions*, American Marketing Association, 1962). The *Macmillan Dictionary of Marketing and Advertising* (2nd edn, 1990) explains further 'a channel consists of all those steps through which a product must pass between its point of production and consumption'.

As economies develop there is an increasing emphasis on specialisation and the division of labour, as a result of which a 'gap' develops between producer and user. The primary purpose of a distributive channel is to bridge this gap by resolving spatial and temporal discrepancies in supply and demand. Irrespective of the extent of these discrepancies, certain essential functions need to be performed which may be summarised as:

1. Transfer of title to the goods involved.
2. Physical movement from the point of production to the point of consumption.
3. Storage functions.
4. Communication of information concerning the availability, characteristics and price of the goods.

5. The financing of goods in transit, inventory and on purchase.

The importance of these functions varies, depending upon the nature of the goods themselves. Physical movement and storage tend to predominate in the case of bulky raw or part-processed materials such as basic chemicals, petroleum products and steel, where price and specification are standardised and the market is comprised of a limited number of buyers and sellers. As the complexity of the product increases the provision of information and product service becomes predominant. In the case of consumer goods, advertising and sales promotion constitute the major communication channel, but industrial goods depend more on personal selling owing to the more heterogeneous nature of the goods involved and the possibility of modifying them to meet end-user requirements. Some indication of the possible complexity of the distribution channel for a commonplace product like the broiler chicken is shown in Figure 9.1.

Reference to Figure 9.1 makes it clear that it is the transfer of ownership which determines channel structure as no reference is made to service organisations that may be involved in the physical movement and/or storage of the product. Rosenbloom (1995, pp. 137–54) emphasises this distinction '... because it is the trading relationship involving the functions of buying, selling and transferring of title where most of the strategic marketing issues emerge' (p. 139). According to Rosenbloom, channel structure has three basic dimensions: the length of the channel, the intensity in terms of the number of intermediaries at each level, and the types of intermediaries involved.

While Figure 9.1 does not include the possibility of direct sale by producer to consumer – the shortest, channel structure – it does make clear the possible complexity and varying length of the channel. As noted above, intensity refers to the number of intermediaries involved at each level or step in the channel. Where only one intermediary is used this is termed *exclusive* distribution; where only a few are used *selective* and where all possible intermediaries are used

Figure 9.1 *British broiler production, flow plan*

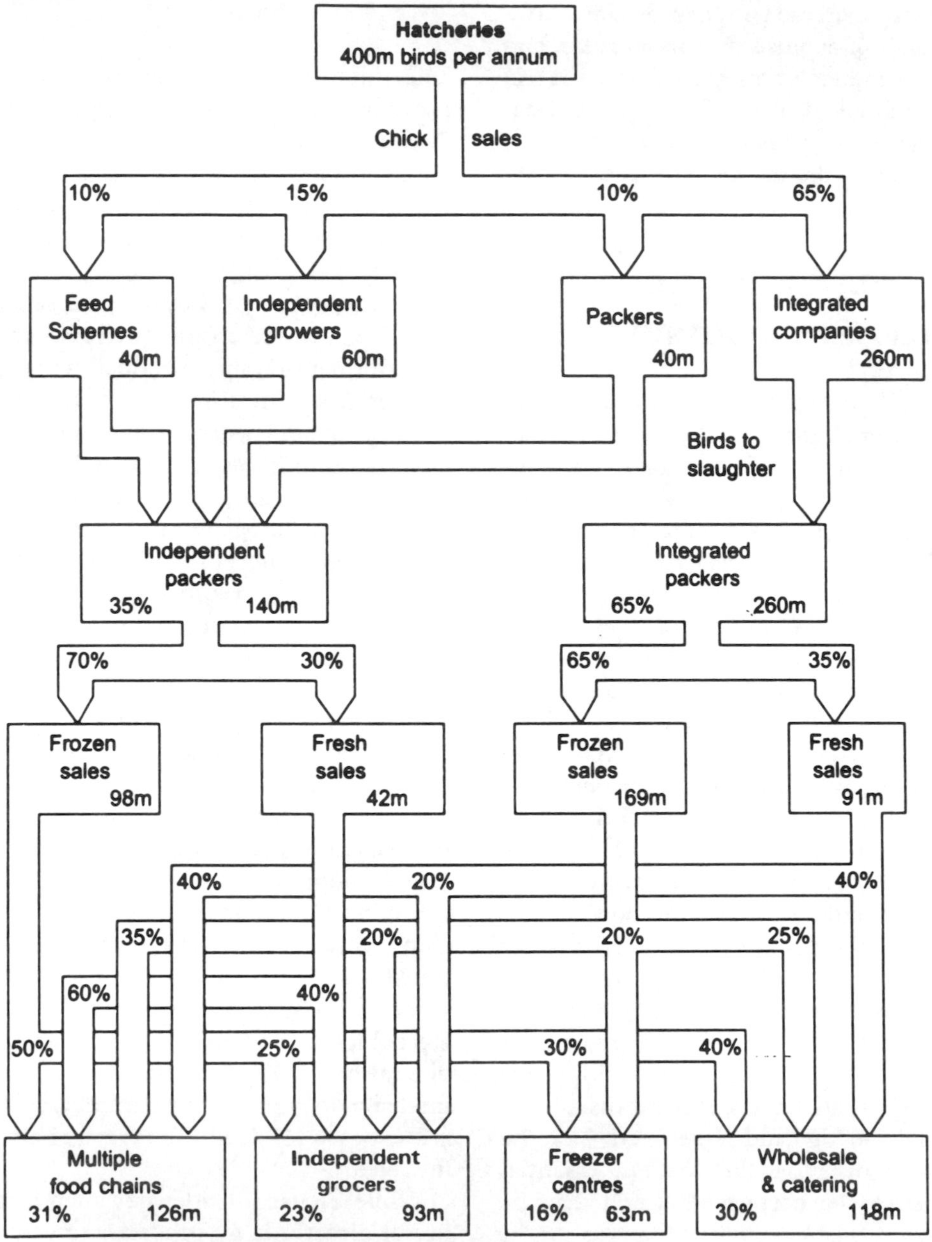

Hatcheries
400m birds per annum

Chick sales

10%   15%   10%   65%

Feed Schemes 40m

Independent growers 60m

Packers 40m

Integrated companies 260m

Birds to slaughter

Independent packers   35%   140m

Integrated packers   65%   260m

70%   30%   65%   35%

Frozen sales 98m

Fresh sales 42m

Frozen sales 169m

Fresh sales 91m

40%   20%   40%

35%   20%   25%

60%   40%   20%

50%   25%   30%   40%

Multiple food chains   31%   126m

Independent grocers   23%   93m

Freezer centres   16%   63m

Wholesale & catering   30%   118m

The flow chart is prepared only as an example, the information contained therein is not an accurate analysis of the broiler industry.
Source: Produce Studies Limited, Newbury, England.

intensive. The types of intermediary involved are usually determined by the nature of the product, although in the case of consumer goods and the development of *scrambled retailing* manufacturers may adopt an intensive approach and sell through as many different kinds of outlets as are willing to carry their product.

Essentially, however, a manufacturer is faced with three basic alternatives when deciding upon a distribution policy:

1. Direct sale;
2. Sale through an intermediary;
3. A 'dual' policy combining direct sale with the use of an intermediary.

☐ *Direct sale*

The major advantage associated with direct sale is that it permits the seller to retain full control over the total marketing process. Its usage is favoured by the existence of:

- A limited number of potential buyers;
- A high degree of geographical concentration of potential buyers;
- A high degree of technical complexity requiring extensive service;
- A high level of technological innovation;
- Stable demand conditions; that is the absence of seasonal and cyclical trends which necessitate stockholding.

Any of these factors in itself may be sufficient to predicate adoption of a policy of direct selling; in combination they are virtually irresistible. Conversely, a conflict between, say, the number of buyers and their geographic dispersion may make direct selling a totally uneconomic proposition – the major disadvantage linked with this approach.

☐ *Sale through an intermediary*

When cost considerations militate against the adoption of direct selling, manufacturers frequently make use of an intermediary who, by acting on behalf of a number of buyers and sellers, is able to perform the necessary functions more economically; that is, the gross margin demanded by the intermediary is less than the on-cost which would be incurred through providing the same services oneself. The advantages and disadvantages of using an intermediary may be summarised as:

Advantages:

1. Cost advantages: use of an intermediary,

   - minimises the cost of a field sales organisation,
   - eliminates warehousing costs,
   - minimises inventory financing charges,
   - minimises sales costs – invoicing, financing or accounts, etc.,
   - minimises the risk of loss through inventory obsolescence,
   - minimises loss through bad debts and reduces the cost of credit control,
   - eliminates local delivery costs,
   - reduces the costs of processing to meet non-standard orders.

2. Coverage. The use of intermediaries allows the producer to reach all potential users without having to incur the fixed costs which would arise if direct selling were used.
3. Provision of service. Intermediaries can provide immediate availability and necessary pre- and after-sales service on a local basis more effectively than many producers.

Disadvantages:

The major disadvantage associated with the use of an intermediary is the loss of direct control over any, or all, of the following:

- Selling effort – Customer selection;
  - Call frequency;
  - Product emphasis;
  - Promotion and missionary selling effort.
- Pricing.
- Delivery.
- Service – Standard and availability.

Clearly, the importance attached to retaining control over these functions will vary from product to product and manufacturer to manufacturer.

☐ *Dual distribution*

In order to try and reconcile the conflict between the desirability of direct contact and the economies offered by selling through an intermediary, many manufacturers have adopted a compromise solution, usually referred to as 'dual' distribution. Under this alternative the manufacturer sells part of his output direct but entrusts the balance of his sales effort to an intermediary. As noted elsewhere, this policy is favoured by the existence of the 'heavy half' phenomenon, where a limited number of users constitute the major demand with the balance fragmented among a large number of small or irregular users.

The major disadvantage associated with dual distribution is the difficulty intrinsic in determining a fair division of the market between producer and intermediary.

Many of these issues will become clear in the following pages where we look at patterns of distribution in more detail.

■ The distribution of raw materials

The term 'raw materials' is often used to describe the physical goods used in manufacturing without distinguishing between natural raw materials and semi-manufactured, or fabricated, materials. For example the raw materials used in the packaging industry – paper, plastics, fibre-board and so on – are the finished goods of other manufacturers in the chemical industry. To avoid confusion the term will be used here to describe materials in their natural state such as coal, wool, wheat and rubber, which are often termed 'primary commodities'.

A broad distinction may be made between those raw materials which occur in a natural state and those which are the result of man's efforts in developing particular types of natural products through agriculture. The distinction is a logical one, for whereas man cannot alter the absolute supply of 'natural' raw materials, he can increase the supply of crops, both in absolute amount and in terms of specific varieties. Accordingly they merit separate treatment.

☐ *'Natural' raw materials*

This category is the one with which the so-called extractive industries are concerned and includes mineral deposits, forest and sea products. It is recognised that it is possible for man to increase the supply of both the latter, just as it may one day be possible to increase the total supply of minerals through deep excavation, or mining them on the moon. In this context, however, they will be treated as being in fixed supply for we have yet to achieve the technological breakthrough which makes such possibilities economically feasible. That this is so is evident in the conservation policies which have been widely adopted.

Another feature which is common to the supply of natural raw materials is that not only is supply fixed in an absolute sense, it is also fixed in the short term if all existing plant is operating at capacity. In other words, supply is not immediately responsive to increases in demand owing to the time-lag between such an increase becoming apparent and resources being diverted to exploit the market opportunity which such excess demand represents. Mines and sawmills cannot be opened overnight, and fishing fleets take time to construct. In the case of minerals the delay is especially protracted as most of the accessible deposits are already being exploited, so that not only do mines have to be opened but road, rail and port facilities also have to be developed. Even reopening disused mines takes time, as is evident from the efforts made in Cornwall during the 1970s and 1980s to cash in on the world shortage of tin.

Because supply cannot readily be increased in the short term, prices for raw materials react very quickly to variations in demand in the way in which economic theory predicts they will. In fact commodity markets are usually used as examples when studying supply and demand because these factors can be clearly distinguished in operation, free from the complications which advertising, sales promotion and the like introduce into consumer goods markets. Owing to the tendency for raw material prices to fluctuate widely with variations in both demand and supply, many attempts have been made to stabilise the functioning of commodity markets – usually with little success as will be seen below.

Salient features of the extractive industries

The extraction of raw materials is usually expensive, and involves considerable capital investment even in the case of the more common materials such as coal, iron ore, basic chemicals and mineral oil. As a result, production of these materials is usually concentrated in the hands of a limited number of firms with the necessary capital and technical resources. From the point of view of the basic industries which process and refine these raw materials, the uncertainties associated with a free market represent a considerable threat to their own security and stability, and predispose them to secure control over a substantial part of their raw material requirements. This is not always possible, however, as many countries limit, or forbid, foreign participation, particularly where they have a monopoly over available supplies. In these circumstances the firm has no option but to buy in the world's commodity markets, the operation of which is very similar to the wheat market described in detail later in this chapter. In an introductory text of this nature it is not possible to consider political interference in the operation of free markets; for example the Arab countries' restriction of oil supplies following the Arab–Israeli conflict in 1973 and the subsequent establishment of OPEC as a producer cartel or the sanctions imposed on Iraq following its invasion of Kuwait in 1990.

The position with regard to the less common raw materials differs in that although production tends to be concentrated for the reasons outlined above, demand is made up of a large number of consumers with limited individual requirements. To satisfy these demands, specialist markets have been developed wherein the processes of concentration, equalisation and dispersion can take place; for example the London Metal Exchange.

In addition to what might he termed the basic raw materials of industry such as oil, chemicals, iron ore and so on, and the rare materials such as gold, silver, tin and diamonds, there is a wide range of materials which occur regularly in nature, and are relatively easy to extract with limited capital equipment. Like many other raw materials they are usually bulky, and the cost of transportation plays a significant role in their marketing. Extraction is closely governed by the proximity of the market to the source of supply and distribution is strictly local, precluding the need for the central markets associated with less common materials. Sand and gravel are examples of such locally distributed materials.

Producer–user agreements

As noted earlier, the inherent instability of commodity markets has stimulated both producers and users to seek some form of agreement to minimise the impact of fluctuations in supply and demand. Under normal conditions the establishment of an agreement is beneficial to both buyer and seller, as it invariably fixes a price bracket for the commodity. Thus, producers can treat the lower limit of the bracket as a guaranteed selling price and plan their output accordingly. Similarly, the buyer can cost his own output in the knowledge that the price of the raw material content cannot exceed the upper limit set by the bracket. However, if supply and demand should get in serious imbalance such agreements are put to a test which few are capable of surviving.

The classic example of the validity of this statement must be the International Tin Council, which was long quoted as the model for such agreements. For many years the council successfully held prices within the limits agreed on by producers and users, through the maintenance of a buffer stock. As soon as the price of tin fell to the lower limit prescribed by the agreement the Council entered the market, and supported it by buying at that price until sufficient excess supply had been removed for the price to rise above the 'floor'. (These are identical to the tactics of the Bank of England in the foreign exchange market.) Similarly, at the other end of the scale, as soon as excess demand or a decline in supply resulted in the price reaching the agreed ceiling, the Council would release stocks until the price fell within the bracket.

A particularly attractive feature of the scheme was that it was self-financing, as the margin between the upper and lower limits was sufficient to cover the stockholding and administrative costs involved. The Tin Council functioned perfectly on this basis until the early 1960s, when demand began to outstrip supply with the result that the market price was invariably near its upper limit. In order to keep the price within the prescribed limits the Council was increasingly called upon to release its stocks, but was never able to replenish them at the lower price. Eventually the inevitable happened and the stocks were exhausted, leaving a free market in which prices spiralled rapidly before stabilising at a more realistic level some £500 above the old limit. It is possible that the market free-for-all might have been avoided if the Council had had more funds at its disposal with which to build up stocks in time of excess supply, or had appreciated the fundamental disequilibrium earlier and raised the market price sooner. As it was, the Council's operations masked the development of imbalance between supply and demand and gave the market a false appearance of stability.

While the Council survived this crisis it collapsed in 1990 and was disbanded.

■ Agricultural products

Agricultural products may properly be regarded both as industrial raw materials and as consumer goods. In that there are significant differences in distribution, depending upon whether crops are sold direct into consumption or to manufacturers for processing it will be convenient to deal separately with these two categories. At the same time there are certain features common to both which deserve consideration prior to a discussion of the salient differences in distribution.

Probably the most striking feature of agriculture is the smallness of the average production unit. Although there has been a consistent trend towards larger unit size in nearly every industrialised country as alternative employment opportunities have become available, this is still true today. In the author's opinion there is unlikely to be a significant decline in the number of small farms and, in fact, it seems reasonable to anticipate that their numbers will increase. As the world's population continues to expand geometrically so will the demand for food increase. At present the economists' calculations are based on average income per acre, from which it is argued that farms are too small to enable the average farmer to attain an adequate standard of living. Further, it is true that increased unit size would permit more extensive use of labour-saving equipment and improve the marginal productivity of capital by comparison with investment in a small farm.

These arguments neglect the fact that the small, intensively farmed unit has a significantly higher yield per acre than the large, mechanised unit – a comparison of average wheat yields as between the United States and Holland reveals that the latter are some 400–500 per cent greater than the former. In the future, as demand outstrips supply, prices will rise and thus make intensive farming not only necessary but also more profitable. If the argument is valid, it would seem that the supply of agricultural products will continue to flow from a large number of small producers albeit of a more sophisticated kind. The current 'green revolution' and the associated interest in natural or organic foods has also seen a revival in the fortunes of the small production unit.

Although agricultural products are usually thought of as being homogeneous, in fact there are considerable variations in quality, and some form of grading process is necessary before they can be offered for sale. Further, crops are perishable and need careful handling and storage to prevent deterioration. Neither of these operations can be performed economically on a small scale, nor with the limited resources at the small farmer's disposal, and a complex distributive network has been developed to facilitate the marketing of crops and foodstuffs.

The causes of market disequilibrium

A commonly observed feature of agricultural markets is the erratic fluctuation of price, particularly in the short term. This instability is essentially attributable to variations in supply, as the demand for most agricultural products is fairly stable and predictable in advance. Obviously, climate is a major cause of supply instability, but its effects are compounded by the behaviour of producers in the manner outlined below.

In the case of many products such as wheat, cotton, rubber and livestock, a high proportion of the total supply is accounted for by large, specialist producers. Allowing for the vagaries of climate, their output tends to be fairly constant and calculable in advance, from which it follows that the major variations in supply must be attributed to the output of the small farmers.

Most land may be used to grow a variety of crops, and the major decision facing the small producer is which crop to plant in order to gain the greatest return; a decision that must be made several months before the crop will be ready for sale. In assessing market opportunity it is natural that the farmer should be influenced by current prices, and there is a strong probability that a large number will independently decide to plant those crops which are currently fetching the best prices. The reason certain crops are fetching above average prices is clearly due to the fact that the existing supply is insufficient to satisfy the total demand, and thus the price mechanism is having the desired effect of encouraging an increase in supply. However, it would be purely fortuitous if the separate decision of thousands of producers to increase planting of a specific crop resulted in an exact balancing of supply and demand. It is nearly certain that the increased supply will depress price and fail to meet the farmer's expectations. Further, the decision to switch from, say, wheat to barley will reduce the supply of wheat and its price will go up, thus encouraging the farmer to increase his acreage under wheat and to decrease planting of barley.

It is the time-lag between the decision to sow a particular crop and its reaching fruition, the inability to go back on the decision once it is made, and the farmer's imperfect knowledge of others' sowing decisions which create fluctuations in supply that disturb market equilibrium.

The impact of the marginal producer

A good example of the manner in which the small farmer determines the final level of supply is afforded by the market for natural rubber.

Between the two world wars the leading rubber-producing countries agreed to limit supply in order to ensure a fair market price for their output; for example the Stephenson Scheme in South-east Asia. The restriction in supply forced prices up and encouraged the peasant farmers in the Dutch East Indies to clear land, which they would otherwise have been unable to cultivate, to plant rubber trees. These trees were not given the same careful attention as is typical of the commercial plantation, and which accounts for the major production costs, they were simply left to grow for the eight to ten years necessary to achieve maturity. As soon as the trees were big enough to tap, native rubber flooded on to the market, causing prices to plummet and the producer agreements to collapse.

The native product is only slightly inferior in quality to the plantation product, and now accounts for about 30 per cent of total supply.

The commercial grower's position is aggravated by the fact that although he is committed to the high fixed costs of maintaining his plantation, the native grower is not, and only taps his trees when the market price justifies the effort. Thus, whenever the market price becomes favourable from the plantation owner's point of view the marginal producers enter the market and force the price down.

Given the possible variations in supply and its diverse origins it is not surprising that man has developed elaborate marketing systems to permit concentration of output so that it may be made available to those with a demand for it. Such marketing systems possess many features in common and the discussion of the market for a single product will help to clarify these. The wheat market in the United States is particularly well documented and will be used as an example here.

□ *The marketing of wheat*

The first stage in the marketing of wheat is concentration at the local elevator by individual farmers. The elevator may be owned by an independent wholesaler, or by the farmers themselves as a cooperative. In either case the elevator will usually offer to purchase the grain outright at central market price, less the cost of freight to the central market and the elevator owner's commission, or, alternatively, to store the grain for a fixed charge. The farmer's decision to sell or store is based on the current price, and expectations as to its future movements, as against the cost of warehousing. (Note: there is an absolute floor to market price determined by Federal Government subsidy. This subsidy is analogous to the guaranteed farm prices offered by the British Government to ensure a minimum level of domestic production prior to entry to the EU when the Common Agricultural Policy came into force.)

Most of the grain in local elevators is resold to manufacturers in the same area, but the balance is sold either to wholesalers in the 'terminal'

markets, for example the 'Wheat Pit' in Chicago, or else sent to commission agents in such centres for sale at the best price available. Dealers at the central market frequently combine the functions of merchants, agents and brokers, unlike other markets where dealers tend to specialise in only one of these functions.

The merchant is usually in business for himself and buys stocks with the intention of reselling them at a higher price, so that his income is determined both by the size of the margin and by the volume of business transacted. By contrast, agents usually act on behalf of a client for a fixed commission, and so may find it more profitable to achieve a high turnover than to withhold supplies until the price rises; similarly, they lack the merchant's incentive to buy at the lowest price. Brokers occupy an intermediate position between merchants and agents as they buy and sell both for clients and on their own behalf. Unlike merchants, however, they rarely take physical delivery or hold stocks.

In order to bring buyers and sellers into physical contact and facilitate the exchange of title to goods, it is usual to find a place specifically designated for this purpose. Usually the dealers who comprise the 'exchange' or 'market' draw up rules to regulate the transaction of business, and to exclude non-members from participation in its operation. Within the market transactions fall into two main categories – spot and future trading. Spot, or cash, transactions concern existing or readily available goods, on which immediate delivery can be effected, while the futures market is concerned with contracts for sale and delivery at some future, and usually specified, time.

In fact the futures contract is not a contract to buy or sell at all, but is an option to buy at an agreed price, at a stated time. From the buyer's point of view an option ensures the future availability of supplies at a fixed, maximum price. If, when the option matures, the market price is less than that negotiated, the option is not taken up, for the commodity can be obtained for less in the open market. Conversely, if the price in the market is higher, the option will be exercised and the seller will have to bear the loss. Naturally, the dealer's success depends on his being able to predict accurately the future level of supply, and setting a price which will be attractive to the potential purchaser while exposing the dealer to the minimum of risk. To achieve this the dealer must secure a continuous supply of accurate market data as the basis for forecasting future price levels. Although some dealing in futures is purely speculative, the majority of dealers depend on it for their livelihood and so base their forecasts on facts rather than hunches. In doing so they perform a valuable service, for they reduce uncertainty concerning both demand and supply in the markets in which they operate.

☐ 'Consumer' crops

Although there is a fairly clear-cut distinction between crops which comprise the raw materials of industry and those which are consumed in their natural state, it is difficult to maintain the distinction if processing is used as the delineating factor. Nowadays the distinction would seem to rest on the necessity for processing as a prerequisite of consumption, rather than the existence or absence of processing. In the case of crops which are usually classified as 'industrial', the common denominator is the fact that they must undergo some physical change before they can be consumed. This change may be relatively minor, as is the case with flour milling, or extensive – if, say, one is converting wool into a suit of clothes. By contrast 'consumer' crops may be used immediately in their natural state but in advanced economies an increasing proportion are now processed in some way or other prior to consumption.

☐ Factors underlying the growth of processing

The volume of agricultural output is ultimately determined by the length of the growing season. Assuming an adequate water supply, temperature is a critical variable. Plants will not grow at or below freezing, and make very little progress until the temperature rises above 40°F. Thereafter, the rate of growth doubles approximately for every 18° increase in temperature, so that the farther one moves away from the equator the shorter the length of the growing season. Thus, from early times, man has been preoccupied with methods of preserving and storing food for out-of-season use.

The slow growth of population until recent times is at least partly attributable to lack of success in balancing excess with famine. The growth of international trade partially alleviated the problem but had to await the development of the steam ship and refrigeration to make any real impact. Similarly, a revolution in farming techniques has greatly increased our ability to increase crop yields and prolong the growing season, but the problems of preservation and storage still exist, and command ever-increasing attention.

Refrigeration is expensive in terms of capital installation, and suffers from the same basic disadvantage as canning and similar methods of preservation – the majority of the good stored is water. Although dehydration eliminates this diseconomy, traditional methods tended to so change the nature of the food that they were largely unacceptable. The development of freeze drying overcame most of the problems associated with satisfactory reconstitution, but the expense was too great to justify general commercial usage. However, research sponsored by the Ministry of Agriculture came up with a method of speeding up the process, and Accelerated Freeze Drying (AFD) was born. The improved process is less costly and has been widely adopted; for example Batchelor's Vesta range and Surprise peas, Nestlé's Gold Blend instant coffee, Cadbury's Smash.

Thus we now have a situation in which the consumer is able to buy highly perishable foodstuffs at any time of the year. Not only that, as methods of preservation have improved costs have fallen, and many 'processed' foods now possess distinct advantages over 'fresh' products. Two obvious advantages are the reduction in waste and the added convenience. Canned, frozen or AFD peas are invariably of uniform quality, which is not the case with peas bought in the pod, and require the minimum of preparation.

The advantages offered by processed foods have had a marked impact on purchasing patterns, and many items traditionally associated with the fresh produce market are now sold through dry-goods outlets; that is, supermarkets and grocery shops as distinct from greengrocers. Retailing forms the subject matter of a later section and will not be discussed here, but a brief description of the traditional channels is called for.

The distribution of fresh produce

Essentially, fresh produce reaches the ultimate consumer by one of the four channels illustrated in Figure 9.2.

The functions of broker, agent and producer exchange are identical with those discussed earlier in connection with the marketing of wheat. The term wholesaler is synonymous with merchant, and is increasingly preferred to the latter designation.

The most direct channel, producer–consumer, is usually only encountered on a limited and local scale, for example door-to-door sales or the stall in the local market, and most growers prefer to sell through conventional retail outlets. Sales direct to retailer fall into three categories:

1. The producer acts as his own wholesaler and establishes direct contact with local outlets.
2. The producer sets up his own retail outlets or, conversely, the retailer with a chain of outlets integrates backwards into production.
3. The producer sells under contract to large retailers; for example the major supermarket chains, Marks & Spencer, BHS and so on.

Few growers are able to dispose of their total output in this way, however, and most sales are made initially to the wholesaler, either direct or through the medium of a broker or agent. Most

urban centres of any consequence have wholesalers who specialise in breaking down bulk supplies into small quantities for resale to the multiple or small retailers in their area. These wholesalers obtain supplies direct on a local basis, but also buy in the central markets from brokers and other wholesalers; for example Covent Garden for fruit, vegetables and flowers, Smithfield for meat, Billingsgate for fish. There can be little doubt that the degree of control exercised by some of the central markets results in diseconomies of which the producer rightly disapproves. Despite the perishability of, say, lettuce, it is difficult to account for the services which increase their value from a farm-gate price of 30p per dozen to a shop price of 40p each. Such excesses go apparently unnoticed by comparison with the criticism levelled at the promotional expenditures of the manufacturer of branded goods.

In order to ensure an adequate supply of certain basic foodstuffs the Government has seen fit to provide incentives for farmers by guaranteeing payment of a minimum price for their output. There are several methods by which this may be achieved, but the most overt and controversial method is through the establishment of a marketing board.

Agricultural marketing boards

The agricultural marketing boards operating in the United Kingdom at the present time were set up under the Agricultural Marketing Acts, 1931–58. The basic features which they have in common are:

- They are producer-controlled.
- They can only come into existence at the request of the majority of producers involved with the production of the commodity concerned; for example milk, hops.
- Their declared object is to secure the best possible return for their members.
- They are committed to improving quality, output, distribution and management within their own field of activity.

Figure 9.2 *The channel of distribution of fresh fruit and vegetables*

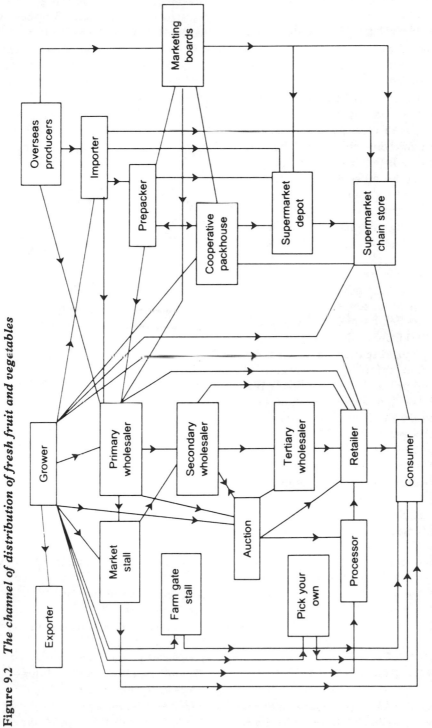

Source: Ministry of Agriculture, Fisheries and Food.

Space does not permit detailed consideration of the organisation and operation of the various boards, which may be obtained from their offices on request, but in view of the fact that the boards are run by producers for producers, some comment seems called for.

In essence the constitution of marketing boards results in the creation of producer-controlled monopolies and, while it is accepted that all monopolies are not necessarily harmful, they do create supply-controlled markets which are the antithesis of the marketing concept. Either the consumer must accept what the producer is prepared to offer, or he must do without. This is tolerable if there are acceptable substitutes for the monopolist's output, for example butter/margarine, or where the product is non-essential, but this is not the case with fresh milk, eggs, potatoes and so on.

The marketing boards pay a standard price to producers for equivalent grades of produce, irrespective of the fact that some are remote from the market and so are being subsidised by those in more economic locations. Similarly, consumers in rural areas tend to subsidise those in urban areas, particularly London, through the adoption of near-standard retail prices. It seems unlikely that maximum efficiency will be achieved so long as all farmers are treated alike and there is little incentive to concentrate on the production of those products which the consumer prefers.

At the time of writing, the following agricultural marketing boards were still operating:

Potato Marketing Board
British Wool Marketing Board

For information on these, readers should make direct contact.

▌The distribution of industrial goods

By contrast with the clearly defined patterns associated with the distribution of raw materials, it is difficult to generalise with regard to the channels of distribution associated with the three main categories of industrial goods – equipment, fabricated materials and supplies. Observation suggests that a number of different channels are used, and that selection is conditioned by a host of factors which are summarised in the following check-list:

☐ *Customer characteristics*

Number of potential users.
Geographical distribution of potential users.
Frequency of purchase.
Average order size.
Distribution of users on the basis of consumption.
Relative importance of product to user; that is, is the product an essential input from the user's point of view, or may its purchase be postponed or delayed?
Degree of user sophistication *vis-à-vis* product characteristics; that is, does the user need technical service, if so, what type?
Credit standing.
Preferred purchasing pattern – a single preference is unlikely to emerge owing to variations in the above factors; for example the need for after-sales service.
Degree of associated service requirements – both before and after sale.

☐ *Middleman characteristics*

Market coverage.
Gross margin.
Proportion of salesmen's time available for selling product.
Degree of technical expertise.
Financial strength and stability.
Stock carrying capacity.
Servicing capability.
Number of substitute products carried.

☐ *Company characteristics*

Size – both absolute, and relative to the industry/market of which it is a member.
Financial strength.
Industry position – leader or follower?
Spatial relationship between plant(s) and major users.
Degree of technical competence.
Degree of specialisation.
Breadth of product line.
Ability to provide desired services.

Environmental and competitive characteristics

The nature of seasonal, cyclical and secular trends in demand.
Degree of concentration in user industry(ies).
Nature and usage of existing distributive channels.
Extent and nature of legal restrictions and regulations.
The impact of taxation, for example on leasing
Government procurement policy.
Consumer needs – in so far as the demand for industrial goods is derived from consumer demand, shifts in the latter will have an impact on the former.

As will be seen in a later chapter, consideration of all these factors plays an important role in determining a firm's distribution policy and results in many diverse alternatives. On the other hand, it is possible to distinguish broadly similar channels operating across the whole field of industrial goods, which suggests that the most useful approach will be to identify the basic structures and illustrate them with actual examples.

Salient features of industrial marketing

Before proceeding to make such a review, however, it will be useful to state some of the salient features which differentiate the marketing of industrial and consumer goods implicit in the 'check-list' outlined above.

Although the basic marketing principles described in this book are felt to be equally applicable to the marketing of all types of goods and services, there are certain differences in degree that condition their relative importance. In the case of industrial goods these differences may be summarised as:

1. *Derived demand.* The demand for industrial goods, and raw materials, is derived from the demand for consumer goods in the sense that any expansion or contraction in the latter will be reflected by a corresponding shift in the former. The more distant the manufacturer is from the production of a specific consumption good, the less direct will be the impact of a change in demand for that good.

2. *Rational buying motives dominate the industrial market.* This is frequently misinterpreted in one of two ways: (a) there is an absence of emotional motives in the industrial purchasing situation, or, (b) consumer purchasing behaviour is irrational. Neither of the above statements is correct: consumers are rational and industrial buyers are influenced by emotional factors, but there is a difference in degree; that is, the industrial buyer will emphasise objective criteria to a greater degree than the average consumer.

3. *Concentration of buyers.* The number of potential buyers for an industrial good is generally far smaller than is the case with consumer goods. Further, industrial buyers tend to be concentrated geographically, for example the cotton and woollen industries. One must be careful not to overstate the importance of this distinction for, clearly, its validity depends upon the precise nature of the product. For example the market for office supplies is both large and dispersed, whereas the market for some consumer goods may be both small and concentrated; for example speciality goods produced on a purely local basis. It is also important to remember that although a national brand

may have millions of users, the producer may concentrate his direct sales and distribution efforts upon a limited number of major buyers, for example wholesalers and grocery chains.

4. *The scale of industrial purchasing is greater*. In absolute money terms this is generally, but not always, true. In a proportionate sense, that is size of purchase, *vis-à-vis* disposable assets, the reverse may often be true.

5. *Industrial products are technically more complex*. Again this is true absolutely but not relatively. The purchaser of a car or television set is faced with a similar degree of technical complexity as the buyer of a computer – in both instances the buyer evaluates performance rather than construction, and is dependent upon the seller for both advice and service.

6. *Industrial buying is a group process*. The same might also be said of the household as a decision-making unit for consumer purchases. It is unlikely that the latter will have formalised evaluation and decision procedures, however, both of which are common in the industrial buying context.

7. *The role of service is greater*. Again this depends upon the nature of the product and the type of service. Immediate availability is a prerequisite for sale of a convenience good – this is rarely the case with even the most common of industrial goods – and consumer durables need after-sales service just as much as many industrial goods.

8. *Leasing, renting, and the extension of credit are important*. This is increasingly true of consumer goods.

From the comments made in respect of these 'distinguishing' factors it is clear that although industrial marketing may differ in degree, there are sufficient points of similarity to permit the transfer of principles and techniques from one to the other. As such, undue emphasis of differences may be harmful if it induces practitioners in either field to neglect thought and practice in the other. In particular, it will become apparent that marketing tactics are largely a function of product and

market, irrespective of whether the specific product be designated 'consumer', 'industrial', or 'business to business', so that a given mix may be equally appropriate to products in either category. Some of the implications for business to business markets are summarised in Table 9.1 taken from *Marketing: Theory and Practice* (Baker, 1995).

☐ *Distributive channels*

As noted earlier, distributive channels tend to cut across arbitrary product/ industry boundaries and attention here will be concentrated on major variations in structure.

Essentially, the same three basic alternatives are open to manufacturers of both industrial and consumer goods, namely:

1. Direct sale to user/consumer;
2. Indirect sale through the medium of a third party;
3. A combination of both direct and indirect sale.

Direct sale offers the greatest degree of control, but can be uneconomic where there is a large number of customers for the product in question. Under these circumstances some form of intermediary may be able to operate at a lower cost by combining the disparate, but complementary, outputs of several manufacturers for resale to small users of such products, for example building materials, office supplies. Distribution through an intermediary, or wholesaler, offers the manufacturer the opportunity to improve his overall profitability, albeit at the sacrifice of some measure of control, and so is frequently used to extend the coverage of the producer's own sales force.

Wholesalers vary considerably in terms of both the nature and extent of the services which they provide, and it is common to draw a broad distinction between 'full' and 'limited' service organisations. The full-service wholesaler usually employs his own sales force, holds stocks from which to make immediate delivery, provides

Table 9.1 *A summary of effects of business market characteristics*

| | Principal consequences for: | | |
Factor	Marketing research	Marketing management	Other functions
1. SMALL/FINITE CUSTOMER NUMBERS	• Identifiable targets • Focused research • Qualitative as well as quantitative approaches	• Personal contact • Relationship cultivation • Potential to react to individual customers' needs	• Need for close liaison with customers for Product/Innovation requirements
2. FEWER BUT LARGER ORDERS	• Need for comprehensive and continual information and intelligence about customers and competitors	• Necessity for competitiveness • Use of relationships/ knowledge to get and remain 'in' • Customer closeness • Predictability of demand	• Irregular demand for specific products • Complexities of plant scheduling and/or inventory carrying • Time a critical variable

3. HETEROGENEITY OF SIZE	• Inappropriateness of small percentage and random samples
	• Focus on stratified/ census techniques
	• Need to secure deep knowledge of major players
		• Segmentation by size/ importance
		• Focus of effort on major players/opinion leaders
		• Customisation of products for major users
		• Risk of ignoring requirements of other segments
			• Requests for priority for major customers/ affecting
			  – production schedules
			  – terms of business
			• Dependence on oligopolistic customer demand
			• Potential proliferation of product varieties

4. CONCENTRATION OF BUSINESS	• Accessibility of populations	• Ease of communication • Structure of sales function • Structure of distribution channels	• Choice of transportation • Use/location of warehouses
5. DERIVED DEMAND	• Complexity of downstream research • Need to research end markets • Familiarity with/use of consumer research techniques	• Need to identify end markets • Multiple product users • Contact with customer; derivation of demand pull as well as supply push strategies • Establishment of *consumer* preferences/ loyalties	• NPD/R&D focus on use applications • Delays in implementing new products due to customer redesign requirements • Need for sustainable demand for end product

Table 9.1 *(continued)*

| Factor | *Principal consequences for:* | | |
	Marketing research	*Marketing management*	*Other functions*
6. RECIPROCITY OF BUYER/ SELLER	• 'Captive' research environment	(a) • Stable customer relationships • Risk of unwanted inertia/'Buyer' pressure (b) • Mutuality of benefit • Repeat business • Loyalty/Relationship development	(a) • Risk sharing • Inertia/brake on corporate R&D development • Potential 'offset' deals (b) • Experience sharing → improved cost effectiveness • Relationship development with corresponding customer functions
7. BUYER/SELLER INERTIA	• Accessibility/regularity of contact	• Relationship building opportunities • Supply chain development • Market stability • Risk of competitor outflanking	• High switching costs • Collaboration in NPD • Risk of lack of innovation
8. TECHNICAL COMPLEXITY	• Multiplicity of uses confuses research environment • Need for access to user markets	• Need for familiarity with specification processes • Involvement in negotiations pre/during/ post transaction • Tendency towards technically qualified sales personnel • Need for detailed comprehension of user environments	• Delays in introducing new products (see Derived Demand) • Multifunctional 'sales' teams • Enhanced importance of process innovation
9. TECHNOLOGICAL/ ECONOMIC	• Need for continual monitoring of end markets	• Understanding of end markets and close relationships with end users and intermediaries • Develoment of more than one operational market • Technology forecasting	• Operational flexibility • Ability to reassess forward orders • Minimise lead times • Maintenance of technological updatedness

Table 9.1 *(continued)*

Factor	Principal consequences for:		
	Marketing research	Marketing management	Other functions
10. RATIONAL/ GROUP BUYING	• Need to gain access to several elements of DMU • Need to employ indirect as well as direct instruments • Increased importance of 'intelligence' • Increased emphasis on intentions/attitude research	• Multilevel communications strategies • Need to identify users and deciders • Need to focus on real motivation of each DMU element • Relationship building at all levels • Development of corporate image of 'customer friendliness'/ 'customer closeness'	• Need for total corporate market orientation • Involvement in major promotional activities, exhibitions etc. • Development of TQM/Total Customer Service • Integration of Production strategies with Marketing

Source: Baker, M. J. (ed.) (1995) *Marketing: Theory and Practice* (London: Macmillan).

information, advice and technical service, and is usually prepared to extend credit. As the name implies, limited-service wholesalers generally perform a restricted function, and often confine themselves solely to stockholding and delivery. In the latter case the manufacturer is responsible for stimulating demand and the provision of technical services.

For the most part manufacturers adopt some combination of both direct and indirect sale and, as will be seen in the chapter on channel policy, the precise mix will depend upon two basic criteria – cost and control.

☐ *The distribution of steel*

Although the manufacturer of steel in the UK is largely concentrated in the hands of a monopoly, which limits competition between separate production facilities, it provides a good example of the need for a complex distributive structure.

Steel is frequently thought of as an essentially homogeneous product when, in reality, it is highly complex and produced in an enormous variety of shapes and to very different specifications, to meet widely disparate end-use requirements. For example mild steel sheet, used in the fabrication of consumer durables such as cars and washing machines, is very different from electrical steels used in transformers and generators, and from high carbon steels used in the machine-tool industry. To simplify matters discussion here will be confined to flat-rolled mild steel producers.

In order to meet specific end-use requirements, an order for flat-rolled mild steel may vary according to any one of the following factors:

- Hot-rolled or cold-reduced;
- Quality/ductility;
- Quantity;
- Thickness;
- Sheet or coil;
- Width (and length in the case of sheets);
- Coated or uncoated – if coated, type and thickness of coating and method of application of coating.

From the user's point of view, each of these factors is highly important and will be specified precisely to meet his exact needs. From the producer's point of view, however, such variants create diseconomies as they interrupt the smooth flow of production and reduce the mill through-put. In turn, the diseconomies created by operating the mill at less than optimum efficiency to meet customer needs are reflected in the producer's price structure. However, beyond a certain point the diseconomies involved in meeting a precise specification become so great that the producer must refuse to accept less than a minimum order quantity (MOQ). The MOQ is determined by a number of complex factors which cannot be discussed here but, over the years, increasing automation has resulted in a gradual increase in the size of the minimum acceptable order. This increase has had little impact on the large-scale user, whose minimum requirements for a given specification are nor-mally far in excess of the MOQ, but could have been a major threat to the user with a limited demand had it not been for the existence of steel wholesalers, or 'stockholders'.

Although some stockholders are subsidiaries of the steel producers, the majority are independent organisations. Given the enormous variety of steel products, all but the largest stockholders find it necessary to specialise in some category, for example tinplate, sheet and plate, structural steels and so on. In essence, the stockholder functions by anticipating the likely needs of small users, which he combines into an acceptable mill order, normally for a 'standard' size. In fact there are no 'standard' sizes, but certain combinations of width and length have been widely adopted as they offer the maximum benefits within the mills' price structure, and so reduce the scrap loss when cutting to the exact size required. To meet the precise size requirements specified by their customers, stockholders install shearing, slitting and shaping machines and, increasingly, are ordering in coil form, which permits them to cut to any length without loss.

In addition to breaking bulk to meet small users' requirements, the stockholder also helps to even out fluctuations in supply and demand. Steel-making is a complex, multi-stage process in which an order may be 'lost' at any stage of manufacture, necessitating a 'remake'. If an order

is rejected at final inspection it can take three to four weeks to replace, assuming that it can be fitted into the mill schedule immediately. Further, production of an exact quantity is a virtual impossibility, so that most orders turn out less than, or in excess of, the specified amount. Steel buyers are familiar with the technological constraints involved in steel production and adjust their buying policies accordingly.

Where a specification is known to be difficult to produce, buyers maintain sufficient stocks to cover the possibility of late or partial deliveries. However, the maintenance of stocks ties up capital, and most buyers reduce their stock levels to the minimum consistent with normal deliveries in the knowledge that temporary shortages may be made good by buying from stockholders. From the producer's point of view the stockholder performs an equally valuable service in absorbing excess supply in the short term. In addition to buying excess production against mill orders that the customer is unpre-pared to accept, the stockholder provides an outlet for cancelled orders and reject materials which the mill would find it uneconomic to reclaim. Thus, through specialisation and local knowledge the stockholder performs a number of valuable functions for both producer and user, at a lower cost than would be possible if they performed these functions themselves.

Concentration ratios as a criterion

(see Chapter 4 for an extended discussion of *industrial concentration*)

The factors which predispose the steel producer to adopt both a direct and indirect approach are typical of many industries with high concentra-tion ratios. (The concentration ratio is an economic concept that is widely used in com-parative industry analyses in preference to the less precise distinction between perfect and imperfect competition.) Concentration ratios take into account both the size and numbers of firms in a market, and are computed by summing the percentage of total sales accounted for by a given number of firms – thus a true monopoly would have a concentration ratio of 100 per cent, while a highly oligopolistic industry might be defined as one in which the four largest firms account for more than 50 per cent of total sales.

For the marketer faced with the decision of selling direct or through an intermediary, the concentration concept provides a useful rule of thumb when applied to purchases by users, as opposed to sales by producers. By ranking firms in terms of their consumption of the product concerned, it is relatively simple to arrive at a measure of concentration and decide whether direct sale is economically feasible and, if so, to what extent. Many analyses of this kind have revealed what has been termed the 'heavy half' phenomenon; that is, 50 per cent of total purchases are accounted for by a small percentage of buyers.

As a generalisation, it is reasonable to state that the higher the concentration ratio the more direct sale is to be preferred, but this does not necessarily mean that the producer will attempt to make *all* sales direct. Consider, for example, the supplies of the motor-car assembly industry, where a small number of buyers account for a very high percentage of total demand. Irrespective of the producer's size, or the nature of his product, he will deal direct with Ford, Toyota and so on. Over time, however, the cars produced by these companies will require replacement parts, but it is unlikely that many components manufacturers will attempt to sell them to every garage and repair shop in the United Kingdom with an uncertain demand for such parts. In consequence, the component manufacturer must decide whether to set up his own regional warehouses, to have distribution to the car manufacturer, or to use the services of motor accessory and parts wholesalers.

Similarly, the manufacturers of standardised parts such as bearings, industrial fasteners or electrical components, and the producers of general-purpose equipment such as bulldozers, fork-lift trucks or lathes will find that a high percentage of sales are accounted for by a limited number of customers. However, unless the producer has a very strong franchise with such major users and can depend upon them consistently to absorb his output, he cannot afford to ignore the multiplicity of small users that make up the balance of the market. The more numerous and geographically segregated the latter are, the less economic direct sale becomes, so that in markets with a very low degree of concentration the producer may well find it necessary to channel his total output through an intermediary. Many operating supplies produced by small, specialised producers fall into this category; for example stationery, hand tools or cleaning materials.

☐ *Manufacturers' agents*

Although attention has been focused on wholesalers as a link between producer and user, many firms prefer to employ agents, either in addition to, or in place of a sales force of their own.

From the manufacturer's viewpoint, the major advantage of employing agents is that he only pays commission on actual sales and so avoids the fixed costs associated with the maintenance of a sales force. Further, agents enter into a contractual agreement with their principal and so are subject to a greater degree of control than is usually possible when selling through an independent wholesaler.

Most agents handle a line of complementary but non-competing products, and operate within a clearly defined territory. The successful agent depends heavily upon his established contacts, and so offers the manufacturer a 'ready-made' salesman when introducing a new product or extending his geographical coverage. On the other hand, agents are not without disadvantage for, as noted when discussing the wheat market, the agent rarely has a complete identity of interest with his principal. This is particularly so when the agent is selling several different products, when he is likely to take the line of least resistance and sell what is in greatest demand, rather than devote his time to missionary selling, that is making cold calls to stimulate demand. Also, unlike wholesalers, the agent does not take delivery of goods, and the manufacturer must maintain and finance a larger inventory than would be necessary if he sold through a wholesaler. Hence, where there are seasonal fluctuations in demand, or the manufacturer is short of working capital, the wholesaler will usually be preferred to the agent.

From the foregoing description it is clear that there is frequently a conflict between the desire for the most economic method of distribution and management's wish to retain control over the marketing of the firm's output. This conflict will be examined in greater detail in Chapter 14, but attention now must be turned to the distribution of consumer goods, or retailing.

The distribution of consumer goods

As noted in the previous section, the demand for industrial goods is derived from the demand for consumer goods. Although this link may sometimes appear tenuous, it is clear that all other productive activities finally depend upon selling goods and services into ultimate consumption. Although several distributive options are open to the consumer-good manufacturer, almost all eventually involve a retail outlet of some type or other, and this section will be largely concerned with the function and operation of such outlets.

Retailing functions

Most dictionaries define retailing as 'the sale of goods in small quantities to ultimate consumers'. As such, the retail outlet constitutes the final link in the distributive chain, and is responsible for the performance of several important marketing functions, namely:

1. The physical movement and storage of goods;
2. The transfer of title to goods;
3. The provision of information concerning the nature and use of goods;
4. The standardisation, grading and final processing of goods;
5. The provision of ready availability;
6. The assumption of risk concerning the precise nature and extent of demand;
7. The financing of inventory and the extension of credit to consumers.

In many instances it is difficult to distinguish exactly where manufacturing ends and retailing begins, owing to the assumption of some of these functions by organisations that are not usually considered to be retailers or, conversely, by the assumption of functions by the retailer which are more often associated with manufacturers. Thus, in recent years there has been an increasing tendency for manufacturers to assume responsibility for the provision of information through extensive advertising and sales promotion campaigns, while many retailers have integrated backwards into wholesaling and even manufacturing activities. In the opinion of one authority, Professor W. G. McClelland (1966) in *Costs and Competition in Retailing*, the distinction must rest on the performance of those functions inherent in the very nature of retailing – the physical movement of goods and arrangement of transfer of title. To a lesser extent, functions (3), (4) and (5) in the above list also serve to distinguish retailing from other forms of manufacturing and distributive activity, and an examination of these five functions follows.

☐ *Physical movement and storage*

As one would expect, there is an enormous variation in the cost of transporting and storing goods depending upon the method of transport used, the length and complexity of the journey, the amount of handling and protection required and so forth. In the case of bulk cargoes for transport by sea, the cost may be as low as £0.01 per ton mile while, at the other extreme, door-to-door delivery of groceries may cost as much as

£60 per ton mile. Clearly, the more homogeneous the cargo and the larger the bulk for delivery at one point, the lower the unit cost incurred. The potential savings inherent in such economies have led in recent years to the growth of larger retail units and the virtual elimination of door-to-door delivery.

Within the retail outlet, recognition of the high costs arising from counter service, both in terms of the duplication of effort in putting goods on display and then fetching them for customers on request, as well as the waste of valuable selling space, have led to widespread adoption of self-service. Competitive pressures, and the ever-growing variety of goods available for sale, have also encouraged the retailer to keep the majority of his stock on display and to depend upon rapid delivery from central warehouses for replenishing his supplies. As a result there has been a strong trend towards the concentration of stocks at the wholesale level, leaving the retailer to stock only those goods for which he feels there is an immediate demand.

☐ *Transfer of ownership*

When one considers the degree of concentration usually associated with the production of goods and the widely dispersed nature of the consumer market, it is clear that few manufacturers will be in the position to undertake direct sale. Thus the need arises for an intermediary to perform this function and effect a transfer of ownership.

In the case of shopping and specialty goods, for example Singer sewing machines, the customers may be prepared to make a special purchasing effort to seek out the nearest distribution point. However, in the case of many convenience goods brand loyalty tends to be low, and maximum distribution is essential to high volume sales. Like the steel stockholder, the retail outlet offers the manufacturer the opportunity to make contact with the consumer at an economic cost. By stocking a line of complementary products the retailer is able to spread the overheads involved in personal selling. Also, by catering to the

separate demands of a large number of individual consumers, he is able to buy in economic quantities from the producer and still further reduce the costs of effecting a transfer of ownership.

From the consumer's point of view, retail outlets greatly facilitate the purchasing decision as they provide the opportunity to inspect and compare both the prices and quality of competing products. The location of retail outlets, and the nature of the goods in which they deal are readily ascertained, whereas the manufacturer's identity and location are not so easy to determine. Similarly, although many manufacturers publicise a recommended selling price, increased competition and the abolition of Resale Price Maintenance have resulted in a situation where the retailer is often the sole reliable source of this information on which so many buying decisions depend. Finally, the retailer often has to break bulk and the price, which represents the consideration given in exchange for ownership of the goods, cannot be determined until the consumer has specified the quantity which he wishes to purchase.

☐ *Ready availability*

Depending upon the nature of the product, consumers are prepared to go to varying lengths to obtain goods to meet their specific needs. Given the number of competing products and outlets, both retailers and manufacturers are highly sensitive to this aspect of consumer behaviour, and adjust their stockholding policies accordingly to offer the desired level of availability.

By definition, a convenience good must be immediately available as the consumer is not prepared to wait to take delivery. From the retailer's point of view the problem is less critical than it is for the manufacturer, as he will usually stock several brands which are acceptable substitutes for one another. However, although convenience goods were defined earlier as those which the consumer buys frequently and with the minimum of effort, the ultimate distinction lies not in the product itself but in the consumer's perception of it, and what may be a convenience good for some may be a specialty good for others. Thus if the housewife is unable to find her preferred brand in one outlet she may well transfer all her custom to another where she can. In that the overall level of brand preference is reflected by the brand's share of the total market, most retailers will stock competing products in the same ratio to one another in the hope of maintaining store loyalty.

In the case of shopping goods, demand is neither so regular nor so predictable as is the case with convenience goods, and the retailer's stock policy, and ultimately his success are based on his judgement of the precise nature of consumer demand. Such decisions invariably create a conflict between the desire to offer a sufficiently wide selection to cater to variations in consumer preference, and the need to hold a sufficient stock of given products to meet the demand for them. A good example of this conflict, shared by both producer and retailer, is the demand for fashion goods in relation to the demand for more conservative styles. The demand for such fashion goods is frequently underestimated, and represents a lost profit opportunity of considerable dimensions. On the other hand, if the retailer overestimates likely demand he will incur additional inventory costs, and may have to sell at a loss to recover his working capital. Although such miscalculations ultimately have an effect on producers' sales, the majority of the risk is carried by the retailer.

☐ *The provision of information*

Retailers supply information to both consumer and manufacturer. In the latter case, the most important information supplied by the retailer is the actual order which he places with the producer, in that it reflects future expectations concerning consumer demand by those in most direct contact with it. However, orders are subject to influence by the manufacturer's salesmen, and may represent wishful thinking rather than informed and objective opinion. Also, in the absence of information concerning stock levels, it is difficult to say whether orders are placed in anticipation of an upswing in demand, or merely to replenish stocks depleted by past demand. Even if the order does accurately reflect changing consumer preferences, it does not give the manufacturer an explanation as to the causes – to obtain such information the manufacturer will have to undertake research.

The provision of information to consumers varies considerably in terms of both amount and quality. Often the most meaningful information provided is the opportunity to examine competing products in close juxtaposition to one another. Price is a more concrete piece of information but, as the advent of the discount house has proved, it is frequently a measure of the retailer's efficiency rather than the value of the product.

Spoken information is still provided by retail sales assistants in many outlets, but consumers would seem to regard much of this information as emanating from a low credibility source; that is, they place little reliance on its accuracy or objectivity. The adoption of this attitude is unsurprising in view of the low status and pay attached to retail selling in general, which is hardly conducive to the recruitment of highly motivated personnel. Hopefully, more retailers will follow the example of pioneers like Boots and Marks & Spencer in upgrading the quality of their employees through the provision of adequate training and incentives. As things stand at present, however, manufacturers are likely to fill the information gap by the continued use of advertising and sales promotion.

☐ *Processing*

The increase of prepacked goods on display in retail outlets is an outward manifestation of the reduced importance of this traditional retailing function. In part this may be attributed to consumer preference, but it is equally due to the manufacturer's desire to make his product identifiable at the point of sale.

In general, it is more economic to pack at the factory than at the point of sale, as the volume of output permits the use of the most productive machines. However, there are a number of important exceptions to this generalisation:

1. Some products may be transported more economically in a completely knocked-down state ('CKD'); for example beds, wardrobes, bicycles.
2. Some commodities may be preserved more easily in bulk form; for example bacon, cheese.
3. In some cases the consumer's exact requirements can only be met by processing at the point of sale; for example 'three lamb chops', 'a pint of mild and bitter'.
4. Packaging can only occur after the customer is satisfied that the goods meet his requirements; for example clothing, fresh produce.

The structure of the retail trade

At a given point in time it is impossible to derive an exact measure of the size and structure of the retail trade in Britain owing to the rapid changes which are taking place. Major changes have taken place in retailing over the last three decades, and the remainder of this chapter will discuss the nature of these developments as well as outline changes in specific sectors – for example, the independent grocers and department stores.

Various social and environmental factors have affected the structure of the retail trade over recent years, affecting not only where goods are bought but also what is bought:

● More leisure time, longer holidays;
● More working wives;
● Increased use of large shopping outlets;
● Less frequent shopping.

These factors, among others, have resulted in the growth of convenience foods and frozen foods. The growth in the consumption of convenience foods has had a major impact on the structure of modern British retailing as it led to the emergence of the supermarket which has affected all forms of retailing.

Overall, the period since the Second World War has been one of increased affluence. Britain became a society with a high demand for consumer goods. By the late 1970s this pattern had begun to change, the demand for consumer durables had slowed down, and there was a small reaction against the increased use of convenience foods with a return to 'natural' foods. Competition between sectors of the retail trade became fiercer as consumers 'tightened their belts'. Some sectors of the retail trade have fared better than others under the competitive pressure.

Some recent changes in retailing are summarised in the following tables. These tables, and many others reproduced elsewhere, are taken from the *Marketing Pocket Book* (1995) published by The Advertising Association in association with NTC Publications Ltd. and are reproduced with their permission. One of the major problems experienced in up-dating text books of this kind is keeping factual data accurate. Given that there is a delay in publishing statistics and a further delay between completing a manuscript and its publication, data are often several years out of date. The only remedy is for the student to note the souce of the tables given and then check the same source for the most recent data. In addition to the *Marketing Pocket Book* NTC publications publish at least eight others which provide a wealth of essential detail for marketers. An order form listing their titles, etc. together with publication details is included at the back of the book. These Pocket Books are essential source material for all serious students of marketing.

In Table 9.2 we summarise the Volume of Retail Sales 1986–94 and in Table 9.3 the Retail Trades in Great Britain.

Table 9.2   *Volume of retail sales 1986–94 (not seasonally adjusted)*

| | *All retailers* (2462) | *Predominantly food retailers* (1035) | *Mixed retail businesses* (171) | *Predominantly non-food retailers* | | | |
				Textile, clothing & footwear (371)	*Household goods* (313)	*Other non-food* (374)	*Non-store retailers/ repairers* (198)
1986	87	90	90	88	80	80	80
1987	92	92	93	93	89	86	100
1988	97	96	99	97	101	94	104
1989	99	99	100	99	102	99	102
1990	100	100	100	100	100	100	100
1991	99	101	99	98	97	95	97
1992	99	104	99	99	97	92	95
1993	102	106	103	103	103	94	96
1994	106	110	105	109	109	98	97

The index has been reclassified on to the Standard Classification of Economic Activities 1992, and rebased using detailed information from the larger 1992 annual retail inquiry.

Index numbers of sales per week (average 1990 prices) 1990 = 100.

Note: Figures in brackets refer to average weekly sales at constant 1990 prices, £ million.

Source: Central Statistical Office, Business Monitor SDM28 Retail Sales.

☐ *Types of retail outlet*

For descriptive purposes, British retail outlets are usually grouped into three main categories:

1. Independent retailers, including small chain stores with nine or fewer branches.
2. Multiple retailers with ten or more branches, but excluding retail co-operative societies.
3. Retail co-operative societies.

The main retail outlets excluded from this classification are department stores, gas and electricity showrooms, and mail order houses.

Independent retailers have declined in recent years, both in shop numbers and in their share of retail trade. This decline is largely attributable to the aggressive price competition from supermarkets and discount houses. (See the later section on the independent grocery trade which gives a more detailed description of the decline of the independents.)

Multiple retailers have enjoyed a period of widespread expansion in the postwar period. The multiples' scale of operation enables them to employ functional specialists, to buy in bulk, and to use their extensive financial resources to acquire the best store locations. Multiple organisations may conveniently be subdivided into three groups:

1. Food chain stores such as Tesco and Sainsbury.
2. Variety chain stores such as British Home Stores, Littlewoods, Marks & Spencer and Woolworth.
3. Speciality chain stores such as Boots, Burtons, Dolcis and Times furniture stores.

Co-operative retail societies are collectively the largest retailer in the United Kingdom but the Co-op has failed to exploit fully the economies of scale open to it and has consistently lost ground to multiple and independent alike over the past quarter of a century. Retail co-operative societies are voluntary, non-profit-making organisations which are controlled by committees elected by customers who are members of the society. In the

Table 9.3 *Retail trades in Great Britain*

I. Analysis by Broad Business and Form of Organisation, 1992

Kind of business and form of organisation	Business number	Outlets number	Retail turnover[1] £m
Total Retail Trade	**219 131**	**318 751**	**137 526**
1 outlet	196 104	196 104	34 839
2–9 outlets	22 221	57 806	14 834
10–99 outlets	682	18 836	16 379
100 or more outlets	125	46 005	71 474
of which co-operative societies accounted for	62	3 583	4 289
Food retailers	**60 119**	**78 606**	**51 462**
1 outlet	55 416	55 416	7 556
2–9 outlets	4 554	11 833	2 879
10–99 outlets	133	3 971	5 770
100 or more outlets	16	7 386	35 247
Drink, confectionery & tobacco retailers	**44 671**	**57 999**	**13 810**
1 outlet	44 758	44 758	8 656
2–9 outlets	1 859	4 695	1 046
10–99 outlets	39	1 226	567
100 or more outlets	15	7 320	3 540
Clothing, footwear & leather goods retailers	**24 923**	**51 319**	**12 428**
1 outlet	20 037	20 037	2 488
2–9 outlets	4 641	13 058	2 382
10–99 outlets	207	5 625	1 874
100 or more outlets	38	12 600	5 685
Houschold goods retailers	**45 532**	**62 648**	**20 881**
1 outlet	49 065	40 065	6 770
2–9 outlets	5 338	12 956	3 547
10–99 outlets	102	3 177	3 180
100 or more outlets	26	6 449	7 384
Other non-food retailers	**36 737**	**52 214**	**12 945**
1 outlet	31 841	31 841	5 995
2 or more outlets	4 896	20 373	6 950
Mixed retail businesses[2]	**3 720**	**11 097**	**24 509**
1 outlet	2 883	2 883	3 252
2–9 outlets	784	2 169	1 648
10–99 outlets	39	1 068	3 444
100 or more outlets	15	4 978	16 165
Hire & repair businesses	**1 430**	**4 868**	**1 490**
1 outlet	1 106	1 106	112
2 or more outlets	324	3 763	1 378

Notes: [1] Inclusive of VAT.

[2] Mixed retail business – Where less than 80% of a business's sales, or 50% in the case of food retailing or hire and repair, fall into the main broad kinds of business, the business is classified as a mixed retail business.

Source: Central Statistical Office, Business Monitor SDA25, Retailing (1991 edition, published by HMSO).

opinion of many it is this factor more than any other which has slowed the growth of the movement by delaying the adoption of modern retailing techniques. As long ago as 1957, the Gaitskell Commission recommended that the Co-op should adopt a new management structure, in addition to the setting-up of more specialised shops and a reduction in the number of societies.

Department stores are another type of retail outlet which has been under increasing competitive pressure from supermarkets, multiples and superstores. Department stores are usually defined as establishments with 24 or more employees engaged in selling clothing, textiles and at least four other major commodity groups. Since 1980 department stores have been classified as mixed retail businesses making it difficult to draw direct comparisons on performance before and after this date. Table 9.2 summarises the pattern of retail sales from 1981–93 by type of business. The number of department stores has stabilised at around 350, with new store openings matching closures. The large national store groups such as House of Fraser, Debenhams, John Lewis, have followed a policy of market repositioning hoping to attract a larger share of the 25 to 40 age group who tend to have the most disposable income. To pull this group away from the variety chain stores, these department stores have modernised and altered their emphasis to one of quality rather than price, improving store ambience and offering co-ordinated product ranges.

☐ *The 'wheel of retailing'*

The 'wheel of retailing' is a major hypothesis concerning patterns of retail development. Advanced by Malcolm P. McNair, a professor at the Harvard Business School, the hypothesis holds that new types of retailers usually enter the market as low-status, low-margin, low-price operators, and gradually acquire more elaborate establishments and facilities involving increased investment and higher operating costs. Finally, they mature as high-cost, high-price outlets, vulnerable to new competitors, and the 'wheel' goes round again.

Although there are a number of exceptions which suggest that the hypothesis is not universally valid, the general pattern of British retail development conforms with it remarkably closely. As a result of wartime restrictions and controls between 1939 and 1952, the normal evolution of the retail trade was brought to a virtual standstill but, with the removal of restrictions, every effort to make up for lost ground was taken. In fact the scale of innovation and the changes in retail structure which have resulted are often referred to as the 'Retail Revolution'.

Stephen Brown (1995) summarises the dramatic structural changes in retailing as the consequence of 6 forces:

- Concentration
- Rationalisation
- Polarisation
- Suburbanisation
- Internationalisation
- Information

We have already referred to the trend towards concentration in retailing with the large multiples accounting for around 70 per cent of all sales. Not only have the major multiples greatly increased their market share at the expense of the independents, but mergers and acquisitions in the multiple sector have seen considerable rationalisation and a significant increase in the share of the largest groups. This trend is reflected in the increased size of the major outlets but has also resulted in a countervailing trend of small convenience stores (see below) which Brown terms 'polarisation'.

The development of superstores is closely linked to the trend towards suburbanisation. Susperstores call for large sites with adequate parking – rarely available in city centres! Brown identifies four major types of development:

1. Regional shopping centres of 400 000 sq ft covered space with several major stores and over 100 outlets.

Table 9.4 *Retailer internationalization: push and pull factors*

Push factors	Pull factors
Mature markets	Fragmented/underdeveloped markets
Intensive competitive pressures	Corporate philosophy to become a global business
Restrictive trading environment	Presence of overseas niche markets
(Impending) saturation in retail floor-space provision	Establish bridgehead for further expansion
Slow economic performance	To employ more fully existing company skills and
Static population growth	strengths

Source: Treadgold and Davies, 1988

2. Sub-regional shopping centres of 200 000–
   400 000 sq ft of covered space, a food superstore, non-food superstore and 20–30 other
   outlets.
3. Retail parks.
4. Stand-alone developments.

A fifth trend of Internationalisation has gathered increased momentum as a result of the
growth of the European Union and the opening
up of the former controlled markets of eastern
Europe. Treadgold and Davies (1988) summarised the factors driving internationalisation
as shown in Table 9.4.

Finally, information technology has had a
major impact on modern retailing and we discuss

these below in the section on Automated Retailing Systems.

Some of the major changes associated with this
revolution are outlined below while their evolution in Europe in summarised in Table 9.5.

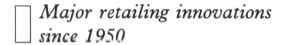

Major retailing innovations since 1950

Self-service

Although the first self-service shop in Britain was
opened in 1942, the wartime restrictions referred
to above delayed its development until these

Table 9.5 *Retail life cycles in EC countries*

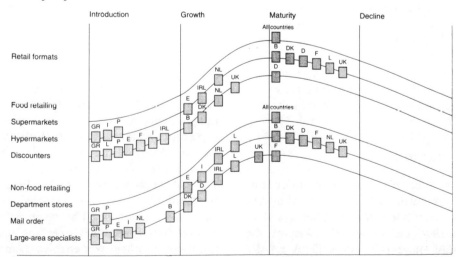

Source: Eurostat (1993: p. 20).

controls were removed: for example there were 10 outlets on self-service principles in 1947; less than 500 in 1950; 4000 in 1957; and nearly 9500 in 1961. There can be no doubt that self-service has been a major factor in improving the productivity of retail distribution, by increasing the utilisation of the available floor area, the carrying of stock on open shelves where it can be selected, rather than in a stockroom, and the reduction in personal service.

Self-service is particularly suited to the sale of branded convenience goods, and thus has had the greatest impact on the food sector, where it has led to the development of supermarkets. Supermarkets are defined as 'self-service shops with a minimum sales area of 2000 square feet and at least three check-outs'. Multiple traders such as Tesco and Sainsbury have been most aggressive in the development of supermarkets and have gradually expanded their product lines from foodstuffs and household requisites such as soap and cleaning materials to include hardware, paint, toiletries and cosmetics and selected soft goods. The supermarkets' scale of operation has permitted them to adopt aggressive pricing policies, and the 'battle of the high street' has forced the independent retailer and wholesaler to join forces to meet the threat through the formation of voluntary chains.

A further development in this area has been the growth of the superstore. The superstore was the natural extension of the supermarket concept. Grocery superstores are defined as stores selling a wide range of food items and other grocery products with at least 25 000 square feet of selling space. In 1994 there were 922 superstores and this number can be expected to increase as superstores become more firmly established in the United Kingdom.

Voluntary chains

The growing success of the multiple outlet rests largely on the integration of both wholesaling and retailing activities. Independent wholesalers had long realised that the growing power of the multiples would place the independent retailer at a competitive disadvantage and that it was only

a matter of time before this group, which comprised their chief customers, would seek to take collective action and set up their own wholesale co-operatives. To forestall such a possibility, the more astute wholesalers took the initiative and organised voluntary chains of independent retailers. Essentially, such chains are based on an agreement whereby the retailer agrees to place a minimum weekly order with the wholesaler; to submit orders by a specified time, often on specially designed forms; and to accept delivery at a prescribed time. In addition many chains, or symbol grocers as they are often called, agree to undertake cooperative advertising campaigns, to adopt a distinctive and uniform decor or 'house style', and to carry 'own brands'. In return for these promises, the wholesaler passes on economies in storage and transportation costs in the form of lower prices, organises joint promotional activities, advises on shop layout and management, and often lends capital for store modification and improvement. Spar, Mace, VG and Londis are examples of symbol voluntary groups in the grocery trade.

While voluntary chains are most active in food retailing they are also to be found in a generally less sophisticated form in other sectors: for example, Vantage and Numark serving the needs of chemists, Interflora, as well as a number of associations in the tobacco, confectionery and hardware trades. However, as the multiples continue to expand their share of the total retail trade one may anticipate further groupings developing among the independents.

The independent grocer

In the years 1971 to 1981 the number of independent grocery outlets almost halved, going from 86 000 to 47 000. This rate of decline was in line with that of all other outlets. However, for the multiples and co-operatives it was part of a policy of rationalisation, and for independents was the outcome of increased competitive pressure. The multiple groups have at least two advantages over the independents: first their buying power enables them to negotiate lower prices and subsequently to sell at lower prices than independents; second they have the advantage of economies of scale accruing to their large scale of operation. The independents' share of sales value and volume reflects this sector's growing difficulties. In the period 1971–81 there was a 38 per cent fall in volume, while the multiples recorded a 57 per cent increase in volume over the same period. The future does not look particularly bright for the independent grocers. In the face of continuing competition from multiples, the independents have had to move towards longer opening hours in order to survive.

Convenience stores

The Marketing Pocket Book has the following information:

CONVENIENCE STORES
There is no official definition of a convenience store but the following criteria provide a generally acceptable description:

- self-service;
- 1,000 to 3,000 square feet selling area;
- parking facilities;
- open seven days a week for long hours;
- a wide range of goods, but limited brand choice, including groceries, CTN products, toiletries, OTC medicines, alcohol and stationery. Other products and services are take-away foods, DIY, toys, video hire, film processing and petrol.

This definition applies to specialist purpose-built convenience stores. Other convenience stores, which do not conform exactly to the full criteria, have developed from grocers, CTNs and petrol stations. Their product mix usually reflects their origin.

Lack of a formal definition makes it difficult to give a precise figure for the total number of convenience stores but it is estimated that there were up to 6,500 in mid-1994, of which about 1,500 fulfil the strict criteria listed above.

Leading operators include:

Ranked in terms of number of outlets

Specialists	
Alldays	393
M & W (Misselbrook & Weston)	161
7-Eleven	51

Grocers	
Spar	2,184
Happy Shopper	2,000
Londis	1,360
Mace	1,137
Costcutter	610
VG (Late Stop)	450
Tates	91
Europa	51
Cullens	23
Petrol Forecourts	
Esso	2,350
BP Express	960
Shell Select	640
Heron (Elf)	535
Texaco (Star Shops)	500
Frost (Save)	236
Murco (Shop-Stop)	220
Conoco/Jet (Jiffy)	165
Total	44
Tesco Express	3
Others	
Dillons	168
Thresher (Food & Drink)	97
One Stop	96
Star News	49
Martin	36
Village Store	29
Forbuoys First	29

Note: All figures as at February 1995 or later.
Source: Verdict Research (0171-404 5042).

Mail order

In the 1970s the mail-order section of the retail trade experienced a period of rapid growth; the sales in 1979 showed an increase of 24 per cent on the previous year. Since then sales have continued to grow from £2335 million in 1980 to £3596 million in 1987 a growth of 54 per cent. However, the index of all retail sales grew by 76 per cent over the same period, indicating the sector is losing ground by comparison.

Mail-order houses fall into two basic categories – general and specialist. The latter usually concentrate on a single product group and are particularly active in the market for seeds, bulbs, plants and small horticultural items. At the other end of the scale, mail order is dominated by the general-line firms with sales well in excess of

£700 million per annum, and including house-hold names such as Littlewood's, Great Universal Stores, Grattan and Freemans. Nearly half the goods sold by mail order are clothing, and another quarter is accounted for by household goods.

Given the extensive network of retail outlets throughout the country, the growth of mail order appears at first sight to be an enigma. In fact, it reflects the marketing skills of the operators who have consistently pursued a policy of high quality, backed by a guarantee of satisfaction that is scrupulously honoured with none of the unpleasantry found in some retail establishments. Add to this the convenience of shopping in the comfort of one's home, and generous credit and repayment terms, and the combination becomes virtually irresistible.

Discount houses

The development of discount houses in Britain was delayed for some years, following their introduction in the United States, owing to the existence of Resale Price Maintenance. Since the abolition of this practice, however, they have become a growing force in the field of retailing.

In the simplest terms a discount house may be defined as a non-food supermarket, and operates on the same principle of low mark-up and rapid turnover. However, firms such as Kwik Save Discount and Asda have extended discounting principles into the food sector. In the first stage of their evolution they tend to concentrate on shopping goods and particularly on consumer durables with a high average margin, which permitted the discounter to offer savings of as much as 50 per cent on recommended retail prices – for example Comet, MFI. The second stage of their evolution has been marked by the turn of the 'wheel of retailing'. Discount houses have upgraded their image by improving the amenities and the range of goods and services offered. Recently there has been a move towards continental-type fresh food discount outlets which, with the renewed interest in 'natural' foods, will undoubtedly expand further.

Franchising

Franchising recently has been a growth sector of the UK economy. It is not a new type of business organisation as its origins can be traced back two hundred years to brewers' 'tied-public house' systems. The recent growth in franchising has been encouraged by the British Franchise Association formed in 1977. The Association offers guidance to prospective franchisees and has done much to stamp out malpractice in the business. In essence a franchise agreement allows an individual to set up in an established business by adopting the name and practices of its originator; for example, Wimpy Bars have a more or less standardised layout and menu. The franchisee usually pays a lump sum to begin with and then pays a continuing royalty to the franchisor. Franchisors exercise varying degrees of control over the operation of franchisees, and provide varying levels of support which preclude generalisation. Given the attraction of running one's own business under the protective umbrella of a franchise offering specialised retailing skills and experience normally accessible only to the large organisation, it is perhaps not surprising that only a relatively small number of UK franchises fail each year. This high success rate is probably due to the great personal motivation of the franchisees and the guidance of the franchisor. Examples of franchise operations can be found in many areas of trade – British School of Motoring, Apollo Window Blinds, Dynorod, Prontaprint, Pronuptia and Youngs. The best-known franchise organisations are probably those in the catering and fast-food sectors – MacDonald's, Burger King, Spud-U-Like, Holiday Inns, Kentucky Fried Chicken and Thorntons all come into this category.

Cash-and-carry wholesaling

Cash-and-carry wholesaling developed out of the independent wholesalers and retailers' desire to remain competitive with the multiple sector. As such it represented an alternative to the formation of voluntary chains which have already been referred to. While the setting-up of a voluntary chain resulted in formal relationship between retailer and wholesaler, cash-and-carry operations place no such restrictions on either party. As the volume of sales and the market share held by the independent grocers has fallen, cash-and-carry operators have been forced to look for new customers and for new, non-grocery lines. The catering trade has become the main cash-and-carry customer, taking over from the independent grocers.

■ Channels of distribution

In broad terms the same channels of distribution noted in respect of the manufacturer of industrial goods are also open to the consumer goods manufacturer, namely:

1. Direct to the ultimate consumer.
2. Direct to the retailer for resale to the ultimate consumer; that is, the retail outlet is regarded as the customer.
3. Indirect sale through the medium of a wholesaler or agent.
4. A combination of any or all of these alternatives.

☐ *Direct sale to ultimate consumers*

Direct sale to the consumer may be achieved by the manufacturer/seller of services in one of three ways:

1. Forward integration into retailing and the establishment of one's own outlets. (Usually it is the retailer who integrates backwards, however.)
2. Mail order selling.
3. Door-to-door selling.

The advantages and disadvantages of each of these alternatives may be summarised as:

1. *Own retail outlets*
Advantages:

(a) Complete control over the selling function: for example price setting, terms of trade, provisions of services, sales training and so on.
(b) Economies of scale in storage, transportation and administration.
(c) The ability to coordinate in-store promotion with advertising and other promotional activities.
(d) Closer contact with the consumers and therefore a better understanding of their needs and preferences.

Disadvantages:

(a) Limited access to the market.
(b) The assumption of all risks.
(c) The need for extensive financial resources to cover both fixed investment and working capital needs.

Examples: Boots, British Shoe Corporation, Burtons, Singer.

2. *Mail order*
Advantages:

(a) Complete control.
(b) Economies of scale.
(c) Access to the whole market, including areas with insufficient population to support conventional outlets.
(d) Consumer convenience.

Disadvantages:

(a) High delivery costs.
(b) High promotional costs.
(c) High costs of building and maintaining an up-to-date mailing list.
(d) Costs of financing credit sales.

Examples: Great Universal, John Moores, Grattan. (Note: although many of the general-line mail-order houses have their own production facilities, a large part of their merchandise represents the output of other manufacturers.)

3. *Door-to-door*
Advantages:

(a) Complete control.
(b) Most effective method of selling certain goods and services where demonstration or complex explanation is necessary: for example vacuum cleaners, insurance policies.

Disadvantages:

(a) Unsolicited calls are viewed with suspicion.
(b) High cost – usually offset by paying low basic salary and high commission.
(c) Difficult to recruit and retain suitable salesmen owing to unattractive working conditions.

Examples: Avon Cosmetics, Kleen-Eze, Prudential Assurance, various publishing houses.

☐ *Direct sale to retail outlets*

In view of the high costs associated with direct sales to the consumer, most consumer-goods manufacturers prefer to sell through some form of independent retail outlet.

Given the number of retail outlets, direct sale might appear totally uneconomic at first sight. On reflection, however, it is clear that a very large percentage of sales are channelled through a very limited number of buying points and the manufacturer can gain direct access to the market through relatively few centralised purchasing agencies (Table 9.6).

As can be seen from Table 9.6 there is a high degree of concentration in several sectors of the UK retail trade. For example, in 1975 Nielsen estimated it was possible to gain access to 75 per cent of the grocery trade through 344 buying points. By 1980, 275 buying points were estimated to control 82 per cent of all purchases but, to reach the remaining 18 per cent of the market one would have had to contact 39 000 additional buying points. The trend continues but whether such an operation is economically feasible requires consideration of the cost and control factors mentioned in the previous section and usually resolves itself into a policy decision on the relative merits of selective, versus extensive, distribution. If the latter is chosen, as it invariably is with mass consumption, widely advertised convenience goods, most manufacturers find it necessary to sell at least part of their output through an intermediary.

☐ *Selling through wholesalers*

The advantages of selling through a wholesaler have already been examined when discussing the

Table 9.6 *Concentration ratios in the UK retailing industry by broad commodity group*

	All sales amount (£m)	The largest five enterprise groups accounted for:		The largest ten enterprise groups accounted for:	
		Amount (£m)	%	Amount (£m)	%
Food	29 080	10 070	34.6	13 805	47.5
Drink, confectionery and tobacco	14 067	2 762	19.6	4 269	30.3
Clothing, footwear and leather goods	16 568	6 080	36.7	8 101	48.9
Household goods	20 318	4 038	19.9	5 970	29.4
Other non-food goods	15 462	3 060	19.8	4 295	27.8
Hire and repair	1 681	1 094	65.1	1 164	69.2

distribution of industrial goods, and will not be pursued further here. In general, manufacturers of consumer goods will find it appropriate to make use of the wholesaler's services under the following circumstances:

1. Where a large number of small, widely dispersed outlets account for a significant share of total sales.
2. Where the manufacturer has limited working capital and is unable to bear the costs of direct selling.
3. Where the manufacturer is new to the market and seeking to gain retail acceptance.
4. Where the manufacturer has an excess supply which could be sold under a wholesaler brand, or where he has no brand of his own.
5. Where demand is irregular and/or seasonal: for example fireworks!
6. Where trade custom has resulted in channel control becoming vested in the wholesaler.

☐ *Automated retailing systems*

A recent report from ICL on *Retailing Tomorrow* opened with the following observations:

> The implications of computer-based systems in the retailing industry are enormous and far-reaching. And they are impacting on every part of the industry – retailers themselves, manufacturers, wholesalers and ultimately consumers too.
>
> In new research and statistical analysis published for the first time here in *Retailing Tomorrow* it is clear that the long-awaited technology revolution in retailing is, at last, happening. Hard evidence shows a massive upsurge in demand from UK retailers for automated systems.

In this section we will examine the benefits associated with automated retailing systems and the forces which are accelerating its take-up and use through the retail sector.

While retailers were among the first organisations to make use of large mainframe computers for central administrative functions, the use of information technology (IT) in individual stores was delayed awaiting necessary developments in both hardware and software. Among these developments may be numbered:

1. Increased standardisation of computer communications.
2. The development of British Telecom's Packet Switched System (PSS) and its X-stream networks enabling easier and more cost-effective transmission of computer signals around the country.
3. The introduction of standardised code-marking (bar coding).
4. The growth of inter-company communications enabling different computer systems to link into one another.

Figure 9.3 *Growth in EPOS market, 1986–93 by number of units installed*

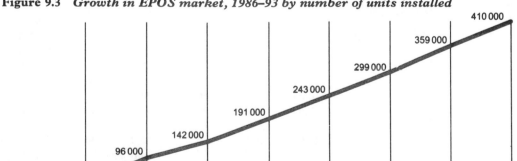

1986	1987	1988	1989	1990	1991	1992	1993
58 000	96 000	142 000	191 000	243 000	299 000	359 000	410 000

Source: ICL, *Retailing Tomorrow*

As a consequence of these developments, the number of EPOS terminals in retail outlets has grown rapidly as can be seen from Figure 9.3 and Table 9.7.

Penetration of EPOS equipment in the UK retail sector as a whole has been spectacular with large and medium-sized retail organisations accounting for the bulk of this growth. Additionally, spending on equipment in the early 1990s was supplemented by a growing level of investment in replacement systems.

The benefits accruing from automated retailing systems may be usefully characterised as 'hard' and 'soft'. Perhaps the most important hard benefit arises from improved stock control and management which allows for lower operating stocks with a better range on display and a greatly reduced need for mark-downs or discounting to shift slow-moving stock. ICL estimate that in the hospitality industry more accurate information can pay for an in-store system within fifteen months and quote the case of a DIY retailer which was able to cut its stock by 40 per cent

without affecting the level of business. In food multiples the use of scanning equipment and EPOS terminals has resulted in greatly improved productivity with a reduction of 19 per cent in checkout labour hours for the same level of business. Checkout operators are able to handle around 25 items a minute which is a 66 per cent improvement compared with a conventional cash register/cash desk operation. Significant savings in labelling, pricing and shelf-filling have also been achieved together with savings in administrative costs due to more accurate reporting.

Another source of hard benefits has been increased cashpoint efficiency with few price identification and price ringing mistakes. Attitudes to these benefits are summarised in Table 9.8.

On the soft benefit side the major gains arise from more and better information on which to make marketing and management decisions. Automated systems also free staff time so they can give more attention to serving customers and thereby enhance perceived service levels. Customers also appreciate the benefits of fewer stock outs and the

Table 9.7 *Penetration of EPOS terminals by retail line of trade*

	1984 (%)	1985 (%)	1986 (%)	1987 (%)	1988 (%)	1989 (%)	1990 (%)
Beer/wine/spirits	15.0	18.0	23.0	30.0	39.0	49.0	57.0
Chemists	1.0	2.0	3.0	6.0	13.0	22.0	33.0
Clothing	5.0	9.0	16.0	25.0	36.0	50.0	65.0
Department stores	47.0	50.0	57.0	65.0	75.0	83.0	88.0
DIY/Home improvement	2.5	12.0	24.0	37.0	51.0	65.0	80.0
Electrical	25.0	30.0	36.0	42.0	51.0	58.0	64.0
Speciality food	3.0	6.0	9.0	13.0	17.0	21.0	27.0
Footwear	2.0	5.0	13.0	22.0	31.0	40.0	50.0
Furniture	4.0	6.0	9.0	13.0	18.0	23.0	30.0
Supermarkets	1.7	4.5	13.0	25.0	39.0	55.0	70.0
Housewares	2.0	10.0	20.0	30.0	37.0	45.0	52.0
Jewellers	15.0	40.0	50.0	60.0	70.0	78.0	85.0
Leisure	20.0	22.0	25.0	29.0	34.0	40.0	47.0
Newsagents	1.0	2.0	5.0	11.0	19.0	27.0	36.0
Variety	10.0	13.0	16.0	20.0	26.0	34.0	46.0
Pubs and restaurants	1.0	2.5	8.0	17.0	28.0	39.0	50.0
Fast food	15.0	21.0	29.0	39.0	51.0	63.0	71.0
Petrol	2.0	6.0	12.0	19.0	29.0	40.0	50.0

Source: ICL estimates. The retail categorisations in the above statistics are based on the line of trade of major UK retail organisations and not on their respective operating philosophies.

Table 9.8 *Benefits of EPOS*

	Very important				Very unimportant
	5	4	3	2	1
(KeyBase: Benefits of introducing EPOS, where 5 = very important and 1 = very unimportant)					
Better stock control	48	28	13	6	4
Improving store level information	39	33	13	9	5
Exercising central management control	23	42	18	13	4
Better staff productivity and planning	14	26	32	20	8
Less stock shrinkage	17	28	30	14	11
Improving promotional planning	7	28	30	24	10
More effective display and store layout	2	19	33	24	22

Note: Numbers are *row* percentages, i.e. number in sample selecting each option.
Source: Research Solutions for ICL, UK Ltd.

provision of more information regarding their purchases. Figure 9.4 is an example of a till receipt issued by a B & Q Supercentre which illustrates the kind of detail available.

☐ *Teleshopping*

In a paper 'Teleshopping: Just Around the Corner?' Ian Miles (1990) examines the reasons underlying the optimistic expectation that tele-shopping is just about to take off and its disappointing development in the UK in recent years. Miles points out that:

> Teleshopping is one of a number of new *transactional services*, such as telebanking (where money is transferred electronically) and telebooking (the ability to reserve, for example, train and theatre seats remotely). These go beyond other new services which make use of computer and telecommunications technology

Figure 9.4 *Example till receipt*

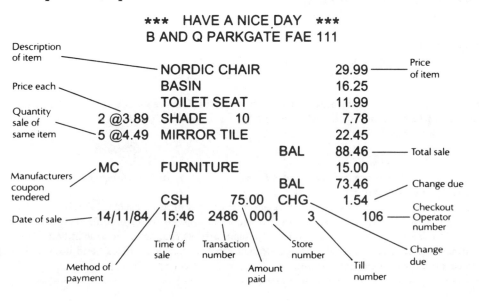

(these are often called *new telematics services*), such as *information services* which allow for mail, conversations, multi-user games.

However, compared with these other kinds of services teleshopping calls for a more significant change in user behaviour and possesses a number of disadvantages which are less off-putting in fields such as telematics. Table 9.9 summarises these drawbacks to teleshopping but also suggests ways of overcoming these barriers.

Although the means of overcoming barriers to the more rapid adoption and diffusion of teleshopping may be identified it seems unlikely that they will be rapidly overcome. Given that shopping is also a social experience which provides a change from the everyday surroundings of the home it would seem reasonable to predict that teleshopping will provide only one of many options and is unlikely to displace in-store shopping in the foreseeable future. That said, a recent report (Inteco, 1995) predicts that by the beginning of the next century teleshopping's impact will be 'as though a bomb has hit the high street'.

In a summary of the Report in *The Sunday Times* (25 June 1995), it is argued that shopping in Britain will change fundamentally in three ways:

- Use of multimedia through personal computers and televisions will allow retailers to display their goods in an appealing way;
- Consumers will be able to order goods via screens;
- 'Digital delivery' will allow items such as videos, newspapers, books, music, banking, travel and medical services to be provided to the home by connecting the PC or interactive TV to telephone, satellite and cable networks.

Of course such changes will require huge investments in new broadband networks as well as the willingness of both sellers and buyers to

---

Table 9.9   *Overcoming barriers to teleshopping*

Overcoming hardware barriers
- Limited text on screen, eyestrain problems: better screens (high resolution, flat screens);
- *Lack of portability of screen and keyboard*: smaller systems, mobile communications, multiple phone sockets/data networks in homes.

Overcoming software/information barriers
- Non-user-friendly interfaces: improved interfaces, using for example 'mice', trackerballs, remote controllers;
- *Cumbersome menu systems*: simulated shopping environments, personalised 'shopping lists', natural language systems;
- *Inferior graphic quality*: photovideotex, video quality images delivered via various media: cable TV, ISDN telephony, 'downloaded' catalogues broadcast on TV and stored on videorecorders, interactive compact disc, satellite broadcasts, etc.

Overcoming social and system barriers
- Limited diffusion of hardware, software and telematics: development of wide range of consumer information technologies (home informatics);
- *Limited choice of services*: expanded range of services as critical mass of users established, and as more retailers use computerised stockholding, ordering and transactional systems, electronic funds transfer, etc.;
- *Problems with delivery schedules*: social innovations, facilitated as economies of scale in delivery possible; flexible delivery times and schedules, neighbourhood deposit centres (e.g. post offices), and household deposit centres (refrigerated post boxes, new types of doors?).

discard current methods and habits. Nonetheless, Inteco forecast that by 1998, 600 000 British households will be able to participate in TV shopping services provided by BT and cable-TV firms. How this will grow is anyone's guess. However, Inteco acknowledges that Prestel floundered in the early 1980s due to the consumer's unwillingness to pay up-front for such a service. Similarly, ownership of PCs is confined to the more affluent so that teleshopping may well be confined to the better off with the necessary hardware/software. The report concludes:

> In spite of early marketing difficulties and the initial low returns on investment, on-line shopping services and interactive television will eventually achieve major success.
>
> This is because consumers will find it hard to resist the low prices for products that are achieved by avoiding retail premises or telesale staff. And for brand and channel owners, the high level of feedback about browsing habits and price enquiries from accurately identified groups of potential customers is very valuable.

Future trends in grocery retailing

In the field of retailing, be it for groceries or financial services, it has long been recognised that convenience and accessibility have had a major influence on consumers' patronage decisions. Accordingly, past decades have seen retailers of all kinds seeking to maximise territory coverage by opening more and more outlets. While this trend is likely to continue in some of the new growth areas it seems much less likely in the field of food retailing where a stable population and static per capita food consumption point to the inevitability of saturation in this market. The consequences of such saturation were the subject of an article by Robert Duke (1991), 'Post-Saturation Competition in UK Grocery Retailing'.

To address the problems of saturation in grocery retailing, particularly between the 'Big Five' of Sainsbury, Tesco, Asda, Argyll and Gateway, Duke proposes the use of a strategic marketing tool called *market leakage analysis* (MLA). MLA is a technique which divides the market into two parts – the company's share of the market and the *leaked* market which the company could serve but currently does not. Figure 9.5 depicts the basis for market leakage analysis and suggests that this can arise from three main causes. In Category A the company does not have a product or service which matches precisely the needs of the consumers comprising this segment. In Category B are potential customers which the firm has been unable to reach due to deficiencies in its marketing communications or distribution strategies. Finally, Category C contains those users which the firm has tried to win and failed. Clearly, each category calls for a rather different strategy.

It seems reasonable to assume that if the market is saturated then there is no potential competitive advantage in Category B as opening still more outlets can only lead to diminishing returns and reduced margins. It follows that opportunities for the future will be concentrated in Categories A and C – extending the product/service mix to match consumer needs better and intensifying one's competitive effort. While such competition has always existed it can only become more acute and focused with the elimination of new outlets as the major source of advantage.

Duke argues that few if any major retailers will wish to attempt a direct frontal assault by opening a new outlet next door to a competitor which suggests that flanking manoeuvres will be the preferred strategy. In the past geographic flanking attacks have predominated, that is find a location with a catchment area with little direct competition, but saturation has closed off this option leaving the 'low price flank', used by Kwik Save and Asda, and defensible differentiation as the basic alternatives. The question is, of course, what will constitute the sustainable competitive advantage which will enable a firm to pursue a differentiation strategy? As Duke points out 'innovative offers in pursuit of differential advantage (price leadership, superstores, own-label, high quality, health, green and so on)... are hard to keep secret and easy to copy, and so, such a

Figure 9.5   *Market leakage analysis*

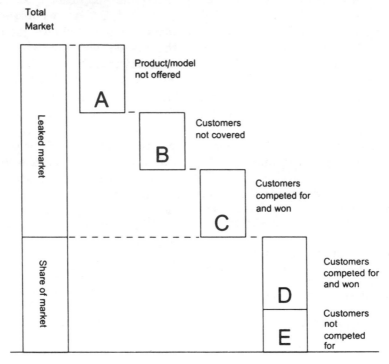

Source: Ohmae (1982).

defensible advantage has largely eluded everyone'. However, Duke goes on to suggest that as resources will not be required for massive store opening programmes so it will be possible divert some of this investment to other purposes, and proposes two general approaches. The first of these is to open new kinds of outlet in a different mould to the existing superstore and the second involves improving the offer made to customers through existing outlets.

In the latter category an opportunity clearly exists in the fifth P of marketing – people. Price competition inevitably led to a reduction in service and staffing levels and the perception of retailing as a poorly paid, low status dead-end occupation. But, as Marks & Spencer, Boots and many others have demonstrated, a well trained, motivated and rewarded workforce plays a major role in developing perceptions of quality and service in the customer's mind.

A second source of defensible competitive advantage is to be found in the adoption and use of new technology such as that available through electronic point of sale (EPOS) systems. While the technology is available to all (at a price) the competitive advantage will lie in the quality of management's interpretation of the data which such systems can generate, particularly in fine tuning the product mix and in their stocking and ordering decision. In addition, the more effective managers will see technology not just as a means of increasing operating efficiency but as an opportunity to redeploy staff into customer support activities.

In the case of new kinds of outlet the experience of the 1980s indicates that while the benefits of one-stop shopping in large, well stocked superstores with good parking facilities were appreciated there was also a need for the traditional corner-shop type of operation with

Figure 9.6 *Grocery multiples' strategic choice grid*

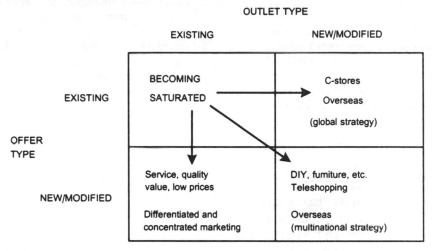

Source: Duke (1991) *Journal of Marketing Management*, vol. 7(1).

long opening hours, stocks of fresh foods and other basic items needed to top-up the weekly shop, and easily accessible without making a major expedition. Convenience outlets – or C-stores are they are now known – have emerged as a major market niche. While the superstores were content to let them develop unchallenged as they concentrated on their expansion of major outlets it would be surprising, now this phase is almost finished, if they did not turn their attention to this sector in the near future. Given that about 80 per cent of a store's operating cost is the cost of goods sold it is clear that the size and scale of the Big Five will give them an almost irresistible advantage if they move into the C-store market.

Taken together Duke sees these possibilities as offering a strategic choice grid as illustrated in Figure 9.6.

An invaluable source of information on retailing is the Economic Intelligence Unit's publication *Retail Business*. Other recommended publications are *Retail and Distribution Management*, *Nielsen Researcher*, *Group Grocer*, *Business Monitor*, *Annual Abstract of Statistics* and the numerous Keynote and Mintel Reports. As already mentioned, perhaps the best source of statistics on all aspects of marketing is the *Marketing Pocket Book* and related titles published by NTC Publications.

Future trends in retailing generally

From the foregoing discussion it is quite clear that major changes have taken and continue to take place in the nature and structure of retailing. Traditionally, consideration of distribution channels, and the discussion of business systems or value chains, would give more attention and emphasis to manufacturers than to retailers as this reflected the balance of power between large manufacturers and small retailers. This position is now largely reversed and, given that the demand for industrial goods is derived from the demand for consumer goods, the emergence of large and very sophisticated retailers means that retailing has grown into a major sub-field of study in its own right. In a book of this kind we can only scratch the surface and readers are referred to the additional readings recommended at the end of the book.

To conclude we can do no better than quote Stephen Brown (*op.cit.*):

The upshot of these dramatic changes is that retailing is no longer the preserve of small, independent shopkeepers relying on the marketing muscle and expertise of their sophisticated suppliers. Retailing is now characterised by large, efficient and expertly managed firms with a strategic outlook and marketing orientation. Retailers dominate the channels of distribution; they are powerful brands in their own right; they engender enormous customer loyalty; and they utilise the full range of marketing mix elements in their pursuit of competitive advantage. Retailing, in short, is no longer one of the *components* of a manufacturer's marketing effort, but the *centre* of its marketing endeavours.   (p. 422)

Summary

This rather large chapter has provided a broadly-based introduction to the subject of Channels of Distribution and has been concerned with the formal systems and structures which have developed to facilitate the movement of goods through the business system or value chain.

To begin with it was noted that in the past distribution has tended to be something of a Cinderella of marketing but, as this chapter has made clear, it now commands close attention. This importance is directly attributable to the functions of the channel which we listed as:

1. Transfer of title to the goods involved;
2. Physical movement from the point of production to the point of consumption;
3. Storage functions;
4. Communication of information concerning the availability, characteristics and price of the goods;
5. The financing of goods in transit, inventory and on purchase.

Basically, a manufacture or producer of goods or services has one or other of three basic alternatives:

- Direct sale;
- Sale through an intermediary;
- A 'dual' policy combining direct sale with the use of an intermediary.

The pursuit of these options was then traced by examining in some detail the distribution of raw materials, the distribution of industrial goods and, finally, the distribution of consumer goods through the retail function. The latter discussion made it clear that the balance of power in distribution channels has shifted significantly in the second half of this century following a revolution in retailing. This shift has had important implications for the management of channels and we return to this topic in Chapter 14 – Channel Management.

We have now completed our review of what we term the Theoretical Underpinnings, which are common to all marketing decisions, and turn our attention to the options available to the marketing manager through manipulation of the marketing mix.

Review questions and problems

1. Discuss the efforts of producers/users of primary commodities to stabilise markets by agreeing upon quotas, price, etc. What are the advantages/disadvantages of such agreements?

2. What factors account for the erratic short-term price fluctuations in market for agricultural products?

3. What advantages/disadvantages have processed foodstuffs over fresh produce, and how has this affected consumer purchasing patterns?

4. There are no fundamental differences between the marketing of industrial and consumer goods. Comment.

5. What basic distributive alternatives are open to the manufacturers of industrial goods? Which do you consider most appropriate to the sale of:

   - Basic chemicals
   - Computers
   - Electric components
   - Machine tools
   - Office supplies
   - Plastic pipe?

   Why?

6. Describe the economist's concept of concentration ratios. How useful is this concept to the marketer – industrial or consumer? In what way?

7. What functions add value to the product, or merely add to its final cost without adding to its value?

8. It is frequently contended that industrial buying is an essentially rational process whereas consumer purchasing is not. State your reasons for agreeing/disagreeing with this statement.

9. Does the industrial market merit special consideration or is it merely a particular application of general marketing principles?

10. Do we understand enough about how buyers and sellers interact in industrial markets to be able to predict industrial buying (or selling) behaviour? If yes, discuss; if no, why not?

11. In industrial marketing there is normally a much closer link between the information-gathering and promotional sides of marketing than is found in consumer goods marketing. Discuss.

12. Evaluate the usefulness of models of the industrial buying process (like Robinson and Faris's buygrid framework) in industrial marketing decisions.

13. Describe the major features which distinguish industrial marketing from consumer markets, and illustrate their implications for marketing management in consumer and industrial companies.

14. There is considerable variation in the retail mark-up on a bar of soap, a household electrical appliance, a suite of furniture and a diamond ring. As all retailers perform the same basic functions why should this be so?

15. In what ways do retailers provide consumers with product information?

16. How well does McNair's concept of the 'wheel of retailing' fit postwar changes in retail distribution in the United Kingdom?

17. What is a 'voluntary chain'? To what do they owe their existence, and what role do you expect them to play in future?

18. What basic distribution alternatives are open to the manufacturers of consumer goods, and what are the major advantages/disadvantages associated with each?

19. Evaluate the factors for and against the establishment of out-of-town shopping centres.

20. The last decade has witnessed an ever-increasing concentration of power into the hands of a reducing number of multiple retailers. Discuss the main ways in which manufacturers have attempted to meet this challenge, indicating what degrees of success have been achieved.

21. Account for the predominance of direct manufacturers-to-user channels in the marketing of capital goods in comparison to the almost pervasive use of some type of middleman in the marketing of consumer goods. What factors determine the choice of channel in each sector?

22. Mail-order marketing has been particularly successful during recent years. How has advertising helped this growth? Your answer should outline the various methods of mail-order operation and use of media.

23. Describe some of the important trends in the retailing sector, and how this might affect marketing.

24. Discuss the possible reasons which might be applicable in the decisions of retailers to develop 'own labels', and manufacturers who refuse to supply 'own labels'.

25. Compare and discuss the relative advantages/disadvantages for a manufacturer of a consumer durable for the distribution of his goods through three of the four methods below:

    (a)   own retail outlet;
    (b)   selective distribution;
    (c)   using wholesalers;
    (d)   franchising.

26. Why are large manufacturers with their own brand willing to supply retailers with a 'retailer' brand? What are some of the consequences of doing so?

27. Explain why effective and efficient inventory management is so important to the physical distribution system.

28. To what extent would you agree with the proposition that contractual vertical marketing systems are the most effective means of controlling the channel?

29. What role can retail alliances play for independent retailers in maintaining competitiveness compared with retail corporate chains? Discuss the advantages and limitations of such retail alliances.

30. In many retail sectors the traditional independent operators are encountering major competition from larger multiple operators. Examine the main areas where the independent operators can compete successfully, using examples to support your answer.

31. Demonstrate how the issue of conflict in distribution channels may affect retailers both horizontally and vertically.

32. Explain what you understand by the expression 'while manufacturers can do away with Intermediaries they cannot do away with their function'. Elaborate your answer with examples.

■ Supplementary reading list

Baker, Michael J. (1975) *Marketing New Industrial Products* (London: Macmillan).

Christopher, Martin (1986) *The Strategy of Distribution Management* (London: Heinemann).

Hill, R. W. (1973) *Marketing Technological Products to Industry* (Oxford: Pergamon).

McGoldrick, Peter (1991) *Retail Marketing* (Maidenhead: McGraw-Hill).

Randall, Geoffrey (1990) *Marketing to the Retail Trade* (London: Heinemann).

Rosenbloom, Bert (1995) *Marketing Channels: A Management View*, 5th edn (Fort Worth: Dryden Press).

Stern, L. W. and El-Ansary Adel, J. (1992) *Marketing Channels*, 4th edn (Englewood Cliffs, N.J.: Prentice-Hall).

West, Alan (1989) *Managing Distribution and Change* (New York: Wiley).

□ *Journals*

Group Grocer
International Journal of Physical Distribution and Materials Management
Nielsen Reporter
Retail Business
Retailing and Distribution Management

Part III
THE MARKETING MIX

■ *Chapter 10* ■

Marketing Research*

Contents

Learning goals

The issues to be addressed in this chapter include:

1. The nature and scope of marketing research.
2. Organising for marketing research.
3. The planning and execution of research.
4. Forms and sources of data, their collection and use.
5. The analysis and presentation of data.
6. The role of marketing research agencies.

After reading this chapter you will be able to:

1. Define marketing research.
2. Explain the scope of marketing research.
3. Discuss the issues involved in the decision to establish a market research department and the role and function of the market research manager.
4. Clarify the distinction between primary and secondary data.

5. Summarise the nature of desk research and list some major sources of external data.
6. Describe the nature of field research and the collection of primary data.
7. Explain the survey methods available to a researcher and the differences between censuses and surveys.
8. Define the nature of sampling and review the types of sample in common use.
9. Illustrate the various methods of making contact with respondents.
10. Review some of the issues involved in the design and use of questionnaires.
11. List the kinds and properties of attitude scales and their use in marketing.
12. Set out the preferred structure and format of market research reports.
13. Describe the role of marketing research agencies and give examples of syndicated research data.

*Readers wishing an extended treatment of this subject are referred to Baker (1991), *Research for Marketing* (London: Macmillan).

■ Introduction

It is not without significance that this chapter is entitled 'Marketing Research' as opposed to the more familiar title 'Market Research', although some might consider it pedantic that a distinction be drawn between the two. It is reasonable to say that most of the published literature on market research is, in fact, concerned with marketing research in that it deals with the question of research in relation to marketing on a much broader front than is implied by the former description. By definition, market research is concerned with measurement and analysis of markets, whereas marketing research is concerned with all those factors which impinge upon the marketing of goods and services, and so includes the study of advertising effectiveness, distributive channels, competitive products and marketing policies and the whole field of consumer behaviour.

☐ *Definitions*

In his *Principles of Management* (second edition), E. F. L. Brech (1954) defines market research as 'the study of all problems relating to the transfer of goods and services from producer to consumer with the aim of producing practical answers consistent with accepted theoretical principles'. At a later point the objective of undertaking research is stated as 'to reduce the areas of uncertainty surrounding business decisions'. Both these definitions indicate a function of much greater scope than is inherent in the more limited concept of the market and analysis of it.

The British Institute of Management has adopted a slightly modified version of the original definition (now superseded) of the American Marketing Association, namely: 'The objective gathering, recording and analysing of all facts about problems relating to the transfer and sale of goods and services from producer to consumer or user.'

The last word in this definition is important for it emphasises that marketing research is equally concerned with industrial goods – a point which is frequently overlooked in definitions which refer solely to consumers, as the latter are usually interpreted as 'ultimate' consumers.

■ The scope of marketing research

Explicit in the introduction to this chapter is recognition of the fact that marketing research is concerned with the scientific investigation of *all* factors which impinge upon the marketing of goods and services. It follows, therefore, that the scope of this function is virtually limitless, and discussion here will have to be confined to those types of research most frequently undertaken in practice.

Essentially, marketing research seeks to provide answers to five basic questions: Who? What? When? Where? and How? The associated question Why? extends inquiry into the area of socio-psychology and is sometimes distinguished as a separate field known as motivation research. (Unfortunately, this title has developed certain undesirable connotations due to the dubious activities of some practitioners.) In practice, marketing research is usually concentrated on a limited number of recurrent problems, often on a continuous basis, which may be classified as follows:

- Market research

  The size and nature of the market in terms of the age, sex, income, occupation and social status of consumers;
  The geographical location of potential consumers;
  The market shares of major competitors, that is brand-share analysis;
  The structure, composition and organisation of distributive channels serving the market;
  The nature of economic and other environmental trends affecting the structure of the market.

- Sales research

  Determination of territorial variations in sales yield;
  The establishment and revision of sales territories;
  Sales call planning;
  Measurement of the effectiveness of salesmen;
  Evaluation of sales methods and incentives;
  Cost–benefit analysis of physical distribution systems;
  Retail audits.

- Product research

  Analysis of the competitive strengths and weaknesses of existing products, i.e. both one's own and one's competitors';
  Investigation of new uses for existing products;
  Product concept testing;
  Product testing;
  Packaging research;
  Variety reduction.

- Advertising research

  Copy research;
  Media research;
  Measurement of advertising effectiveness.

- Business economics
  Input–Output analysis;
  Short- and long-range forecasting, that is based on trend analysis;
  Price and profit analysis.

- Export marketing research

  Any or all of the above where relevant.

- Motivation research

This check-list is by no means comprehensive but serves as an outline of the possible scope of research activities. Although research in most of the above areas is concerned with the recording of fact, qualitative research into the nature of attitudes and opinions is also appropriate in a number of instances, for example product concept testing.

Organising for marketing research

In view of the frequent references to the increasingly competitive nature of the business environment one might expect that the majority of firms would have a marketing research department – in fact, remarkably few do. Recent data are hard to come by but a survey by the BIM in 1966 achieved only a 40 per cent response from the 265 companies contacted – presumably because the majority had no research department as such. However, it would be erroneous to assume that this implies a correspondingly low usage of research findings, as a large part of marketing research is carried out by specialist organisations. It is also true that many companies have departments which are performing a marketing research function although identified by some other title such as Economic Intelligence. The BIM survey, *Marketing Organisation in British Industry* (1970), would seem to confirm this view in that it indicated that 74 per cent of the respondents undertake marketing research but only 38 per cent of the respondents have appointed somebody full time to this activity. However the most up-to-date findings, which relate to research undertaken during the 1970s and 1980s, would suggest that comparatively few firms have their own marketing research function or indeed make use of any formal marketing research. In *Marketing and Competitive Success* Baker and Hart (1989) comment as follows:

> Throughout the seventies market research was frequently associated with higher export performance (ITI Research, 1979, British Institute of Management (BIM), 1975 and Rollason, 1971). Such findings were confirmed in a recent study carried out by Baker and Abou-Zeid (1982), where 86 per cent of companies with a Queen's Award for export achievement carried out export market research. The most popular method of conducting market research was to use salesmen, while agents and government sources were less popular means of providing information. The major use to which the information was put was in selecting the foreign

markets, while other uses were providing market information and identifying the required adaptation to suit the needs of these markets.

Cross-national comparisons have also highlighted the importance of market research to competitive success. For example, Connell (1979) describes how innovation in Japanese firms is typically initiated by sales and marketing personnel in the light of identified customer needs. This, along with other factors which emphasise customer interaction and interdepartmental cooperation in product development, distinguished Japanese firms from British firms.

Recent empirical work in the UK also lends weight to the argument that market research plays an important role in successful companies' marketing operations. Takeuchi and Quelch (1983) quote examples of successful companies who constantly monitor product quality from the buyers' point of view. The market research tactics involved include:

● Conducting customer satisfaction surveys;
● Tracking and recording all complaints and problems;
● Having a questionnaire completed by all customers returning goods;
● Carrying out extensive field tests on new products;
● Analysing warranty claims;
● Assessing the condition of goods received by administering a questionnaire.

Alexander (1985) shows that the use of qualitative market research by three companies (studied by her in some depth) generated information which was used to move beyond existing product concepts and to translate market requirements into innovative, successful designs. In the study by Walsh and Roy

(1983), into the practices and policies of winners of the Design Council Awards, all award-winning companies paid attention to market research, and many ideas for new market opportunities, as well as design evaluation, came from market or customer research. Finally, Hooley and Lynch (1985) report that successful companies made much greater use of all types of market research than did less successful ones. Table 10.1 summarises the types of market research used by both High-fliers and Also-rans.

It is logical to hypothesise, in view of the above information, that market research has a positive influence on company performance. Given the dictate of the marketing concept – that the customer is the focus of the company – it is axiomatic that market research be included in the company's operations.

However, investigation of the existence and effectiveness of market research has been called into some question. Criticism by Ames (1970), Wilson (1984) and King (1985), among others, has emphasised that counting the number of heads in marketing research departments, or estimating market research budgets, focuses on the 'trappings' of marketing, not its 'substance'. Small low-budget research teams may be as effective in gaining an understanding of customers' needs, wants and perceptions as a larger organisation.

Based upon their survey Baker and Hart found that above-average companies made significantly greater use of market research than below-average companies as shown in Table 10.2.

Some indication of the magnitude of expenditure on marketing research is provided by Table 10.3 which also contains data on users of market research and number of research agencies.

Table 10.1   *Frequent use of market research techniques*

	Sample	*High-fliers*	*Also-rans*	*Significance*
Sample size	1504	175	1329	'T'
Customer surveys	26.9%	33.7%	26.0%	0.05
Qualitative research	24.7%	30.9%	23.9%	0.0
Field experiments	18.5%	26.9%	17.4%	0.0
Laboratory experiments	12.4%	20.6%	11.3%	0.001

Source: Hooley and Lynch (1985), 'Marketing Lessons from UK's High-flying Companies', *Journal of Marketing Management*, vol. 1, no. 1 (Summer).

Table 10.2 *Market research on above-average and below-average companies*

Research type	Above-average companies (%)	Below-average companies (%)	Variation (%)
In-house	52	31	+68
External	69	47	+47

Note: Significant at the 5 per cent level.

Table 10.3 *Expenditure on market research*

	Value of GB commissioned market research					
	1989	1990	1991	1992	1993	1994
AMSO members' turnover £m	230	265	266	293	285	325

Note: The AMSO accounts for more than two thirds of all market research conducted in the UK

AMSO members' source of income by client's business 1994

	£m	%		£m	%
Food/soft drinks	42.4	+11	Alcoholic drinks	13.7	−11
Public services & utilities	30.1	+13	Household products	13.4	—
Media	30.0	+13	Travel & tourism	10.7	+7
Financial services	26.0	+45	Advertising agencies	9.6	+12
Pharmaceuticals	21.4	+17	H'hold durables/hardware	3.8	+92
Business & industrial	18.6	+26	Oil	3.8	+13
Vehicles	18.2	+26	Tobacco	3.6	+73
Health & beauty	18.1	+11	Other direct clients	26.9	+13
Govt., public bodies	16.7	−5	Other AMSO cos. (mainly		
Retailers	14.8	+13	subcontracted fieldwork)	3.3	—

Nature of AMSO members' fieldwork

	1993	1994		Percentage of total 1993	1994
Personal interview	52	48	Group discussion	11	9
Telephone interview	16	19	Self-completion/postal	9	9
Hall test	12	12			

Source: Association of Market Survey Organisations, 1995.

The decision to set up one's own marketing research department clearly depends upon an evaluation of its potential contribution to the firm's overall operation. Such an evaluation is essentially qualitative, and will vary from firm to firm, precluding the statement of hard-and-fast rules. For our purpose it will suffice if it is assumed a decision has been made to establish such a department and attention concentrated on the factors which must be taken into account. These may be summarised as:

1. The role and function of the department;
2. Its position within the organisation structure;
3. The role and function of the department manager.

Role and function of the department

From the checklist covering the scope of marketing research it is apparent that a very large department would be necessary to cover all the areas mentioned. If a firm is undertaking research for the first time it would be well advised to draw up a list of priorities and content itself with attempting to achieve only the more important in the first instance. This does not mean that all other research must be discouraged absolutely, as too rigid lines of demarcation can only lead to an inflexible approach and the neglect of lines of inquiry complementary to the main purpose of the research.

All too often firms make the mistake of handing over responsibility for the maintenance of routine records to the newly formed marketing research department. The transfer of such records invariably creates both friction and inefficiency – it hinders the operation of the department which depends upon such records for its routine operation, for example sales, and diverts the marketing research department from its main function – research. In that much routine work involved in the compilation and maintenance of records will have preceded the setting up of a specialist research department it is best if the various divisions retain this function, making the data available as and when required. In order to avoid both duplication and fragmentation of effort, each department's responsibility should be clearly stated, and only those returns essential to the marketing research department's internal research efforts should be submitted. That said, the creation of computerised information systems greatly enhances the free flow of information within an organisation and offers the market research department almost instant access to all stored data relevant to its function.

Organisational positioning

The positioning of the marketing research department within the organisation depends very largely on the existing structure. As a generalisation, the department should have direct access to the managing director, as it is performing a staff function and, in many instances, is providing the chief executive with the raw material upon which policy, as opposed to operating decisions, will be made. In the larger organisation, with executive directors in functional appointments, the marketing director may well be delegated responsibility for directing the efforts of the research department and deciding which reports should be submitted to the chief executive. Even so there is a strong case for a 'dotted line' relationship between the managing director and the department to ensure that reports that are critical of a particular aspect of the firm's activities are given a hearing, and to avoid straining relationships between the marketing and other functional directors. Further, the managing director is concerned with the overall effectiveness of the firm and so is in a better position to see the implications of research findings without becoming subjectively involved with the possible effect on an individual department.

Some writers recommend that the manager of the marketing research department should be of equivalent status to the managers of the major operating divisions, but it is felt that this is unrealistic in view of the discrepancy in size and responsibility that usually exists. Provided the manager has access to the board of directors his status should be directly related to the importance accorded the department within the organisation as a whole.

The role and function of the marketing research manager

The job specification of the marketing research manager will vary, depending upon the size and function of the department and the degree of external control and direction. In all cases, however, the manager must be technically competent and possess personal integrity. Technical competence includes not only experience and skill in marketing and analytical techniques but also the ability to translate management problems into viable research projects capable of implementation within the constraints imposed by time, and the available budget.

Personal integrity requires that the marketing research manager interpret findings objectively in accordance with generally accepted principles of scientific inquiry. 'Lies, damned lies and statistics' can only enjoy currency so long as the unscrupulous use 'facts' to support preconceived conclusions by judicious selection, manipulation and presentation – 'massaging the data', in research jargon.

In addition to these essential requirements the manager should also possess those skills common to all managerial positions – administrative ability, an understanding of human behaviour and the ability to communicate effectively.

The planning and execution of research

Marketing research activity falls into two main categories – continuous and *ad hoc*. Marketing is an on-going process in a dynamic environment, and continuous research is essential if the firm is to remain informed of changes in the demand determinants outlined in Chapter 5 and be able to modify its policies accordingly. Much data of this type is collated by specialist organisations and government departments, but is often too generalised to meet the individual firm's specific requirements and needs to be supplemented by 'in-house' research.

However, many marketing situations are unique, for example the introduction of a new product, and demand a specific or *ad hoc* investigation. Such research invariably follows a clearly defined sequence which includes the following stages:

1. Recognition of the need for research;
2. Analysis of the parameters which predicate this need – problem definition;
3. Exact statement of the objective of the research;
4. Formulation of an experimental or survey design based on the analysis of Stage 2;
5. Data collection;
6. Tabulation and analysis of data;
7. Interpretation of results and the formulation of conclusions and recommendations;
8. Preparation and presentation of a report containing the findings;
9. Evaluation of results of action initiated on basis of research findings, that is 'feedback'.

Clearly, continuous research must follow the same procedure in the first instance, but the first four stages will be omitted subsequently.

Primary and secondary data

The data collection phase of a research investigation draws on two main sources of information, which are distinguished as primary and secondary sources. Secondary sources consist of existing data and should always be examined first. Frequently, however, such data have been collected for purposes peripheral to the researcher's main line of inquiry and so need to be supplemented by the collection of new, or primary, data. These differences in the source of data are recognised in the distinction between Desk Research and Original, or Field, Research.

Desk research

Desk research into secondary data sources is a common-sense preliminary to any field research. Not only is it possible that the required information is already available, albeit in a form which requires retabulation, but also such research is essential to indicate the precise nature of the data to be obtained by survey or experimentation. Further, published sources are more accessible and offer savings in time and money if properly used.

Logically, desk research should begin with the firm's own records. It was argued earlier that the responsibility for maintaining records should be left in the hands of the individual departments, but it is the marketing research department's responsibility to ensure a sufficient degree of uniformity to permit collation of these records into a common data base for the firm as a whole. The area in which records are usually maintained from which to compile such a data base normally include:

1. Purchasing – stock levels, unit costs, usage rates, etc.
2. Production – output, material, labour, inventory, physical distribution and overhead costs, machine utilisation, etc.
3. Personnel – wage costs, turnover, efficiency levels, absenteeism, etc.
4. Marketing – promotional and administrative expenditures, market and brand data, etc.
5. Sales – by product volume, value, contribution to profit, order size;
   – by type of outlet/customer;
   – by area and by salesman.
6. Finance – all cost and accounting data.

In addition to these internal data, the researcher also has access to a large number of external sources, which may be conveniently grouped into five main categories:

1. Government – domestic and foreign.
2. Universities and non-profit research organisations; for example the *Oxford Bulletin of Statistics*.
3. Trade associations, e.g. British Institute of Management.
4. Academic and professional journals, the trade press.
5. Commercial research organisations; for example Attwood Statistics, Economist Intelligence Unit, Gallup, Nielsen, Dun & Bradstreet, Kompass etc.

The publications of government departments are far too extensive to permit full documentation, and only a few may be detailed here. A comprehensive list is contained in the *List of*

Principal Statistical Series and Publications which is number 20 in the *Studies in Official Statistics* published by HMSO. The more important Government sources are:

Annual Abstract of Statistics
British Labour Statistics Year Book
Business Monitor
Censuses of Distribution, Population, and Production
Department of Employment Gazette
Economic Trends
Family Expenditure Survey
Financial Statistics
General Household Survey
Guide to Official Statistics
Monthly Digest of Statistics
National Food Survey
Overseas Trade Statistics
Regional Trends
Report on Censuses of Production
Report on Censuses of Distribution
Social Trends
Statistical News
Trade and Industry
UK Balance of Payments 'Pink Book'
UK National Accounts 'Blue Book'

Commonly used international sources include:

Balance of Payments Year Book (IMF)
EU, EEC and ECSC publications
International Financial Statistics (IMF)
International Labour Review
International Travel Statistics
International Reports on Cotton, Sugar, Tea, Tin, etc.
UN Year Book of National Accounts Statistics
UN Year Book of International Trade Statistics
UN Demographic Year Book
UN Direction of International Trade
UN National Statistical Yearbook
UN Statistical Papers
Yearbook of International Trade Statistics
Yearbook of Fisheries
Yearbook of Forest Product Statistics
Yearbook of Food and Agricultural Statistics
Yearbook of Labour Statistics

An extensive listing of foreign sources is to be found in the Stationery Office publication *International Organisations and Overseas Agencies Publications.*

In the *Companion Encyclopedia of Marketing,* Christopher West (1995, p. 350) claims that a diligent search of secondary sources can be expected to yield data on:

- Population size, structure into geodemographic groups and growth;
- The structure of distribution and the importance of various channels;
- Total sales, imports and exports of products;
- Imports and exports by origin and destination;
- Products available and their specifications;
- New product launches;
- Sources of supply;
- New contracts and successful bidders for outstanding contracts;
- List prices;
- Advertising expenditure by product, industry sector and supplier;
- New market entrants;
- Staff movements;
- Financial performance of suppliers.

When using published sources it is important to ascertain the method employed in the compilation and tabulation of the data, and to avoid direct comparative analysis where this differs. Further, such data should only be used when the researcher has satisfied himself as to their validity, reliability and homogeneity.

Field research

When all published sources have been evaluated, the research issue may still remain unanswered, although much more clearly defined. As noted earlier, desk research is often incapable of providing answers to highly specific problems, but it will often indicate factors which have proved important in similar situations in the past. None the less, there are a number of areas in which field research is usually necessary, and these may be summarised as:

- Advertising research – the effectiveness of advertisements *per se*; that is, copy testing, and media research – usage, coverage and so on.
- Consumer research – investigation of the factors underlying consumer choice and preference.
- Distribution research – effectiveness of alternative channel structures, methods of handling and so forth.
- Packaging research – colour, design, size, shape, informational content and so on.
- Product research – concept testing, acceptability of new product offerings, development of user and non-user profiles, and so forth.

▎ Quantitative or qualitative?

Before deciding what kind of data one requires and how to collect it it is necessary to consider whether one requires quantitative or qualitative data or, possibly, both.

For many years the distinction between qualitative and quantitative research was frequently presented in a polarised way as if these were alternative strategies. In *Research for Marketing* (Baker, 1991, pp. 32ff) we present a table which appears to suggest that quantitative and qualitative research may be regarded as polar and mutually exclusive alternatives, as can be seen from Table 10.4.

But, as our discussion then points out, more recently a more balanced approach has emerged in which both kinds of researcher admit the contribution of the other. In parallel with this trend (or perhaps because of it) there has developed a growing recognition amongst the users of research that qualitative research is essential to address questions of what, how (process) and why, while quantitative research is appropriate to answer questions of whom, where, when and how (quantity).

In very broad terms one should use qualitative research:

Table 10.4 *Qualitative versus quantitative research*

Qualitative	Quantitative
Soft	Hard
Dry	Wet
Flexible	Fixed
Grounded	Abstract
Descriptive/exploratory	Explanatory
Pre-scientific	Scientific
Subjective	Objective
Inductive	Deductive
Speculative/illustrative	Hypothesis testing
Political	Value free
Non-rigorous	Rigorous
Idiographic	Nomothetic
Holistic	Atomistic
Interpretivist	Positivist
Exposes actors' meanings	Imposes sociological theory
Phenomenological	Empiricist/behaviour
Relative case study	Universalistic survey
Good	Bad
Bad	Good

Source: P. Halfpenny (1979), 'The Analysis of Qualitative Data', *Sociological Review*, 27 April.

1. To define the parameters of the market;
2. To understand the nature of the decision-making process;
3. To elicit attitudinal and motivational factors which influence behaviour;
4. To help understand why people behave the way they do.

Overall, qualitative research is best suited to areas needing a flexible approach while quantitative research is necessary to define more precisely the issues identified through qualitative methods. According to Peter Sampson (1967) the areas calling for a flexible approach may be summarised as:

1. Concept identification and exploration;
2. Identification of relevant behavioural attitudes;
3. Establishing priority among and between categories of behaviour, attitudes and so on;
4. Defining problem areas more fully and formulating hypotheses for further investigation.

More recently, Wendy Gordon and Roy Langmaid (1988) have suggested that the most important areas for qualitative research are:

- Basic exploratory studies;
- New product development;
- Creative development;
- Diagnostic studies;
- Tactical research projects.

Exploratory studies are usually called for when seeking to identify market opportunities for new product development, to monitor changes in consumption patterns and behaviour, to help define the parameters and characteristics of newly emerging markets or when seeking to enter established markets of which one has no prior experience. Gordon and Langmaid (1988) indicate five specific types of information which may be obtained from studies of this kind, namely:

1. *To define consumer perceptions of the market or product field* in order to help understand the competitive relationships between different types of product and/or brand in any product category – from the consumer's point of view rather than the manufacturer's.
2. *To define consumer segmentations in relation to a product category or brand*; for example psychographics and life-style segmentations.
3. *To understand the dimensions which differentiate between brands,* specifically on the basis of rational criteria and emotional beliefs. Where objective differences can be developed between products, rationality will predispose consumers to select these which conform most closely with their own preferences or criteria. Unsurprisingly, objective differences are comparatively easy to emulate with the result that emotional beliefs have come to

play an increasingly important part in purchase decisions – industrial as well as consumer.

4. *To understand the purchase decision-making process and/or usage patterns.*
5. *Hypothesis generation.*

As a broad generalisation, then, qualitative research is an essential prerequisite to most quantitative research in that it will help clarify the issues to be addressed, the parameters to be defined and measured and the likely relationships between them

The distinction between quantitative and qualitative research and their mutual dependence, was illustrated by an article by Johannson and Nonaka (1987) entitled 'Market Research the Japanese way'. In this article, the authors report Japanese disdain for the volume of formal market research, conducted in the USA. They point out that when Sony researched the market for a lightweight portable cassette player the results indicated that consumers would only buy one with a recording facility. Akio Morita ignored this finding and the Walkman is history. Citing examples such as Matsushita and Canon the authors report how Japanese companies depend upon a combination of 'soft data' about shipments, inventory levels and retail sales. However, the authors also cite evidence of Japanese failures in American markets which they attribute to a lack of understanding of the attitudes and opinions of American consumers which could have been established by use of some of the survey techniques which they have eschewed. The conclusion is that both kinds of research are called for. Clearly with highly innovative and novel products it is unlikely that consumers could conceptualise the possibilities for a portable, personal entertainment system such as the Walkman. But, once the technological possibilities have become apparent and markets begin to grow and mature then the need to segment markets and position products will call for the kind of quantitative data which is unavailable when developing wholly new product concepts.

 # The collection of primary data

Original data may be collected by one, or a combination, of three methods – observation, experimentation and sample survey. Observation is the simplest, but usually least satisfactory, alternative and consists essentially of observing the processes associated with the factor under investigation. A good example of this approach is the measurement of customer flow patterns within retail outlets, from which many principles of store layout have been derived.

Observational techniques depend heavily on the skill and objectivity of the observer, and suffer from the need for secrecy if behavioural patterns are not to be disturbed as a result of the subject's awareness that he is under scrutiny. Further, overt behaviour rarely throws much light on the subject's motivation and decision processes, and it is these that one is usually trying to determine.

Experimentation avoids the lack of control common to observational methods and is usually less expensive to undertake than a sample survey. Several examples of experimental method are contained in the section on 'Laboratory Techniques' in Chapter 16 and make it clear that the major drawback lies in the difficulty of replicating normal behaviour in the laboratory setting. In part this may be overcome by conducting such experiments in their normal context, for example testing pack design by putting the test item(s) on display in a shop. However, if the results of such tests are to be taken as valid it is necessary to hold constant all variables other than that which is actually under test. Difficulties in identifying both the nature and effect of other variables may be largely overcome by repeating the experiment a sufficient number of times to permit the derivation of an average or representative results, and through the use of controls. A control often consists of running an experiment identical with the test situation with the exception of the test variable, on the assumption that any differences which arise are due to this variable.

Measurement of a single variable can be both expensive and time-consuming, in view of the large number of variables which may require testing. For example in the case of a new pack one may wish to isolate the separate effect of name, colour, size, shape, information value and so on, as well as the total effect. Techniques such as Latin Square and Factorial Design have now been developed which permit multiple variable analysis of this sort, and most modern statistics texts detail their use, for example M. J. Moroney (1956), *Facts from Figures*. A more specific treatment is to be found in Cox and Enis's (1973) *Experimentation for Marketing Decisions*, and in Rothman (1986).

Probably the most familiar method used in the collection of primary data is the sample survey. Survey method and sampling are both subjects on which a number of specialised texts have been written, and only the briefest coverage can be attempted here.

Census versus sample

As will be seen, marketing researchers have access to a wide selection of survey methods and, subject to time and financial constraints, their choice will be dictated by three separate considerations:

1. Respondent selection;
2. The means of establishing contact with respondents;
3. The information required and the means of obtaining it;

Theoretically, the ideal method of collecting primary data is to undertake a census of the whole population possessing the attribute to be investigated. In practice such an exercise is near impossible and only practicable where the population, in the statistical sense of all units belonging to a clearly defined group, is both small and readily accessible. Thus, although one might successfully conduct a census of a narrowly defined population such as 'all students registered in the first year

marketing course at X college', if one were to extend the population to all students in the college, or 'all students of marketing', it is almost certain that one would be unable to establish contact with some members of the population.

Even assuming one could complete a census of a large population, the cost would be enormous and the data so extensive that it would be out of date before it could be collated and analysed, for example the 1960 Census of Population was not published until 1964, and the 1970 Census until 1973. For these reasons most researchers content themselves with a representative sample of the population which they wish to study.

Once the marketer has precisely identified the population to be studied, for example 'the market for instant cake mixes', the researcher can set about the construction of a sample design which will yield the desired information within the ever-present time and budgetary constraints.

Sampling

Sampling is based on two fundamental principles of statistical theory which are usually termed 'The Law of Statistical Regularity', and 'The Law of Inertia of Large Numbers'. The first law holds that any group of objects taken from a larger group of such objects will tend to possess the same characteristics as the larger group. The second law holds that large groups are more stable than small groups owing to the compensating effect of deviation in opposite directions.

On the basis of these and similar principles, one can determine the size and composition of a sample which will yield a desired level of accuracy while allowing for, and eliminating, possible sources of error. In fact, a properly designed and executed sample may prove to be more accurate than a poorly conducted census.

In most instances, the researcher wants some measure of the reliability of the data he has collected, and so will select a sample design based on probability theory such that the chance that any given unit will be selected may be assigned a definite, non-zero probability. There are many types of probability-based sample design, including simple random sampling, stratified samples, cluster samples and multi-stage samples, and the interested student should consult Moser and Kalton's (1971) *Survey Methods in Social Investigation,* for a clear and concise exposition of their nature, usage and so on or Chapter 4 'Sampling' by Martin Collins in the *Consumer Market Research Handbook* (3rd edn, 1986).

Although some form of probability sample is essential if the results are to be used for predictive purposes, there is often a need for a 'quick and dirty' survey as a preliminary to such a sample, to clarify basic issues, or to provide generalised information required in a hurry. To this end three types of non-probability sample are sometimes used – the convenience sample, the judgement sample and the quota sample.

Convenience sampling consists of soliciting information from any convenient group whose views may be relevant to the subject of inquiry. Thus, one might stop passers-by on the street to ask their views on parking meters and off-street parking to get a feel for the subject, and as a basis for formulating more precise questions to be asked of a representative sample.

Judgement sampling is a slightly more refined technique in that respondents are selected on the basis of the interviewer's subjective opinion that they constitute a representative cross-section of the population to be investigated.

Quota sampling represents a distinct improvement on both these approaches in that the respondent 'type' is specified on the basis of characteristics of the population at large. Each interviewer is then assigned a quota and solicits information from people who meet the specification. Clearly, the more detailed the latter is, the more representative will be the data; for example if the quota calls for ten middle-class housewives between 20 and 35 years old, with at least one child under school age, there is a precise specification that can easily be met by visiting a residential suburb and interviewing young women pushing prams or push-chairs. In a number of cases, well-designed and well-executed quota samples have achieved results comparable to much more expensive probability samples. However, such verification can only be established in retrospect and is no basis for accurate prediction.

Establishing contact with respondents

Once respondents have been identified from the sampling frame, that is a list of all members of a given population, the researcher may establish contact by one of three methods – personal interview, mail questionnaire or telephone interview.

Taking these in reverse, it is clear that the telephone possesses the major disadvantage that private subscribers represent only a proportion of all households and tend to be concentrated in the higher socioeconomic groups. These factors can be overemphasised however, and researchers are becoming increasingly aware of the advantages of the telephone for quick, low-cost interviews. This is particularly true in the field of industrial market research, where the compulsion to answer the phone can often secure an otherwise unobtainable interview, or where one wishes to limit investigation to members of the higher socioeconomic groupings.

To be effective telephone interviews should be both short and explicit. If they are not the interviewer runs the risks of respondent confusion and of having the interview terminated before it is complete. In the United States, where a higher proportion of households have telephones, this method is widely used to monitor reaction to radio and television programmes and to measure advertising recall.

The mail survey possesses the advantage that it enables the researcher to reach any household or business establishment in the United Kingdom at very low cost. It also avoids the problem of interviewer bias. Unfortunately, the ability to contact an individual does not ensure his cooperation, and mail questionnaires suffer from very high refusal rates – a 50 per cent response would be considered excellent. In part this may be overcome by increasing the number of potential respondents, but one cannot escape the possibility of bias which arises from respondent self-selection; that is, it is reasonable to argue that people who do complete mail questionnaires are different from those who will not. As with the telephone interview, there is also the possibility of misinterpretation of the actual questions asked, and although this may be reduced by using short, simple questions, the value of the information obtained is correspondingly reduced.

It is because of the disadvantages associated with telephone and mail questionnaires that the personal interview remains the most popular survey technique, despite its high cost. The use of trained interviewers invariably produces a high percentage of acceptable returns with a low refusal rate. The ability of the interviewer to clarify ambiguities improves accuracy, permits the use of longer and more complex question-naires, and greatly reduces the problem of respondent self-selection. Further, the inter-viewer may be able to obtain additional informa-tion from observations, for example type of housing, possession of durables, and so on. The major disadvantages of personal interviewing are high cost and the shortage of trained interviewers which increases the possibility of interviewer bias; for example the interviewer may 'lead' the respondent, or simply record the answers inac-curately. However, many of the problems involved in data collection may be minimised through good questionnaire design. (A full treatment of the above issue is to be found in Joan McFarlane-Smith's (1972) *Interviewing in Market and Social Research*, and in the *Consumer Market Research Handbook*, Chapter 6, 'Inter-viewing and Field Control' by John F. Drakeford and Valerie Farbridge (1986).)

Tables 10.5 and 10.6 summarise some of the advantages and disadvantages of different kinds of interview and interviewing methods.

■ Questionnaires

Most formal questionnaires are structured so that they may be administered easily to a large number of respondents, and to simplify subse-quent analysis. Conversely, unstructured ques-tionnaires are of great value when one is seeking to get the feel of a problem, but they are difficult to interpret owing to the differences in emphasis and meaning which arise when respondents are

Table 10.5 *Advantages and disadvantages of different types of interviews*

	Advantages	Disadvantages
Standardised or structured interviews	Interviewer briefing and training simplified Less scope for interviewer bias Less interviewer variation Classifying, coding and analysis simpler Results comparable Higher reliability Greater opportunity for measurement	Questions must be simple and (usually) closed Data lack depth Lower validity Cannot probe Cannot obain clarification of ambiguity Interviewers need skill and training Interviewer bias may increase
Depth focused or unstructured interviewers	Question can be deep searching Data rich and full High degree of validity Probing possible Can obtain clarification of ambiguities	Greater interviewer variability Result often not comparable Reliability questionable Less scope for measurement

Source: Hart, S. J. (1987), 'The Use of the Survey in Industrial Marketing Research', *Journal of Marketing Management*, 3 (Summer), p. 31.

Table 10.6 *Preferred data collection methods under different survey conditions*

Conditions of survey			Possible data collection method(s)			
Funds	*Time*	*Type of data*	*Personal Interview*	*Mail*	*Telephone*	
Restricted	Restricted	Few items			x	Assuming telephone population representative
Restricted	Restricted	Much information	x			If funds permit
Restricted	Ample	Few items		x	x	Assuming telephone population representative
Restricted	Ample	Much information	x	x		Non-respondent follow-up needed
Restricted	Ample	Few items		x	x	
Restricted	Ample	Much information		x		
Ample	Restricted	Few items	x		x	Assuming telephone population representative
Ample	Restricted	Much information	x			
Ample	Ample	Few items	x		x	Assuming telephone population representative
Ample	Ample	Much information	x			
Ample	Ample	Few items	x	x	x	
Ample	Ample	Much information	x	x		Either joint or one method alone

Source: Hart, S. J. (1987), The Use of the Survey in Industrial Marketing Research, *Journal of Marketing Management*, 3 (Summer).

allowed free choice of vocabulary. In either case, the questionnaire may conveniently be considered to consist of four basic elements.

First, all questionnaires must be identifiable and so must be given a title and a distinctive number. Further, where the questionnaire is to be administered by an interviewer, provision should be made for recording the date and time of the interview, the place where the interview took place, and the interviewer's number and signature.

Second, all questionnaires should make provision for the recording of basic respondent data as a basis for subsequent classification, and to permit comparative analysis with other surveys. These data may be obtained partly by questioning and partly by observations, and should include: age, sex, social class, occupation of head of household, marital status, family size and composition, level and type of education. Optional, but useful, data are: name and address, owner or tenant of property, type of property, ownership of consumer durables. Income is obviously a desirable piece of information, but many respondents consider such questions too much of an intrusion on their privacy and either refuse to answer or exaggerate. If personal questions of this type are to be asked, it is best to leave them until the end of the interview to avoid antagonising the respondent and possibly securing an incomplete interview.

Third, the questionnaire should contain control questions to check on respondent consistency and to ensure that it has been administered or completed in accordance with the instructions given. The form of such questions depends on the nature and subject matter of the survey.

Finally, the questionnaire must contain questions that will elicit the information required to provide answers to the problem under investigation.

☐ *Question design*

Questions may be dichotomous, multiple choice or open-ended. Dichotomous questions require a straight yes or no answer and are easy to ask, understand, record and analyse. On the other hand a large number of questions will be necessary if detailed information is required, and the responses will not reveal possible shades of meaning. Thus, although they are useful for securing factual data, for example 'Do you have a refrigerator?', they are of limited value when seeking opinions or attitudes, when multiple choice questions are to be preferred. As the name implies, multiple choice questions offer the respondent a number of alternatives and so permit the collection of more detailed and accurate data, for example 'How often do you use Whizzo?'

> At least once a week ...
> Once a fortnight ...
> Once a month ...
> Less than once a month ...
> Never ...

Similarly, one can obtain a measure of the strength of opinions or attitudes, for example 'Old age pensions should be increased.'

> Strongly agree ...
> Agree ...
> Disagree ...
> Strongly disagree ...
> No opinion ...

Some form of pilot survey is usually necessary to ensure that an adequate list of alternatives is offered, and 'All', 'None', or 'Don't know' should be included if the alternatives are not mutually exclusive. In recent years a number of sophisticated techniques, such as multi-dimensional scaling, have been developed to improve the quality of the data obtained through the use of multiple choice questions.

Open-ended questions give the respondent complete freedom in answering and so yield the maximum information, as well as eliminating interviewer bias. They are very useful in situations where it is impossible to formulate all possible alternatives, or shades of opinion, and reveal many facets of the respondent's attitudes and behaviour beyond the scope of dichotomous or multiple choice questions. On the other hand there are several disadvantages. The answers have to be recorded verbatim, for subsequent editing and analysis, to avoid the possibility that the interviewer is only recording what he considers significant. In addition, much of the data may be irrelevant, or become so, through the need to group it into categories for purposes of analysis.

In so far as is possible, all questions should be clear and unbiased, and phrased in terms which are meaningful to the likely respondent. To meet these requirements each question should be formulated in the light of the information which it is hoped to elicit. For example if one is investigating smoking habits there are a number of possible dimensions along which data may be secured, and it is pointless to ask a multiple-dimensional question, 'What kind of cigarettes do you smoke?', which may be answered in terms of brand, price range, whether tipped or not, and so on. Similarly, the question 'Why do you smoke brand X?' may be answered in terms of quality, price or satisfaction, all of which are interrelated and so give no clear indication of the salience of such factors taken in isolation.

The sequence in which questions are asked also has an important bearing on the value of the data obtained. Most respondents are nervous or suspicious initially, and so should be asked simple questions of a non-personal nature. Conversational questions, for example. 'Have you lived here long?', and those which seek the interviewee's preference, for example 'Do you like making cakes?', often help to break the ice, as well as leading naturally into more specific questions. Sequence is also important, in that each answer inclines the respondent to make use of the same ideas in answering subsequent questions, for example, if you ask questions about price, followed by questions on reasons for brand preference, price will usually be stated as a major reason. Similarly, if you ask women questions about fashions, followed by questions on their attitude to advertising, you will get many more favourable responses than you would if you had omitted the questions on fashions.

Questionnaires should always be field tested before use to ensure that they meet the criteria outlined above.

The standard references on questionnaire design are A. N. Oppenheim (1967) *Questionnaire Design and Attitude Measurement*, and S. Payne (1951) *The Art of Asking Questions*. An up to date discussion appears as Chapter 5 of 'Questionnaire Design' by Jean Morton-Williams (1986).

■ Attitude scales

While the precise nature of the link between attitudes and behaviour is subject to debate there can be no argument that attitude is one of the most important and pervasive concepts in marketing. This concept has been discussed earlier (Chapter 6) and the purpose here is to review some problems associated with the measurement of attitudes.

Many of the problems of measuring attitudes are inherent in the concept itself and in the varying interpretations of it by different theorists. However, as Gilbert A. Churchill Jr (1976) observes in *Marketing Research: Methodological Foundations*, there is substantial agreement on the following:

1. Attitude represents a predisposition to respond to an object, and not the actual behaviour toward the object. Attitude thus possesses the quality of readiness.

2. Attitude is persistent over time. It can change to be sure, but the alteration of an attitude, which is strongly held, requires substantial pressures.

3. Attitude produces consistency in behaviour outcroppings. Attitude is a latent variable that produces consistency in behaviour when manifested. This consistency occurs whether the manifestations are in the form of verbalizations about the object, or approach or avoidance of the object.

4. Attitude has a directional quality. It connotes a preference regarding the outcomes involving the object, evaluation of the object, or positive–neutral–negative affectations for the object.

Of these four clusters of attributes it is the latter which poses the strongest need for measurement through the assignment of some form of number which reflects the directional nature of an attitude. This object is achieved through scaling but one must be careful to determine the nature of a scale before jumping to too hasty a conclusion of the interpretation to be placed upon it.

In brief there are four types of scale, nominal, ordinal, interval and ratio, and their properties may be summarised as:

1. *Nominal scales*. This is the weakest form of scale in which the number assigned serves only to identify the objects under consideration. Library classification schemes employ nominal scales, as does the Standard Industrial Classification (SIC) such that members of the same class will be assigned the same number but each class will have a different number. By extending the number it is possible to achieve finer and finer distinctions until a unique number is assigned to a specific object, for example a telephone number.

2. *Ordinal scales* seek to impose more structure on objects by rank ordering them in terms of some property which they possess such as height or weight. As with nominal scales identical objects are given the same number but the ordinal scale has the added property

that it can tell us something about the *direction* or relative standing of one object to another; for example 1 may represent the smallest member of a group such that we can safely say that 2 is bigger than 1, 5 is bigger than 2 and 17 is bigger than 5. However, this is all we can say (other than reversing the scale) and in order to be able to draw conclusions about differences between the numbers we must know something about the interval between the numbers.

3. *Interval scales* have this property in that they are founded on the assumption of equal intervals between numbers; that is, the space between 5 and 10 is the same as the space between 45 and 50 and in both cases this distance is five times as great as that between 1 and 2 or 11 and 12, and so on. However, it must be stressed that while we may compare the magnitude of the differences between numbers we cannot make statements about them unless the scale possesses an absolute zero, in which case we would have a ratio scale.

4. *Ratio scales*. Ratio scales are the most powerful and possess all the properties of nominal, ordinal and interval scales, while in addition they permit absolute comparisons of the objects; for example 6 feet is twice as high as 3 feet, and six times as high as 1 foot.

The above discussion is essentially descriptive – for a discussion of the mathematical properties of the various scales one should consult *Research for Marketing Decisions*, by Paul E. Green and Donald S. Tull (1978).

☐ *Scaling methods in marketing*

Marketing researchers have borrowed a number of different scaling techniques from the behavioural sciences, among which the most important are:

● Thurstone's comparative judgement technique;

● Likert scales;
● Guttman Scales;
● The Semantic Differential;
● Q-sort technique.

Thurstone scales were first introduced by L. L. Thurstone in 1928 and have been very widely used ever since. In essence a Thurstone scale is an attempt to construct an interval scale by selecting a set of statements about a subject which range from very favourable to very unfavourable expressions of attitude towards the subject with each statement appearing to be equidistant from those on either side of it. Scales may contain eleven, nine or seven statements, which are chosen by a panel of judges from a pool so as to achieve the property of equal-appearing intervals, and respondents are asked to select the statement which most accurately reflects their attitude. A score is assigned to each statement and is used, often in conjunction with scores for other sets of statements, in order to provide a summary statement of attitude towards the object of inquiry.

Likert scales differ from Thurstone scales in that respondents are presented with a series of statements and asked to indicate their degree of agreement/disagreement with each. Respondents are usually offered five categories – Strongly Agree, Agree, Uncertain, Disagree, Strongly Disagree, though three or seven divisions are used by some researchers – and are asked to select the position corresponding most closely with their opinion. By scoring a series of statements on a given subject, for example qualities of a brand, content of an advertisement, it is possible to construct a generalised attitude towards the object with an indication of the *intensity* with which the attitude is held.

Guttmann scaling represents an attempt to ensure a highly desirable property of an attitude scale which is only partially achieved by the Thurstone and Likert methods – the property of unidimensionality; that is, all the statements used belong to the same dimension. The construction of Guttmann scales is more complex and laborious than for Thurstone and Likert scales and is described at some length by Moser and Kalton

(1971) in *Survey Methods in Social Investigation* – as are all the other methods referred to here. However, relatively little use is made of the method in marketing research.

In contrast the Semantic Differential technique developed by Osgood *et al.* (1952) in *Method and Theory in Experimental Psychology*, is very widely used, largely because it is much simpler to construct than any of the scales discussed so far and yet yields a very high measure of agreement with these more elaborate measures. The method consists of a series of bipolar adjectives (strong–weak, good–bad, etc.) separated usually by between five to nine points. The respondent is asked to check-mark the point which best indicates their attitude. Scale positions are sometimes qualified, for example:

Extremely good. Very good. Fairly good. Neither good nor bad. Fairly bad. Very bad. Extremely bad.

However, such qualification tends to discourage selection of the extreme positions.

☐ *Multidimensional scaling*

All the scales discussed so far use a single number to represent a person's attitude – or, as Churchill (1976) puts it, 'a linear compensatory model'. Such a model rests upon the basic assumption that attitude is unidimensional such that we balance negative and positive factors in arriving at a single summary statistic.

In recent years, marketing researchers have challenged this basic model and have argued that attitude is multidimensional. In turn this requires a concept of a multidimensional space rather than a unidimensional scale and considerable effort and ingenuity has been devoted to developing measures of this space.

The basic characteristic of multidimensional scaling is that respondents are asked to make judgements concerning the degree of similarity/distance between pairs of stimuli using a scale which may be either *metric* (interval or ratio scale) or *non-metric* (ordinal scale). A particularly attractive feature of non-metric multi-dimensional scaling is that it converts an ordinal input into an interval scale or metric output. Thus as long as the respondent can rank order all the stimulus pairs it is possible to convert such 'greater than', 'less than' statements into absolute statements concerning the status of all the objects.

Multidimensional scaling is based upon sophisticated mathematical techniques, a full discussion of which is to be found in Paul E. Green and Frank J. Carmone (1970) *Multidimensional Scaling and Related Techniques in Marketing Analysis*, or *Theory and Methods of Scaling* by Warren Torgenson (1955). However, for normal use packaged computer programs such as M-D-SCAL are available which require only basic mathematical skills. 'Multivariate Analysis of Market Research Data' by C. Holmes (1986) provides a more recent source.

■ Presentation of findings

Space limitations preclude consideration of field interviewing procedures, and the techniques used in collating, tabulating and analysing the data collected. Once these steps have been completed, the findings, and recommendations based on them, must be presented in the form of a report.

Most research findings have to be presented to two distinct groups – general management and research specialists – and the different needs and orientation of these groups usually requires the preparation of two separate reports. The first of these consists of a fully documented technical report, while the second consists of a short but detailed account of the major findings, conclusions and recommendations abstracted from the first.

The Market Research Society has adopted the following standards as constituting the minimum acceptable content of a survey report:

1. The purpose of the survey;
2. For whom and by whom the survey was undertaken;

3. General description of the universe covered;
4. Size and nature of the sample, including a description of any weighting methods used;
5. The time when the field work was carried out;
6. The method of interviewing employed;
7. Adequate description of field staff and any control methods used;
8. A copy of the questionnaire;
9. The factual findings;
10. Bases of percentages;
11. Geographical distribution of the interviews.

In order to ensure that a technical report satisfies these minimum requirements and presents the material in a logical sequence, many organisations have adopted a formal layout on the following lines:

1. *Introduction* Title of the report; Name of sponsor; Title of research organisation; Date of publication.
2. *Table of Contents*
3. *Preface* Stating terms of reference, and acknowledgements where appropriate.
4. *Statement of purpose* This generally consists of an elaboration of the terms of reference contained in the preface. It should outline the general nature of the problem to be investigated and the specific hypotheses on which the research was based.
5. *Methodology* This section should outline the stages through which the project passed, step by step, and include a statement of the definitions adopted, the research techniques employed, the sources of data used, details of sample size and composition, a description of the methods of analysis employed, and any explanatory observations deemed necessary by the researcher.
6. *The findings* This section consists of an abstract of those data considered relevant to the problem under investigation.
7. *Conclusions* Those drawn from the findings.
8. *Recommendations* Based on the conclusions.

9. *The appendices* These should include a detailed account of the sample design and its theoretical reliability; a copy of the questionnaire and instructions to interviewers; detailed statistical tables; the bibliography and glossary of terms if appropriate; details of any tests of reliability, theoretical proofs and so forth.

In reports intended for line management as opposed to other researchers it is common to find that the conclusions and recommendations follow immediately after the statement of purpose or terms of reference, and the description of the methodology is consigned to the appendices. Reports of this nature usually also include a single-page statement of the basic purpose and findings entitled Management or Executive Summary.

 ## The role of marketing research agencies

It was stated earlier that many companies utilise the services of independent marketing research agencies, either to supplement their own research effort or as a substitute for a research department of their own. To provide these services, most independent agencies are capable of undertaking 'all aspects of the research process' described above, and act in both an advisory and executive capacity.

In addition to undertaking *ad hoc* research on behalf of client firms, some of the bigger organisations specialise in documenting a particular area of marketing on a continuous basis. The findings from such research are usually incorporated in standardised reports which are circulated to subscribers at regular intervals. A well-known example of such a service is the Inventory Audit of Retail Sales, which is often referred to as the Nielsen Index, after its originator.

Once the manufacturer's products leave his factory there is invariably a time-lag before they are purchased and consumed. The longer

Table 10.7 *Nielsen Food Index*

	The Nielsen Food Index measures the performance of product categories sold in grocers. A grocer is defined as a retail outlet with at least 20% of its total turnover in groceries and/or provisions, and a larger proportion of turnover in no other commodity unless it is one or a combination of the following: off-licence trade, bakery goods, or tobacco.
Sample size	831 grocery outlets in England, Scotland and Wales. These have been selected to allow analysis of patterns of trading by shop type and 9 regions.
Audit frequency	Audits are carried out every 2 months.
Report contents	For each brand, size, flavour, etc., specified by the client and an 'all other' section.

CONSUMER SALES and Shares	Units Sterling Average sales per shop handling Weighted average sales per shop handling
RETAILER PURCHASES and Shares SOURCE OF DELIVERY	Units Co-ops Multiples direct v. other Independents
RETAILER STOCKS and Shares	Units Average stocks per shop handling Units in forward selling area
STOCK COVER	Days/weeks/months supply
PRICES	Average retail selling prices
DISTRIBUTION Shop, all commodity and product class turnover weighted	Handling Total out-of-stock Out-of-stock in selling area Purchasing Merchandising
ADVERTISING	Press, magazine and TV expenditure Group promotions

Subdivisions in the report

SHOP TYPES	NIELSEN REGIONS
All grocers	London
Co-operatives	Anglia
Multiples	Southern

Major multiples – Argyll, Asda,
                    Fine Fare,
                    International,
                    Sainsbury,
                    Tesco
	Wales, West and Westward
	Midlands
	Lancashire
	Yorkshire
	Tyne Tees

Other multiples	Scotland
Total independents	
Major symbols – Mace, Spar, VG, Wavy Line	
Other independents	
Superstores – over 25 000 sq ft	

this time-lag, the more difficult it becomes for the producer to exercise control over supply to meet variations in demand and modify his production to maximise profit. The Inventory Audit helps reduce these uncertainties by monitoring both sales and stock levels for three major product groups – food, drugs and pharmaceuticals. The actual audit is made in a representative sample of outlets, carefully selected from the population of all retail outlets stocking the three product groups. Each outlet enters into an agreement with Nielsen's under which all invoices are retained for inspection and auditors are permitted to take physical stock on the premises. By the simple process of adding goods invoiced to opening stock and deducting closing stock, sales of each item may be determined. These data are then circulated to subscribers, together with information covering the number of outlets stocking given brands, prices, average order sizes, merchandising schemes, etc. A fact sheet issued by Nielsen for their Food Index is reprinted as Table 10.7.

AGB Superpanel is a panel of 8500 households in which all individuals regularly record purchase data on a wide range of packaged grocery, household, fresh food, toiletry and other personally purchased products. The panel is representative of Great Britain, with regional samples sufficiently large to permit separate reporting on ten ITV regions and is run by AGB Market Information.

Data collection is via a personal data terminal (p.d.t.) equipped with a light pencil, which panel members use to 'wand' the bar codes of their purchases, entering the price manually. Information on the retailer used and on unpackaged items without bar codes is obtained from specially created codes in a patented code book. The p.d.t is kept in a modem linked to the power supply and a telephone socket and data are polled overnight. The technique enables achievement of unprecedented levels both of data accuracy and speed of collection.

The following data are obtained about each panel home and each purchase within the audit field made by these households.

The home
1. Age of housewife
2. Size of household
3. Social class
4. With or without children
5. Claimed housewife weight of ITV viewing
6. Cat/dog ownership
7. Ownership of refrigerator
8. Washing machine ownership
9. Ownership of deep freezer
10. Ownership of colour television
11. Full-time working, part-time working or non-working status of housewife
12. Terminal age of education of housewife

The purchase
1. Brand name
2. Size
3. Flavour/variety
4. Actual price paid
5. Weight of purchase
6. Quantity bought
7. Name and address of shop
8. Type of shop

Subscribers to the Superpanel service receive standard four-weekly reports on their selected product fields, for the country as a whole and each ITV region separately. They include the following information.

1. Total consumer expenditure – for the total market, for each brand and for each size an estimate is made of consumer expenditure at actual retail prices and an estimate of volume is made.
2. Market shares – gives share of total market held by each itemised brand.
3. Product penetration – gives the percentage of households buying each brand at least once during the four-weekly period.

All data relating to each household and individual's weekly purchasing are retained by AGB and can be provided in various forms according to the particular marketing situation which needs to be analysed.

The principal types of special analysis are weekly purchasing, brand profiles, repeat purchasing brand share predictions, brand switching and source of purchase.

Other forms of analysis relating to test marketing product usage, television viewing, effectiveness of coupons, samples and special offers and cross-matching of purchasing and media data can be provided.

Other well known sources of continuous research data are the British Market Research Bureau's Target Group Index and G & A's Home Audit. Further details of these panels are to be found in Peter M. Chisnall (1992) *Marketing Research*, 4th edn.

Database marketing (DBM)

One of the most valuable assets a company possesses is its knowledge of the identity and location of actual and potential customers. Such information constitutes a database. In recent years developments in computing capacity and information technology have led to the recognition that the customer database is ideally suited to the new technology and resulted in the emergence of the new field of database marketing.

In his book *Marketing Management and Information Technology* Keith Fletcher (2nd edn, 1995) examines the application of IT to the whole process of marketing management and its specific application to particular marketing functions and tasks. In Chapter 10 of that volume he examines the topic of sales decisions and includes a comprehensive review of DBM. While it is stated that there is no agreed definition of DBM, that offered by Stone and Shaw (1987) captures well its essential characteristics, namely:

> DBM is an interactive approach to marketing communications, which uses addressable communication media (such as mail, telephone and the sales force) to extend help to its target audience, to stimulate demand, and to stay close to them by recording and keeping an electronic database memory of customer, prospect and all communication and commercial contacts, to help improve future contacts.

The key point is that the power of electronics aided and abetted by developments in telecommunications have made it possible to increase the power of the database far beyond that which was possible when depending upon a manual system. To be fully effective, however, it must be possible for the user to interact with or relate to the database (hence *relational database*) and match any variable with any other in order to develop and exploit the potential for distinctive and focused marketing efforts. It is this use of a database for marketing planning which distinguishes DBM from *direct marketing* with which it is often confused. Specifically, direct marketing embraces 'any activity which creates and profitably exploits a direct relationship between the company and the prospect (Ogilvy and Mather, 1985) and tends to focus on the communication opportunities for this such as the new electronic media, telephone selling and direct response advertising' (Fletcher, 2nd edn, 1995). From this definition it is clear that direct marketing will benefit greatly from the existence of a relational database as this will increase significantly the ability to pinpoint specific targets with unique messages but much direct marketing is developed using customer databases which do not possess this property; that is, DBM requires a more sophisticated database than is necessary for basic direct marketing.

While DBM is a suitable base for all kinds of marketing communication and effort it is particularly suited for use with the telephone. Recognising this fact British Telecom publish annually a TMS (Telephone Marketing Services) *Direct Marketing Handbook* which is available from them, and which contains excellent coverage of most aspects of direct marketing. In an article entitled 'The Emergence of Marketing Databases and their Uses' Tony Coad (1990) offers the following guidelines on what he looks for in a marketing database:

> Firstly, a Marketing Database contains the names and addresses of a company's customers, with as much individual characterisation as possible.
>
> When building consumer databases for example, each responding customer can be distinguished by their demographic and lifestyle attributes.

My Company, NDL International has built over 60 consumer marketing databases for major UK companies, characterising individual customers by their individual demographic and life style qualities.

Such detail – whether of individual consumers, or individual businesses – enables us to search for common characteristics among customers that relate to purchase behaviour. If we did not characterise each customer we would not be able to distinguish between them. We then could not use our database to reach people on the basis of their individuality or to help us understand the separate market segments that exist in nearly all markets.

Secondly, we need to distinguish between our customers on the basis of their purchase behaviour. This is the what, when, how much, why, where of their purchase history.

We now have all the data we need effectively to operate a marketing database. We can track purchase behaviour by the profile of that customer, so, in theory can:

- Find out where customers for Product X live.
- See how customers for the standard model differ from those of the full-feature version.
- Find out which types of customer pay the top price for a product or service.
- See which sort of people buy at different outlets then vary our point of sale accordingly.
- Make sure that the people who are actually buying our product are those we had in mind when promoting it.
- Identify prospect names and addresses, and individual lifestyles as a point of contact.

With the data, we can track purchase behaviour and profile the types of customer exhibiting that behaviour. But of course marketing databases need to present data in a form digestible to marketers, so...

...The third characteristic of a marketing database is that it should be based on relational software. This will enable any piece of data to be retrieved in any sequence and placed in any combination. Hierarchical database software does not allow this so we cannot readily identity segments and then relate those segments to names and addresses. And we should make our consumer database address-based.

Thanks to the Post Office's Postal Address File we have a means of standardising addresses – which means we can recognise duplicate entries – and can attach data from a variety of sources to the correct household with confidence.

The fourth characteristic of a marketing database is its geography. It has to be all in one place, not scattered around the company, probably on incompatible installations.

Fifthly, the output must be user friendly. Reports must be customised, friendly and rapid. Better still the output should be capable of being accepted by marketers who need not be systems analysts. PC-based output, rich in opportunities for statistical analysis, is ideal.

The sixth characteristic of a marketing database is obvious. It must belong to the marketing department and be an effective source of influence over major marketing decisions. An installation which is really part of some other function or department will never be satisfactory. The Marketing Database is now – and potentially – too important a resource to be at the wrong end of another department's priorities.

The TMS *Direct Marketing Handbook* contains a wealth of practical advice and information and is recommended for those wishing to pursue the topic in greater detail than is possible in a basic textbook.

The application of Bayesian techniques to marketing research

Traditionally, marketing research has employed a methodology based on classical statistics as exemplified by the principles stated in the section on sampling. In recent years, however, increasing attention has been given to the Bayesian, or subjective, approach to probability which incorporates the decision-maker's personal feelings regarding the likely occurrence of specified events.

The aim of marketing research is to reduce uncertainty concerning the outcome of future events or a given course of action. It is clear, however, that even the most extensive research is unlikely to result in perfect information and that even if it did, the value would not be justified by the cost. Thus, even when the results of research are available to him, the decision-maker will still be faced with some degree of uncertainty and the value of the Bayesian approach lies in its ability to quantify such uncertainties and incorporate them in an analysis of the problem. In practice, many managers make use of subjective probabilities in an informal way and always have, for example, the sales manager forecasting next year's sales adjusts the individual salesman's estimates on the basis of his own opinion of their likely accuracy; the production manager decides to use a substitute material to meet an urgent order because he feels the chances are eight out of ten it will work.

Although the Bayesian approach is rejected by many classical statisticians, it is the author's opinion that it is a valuable technique when properly applied. While it is beyond the scope of this book, the student is recommended to consult one, or all, of the following:

1. 'Better Decisions with Preference Theory', John S. Hammond III (1967); the 'best' short introduction to the use of subjective probabilities in analysing real-world problems.
2. *Analysis of Decisions Under Uncertainty*, Robert Schlaifer (1969); an introductory text by one of the pioneers in the field. It is difficult to follow, but involves no sophisticated mathematics. Well worth the effort of the several readings usually necessary to achieve understanding.
3. *Research for Marketing Decisions*, Paul E. Green and Donald S. Tull (1978), integrates both traditional and Bayesian approaches, as well as covering most of the new research techniques. Strongly recommended to the student who wishes to specialise in marketing research.
4. 'Making Decisions in Marketing', T. Cass (1968, pp. 15–24), *Marketing Forum* is a 'home-grown' review article based largely on Schlaifer's book.
5. Chapter 12, 'Marketing Research', in *Marketing Strategy and Management* (M. J. Baker, 1992), pp. 299–312.

Marketing information systems and the use of information technology

The paradox of information technology is that whilst the phrase is upon everyone's lips there is surprisingly little of it to be found in practice save in a relatively uncomplicated and unsophisticated form. Thus whilst there are frequent references to the concept of the paperless office 'one per desk' (a reference to the fact that every manager and office worker would have a personal computer or terminal on their desk) electronic mail and the like all the evidence points to an explosion in the volume of paper-based information in circulation. This phenomenon is reflected in Figure 10.1, which is taken from *Industrial Market Research Handbook* (Hague, 1987), a representation of life-cycles in methods of copying and shows that with the advent of xerography there has been an exponential growth in the demand for copied material. Similarly the growth of information technology, which has been defined by the Department of Trade and Industry as 'the acquisition, processing, storage and dissemination of vocal, pictorial, textual and numeric information by a microelectronics based combination of computing and telecommunications', was projected to lead to mass unemployment in office based occupations. However, the job of clerk is now the single largest occupation in the United States of America and continues to grow. Just 100 years ago the single largest source of employment was farm work which is now well down in the list of major occupations. Indeed, this trend is to be observed throughout the world where employment in knowledge and service based occupations is displacing all forms of manual occupation in terms of size and importance.

Applications of information technology

Consideration of these trends would seem to suggest that information technology will have a

Figure 10.1 *Life-cycles in methods of copying*

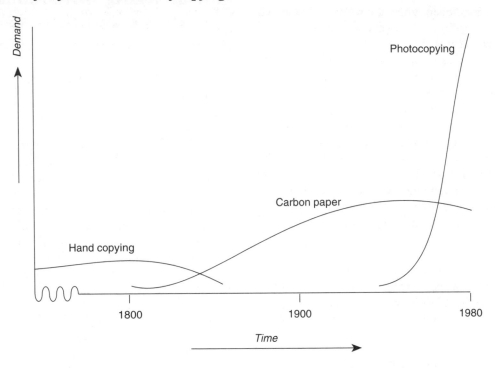

very similar impact but as an innovation it is still at a very early stage in its life-cycle. In the great majority of instances the application of computing to business decision making has been confined to an extension of earlier data processing applications. Lucey (1987) suggests that:

> computers can be used to best advantage for processing information which has the following characteristics: a) a number of interacting variables b) speed is an important factor, c) there are reasonably accurate values, d) accuracy of output is important, e) operations are repetitive, f) large amounts of data exists.

These conditions or characteristics describe well the accounting and other records kept by commercial organisations. It is to these applications which the power of the computer has been harnessed, a development which is unsurprising on the grounds that 'innovations pursue the line of least resistance'. In other words innovations will be adopted most quickly where they can be substituted most effectively for an existing method or solution to a consumption need. It

seems likely, therefore, that having established the benefits which computing can bring to business management the extension of computing and telecommunications from basic database and data handling applications into decision support systems (DSS) will soon follow.

Lucey (1987) states that:

> there is abundant evidence from numerous surveys both in the UK and USA that existing MIS, often used in advanced computer equipment, have had relatively little success in providing management with the information it needs. The typical reasons discovered for this include the following:

- lack of management involvement with design of the MIS,
- narrow and/or inappropriate emphasis of the computer system,
- undue concentration on low level data processing applications particularly in the accounting area,
- lack of management knowledge of computers,
- poor appreciation by information specialists of management's true information requirements and of organisational problems,
- lack of top management support.

Support for these findings is to be found in a recent case study describing the development of home office banking systems (HOBS) by the Bank of Scotland. Writing in the Summer 1989 edition of the *Journal of Marketing Management*, Lannon and Scarborough discovered that the application of IT in the bank was being impeded for most of the reasons cited by Lucey. Perhaps the major problem of all was that management was seeking to use IT in a tactical way and was ignoring its strategic potential. Given that the Bank of Scotland has very few outlets in England and Wales and its wish to move into this market required either that it replicated the branch network of the other major competitors or that it provided an alternative means of access to the banking services which it had to offer. HOBS offered this potential. It is interesting that Lannon and Scarborough report senior management in the Bank of Scotland as stating that this was an area where no marketing research could provide any sensible input to the strategic decision. But, once top management had perceived the opportunity IT offered it adopted it as a main plank in its competitive strategy.

Indeed it is probably true to say that the organisations with the greatest experience of the application and management of information technology are the world's major financial institutions. Consideration of their experience underlines that while return on their investment has been disappointing there is equally wide agreement that *not* to have invested would have resulted in a loss of competitive edge and a decline in market position. Much the same is likely to be true of the adoption of IT in marketing and market research – while such investment may lead to only a transient comparative advantage failure to invest could lead to a permanent loss of market share.

While banks may have come late to marketing they have responded with enthusiasm. Further, because of their experience with large scale data processing with account management they are familiar with the potential of information technology and have the resources to extend it to the marketing realm – particularly in the growing

battle for 'retail' financial services. In doing so they face two major problems. The first has already been referred to in our comment on Lannon and Scarborough's case study, namely, the organisations and attitudinal barriers to extending IT from a control function to an input to decision making. The second is that early entrants to the field of information technology often face significant problems and expense in updating their software. As Alan Kane observed in a *Financial Times* survey (3 December 1987)

> the banks, trusts and building societies have a common software problem. They have an abundance of elderly software, most of it creaking at the joints and out of tune with today's competitive requirements.
>
> Their files, for example, are mainly arranged by account rather than customer. Such an arrangement makes it extremely difficult to readily extract information about customers for the purposes, for example, of special product initiatives or cross selling.

As with other realms of marketing the main challenge is the development of an integrated database. In 1987, for example, Lloyds Bank announced an initial commitment to invest £570 million to upgrade all the bank's branch technology and build a new integrated voice and data network (*Financial Times*, 3 December 1987). Among the main benefits expected from the project are speedy and integrated access to any customer file, improved marketing information, sales prompts, assistance with lending control and the ability to provide self service banking and interfaces with Lloyds' other systems. According to the *Financial Times*:

> Using a computer to assemble and analyse information such as customer age groups, income levels, occupations, savings, home ownership and so on, provides a valuable marketing tool. Successful targeting of different age and income groups for such services as pension schemes, mortgages, life assurance policies and savings plans depends on first identifying the relevant groups and having on file sufficient information to target accurately.

Clearly the same is true of marketing any other good or service and emphasises the importance of creating or gaining access to suitable databases.

From the above discussion it is clear that information technology is an enabling innovation in that it allows some tasks to be done more easily, more quickly, more efficiently and, possibly, more effectively. In his contribution to *The Marketing Handbook* (Thomas, 1989) Alan Melkman proposes four broad areas of IT application as shown in Table 10.8. These may be described as follows:

1. *Enhancing operating efficiency* '...those marketing activities which are already carried out in one form or another within the company. Typically, these include maintenance of customer records, budgeting, preparing and making presentations and analysing sales statistics, scheduling meetings and so on'.
2. *Changed methods* '...enabling the Marketing Department to carry out internal functions which were not possible before'. This will usually start with an extension of applications in the first quadrant such as using databases for segmentation and positioning studies, more sophisticated forecasting and modelling, better and faster communication with a field sales force, etc.
3. *Enhancing customer service* This will be made possible by better and faster communication with customers the application of CATI to obtain timely and relevant data on changing market needs, etc.
4. *Marketing innovation* The use of video cassettes to make sales presentations and demonstrate product use, access to and use of large on-line databases such as DataScan, Information Line and Dialog; direct mail services, market identification studies such as Pinpoint, Acorn and Market Location. EPOS (Electronic Point of Sale) has already had a significant impact on retail store management and is likely to develop into EFTPOS (Electronic Funds Transfer at Point of Sale). Reference has already been made to HOBS

Table 10.8 *An IT applications framework*

		Marketing activities	
		existing	new
Focus of activity	Internal	1 Enhancing operating efficiency	2 Changed methods
	External	3 Enhancing customer service	4 Market innovation

and it can only be a matter of time before other financial service institutions follow suit. Similarly the growth of cable and satellite television is likely to increase the growth of telemarketing.

Melkman's four areas of IT application illustrate the likely sequence which organisations will follow in exploiting the potential benefits of information technology. A constant and recurring theme of this book is that increased competition has resulted in much greater awareness of the value of timely and relevant data. In parallel with other changes these have helped to accelerate the take up of IT. Amongst these changes may be numbered:

(a) The availability of much less expensive hardware.
(b) The availability of much more sophisticated software.
(c) Greater user friendliness in both.
(d) Growing familiarity with visible applications and all the output of IT based systems, e.g. detailed retail receipts generated by EPOS systems, access to and use of automatic telling machines (ATM), extensive use of word processing, etc.
(e) The availability of more skilled and trained manpower.
(f) The establishment of specialist service and software houses.

Review questions and problems

1. What factors, and what sources, would you take into account in preparing a forecast of the potential market for:

   (a) A new 'snack' food?
   (b) Frozen TV dinners?
   (c) A combined refrigerator/freezer unit with a capacity of 14 cubic feet?
   (d) Computer time sharing services?
   (e) Industrial catering equipment?

   Make whatever assumptions you like about the 'product', but state them clearly.

2. Under what circumstances would you consider a non-probability sample a useful and valid market research technique? What disadvantages do you associate with such samples?

3. Compile a short questionnaire:

   (a) For sampling the opinion of industrial users on the benefits of containerisation.
   (b) To elicit the opinions of housewives about freeze-dried coffee. You should stipulate how the questionnaires are to be administered and to whom.

4. What is market segmentation? What variables would you use in segmenting the market for:

   (a) Detergents?
   (b) Fractional horse power electric motors?
   (c) Motor cars?
   (d) Vacuum cleaners?

5. Provide an explanation of the following methods of structuring samples for market research surveys:

   (a) Systematic sampling;
   (b) Cluster sampling;
   (c) Area sampling; and
   (d) Quota sampling.

   In each case, give an example of a marketing situation in which the particular method could be most effectively employed.

6. Formulate the main rules to be kept in mind when designing a questionnaire. How important is question order in securing a satisfactory response?

7. Describe the main guidelines to be followed when framing market research questionnaires to be administered by interviewers to a large sample of respondents.

8. Qualitative research is often criticised as producing results subject to the bias of the investigator. How far do you think this is dangerous, and what compensating advantages do you see in the qualitative approach?

9. Give a definition of an 'attitude', and discuss the difficulties of providing such a definition. Why do marketing researchers concern themselves with attitude measurements?

10. Users of a motorway service area on leaving are to be interviewed to find out, among other things, whether their decision to shop at that particular service area was dependent on their immediate need for petrol or refreshment, the distance or time since their last stop (and where that was), or on other factors. Draft a section of a face-to-face questionnaire designed to establish which of these was or were most influential, and which facilities the respondent in person has used in the current visit. Do not show any coding data or any introductory section.

11. It has been said that the art of management consists of 'taking account simultaneously of the inner workings of the firm and its interaction with external forces'. Describe the contribution of marketing research to the understanding of these external forces.

12. What are the similarities and differences between market research for major capital plant? How would you account for the differences?

13. What are the essential stages in developing a proposal for market research? What differences would you expect to see in a proposal for industrial market research compared with a proposal for consumer market research?

14. What useful information could you hope to obtain through market research when planning to enter the market with a totally new product, based on a recent invention, about which the marketplace has no knowledge?

15. Distinguish between primary and secondary marketing research data. What are the main sources of data in each case?

16. It has been said that the initial research showed that there was no market for a dry-copying machine. However, Rank Xerox ignored the findings and proceeded to establish a successful international company based on the dry-copying concept. How would you explain this contradiction and does it invalidate the use of marketing research data as a planning tool?

17. Discuss the advantages and disadvantages of using the in-depth interview technique to undertake primary market research.

18. Describe and justify the survey methodology you would use in each of the following situations:

   (a) Research on the use of under-arm deodorants to assist in the development of new product ideas.

   (b) Research on consumer reactions to a new type of video recorder.

   (c) Research to assist in the design of a petrol station forecourt.

19. Detail the advantages and disadvantages of using a market research agency to undertake primary research.

20. Explain why and under what conditions a researcher might choose to select a qualitative rather than a quantitative approach to data collection. Use illustrations to support your line of argument.

21. What difficulties is a marketing research agency likely to encounter when undertaking consumer research for a new insurance product? How can these difficulties be overcome?

22. Using examples, evaluate how marketing research could help in the launch of a newly packaged consumer good.

Supplementary reading list

Baker, M. J. (1991) *Research for Marketing* (Basingstoke: Macmillan).

Baker, M. J. and Hart, S. (1989) *Marketing and Competitive Success* (London: Philip Allen).

Chisnall, P. (1992) *Marketing Research*, 4th edn (Maidenhead: McGraw-Hill).

Crimp, Margaret (1990) *The Marketing Research Process*, 3rd edn (Englewood Cliffs, N.J.: Prentice-Hall).

Enis, Ben M. and Broome, Charles L. (1973) *Marketing Decisions: A Bayesian Approach* (Glasgow: International Textbooks).

Fletcher, Keith (1995) *Marketing Management and Information Technology*, 2nd edn (London: Prentice-Hall).

Green, Paul E. and Tull, Donald (1993) *Research for Marketing Decisions*, 6th edn (Englewood Cliffs, N.J.: Prentice-Hall).

Kinnear, T. C. and Taylor, J. R. (1987) *Marketing Research: An Applied Approach*, 3rd edn (London: McGraw-Hill).

Parasuraman, A. (1991) *Marketing Research*, 2nd edn (Reading, Mass.: Addison Wesley).

Tull, D. S. and Hawkins, D. I. (1990) *Marketing Research: Measurement and Method*, 5th edn (West Drayton: Collier Macmillan).

Worcester, R. M. and Downham, J. (1988) *Consumer Market Research Handbook*, 3rd edn (London: Van Nostrand Reinhold).

Chapter 11

Product* Policy, Planning and Development

Contents

Learning goals

The issues to be discussed in this chapter include:

1. The need for and nature of product policy.
2. The concept of the product life-cycle.
3. The definition of what constitutes a new product and the role of new product development (NPD).
4. The NPD strategies open to the firm and the nature of the NPD process.
5. Organising for NPD.
6. The concept of the product portfolio.

After reading this chapter you will be familiar with:

1. The central role of the product or service as a key element in achieving and sustaining competitive success.

2. The view that change is inevitable and that progress is achieved by the continuous substitution of new and improved solutions to consumer needs such that all products and industries follow a life-cycle from birth through growth to maturity and eventual decay.

3. The *process* of new product development through which firms identify market opportunities and develop new products to exploit them.

4. The *procedures* followed to screen ideas and translate these into successful new products.

5. Some alternative organisational structures for encouraging and managing NPD.

6. The need for a firm to develop a portfolio of products each at different stages of the life-cycle to ensure its survival and long-run success.

---

* While the emphasis here is on physical products and a separate chapter (22) deals with the special case of services, in most instances products may be regarded as synonymous with services throughout this chapter.

■ Introduction

A cardinal principle of marketing is that firms should seek to determine the multidimensional nature of consumer demand, and then deploy their resources in the creation of products which will satisfy these demands. Acceptance of this principle recognises that the firm's ultimate success, whether measured by total profits, return on investment, market share or any other criterion, is largely dependent upon its product policy.

Earlier (Chapter 3, Demand and Supply), we looked briefly at the 'product' in theory and practice. In this chapter we extend this preliminary review into a consideration of the product as one, and perhaps the most important, of the 4Ps. To begin with we discuss the role of the product and its relationship to user needs and practices. Next, we examine the role of product policy and return to the concept of the product life-cycle (PLC) also introduced in Chapter 3.

The PLC concept underlines the inevitability of change in the market place as a result of innovation and competition. As a consequence firms must constantly seek to improve on existing products and look for new ones. Accordingly, we seek to define what constitutes a 'new' product prior to a look at the role of new product development (NPD) and the importance of new products. While a firm can modify or extend its product line in a number of ways, all of these are the outcome of a process with a number of distinctive stages usually distinguished an Exploration, Screening, Business Analysis, Development, Testing and Commercialisation. Each of these phases is discussed briefly and raises issues concerning the organisation of NPD activities.

To conclude the chapter we introduce the idea of product portfolio analysis and the importance of having a clear policy for removing or eliminating declining products from the product line.

■ The role of the product in marketing

For many years previous to the birth of the electronic watch, a classic case study in the armoury of any business school teacher offering a course in Business Policy, General Management or Marketing strategy was 'Hamilton Watch'. Almost without exception the first question posed on this case study was 'What is a watch?', and the answer would encompass a wide range from 'a scientific instrument for measuring time' through 'a gift' to 'a status symbol', thus allowing the instructor to make *the* basic point about any product, namely, that it is a bundle of attributes and that it is the need and perception of the consumer or user which will determine which of these definitions is most apposite in any given set of circumstances. Such an insight is fundamental to the marketing concept, underlies the reason why product differentiation became the basic competitive strategy in the 1920s and explains why market segmentation has assumed such importance in the mature and saturated markets of the advanced industrialised economies.

As we attempted to show in Chapter 6, when addressing the question of how buyers select between alternatives, choice behaviour is conditioned by both objective and subjective factors. In recent years recognition that the objective factors which are intrinsic to the product (performance and price) are relatively easy to copy has led to much greater emphasis upon the qualitative and subjective dimensions which will become determinant when objective parity is perceived to exist. We say 'perceived' advisedly for our analysis has shown that people have difficulty in distinguishing very small differences to the extent that in business a useful working rule-of-thumb is that a difference must be at least 10 per cent between the objects which are being compared if it is to become 'noticeable'; that is, 10 per cent bigger, smaller, faster, more efficient and so on.

Two consequences flow from this:

1. Producers wrongly assume that small differentiating features will be perceived when they won't, with the result that:
2. Greater emphasis is given to creating subjective differences between competitive products through service and promotional efforts.

The net outcome of these trends is that the recent literature on marketing has tended to give little specific attention to product characteristics and product differentiation and has concentrated more upon user characteristics and market segmentation. Such a change in emphasis is believed to have gone too far, for the simple reason that objective differences are easier to develop, control and sustain than subjective differences and, if they exist, will largely eliminate the need to try and create such subjectives differences.

As H. U. Thompson (1962) observed in his book *Product Strategy*, 'You can change products: it is a comparatively simple matter of decision and cost. You can't change people – but you can influence them – but seldom if ever cheaply. It is far easier – and thus far more economical – to find out what people want and to supply it than it is to influence them to want what you make'. A sentiment echoing those of Ries and Trout on 'Positioning'.

Support for the view that too much attention has been given to market 'need' as opposed to product content is to be found in a forceful article by Bennett and Cooper. Citing the automobile industry as a microcosm of the American economy Bennett and Cooper claim that lower cost and better fuel economy are simplistic explanations of the 30 per cent market share secured by Japanese and European imports. In their view 'The Europeans and Japanese car makers have simply been better competitors; they anticipated market needs; they built a better product – one that is more reliable, has better workmanship, and is better engineered; and they did it effectively. In short, these manufacturers delivered better value to the American consumer.'

Several similar instances (TV tubes, motorcycles and so forth) are cited and lead to the conclusion that:

> The failure to deliver product value to the customer is the prime reason for this lack of competitiveness. Twenty years of adherence to the marketing concept may have taken its toll of American enterprise. The marketing concept has diverted our attention from the product and its manufacture; instead we have focused our strategy on responses to market wants and have become preococupied with advertising, selling, and promotion. And in the process, product value has suffered.

Similarly it is a truism to state that consumers will always prefer a better product at the same price or the same product at a lower price, but both observations underline the importance of trying to create objective product differences before resorting to the intangible and subjective elements. Satisfaction is the end, but the product or service is the means by which it is achieved. As Lawrence Abbott (1955) has pointed out, 'what people really desire are not the products but satisfying experiences', but 'experiences are attained through activities. In order that activities may be carried out physical objects or the services of human beings are usually needed. Here lies the connecting-link between man's inner world and the outer world of economic activity. People want products because they want the experience-bringing services which they hope the products will render.'

User needs and product characteristics

Ultimately it seems to me to be irrelevant whether one first identifies user needs and develops product characteristics to match them or, alternatively, creates a product and then seeks out customers whose needs match these characteristics. In the final analysis the process is circular and subject to continuous adjustment. That said, there will be clear benefits if one can spell out some of the basic dimensions of user needs as this will make it that much easier to develop the appropriate product characteristics. A very helpful approach to this process is to be found in a monograph published by the Design Council by Rothwell, Gardiner and Schott (1983) which provides a framework for this section.

Rothwell *et al.* argue that user needs can be thought of as having four dimensions which they define as follows:

- *Need elements*: An indication of the overall price and specific performance characteristics required by customers.
- *Need intensity*: A measure of the degree of importance given to each need element by potential users.
- *Need stability*: A measure of the degree to which the need remains unchanged over time.
- *Need diffusion*: A measure of how widely felt the need is. This defines the size of the potential market.

Thus 'need elements' define the properties which a product must contain and/or deliver while 'need intensity' specifies the relative importance which consumers will attach to any given element. As we have seen when analysing how buyers choose, many properties are assumed to exist as they are intrinsic to the product and it would not qualify for consideration at all if it didn't possess them. Further, buyers will often use a single performance or benefit criterion as a surrogate for a large number of individual product characteristics when assessing suitability or fitness for purpose; for example, few buyers of machine tools will evaluate the metallurgical analysis of the materials used nor the precise tolerances used in constructing the tool – they will assess its suitability in terms of its output potential. By the same token the purchaser of a TV set rarely inquires into the nature of the electronic gadgetry contained in the 'box'; he is concerned with the quality of the sound and picture which these components deliver. Of course there will always be exceptions to these generalisations and it is for this reason that it is felt more attention should be given to spelling out the product's characteristics, for only by cataloguing them fully will we be able to establish whether our product possesses features others don't and, if so, whether these features will have appeal to a sufficient number of potential customers to constitute a viable market segment.

In Table 11.1 an attempt has been made to provide a consolidated listing of product

Table 11.1 *Product characteristics*

| Technical | Economic | |
	Non-price	Price
Size	Servicing costs	List price
Shape	Availability of parts and service	Sale price
Weight	Running costs	Net price after trade-in allowance
Consistency	Breakdown costs	Financing or leasing arrangements
Materials used in construction	Depreciation	Discounts
Complexity	User training facilities	Sale or return
Power source	Instructions	Special offers
Power output	Delivery	
Speed/Production rate		
Reliability		
Flexibility/Adaptability		
Ease of use		
Ease of maintenance		
Safety		
Appearance/Design features		
Smell		
Taste		

Source: R. Rothwell, P. Gardiner and K. Schott (1983), *Design and the Economy* (London: The Design Council); J. R. Evans and B. Berman (1982), *Marketing* (New York: Macmillan).

Figure 11.1 *Bar chart showing need elements and need intensity*

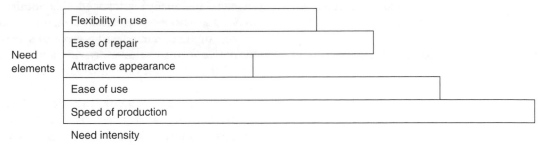

Source: R. Rothwell, P. Gardiner and K. Schott (1983), *Design and the Economy* (London: The Design Council).

characteristics or attributes to act as a check list for assessing existing or proposed new products. Several sources have been used in an attempt to make the listing suitable for all categories of products.

In Figure 11.1 we reproduce a simple bar chart which illustrates well how need elements and need intensity can be combined to give a quick visualisation of the product configuration desired by a particular market segment. Such pictograms should be constructed for each market segment and, when combined with an evaluation of the need stability and need diffusion, will enable the planner to decide which offer the best opportunities in terms of their own aspirations and supply capabilities.

While physical attributes are a necessary condition for purchase they are not usually sufficient, particularly where there is little to distinguish one physical product from another. In these circumstances our model of buyer behaviour predicates that subjective/behavioural influences will become determinant in enabling the individual to discriminate between competitive offerings. As we noted earlier, the creation of subjective perceived differences is likely to prove more difficult and more costly than the creation of objective differences, but the likelihood of being able to achieve this will be greatly enhanced if one adopts a marketing approach and defines one's products in terms of the benefit/satisfaction it provides rather than the function it performs. Levitt first propounded this philosophy in his famous 'Marketing Myopia', but elaborated on it in a subsequent contribution entitled 'The Augmented Product Concept' (1983) in which he wrote:

> One million quarter-inch drills were sold not because people wanted quarter-inch drills, but because they wanted quarter-inch holes.

Levitt also quoted the President of Melville Shoes as saying:

> People no longer buy shoes to keep their feet warm and dry. They buy them because of the way the shoes make them feel – masculine, feminine, rugged, different, sophisticated, young, glamorous, in. Buying shoes has become an emotional experience. *Our business now is selling excitement rather than shoes.*
>
> (my emphasis)

This, of course, is an extreme statement and not to be taken too seriously. Clearly, people still do buy shoes to keep their feet warm and dry and have quite clear expectations as to the function shoes must perform. But, the point is well made that different images and associations may well encourage people to buy more shoes, to suit different moods and situations, than are required for the sole purpose of protecting one's feet.

■ Product policy

A firm's product policy is fundamental to the whole operation of the business. Most new companies are conceived to produce a specific product or group of products, and it is this decision which dictates the industry to which they will belong, the markets they will serve, and the nature and extent of the resources, methods and techniques they will employ. These factors often tend to be overlooked, however, for most companies are long-established members of a given industry and inextricably linked with their product line. Similarly, it is often erroneously assumed that companies are irrevocably committed to their current product mix, which ignores the fact that apart from certain highly specific capital equipment, most corporate resources may be put to other uses.

The latter assumption may be attributed to the fact that companies rarely do undertake a radical change in product policy, even when environmental changes indicate that they should – a fact which prompted Theodore Levitt (1960) to write the now classic 'Marketing Myopia'.

Levitt's thesis is that companies take too narrow a view of their market because they think in terms of their product offering, rather than in terms of the fundamental needs which these products satisfy. Thus the American railroads thought of themselves as the ultimate development in overland transportation, and failed to respond to the invention of the internal combustion engine which gave us the car, lorry and aeroplane. If the management of the railroads had thought of themselves as being in the 'transportation business', then doubtless they would have integrated these new methods of moving goods and people into their existing network. As it was, the expanding demand of a rapidly growing economy masked the impact of the new competition and lulled the railroads into the complacent belief that they could look forward to continued and uninterrupted growth. Even when the threat was appreciated the railroads chose to compete head-on, failing to realise that they could not hope to duplicate the speed and convenience offered by their rivals, with the result that until recently they have appeared to be members of a dying industry. Now, however, as the result of a

belated appreciation of the marketing concept, railways in many advanced economies are enjoying a new lease of life as a result of careful analysis of their comparative strengths *vis-à-vis* alternative forms of transportation and a strategy of positioning based on realistic market segmentation.

The writings of Levitt and Peter Drucker, among others, have given us the concept of corporate strategy which, in essence, consists of a statement of the firm's objective, and the mix of policies to be used in the attainment of that objective. A first step in the formulation of a corporate strategy is to answer the questions 'What business are we in?' and 'What business do we want to be in?' Declining industries have invariably failed to define their business in sufficiently broad terms. Had the railroads thought of themselves as being in the 'transportation business' it is reasonable to assume that they would have been responsive to the development and introduction of new methods of transport, irrespective of whether they involved rails and locomotives.

Gulf Oil exemplifies the broad viewpoint in that it has defined its role as 'servicing the travelling public'. Although the company's past growth depended largely upon the refining and sale of petroleum products to motorists, Gulf recognised that developments in fuel cell technology and growing concern over air pollution may be sounding the death-knell of the petrol engine. The motor car represents only one stage in the evolution of personal transport, however, and it is clear that people will continue to travel even though we may not be able to predict the exact nature of the next development. While travelling, people have a need for both rest and refreshment, and to meet this continuing need Gulf developed a nation-wide network of Holiday Inns (now divested and operated as a franchise).

Hopefully, this example makes it clear that by defining the business they are in, and want to be in, Gulf did not commit themselves irrevocably to a given product mix, but will modify their product offering in the light of changes in consumer demand – this is their product policy.

The concept of the product life-cycle

The above examples clearly indicate that, over time, man develops new and better ways of satisfying basic needs, with the result that as new products are introduced, established products become obsolescent and eventually pass into oblivion. In time the cycle repeats itself, and the once new product suffers the fate of the product which it originally replaced. In many ways this process resembles the human life-cycle, with its phase's of birth, growth, maturity, senility and death, and has given rise to the concept of the product life-cycle.

The first stage in the product life-cycle is represented by its introduction into the market. As with human beings, this is a critical stage, for the product has little to protect it from the hostile environment into which it is introduced. (Fortunately, medical science has been more successful in protecting new-born offspring than has the marketer!) Assuming survival, new products enjoy a period of increasing demand and rapid growth, but as most innovations are merely substitutes for existing products, other manufacturers will react strongly to the newcomer, and their own decline in market share, stemming the newcomer's growth. However, as the superiority of the new substitute becomes apparent many suppliers will switch to it to protect their market share accelerating the adoption of the new product and the decline of the old. The levelling out of demand for the new product represents the onset of maturity.

In time, other new products will enter the market offering advantages over the now mature product, which will experience a decline in demand as consumers switch their allegiance. This phase has been characterised as senility or decay. Classically the product life-cycle is represented as having four basic phases as represented in Figure 11.2.

If the stylised PLC shown reflects reality then clearly the change in the inflection of the curve at A heralds rapid exponential growth, at B a levelling off of demand, at C a diminution that suggests either product rejuvenation or replacement. Although the utility of the PLC concept is occasionally challenged by sceptical practitioners their criticisms tend to reflect their own failure to understand its meaning, and to the rather naive assumption that all products will exhibit perfectly symmetrical S-shaped curves.

Figure 11.2 *Stages in the product life-cycle*

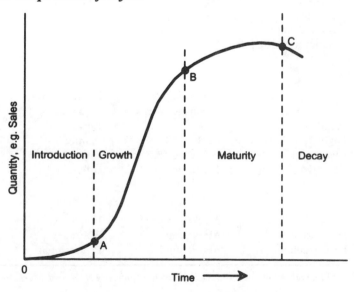

In fact, consideration of a number of other areas reveals that some form of exponential function (represented graphically by a cumulative S-shaped curve) is typical of the manner in which objects or ideas spread or diffuse through populations of 'adopters'. Elsewhere (Baker, 1975, in *Marketing New Industrial Products*), I have argued that the consistent and pervasive nature of the diffusion process approximates a law of nature and reflects an underlying process such that if one can initiate diffusion it will proceed to some extent automatically thereafter due to the 'bandwagon' or 'contagion' effect.

In the context of new-product marketing we find that success is usually defined in terms of achieving a predetermined sales target within a specified time period. It follows that the sooner one can achieve an initial sale the sooner diffusion will commence. In essence the logic is that proof of a sale adds conviction to the selling process, while word-of-mouth recommendation or pure visibility, for example a new car at the kerbside, will accelerate awareness of the new product's existence and so improve the probability of further purchases.

Put very simply then, success or failure is highly dependent upon the speed with which we can achieve initial sales and the lesson to be learned from the concept is that effort to pre-identify 'early adopters' is essential to long-run success. In the particular, however, it is impossible to be highly specific about the particular characteristics of early adopters in different contexts and situations as has been demonstrated by the lack of correlation between the findings of various research studies.

Table 11.2 *Product life-cycle: implications for marketing*

Product life-cycle	Introduction	Growth	Maturity	Decline
Characteristics				
Sales	Low	Fast growth	Slow growth	Decline
Profit	Negative	Rapid rise	Falling margins	Declining
Cash flow	Negative	Moderate	High	Moderate
Strategy				
Objective	Aggressive entry	Maximize share	Boost profits	Milk product
Focus	Non-users	New segments	Defend share	Cut costs
Customer targets	Innovators	Early adopters	Majority	Laggards
Competitor targets	Few, pre-empt	Growing number	Many	Declining
Differential advantage	Product performance	Brand image	Price and service	Price
Marketing mix				
Product	Basic	Extensions & enhancements	Differentiation, variety	Rationalize range
Price	High	Lower	Low	Stabilizing
Promotion	High	High	Falling	Low
Advertising forms	Awareness	Brand performance	Loyalty	Selective
Distribution	Selective	Intensive	Intensive	Rationalize
Organization				
Structure	Team	Market focus	Functional	Lean
Focus	Innovation	Marketing	Efficiency	Cost reduction
Culture	Freewheeling	Marketing led	Professional	Pressured

Source: Peter Doyle (1976), 'The realities of the Product Life Cycle', *Quarterly Review of Marketing*, Summer, pp. 1–6.

Such a lack of correlation does not invalidate the utility of the concept – it merely emphasises the need for persons well versed in their own product–market interface (however we define 'product' and 'market') to apply their experience and knowledge in seeing how such a basic idea can be of use to them.

Unlike the human life-cycle, however, one cannot predict the length of any of the phases of the product life-cycle – certainly there are not the equivalent of actuarial tables for new products. Further, marketers have the option to practise euthanasia and quietly dispose of products which fail to live up to expectations, or, alternatively, to prolong the life-cycle through a rejuvenation process. The analogy is a useful one, provided that one bears in mind that it is a generalisation and says nothing specific about the duration of any given phase. However, by monitoring changes in demand, one can predict the onset of growth, maturity and senility, and vary one's marketing inputs accordingly; for example, reduce the level of advertising expenditures during growth and emphasise production and physical distribution; step up the amount of sales promotion at the onset of maturity; retire the product when senility sets in. Table 11.2 provides a useful summary of how various characteristics such as cash flow and competition vary in accordance with the stages of the product life-cycle and their implications for managing the marketing mix.

■ What is a 'new' product?

The first stage in the product life-cycle posits the introduction of a new product – the question is, 'What constitutes a new product?' There can be no hard-and-fast answer, for newness is essentially a subjective concept that depends upon one's state of knowledge or, in the case of a firm, its current range of activity. It is possible to distinguish a spectrum of newness ranging from an invention, which Mansfield (1966) has defined as 'a prescription for a new product or process that was not obvious to one skilled in the relevant art at the time the idea was generated', to a minor change in an existing,

widely known product, for example the addition of a new blue whitener to a detergent.

For the purpose of this book a new product will be considered anything which is perceived as such by the consumer, or with which the firm has no previous experience. The former permits the inclusion of variants in existing products, and their packaging, as well as totally new products such as satellite television, body scanners or laptop computers. The latter acknowledges that production of an existing product with which the firm has no previous experience raises the same marketing problems as does a totally new product. Further, it may also be perceived by consumers as a new product; for example the sale of home furnishings under the 'St Michael' brand by Marks & Spencer.

The importance of product development in the firm's marketing strategy was introduced in Chapter 3 when we proposed that a firm has only a limited number of strategic alternatives which it can choose from (pp. 63–5). This view was supported by Ansoff's 'Growth Vector Matrix' which sees product development as one of only four options available to the firm. (In passing, it should be noted that research by Baker and Hart (1989) showed that the most successful firms do not regard these strategies as mutually exclusive but seek to increase market penetration while, simultaneously, developing both new products and markets.) It is for this reason that we regard new product development as being at the very heart of the organisation's strategy.

It is also important to remember that the introduction of new products creates problems for buyers in that it requires them to reconsider their existing attitudes and patterns of behaviour. Many of these problems were looked at in Chapters 6 and 7 concerning consumer (individual) and organisational buyer behaviour respectively.

⃞ *The role of new product development*

Although it is impossible to predict the life span of a given product, there is an inevitable certainty that it will eventually be replaced by the introduction of a new substitute or even made totally obsolete as the result of technological innovation.

In Chapter 5 it was stated that branding developed in its present form as a result of the realisation that many mass markets were faced with the possibility of over-supply, such that the individual manufacturer could only protect his position by distinguishing his output from that of his competitors. Many critics of advertising would argue that the claimed differences between brands are more a figment of the copywriter's imagination than a reality, and still view products such as detergents and canned peas as homogeneous. This view is admissible if one adopts a narrow definition of a product, based solely on the function that it performs in terms of objective and quantifiable criteria. However, from the arguments advanced concerning newness, it is clear that the consumer's perception is modified by subjective considerations which are not amenable to quantification. Thus a relatively minor change in a product's composition or marketing may assume major significance in the user's eyes and

result in a marked shift in demand for that product. It is argued, therefore, that branding can only succeed as a competitive strategy given the existence of perceived differences.

If this is so it follows that a competitive market will be characterised by a continual effort to develop such differences. Clearly, the producer who succeeds in distinguishing his product from that of his competitors, through the creation of a new and desirable attribute, will enjoy an advantage which will enable him to expand his sales and share of market. Such an advantage is in the nature of a monopoly, which may last for years if protected by a patent, for example the Polaroid camera and film, or be eroded overnight by imitative innovation, for example enzyme active detergents.

The role of new product development is the creation of such competitive advantages.

Over the years the American consulting firm Booz-Allen & Hamilton has pursued the objective of seeking to understand the management approaches that result in competitive advantage with a particular emphasis upon the role of new

Figure 11.3   *Strategic roles for successful new products*

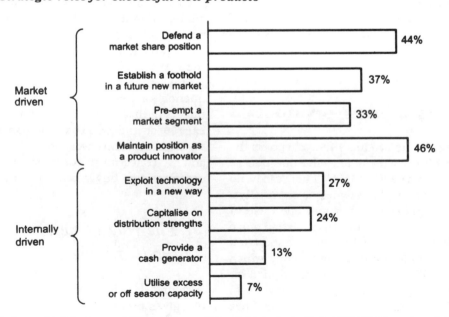

Source: Pierre Rodocanachi, 'The Successful Management of New Products in the 1980s', ESOMAR seminar, Athens, Nov. 1983.

product development. In a paper given to the Esomar seminar on New Product Development (Athens, November 1983) entitled 'The Successful Management of New Products in the 1980s', Pierre Rodocanachi presented the findings of their most recent research based upon in-depth interviews with top management of large and medium sized companies in the United States and Europe, complemented by a comprehensive mail survey of corporate executives and product managers of *Fortune 1000* companies. According to this research new products play an important and diverse role in the firm's overall strategy as can be seen from Figure 11.3. These objectives are considered to be just as valid today.

☐ *The importance of new products*

Any attempt to measure the contribution of new products to a firm or industry's growth and profitability is bedevilled by a lack of consensus as to what constitutes a new product. Similar

difficulties also exist when one seeks to measure the failure rate of new product introductions.

Ignoring the problems of data comparability for the present, two valid generalisations may be advanced:

1. Firms are increasingly dependent upon new products for the maintenance and expansion of sales.
2. A large proportion of new product introductions are failures in the sense that they do not achieve the expected sales level, and are withdrawn from the market.

The first generalisation is supported by Figures 11.4 and 11.5, and by the data reported in Table 11.3, based on a survey of a representative cross-section of UK industry in 1974. Although more recent hard data is not available, the anecdotal evidence drawn from trade magazines and so forth confirms this general pattern.

Estimates of new product failure rates vary enormously from the oft-quoted level of 80 per cent (Ross Federal Research Corporation, quoted

Figure 11.4 *Consumer goods manufacturers' dependence on new products*

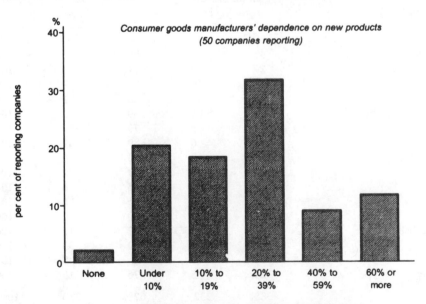

Figure 11.5 *Industrial goods manufacturers' dependence on new products*

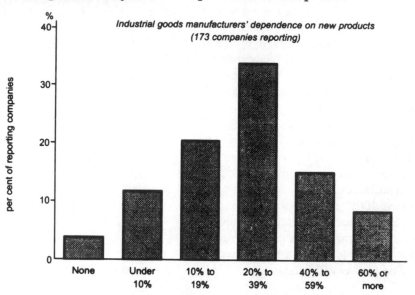

Source: *The Marketing Executive Looks Ahead*: 'Experiences in Marketing Management' 13, National Industrial Conference Board, 1967.

Table 11.3 *Inter-industry variations in dependence on new products*
(Where does the largest proportion of your sales come from?)

Industry	Products launched within the last five years		Products launched more than five years ago		Totals	
	%	n	%	n	%	n
Building and construction	45	13	55	16	100	29
Chemicals/allied products	29	12	71	30	100	42
Clothing	67	19	33	9	100	28
Electrical machinery	38	13	62	21	100	34
Engineering/general machinery	41	71	59	102	100	173
Fabricated metal	21	8	79	30	100	38
Food, drink, tobacco	11	6	89	49	100	55
Furniture and fixtures	57	8	43	6	100	14
Iron and steel	21	6	79	22	100	28
Leather	54	7	46	6	100	13
Paper	24	5	76	16	100	21
Plastics	50	9	50	9	100	18
Printing and publishing	38	8	62	13	100	21
Textiles	50	33	50	33	100	66
Miscellaneous	64	9	36	5	100	14
Stone, glass, clay	24	5	76	16	100	21
Total	38%	232	62%	383	100%	N = 615

Source: M. J. Baker and S. T. Parkinson (1974), 'An Analysis of the Significance of Innovation', Appendix to *S.S.R.C. Report*.

in the *Wall Street Journal*, 5 April 1961), to an absolute low of 7 per cent (A. C. Nielsen Company, *How to Strengthen Your Product Plan*, 1966) if the firm makes full use of the screening and testing procedures described below. According to *Marketing Week* magazine (8 October 1994) some analysts believe that 80 per cent of new products fail. The reason for failure is that they basically do not address a real customer need. The new product development process is crucial to success. A Brand Development Business survey showed that 82 per cent of fast moving consumer goods (fmcg) companies saw new product development (npd) as the key to growth. However, in practice the term npd is loosely applied and most of the new products launched by companies are merely extensions of those already in existence. For obvious reasons this is a cheaper and less risky alternative to a completely new product. For example by launching gravy granules Bisto were able to make use of a product improvement but still associate the product with the company's traditional reputation and image.

Alternative new product strategies

Relatively few new products emanate from totally new companies, and attention here will be focused on the established firm with an existing product line. Such firms vary in their willingness to innovate and develop new products, and are usually categorised as 'leaders' and 'followers'.

Many industries which are highly concentrated or oligopolistic in structure are dominated by one or a small number of firms which determine the competitive character of the market along such dimensions as price, quality, distribution policy and innovation. These firms are the leaders. The remaining firms are thought of as followers in that they imitate the policies of the leaders and rarely possess a sufficient market share to affect industry practice through independent action. (Although this is not the place to enter into a discussion of the evils of monopoly/oligopoly, there is a considerable body of evidence which suggests that small firms in an industry are the most innovative, and it would be wrong to assume that it is always the industry leader who stimulates innovation.)

Whether a firm is a leader or follower, there are several distinct ways in which it can add to its product line which may be summarised as:

1. Modification of an existing product; for example, addition of a new ingredient in a detergent, toothpaste or cake mix; increase in the cubic capacity of a car engine, adoption of disc brakes, and so on.
2. Addition of a complementary product; for example, a new brand of cigarette, a new flavour in a food or beverage; the development of a new model of car.
3. Entry into an existing market new to the firm; for example, Cadbury's entry into the cake market; Rank Organisation's entry into the office-equipment market.
4. Development of a new market through the introduction of a totally new product; for example the Polaroid camera, television, computers.

These alternatives are listed in ascending order of risk. The first strategy usually entails a low level of risk, and is frequently in response to overt public demand. Thus, offering variants of their standard models improve a car maker's competitive position but requires comparatively little additional investment by the firm.

The second strategy involves a greater degree of risk, as the firm has no previous direct experience of the production and marketing of the new item. However, in so far as it is a complementary product, previous experience with similar products and markets will be almost directly relevant and reduce the risk accordingly.

Entry into an existing market of which the firm has no previous experience is unlikely to be viewed favourably by the companies currently sharing that market. Thus the new entrant's inexperience is compounded by the aggressive reaction of competitors, and involves a still higher level of risk.

The fourth alternative exposes the firm to a completely unknown situation, added to which the value of fundamentally new products may take years to establish owing to the innate conservatism of the potential user. Further, it is only when a product achieves wide-scale trial that many of its limitations become apparent, which may involve the innovator in many years of adjustment and modification. At the end of this time another firm may well enter the market which the innovator has developed and deprive him of the fruits of his labours; for example IBM in the computer market.

The sources of new product failures identified by Cooper (1975) and Cooper and Calantone (1979) are summarised in Table 11.4. While these results may seem dated they have been confirmed in numerous studies since both by Cooper and other researchers.

Table 11.4   *Reasons for new product failure*

Product characteristic	Percentage of failures
The better mousetrap no one wants (innovative, unique products rejected by the market)	28
The me-too product meeting a competitive brick wall (similar to products on the market already meeting customer needs)	24
Competitive one-upmanship (me-too products hurt by the concurrent introduction of similar ompetitive products)	13
Environmental ignorance (products not well-suited to customer needs)	7
The technical dog product (technically new products not performing)	15
The price crunch (products well-suited to customer needs but priced too highly)	13

Source: R. G. Cooper (1971), 'The Dimensions of Industrial New Product Success and Failure', *Journal of Marketing*, vol. 43 (Summer).

■ New product development

Despite the risks involved, new product development is a competitive necessity and has prompted many companies to evolve formalised procedures for dealing with the complexities and uncertainties inherent in the process. In the survey undertaken by Booz-Allen and Hamilton (1982), strong support was found for a six-stage process represented diagrammatically in Figure 11.6.

It should be emphasised that the Booz-Allen and Hamilton process model is a greatly simplified one. While it is reproduced in most textbooks, sometimes with considerable elaboration to reflect more stages, it must be recognised that it represents the *logic of the process* rather than the reality. In the real world new product development frequently involves much back tracking and many feed-back loops. It would also be more accurate to show the process as *circular* (evolutionary) rather than *linear*. That said, the model has the great virtue of identifying the key stages through which every new product must pass before it reaches the customer. Further, by isolating the stages it has thrown into sharp relief the fact that costs increase rapidly as one moves from the exploratory and creative phases into the development and marketing activities. This was reflected in the 1982 survey which indicated a significant change of emphasis from the findings of the 1968 study. Specifically: 'Companies now conduct far more up-front analyses than in the past. Specific strategies are delineated. Ideas and concept generation are focused. Screening and evaluation are more rigorous, more attuned to strategic and performance considerations. On the whole, the up-front process receives more attention.'

⬜ *The location of new product ideas*

To be effective, any search for new product ideas should be structured, in the sense that efforts should be directed towards a specific area and

Figure 11.6   *Six stages of product evolution*

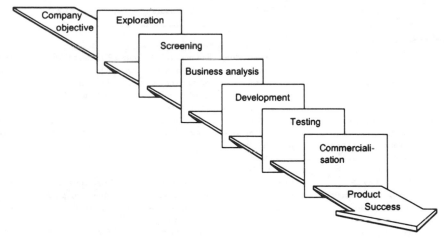

Source: Booz-Allen & Hamilton (1982) *New Products Managment for the 1980s* (New York: Booz-Allen & Hamilton).

pursued systematically. Most firms possess some special skill or 'distinctive competence', and it is this which they should seek to exploit in developing new products. Thus, if a firm has developed a reputation for precision engineering it should seek to build on this strength, rather than branch out into mass-produced, fabricated products, Although there are cases of firms which have achieved success following a radical departure from their original product policy, the author would argue that this is attributable to their developing a distinctive competence they previously lacked or had failed to exploit.

The adoption of search criteria is essential if the firm is to avoid wasteful exploration of the multiplicity of sources open to it. Such sources may be internal or external to the firm.

Internally, every member of the company is a potential source of new product ideas, and company suggestion schemes have thrown up many more valuable suggestions than they are generally credited with. Many companies now have their own Research and Development Department, specifically charged with developing in-house projects, in addition to which Sales, Marketing and Production usually have distinct ideas of how the current product line could be improved or extended.

Externally, the firm's distributors and customers are frequently a fruitful source of ideas, as are the product offerings of one's competitors. Another major source is the published literature of the universities and professional bodies, the technical and trade press, and the various government research departments. Much of the information to be gleaned from these sources is incapable of immediate application but is sufficient to stimulate further investigation – the AFD process described earlier in Chapter 9 is a clear exception to this generalisation.

The major source of ideas for radical innovations is undoubtedly the private inventor, whose work may be reviewed by consulting the Patent Office files or the weekly *Official Journal*. (Few inventors appreciate the commercial potential of their ideas, and those that do frequently meet with a cool reception from potential manufacturers, for example Xerography and the Hovercraft, but nearly all patent their ideas.)

☐ *Screening new product ideas*

In drawing up a short-list of product ideas for detailed investigation the search criteria

Table 11.5 *Factor and subfactor rating for a new product*

		Very good	*Good*	*Average*	*Poor*	*Very Poor*
1.	**MARKETABILITY**					
A.	*Relation to present distribution channels*	Can reach major markets by distribution through present channels	Will have to distribute by distribution mostly through present channels, partly through new channels	Will have to distribute equally between new and present channels, in order to reach major markets	Will have to distribute mostly through new channels, in order to reach major markets	Will have to distribute mostly through new channels, in order to reach major markets
B.	*Relation to present product lines*	Complements a present line which needs more products to fill it	Complements a present line that does not need, but can handle, another product	Can be fitted into a present line	Can be fitted into a present line but does not fit entirely	Does not fit in with any present product line
C.	*Quality/price relationship*	Price below all competing products of similar quality	Price below most competing products of similar quality	Approximately the same price as competing products of similar quality	Price above many competing products of similar quality	Priced above all competing products of similar quality
D.	*Number of sizes and grades*	Few staple sizes and grades	Several sizes and grades, but customers will be satisfied with few staples	Several sizes and grades, but can satisfy customer wants with small inventory of non-staples	Several sizes and grades, each of which will have to be stocked in equal amounts	Many sizes and grades which will necessitate heavy inventories
E.	*Merchandisability*	Has product characteristics over and above those of competing products that lend themselves to the kind of promotion, advertising, and display that the given company does best	Has promotable characteristics that will compare favourably with the characteristics of competing products	Has promotable characteristics that are equal to those of other products	Has a few characteristics that are promotable, but generally does not measure up to characteristics of competing products	Has no characteristics at all that are equal to competitors' or that lend themselves to imaginative promotion
F.	*Effects on sales of present products*	Should aid in sales of present products	May help sales of present products; definitely will not be harmful to present sales	Should have no effect on present sales	May hinder present sales some; definitely will not aid present sales	Will reduce sales of presently profitable products
II.	**DURABILITY**					
A.	*Stability*	Basic product which can always expect to have uses	Product which will have uses long enough to earn back initial investment plus at least ten years of additional profits	Product which will have uses long enough to earn back initial investment plus several (from five to ten) years of additional profits	Product which will have uses long enough to earn back initial investment plus one to five years of additional profits	Product which will probably be obsolete in near future
B.	*Breadth of market*	A national market, a wide variety of consumers and a potential foreign market	A national market and a wide variety of consumers	Either a national market or a wide variety of consumers	A regional market and a restricted variety of consumers	A specialised market in small marketing area
C.	*Resistance to cyclical fluctuations*	Will sell readily in inflation or depression	Effects of cyclical changes will be *moderate*, and will be felt *after* changes in economic out-look	Sales will rise and fall with the economy	Effects of cyclical changes will be *heavy*, and will be felt *before* changes in economic out-look	Cyclical changes will cause extreme fluctuations in demand

Continued on next page

Table 11.5 *(continued)*

	Very good	Good	Average	Poor	Very poor
II. DURABILITY *(continued)*					
D. *Resistance to seasonal fluctuations*	Steady sales throughout the year	Steady sales – except under unusual circumstances	Several fluctuations, but inventory and personnel problems can be absorbed	Heavy seasonal fluctuations that will cause considerable inventory and personnel problems	Severe seasonal fluctuations that will necessitate lay-offs and heavy inventories
E. *Exclusiveness of design*	Can be protected by a patent with no loopholes	Can be patented, but the patent might be circumvented	Cannot be patented, but has certain salient characteristics that cannot be copied very well	Cannot be patented, and can be copied by larger, more knowledgeable companies	Cannot be patented, and can be copied by anyone
III. PRODUCTIVE ABILITY					
A. *Equipment necessary*	Can be produced with equipment that is presently idle	Can be produced with present equipment, but production will have to be scheduled with other products	Can be produced largely with present equipment, but the company will have to purchase some additional equipment	Company will have to buy a good deal of new equipment, but some present equipment can be used	Company will have to buy all new equipment
B. *Production knowledge and personnel necessary*	Present knowledge and personnel will be able to produce new product	With few minor exceptions, present knowledge and personnel will be able to produce new product	With some exceptions, present knowledge and personnel will be able to produce new product	A ratio of approximately 50–50 will prevail between the needs for new knowledge and personnel and for present knowledge and personnel	Mostly new knowledge and personnel are needed to produce the new product
C. *Raw materials' availability*	Company can purchase raw materials from its best supplier(s) exclusively	Company can purchase major portion of raw materials from its best supplier(s), and remainder from any one of a number of companies	Company can purchase approximately half of raw materials from its best supplier(s), and other half from any one of a number of companies	Company must purchase most of raw materials from any one of a number of companies other than its best supplier(s)	Company must purchase most or all of raw materials from a certain few companies other than its best supplier(s)
IV. GROWTH POTENTIAL					
A. *Place in market*	New type of product that will fit a need presently not being filled	Product that will substantially improve on products presently on the market	Product that will have certain new characteristics that will appeal to a substantial segment of the market	Product that will have minor improvements over products presently on the market	Product similar to those presently on the market and which adds nothing new
B. *Expected competitive situation – value added*	Very high value added so as to substantially restrict number of competitors	High enough value added so that, unless product is extremely well suited to other firms, they will not want to invest in additional facilities	High enough value added so that, unless other companies are as strong in market as this firm, it will not be profitable for them to compete	Lower value added so as to allow large, medium and some smaller companies to compete	Very low value added so that all companies can profitably enter market
C. *Expected availability of end users*	Number of end users will increase substantially	Number of end users will increase moderately	Number of end users will increase slightly, if at all	Number of end users will decrease moderately	Number of end users will decrease substantially

Source: John T. O'Meara, Jr (1961), 'Selecting Profitable Products', *Harvard Business Review* (Jan–Feb), pp. 83–9.

mentioned earlier will also help reduce the need for subsequent screening, that is weeding out of marginal ideas. Such criteria usually require that:

- The product will meet a clearly defined consumer need;
- The product is consistent with the firm's production and marketing policies;
- The product will utilise the firm's existing skills and resources;
- The product will contribute to the firm's long-run profitability.

Once a short-list has been compiled, the next step is to evaluate each product's potential. To ensure consistency, many firms make use of a factor-rating table similar to that reproduced in Table 11.5 which suggests the use of five ratings, ranging from Very Good to Very Poor, for seventeen different factors. By assigning a value, for example 10, 8, 6, 4 and 2 to the rating, and by weighting the factors in terms of their relative importance to the firm, it is possible to compute a score for each product idea and limit further investigation to the highest scoring ideas.

Given the revised short-list, the next step is a detailed feasibility study based on tests of the product concept. Such tests may have been made already, but if not, it is essential that they be undertaken prior to detailed market studies and the finalisation of prototypes. In its original form the product concept represents the marketer's perception of a product which will satisfy a specific consumer want, and may differ considerably from the consumer's own perception of what is required. As it is the latter who ultimately decides whether the product will be a success, reconciliation of any discrepancy is vital. Further, outlining the broad characteristics of a new product to a potential consumer may well stimulate the latter to suggest specific attributes previously unthought of.

In some instances the product concept is too complex to be tested verbally, and some form of mock-up or prototype must be used to communicate the idea and gain consumer reaction. For example, the concept of a cordless telephone or a pick and place robot may be difficult to convey in words but eminently simple to demonstrate.

Once management is satisfied that the basic idea is indeed consistent with its policies, and within its engineering and production capabilities, it should formulate a product concept; that is, a precise statement of the need the product will fill and the form it will take. Based on this statement the marketing research department can

Figure 11.7 *Mortality of new product ideas (by stage of evolution)*

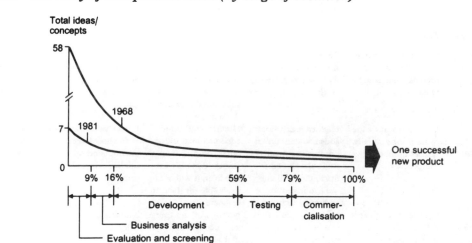

Source: Pierre Rodacanachi (1983), 'The Successful Managment of New Products in the 1980s', Esomar Seminar (Athens, November).

develop a profile of the potential market and the production department can estimate unit cost at various levels of output. (The latter may necessitate the construction of a prototype(s).) Utilising these data, the marketing department can then develop its own estimate of the costs associated with varying levels of market penetration.

The emphasis upon 'front-end' analysis referred to earlier has had a dramatic effect upon the mortality of new product ideas as can be seen from Figure 11.7, reproduced from Rodocanachi 'Successful Management' which compares the findings of the 1968 and 1981 Booz-Allen studies.

Despite this increased emphasis upon evaluation and screening it appears that the UK and USA still lag considerably behind Japan in the attention given to this phase, which suggests that still more effort will be applied to it in future.

☐ *Business analysis*

Once the firm has isolated those concepts which appear to have potential for development it needs to undertake a business analysis to test its commercial viability.

Of necessity any assessment of a new product's potential will require the firm to undertake a certain amount of research. To begin with it will need to define the market segment which it intends to target. It will then have to establish the size and potential of this segment, of any competition and the strength/performance of these competitors and decide upon its own positioning (see Chapter 8).

Internally, it will have to prepare forecasts of the costs of developing and marketing the new product or service, and then develop various scenarios for entering the market. Based on these scenarios it will develop forecasts of sales volume/market share so that it can decide whether or not to proceed.

New product introductions represent an investment opportunity for the firm, and it is essential that such opportunities be evaluated in the light of all other possible uses of the firm's resources. In the normal course of events a company is faced with a disparate collection of investment opportunities, and so must develop a common denominator with which it may rank dissimilar projects in order of preference. The discounted cash flow (DCF) technique has been widely adopted for this purpose.

The basic principle upon which the DCF technique is based is recognition of the fact that a currently available sum of money can be invested to generate a stream of future earnings. Thus £1 invested today will be worth £1.10 a year hence if the return on investment is 10 per cent per annum. Conversely, £1 received a year hence is only worth £0.90 today if it could be invested at 10 per cent. By applying the DCF technique one can make direct comparisons of investment opportunities with very dissimilar future cash flows and select the one with the highest net present value. Naturally, the method is not infallible, as it is very dependent upon the accuracy of the predicted future cash flows. The more distant these are the less accurate they become – a factor which partially accounts for the popularity of payback and similar methods which emphasise the time in which the original investment will be recovered. Many students will be familiar with these techniques already: those that are not are recommended to refer to *An Insight into Management Accounting* by John Sizer (1989).

At this stage of the new product evaluation procedure it is unlikely that sufficient information exists to permit a detailed comparison of proposals, but even a rough computation will help reduce the list.

☐ *Product developement and testing*

If the business analysis indicates a profitable market opportunity then the firm will commit resources to physical development and testing. This phase of the NPD process frequently involves iterations with the preceding Business

Figure 11.8 *New product development structures*

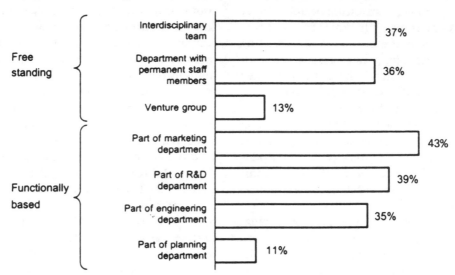

Source: Booz-Allen & Hamilton (1983).

Analysis stage as more and better information about cost and performance becomes available allowing further refinement of forecasts.

In view of the high risks associated with new product introductions, field testing should logically precede firm commitment to large-scale production and marketing. Product testing consists of an objective appraisal of the product's performance, free of subjective associations created by other elements of the marketing mix, for example price, packaging, brand image and so on. It should not be confused with test marketing, which includes consideration of these factors.

The precise nature of a product test obviously depends upon the product itself but, essentially, all seek to determine how well it will perform in actual use. Certain product attributes are capable of precise measurement, for example the efficiency of an engine, the life of an electric light bulb; whereas others depend upon consumer preference and defy exact quantification, for example the taste of a food or beverage. Recognised tests exist for the measurement of most items included in the product specification and subsequently incorporated in the description of the goods as offered for sale. With the passing of the Trade Descriptions Act 1968, the importance of ensuring the accuracy of such quantitative statements became a matter of law rather than conscience. This Act makes it an offence to use a false trade description, which is defined as covering:

- The composition, quality, quantity, and size of goods.
- Their suitability and fitness for any particular purpose.
- Their testing or approval by any person.
- The method, origin, date of manufacture, production or processing.
- Their history and previous ownership.

Under the provisions of the Act, the use of a false description becomes a criminal offence punishable by fine and/or imprisonment, whereas previously misrepresentation was only actionable in a civil action.

As noted, however, many product qualities are a matter of individual perception and preference, the incidence of which can only be established through actual trial. In practice a number of experimental methods have been developed, some of which will already be familiar to the reader as a result of their incorporation in television commercials.

In that the manufacturer is seeking to establish how his new offering will be perceived by the consumer, a commonly used test involves comparison with a leading competitive product. The detergent advertisement which shows two halves of a badly stained article washed in an identical manner, except for the fact that one powder is Spotto and the other Brand X, is an example of such a paired comparison. Although scientifically valid, a successful rating on a blind test in which the new product is identified solely by a code number is no guarantee of market acceptance. The purpose of such tests is to test a specific variable such as taste, texture, washing power and so forth, and thus requires that all other variables be held constant. In the real world the consumer does not normally select a product along one dimension alone, even though a single factor such as washing power may predominate. Products are bundles of attributes which are viewed collectively and which create their own associations in the mind of the potential user, so that a preference for A over B based on a single variable may be reversed when all the variables are taken into account. Thus, although a successful product test is an essential preliminary to continued development, it is not conclusive evidence of market success, and many producers will only make a final decision on the product's future after large-scale market testing.

☐ *Test marketing*

Basically, test marketing consists of launching the product on a limited scale in a representative market, thus avoiding the costs of a full-scale launch while permitting the collection of market data which may subsequently be used for predictive purposes.

In practice the term 'test marketing' tends to be used loosely, and it is important to distinguish the original concept, as outlined above, from two associated techniques commonly confused with it.

The first of these is often referred to as pilot marketing, and fulfils the same function for the marketer as the pilot plant does for the production engineer, that is it tests the feasibility of the proposed course of action. In many instances companies become so involved with the development of a new product that by the time successful product tests have been completed they feel irrevocably committed, and any course of action other than full-scale marketing is unthinkable. However, companies of this type are usually aware of the critical importance of a well-designed and co-ordinated marketing plan, and so test its feasibility in practice prior to full-scale operations. pilot marketing on a regional basis may also serve to give the firm valuable marketing experience while commissioning new plant to meet the anticipated demands of a national market.

The other practice often confused with test marketing is the testing of mix variables, that is measuring the effect of changes in the test variable, all other variables being held constant, for example copy testing. Such tests are often used to improve the marketing of existing products, and should not be confused with the true test market in which the collective impact of all variables is being tested simultaneously.

It is clear that if test market results are to be used to predict the likely outcome of a full-scale national launch, then the test market must constitute a representative sample of the national market. Despite the claims of various media owners it is equally clear that no such perfect microcosm exists and that test marketing is of dubious value if undertaken for predictive purposes alone. In addition to the dangers inherent in scaling up atypical test market results to derive national sales forecasts, many marketers feel that test marketing increases the risks of aggressive competitive reaction in an attempt to nip the new product in the bud. Test market validity depends heavily on the assumption that trading conditions in the market are 'normal', and it follows that any departure from such conditions will bias the results. Competitors learn quickly of test marketing operations and typically react in one of two ways. If the new product closely resembles existing brands, the manufacturers of these brands will usually step up their advertising and sales promotion in the test market to maintain existing brand loyalties and prevent the new entrant getting a foothold. These tactics also ensure the existence of 'abnormal' trading conditions during the test period. Alternatively, if the new product represents a radical departure from existing products, competitors can easily monitor its test market performance while developing their own substitutes. If the test results seem promising the imitative innovator may well enter the national market at the same time as the originator of the idea – if not before!

For these reasons many manufacturers now undertake more exhaustive tests of the mix variables and omit the test market stage altogether. This approach is strongly favoured by Japanese companies. If the new product is launched on a limited scale initially, more often than not it is in the nature of a feasibility study rather than in the hope of obtaining hard data from which to predict the outcome of a national launch.

Evidence to support this view was provided by Eleanor Tracy (1984) in an article, 'Testing Time for Test Marketing'. According to the author:

Revolution is coming to test marketing. Not so long ago it was heresy for a U.S. company to introduce a new product nationwide without reams of test results gleaned from 3 per cent of the population over at least a year. But traditional test marketing is slow, expensive, and open to spying and sabotage. So some consumer goods companies now use a much smaller sample over a much shorter time to probe the market. Sometimes they bring out a new product without test marketing it at all.

Procter & Gamble, which practically wrote the primer on test marketing, is a leader in changing the rules. The Cincinnati giant tested its new encapsulated aspirin, Encaprin, for only three months in one market before rolling out nationwide in June. It put Folgers instant decaffeinated coffee on U.S. shelves without test marketing. Other companies shunning the conventional test-market route: Quaker Oats with Chewy Granola Bars and chocolate-covered Granola Dipps; Sara Lee, a division of Consolidated Foods, with frozen croissants; and Campbell Soup with its Pepperidge Farm Star War Cookies. This

year Pillsbury introduced Milky Break Bar, a cream-filled chocolate-covered wafer, without test marketing, even though it was the company's first venture into the ready-to-eat snack market.

In addition to test marketing being 'slow, expensive, and open to spying and sabotage' its demise is being hastened by the availability of alternative methods for assessing likely market response. Among these alternatives the simulated test market and scanner-based test marketing are the most popular and widely used techniques.

In a simulated test market consumers are recruited in retail outlets, asked to read an advertisement about a new product and given a free sample of it. Subsequently, the consumer is asked to rate the product (by means of a telephone interview in the USA) and these data are used to predict market response by means of a computer programme. Apparently this method is quite successful at weeding out potential failures for a modest investment ($40 000) but is less good at predicting actual potential.

A more sophisticated approach is the scanner-based test in which consumers in selected markets get an identification card which is presented at the retail check-out. Using the product codes a record is made of purchase, without the consumer or competitors knowing which product(s) are being tested, which enables prediction to be made about take-up and sales potential.

Despite the availability of less expensive and less obvious test marketing methods all the evidence supports the *Fortune* article cited earlier that many firms now skip this phase in the process. The main factor behind this is undoubtedly what is referred to as 'time-based competition' or 'time to market'.

At several places we have commented on the impact of accelerating technological innovation and intensifying competition. Taken together these trends have led to shorter product life cycles and so put a premium on faster product development and early market entry. It is also believed that greater emphasis on the earlier creative and research based phases of the NPD process has done much to improve the likelihood of success without the penalties of the traditional test market.

☐ *Commercialisation*

The final phase of the NPD process is commercialisation when the product is launched in the market, thus initiating its life-cycle, and it is this phase which is the main focus of *Market Development*. As can be seen from Figure 11.9, commercialisation increases the firm's financial commitment by several orders of magnitude. Capacity must be installed to cater for the anticipated demand; inventory must be built up to ensure that supplies can be made available to the distribution channel; intensive selling-in must take place to ensure widespread availability at the point of sale or to canvass orders from prospective buyers; maintenance and servicing facilities may be necessary and a large promotional investment will be needed to create awareness of the new product's existence. Given the importance of this phase, one might reasonably expect discussions of it to dominate texts dealing with the subject, but it only requires a cursory examination to reveal that this stage rarely receives equal treatment with the preceding phases and attracts comparatively little attention.

In recent years organising for NPD has received considerable attention. Linear process models, such as the one described here, have often led to a perception that each phase is a discrete activity and the prime responsibility of

Figure 11.9 *Cumulative expenditures in NPD*

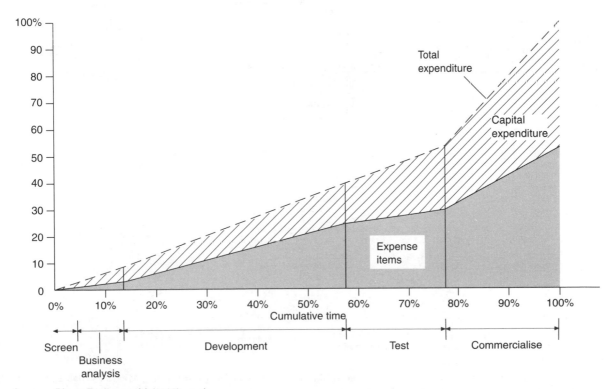

Source: Pierre Rodocanachi (1983) *op cit.*

different functional experts. Thus, marketing may initiate the process by identifying potential products but these get passed to R&D and Engineering to see if they're feasible technically. If they are, then Finance will be asked to test their commercial feasibility after which they will go to Production for physical development. Finally, the new product will be handed over to Marketing again for commercialisation.

This tendency to compartmentalisation leads to what has been termed a 'pass the parcel'

approach with a lack of ownership and sense of urgency. Analysis of Japanese NPD suggests a quite different approach, with considerable overlap and integration of the phases, which has been likened to a rugby team rather than a relay race. To facilitate this team approach the practices of parallel processing and simultaneous engineering havebeen widely adopted.

In collaboration with Professor Susan Hart, the author has developed a more sophisticated model of new product development which we

Figure 11.10 *An example of the early stages of the multiple convergent process*

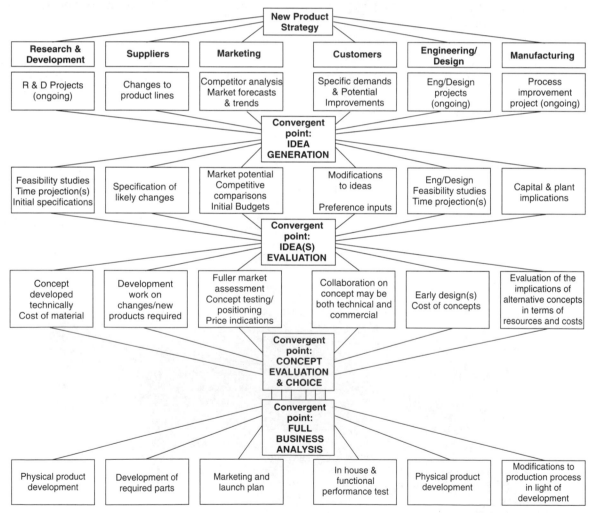

Source: Hart, Susan J. (1995) 'New Product Development' in *Marketing Theory and Practice*, ed., Michael J. Baker (3rd edn) (Basingstoke: Macmillan).

have called Multiple Convergent Processing (MCP). The MCP model sees the Booz-Allen Hamilton model as the spine of a complex set of interrelated and interdependent activites. In other words, a *critical path*, Developing this concept further we conceive of all the firm's functions working simultaneously and in parallel on new product development with the convergent points providing the necessary focus and integration. An example of the early stages of the MCP is shown in Figure 11.10.

Organising for new product development

In Chapter 19 (Organising for Marketing) passing reference is made to compromise structures suited to new product development. In the 1981 Booz-Allen survey this issue was given considerable attention and revealed the existence of two broad approaches described as free standing and functional. As can be seen from Figure 11.8, free standing approaches, which consist of an independent team, can be sub-divided into three main types while teams based in a functional department are of four main types.

According to Rodocanachi, 'Successful companies tend to use more than one organisational concept, mixing and matching not only the approach but the types of skills and leadership elements of the team.' Based on this observation three basic organisational approaches are identified as illustrated in Figure 11.11.

These approaches are described as follows:

The first is the entrepreneurial approach, typically used for developing new-to-the-world products. The structure requires an interdisciplinary venture team and a manager with the ability to integrate diverse functional skills. This is an autonomous new products group, usually reporting to a general manager. Success requires involvement of, and strong commitment from, top management. Typically, the process, the management structure, and the requirements for formal business planning are less rigid than other approaches. Usually, an incentive system promotes risk taking by rewarding handsomely for success.

The second is the collegial approach, typically used to enter new businesses or add substantially different products to existing lines. This approach requires strong senior-management support and participation in decision making, a commitment to risk taking, and a formal new products process to guide the effort and ensure discipline. It also requires a clear commitment to provide whatever is necessary for success and for expediting decisions.

The third is the managerial approach. This is the standard process used for existing business management. It involves strong planning and heavy emphasis on functional leadership to drive new products in manufacturing, distribution, marketing, or the like. It tends to be a rigid new products process involving

Figure 11.11 *New product organisation*

Approach	Skill mix	Leadership
• Entrepreneurial	• Interdisciplinary venture team	• Integrative manager
• Collegial	• New Product specialists	
	• Marketing R&D	• Functional manager
• Managerial	• Specific functions	

Source: Pierre Rodocanachi (1983) *op. cit.*

many levels of management, quick promotion of successful new product managers, limited risk incentives, and rigorous application of financial criteria.

The more successful companies match all of the elements just discussed to specific new products opportunities. The organizational approach and extent of top-management support vary, based on the specific needs of each new products opportunity. As the newness of the product increases, the entrepreneurial, integrative focus of the team increases, along with the involvement and support of top management.

An analysis by *Fortune* (15 October 1984) of 'Eight Big Masters of Innovation' confirms this need for organisational flexibility when it reported:

New models of corporate organization are emerging at the innovative companies. To retain an entrepreneurial feel for their markets, most of them work hard to stay highly decentralized. 3M, for example, encourages a process analogous to cell mitosis: as they develop new products, units of the organization subdivide into new units. At Campbell Soup, $3.3 billion in sales is spread among 52 so-called strategic business units.

The ability to make use of the market information gleaned by decentralized operations seems to depend on compressing the lines of communication between the chief executive and the middle manager. Apple achieved this by flattening its organization chart: fully 15 people report to Chief Executive John Sculley, and a line manager of modest responsibility is rarely more than three reporting levels away.

All these companies believe in keeping their management ranks lean, but even those with relatively thick layers of management have developed ways of keeping management in touch.

■ Product portfolio analysis

Thus far the discussion has tended to look at products, and especially new products, as if every firm produced only a single product. In reality most firms have a range or portfolio of products each of which may be at a different stage in its life-cycle. It is recognition of this which led the Boston Consulting Group to propose a diagnostic procedure for analysing the comparative and collective performance of different products in a firm's range which has since become famous as the 'Boston Box'. While several variants of the Boston Box have been proposed they all rest on two fundamental propositions, namely that the 'competitive value of market share depends on the structure of competition and the stage of the product life cycle' (see G. S. Day (1977), 'Diagnosing the Product Portfolio').

The importance of taking into account the stage which a product (or industry) has reached in its life-cycle is fundamental to the whole concept and practice of marketing. As we saw in Chapter 1 when reviewing the evolution of the marketing concept, survival depends upon understanding and satisfying the needs of customers and realisation and acceptance of the fact that over time these needs will change, often due to the action of marketers; hence, the product life-cycle. If, then, we accept the inevitability of the PLC it follows that even where we are concerned with a basic product such as steel with a life span of decades we would be unwise to assume that any particular formulation or, more important, method of manufacture is immune to competition and replacement. To guard against this possibility product differentiation has become a key competitive strategy and new product development an essential activity, so that even the overtly single product firm should have a range of products at different stages of development.

The emphasis upon market share as a surrogate for profitability has been extensively documented since the publication of the PIMS (Profit Impact of Market Strategy) analysis by the Marketing Science Institute based on a technique developed by General Electric. However, as Day points out, in many situations market share is a poor proxy as its use rests on the assumption that all competitors 'have the same overhead structures and experience curves, with their position on the experience curve corresponding to their market share position'. Thus market share indicates *relative* profitability between firms in direct competition (Ford *vs* General Motors) but neglects factors which affect *absolute* profit performance when comparing dissimilar products.

Day cites a number of other pitfalls in using portfolio analysis and the issue is discussed in considerable detail in Alan Morrison and Robin Wensley (1991), 'Boxing up or Boxed in? A Short History of the Boston Consulting Group Share/ Growth Matrix', which the student should consult for details. However, the purpose here is to introduce a conceptual approach which has secured extensive support among practising managers for at least the three reasons cited by Day:

> They [managers] are first attracted by the intuitively appealing concept that long-run corporate performance is more than the sum of the contributions of individual profit centres or product strategies. Secondly, a product portfolio analysis suggests specific marketing strategies to achieve a balanced mix of products that will produce the maximum long-run effects from scarce cash and managerial resources. Lastly the concept employs a simple matrix representation which is easy to communicate and comprehend.

A typical example of this matrix is reproduced as Figure 11.12 using market share and market growth (a proxy for stage in the PLC) as the relevant parameters. In this matrix no values are attached to market share or growth rate although these will usually be included when assessing the comparative performance of one's own products against those of the market leader. Hence the purpose is solely to distinguish the four basic categories of product, the desired movement of businesses over time, and the likely movement of cash between them.

Wildcat businesses (also known as problem children) represent products at the beginning of their life-cycle where hopes run high and expectations of rapid growth and profitbaility encourage the firm to invest heavily in its new product despite uncertainty as to its eventual success. Clearly, the hope is that by so doing the product or business will get on to the rapid growth curve when sales expand exponentially and costs and overheads decline rapidly as a result of economies of scale and growing experience. At this stage of market development

Figure 11.12 *The product portfolio*

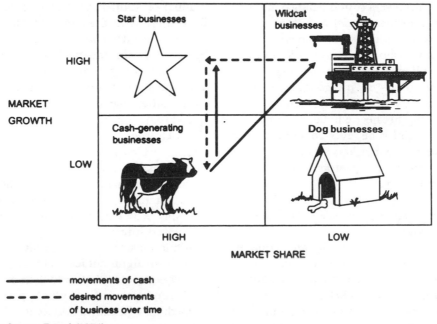

Source: The Conference Board (1974).

competition is fierce as firms jockey for position to become 'stars' and seek to secure cost and price advantages which will enable them to secure the dominant share of the new market.

To achieve this all the cash generated has to be ploughed back into the business together with the profits from the products at the mature stage of their life-cycle represented as cash cows. Finally, while the transition from cash cow to dog is not a desired move the PLC concept tells us that this is inevitable as the mature phase degenerates into decay and senility with declining growth and profitability.

As noted in a 1974 report from the Conference Board, the construction of product portfolios has significant implications for the firm's corporate planning, namely:

1. Careful and continuous watch must be kept on competitors in the star businesses, lest any of them gains leadership in market share.
2. For the corporation as a whole, the overriding objective should be to maximise the net present value of the portfolio of businesses over the planning period, subject to the constraints of financial or other corporate policies.
3. It is vital to achieve a sound balance in terms of financial and managerial resources among cash cow, wild cat and star businesses.
4. The family of businesses is dynamic. In time, wild cats will become stars – or dogs. Stars will become cows – or, if inadequately nourished – dogs. Eventually, new stars or new wild cats will be needed; hence corporate management must be ever-concerned with new products, new markets and acquisitions. It should strive to postpone indefinitely corporate maturity.

While it is not possible to pursue these issues in greater detail in an introductory text, it should be clear that *Product Policy, Planning* and *Development* is at the very heart of the marketing process. Indeed, we can safely say that the best marketing advice we can offer is 'Build a better product at the same price as your competitor or the same product at a lower price.' While achievement of this ideal will not eliminate the need for the other elements of the marketing mix – distribution and promotion – it will go a long way to ensuring success.

Similarly, space limitations preclude discussion of the actual management of the product as it progresses through its life-cycle – particularly the variations in emphasis upon the mix elements both individually and together. However, an extended treatment of these issues is to be found in *Marketing Management and Strategy* (Baker, 1992).

☐ *Managing the decline phase*

Given that most new products are substitutes for existing products – hence the popularity of the 'what business are we in' approach to long-term strategic planning – one should not be surprised if cumulative sales curves are reasonably symmetrical. In other words all the factors which may delay or accelerate a new product's acceptance are just as likely to work for or against it when a substitute for it is subsequently introduced to the market. However, whether or not one anticipates that the decline phase of the life-cycle will be gradual or sudden one must have a clear policy for dealing with the ailing product.

Until recently comparatively little interest has been shown in the decline phase and in 1984 there were only about five articles which dealt with the subject in any depth and most of these were rather dated and failed to address adequately the practical problems of implementation. However in the early 1980s my former colleague George Avlonitis published a number of articles on the topic dealing with both the theoretical considerations and the practicalities using extensive research into the UK engineering industry as an empirical foundation and launched a renewed interest in the topic.

While most writers on product elimination see it as a straight choice between phasing it out slowly – variously referred to as milking, harvesting, run-out and product petrification – and immediate withdrawal. Avlonitis (1983) identifies two further alternatives:

1. Drop from the standard range and reintroduce as a 'special'.
2. Sell out to another manufacturer ('Divert').

Avlonitis believes that the ability to reintroduce a product as a special is probably unique to the industrial market, but otherwise the strategies would seem to be equally appropriate to both consumer and industrial products. That said, such evidence as there is points to a tendency for industrial goods to be phased out gradually while consumer goods are more prone to immediate withdrawal.

Of course much will depend on whether the seller's production equipment is specific or non-specific and the extent to which it has been depreciated. Where the production equipment can be put to other uses or is near the end of its useful life an immediate drop decision is much more likely than a slow phase-out and vice versa. Further, in the case of durable goods the seller will have to give careful attention to service and maintenance obligations and the provision of spare parts and components. For such products Avlonitis provides a very helpful flow diagram of the product-elimination decision and this is reproduced as Figure 11.13.

Once it has been decided to phase a product out then the guiding principle must be to extract the maximum benefit at the minimum cost and Luck and Ferrell (1979) provide an excellent set of strategic steps for accomplishing this:

1. Simplify the product line to the best selling items and, if workable, those that yield the higher gross profit margins.
2. Dress up the product with relatively inexpensive styling and feature changes that create a fresh impression.
3. Bring all marketing efforts into a narrower focus by determining which portions of the market are the heavier and more loyal users or are best served by the existing product. Make limited resources go further in concentrated markets, including selectivity in advertising media and sharper tailoring of appeals.
4. Concentrate also on market areas and on distributors that have the best potentials. If the specific types of buyers being promoted consider the old brand as speciality in shopping behaviour, exclusive distribution agreements may obtain dealer support.
5. Offer special bonuses or other rewards for pushing of the product by distributors and their sales personnel.
6. Limit the always costly personal sales calls to only the best outlets or buyers. Substitute more telephone or mail ordering for personal calls.
7. Utilise more economical wholesale channels by shifting to agents that are shared with other products.
8. Trade down the product to lower price buyers through price reductions made possible by austerity actions.

Review questions and problems

1. Why is the firm's product policy of such central importance to its continued growth and development? Describe a declining firm or industry, and suggest how it might improve its fortunes by adopting a macro view of is markets.
2. Describe how the product life-cycle concept might be of operational use to the marketer.
3. Suggest a system for classifying 'new' pro-ducts. What are the parameters on which your classification rests, and how were they selected?
4. What advantages do you perceive in being (a) a leader, (b) a follower, in terms of product innovations?
5. Design a rating table for evaluating new product ideas, specifying the industry in which the table is to be used.
6. How would you product test:

    (a) An instant soup mix?
    (b) A new plastic resin?
    (c) A new model car?

7. Summarise the advantages/disadvantages of test marketing.

Figure 11.13 *A sequential flow diagram for the implementation of the product-elimination decision*

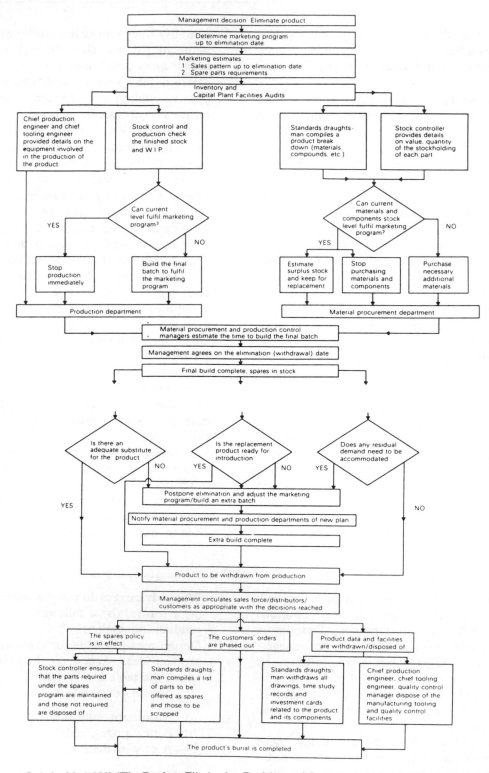

Source: George J. Avlonitis (1983) 'The Product-Elimination Decision and Strategies', *Industrial Marketing Management*, 12, pp. 31–43.

8. Is the fact that intuition and judgement are important factors in the development of new products a valid argument against the use of formal sequential procedures in this area?

9. Distinguish between product and market testing. Explain the contributions and limitations of each in both the consumer and the industrial goods fields.

10. Is it possible to reconcile grocery manufacturing companies' continuous introduction of new products with a supermarket policy of variety reduction?

11. Define 'product policy'. What is the role in product strategy of the product life-cycle? Under what circumstances would it be advisable to try to arrest a declining sales curve? Discuss the alternatives to atempting to arrest such decline.

12. Explain the significance and implications of the timing of a new product launch.

13. What scope is there, in your view, for the successful introduction of strict management control and evaluation procedures in the area of product planning and new product development?

14. Outline the major 'steps' in the new product evolutionary cycle, and assess the extent to which these are amenable to systematic organisation, management and control.

15. Comment on the value of a systematic approach to new product development. Can such development be planned?

16. Discuss the benefits that accrue to a company in setting up a system of regular, detailed product marketing plans.

17. Examine the limitations of test marketing exercises as a guide to full-scale product launch.

18. The rate at which new products are introduced into the marketplace has increased greatly in the last decade. This has been attributed to: (a) evidence of economic progress, OR (b) an increase in planned obsolescence. Develop an argument supporting ONE of these stands.

19. New product development may be just as important for non profit organisations as it is for business organisations. Discuss.

20. How can diffusion theory be used to improve the chances of a successful new product launch?

21. Identify and evaluate the strategies a company could adopt to extend the life cycle of a product.

22. Critically appraise the usefulness of the product life-cycle concept to marketing management.

23. How is the marketing mix likely to differ between the maturity and the decline stages of the product life cycle?

24. Explain how markets may use the Boston Box matrix in planning for marketing.

25. Assess the strengths and weaknesses of the Booz-Allen and Hamilton model of new product development process. In the light of your assessment, how far do you consider that the wide acceptance and citation of this model are justified?

26. When seeking to develop and launch an innovative, high technology product on to the market, what strategic and tactical considerations should a company take into consideration?

27. Identify the stages of the New Product Development Process. Explain why it is important to have managerial support throughout the process.

28. To what extent can the risk of failure in new product development be reduced by a sound evaluation and testing process?

▮ Supplementary reading list

Baker, M. J. (1975) *Marketing New Industrial Products* (London: Macmillan).

Baker, M. J. (1983) *Market Development* (Harmondsworth: Penguin).

Baker, M. J. (ed.) (1979) *Industrial Innovation: Technology, Policy, Diffusion* (London: Macmillan).

Baker, M. J. and McTavish, R. (1976) *Product Policy and Management* (London: Macmillan).

Bureau, J. R. (1981) *Brand Management* (London: Macmillan).

Choffray, J. M. and Lilien, G. L. (1980) *Marketing Planning for New Industrial Products* (New York: Wiley).

Crawford, C. M. (1993) *New Products Management*, 4th edn (Homewood, Ill.: Irwin).

Hisrich, R. D. and Peters, M. P. (1991) *Marketing Decisions for New and Mature Products*, 2nd edn (New York: Maxwell Macmillan).

Johne, Axel and Snelson, Patricia (1990) *Successful Product Development* (Oxford: Blackwell).

Pessemier, E. A. (1977) *Product Management: Strategy and Organisation* (New York: Wiley).

Rothwell, R. and Zegweld, W. (1985) *Reindustrialisation and Technology* (London: Pitman/Longman).

Twiss, B. C. (1992) *Managing Technological Innovation*, 4th edn (London: Pitman).

Wind, Yoram, J. (1982) *Product Policy: Concepts, Methods and Strategy* (Reading, Mass.: Addison-Wesley).

■ *Chapter 12* ■

Packaging

Contents

Learning goals

The issues to be discussed in this chapter include:

1. The basic functions of packaging desired by consumers and distributors and required by law.
2. The use of packaging as a variable in the marketing mix.
3. Environmental concerns and trends in packaging development.

After reading this chapter you will be familiar with:

1. The protective information and usage functions looked for in packaging by consumers and distributors.
2. The legal requirements covering disclosure of information on packaging (UK and EU).
3. The use of packaging as a marketing mix variable and source of competitive advantage.
4. Ways in which a growing concern for environmental matters is influencing attitudes to the use of packaging materials.

■ Introduction

Surprisingly few introductory marketing texts devote much attention to the role of packaging as an element in the marketing mix. When one considers that total packaging industry sales amounted to over £8400 million in 1990, and have risen steadily since, it is clear that packaging costs are a major marketing expenditure and deserve fuller treatment.

The present lack of attention is partially attributable to the tendency to classify packaging as a production cost, so that it is seldom isolated in the way that expenditures on advertising and promotion are. In part it is also attributable to the practical function which the pack performs, which tends to shield it from public scrutiny of the type directed at promotional expenditures whose practical virtues are less easily discernible. In reality packaging costs often exceed all other marketing costs and, in some instances, constitute the major element of total cost, for example cosmetics. These facts were emphasised by a cost analysis of the items in a household food basket in which it was found that while advertising only accounted for 2 per cent of the total cost packaging materials were responsible for 22 per cent or eleven times as much. In the same vein the chairman of Teacher's the whisky producers was quoted in the *Financial Times* in June 1973 as stating 'In spite of stringent control in purchasing materials at the lowest possible cost consistent with quality, the value of the packaging material in a standard case now exceeds that of the whisky.' The same is true today.

Although more recent data are hard to come by, it is clear that the trend for packaging to comprise an increasing proportion of the total cost of convenience goods continues. In an article in *Retail and Distribution Management* (Mar–Apr 1974) reference was made to the rapidly increasing costs of packaging raw materials, together with the observation that 'We may soon reach the situation where the plastic and cardboard wrapper around four tomatoes or half a dozen nails costs more than the goods involved.' In absolute terms it is quite clear that packaging costs have increased significantly in recent years, as can be seen from Table 12.1.

Nowadays packaging is an extrinsic product attribute which is seen to have as much influence on the buyer's perceptions and behaviour as other such attributes as price, brand name and level of advertising. In this chapter we look first at basic packaging functions and the requirements which packaging must satisfy – distributor, consumer and legal. We then review packaging as a discrete variable in the marketing mix and conclude with a discussion of future trends.

■ Basic packaging functions

The basic function of any pack is to protect its contents in transit, in storage and in use. This criterion will play a major role in determining the shape, size and materials used, but in recent years there has been a tendency to subordinate such practical aspects to design and promotional considerations. In most cases there will be little or no conflict between the physical characteristics considered desirable by manufacturers and distributors and the promotional and design elements demanded by consumers. However, it will be useful to consider the requirements of these two groups separately to emphasise the varying nature of their needs.

□ *Distributor requirements*

As noted, the prime function of any pack is to protect the contents. From this it follows that pack design will depend very largely on the nature of the contents in terms of their value, physical composition and durability. In addition one must also take into account the length of the distribution channel, the amount of handling which the container will receive, and variations in climatic conditions which may he encountered between the point of manufacture and sale.

Table 12.1   *Value of packaging products sold in UK (equivalent)*

	1986 £m	1987 £m	1988 £m	1989 £m	1990 £m	1991 %
Paper and pulp	606	636	709	731	771	9
Board	1902	2111	2322	2572	2645	31
Plastic	1482	1707	1982	2229	2274	27
Metal	1552	1632	1809	1833	1835	22
Glass	430	437	447	465	510	6
Wood	271	324	344	368	383	5
Total	6243	6847	7613	8202	8418	100

Source: *The Marketing Pocket Book* (1995).

Most small items are bulk-packed in some type of outer container capable of withstanding the anticipated degree of rough handling. However, such containers can only reduce the shock of mishandling, so that the individual packs must also be capable of resisting such punishment. An example of the degree of protection necessary is provided by the findings of the Printing, Packaging and Allied Trades Research Association that containers which one man is just capable of handling are likely to be dropped from a height of three feet somewhere in transit. This distance corresponds to waist height, or the level of a lorry tailboard, and requires that containers should be able to withstand an equivalent shock. It was also found that heavier packages tended to receive more careful handing as two men were needed to lift them or else mechanical handling methods were used, for example fork-lift trucks. Such methods are widely used now, and it is in the packer's interest to determine the capacity of such equipment and take it into account in establishing bulk pack size and weight. Modifications to containers to satisfy mechanical handling requirements may well increase their intrinsic cost, but such costs are invariably more than recouped through a reduction in the amount of handling required.

Breakage in transit due to rough handling is only one aspect of protection, and equal attention must be given to spoilage from other causes. Foremost among these are moisture, fungus, insects and exposure to sunlight.

Transportation and storage costs are usually computed on the basis of weight and/or volume, and it is clearly in the manufacturer's interest to use packages which make maximum use of a given space. At the retail level the space/volume factor takes on added importance, as it directly affects the number of different items which can be put on display. Sales per square foot, or per linear foot of shelf, are frequently used measures of retail productivity, and it is clear that retailers will avoid packs which occupy a disproportionate amount of space in relation to their value. However, the retailer, like the manufacturer, recognises that purely physical properties must be modified in the light of consumer preferences,

and so may be prepared to subordinate these in favour of packs with greater promotional appeal.

☐ *Consumer requirements*

Reference has already been made to the fact that the packaging of consumer goods was originally a retailing function but that competitive pressures, and the growth of branding, resulted in the manufacturer assuming responsibility for it. Through the adoption of a distinctive pack and brand name, the manufacturer is able to differentiate his product at the point of sale and to develop advertising and promotional strategies designed to create consumer preference for his output. Further, by packaging the product himself the manufacturer is able to exercise much greater control over the condition in which the ultimate consumer will receive it, and so avoid dissatisfaction arising from poor storage and packing at the retail level.

Essentially, consumers want products, and have little direct interest in their packaging *per se*. In many instances, however, the satisfaction to be derived from a product is dependent upon its packaging, and consumers are receptive to both technical and aesthetic improvements in pack design. Many competing products are incapable of differentiation on the basis of objective criteria, and in these instances packaging and promotion often constitute the sole distinguishing features upon which the product's success or failure depends.

A clear example of this is the United Kingdom sardine market. Some years ago a number of fish packers in Britain offered a variety of brands of sardines in competition with Scandinavian and Portuguese imports. Although sardines tend to be associated with the latter countries, the domestic product was competitively priced and secured a strong following among those who could perceive no difference in product quality – real or imagined. As a group, however, sardine eaters became increasingly frustrated by the difficulties associated with opening the conventional pack, as the tag frequently broke when the key was turned, facing them with the almost impossible task of opening the tin with an ordinary tin-opener. In part the trouble was due to the fact that few people used the key correctly, but it was also due to the lock-seamed construction of the can which required that the tag be sufficiently strong to tear open a double thickness of material at the seam. The Scandinavians overcame this problem by adopting aluminium lids, while the Portuguese soldered the lid to the body, leaving a line of weakness which opened easily. Neither course was open to the British packers – aluminium is much more expensive than in Scandinavia, and high labour costs precluded following the Portuguese practice. Consumers responded enthusiastically to the new pack and the domestic share of market sagged dismally owing to the inability of the United Kingdom packers to duplicate the improved container at a competitive price. Ease of opening is clearly a significant consumer 'plus'.

Conventional demand curves indicate that as price falls the volume demanded will increase. In theory this relationship is continuous and we can establish the volume which will be demanded at any given price. In practice prices are discrete and should properly be represented by a 'stepped' demand curve. However, theory suggests that if the manufacturer can offer his product at a lower price he will be able to increase demand, and this is frequently achieved by offering the consumer a variety of different sizes. In addition to catering for variations in household size and usage rates, a range of pack sizes enables the manufacturer to reach consumers with limited purchasing power. As the retired population expands less perceptive marketers will increasingly come to appreciate that lifelong consumption patterns may well have to be modified as inflation reduces the purchasing power of fixed retirement incomes. It would be naive to expect manufacturers to offer small packs at a price proportionate to the 'standard' size in view of the high proportion of fixed costs incurred irrespective of unit size. None the less, the provision of non-standard pack sizes is not only good marketing, it is a socially desirable activity.

Many products are not consumed immediately the package is opened but are used over varying periods of time. To prevent spoilage, such products must be packed in resealable containers, the most familiar of which are the screw-top bottle and jar, and the lever-lid can. Screw-top jars have long been in use for the packaging of products containing sugar, such as jam, which are susceptible to mould when exposed to the atmosphere. However, cheap metal screw caps have only recently come into their own as bottle closures as an alternative to the crown cork. The latter suffers from the disadvantage that it is difficult to remove without an opener and cannot be reused unless fitted with a plastic insert, which greatly reduces its cost advantage as a closure. Lever-lid cans are widely used for packaging hygroscopic materials such as dried milk, instant coffee, cocoa and health salts, but are losing ground to plastics for certain applications. Although ease of opening and reclosure are desirable, many mothers want a pack to be stable and 'child-proof', to prevent accidents to young children, and will show a preference for packs with the latter attributes.

Visual appeal is also an important aspect of pack design, particularly in the case of products of a luxury or semi-luxury nature where the pack itself may add to the image of product quality which the manufacturer is seeking to create. Some critics have argued that elaborate and expensive packaging is used to disguise inferior products, or to permit the seller to inflate the true worth of the product. Neither claim will sustain much examination, for poor packaging is almost always a good indicator of a poor product, and no amount of packaging can disguise a poor product for long. Similarly, few consumers are prepared to pay more for a product solely on account of its packaging unless such packaging will add to their enjoyment of the product itself – After Eight Mints are a classic example, and it is irrelevant if the added satisfaction is purely subjective to the consumer and incapable of objective measurement.

Finally, consumers demand packages which satisfy their information needs. Certain information is required by law, for example statement of weight and composition of product, although frequently the latter is expressed in language incomprehensible to the average consumer. In addition to this basic information, consumers favour a clearly marked price (now largely a retailer responsibility since the abolition of Resale Price Maintenance), information on how the product should or may be used, and, preferably, some view of the contents themselves.

□ *Legal requirements*

In addition to providing a distinctive and appealing means of identifying and protecting, the pack must also provide the user with information concerning its contents. Some of this information may be required by law. The production and design of packaging is influenced by the ever-increasing amount of information which by law must appear on it. Two examples are given of the nature of product information required:

1. *Food products* in general must be marked with:
   - A description of the contents;
   - An indication of the physical form of the food;
   - A list of ingredients in order of weight;
   - Any food which is characterised by the presence of a particular ingredient must have a declaration of the percentage contents of that ingredient;
   - An indication of any storage conditions and its minimum durability;
   - Any necessary instructions for use.

2. *Cosmetics* must be marked with:
   - Name and address of an EU seller or manufacturer – batch number;
   - Description of product;
   - Any relevant expiry date;
   - Warnings or cautions necessary;
   - Required references to particular ingredients.

There is strong pressure for more information – America and Germany already have ingredient declarations on cosmetic products.

The rights to package designs are another legal aspect of packaging. In today's market where products are sold by the shape of the packaging as much as anything else, design registrations can be very valuable, especially in the areas of wine, spirit, toiletries and cosmetics packaging. Other means of securing the legal rights over a product package include the following:

- Patent Rights – for a new invention or application.
- Copyright – provided the existence and ownership can be proved this is a powerful weapon against imitators.
- Trademarks – may assist in distinguishing packaging from that of competitors. Directories are available in most technical libraries. For information on existing trade names, see for example, Brenda M. Rimmer *Trade Marks: A Guide to the Literature and Directory of Lists of Trade Names* (British Library; Science Reference Library, Occasional Publications, 1976).

To secure ownership of these legal rights you must:

1. Identify the designer. You must know who made the design, are they an employee or contracted labour? One person or several?
2. Ensure that the rights have been assigned to you. There should be a standard clause in contracts of employment concerning the ownership of copyrights. Formal assignment documents for employees and contracted workers may be advisable.
3. Keep the original drawings. A file should be kept with the history of the development of the packaging and signed, dated original drawings.

Britain's membership of the EU has had its effect on the legal requirements for packaging – new rules have been agreed for the labelling of packaged food and drink products, and these new labels appeared in British shops in 1983. The most important change was that all products had to list ingredients, including additives. The Food and Drinks Industry Council had anticipated the confusion that this might cause, and published an explanatory leaflet listing the purpose of every food additive. For example, butylated hydroxy-toluene prevents oils on crisps and fried snacks going off, sodium nitrate gives bacon a long storage life and its pink colour, and monosodium glutamate is a flavour enhancer used in prepared meats and savoury foods.

Another effect of Britain's membership of the EU is in the area of unit pricing. This is a system of selling products in standardised pack sizes and marking on the pack the price per unit of quantity and the actual price. This promotes easy compar-ison of products by consumers and thus should lead to fair competition. The current EU status on unit prices is an optional directive concerning prescribed quantities on a wide range of products and a mandatory directive concerning unit pricing on foodstuffs. There are constant pressures to expand this to other products. Some EU countries, for example Germany, enforce prescribed quan-tities; however, others including the UK regard this regulation with caution, preferring to operate without these regulations. Some products, how-ever – for example, bread, jam, tea and canned products – have long had standardised pack sizes.

We have discussed here a few of the existing and future legal requirements for packaging. It is impossible to generalise any further as there is no complete summary of legal requirements in existence at present, only partial summaries as the legal requirements will vary by type of product. Specialised advice should be sought on this from any of the trade bodies and institutions concerned.

The resolution of conflict between distributor/user requirements

Such conflict as does exist between user and distributor requirements is almost invariably resolved in favour of the user. Diseconomies in weight/volume relationships due to the use of odd-shaped containers, and losses due to breakages can often be minimised through the use of standardised outer containers. However, the manufacturer can only afford to incur such additional costs if the consumer is prepared to pay a premium for the added benefits received.

Similarly, retailers are more concerned with turnover and gross margins than with the actual number of units on display. If it can be shown that although a promotional pack may occupy twice the space of a conventional container it will generate increased demand or help build store traffic, then the retailer will usually cooperate in the promotion; for example Pyrex coffee jugs filled with instant coffee.

However, manufacturers are not unresponsive to retailer demands and many new packs have been developed as a result of pressure from the big food chains, especially those employing self-service. Self-service has largely replaced counter service owing to the lower operating costs possible through the elimination of sales assis-tants. This in turn has stimulated manufacturers to develop new packaging materials to help the product sell itself and lead to the elimination of many traditional practices.

In the former category may be included plastic bottles, first introduced in 1964 by ICI, alumi-nium foil, bubble-packs, and shrink-wrapping for prepackaged meats, and so on. In the latter category the one-trip bottle was developed to encourage supermarkets to carry carbonated bev-erages, which they had virtually dropped owing to the diseconomies associated with returning deposits and handling empty bottles. Innovation has not been confined to the development of new materials alone, and many improvements have been made in the use of traditional materials. Lightweight tinplate has reduced both the cost and weight of cans and closures, while increased strength has permitted the development of the aerosol, sales of which now amount to hundreds of millions every year. The difficulties described earlier in connection with sardine cans have now been overcome with the development of the Ziehfix can in which the lid is attached to the body by a rubber sealing ring and is easily stripped off. (It is doubtful if this innovation would have saved the sardine packer, for such cans cost more to manufacture than a conventional can. For a distinctive product such as John West's kipper fillets the added cost would appear to justify the convenience, however.) Similarly, the strip-top beer can has combined the advantages of two competing materials – aluminium and tinplate.

The package as a marketing variable

In an article in the *Wall Street Journal* Alecia Swasy (1989) posed the question 'Sales lost their vim? Try repackaging', and claimed that packaging represents the last five seconds of marketing. By this she meant that the final decisions of which fast moving consumer good to buy are usually made at the point of sale when faced with an array of objectively similar packaged goods which can only be differentiated by their price, brand and packaging – the extrinsic product attributes referred to in the Introduction.

Comparatively little research has been done into 'packaging as an extrinsic product attribute' but Robert Underwood (1993) presented a paper on this subject at the AMA Winter Educators' Conference. The references cited are to be found in this paper.

Underwood quotes Schlossberg (1990) who argues that the importance of packaging as a marketing variable can be summarised by three numbers: '25 000 or the number of items in a typical grocery store; 20, or the average number of minutes a consumer spends shopping in such a store; and 80, or the percentage of shoppers who make a final decision on what they're buying while in the store'. Underwood then reviews the small number of studies which have explored the role of the package as a cue to product quality as the basis for his own research. In his view the attributes of a package such as colour, design, type of container and so on create utility for a

consumer and these 'package utilities' influence the consumer's overall perception of utility (or value) which is essentially a measure of the satisfaction of consumer wants and/or needs.

Underwood proposes a conceptual model which recognises five utilities – Functional, Symbolic, Informational, Aesthetic and Structural – the first four of which are of direct importance to the consumer while the last refers to the benefits the package provides to distributors; for example ease of shopping, handling and storage. The other four utilities are defined as follows:

- *Functional* package utility is the benefit consumers derive from a product's package performing five key functions: facilitating usage, easing disbursement, providing security and protection, accommodating storage for product re-use, and allowing re-use of the actual package.
- *Symbolic* package utility is defined as internally generated feelings engendered by a product's package including self-enhancement, role position, group membership, and ego identification. Such symbolic meanings are frequently communicated by the product's package. For example, in the USA there are over 700 brands of perfume and cologne. In such a saturated market, packaging is seen as essential in communicating symbolic values or image and attracting the consumer's attention at the point of sale.
- *Informational* package utility is derived from the quantity and quality of information provided. As noted earlier this includes factual information, often required by law, as well as the brand and imagery associated with it, advice on use, and so forth.
- *Aesthetic* package utility derived from the sensory benefit conveyed by the design, shape, colour, texture and so on of the package.

Underwood describes each of these utilities or attributes in some detail in establishing a series of propositions as to how they influence consumer perception and, possibly, behaviour. However, this is a theoretical model and, while the propositions seem eminently sensible, they still require to be operationalised and validated. Nevertheless, there are numerous case histories which lend support to the view that the package has a major influence on consumer decisions.

In recent years a number of articles have appeared describing how manufacturers have used packaging as a competitive weapon in their marketing strategy. The one-trip bottle was adopted by Schweppes in an attempt to recapture the market share lost to Beechams, who had capitalised on the supermarkets' unwillingness to handle returnable bottles by introducing the Hunt range of 'mixers' in cans. After Eight Mints' luxury image was born out of careful pack design backed up by an effective advertising campaign. Van den Bergh commissioned Rockwell glass to design a streamlined, lightweight bottle for their Tree Top line of fruit squashes to give it added appeal at the point of sale.

The contribution of packaging (reinforced by effective promotion) to the expansion of an established brand is exemplified by no. 6 in the series 'Marketing Case Studies from ITV Advertisers', which describes the campaign to reposition R. Whites Lemonade following its merger with Canada Dry in 1980. As the case study reports:

Currently over two billion litres of colas, mixers and other carbonates worth just over £1 billion are consumed in the UK. 'Other Carbonates' account for 61 per cent of volume and 49 per cent by value.

Although the Soft Drinks Market is now fairly static overall, following a period of steady volume growth in the 1970s, certain sectors are continuing to develop. Thus, whilst on-licence sales have been particularly affected by the recession, the take-home sector of the market is continuing to expand.

Grocery outlets are increasing their hold on the take-home market but traditional distribution through off-licences and CTNs remains important for all forms of carbonated soft drinks.

Lemonade accounts for around 80 per cent of sales of the 'other carbonates' grocery sector of the market.

In line with the growth of the grocery sector has been the growing importance of 'own label' and a comparable increase in marketing and promotional activity by the major brands. Distribution trends have also had a major effect of packaging, particularly in terms of the development of plastic bottles able to contain carbonated drink (polythene terephalate, or PET as they are known in the trade). These bottles are not only easy to handle but, due to their lightness, facilitate larger sizes. Recently there has also been a rapid expansion in sales of the new $\frac{1}{4}$-litre can.

All in all, therefore, an increasingly competitive market where the large brands are fighting it out with each other and 'own label'.

Canada Dry Rawlings Limited

R. Whites Lemonade is marketed by Canada Dry Rawlings, a company formed by the merger of Canada Dry (UK) Limited, and R. Whites & Sons Limited/H. D. Rawlings Limited, in 1980. These companies represent the soft drinks interests of Bass and Whitbread, Bass Limited owning 65 per cent and Whitbread and Company Limited 35 per cent.

Canada Dry Rawlings Limited is the third largest company in the British Soft Drinks industry. The formation of the Company means it has historic strengths in brands for each sector of the Soft Drinks market. Canada Dry Mixers, Rawlings Fruit Juices, Squashes and Cordials, R. Whites flavoured carbonates, Bass, Pilsner and Cyder Shandies, Barbican alcohol free lager, and Buxton Spring Waters. This means that Canada Dry Rawlings offers a soft drink range that is second to none for variety and quality.

R. Whites lemonade

Since 1978 R. Whites has been relatively dormant, and packaging developments within the soft drinks market has not been pursued. After the merger in 1980, the company capitalised on these trends and introduced $1\frac{1}{2}$-litre PET bottles in late 1981. This pack proved to be a great success, especially in the multiple sector of the trade, and was followed in early 1982 by the introduction of the 2-litre pack. This was followed in April 1982 by the repackaging of the litre non-returnable glass bottle in a new lightweight bottle with a pre-printed wrap-around label. At the same time the R. Whites canned carbonate range was reintroduced in the new $\frac{1}{4}$-litre can.

The launch of the new packs spearheaded a massive sales and distribution drive, and at the same time the brand received overall support from television advertising in London, South and Midlands – currently the strongest sales areas for R. Whites Lemonade.

Recall of the campaign to increase awareness showed an improvement from under 20 per cent to around 60 per cent, but more important still, sales improved significantly, particularly for the $\frac{1}{4}$-litre can and $1\frac{1}{2}$-litre PET bottle, underlining the importance of using packaging as an important variable in the marketing mix.

An article by Ludo Pinxt (1984), 'A Nation of Importers', provides several powerful examples to support the author's claim that:

Britons spend £40.85 bn on food and drink every year but British food manufacturers are missing out on a large chunk of this business by failing to recognise the need for new products. The result is that European companies are taking the business with more interesting products, more imaginatively packaged and displayed.

Given that true innovations in foodstuffs are few and far between it is clear that processing and packaging play the critical role in a food company's marketing strategy, as Pinxt's examples clearly demonstrate.

Take coffee cream, which is a basic German supermarket line. The product cannot alter, but the presentation can. One maker now markets its product in a vacuum-formed container that is made in the shape of a lidded jug which works better and looks different. The result is product advantage for the manufacturer and added value for the consumer.

Pinxt also draws attention to the fact that canners of fish products like John West and Carnation have done nothing to add any excitement to standard products like tuna fish, while Saupiquet, a continental producer, offers six varieties (tuna and capers, and so forth) as well as four tuna snack dishes. However, product modification is only part of the story:

With Saupiquet it was not just a product change, but a packaging change as well. Canning is seen as an outmoded concept in the UK, but this is because UK food processors have been slow to take up new packaging methods.

Saupiquet sells its new snack range in new canning packs that do away with the concept of the old hard-to-open can. The process, now well accepted in Europe, involves preprinting the entire pack design, including the top, on to a flat sheet of metal, then punching it into a can shape. This provides more scope for graphics and branding, and also makes it possible for the base to become a single ring-pull section, which does away with the need for a special opener. The new snack lines have become an instant meal purchase, competing with other forms of takeaway food.

Saupiquet produced a different product, differently packaged and displayed. The process is not unknown in Britain, but while cans of this type are seen in provincial supermarkets, the contents are invariably imported patés, salads, fish and processed meat products. When shown to a senior UK food marketing manager recently, the pack was dismissed with the claim that it could not be done. It can be done, and is being done, along with a wide variety of other technical advances in Europe, with the result that even very basic or familiar products can be re-presented with great success to consumers in the marketplace.

It is not true to say that the British won't try anything new. The concept of the wine box was taken from Australia and refined in the UK as a new marketing concept. But why not a variety of plastic containers to create product advantage and difference? All are in use on the Continent.

Multiple packaging

And why not more multiple packaging to create more choice and demand? In France and Germany, yogurt makers package up six, even twelve, different flavours in one multiple pack. The purchase appears different from endless plastic cartons, and gives consumers the opportunity to try different flavours which, individually, they might not choose.

Enlightened UK marketers show what can be achieved, with imagination. Long Clawson Dairy, a fast-growing cheese company in Leicester, acknowledges that its success in its first year of exporting – worth £1m – was learned from continental rivals. Marketing manager Keith Tate says: 'We have learned an awful lot, in a short space of time, from continental cheese suppliers, who pay particular attention to packaging.' And £1m on a total turnover of £11m is new business worth learning about.

In Holland, Denmark, Italy and France, the designer is always designing for markets other than the home market, pushed by marketing managers constantly looking across borders for new business. Britons tend to wait for someone else to prove a new idea, and then produce a me-too. Why wait for the

Danes to import crispy fried onions such as the recent Mr Funions range?

The UK attitude of 'I don't believe it can be done' is replaced on the Continent with 'This is what we want. Find a way of getting it done.' It can be as simple as repackaging existing products – peas and carrots look tantalising in glass jars in French supermarkets even though the product is the same as the discredited canned peas and carrots in the UK.

It is a matter of approach – an approach which argues that the market is constantly looking for new products, whether new or apparently new, and that it is better to get in first, rather than come along later with a me-too. Me-too can be too late.

(Pinxt, 1984)

Many of the innovations cited in this article have now been adopted by British food manufacturers, but the advice remains sound. In a crowded market place packaging and presentation at the point of sale may be the sole means of attracting attention and purchase. The need for continuous innovation is obvious.

▌ Future trends in packaging

Major changes in the areas of packaging systems and materials are few and far between because the problem is not only to develop a new idea, but that it should be of enough consequence to merit a change from the existing method of packaging. A change usually involves a good deal of capital expenditure, and this is the main factor which helps to maintain the status quo.

Today, however, there is a growing cost differential between the packaging currently being used and their possible substitutes. This can be shown by the amount of energy used in the creation of packaging materials.

Energy content: Glass pack   6542 kj per unit
                  Metal pack   5191 kj per unit
                  Bag in box* 3046 kj per unit

(* carton containing powdered or granulated products)

The actual costs will very approximately reflect these differences.

One development which is threatening the glass industry is PET (polyethylene terephthalate), a type of polyester. This is mainly produced in Britain by ICI and is increasingly being used in the USA, Britain and Japan, especially in the area of non-returnable soft drinks bottles. In 1982 in Britain for the first time PET took a larger share of the soft drinks packaging trade than glass; 15 per cent PET, 12 per cent glass. This growth is expected to continue, as PET is expanding into other packaging fields such as beer, wine and fruit drinks and was used in 1983 for the first time as a container for spirit miniatures by international airlines. This is because of the substantial weight reduction – PET miniatures weigh 9 gm compared with 63 gm for a glass container, and this leads to savings on fuel for the airlines.

It was predicted by V. Wolpert, a London analyst of plastics packaging materials, that glass will be forced into narrower areas such as bottles for medicines, cosmetics and pharmaceuticals. Similarly, in *Packaging Today* (October 1982), L. Fennelly declared: 'Two decades from now the glass container industry will be a small specialist area of packaging in cosmetics and decorative packs, and in quality segments of larger markets.' The glass manufacturers, however, are not simply waiting for the predicted end to come, but are employing some defensive measures to reduce production costs. The most widely publicised cost-cutting exercise has been the spread of recycling schemes and bottle banks. The Glass Manufacturers Federation represents the UK's 10 bottle manufacturers and began the bottle bank scheme in 1977. This scheme was started as a direct result of pressure from environmentalist groups. However, the industry soon began to realise that what had started as a defensive move was making good business sense. The Federation's Assistant Director, K. Stott said (*Sunday Times*, 2 May 1982): 'At that time there was a groundswell of feeling in Europe against non-returnable bottles, and it seemed that legislation was imminent.' And 'It has gone much better than we hoped, from being an act of environmental

Figure 12.1 *An example of a European article numbering code*

5 000114 201213

responsibility it has become a major part of the industry.' The scheme is helping to bring down energy costs by increasing the amount of waste glass in the initial melting process. Every 10 per cent of cullet (waste glass) which is added to traditional glass making materials saves 2 per cent on energy costs. Other-cost saving measures are also being adopted, such as reducing the amount of glass used in making a bottle.

The 1970s saw the increasing use of electronic devices to improve the efficiency of day-to-day marketing activities. One of these innovations is the *European Article Numbering system* (EAN), used in food retailing. This system started in Britain in 1977, and originated in the USA in the early 1970s under the name of the Universal Product Code system (UPC). This is a system of incorporating a 13-digit item identification number, both in decimal characters and bar code form, into the product packaging. See Figure 12.1 for an example of an EAN code for a coffee creamer. This code, marked on the packaging, is read by an optical scanner at the supermarket checkout desk, which retrieves the price and product description and displays this to the shopper whilst printing out this information onto the receipt (see Chapter 9).

The EAN system is in use in food retailing in Europe, Australia, Japan and South Africa. America and Canada are the only countries operating the UPC system which has a 12-digit code. This 12-digit UPC code did not have sufficient capacity for use as a world-wide system, hence the adoption of the 13-digit code. However, both the American system and the EAN system are very nearly compatible and the majority of scanning devices being used can scan 12 or 13-digit codes.

The system has benefits in inventory control, checkout productivity and it eliminates the need for marking the price on every item in the shop. Prices are displayed near the item on the shelf. The retailer can analyse the performance of new items, advertising and the comparative performance of similar items in different supermarkets. A list of possible benefits are set out in Table 12.2.

Table 12.2 *Potential benefits to food retailers from adoption of UPC-orientated systems*

Front-end benefits	*Merchandising benefits*
Improved throughput	Point of sale movement data
Checker productivity	Advertising analysis
Reduced misrings	Vendor analysis
Tender reconciliation	New item performance analysis
Cash reporting	Location analysis (for within and between stores)
Store funds control	Price management
Check authorisation	
Store operation benefits	*Inventory management benefits*
Eliminates price marking and re-marking	Shelf space allocations marking
Permits routine ordering	Reduced out-of-stock
Reduces shrinkage	Reduced backroom inventory
	Warehouse and Transportation workload balancing

Source: IBM Corporation, 1975.

The December 5 issue of *Marketing News* (1994) carried a short article which emphasised many of the points made earlier about packaging's role in the marketing mix. It also pointed to the impact which retail trends are having on package design. Among these are:

- *Lifestyle purchasing* As more and more consumers look for products which reflect a desired lifestyle packaging is being used increasingly to communicate these values.
- *Eroding brand loyalty* As private labels, generic brands and discounting have eroded traditional brand share manufacturers are redesigning their packaging to reposition their brands and emphasise their intrinsic values.
- *Shelf information overload* As the number of products increases – there are twice as many on supermarket shelves as there were 10 years ago – distinctive packaging is critical to consumer recognition/attention.
- *Line extensions* In the face of product proliferation and intensive competition many producers use their existing brands and identities when introducing new products (line extensions). Package design has a major role to play in establishing links between the old and new product.
- *Declining marketing budgets* As recessionary forces have bitten into promotional budgets the package has increased in importance as a communication variable.

■ Environmental concerns

In its August 1990 issue, *Which* magazine examined a number of issues related to packaging including the incidence of misleading and excessive packaging, problems with opening packaging and environmental concerns.

In terms of environmental concerns *Which* claim that packaging makes up around a third of the rubbish by weight which we put in our dustbins. Of course, packaging plays an important role in the protection, distribution and marketing of products, as discussed earlier in the chapter, but it also impacts on the environment in a number of ways. First, packaging consumes scarce natural resources some of which are non-renewable. Second, the manufacture of packaging materials consumes energy (itself a natural resource) which generates carbon dioxide emissions which contribute to the 'greenhouse' effect. Third, it results in waste, which has to be disposed of, and litter which has to be cleaned up.

In total the UK consumes about six million tonnes of packaging a year which is equivalent to about six billion glass containers, 14 billion cans and 700 000 tonnes of plastic. Paper and cardboard make up the balance. In theory all these materials can be recycled but in practice only a fraction is. In the case of glass the UK recycles about 20 per cent, 10 per cent of cans, 30 per cent of paper and cardboard and less than 1 per cent of plastic. Many European countries have better records than this, for example Germany recycles 40 per cent of its glass bottles and the Netherlands 60 per cent, and the UK government has set a target for 50 per cent of recyclable household waste to be recycled by the year 2000. Given that the *Which* survey indicated that 59 per cent of the respondents said they would be more likely to buy a particular brand of a product if the packaging was less likely to damage the environment, against 20 per cent who said they would not, the Government's target would seem achievable and with obvious implications for marketers.

We have briefly covered some of the current and future trends in the packaging materials industry, concentrating on the area of consumer goods packaging. For further information on this and other areas of packaging the reader should regularly consult the trade press.

Review questions and problems

1. What considerations would you take into account in selecting the basic packaging material, e.g. tinplate, glass, etc., for the following items (stipulate the material to be used and the reasons for your choice in rank order of importance, i.e. cost, strength, etc.)

   - Breakfast cereal
   - Jam
   - Hand cream (a) standard quality
   -            (b) de luxe quality
   - Frozen vegetables
   - Chocolates
   - Panty-hose
   - Men's shirts
   - Instant coffee
   - Salt
   - Shampoo.

2. A well-known book on packaging is entitled *The Silent Salesman*. Discuss.

3. Summarise: the consumer's requirements of a satisfactory pack; the retailer's requirements.

4. Select any three well-known consumer products and analyse packaging's contribution to their marketing.

5. What contribution can motivation research make to the packaging decision? Quote specific examples to illustrate your answer.

6. Account for the increased importance of packaging as an element in the marketing mix of a typical fast-moving consumer good in recent years.

7. Packaging plays a major part in the promotion of branded products. Discuss this contribution in the light of growing dissatisfaction from conservationists and consumerist interests throughout the world.

8. Write an essay on the social psychology of colour in packaging and sales promotion.

Supplementary reading list

Baker, Michael J. (1983) *Market Development* (Harmondsworth: Penguin).

Booth-Clibborn, E. (1993) *British Packaging Now* (Internos Books Ltd).

Briston, J. G. and Veill, T. J. (1972) *Packaging Management* (London: Gower).

Kline, C. H. and Co. Inc. (1972) *Modern Packaging Encyclopaedia* (New York: McGraw-Hill).

Paine, F. A. (1962) *Fundamentals of Packaging* (London: Blackie & Son).

Pilditch, J. (1973) *The Silent Salesman* (London: Business Books).

■ *Chapter 13* ■

Pricing and Price Policy

Contents

Learning goals

The issues to be addressed in this chapter include:

1. The role of price in competitive strategy and the marketing mix.
2. The importance of price in competitive strategy and the marketing mix.
3. The nature of internal and external factors influencing the pricing decision.
4. The establishment of pricing objectives.
5. Methods of pricing.
6. The selection of a pricing strategy.
7. Perception and pricing.
8. An alternative model of pricing behaviour.

After reading this chapter you will be able to:

1. Explain why pricing has often been relegated to a secondary role in competitive strategy and the marketing mix.

2. Identify some reasons why pricing may receive more attention in the 1990s.
3. Describe and analyse the influence and impact of both internal and external factors on price determination.
4. Discuss pricing objectives.
5. Understand price 'formulas' or methods and give their advantages and disadvantages.
6. Explain the two main pricing alternatives, and suggest where each would be used.
7. List pricing strategies used in practice and give some reasons for their use.
8. Identify the influence of perception on the pricing decisions of both buyers and sellers.
9. Consider and evaluate a dynamic model of pricing behaviour.

■ Introduction

As we saw in Chapter 5 when discussing Demand and Supply, price is the mechanism which ensures that the two forces are in equilibrium. In other words, if demand exceeds supply then the price will rise to the point where the volume demanded by those willing and able to pay that price is equivalent to the volume available. Conversely, if supply exceeds demand then prices will fall until sufficient new buyers have entered the market to ensure the consumption of the available supply. Thus it is the price mechanism which determines whether firms will wish to enter or leave a given market because of the returns which may be earned on a given investment of resources. It follows that if all markets were perfect and infinitely flexible then the return on investment would be the same in them all.

Of course these conditions do not prevail and the aim of the investor/entrepreneur is to get out of industries where returns are falling and into those where they are rising – usually because demand exceeds supply. But what will happen if the overall capacity to supply exceeds the overall capacity to consume? The answer is obvious – in the short run, factors of production will be surplus to requirements and become idle, as happened during the recessions in Britain in the 1980s and 1990s where over 2 million people are unemployed at the time of writing. During a recession and in the short-to-medium term at the microeconomic or firm level, the emphasis is more than ever on survival and the need to ensure that revenues, which depend upon the volume sold and the price earned, exceed the costs of producing, distributing and selling that volume. Clearly, costs and prices must be primary considerations in the development of a marketing strategy.

The present propensity to produce more than we can consume is not entirely new, for as we saw in the opening chapter, it was the threat of such a situation at the beginning of this century which led to the 'rediscovery' of the marketing concept. It also led to the emergence of product differentiation supported by promotional effort as the preferred competitive strategy. Foremost among the reasons for this change of emphasis from a concern with producing the largest volume at the lowest cost, was recognition of the fact that if products are perceived as homogeneous then consumers will prefer the lower-priced offering and that economies of scale will invariably mean that the firm with the largest output will have the lowest costs and so be able to undercut its rivals. More correctly it is the firm with the largest market share which will enjoy the maximum benefits of the scale and experience effects and it will use its cost advantage to maximise its returns and/or dominate its immediate competitors. In such a situation the firm with a lesser market share either has to accept the going market price or it can seek to position its product in such a way that it will be perceived as different by a sufficient number of customers so that in effect it will have its own little monopoly and can charge a differentiated price (hence, *monopolistic competition*). It is for these reasons that while price occupies a central role in economic theory, in marketing it tends to be relegated to a secondary role and much more attention is given to other elements of competitive strategy and the marketing mix. This is born out by the findings of numerous surveys. For example, during 1990 Cath Byrne of Strathclyde University undertook a survey in several European Countries on behalf of Honeywell Ltd in which she asked respondents to identify their key purchasing criteria. The results were as follows:

Key factors:	Technical ability, quality.
Very important:	Flexibility, reliability, delivery scheduling, ordering convenience.
Important	Price, personal contact, service.
Quite important:	Reputation, innovations, after-sales service, previous contact.
Not at all important:	Image, location, payment terms, salesmen.

Similarly Ughanwa and Baker (1989, p. 84) *The Role of Design in International Competitiveness*, found price ranked third out of 16 critical success factors behind 'Performance in operation' and 'Reliability'. Results such as these may be accounted for by one or more of the following reasons:

1. Perfect competition prevails. Under these circumstances the firm cannot have a 'price policy', it must accept the market price.
2. Under conditions of imperfect competition there is a tendency towards 'rigid prices', and for competition to be concentrated on non-price elements such as product differentiation, advertising, service, and so on. Thus

competitors prefer to avoid direct price competition, which could lead to a price war, and adopt the price level of the industry leader.

3. The construction of a demand schedule is considered impossible owing to the enormous number of interacting variables which condition consumer preference. Even if it were possible to quantify demand at various price levels the value of the information would not justify its cost, thus a trial and error approach, or acceptance of the 'going rate', is to be preferred.

4. Marketers lack an adequate understanding of the theoretical concepts and so avoid the complexities involved in developing a 'scientific' price policy.

In every field of marketing activity the suppliers emphasis upon new product development and differentiation confirms their reluctance to compete on price alone. That said it is clear that no seller can ignore the price dimension, albeit that, as the composite model of buyer behaviour proposed in Chapter 6 indicates, consumers will place more emphasis upon fitness for purpose in short-listing products for possible purchase. The more similar the products the more important price will be in determining the final choice, and only if both product and price are very similar indeed will the subjective association created by promotion have a significant influence on that decision.

The paradox is, therefore, that while price may not be the most important element in competitive strategy, and receives comparatively little attention in the marketing literature, it can never be far from the strategists' thoughts. In other words, a competitive price is a necessary but not sufficient condition for marketing success. Further, in the short term, price may be the most effective tactical weapon, as we shall see later in this chapter and also when considering the role of sales promotion particularly in a recessionary environment.

Indeed the results of a survey of 'The Relevance of Price Theory to Price Practice' by Hanna Said (1981), undertaken at the depth of a recession provided results which are at variance with those of nearly all other recent studies as can be seen from Table 13.1.

Table 13.1 *The relative importance of marketing activities in all types of products*[a]

	Rank 1,2	Rank 3,4	5,6	Resultant Rank	n
Pricing*	63%	27%	10%	1	357(100%)
Customer service	51%	34%	15%	2	306(100%)
Product research and development	41%	31%	28%	3	274(100%)
Product services	40%	38%	21%	4	207(100%)
Sales management	28%	38%	34%	5	264(100%)
Physical distribution	23%	36%	41%	6	173(100%)
Advertising and sales promotion	20%	30%	50%	7	173(100%)
Marketing research	25%	24%	51%	8	140(100%)
Marketing cost, budgeting and control	19%	24%	48%	9	123(100%)
Distribution channels control	21%	32%	47%	10	81(100%)
Extending customer credit	15%	38%	47%	11	81(100%)
Public relations	13%	33%	54%	12	66(100%)

[a] Based on 244 industrial goods, 55 durable goods and 108 non-durable goods.

* To be read: 63 per cent of 357 producers of industrial, durable and non-durable goods ranked pricing as the most important policy area

n = number of mentions

Source: Hanna A. Said (1981), 'The Relevance of Price Theory to Price Practice', unpublished Ph.D. Dissertation, University of Strathclyde.

In Said's view, 'These differences may be accounted for by today's inflation which may lead firms to perceive price as the most important element of strategy. It can also be explained by the fact that this study is mainly concerned with pricing and our respondents probably are those who think that pricing is of more importance so they 'perceived it to be the most important area'. Certainly, the survey by J. Hooley, C. J. West and J. E. Lynch (1983), *Marketing in the UK: A survey of current practice and performance*, supports the general view, as can be seen from Table 13.2. However, Simon's 1986 survey would seem to support Said as can be seen from Table 13.3 and he suggests a number of reasons why the significance of price has increased in recent years which may be summarised as follows:

1. High inflation rates have led to higher price consciousness.
2. Stagnating or declining real incomes have induced consumers to switch to cheaper products.
3. Increased competitive pressure (and the difficulty of sustaining an advantage through differentiation) has enhanced the role of price particularly in industrial markets.
4. Aggressive pricing is a major competitive weapon in buyers' markets as suppliers seek to maintain market share.
5. New competitors use aggressive pricing strategies to break into markets and secure a foothold, for example Japan, Korea.
6. Consumerism and legislation on competition (see Chapters 4 and 23) have resulted in

Table 13.2   *Importance of factors in gaining business related to product category*

Factor place 1, 2 or 3 in importance	All companies	Product category				
		Consumer durables	FMCG	Repeat industrial	Capital industrial	Services
Product performance	74.7%	63.9% (86)	77.9% (104)	84.0% (112)	91.9% (123)	61.7% (87)
Product design	43.1%	57.4% (133)	42.2% (98)	38.4% (89)	59.4% (136)	34.9% (81)
Consumer research	10.6%	11.1% (105)	14.4% (136)	5.4% (51)	4.8% (45)	13.4% (126)
Sales force management	32.2%	28.6% (89)	31.5% (98)	34.5% (107)	33.5% (104)	32.1% (100)
Advertising and promotion	28.9%	41.2% (143)	48.1% (166)	15.7% (54)	9.5% (33)	27.6% (96)
After-sales service	26.3%	20.9% (79)	10.7% (41)	29.6% (113)	39.6% (151)	31.4% (119)
Pricing	53.3%	61.2% (115)	58.6% (110)	63.3% (119)	46.0% (86)	43.3% (81)
Distribution	25.0%	32.4% (130)	36.0% (144)	37.9% (152)	14.8% (59)	10.7% (43)
Finance and credit	8.3%	8.3% (100)	9.0% (108)	10.2% (123)	10.1% (122)	6.0% (72)
Transport and storage	5.7%	5.1% (89)	7.3% (128)	9.4% (165)	3.4% (60)	3.5% (61)
Public relations	10.7%	6.1% (57)	7.8% (73)	6.3% (59)	5.2% (49)	19.0% (178)

Source: G. J. Hooley, C. J. West and J. E. Lynch (1983), *Marketing in the UK: A Survey of Current Practice and Performance*, Institute of Marketing.

Table 13.3   *'Pressure' in various marketing areas as perceived by managers*

	Europe	USA
Pricing	78.0	80.6
Product quality	73.6	63.3
New products	68.2	78.5
Internal staffing and training	67.6	67.1
Selling costs	67.2	70.4
New competition	64.2	55.0
Government regulation	63.0	50,1
Product differentiation	62.6	62.6
Distribution	60.4	64.6
After sales service	53.8	66.4
Advertising	47.8	56.4

Source: USA, *Marketing News*, 11 June 1986, p. 1; Europe, Author's study 1986.

greater market and price transparency and encouraged buyers to compare price and quality more systematically.

More recent evidence is not as detailed as that reported in the preceding studies undertaken in the 1980s. However, such evidence as there is underlines the conclusions of both Said and Simon that, under conditions of excess supply or depressed demand (recession), competition intensifies and price assumes increased importance as a competitive weapon. Indeed in the UK in 1996 there is much anecdotal evidence to suggest that sellers' continued use of price as a major marketing factor has resulted in a situation where consumers give it much more attention than hitherto and believe that further discounts or price cuts will always be forthcoming. In other words, current practice has led to a situation which could be characterised as 'cutting your competitor's throat and bleeding to death yourself'. The inevitable consequence (as predicted by economic theory) is that the least efficient and least effective producers will go to the wall.

In developing a price policy it is clear that one has to consider both the external environment in which one has to compete and also the internal factors which condition and control the courses of action open to the firm. A brief review of these follows.

 # External price determinants

A major determinant of price policy is the structure of the market in which the firm is selling its output. Many authors tend to confuse industry structure with market structure, and limit their attention to the size and number of firms engaged in creating perfect substitutes. Thus it is common to find references to monopolistic and oligopolistic industries when the total output of a given product is concentrated in the hands of one, or a few, firms. Although it is acknowledged that the true monopolist is a price-maker, and that oligopolistic industries frequently exhibit price rigidity owing to the price leadership of a dominant firm, it is felt that the industry view oversimplifies the true situation.

Conventionally, the industry approach would distinguish the manufacture of aluminium, steel, glass, paper and plastics on the basis that their output possesses different physical properties and is the result of distinctive production processes. Each would be classified as a separate industry, yet all compete with one another for the packaging market. This suggests that one must take into account not only the prices of perfect substitutes but also the prices of all goods which compete for the same market and can be used to satisfy the same basic wants. Certainly no self-respecting buyer is going to confine his attention to a single material when several acceptable alternatives are available, and the technique of value analysis has been developed largely to permit comparative cost analysis of competing substitutes.

If the above arguments are accepted, then it follows that the firm must look beyond the narrowly defined industry of which it considers itself a member, and should evaluate the price structure of its end market and the policies of all firms/industries operating in that market. (In the language of the economist, one must analyse the cross-elasticity of demand.)

The second major external price determinant is best summarised by the economist's concept of elasticity. Essentially elasticity measures the responsiveness of demand to changes in price, i.e. it is a measure of price sensitivity. Thus if a 1 per cent change in price results in a change in the amount demanded of more than 1 per cent demand is said to be elastic, if less than 1 per cent then demand is inelastic, and a directly proportionate change indicates unitary elasticity. Elasticity of demand is conditioned by the importance of the product in the consumer's scale of preferences, by the disposable income of existing and potential consumers, by the existence of substitutes and a number of other, lesser factors. As a summary measure it is of great value in determining the firm's basic attitude to price – if demand is elastic pricing will be a major policy area, if inelastic it will be of secondary consequence.

Thirdly, the firm's pricing policy will be influenced by government policy as expressed in the extant and proposed legislation in such areas as price maintenance, monopolistic practices, minimum performance standards for products, and so on; for example the introduction of cut-price detergents by Procter & Gamble and Lever Brothers following the Monopolies Commission recommendation to this effect.

Internal price determinants

The major factor conditioning the firm's price policy is its own definition of the business it is in, for this will determine the products it will produce and the nature of the markets it will seek to exploit. The product mix identifies the firm with an industry, while its market specifies the firms, industries and products with which it will compete, and the dimensions along which it will compete.

Traditionally, the firm's success has been measured by its profitability, which is simply a measure of the amount by which income exceeds expenditure. If, as implied earlier, the majority of firms accept the going market price, it is evident that profits will depend very largely on the firm's ability to minimise expenditures or costs. To this end considerable effort has been devoted to the development of sophisticated cost measurement and control systems, and management is often happier to immerse itself in the tangible realities of such systems that grapple with the complexities of price determination. Further, both shareholders and the Government require the firm to account for the way in which it spends its income, and so emphasise the need for detailed cost analyses and statements. As will be seen below, such data are widely used in the formulation of prices.

The third internal constraint on the firm's price policy is the nature and extent of its corporate resources, which are discussed in Chapter 19 and will not be reiterated here.

It follows from the brief outline above that the price-setter's discretion is circumscribed by a number of factors, admirably summarised by Joel Dean (1951) as:

1. The number, relative sizes and product lines of competitors who sell products to do the same job.

2. The likelihood of potential competition.
3. The stage of consumer acceptance of the product.
4. The degree of potential market segmentation and price discrimination.
5. The degree of physical difference between the seller's product and those of other companies.
6. The opportunities for variation in the product–service bundle.
7. The richness of the mixture of service and reputation in the product bundle.   (p. 402)

■ Pricing objectives

In an article entitled 'How to Price for Maximum Profits', Jules E. Anderson (1956) quotes a survey by the National Industrial Conference Board which revealed that only 4 out of 155 leading US manufacturers used a clear-cut, written procedure in setting prices. Although dated, these findings tend to confirm a widely held belief that most firms lack clearly defined, explicit pricing objectives and formalised pricing procedures. It is the author's opinion that this belief is erroneous, and based upon faulty data derived from poorly designed surveys. This opinion tends to be supported by the findings of more sophisticated researchers, in particular those of Robert Lanzillotti (1956) in 'Pricing Objectives in Large Companies', and W. Warren Haynes (1962) in *Pricing Decisions in Small Business*, both of whom have undertaken extensive field research into the firm's pricing objectives.

Lanzillotti's findings were: 'The most typical pricing objectives cited were: (1) pricing to achieve a target return on investment; (2) stabilisation of price and margin; (3) pricing to realise a target market share; and (4) pricing to meet or prevent competition.' The main conclusions drawn from this study are considered sufficiently significant to be quoted verbatim, namely:

The general hypothesis which emerges is that (a) the large company has a fairly well-defined pricing goal that is related to a long-range profit horizon; (b) its

management seeks – especially in multiproduct multimarket operations – a simultaneous decision with respect to price, cost, and product characteristics; and (c) its pricing formulas are handy devices for checking the internal consistency of the separate decisions as against the general company objective. Under this hypothesis no single theory of the firm – and certainly no single motivational hypothesis such as profit maximisation – is likely to impose an unambiguous course of action for the firm for any given situation; nor will it provide a satisfactory basis for valid and useful predictions of price behaviour (pp. 938–9).

It seems reasonable to conclude that the pricing policies are in almost every case equivalent to a company policy that represents an order of priorities and choice among competing objectives rather than policies tested by any simple concept of profit maximisation (p. 939).

Another relevant aspect of the data for theoretical analysis is the conception of the market held by managements of large corporations. Individual products, markets, and pricing are not considered in isolation; the unit of decision-making is the enterprise, and pricing and marketing strategies are viewed in this global context. Because of the tremendously complex joint-cost problems and lack of knowledge of actual relationships between cost and output or sales, on the one hand, and the joint-revenue aspects of multiproduct companies, on the other, pricing is frequently done for product groups with an eye to the over-all profit position of the company. This means that costing of products ends up as a result of price policy rather than the reverse. In view of the various external pressures on the company and the nature of the strategy of the enterprise, it is doubtful if price would have any closer relationship to actual costs were detailed cost data available to management. The incentive to realise target rates of profit for the long haul better suits the objectives of management-controlled companies than any desire to profiteer or seek windfall profits (p. 940).

From these conclusions it is clear that firms do establish pricing objectives, even though they may not be stated explicitly. Frequently such objectives are implicit in the company's overall objective, in other cases they may take the form of a generalised statement such as:

'All prices must cover fully allocated costs.'
'Prices will not exceed those asked by immediate competitors.'

'Prices will be set which will discourage the entry of new firms into the market.'

'All prices must yield a return of investment not less than X per cent.'

In the analysis by Said, referred to earlier, the findings did not support conventional price theory which assumes that profit is the sole and principal motivation of business firms. Indeed her evidence suggests strongly that firms are motivated by many objectives simultaneously related to profitability, security and sales. As can be seen from Figure 13.1, survival is seen as the most important goal, followed by short-term profits, liquidity, medium-term profits, market share, sales revenue, with long-run profits seen as of relatively little importance. Not evident from the figure but of considerable interest is the fact that divisional managers and accountants placed much more stress on short-term survival/liquidity/profit goals than did managing directors and marketing managers who took a longer-term perspective and emphasised market share and long-run profitability.

In *Marketing: Theory and Practice* (Baker, 1995) Professor Adamantios Diamantopoulos provides an authoritative overview of the subject of pricing and summarises the findings of research into pricing objectives into a Table which is reproduced below as Table 13.4. (This chapter, and indeed all the chapters in *Marketing: Theory and Practice* are strongly recommended for reading in conjunction with this book.) In his commentary on Table 13.4, Diamantopoulos points out that firms seek to achieve multiple objectives through their pricing policies; that while some sort of profit goal enters the objective function of virtually all firms, its exact formulation can vary substantially; that sales revenue and market share dominate volume objectives; that there is little support for short-run profit maximisation but there is for long-run profit maximisation; overall, however, firms seek to earn 'satisfactory' profits.

Figure 13.1 *Values of importance quoted to pricing objectives*

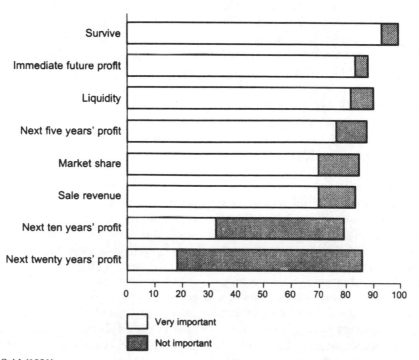

Source: Hanna A. Said (1981).

Table 13.4 *A taxonomy of pricing objectives*

Profit	*Volume*	*Financial*
● Money Profit	● Market Share	● Cash Flow
● Gross/Net Margin	● Sales Volume	● Earnings per Share
● Contribution Margin	● Sales Revenue	● Price Earnings Ratio
● Return on Sales	● Sales Growth	● Dividends
● Return on Costs	● Capacity Utilisation	
● Return on Capital Employed		
● Return on Net Worth		
● Profit Growth		
Competition-Oriented	*Customer-Oriented*	*Miscellaneous*
● Matching/Undercutting competition	● Fair Price Levels	● Projection of High Quality Image
● Avoidance of Price Wars	● Goodwill	● Avoidance of Government Intervention
● Limit Entry	● Value-For-Money	● Survival/Security
● Price Stability	● Full Price Range	
● Money Profit	● Price Maintenance in the Channel	

Source: A. Diamontopoulous in Baker (1995).

Pricing formulas and methods

Even though the firm may not have committed itself to a formal statement of price policy, in practice its pricing behaviour is usually sufficiently consistent to permit identification and classification. Observation indicates that there are a limited number of pricing formulas, or methods, in general use, and these may be classified as:

Full-cost or cost-plus pricing

In simple terms, all this involves is the addition of a predetermined margin to the full unit cost of production and distribution, without reference to prevailing demand conditions. In practice, it is doubtful if the firm can establish its true unit cost in advance, owing to uncertainty as to the volume it can make/sell. Broadly speaking, all costs may be classified as fixed or variable. Fixed costs are incurred irrespective of the volume of output and are the result of management policy, for example the depreciation of fixed assets, the level of selling, general and administrative overheads,

while variable costs fluctuate more or less directly with the volume of output, for example raw material and labour costs. In that unit cost is computed by dividing total cost by output in units, it is clear that this can only be established when the two quantities are known. The price-setter may forecast sales volume and compute unit cost on the basis of this estimate, adding the predetermined margin in order to arrive at a price. It would be purely fortuitous if demand at this price were to coincide exactly with the available supply, with the result that the seller will either be left with unsold units or else will sell his total output at a lesser profit than could have been obtained. Further, as Lanzillotti implies, the allocation of fixed costs to given products tends to be arbitrary, so that the unit cost used as the basis for a price may bear no relation to true cost at all.

Although cost plus a fixed margin may be a valid method to adopt when deciding whether to enter a new market, most sellers would be prepared to vary this price in the light of potential consumer reaction to it, implicit in current market prices. If this is so, then the price-setter's decision rule is rather different from that generally associated with full-cost pricing – cost plus

Table 13.5 *Drawbacks of cost-plus pricing*

- Difficult, in advance, to determine such costs as construction, material price changes, and similar costs
- Difficult to allocate joint costs to specific products
- Not based on realistic profit goal or market share objective
- Ignores elasticity of demand
- Generally disregards competition
- Buyers are more concerned about the cost and value of product to them than about production and selling costs to supplier
- Does not distinguish between out-of-pocket and 'sunk' costs*
- Difficult to determine 'fair' return
- Ignores capital requirements and return on investment
- Many costs vary with volume, and volume depends on price charged

*Those which are spent, regardless of production level.

Source: John Winkler (1991), 'Pricing' in M. J. Baker (ed.), *The Marketing Book*, 2nd edn (London: Heinemann), Chapter 16.

a predetermined margin is not the price, it is a minimum acceptable price and the actual price adopted may be any amount greater than this. This being so, it is erroneous to contend that prices based on cost takes no account of consumer demand. However, cost-plus pricing has a number of drawbacks admirably summarised by John Winkler in Table 13.5.

Break-even analysis

Break-even analysis utilises the concepts of fixed and variable costs, and enables the price-setter to investigate the implications of any number of price–volume alternatives.

The first step in a break-even analysis is to compute the firm's total cost curve by adding

Figure 13.2 *Break-even chart*

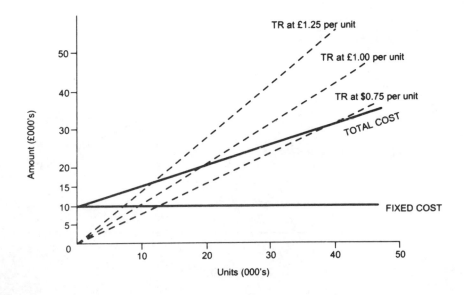

the variable costs incurred at different levels of output to the fixed costs; for example, if fixed costs (FC) = £10 000, and unit variable cost (VC) = £0.25, then total cost (TC) = £10 000 + £0.25x where x = the number of units produced. The next step is to compute total revenue (TR) curves for the range of prices under consideration and plot these graphically as shown in Figure 13.2.

Clearly the 'break-even' point for a given price lies at the intersection of the total revenue curve for that price and the total cost curve; for example, with a price of £0.75 the firm will break even at a sales volume of 40 000 units. On its own, this information is of little value to the price-setter, unless he has some feeling for the likely volume of demand over the range of prices for which he has calculated break-even points. In reality, the price-setter will usually have at least a preliminary analysis of the potential market for the product, from which he may derive a hypothetical demand curve as shown in Figure 13.3.

By reference to the demand curve it can be seen that at a price of £0.75, 36 250 units will be demanded and the firm would incur a loss.

Closer inspection would seem to indicate that the best price is £1.00, at which 20 000 units will be sold.

Marginal costing/contribution analysis

Break-even analysis allocates fixed costs to a product at a predetermined rate in such a way that, collectively, the firm's products will absorb the firm's total fixed costs. Many price theorists contend that this conventional accounting approach can lead to incorrect decisions, and advocate the adoption of techniques based on marginal analysis as developed by economists.

In essence the marginal approach states that one should ignore fixed costs and concentrate on the relationship between variable cost and revenue, usually termed the 'contribution'. For example, if the variable cost of producing a unit is £0.25 and this unit may be sold for £0.50, then the contribution is +£0.25. It is understood that contribution means 'contribution to fixed costs, variable marketing costs, and profits', and the firm's objective in setting price should be to

Figure 13.3 *Hypothetical demand curve*

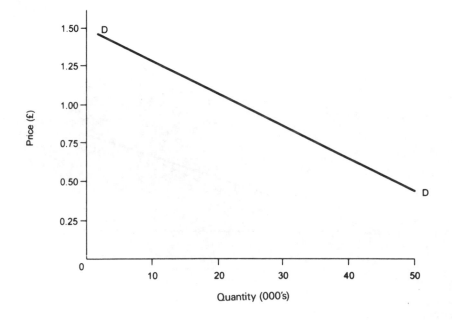

maximise the total contribution. If average unit cost is used as a criterion, then it is likely that the firm will reject any price less than average cost, and so forego the contribution which sale at such a price would generate. A simplified example will help clarify this point.

During the day many trains in the London area carry only a few passengers, and it seems clear that the revenues earned must be less than the average cost of running a train. Ignoring the social responsibilities of a public transportation authority, such a practice seems economically suicidal. However, marginal analysis reveals that elimination of these services would lead to lower profits (bigger losses!), in that the incremental cost incurred in running a train is negligible. The fixed investment necessary to cope with rush-hour traffic flows has already been made

Figure 13.4 *Pricing – an example of decision criteria*

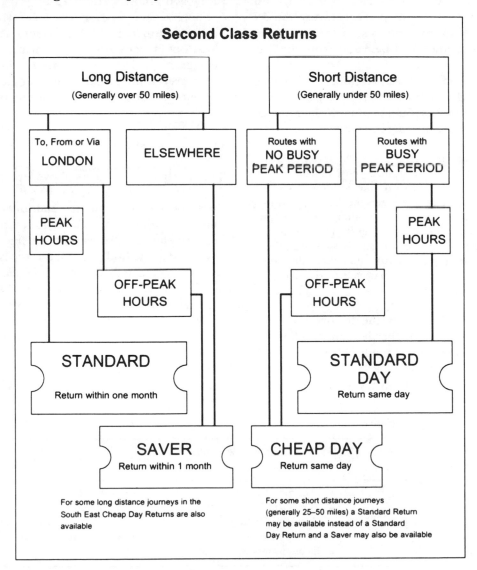

Source: *Railnews*, October 1984.

and is a 'sunk' cost; maintenance and engineering crews have to be paid to keep the rolling stock and track in good repair, as do railwaymen to operate the signals, drive the trains, and so on. While it is true that some of the latter may work a split shift, the majority do not, and two shifts must be employed as a minimum. Thus, running off-peak trains adds little to the fixed costs to which the transportation authority is committed if it is to provide reasonably adequate commuter services –the cost of the power used and a slight increase in maintenance and operating cost. Provided that sufficient passengers use the off-peak services to cover the cost of these variables, then a contribution will be earned towards fixed costs.

An article in *Railnews* (October 1984) illustrates how British Rail used these principles in seeking to maximise its revenue through a carefully thought-out pricing strategy:

A new range of rail fares is to be introduced next May to make ticket categories more understandable, and bring prices more into line with our markets.

By introducing the changes, the passenger business aims to increase revenue, encourage off-peak travel and compete more effectively in the travel market.

Earnings are expected to increase by £10 million – £15 million a year, mostly on Inter-City travel. Passenger-miles are also expected to rise about 500 million miles a year.

Figure 13.4 illustrates the factors taken into account in arriving at the decision to offer four basic fares – Standard, Standard Day, Saver, and Cheap Day – and provides a clear example of how a once-declining industry is using marketing

principles to restore its fortunes. (While British Rail now use a different fare structure it follows similar principles in seeking to optimise revenue from a combination of peak and off-peak pricing.)

Many managers find it difficult to ignore fixed costs and so make incorrect decisions. The argument that a firm has spent £x million in developing a product, and so must continue with its production and sale in the face of unfavourable use reactions, is a classic example. The best advice in such a situation might well be 'Don't throw good money after bad'.

Contribution analysis does not simplify the problems inherent in forecasting demand and costs, but it does ensure that management does not reject projects which would improve the firm's overall profitability solely because they are not self-supporting on an average cost basis.

Other methods

The methods described above are those most frequently encountered in practice. However, they possess many faults and difficulties and numerous other approaches and techniques have been developed. Diamantopoulos (*op. cit.*) classifies pricing methods into three types which he calls Cost-oriented, Demand-oriented and Competition-oriented as summarised in Table 13.6.

In commenting on these methods Diamantopoulos observes that in most cases firms use more than one method. For example, for routine pricing decisions they will use cost-plus; for special situations, for example to win a large order they might well use contribution pricing.

Table 13.6 *Pricing methods*

Cost-oriented	Pricing Methods Demand-oriented	Competition-oriented
• Cost-plus Pricing	• Marginal Analysis	• Product Analysis Pricing
• Contribution Pricing	• Trial and Error Pricing	• Value Pricing
• Target (ROI) Pricing	• Intuitive Pricing	• Price Leadership/Followership
• Price-minus Pricing	• Market Pricing	• Competitive Parity Pricing
• Return on Costs	• Monopsonistic Pricing	

Source: A. Diamontopoulous (op. cit.).

With regard to *type* of pricing method cost-oriented approaches are characterised by an emphasis on covering some combination of cost element; demand-oriented methods focus on the customer and their likely reaction to price while competition-oriented approaches are concerned with competitive reaction.

Diamantopoulos confirms that cost-oriented methods predominate in industry with cost-plus being the most popular. Market pricing – charging what the market will bear is the second most popular approach with following the market leader third. The use of the other methods is limited and tends to reflect special circumstances. Elsewhere, Diamantopoulos and Mathews (1995) in *Making Pricing Decisions* has observed that:

> Undoubtedly, the most important conclusion permeating the entire spectrum of findings [into price research] is that pricing behaviour is situational in nature, i.e. influenced by the specific organizational and market setting at hand. The impact of organizational factors is reflected in (a) the structure of price responsibility within the firm and (b) the kind of informational inputs and approaches utilized in price-setting. The impact of the market environment, on the other hand, is reflected in the different market and competitive conditions associated with the various product markets served by the firm

which, in turn, gives rise to differences in practically all areas of price decision-making. In this context, it was demonstrated quite conclusively that the nature of the market environment impinges upon (a) the importance attached to short- as well as long-run pricing objectives, (b) the suitability of alternative pricing methods, (c) the frequency and timing of price changes, (d) the effectiveness of promotional price-cutting, (e) the demand curve perceptions of decision-makers and (f) the appropriateness of different new product pricing strategies. A summary picture in provided in Table 13.7.

Some insight into current practice was provided by project MACS (Baker and Hart, 1989) as indicated by Figure 13.5.

Information on pricing methods and the use of cost in price setting is to be found in Said's (1981) thesis 'Relevance of Price Theory' and is reproduced in Tables 13.8 and 13.9. From these tables the following conclusions may be drawn:

1. Considerable attention is given to cost even when prices are not finally based on cost.
2. Full-cost methods are used much more extensively than marginal cost methods.
3. Firms are flexible in their approach to pricing with the great majority varying their profit margin to reflect market conditions.

Figure 13.5 *Pricing in successful and less successful companies*

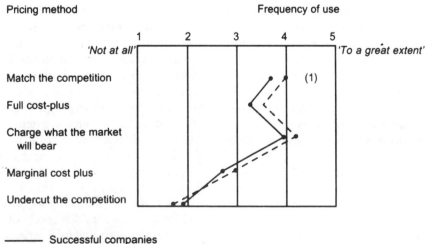

——— Successful companies
– – – Unsuccessful companies
(1) Significant at the 5 per cent level

Table 13.7 *Influence of the market environment on pricing behaviour*

Market characteristics	Pricing objectives	Pricing methods	Price changes	Price–volume relationships	New product pricing strategies
Market growth	•				
No. of competitors	•			•	•
Market concentration	•			•	
Product substitutability	•	•	•	•	•
Market price sensitivity	•	•	•	•	
Price competition	•	•	•	•	
Non-price competition	•	•		•	
Competitive price-cutting	•		•	•	

Source: A. Diamantopoulous (1995) *Marketing Pricing Decisions.*

■ Pricing strategies

In *Price Management*, Henry Simon (1989) confirms that while it is the product which provides value, benefit or utility it is price which enables one to make comparative assessments between different products and it is this alone which 'determines the amount a customer must sacrifice to acquire a product'. However, in addition to its importance in establishing the price value relation, Simon cites six reasons why price is an important element in the marketing mix.

1. Price elasticity is 20 times greater than advertising elasticity; that is, a 1 per cent change has a sales effect 20 times as big as a 1 per cent change in advertising expenditure.
2. The sales effect of a price change is often immediate, and so measurable, while changes in other mix variables are usually lagged and difficult to quantify.
3. Price changes are easy to effect compared with varying other mix variables.
4. Competitors react more quickly to price changes.
5. Price does not require an initially negative cash flow as do other marketing expenditures such as advertising which have a lagged effect.
6. Price and the product are the only two mix elements which feature significantly in strategic planning concepts.

So far, attention has been focused on quantitative aspects of price determination and little consideration given to the qualitative factors which shape the final pricing decision. Given the difficulties involved in constructing a demand schedule, pricing formulas can only give a broad indication of the range within which the desired sales volume might be achieved. Hence, the final price decision must depend upon a judgmental assessment of the impact of a given price strategy. In broad terms there are two alternatives open to the marketer – a high price approach aimed at 'skimming the cream' off the market, and a low price strategy aimed at pre-empting a significant share of the total market.

High price strategies are appropriate to mature or saturated markets, which show a degree of segmentation on the basis of quality, design features and so forth, or to the introduction of a product which differs significantly from anything currently available. In the case of existing markets, consumers in the higher income groups are often prepared to pay a premium for products which are differentiated from those appealing to the mass market; for example a Rolls-Royce or Toyota Lexus compared with a Renault or a Ford Escort. Owing to the limited demand at the higher prices, a small, high-quality producer can maintain a profitable level of sales without building up a sufficiently large market share to attract the competition of firms catering to the mass market. This does not mean that the latter

Table 13.8 *Pricing methods*

| | Extent of using the method | | | | | | (a) Total response | | |
	Very great extent	Great extent	Moderate	Little extent	Very little	Not applicable	x	n	N
(1) Domestic market									
Adding a percentage to cost (cost plus)	*87(29%)	30(10%)	52(18%)	33(11%)	52(18.0%)	42(14%)	3.199	296(100%)	356
Fixing required gross profit margin on selling prices	84(29%)	50(17%)	53(19%)	22(8%)	49(17.0%)	28(10%)	2.951	286(100%)	356
Prices to realise a specified level of profit on sales	62(23%)	57(21%)	54(20%)	33(12%)	37(13.5%)	31(11%)	3.069	274(100%)	356
Following market leader	28(10%)	27(10%)	43(16%)	45(17%)	62(23.0%)	66(24%)	4.048	271(100%)	356
Charging what the market will bear	161(50%)	73(22%)	43(13%)	13(4%)	24(7.4%)	12(4%)	2.086	326(100%)	356
(2) Export									
Adding a percentage to cost (cost plus)	72(34%)	22(10%)	29(14%)	18(9%)	27(13.0%)	41(20%)	3.139	209(100%)	275
Fixing required gross profit margin on selling prices	49(25%)	25(13%)	42(21%)	20(10%)	32(16.0%)	30(15%)	3.258	198(100%)	275
Prices to realise a specified level of profit on sales	37(20%)	3(17%)	33(17%)	19(10%)	31(17.0%)	35(19%)	3.420	188(100%)	275
Following market leader	11(6%)	16(9%)	21(12%)	22(12%)	42(23.0%)	68(38%)	4.511	180(100%)	275
Charging what the market will bear	126(55%)	31(14%)	25(11%)	11(5%)	17(7.0%)	18(8%)	2.193	228(100%)	275

* To be read 87(29%) out of 296 companies use cost plus in the home market to a very great extent.

(a) The greater the mean, the less the extent of using the method

X = the arithmetic mean

n = number of valid observations

N = number of cases included in the sample for export = number of firms' exports

Source: Hanna A. Said (1981), 'The Relevance of Price Theory to Price Practice', unpublished Ph.D. dissertation University of Strathclyde.

Table 13.9   *Type of cost used for different pricing methods*

	Full cost	Marginal cost	Do not use cost	n	N
Domestic market					
Adding a percentage to cost (cost plus)	69% (175)*	28% (70)	3% (9)	100% (254)	356
Fixing required gross profit margin on selling price	75% (192)	22% (57)	3% (9)	100% (258)	356
Target pricing	73% (178)	24% (57)	3% (8)	100% (243)	356
Following market leader	75% (153)	21% (43)	4% (9)	100% (205)	356
Charging what the market will bear	71% (224)	25% (78)	12% (9)	100% (311)	356
Export					
Adding a percentage to cost (cost plus)	59% (99)	39% (65)	2% (4)	100% (168)	275
Fixing required gross profit margin on selling price	65% (99)	31% (53)	4% (6)	100% (168)	275
Target pricing	64% (97)	33% (51)	3% (5)	100% (153)	275
Following market leader	55% (73)	30% (34)	4% (5)	100% (112)	275
Charging what the market will bear	64% (133)	33% (70)	3% (7)	100% (210)	275

* To be read 69 per cent (175) of 254 firms which use cost plus refer to full cost in deciding their selling prices

n = number of valid observations

N = number of cases included in the sample

Source: Hanna A. Said (1981), 'The Relevance of Price Theory to Price Practice', unpublished Ph.D. dissertation University of Strathclyde.

type of firm will not diversify into the high price segment to make fuller use of its resources, as did Ford with its purchase of Jaguar, but the established reputation of the quality producer will provide a high degree of protection against such competition.

Skimming the market is also attractive to the firm with a new and unique product. As noted earlier, new product development invariably represents a considerable investment on the part of the innovator, and a high initial price offers the opportunity to limit the costs of launching the product into the market while earning monopoly profits. A good example of such a strategy is the launching of the Polaroid Land camera, which was originally put on the market at a price of around £100, with very limited distribution and promotion. The novelty of a camera which could produce a finished print within a matter of seconds attracted a lot of free publicity, as well as being something of a status symbol because of its price. As demand at the initial high price was exhausted, Polaroid lowered prices and 'slid down the demand curve', with the result that a basic camera is now available at around £10. It is interesting to note that in the United States, where the camera was developed and first put on sale, a rather different strategy was adopted and the camera offered originally at a relatively low price. The reasoning in this instance was that the purchase of a camera tends to be once and for all, whereas there is a continuing market for film, thus the more cameras that were sold the greater would be the demand for film. As the film was unique, and protected by patents, competition from other manufacturers such as Eastman-Kodak was precluded and offered greater long-run profitability, provided sufficient cameras could be sold.

When adopting a skimming strategy, with the intention of subsequently reducing price to appeal to a wider market, it is important not to create ill will by reducing price too quickly. This danger may be reduced by differentiating the appearance of the product and offering it as a 'stripped-down', or economy model. The use of this strategy is to be seen in the marketing of PCs and electronic calculators, as well as camcorders, mobile phones, and so on.

A low price policy recommends itself in a number of circumstances, pre-eminent among which is entering a market with a high price-elasticity of demand. The newcomer will have to achieve a certain level of sales in order to break even, and in the short run may only be able to wrest sales from existing products through the medium of an attractive discount on current prices. Penetration pricing, as this strategy is sometimes termed, usually involves the firm in accepting a loss initially, while achieving sampling of the product and the development of brand loyalty. As suggested earlier, however, few firms are willing to buy market share openly for fear of setting off a price war, and a penetration policy is usually disguised as some form of sales promotion, for example price-off labels, coupons, and so on. Where the firm possesses a cost advantage it has little to fear from a low price strategy, but it is rare that a new entrant into a market can undercut the existing brand leaders owing to the economies of scale open to them. In fact, contrary to popular belief, oligopolists often practise a low price policy to discourage the entry of new competitors into the market.

In 1954, E. R. Hawkins elaborated on these two basic strategies when he listed the pricing policies described by 'marketing specialists'. These policies may be summarised as:

1. *Odd pricing* – that is, the adoption of prices ending in odd numbers. This policy is notably prevalent in food retailing, and is also used extensively on low ticket items in general. The adoption of such prices implies the existence of a stepped or discontinuous demand curve; that is avoidance of intermediate prices ending in round numbers suggests that the price-setter believes that demand is totally inelastic at that price, for example reducing an item from 25p to 24p would not increase demand so price is reduced to 23p.

2. *Psychological pricing*. This differs from odd pricing in that the price need not be an odd number but merely one that has an apparent psychological significance for the buyer; for example 95p instead of £1.

3. *Customary prices*. Such prices are fixed by custom; for example the old 6d bar of chocolate. Like the first two strategies the adoption of such prices assumes a kink in the demand curve. (The abolition of resale price maintenance and inflation seem to have seen the demise of customary prices for products like shoes and confectionery where they were formerly commonplace. However, 'psychological' prices still prevail, and 99p seems to have assumed a particular significance in this context. However, with the disappearance of 1p and 1 cent coins in many countries this will have to change!)

4. *Pricing at the market/meeting the competition*. This strategy presumes a marked inelasticity of demand below the current market price, such that a price reduction would not be justified by increased sales revenues. This approach is frequently adopted to avoid price wars.

5. *Prestige pricing*. This strategy implies a skimming approach in which the seller gives prestige to his product by asking a price well in excess of those asked for near perfect substitutes; for example Estée Lauder cosmetics, After Eight Mints.

6. *Price lining*. This policy of adopting specific prices for certain types of merchandise is common among retailers and is closely related to both psychological and customary prices; for example women's dresses, nylon stockings.

7. *Geographic pricing*. This policy is sometimes used where the marketer serves a number of distinct regional markets and can adopt different prices in each without creating consumer or distributor ill will. Petrol is priced in this way, depending on the distance of the garage from the nearest bulk terminal.

8. *Dual pricing strategy*. The marketer sells the same product at two or more different prices. Within the same market it is necessary to use different brands, but in distinct regional markets it may be possible to justify price differentials on the grounds of varying distribution costs, cf. petrol.

The arguments for skimming and penetrating strategies are admirably summarised by Simon (1989) in Table 13.10.

In the Introduction to this chapter it was noted that pricing tends to be relegated to a secondary role in the formulation of competitive strategies. To a large degree this is due to the fact that price is highly visible and readily understood by consumers and competitors alike, whereas other elements of the marketing mix are less capable of direct and objective assessment.

However, as was noted in the Introduction to this chapter, an increasingly competitive climate has resulted in much more attention being given to the use of price as both a tactical and strategic weapon. An extended discussion of the topic is to be found in A. F. Millman's 'Price Wars' (1983),

in which he cites several markets where price has been used extensively as a competitive weapon – retailing, airline seats, petrol, motor cars, cross channel ferries, and so on. In some cases, such as Tesco's *checkout* campaign, the results have been spectacular and beneficial; in others, such as Freddie Laker's *Skytrain*, they have been spectacular and fatal.

In his analysis Millman covers a number of issues not discussed here including the attitudes to risk of marketing executives and the legal implications of the Resale Prices Act of 1976. He also makes a useful distinction between price wars and price attrition and argues that the latter 'are characterised by long periods during which the total price *package* is gradually worn down' interspersed with short bursts of high activity. By contrast a price war is 'typically the result of a battle for market share which can easily get out of hand if there is no pressure group or check mechanism with sufficient mobility and authority to restore order'.

It was Fellner who described price as 'the blunt instrument of competition'. Under the right conditions its use may bring quick and

Table 13.10 *Arguments for skimming and penetration strategies*

Skimming strategy	*Penetration stra# strategy*
• High short-run profits little affected by discounting • Quick pay-back for real innovation during the period of monopolistic market position, reduces long-run competitive risk, quick amortisation of R&D expenses • High profit in early life-cycle phases, reduces the risk of obsolescence • Allows for price reduction over time • Avoids the necessity of price increases • High price implies positive prestige and quality • Requires fewer financial resources • Requires lower capacity	• High total contribution through fast sales growth in spite of low unit contribution margins • Takes advantage of positive intrapersonal (consumer goods) or interpersonal (durable goods) carryover effects, builds up a strong market position (with the potential of higher prices and/or higher sales in the future) • Takes advantage of short-run cost reductions through (static) economies of scale • Allows for fast increase of the cumulative quality by accelerating the experience curve effect. Achieves a large cost advantage that competitors will find difficult to match • Reduces the risk of failure; low introductory price gives some assurance of low probability of failure • Deters potential competitors from market entry, or delays their entry

Source: H. Simon (1989), *Price Management* (Amsterdam: Elsevier Science Publishers).

beneficial results but you are more likely to remain in good health if you can avoid being the victim of price warfare.

■ Perception and pricing

In Chapter 6 we proposed a composite model of buying behaviour which placed considerable emphasis upon the mediating influence of selective perception in determining not only what cues or stimuli are given conscious attention but also on the interpretation given to the information. It is the phenomenon of selective perception which modifies the strictly economic explanation of the manner in which demand will react to supply at different prices and so may be seen to contradict the concept of 'economic rationality'. According to the latter concept buyers will always select the supplier offering the lowest price but, in reality, the market for many goods and services will contain a variety of different prices for superficially similar offerings. The explanation is, of course, that even if the offerings are objectively perfect substitutes one for another buyers may perceive them subjectively as being different. Much of the effort of competing suppliers is directed specifically at achieving such perceived differences through the creation of reputation, brand loyalty and the augmentation of the core product.

Simon (1989) devotes a chapter to the subject of 'Price Management and Psychology' and provides a comprehensive summary of the variables which influence price perception and evaluation which is reproduced as Table 13.11.

From Table 13.11 it is clear that a multiplicity of factors bear upon the buyers' (both consumer and industrial) perception of price. In addition, their relative influence may well vary from one buying decision to the next as a consequence of changes in the buyers' status and/or the circumstances or context in which the decision has to be made. Thus, while there has been much research which suggests that buyers (particularly individual consumers) have poor price recall it would be wrong to assume that this reflects price insensitivity or lack of consideration for price in making a buying decision. Indeed, there is also a considerable body of research which indicates that at the

Table 13.11 *Variables which influence price perception and evaluation*

Motivational variables	Cognitive variables	Situation variables
• personal involvement • striving for – social recognition – quality – cognitive consistency – shopping convenience – saving	• ability to compare quality • ability to remember and compare prices • experience • trust in the supplier • self-confidence • application of simplified decision rules (brand loyalty, etc.)	• way of exhibiting price (form and quality, etc.) • mode of payment • time pressure • competitive products and prices • complexity of purchasing task • variability of prices • price labelling • product use • financial situations of buyers • price image of the store

Source: H. Simon (1989), *Price Management* (Amsterdam: Elsevier Science Publishers).

time when a buyer makes a purchase decision they have a good feel for what is available in the market place so that the decision is 'rational' in terms of what the buyer is seeking to optimise at that precise time and in that specific context.

Of particular interest in terms of the psychology of pricing is the case where the price itself becomes of major importance in influencing the prospective buyer's perception of the quality of the offering. Simon provides an excellent overview of the evidence that price is used as an indicator of quality and cites Zeithman's (1988) finding that much of this is contradictory. That said, and despite the lack of much empirical support, Simon (1989) proposes 16 conditions or contexts where 'we expect the phenomenon...' to occur, namely:

Conditions under which quality will be inferred from the price.

1. Brand and manufacturer names do not play an important role, for example rugs, furniture.
2. Consumers have little or no experience:

   - Because the product is new. Note that the quality indication is effective only if the new product is not a genuine innovation which is beyond the existing reference system.
   - Because the purchase interval is long; that is, for infrequently purchased 'low involvement' products.
   - Because it is not usual for people to share their experience with the product.

3. Objective quality is difficult to evaluate:

   - Because of the technical complexity.
   - Because of the particular importance of such attributes as durability, reliability, and so forth.

4. Considerable quality differences are perceived.
5. Price itself is an important product attribute.

   - Prestige products (Snob, Veblen effect).

   - Use or display of the product are associated with social risk (wine, liquor, cosmetics, fashion products, clothing, gifts, and so on).

6. Absolute price is not too high. For very expensive products, the search for objective quality information can be rewarding. In other words, the reliance on price alone can be costly.

With respect to situational conditions, the role of price as quality indicator is the greater, thus:

7. The greater the time pressure is during the purchase.
8. The more complex the purchase task is.
9. The lower the price transparency is (for example with respect to the variation of prices for the same product).
10. The more the buyer trusts the supplier of the price information.

With respect to personal characteristics, price-dependent quality evaluation should be the most important, thus:

11. The less self-confident the buyer is.
12. The less frugal the buyer is.
13. The stronger the desire is to purchase quickly and conveniently.
14. The stronger the desire is to avoid cognitive dissonance.
15. The better the economic situation of the household is.
16. The less product-related information the buyer has.

The important point to be made here is that if these are widely held expectations (and we believe they are) then they will have an important bearing upon the way in which suppliers set their prices.

In other words, if these 'hypotheses' reflect the pricing decision maker's perception of the situation then it is this which will govern his pricing decision. Similarly, under the conditions proposed by Simon, it would seem to make a lot of sense for the buyer to use price as an indicator of quality where the opportunity cost of getting better information is very high together with the perceived risk of making the wrong decision. Hence, while IBM equipment is often 25 per cent more expensive than comparable competitive products there is considerable support for the view that 'Nobody ever got fired for buying IBM'.

A strategic pricing framework

In the *Journal of Consumer Marketing* Hugh Cannon and Frank Morgan present 'A Strategic Pricing Framework' which conceptualises pricing outcomes or objectives as a function of pricing strategies constrained by environmental factors. The essence of their framework is reproduced in Figure 13.6 and provides a very useful summary of the key issues to consider in pricing decision making.

The model comprises three central elements:

- A series of rules (R);
- A selection of pricing methods (P);
- A set of possible pricing objectives (O).

Readers should consult the original source for the precise definitions used by the authors but in broad terms P1 and P2 (target profit and cost-plus pricing) are both variants of cost-based methods. P3 and P4 (perceived value and going-rate pricing) are based upon what the market will bear, while P5 (sealed bid pricing) and P6 (negotiated pricing) are self-explanatory. Similarly, the rules and objectives are fairly clear, the point about the first rule being that if the customer is small then it is unlikely the seller would entertain sealed bid or negotiated prices (P5 and P6) so these are eliminated from the feasible set. Otherwise one proceeds through the decision tree using the rules and objectives to help one select a preferred pricing method.

An alternative model of pricing behaviour

Based on her extensive analysis of pricing behaviour, Said offers us an alternative model in Figure 13.7, which she describes as follows:

As a first step, there is the decision about objectives which business firms seek to achieve through their pricing policy.

The process of price determination comprises both the firms' approach to pricing and the techniques used, which includes the following:

- Decisions concerning the methods of pricing either cost or not cost related;
- Decisions concerning methods of costing for pricing purposes;
- Decisions concerning profit policy, the techniques used in calculating profit margins and their flexibility between products;
- Decisions concerning price changes in response to demand and cost fluctuations;
- Decisions concerning price review;
- Decisions concerning pricing systems to be used;
- Decisions concerning discount structures to be operated.

As suggested in the model, pricing behaviour is a function of a complex of objective and subjective variables. The objective variables indicated in the model are the type of product, methods of production, methods of distribution, industry sector and size. The subjective variables are the choices made by executives responsible for pricing and the type of respondent manager.

To begin with pricing objectives, the model shows a link between pricing objectives and industry sector, type of manager responsible for pricing decisions and type of respondent manager.

Firms' approach to pricing and techniques used are functions of all these objective and subjective variables combined with pricing objectives. More specifically:

- There is an association between the pricing methods used in business firms and their pricing objectives, the type of product they produce, the methods of production and distribution they use, the industry sector they fall in, and the type of manager responsible for setting prices.

Figure 13.6 *A strategic pricing decision model*

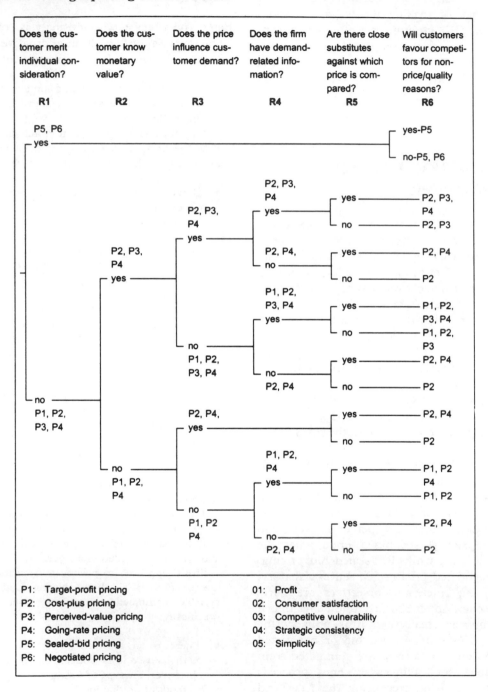

P1:   Target-profit pricing
P2:   Cost-plus pricing
P3:   Perceived-value pricing
P4:   Going-rate pricing
P5:   Sealed-bid pricing
P6:   Negotiated pricing

O1:   Profit
O2:   Consumer satisfaction
O3:   Competitive vulnerability
O4:   Strategic consistency
O5:   Simplicity

Figure 13.7 *A model of pricing behaviour*

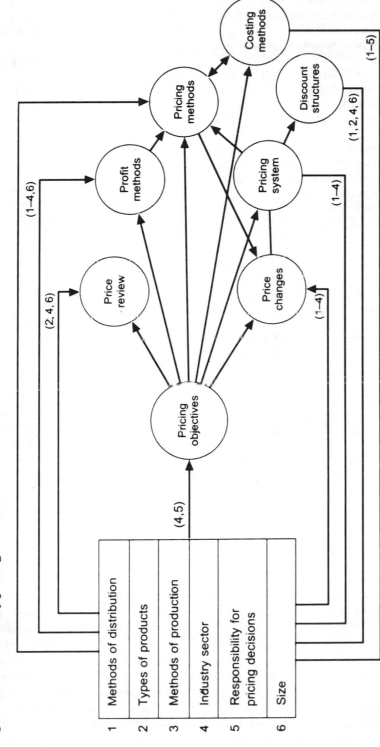

Source: Hanna A. Said (1981).

- There is an association between the costing methods used in business firms and their pricing objectives, pricing methods, the type of product, methods of production and distribution, industry sector and the type of manager responsible for pricing.
- There is an association between profit policy employed by a business firm and its pricing objectives, pricing methods, type of product, methods of production and distribution, industry sector and size.
- There is an association between price changes and pricing objectives, pricing methods, type of product, methods of production and distribution, industry sector and pricing systems.
- There is an association between firm's policy in reviewing prices and pricing objectives, pricing methods, type of product, industry sector and size.
- There is an association between pricing systems employed by firms and their pricing objectives, the type of product, methods of production and distribution and industry sector.
- There is an association between discount structures operated by business firms and their pricing systems, type of product, methods of distribution, industry sector and size.

As shown in the model, the relationship between the different aspects of pricing behaviour is cross-sectional or one way, which indicates the case in a static analysis. However, over time these associations will show a two-way relationship, indicating a dynamic state and the adjustment of policy and practice in the light of experience. For example, a price review can result in a change in the firm's pricing objectives, which in turn will cause a change in its profit policy, pricing methods, pricing systems, price changes and so on. A change in profit policy can cause a change in pricing objectives, pricing methods, costing methods, etc. Also a change in costing methods can cause a change in pricing methods, which in turn influence profit policy, pricing objectives and consequently all the process of pricing.

This model might fill an existing gap in the pricing literature on two counts:

First, it suggests a link between pricing behaviour and certain variables which play an important role in pricing, but which have received little attention previously.

Second, while recognising the interdependence and interrelationship of the various aspects of the pricing process, it considers them to be influenced significantly by the firms' overall pricing objectives, of which there may be several, and so conditioned by them.

These two points suggest the complexity of pricing decisions, which is emphasised by Livesey, Oxenfeldt, Tucker, Hague, and many others, that pricing decisions constitute a complex web, and that successful pricing requires an awareness of the many interrelationships among pricing decisions.

Summary

In this chapter we have examined the role of price as a key variable in the marketing mix. Traditionally, economic theory sees price as the mechanism which brings supply and demand into equilibrium. However, theories of competition designed to explain how price achieves this tend to contain a number of simplifying assumptions which clearly do not exist often in the real world. The assumption that people are homogeneous and so are willing to accept homogeneous products obviously contradicts reality. If it were true then the most efficient firms would undoubtedly dominate the market as their efficiency would enable them to offer the lowest price. With nothing to distinguish one supplier's offering from another's then buying at the lowest price is the only logical outcome and all industries would be monopolistic or oligopolistic in character.

Because user needs and wants differ there is an opportunity to escape the rigours of price competition by differentiating the product or service offering. Thus much of recent marketing thinking and practice has focused on the development of a sustainable differential advantage through non-price factors. However, in recent years characterised by recession and intensive competition many producers and sellers have turned to price as a competitive weapon in their attempts to hold or build market share. One consequence of this is that many buyers' perception of price has changed. Formerly, price was seen to be fixed. Now, it is seen as variable and negotiable – a change which has important implications for marketing managers.

Against this background we have looked at the major price determinants – internal and external – and their influence on pricing objectives. Following Diamantopoulos we have classified these as falling into six categories:

- Profit related;
- Volume related;

- Financially related;
- Competition-oriented;
- Customer-oriented;
- Miscellaneous.

In order to achieve their pricing objectives, organisations have access to a number of formulas or methods. These we reviewed in some detail paying particular attention to cost and competition based approaches. In turn, this led to a consideration of pricing strategies with penetration or skimming seen as the basic options. Next, we looked at how the buyer's perception of price influences their buying behaviour and particularly how price affects perceptions of quality. Finally, we proposed an alternative model of pricing behaviour developed from empirical research undertaken at Strathclyde University.

In the next chapter we turn our attention to the third P in the marketing mix with a discussion of the role and nature of channel management.

Review questions and problems

1. Summarise the major factors that should be taken into account in developing a price policy.
2. Discuss the advantages/disadvantages of each of the price 'formulas' discussed in the text.
3. Under what circumstances would you recommend (a) a 'skimming' approach, (b) a 'penetration' policy? Identify a current example of each and document the reasons which you believe prompted its selection.
4. Discuss the importance of price as an 'indicator of quality'.
5. What relevance have the concepts of the product life cycle and market segmentation for pricing policy?

6. Describe three ways in which product pricing policy can be used as a means of creative marketing.
7. Explain the statement that optimal pricing policies should be based upon a combination of contribution analysis techniques and a marketing-oriented view of customers.
8. Describe the uses of break-even analysis as a tool of effective marketing management.
9. Explain and comment on the view that optimal price is that price which best services the central aims of the business.
10. What have recent studies revealed about the effect of price differentials on consumers perceptions of product quality?

11. In *How British Industry Prices*, the authors found that 63 per cent of the firms investigated used the absorption (full) costing approach to establish the cost and selling prices of their products.

12. A surprisingly large number of companies relegate price policy to a secondary role in the planning of their marketing strategy. What factors might cause a company to act in this way?

   (a) What are the problems which can arise when this method is used to calculate the selling price?

   (b) Discuss the use of marginal (direct) costing and indicate how this method can be particularly important during a period of depressed economic conditions.

   Illustrate your answer with simple numerical examples.

13. How do contribution analysis and break-even analysis relate to each other? What use is made of them in marketing?

14. Tooth-i-Pegs Ltd make and sell 100 000 toothbrushes per month at 40p each. The total unit cost is 38p and fixed costs amount to £10 000 per month. Market research has revealed that there would be an increase in sales to 125 000 brushes per month if the price was reduced to 38p per brush. Assuming that there is excess manufacturing capacity available, should Tooth-i-Pegs Ltd reduce its selling price? Prepare an advertising and marketing plan.

15. Write notes on FOUR of the following: (i) mark-up pricing, (ii) target pricing, (iii) price discrimination, (iv) loss-leaders, (v) prestige pricing.

16. What is means by the term 'penetrating pricing?' Under what circumstances is as company *most* likely to use this type of pricing?

17. In determining a pricing policy, why is it important to evaluate competitors' prices? Detail the likely outcomes if a firm did not take competitors' prices into consideration, when determining the price of their product.

18. What is meant by the term price skimming? Under what circumstances might this be the most optimal pricing strategy to follow?

19. To what extent would you support the view that the British shopper has become more conscious about the value for money in recent years? Use examples to support you answer.

20. In price discounting, the principle should be that if you give something away, you've got to get something back. Discuss this proposition using examples.

Supplementary reading list

Benke, R. L. and Edwards, J. D. (1981) 'Transfer Pricing Techniques and Uses', NAA, 1981.

Blackman, Jules (1953) *Price Practices and Price Policies* (New York: Ronald Press).

Dean, Joel (1951) *Managerial Economics* (Englewood Cliffs, N.J.: Prentice-Hall).

Gabor, A. (1977) *Pricing Principles and Practices* (London: Heineman).

Marshall, A. (1980) *More Profitable Pricing* (New York: McGraw-Hall).

Price Commission Reports

Simon, H. (1989) *Price Management* (Amsterdam: Elsevier).

Winkler, John (1986) *Pricing for Results* (London: Pan Books).

■ *Chapter 14* ■

Channel Management

Contents

Learning goals

The issues to be addressed in this chapter include:

1. The functions of the distributive channel.
2. The determinants of channel policy.
3. The selection of a distributive channel.

After reading this chapter you will be able to:

1. List the five essential functions performed by a distribution channel.
2. Review the advantages and disadvantages of the three basic alternatives available when selecting a distribution policy

   ● direct sale;
   ● sale through an intermediary;
   ● a dual policy.

3. Explain the channel policy decision in terms of the resolution of conflict between cost and control.
4. Summarise the factors to be considered when selecting a distribution channel.

■ Introduction

In Chapter 9 we discussed 'Channels of Distribution, in some detail. In that chapter our intention was to *describe* the functions of distribution channels and then elaborate these by looking at the existing patterns for raw materials, industrial and consumer goods. In this chapter the emphasis is upon distribution as an element of the marketing mix which the marketer has to consider when developing a marketing plan.

To begin with we offer some definitions as a basis for a discussion of channel structure. Next, we consider some of the determinants of channel policy which influence the channel decision and the selection of a particular strategy. Having chosen a channel it is necessary to manage the relationship with intermediaries which raises issues of conflict, control and performance measurement. To conclude the chapter we summarise some current trends and look briefly at the subject of logistics or physical distribution.

■ Defining the channel

Earlier (p. 184) we introduced the concept of the business system as the forerunner of the currently popular idea of the 'value chain'. This concept traces the flow of goods from the extraction of raw materials/growth of primary commodities through processing and fabrication into industrial or consumer goods and their sale into ultimate consumption along with those services necessary to facilitate consumption. In tracing this flow we identified a number of functions which have to be performed which we summarised as (p. 185):

1. Transfer of title to the goods involved.
2. Physical movement from the point of production to the point of consumption.
3. Storage functions.
4. Communication of information concerning the availability, characteristics and price of the goods.
5. The financing of goods in transit, inventory, and on purchase.

The performance of these functions adds value – hence value chain – and involves the performance of a number of specialised tasks.

In *Marketing: Theory and Practice* Sean Ennis (1995) cites Bowersox & Cooper's definition of a channel as 'a system of relationships among businesses that participate in the process of buying and selling products and services' (p. 199). From this definition it is clear that the authors conceive of channels comprising a number of members each responsible for specific tasks. As can be seen from Figure 14.1 this is usually the case although it can also be seen that in some instances manufacturers will seek to establish direct contact with their customers.

From Figure 14.1 it is clear that channels can vary considerably in their complexity and the basic issue is whether the manufacturer should seek to perform the functions involved or transfer/delegate these to one or other kind of specialist who will mediate (hence, intermediary) between them and the ultimate customer. We return to this issue later when discussing cost and control in distribution channels. However, the reader may wish to refer back to Chapter 9 where we summarised some of the advantages and disadvantages of direct sale and selling through intermediaries.

■ Factors influencing channel structure

With rare exceptions most producers will find themselves faced with a number of different channels through which they might seek to reach their target market. Some understanding of the broad influences which give rise to these different channel structures will provide a useful insight when deciding which of the alternatives to use.

In reviewing various explanations of channel structure Lambert (see Figure 14.1) notes that there is no consensus of opinion, with some theories stressing the product life-cycle, others the characteristics of goods and still others the size of firm. Among these theories perhaps the most detailed and best-known is that put forward by Bucklin (1968) which rests upon the economic relationships between channel members and the concepts of substitutability, postponement and speculation.

According to Bucklin marketing functions are substitutable for one another in much the same way as the basic factors of production and 'This substitutability permits the work load of one function to be shrunk and shifted to another without affecting the output of the channel'. He continues later: 'In essence, the concept of substitutability states that under competitive conditions institutions of the channel will interchange the work load among functions, not to minimise the cost of some individual function, but the total costs of the channel.'

Postponement and speculation are the converse of each other in that the principle of postponement 'states that changes in form and inventory location are to be delayed to the latest possible moment' while 'the principle of speculation holds that changes in form, and the movement of goods to forward inventories, should be made at the

Figure 14.1 *Alternative channels of distribution*

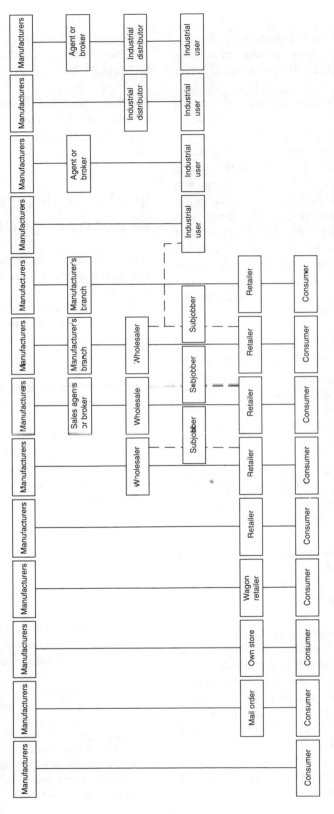

Source: D. M. Lambert (1978), *The Distribution Channels Decision* (New York: The Society of Management Accountants and National Society of Accountants).

earliest possible time in the marketing flow in order to reduce the costs of the marketing system', for example through economies of scale.

Based upon these three principles, Bucklin argues that consumer demand will determine what services are required and what value is placed upon them, and this will result in the evolution of the most efficient and cost-effective channel structure. Thus for convenience goods ready and widespread availability is a *sine qua non* and we are likely to find the producer using multiple channels involving both direct and indirect sales to achieve the maximum market coverage. Conversely, for the many industrial goods and consumer shopping goods the variation in consumer demand will lead to greater postponement so that precise needs can be articulated and will frequently result in shorter buyer and seller.

However, as producers and distributors jockey for position to satisfy the ultimate customer one must anticipate an ebb and flow in the competitive standing of the channel members. Lambert provides a useful synopsis of Bruce Mallen's (1977) analysis of the competitive forces which are likely to result in structural change in the channel, as follows:

1. A producer will spin-off a marketing function to a marketing intermediary(s) if the latter can perform the function more efficiently than the former.
2. If there are continual economies to be obtained within a wide range of volume changes, the middleman portion of the industry (and perhaps individual middlemen) will become bigger and bigger.
3. A producer will keep a marketing function if the producer can perform the functions at least as efficiently as the intermediary.
4. If a producer is more efficient in one market, the producer will perform the marketing function; if in another market the middleman is more efficient, then the middleman will perform the function.
5. If there are not economies of scale in a growing market, more firms may be expected to join the channel.

Of course, changes in the competitive standing of producers and distributive intermediaries will be subject to the complex interplay of the environmental forces reviewed earlier and underlies the importance of monitoring these if one is to select the most efficient channel – a subject to which we turn next.

Major determinants of channel policy

Fundamentally, the channel decision requires resolution of the often conflicting forces of cost and control.

Cost is readily understood even if it is sometimes difficult to quantify, and several aspects of control have already been stated. However, the concept of control must be broadened to recognise the fact that a firm's ability to exercise control is a function of its competitive strength *vis-à-vis* other channel members. Thus it is usual to find that one member of the distributive channel dominates its practices and is regarded as the 'locus of channel control' (see Louis P. Bucklin (1968) 'The Locus of Channel Control'). In general the dominant members are either producers or users/consumers, but there are situations where a channel intermediary may be dominant and so condition the structure and operation of the channel. The latter situation is most likely to occur where both producers and users are small and the market is geographically dispersed, and is equally true of retailer/wholesalers in the consumer goods market as it is of the industrial goods wholesaler. Overall, dominance or control is determined by a number of factors which may be summarised as:

Buyer/seller concentration ratios in terms of production/consumption, and spatial relationships.

Technical complexity. In the case of technically complex products, dominance will be conditioned by the relative sophistication of the producer *vis-à-vis* the intermediary and/or user. Thus a small firm may exercise considerable influence over much larger users or intermediaries.

Service requirements – the more complex these are the more likely it is that the producer will exercise control.

In the final analysis, however, the determining factor is economic advantage; that is, which channel member can perform the necessary channel functions at the lowest cost consistent with the required degree of efficiency. At a given point in time the structure of a trade channel serves as a rough and ready guide as to the relative efficiency of its members, but it is clear that over time environmental changes may predicate the adoption of an alternative structure to better meet the needs of users/consumers. Similarly, lack of control may persuade a channel member to modify his policies in order to protect his position – a tendency which is implicit in Galbraith's concept of 'countervailing power'.

Examples of competitive reaction within the distributive channel are well documented in the field of consumer goods but less so in the industrial sphere. The growth of dominant retailing institutions was noted in Chapter 9, together with the response of the independent wholesaler whose livelihood was threatened, and similar trends are to be observed in industrial markets.

Among the latter may be noted the adoption of contract purchasing, also known as systems contracting, stockless purchasing, automatic ordering or 'Just in time' (JIT) purchasing. Under this system, buyers negotiate contracts for the continued supply of standard requirements from a single source at a fixed price. Effectively, this reduces the actual stock of parts, supplies or components to the absolute minimum consistent with day-to-day operations, and transfers the inventory costs and risk of obsolescence to the supplier. Such contracts are invariably based upon a total cost analysis rather than on a basis of minimum price. Associated with contract purchasing there is a growing trend in the United States towards computerised ordering systems in which standardised and routine orders are placed direct with the supplier (producer or wholesaler) through the medium of electronic data processing equipment, for example Data Phone, WATS-line and Flexowriter. In that these practices not only

result in operating economies but also free the purchasing agent to devote more time to non-routine buying decisions, they are resulting in a fuller and more sophisticated evaluation of competitive offerings. In the UK, Kwik-fit operates such a system for all its outlets.

To counteract the growing sophistication of buyers, many sellers have switched to systems selling, in which they offer a complete 'package' of related products and services which would formerly have been purchased from a variety of different sources. Similarly, the appointment of market managers, as opposed to product managers, recognises the need to adapt marketing practice to the specific needs of different end-use markets.

☐ *The channel decision*

Whether one accepts profit maximisation as the basic corporate objective or not, it seems reasonable to affirm that uncertainty about the future business environment and the competitive activity of other firms will predispose the firm to reduce costs to the minimum level consistent with achievement of its own stated objective. If this is so, then the channel decision may be viewed as a three-stage process. The first stage consists of a qualitative assessment of the environmental opportunity which the firm is best suited to exploit, conditioned by less tangible objectives such as 'To build the best product' or 'To provide the best after-sales service'.

Once the broad strategy has been determined, management must decide which mix of policies offers the optimum probability of attaining the desired result. Such decisions cannot be made in isolation, for the success of a strategy demands that the separate marketing policies in respect of price, distribution, promotion, and so forth be synthesised into a consistent and cohesive whole. Usually, however, one variable will take pre-eminence over the others by virtue of the basic strategy decided upon – the 'strategic variable'. For example, if the basic strategy is to sell mass consumption convenience goods, extensive or mass distribution may well be considered the key or strategic variable, and will condition policies adopted in respect of other mix elements. Similarly, if the basic strategy is to build a reputation for high product quality the product itself will become the strategic variable, and probably result in ,a high price, selective distribution policy.

In order to decide which distribution channel or combination of channels is to be preferred the marketer should then quantify the costs associated with the available alternatives. This analysis should be based initially on a check-list similar to that in Chapter 9, followed by a detailed cost breakdown for direct sale to the number of accounts thought to be necessary to achieve the desired sales volume. Such a breakdown would normally include consideration of the following:

- Number and geographical distribution of accounts;
- Number of calls per account adjusted to allow for potential order size;
- Average sales per call;
- Average time per call;
- Number of salesmen necessary to achieve the optimal call pattern;
- Salaries and commission payable;
- Travelling and administrative costs incurred;
- Costs of holding inventory;
- Costs of financing receivables;
- Costs of extending credit;
- Costs arising out of bad debts;
- Costs of providing necessary services;
- Costs of invoicing, order processing, expediting, and so forth;
- Transportation costs.

On the basis of such a cost analysis one may then compute the average selling, general and administrative costs per unit sold, and compare this with the gross margin asked by intermediaries for providing the same services and market coverage. Obviously, if the margin asked is greater than the average unit cost, direct sale will appear more attractive, and vice versa. The outcome of such an analysis is rarely clear-cut, however, and even when it does appear so it does not necessarily

represent the optimal strategy. The latter may only be determined effectively on a marginal or contribution basis, which in turn will usually require the use of a computer to cope with the enormous number of possible combinations and permutations.

 # Vertical marketing systems

To this point, the discussion of distribution channels has conformed with the traditional view that members of such channels are autonomous and independent organisations which are pursuing their own individual objectives. Where these objectives are not congruent there is the potential for *conflict* and, to try and avoid this, the channel members with the greatest leverage will seek to superimpose their goals over other members and assume *control* of the channel. Thus, as we have seen, conflict and control are major issues in selecting a distribution policy. Further, and implicit in the word 'superimpose', there has been the expectation that channel conflict will be resolved by competition rather than cooperation.

In many cases competition between channel members leads to inefficiencies and lost profit opportunities. To avoid this, an alternative, more co-operative form of organisation has begun to emerge in recent years and has been designated the *vertical marketing system* (VMS). According to the Macmillan *Dictionary of Marketing and Advertising* (1990) a VMS is 'A marketing channel which has achieved some degree of vertical integration involving some central control of operational practices and programmes'. Nylen (1990) elaborates on this definition by suggesting that VMSs differ from conventional channels in four important respects:

1. VMSs use centrally prepared marketing programs.
2. Whether or not the members of a VMS are independent of each other, their activities are directed by this central program.

3. In a VMS, marketing functions are assigned to units on the basis of efficiency and effectiveness rather than on the basis of traditional roles and precedent.
4. The members in a VMS accept closer control than is usual in a conventional channel, with the result that VMSs tend to be more stable.

Following the publication of a paper by Bert C. McCammon Jr it has been customary to recognise three main types of VMS – *Administered*, *Contractual* and *Corporate*. The difference between three three kinds of system is determined primarily by the means used to exercise control over the members. In an *administered* system a channel leader (sometimes termed the *channel captain*) has sufficient power to persuade the other members of the benefit of cooperation. In order to enjoy this power the leader will normally be the organisation which enjoys the strongest customer franchise. For most food products this now means the major multiples will set the lead although major brands like P&G, Lever Bros, Heinz and so on, will be able to moderate this power and are likely to give the lead in the channels which involve the smaller retailer chains and independents. Either way the leader of an administered VMS will be expected to spell out the terms of trade within the channel (discounts, allowances, trading areas and so forth) in order to provide the incentives necessary to keep the channel intact.

The second type of VMS is the *contractual* system in which the relationships between members tend to be more formalised and spelled out in official contracts. Three main kinds of contractual VMS may be distinguished – retail co-operatives, wholesale co-operatives and franchises. Retail co-operatives occur when independent retailers take the initiative to band together and set up their own wholsesaling intermediary. Conversely wholesaler co-operatives occur when smaller wholesalers band together to secure the benefits of bulk buying power through pooled purchases as well as the benefits of professional advice, joint branding and advertising, etc. commonly associated with both kinds of co-operative.

Franchises occur where the owners of products or services licence others to wholesale or retail them under the franchiser's name in exchange for the payment of a fee. Car dealerships, fast food outlets and soft drinks like Coca-Cola are probably the best known example. Franchises also depend upon a contractual relationship, but differ from retail and wholesale co-operatives which are forms of backward integration by intermediaries whereas franchises are cases of forward integration by producers.

Finally, *corporate* VMSs exist where a firm integrates vertically, either backwards or forwards, and so becomes responsible for the product/service from its initial conceptualisation/production right through to its consumption and after-sales service.

Nylen (1990) summarises the advantages and disadvantages of VMSs as follows:

- *Advantages*

    1. Distribution economies.
    2. Marketing control.
    3. Stability, reduction of uncertainty.

- *Disadvantages*

    1. Loss of incentive.
    2. Investment requirements.
    3. Inflexibility.

Nylen continues to suggest that the choice between VMS and conventional systems depends largely on the answers to six questions.

1. What level of power does the firm have?
2. What is the potential for economies?
3. How much marketing cooperation is needed?
4. Are appropriate channel members available?
5. Is there potential for competitive differentiation through the channel system?
6. Is there a competitive threat from integrated systems?

Clearly, the answers to these questions (like so many in marketing) will call for both formal analysis and the exercise of judgement.

Ennis (1995) describes a number of variations of Vertical Marketing Systems as follows:

- *Corporate vertical marketing system*: These exist when the various channel members participating within the chain are owned by one organisation. This can occur through forward integration – where a manufacturer acquires or sets up its own wholesaling or retailing structure; or through backward integration – where a retailer or wholesaler owns its own supplier base.

- *Contractual vertical marketing systems*: The main distinguishing feature of this form of arrangement is that the relationships are formalised through a contractual agreement. This specifies the precise functions and responsibilities of each member. Typical examples of this type of structure are franchises, exclusive dealerships, and joint ventures. There is a marked absence of ownership in this situation (as compared to corporate arrangements).

- *Alliances*: Bowersox and Cooper (1992) suggest that this structure is characterised by a voluntary form of extended organisations – where two or more firms agree to develop close working relationships. At a basic level this can be described as a partnership – without necessarily producing changes or modifications in the individual way in which the parties conduct their operations. Clearly this may change over time, where parties are willing to alter their practices as they perceive individual and mutual benefits accruing. This type of structure can be described as a *strategic alliance*.

- *Administered vertical marketing systems*: Marketing institutions in such systems generally pursue their individual goals and have no formal organisational structure to bind them together. The marketing programme, on the other hand, allows these organisations to collaborate informally on the goals they do share (Stern *et al.*, 1989). While an attempt is made to inculcate a systematic approach to the planning and coordination of certain marketing activities on the part of the channel participants, the approach is to the individual rather than to the overall channel (p. 204).

■ Channel management

By now it should be clear that the selection of a distribution channel is a key issue for marketing management. Martin Christopher (1992) in *Logistics and Supply Chain Management*, cites four factors which emphasise the importance of channel management, namely:

- The customer service explosion;
- Time compression;
- The globalisation of industry;
- Organisational integration.

Clearly, the channel of distribution offers significant opportunities to add value through the creation of additional services and time and place utilities. Similarly, global competition and the creation of major trading blocs like the EU, LAFTA, NAFTA and so on, has given added emphasis to the importance of efficient and effective distribution as a source of competitive advantage. Taken together these forces call for improved coordination and integration of the firm's functions to ensure the creation and delivery of customer satisfaction. In turn, these issues throw into sharp relief the fundamental question of whether one should seek to establish direct contact with the customer or work through an intermediary or intermediaries.

We have already noted that the growing power of retailers has done much to erode the manufacturer's franchise with the ultimate consumer (Chapter 9). To restore this loss of franchise many manufacturers have sought to integrate forward into distribution, deal direct, and/or increase their promotional effort to communicate directly with end users in order to 'pull' their products through the distribution channels. Vertical marketing systems also offer greater opportunities for integration of distributive functions. However, as we have seen in this chapter, distribution channels are all about relationships between the members and the exercise of power and control with the potential for conflict these create. (Ennis, *op. cit.* discusses these issues in some detail.

Whatever the final solution, the producer will want to measure the performance of the channel and this will usually call for a combination of quantitative and qualitative measures; for example sales, inventory levels, delivery, customer satisfaction and so forth. Readers should consult one of the specialised texts for information on the selection and use of appropriate performance indicators.

Physical distribution

Physical distribution, or logistics as it is sometimes termed, is also a specialist topic in its own right to which only limited reference can be made in a general, introductory text of this kind.

As the term implies, physical distribution is concerned with the movement, handling, storage and delivery of raw materials, fabricated materials, components and sub-assemblies, and finished goods. All of these possess value but they also represent capital tied up in inventory or stocks. While the appropriate level of stocks will vary according to one's position within the business system, or value chain, and the nature of the industry/market, efficiency and effectiveness will depend very much on keeping stocks to a minimum and turning them over as quickly as possible. Recognition of this underlies the current emphasis on '*just-in-time*' or JIT techniques, and has resulted in much closer attention being given to physical distribution.

Kotler (1988) has summarised the key decisions as:

- *Order processing* – how should orders be handled?

- *Warehousing* – where should stocks be located?
- *Inventory* – how much stock should be kept on hand?
- *Transportation* – how should goods be shipped?

Each of these functions may have an important impact on customer service and satisfaction levels and calls for careful analysis, planning and control. Suggestions for further reading are given in the appendices.

Current trends

Rosenbloom (1995) in the *Companion Encyclopedia of Marketing* identifies five trends that have affected channels of distribution in recent years as:

1. More strategic emphasis by firms on channels of distribution.
2. Partnerships and strategic alliances gaining more ground.
3. Continued growth of vertical marketing systems.
4. Growing power of retailers in distribution channels.
5. Greater role for technology in channels of distribution.

With the exception of partnerships and strategic alliances we have covered all the above issues either in this Chapter or Chapter 9. Partnerships and strategic alliances are becoming more commonplace in virtually every field of business activity and mark an important departure from the more combative and adversarial attitudes of yester-year. Undoubtedly, this trend owes much to the emphasis on relationship marketing discussed at some length in Chapter 1.

Summary

While Chapter 9 was concerned primarily with describing channels of distribution as an important element in the marketing environment this chapter has focused on distribution as an element in the marketing mix.

The chapter opened with a definition of the marketing channel and a reprise of the functions discussed in Chapter 9. Next we reviewed the forces which influence the structure of marketing channels, including the often conflicting forces of cost and control which also act as major determinants of channel policy. A discussion of the channel decision followed in which we looked at the multiplicity of factors which influence the marketer's selection of a distribution channel.

The following section examined a relatively new development – the Vertical Marketing System (VMS) which represents greater cooperation and collaboration between members or higher levels of integration in vertically integrated organisations. Brief reviews of channel management, physical distribution and current trends concluded the chapter.

Review questions and problems

1. Rank the 'essential distributive functions' cited in the text in order of importance for each of the following:

    (a)   Steel stockholder;
    (b)   Primary commodity wholesaler –
        (i)   perishable goods;
        (ii)   non-perishable goods.
    (c)   Packaged-food wholesaler;
    (d)   'Main' car dealer.

2. Which distribution policy do you consider most appropriate to the sale of the following products:

    ● Car accessories;
    ● Car tyres;
    ● Ethical pharmaceuticals;
    ● Household cleaning materials;
    ● Luxury cosmetics;
    ● Industrial robots?

    Stipulate the assumptions underlying your selection of a given policy and cite actual examples wherever possible.

3. Discuss the impact of vertical integration on the structure of traditional distribution channels.

4. Selection of a distribution policy invariably demands a compromise between cost and control. Discuss.

5. Evaluate the possible effect of mail order, automatic vending and door-to-door selling on retail distribution in the coming decade.

6. How can a manufacturer evaluate the following choices in the construction of a marketing/distribution system:

    (a)   Own retail sales force and direct delivery with own transport system.
    (b)   Own retail sales force and commercial warehousing/delivery service.
    (c)   Wholesale salesmen and own transport system delivering to wholesalers only.
    (d)   Any other combination.

7. Describe the variables which affect the design of distribution channels and comment on their relative importance.

8. What are the possible sources of innovation in distribution, describing some you are familiar with, and comment on the process of adoption or of rejection.

9. Describe the variables which affect the choice of distribution channels by a manufacturing firm.

10. Argue the case for managing the physical distribution of a company's products as an aspect of its marketing strategy.

11. What problems are inherent in producing a definition of the term 'channel of distribution'?

12. What do you understand by the total distribution cost concept? Outline the scope of the constituent centres involved and relate the importance of an understanding of the concept to the marketing manager.

13. Discuss the major considerations in designing a channel system.

14. Why is the decision about the type of channel system to be used by a manufacturer often critical to marketing success?

15. By what criteria would you judge the efficiency of a particular channel of distribution?

16. Identify and discuss some of the factors that should increase the trend towards vertical marketing systems.

17. Give reasons as to why an effective distribution strategy can give a firm a differential competitive advantage.

18. 'Without purposive co-ordination, motivation and direction, channels are doomed to failure, irrespective of the way they are structured' (Stern & Ansary). Comment.

19. Discuss fully the proposition that the key concern and source of conflict in distribution channels is with the management of inventories and logistics. Use examples where possible to illustrate your answer.

Supplementary reading list

Baker, Michael J. *et al.* (1983) *Marketing Theory and Practice*, 2nd edn (London: Macmillan).

Bowersox, D. J. and Closs, D. J. (1966) *Logistical Management*, 4th edn (Boston: McGraw-Hill).

Bucklin, Louis P. (1966) *A Theory of Distribution Channel Structure* (Berkeley, CA: Institute of Business and Economic Research).

Clewitt, Richard M. (ed.) (1954) *Marketing Channels for Manufactured Products* (Homewood, Ill.: Irwin).

Mallen, B. (1977) *Principles of Marketing Channel Management* (Lexington, MA: Lexington Books).

Stern, L. W. and El-Ansary, A. I. (1977) *Marketing Channels* (Englewood Cliffs, N.J.: Prentice-Hall).

See also texts for Chapter 9, Patterns of Distribution.

☐ *Journals*

European Journal of Physical Distribution
Journal of Marketing Management
Marketing
Retail and Distribution Management

■ *Chapter 15* ■

Marketing Communications

Contents

Learning goals

The issues to be discussed in this chapter include:

1. The definition of communication and basic models of the communication process.
2. The way in which advertising works.
3. The role of communication in the marketing mix.
4. Marketing communications as information processing.

After reading this chapter you will be familiar with:

1. The concept of a channel of communication linking communicators with an intended audience.
2. The view that effective communication is the consequence of a process similar to that described in the hierarchy of effects models; that is moving an audience from unawareness to awareness, interest and action.

3. The distinction between personal and non-personal influence and their combination in the theory of the two-step flow of communication.
4. The paradigm of the innovation-decision process comprising the four stages of *knowledge*, *persuasion*, *decisions* and *confirmation* and its use in planning and communication strategy.
5. The nature of opinion leadership and the characteristics of opinion leaders.
6. The influence of source effect.
7. The concepts of consonance and dissonance.
8. The relationship between message and medium.
9. The role of communications as a marketing mix variable.
10. The view of marketing communications as a form of information processing in which consumers play an active role.

Introduction

In the view of some authors (see for example M. Wayne DeLozier (1976), *The Marketing Communications Process*) all the marketing-mix variables and indeed all company activities may be regarded as marketing communication variables. Conversely, E. J. McCarthy and William D. Perreault Jr. (1984) in *Basic Marketing* take a more narrow approach and regard marketing communications as the *promotional* activities of personal selling, and mass selling, which they see as comprising advertising and publicity, and sales promotion.

In the *Companion Encyclopedia of Marketing* Keith Crosier (1995) answers his own rhetorical question 'What is marketing communications?' by defining seven varieties of marketing communication as follows:

1. *Advertising* communicates via a recognizable advertisement placed in a definable advertising medium, guaranteeing exposure to a target audience in return for a published rate for the time or space used.
2. *Publicity* communicates via a news release to definable news media in the hope of secondary exposure to a target audience in return for a published rate for the time or space used.
3. *Packaging* communicates via display, guaranteeing exposures to a potential customer at the point of sale but not normally to a wider target audience.
4. *Personal selling* communicates person to person via a sales pitch by a sales representative to a prospect, or by a sales assistant to a customer, guaranteeing exposure to a selected individual within a target market.
5. *Direct marketing* communicates person to person but through an intervening channel, such as the post (a mailshot or mailing), door-to-door delivery (a mail drop), the telephone (telemarketing) or a fax line (no specific description yet), guaranteeing exposure to a selected individual within a target market. For many years, the only form of direct marketing in use was direct mail.
6. *Sponsorship* communicates via explicit association of a product or service with an entity, event or activity, in the expectation of secondary exposure to a target audience through identification during associated media coverage.
7. *Sales promotion* communicates via a variety of promotions not encompassed by any of the definitions above, each aiming for exposure to a target audience and some furthermore offering an incentive to respond actively.

Our own discussion will incline towards the latter, narrower, functional treatment as it is felt to be more appropriate to an introductory text. However, an attempt will be made in this chapter to put this basically factual and descriptive treatment into a theoretical perspective by reviewing some of the major concepts and ideas which have found their way into the marketing literature in recent years.

To this end the chapter begins with a definition of communication and proceeds to examine some of the basic models of the communication process in current circulation. References will be made to the role of attention and perception as prerequisites of action by the receiver – usually in the form of some attitudinal or behavioural change, or both – as well as to the relevance of learning theory to the propagation and understanding of marketing communication. Both these topics were introduced in Chapter 6 ('Consumer Behaviour').

The chapter then looks more closely at some of the major components of any marketing communication – the source, the message and the medium – and concludes with a discussion of the role of communication in the marketing mix. Finally, we examine a suggestion by Crosier (1983) that we should abandon traditional models of the kind discussed in this chapter in favour of an alternative explanation based upon information processing theory.

Communication defined

Wilbur Schramm (1995) defined communication as 'the process of establishing a commonness or

Figure 15.1   *Simplified communication model*

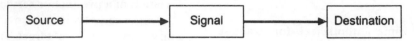

Source: Schramm, Wilbur (1995) *The Process and Effects of Mass Communication* (Urbana, Ill.: University of Illinois Press).

oneness of thought between a sender and a receiver'. Central to this definition is the concept that for communication to occur there must be a transfer of information from one party – the sender – which is received and understood by the other party – the receiver. In other words both receiver and sender play an active role in establishing communication – a fact which is given particular point when one considers that the average consumer is estimated to be exposed to approximately 3000 promotional messages a day but only receives nine of these messages. My colleague Keith Crosier has drawn to my attention the fact that while I assert that 'both receiver and sender play an active role' this is not clear from Schramm's model nor the pictorial representation of it in Figures 15.1 and 15.2. I agree – in fact the arrows in the figures tend to convey unidirectionality and cast the destination in a passive 'receiver' role. I do not believe Schramm intended this, and I certainly do not, in that my composite model of consumer behaviour described in Chapter 6 stresses strongly the point just alluded to – it is the receiver who decides whether or not to 'switch on' and thus plays an active role in the process. This point is of particular importance as much of the criticism of advertising rests on the assumption that promotional activity is something done to or exercised on passive consumers with no opportunity to control or influence the process.

Pictorially the simplest model of the communications process is shown in Figure 15.1. However, this simple model ignores the fact

that it is necessary to convert ideas into a symbolic medium to enable them to be transmitted via a communication channel. To allow for this we must introduce two more elements into the model – encoding and decoding – as shown in Figure 15.2.

As Schramm points out, this model can accommodate all types of communication so that in the case of electronic communication the encoder becomes a transmitting device – microphone, teletype, and so on – and the decoder a receiver – radio or television set, telephone, and so on. In the case of direct personal (face-to-face) communication then one person is both source and encoder while the other is decoder and destination and the signal is language. It follows that if an exchange of meaning is to take place, then both source and destination must be tuned in to each other and share the same language. Put another way, there must be an overlap in the field of experience of source and destination – which Schramm illustrates in Figure 15.3.

We must also recognise that all communication is intended to have an effect and introduce the notion of *feedback* into our model of communication, for it is through feedback that the source learns how its signals are being interpreted. In personal communication feedback is often instantaneous through verbal acknowledgement or gesture; but in impersonal communication through the mass media it may have to be inferred from other indicators, for example audience size, circulation, readership, or monitored by sampling opinion.

Figure 15.2   *Communication channel model*

Source: Schramm, Wilbur (1995) *The Process and Effects of Mass Communication* (Urbana, Ill.: University of Illinois Press).

Figure 15.3 *Communication channels*

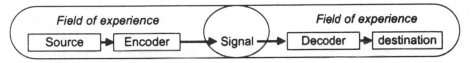

Source: Schramm, Wilbur (1995) *The Process and Effects of Mass Communication* (Urbana, Ill.: University of Illinois Press).

The final element in Schramm's model, which is not immediately apparent from the figures other than in the existence of arrows linking the other elements, is the *channel* or, more correctly channels, for messages are rarely transmitted through a single channel. Thus in personal communications it is not merely the words which convey the message but the intonation of our voice and the gestures which accompany them although some might regard these as coding rather than channels. In the field of marketing communication then the channel tends to have the specific connotation of the *media classes* which are the subject of more extended treatment in the next chapter.

The marketer's version of Schramm's model employs slightly different terminology, but contains all of the following elements (see C. Shannon and W. Weaver, 1962, *The Mathematical Theory of Communication*):

Who...	says what...	how...
Communicator	Message	Channels
to whom...	with what effect	
Audience	Feedback	

Kotler defines these basic elements as follows:

Communicator: The sender or sources of the message;

Message: The set of meanings being sent and/or received by the audience;

Channels: The ways in which the message can be carried or delivered to the audience;

Audience: The receiver or destination of the message.

From his model Schramm derives four basic 'conditions of success in communication... which must be fulfilled if the message is to arouse its intended response'. These are:

1. The message must be so designed and delivered as to gain the attention of the intended destination.
2. The message must employ signs which refer to experience common to source and destination, so as to 'get the meaning across'.
3. The message must arouse personality needs in the destination and suggest some ways to meet those needs.
4. The message must suggest a way to meet those needs which is appropriate to the group situation in which the destination finds itself at the time when they are moved to make the desired response.

Consideration of these four requirements should strike a receptive chord in the memory of the reader who is methodically working their way through the book, for they echo closely points discussed in Chapter 6 concerning hierarchy-of-effects models in consumer behaviour. In fact Schramm's four conditions are very similar to Strong's basic AIDA model – Attention, Interest, Desire and Action. It will be useful, therefore, to recapitulate on this earlier discussion but specifically in the context of marketing communications. In doing so we will first provide a broad overview and then pick out certain key concepts for a fuller discussion, namely diffusion theories, opinion leadership and the two-step flow of communication, source credibility and cognitive consonance and dissonance.

How marketing communication works

One of the earliest explanations of how advertising works is based upon the stimulus–response theory of learning in which advertising is perceived as a stimulus and purchasing behaviour the intended and desired response. However, it is clear that advertising, even when very intense does not lead automatically to purchase and it was postulated that the act of purchase is the culmination of a whole sequence of events. If this is so then it is argued that advertising's role is to move people up the steps from a state of unawareness to purchase and a number of models of varying levels of sophistication have been put forward including Strong's AIDA model (Attention, Interest, Desire, Action), Lavidge and Steiner's 'Hierarchy of Effects' Model (Awareness, Knowledge, Liking, Preference, Conviction, Purchase), and Roger's 'Innovation Adoption' Model (Awareness, Interest, Evaluation, Trial, Adoption). (See p. 117.)

The models referred to above are all old (the most recent is 1961) and relate specifically to personal communication rather than the broader field of marketing communication which is our concern here. Keith Crosier (1995) addresses this issue directly in Chapter 6 of the companion volume *Marketing: Theory and Practice* and the reader is strongly advised to consult this for a much extended discussion of marketing communications in general and the role of hierarchical models in the particular. However, all these models suggest a sequence of events which observation and experience often contradict, particularly in the case of low involvement and/or impulse purchases, and Crosier underlines the trenchant criticisms of, *inter alia*, Copland, Palda, Krugman, Ehrenberg and Ray. Indeed this conflict of opinion is but another manifestation of the conundrum as to whether attitude change leads to behavioural change or vice versa, there being substantial evidence for both schools of thought. However, notwithstanding this conflict of opinion, it is clear that most advertisers find the learning model intuitively appealing and often set objectives in terms of moving potential customers up the various steps from unawareness to purchase.

Two basic problems may be identified immediately: first, audiences are comprised of persons who differ from each other in many demographic and psycho-social respects; second, there is likely to be considerable variation in the levels of knowledge and awareness of different members of the audience at any given point in time. As a consequence individuals will vary in their response to the advertisers' message and the channels through which it is communicated. It follows that insight into the understanding of how such variance occurs is of vital importance in designing marketing communications.

Many communication experts subscribe to McLuhan's (1965) thesis that 'the medium is the message', and so would argue that once a target audience has been identified the primary decision is selection of the medium or channel to be used. Conversely others point out that media planning is a complex activity only because there are so many similar media that choice between them is difficult. This being so, then it is the message which must be selected first and this will help identify the most appropriate medium to reach the target audience. In reality, however, it seems that both approaches are used and that preference is 'situation-specific' – but, on balance, the channel seems to exercise the greater influence and will be dealt with first.

In general, channels may be divided into two major categories: *personal and non-personal*. As the name implies personal channels embrace all those situations in which a direct, face-to-face communication takes place, while non-personal channels comprise all media through which messages are transmitted *without* face-to-face communication, for example press, television, exhibitions, and so on. The available evidence suggests that both types of channel have a role to play and it is usually held that non-personal media are most effective in establishing awareness and interest, while personal influence is necessary to move the members of an audience up the hierarchy through desire to action. Further, it has been found that personal influence is most effective in high-risk purchase situations; that is, where the consumer is expending relatively large amounts and purchases infrequently (shopping goods) or where the product/service has social connotations which link brands with social groups (speciality goods). (The obverse of this is that mass communication is most appropriate for convenience goods.)

As indicated, however, it is usual to find a combination of both personal and non-personal channels used in a given campaign. Research by Lazarsfeld (1944) showed that impersonal channels are often mediated in their effect by personal channels – the so-called 'Two-step flow of communication'. According to this model certain members of the population act as filters and amplifiers for messages and these persons have been designated *opinion leaders*. It follows that if the two-step model applies then the communicator should identify the *opinion leaders* and transmit their messages through them. Often opinion leaders are best reached via impersonal channels and themselves become a personal channel performing the role of unpaid salesmen.

Clearly, the achievement of direct face-to-face communication could be expensive and impersonal channels help reduce the cost of conveying messages to consumers. However, many messages transmitted through the mass media compete for our attention and most of these are screened out by the psychological defence mechanisms of selective *perception*, *distortion* and *retention*. As a result the power of mass communication as a persuasive influence is largely discounted nowadays and the mass media are seen primarily as leading to learning and reinforcement over time. Further, different media act in different ways and the skill of the media planner lies in selection of the medium or combination of media best suited to the audience they are seeking to reach

Reference has been made to the message on several occasions and its importance is obvious, for, as Kotler says, it is the means 'by which the communicator attempts to make the product meaningful and desirable to the buyer'. Perhaps the most important point about the message is that it should be designed so that it is meaningful to the recipient after the distortion which will inevitably occur on transmission through the

chosen channel or channels and its selective screening by the audience. It follows that the message is an infinitely variable element in the communication process, as it must be tailored to the differing needs and levels of knowledge/experience of a constantly changing audience. However, two broad schools of thought exist concerning message structure and content, one favouring *consonance* (that is conforming with held beliefs, aspirations, and so forth – 'pleasant' messages) , the other *dissonance* (that is contrary to held beliefs and so creating discomfort or dissonance). We return to these concepts later in the chapter.

The final element is the communicator himself. Their influence is both direct – identification of audience, selection of channel, choice of message – and indirect – the way they are perceived by the audience as the source of the message (the 'source effect'). Again, it is important to stress that the source is not necessarily the communicator but rather the origin of the message as perceived by the audience (cf. the testimonial advertisement). In turn the audience's perception of the message will be governed by its interpretation of the *source credibility* – a concept developed by Kelman and Hovland and seen as comprising two elements – expertness and trustworthiness. Fundamentally the precept is 'the higher the source credibility the greater the effectiveness of the communication'. However, source effect decays over time and must be reinforced through repetition. Further discussion of source effect is to be found on pp. 351–3.

■ Diffusion theories

In discussing hierarchy-of-effects models in Chapter 6 reference was made to Everett Rogers's five-step adoption model – awareness, interest, evaluation, trial, adoption – which has been used extensively in many studies of new product marketing and marketing communications. However, Rogers' basic model has been subject to a number of criticisms. Specifically, it suggests that adoption is a consequence of the process when in fact the decision might be to reject the innovation, or even to 'wait and see', that is deferred rejection/adoption. Second, the five stages need not occur in the sequence proposed (cf. impulse purchasing) and it seems likely that evaluation is not a discrete phase but takes place throughout the process. Further, in many instances the trial phase may be omitted. Finally, some critics have pointed out that adoption (purchase of a product) is not the final stage in the process, as post-adoption activity will occur leading to feedback which will influence subsequent behaviour.

To meet these criticisms Rogers joined forces with Floyd Shoemaker (1971) and proposed a revised 'paradigm of the innovation–decision process' containing four stages:

1. *Knowledge*:   The individual is aware of the innovation and has acquired some information about it.
2. *Persuasion*:   The individual forms an attitude, pro or con, towards the innovation.
3. *Decisions*:   The individual performs activities which lead to an adopt-reject decision about the innovation.
4. *Confirmation*:   The individual looks for reinforcement regarding his decision and may change their earlier decision if exposed to counter-reinforcing messages.

Clearly this model is more flexible and less mechanistic than the original and permits the accommodation of the criticisms outlined earlier. Diagrammatically the model appears as shown in Figure 15.4. The reader will be familiar with the antecedent variables, for these were reviewed in Chapter 6, so attention will be focused on the process itself. However, before doing so it will be useful to introduce the concepts of *adopter categories* and *diffusion*.

Under another name (the concept of the product life-cycle, PLC – see pp. 265–7) the diffusion process is one of the most familiar and fundamental of marketing ideas. In essence the PLC and cumulative adoption curves are the same and show that after a slow initial start sales grow rapidly and then begin to level off until saturation is achieved. If these sales are plotted against elapsed time from introduction of an innovation, then a normal distribution results and this has lead to attempts to analyse and classify the adoption/buying behaviour of individuals in terms of the properties of the normal distribution. Figure 15.5 illustrates this.

It follows that if we are able to identify beforehand certain individuals as being more receptive to a given innovation, then we should be able to accelerate adoption by focusing our initial marketing efforts upon them. In turn, because the diffusion process is probabilistic, this will accelerate the whole diffusion process and result in enhanced profitability.

Returning to the process of adoption it has been determined that certain communication mixes are more appropriate than others at different stages and this knowledge is of great value in planning a communications strategy.

The *knowledge stage* is one of awareness and preliminary information-seeking in which impersonal sources tend to dominate. Other things being equal one could conceive of a situation in which all potential buyers of a new product were exposed to information about it simultaneously but because of selective perception and distortion relatively few would react to the information. Early adopters are those who do react quickly and they have been found to possess a number of characteristics which distinguish them from later adopters. Specifically, they make it their business to be well-informed and so make greater use of mass media and personal sources of information – both social and professional (that is sales personnel or 'change agents') – and they also tend to be better-educated, extrovert and more cosmopolitan than later adopters.

The second stage in the process is that of *persuasion*, in which the potential user moves from a state of neutral awareness to the development of an attitude towards the new object. In my model (pp. 132–4) this change is initiated by 'precipitating circumstances' and leads to formal evaluation of possible solutions to the felt need. In the Rogers and Shoemaker model this evaluation is based upon the perceived characteristics of the innovation – relative advantage, compatibility, complexity, trialability and observability. At

Figure 15.4 *Paradigm of the innovation decision process*

(Note: A modified version of this figure is to be found in Everett M. Rogers (1983), *Diffusion of Innovation*, 3rd edn (New York: Free Press), p. 165.

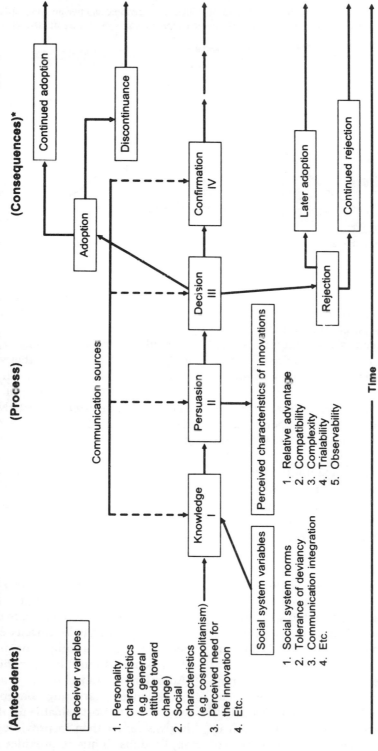

*For the sake of simplicity we have not shown the consequences of the innovation in this paradigm but only the consequences of the process.

Source: Everett M. Rogers with Floyd Shoemaker (1971), *Communication of Innovators*, 2nd edn (New York: Free Press).

Figure 15.5 *Adopter categorisation on the basis of innovativeness*

(The innovativeness dimension, as measured by the time at which an individual adopts an innovation or innovations, is continuous. However, this variable may be partitioned into five adopter categories by laying off standard deviations from the average time of adoption.)

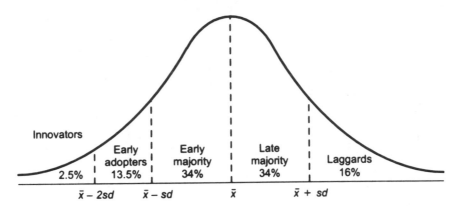

this stage prospective users will seek to extend their information base and make greater use of personal sources. It is at this juncture that opinion leadership assumes great importance as the potential user will seek the advice of those they see as knowledgeable about the item under consideration.

Relative advantage is defined as 'the degree to which an innovation is perceived as better' than an existing idea or object and it is stated that the higher the relative advantage the greater the likelihood of adoption. Compatibility and complexity are self-explanatory and tend to vary inversely with one another; that is, the more compatible an object is with one's field of experience, attitudes and value structure, and so on, the less complex it is likely to seem and vice versa. Trialability, or the extent to which an individual can try out an innovation before coming to a decision, is an important factor in reducing perceived risk and an aid to speeding up decision-making (it works both ways!). Finally, observability refers to the visible effectiveness of the innovation.

While these perceived characteristics enjoy wide currency I am not overly fond of them myself. For example, relative advantage is really a catch-all for all the other characteristics and it is tautologous to state that the greater the perceived

advantage the faster the adoption – even the clinically insane act in the manner which maximises their own perceived self-interest however misguided some people may regard it. Accordingly the reader is warned that while the concept is appealing one must beware that it is not meaningless due to circularity of definitions; for example, the greater the relative advantage the faster adoption but the faster the adoption the greater the perceived advantage. Certainly it is difficult to operationalise the concept, for the perception of characteristics tends to be individual-specific.

Following their evaluation the potential user will make a decision to adopt or reject which, as the model shows, is open to subsequent modification; that is, an adopter may continue in use or reject and vice versa for a rejector. Once made the decision is subject to *confirmation*, in which the person seeks to validate the rightness of their decision and therefore alleviate any post-decision cognitive dissonance (discussed below). This being the case it might be more accurate to show confirmation following the actual decision: 'Adoption' or 'Rejection'.

Like many marketing concepts Rogers' diffusion model is most valuable for the insights which it gives rather than in providing direct practical applications. Thus it provides a framework for organising one's thinking about the decision process and the stages which the individual goes through which can be related to the specific features which distinguish a particular marketing problem.

Opinion leadership and the two-step flow of communication

Early models of communication regarded both impersonal sources (the mass media) and personal sources as establishing direct contact with an audience – the so-called 'hypodermic effect'. Belief in this model leads to speculation concerning the influence of the mass media upon voting behaviour – thus the undertaking of one of the most celebrated pieces of communication research, reported in Paul F. Lazarsfeld *et al.*'s (1944) *The People's Choice*.

Lazarsfeld and his colleagues set out to study the influence of the mass media on individual voting behaviour in the 1940 presidential election in the United States. Contrary to expectations it was found that influence did not flow directly from a medium (press, radio, and so on) to an audience but was channelled through an intermediary who was designated the 'opinion leader'. It was this finding which gave rise to the two-step model which has had a significant influence on communication research and practice ever since. However, it must be emphasised that the two-step hypothesis does not exclude the possibility of a direct flow (one step) and its main contribution is in introducing the mediating effect of personal influence on impersonal communications. Thus nowadays the mass media are regarded primarily as *information* sources and considerable attention is focused upon the nature and behaviour of opinion leaders – how to identify them and how to communicate effectively with them. Engel *et al.* (1978) emphasise that contemporary models of social influence are built on a multi-stage interaction model in which the mass media can prompt seekers of information to approach opinion

leaders and vice versa. But while opinion leaders do not *mediate* the flow of information their potential influence as personal sources remains significant.

In simple terms an opinion leader is one to whom others turn for information and advice. However, it must be emphasised that in the usual marketing context opinion leaders are not a distinct and easily classified group in the sense in which Cabinet Ministers or Managing Directors of major companies are. More often than not opinion leaders are people just like you and me, for if they are to be effective at a personal-influence level they must be accessible, which implies that they are members of reference groups with which people have contact. In fact most reference groups develop around shared interests and some members will be seen as more influential than others in the context of that interest. But we belong to many reference groups and leader and follower roles may be reversed; for example, the captain of the football team may well seek the first reserve's opinion on the merits of hi-fi systems. It is this tendency which makes identification of opinion leaders difficult but, despite this, a number of studies have been completed which permit some generalisations to be made. Writing in 1971, Thomas S. Robertson in *Innovative Behavior and Communications* offered those shown in Table 15.1.

Table 15.1 *Summary profile of opinion-leader traits*

Characteristics	Findings
Age	Varies by product category
Social status	Generally same as advisee
Gregariousness	High
Cosmopolitanism	Limited evidence that higher than advisee's
Knowledge	Generally greater for area of influence
Personality	No major distinguishing traits
Innovativeness	Higher than advisee's

Source: T. S. Robertson (1971), *Innovative Behavior and Communications* (Holt, Rinehart & Winston), p. 179.

Research in the past two decades has done nothing to modify significantly these generalisations and Elihu Katz's summary (cited by Robertson, *Innovative Behavior*, p. 180), made in 1957, would still seem to be valid:

> influence is related to (1) *personification of certain values* (who one is), (2) *competence* (what one knows), and (3) *strategic social location* (whom one knows). To the extent that an individual represents or personifies group values, he stands a better chance of leadership. Thus if the group emphasises an 'in' manner of dress, the person who dressed most accordingly may well be influential. Again, to the extent that an individual is highly knowledgeable, he stands a better chance of leadership. Finally, to the extent that an individual is available and active in the everyday interpersonal communication process, the better his chance of leadership.

Engel *et al.* (*Consumer Behavior*, 1978) conclude from their survey of the available evidence that opinion leaders gain satisfaction from one or more of five basic motivations – product involvement, self-involvement, concern for others, message involvement, and dissonance reduction. Conversely people accept opinion leadership where there is limited alternative information available, where their own knowledge is inadequate, where there is a high degree of perceived risk and, of course, because there is little or no cost to such information.

From the above summary it follows that marketers must identify the opinion leaders for their own product/service category. Certain of the generalised traits outlined above will assist in this identification, as will the trait of innovativeness. It is also clear that opinion leaders maintain their status, which gives them satisfaction, from being well-informed and so are likely to make greater use of both personal and non-personal sources of information.

■ Source effect

As the basic model of communication makes clear, all communication originates from a source and this source has a marked bearing upon the subsequent interpretation of the message. In a marketing context it is important to distinguish between the true source – the organisation which is responsible for the generation of the message and pays for its communication in promotional channels – and the perceived source, which is the consumer perception of its origin. This distinction is important because we (consumers) often identify messages with the communicator (sales agent, personality in the television commercial) or the channel (*Good Housekeeping*, *Reader's Digest*, Radio Clyde) rather than the company 'behind' the message.

A great deal of attention has been given to source effect and extended discussions are to be found in several of the texts cited. Typical of these is DeLozier (1976) in *The Marketing Communications Process* who provides the following summary:

1. In general, a source is more persuasive when his audience perceives him as high, rather than low, in credibility.
2. A source's credibility, and thus his persuasiveness, is reduced when his audience perceives that the source has something to gain from his persuasive attempts (intention to manipulate).
3. Over time the opinion change attributed to a high-credibility source decreases, whereas the opinion change induced by a low-credibility source increases, resulting in about the same level of retained opinion change for both low and high-credibility sources.
4. Reinstatement of a high-credibility source time after his initial message presentation results in higher opinion change retention than if no reinstatement occurs; whereas reinstatement of a low-credibility source some time after his message presentation results in lower opinion change retention than if no reinstatement occurs.
5. The low-credibility source can increase his influence by arguing for a position which is against his own self-interest.

6. A communicator increases his influence if at first he expresses some views already held by his audience, followed by his intended persuasive communication.

7. A communicator increases his persuasiveness if at the beginning of his message he states that his position on the topic is the same as that of his audience, even though he may argue against that position.

8. The more similar members of an audience perceive the source to be themselves, the more persuasive the communicator will be.

9. What people think of a communicator's message affects what they think of him (his image).

10. A source is more persuasive when he holds a positive, rather than a negative, attitude towards himself, his message and his receiver.

11. The more powerful and attractive a source is perceived to be, the more influence he has on a receiver's behaviour.

As Keith Crosier has pointed out to me, one must treat such apparently authoritative statements with considerable circumspection, for much of the evidence on which they are based is derived from situations far different from those encountered in the market place (for example students' reactions to views communicated by their professors). For an extensive and up-to-date interpretation of marketing communications as such, then students are strongly recommended to supplement this chapter with Chapter 13 of *Marketing: Theory and Practice* (1995).

☐ *Consonance and dissonance*

At various places in the text reference has been made to dissonance and it will be useful to indicate the role this concept has to play in marketing communications.

In the discussion of perception (pp. 149–152) it was indicated that we seek to organise perceived stimuli (cognitions) into coherent and consistent patterns which are in accord with our knowledge, beliefs and attitudes – in other words we are seeking a state of *consonance*. If two cognitions are not consonant, they may be either irrelevant, that is they have no relationship to one another, or dissonant, that is in conflict with each other. Clearly dissonant cognitions create a state of psychological tension which the individual will seek to avoid, reduce or eliminate. It is also clear that in any choice situation there is a potential for dissonance, as the recognition of choice implies alternative solutions to a perceived need. In many consumer purchasing situations these alternatives are very similar and the propensity for dissonance is correspondingly greater.

Attention was first focused upon this phenomenon by the publication of Leon A. Festinger's (1957) *A Theory of Cognitive Dissonance*, and has been the subject of much interest ever since. It is generally agreed that dissonance can arise from one of three basic causes – logical inconsistency, a conflict between attitude and behaviour or two behaviours, and when a strongly held belief is contravened or negated. Faced with a state of dissonance we tend to use a number of approaches to remove the state, and all these contain elements of selectivity. *Avoidance* is a clear example in which we screen out stimuli which conflict with our preferred interpretation (this can occur both before a decision and after and may be subconscious), while in the case of *rationalisation* we interpret the stimuli to suit our preferred belief (cf. the example of the American football match on p. 151). Alternatively we can *seek additional information* which supports our choice – again on a selective basis or forget or suppress the inconsistent information we have. It follows that dissonance can occur at any stage of the purchase decision, though most interest has been shown in the post-purchase phase when commitment has been made to a particular choice, and is likely to be most acute in the case of major purchase decisions.

In a paper given at the 1970 Market Research Society Annual Conference ('The Complementary Benefit Principle of How Advertising Works in Relation to the Product') Peter Hutchinson suggested that the existence of cognitive dissonance has two basic lessons for practitioners:

1. Perfect in manufacture those product benefits which are readily available.

2. Advertise those attributes which are not immediately observable or easily learned.

The first recommendation underlines the importance of ensuring that those dimensions on which direct comparisons can be made are highly developed in one's product, while the second emphasises the need to provide the potential user with additional reasons for preferring your alternative to all the others.

☐ *The message and the medium*

Earlier in the chapter reference was made to Schramm's four basic conditions for successful communication, all of which involved the basic element of communication – the message. The message is the subject of a separate chapter in DeLozier (1976) and this source should be consulted for a full discussion of the topic. Only a brief overview can be presented here.

There are three dimensions of messages which demand particular attention – structure, appeal or content, and the symbolic code (words, music, gesture, and so on) in which the message is couched.

The structure of a message embraces three main considerations – whether it should be a one-sided or two-sided presentation, the sequence in which information should be presented, and whether a conclusion should be offered. In fact there is no single preferred structure, for this will vary according to the audience. For example, one-sided messages are most effective with people who agree with the source, are poorly educated and unlikely to be exposed to any counter-arguments, while a two-sided message is better suited to convert persons inclining to an opposite opinion, better educated and likely to be exposed to counter-arguments Similarly, in the case of sequence some messages are more effective when they build up to a climax (high audience interest), others to an anti-climax (low audience interest), while in the case of two-sided arguments controversial material is most effective when pre-

sented first (the *primacy* effect) and bland or uninteresting information is favoured by *recency*, that is the material presented last is more effective. Finally, while messages are in general more effective if a conclusion is presented, this applies more to persons of low intelligence than persons of high intelligence and is less so. In all cases where the source is seen as having a vested interest in the conclusion. Much of the same applies where drawing a conclusion would insult the audience's intelligence.

In the case of message appeal, DeLozier cites six alternative approaches – fear, distraction, participation, emotion *versus* rational, aggression arousal, and humour. Of these the most controversial are the use of fear appeals and distraction methods. Much criticism has been levelled against advertisements for consumer products which suggest that non-possession will lead to loss of status or social unacceptability (for example deodorants), while the use of fear is widely supported in health and safety advertising. Distraction is also criticised on the grounds that it diminishes/influences critical judgement concerning the prime subject of the communication, for example the expense-account lunch or the use association in consumer advertisements. Overall the evidence regarding the efficiency of different message appeals confirms that it is situation-specific and must be varied in light of the circumstances they are expected to encounter.

Some mention has already been made of the symbolic code in which a message is couched. Here the evidence is more clear cut and indicates that while choice of words can have an important bearing upon the interpretation of a message, non-verbal communications are often more important in conveying ideas and meaning than words alone. The validity of this is readily apparent in television commercials when sound and movement can be combined to enhance the impact of the purely verbal message to be put across.

At this juncture no reference will be made to the advertising media through which a message is conveyed to an audience, as this is discussed at some length in the next chapter.

The role of communication in the marketing mix

As a process marketing is firmly founded on the assumption of effective two-way communication – of consumers telling firms what they want and firms informing consumers what they have to sell. In this sense communication is central to everything the firm does and pervades all its activities. However, when we speak of marketing communications we do so in the more restricted sense of those functional activities which are collectively known as 'promotion' – advertising, personal selling, public relations and sales promotion. Each of these topics is treated at some length in the chapters which follow but before turning to these it will be useful to summarise the basic objectives of promotional strategy.

Martin Bell (1972) in *Marketing: Concepts and Strategy*, rightly observes that each item on an exhaustive list of promotional objectives would need a chapter to itself and contents himself by selecting seven for specific mention:

1. Increase sales;
2. Maintain or improve market share;
3. Create or improve brand recognition, acceptance or insistence;
4. Create a favourable climate for future sales;
5. Inform and educate the market;
6. Create a competitive difference;
7. Improve promotional efficiency.

Clearly there is considerable overlap between these seven objectives but the distinction between them is important because emphasis upon any one will tend to lead to a different *promotional mix* being required. For example, creating a favourable climate for future sales is most appropriate for industrial products and consumer durables where there is a long repurchase cycle. Thus customers need to have the wisdom of their previous purchase confirmed in order to reduce post-purchase cognitive dissonance and will also

respond favourably to advice on how to get the best out of their purchase. Conversely if one is seeking to win customers from other manufacturers, then one may be seeking to engender cognitive dissonance by suggesting the currently preferred brand is inferior to your own. To achieve these objectives it will often be necessary to use different messages and different channels – a requirement which will only be apparent if one has carefully defined the objective in advance.

Bell also cites five key conditions which favour the use of promotion in the marketing mix:

1. A favourable trend in demand;
2. Strong product differentiation;
3. Product qualities are hidden;
4. Emotional buying motives exist;
5. Adequate funds are available.

While a favourable trend in demand will usually result in a greater apparent return on one's promotional investment, it should not be overlooked that maintaining sales under conditions of stagnant or declining demand is equally and sometimes more important. Similarly, while the existence of strong product differentiation will allow clear distinctions to be drawn with competing products, it must also be remembered that the greater the departure from known and trusted concepts, the greater the intrinsic resistance to change. For these reasons it often happens that the most effective promotions are those which communicate hidden product qualities (purity, taste, durability, and so forth) which can only be recognised in use, coupled with promotions which appeal to emotional buying motives. (As noted in my model of buying behaviour in Chapter 6, faced with a need to discriminate between two objectively similar competitive brands, the subjective/emotional factors may be trivial but determinant.) Finally, it is a truism to extol the need for adequate funds but it is a factor which is often overlooked, as will be noted when discussing advertising appropriations in the next chapter.

Marketing communications as information processing

In earlier editions reference was made to the eclectic nature of the foregoing review of marketing communications which was supported by a recommendation that the reader consult the named sources for a fuller treatment. At several places reference has been made to Keith Crosier who has made many helpful and cogent criticisms which I have attempted to accommodate in this revision. However, his most radical suggestion – that I completely restructure the chapter – I have chosen largely to ignore, on the grounds that he is concerned with the latest state of the art in marketing communication theory whereas my perception of an introductory text book is that it must record and analyse the received wisdom and practices which enjoy common currency. That said it is also important that the reader should be exposed to the latest thinking and this section examines Crosier's argument, referred to in the introduction to the chapter, that we abandon traditional theories in favour of one based on information processing.

Clues to Crosier's thinking are to be found in Chapter 13 of the *Marketing: Theory & Practice* (1995, 3rd edn), but even this recent contribution lacks the integrative framework which becomes possible by using information processing theory. Thus his proposals are to be found in an article entitled 'Towards a Praxiology of Advertising' (Crosier, 1983), the abstract of which states:

> This article argues for the need to abandon traditional models of advertising effect, if a theory is to be developed which is capable of fitting the observable reality that people use advertisements deliberately rather than being used by them. Using information processing theory as the best available organising principle, it proposes a number of candidate elements of a future, fully grounded theory of advertising.

In the opening paragraph we are told that 'Praxiology is the study of human action. The term is used here to express the crucial idea that people voluntarily and deliberately consume and use advertisements, in contrast to the commonly implied alternative that advertising manipulates people.' Crosier then goes on to argue that:

> Where advertising is concerned the prevailing grand theory is operant conditioning, expressed in the form of various hierarchical models of advertising effect all implicitly conforming to the stimulus–response – or at best stimulus–organism–response – paradigm of human behaviour. In the half century since Pavlov died at the age of 87, the social and cultural influences upon response to stimuli such as advertisements have of course changed considerably.

Thus we need to reconsider the relevance and applicability of this model by observing how people actually behave when reacting to modern advertising.

As we have inferred earlier, 'The conversation and publications of advertising practitioners, social critics of advertising, consumerists and politicians very often hinge upon an important implicit hypothesis: that advertising is something powerful firms do to powerless (though sometime stubborn) consumers.' But this is an assumption rejected by our earlier composite model of buying behaviour and by Crosier's conceptualisation of Advertisement Processing Behaviour reproduced as Figure 15.6.

In support of his model Crosier cites Sternthal and Craig's (1982) proposal that purchase and consumption decisions are viewed in terms of how individuals acquire, organise and use information. According to this view, consumers are active seekers and users of information although they may indulge in such behaviour for purposes other than specific product purchase decisions. (Crosier proposes six other uses in addition to 'hard' information – entertainment, added value, implied warrant, reassurance, involvement, vicarious experience.) Thus without departing entirely from the classical operant conditioning or stimulus–response process implicit in the hierarchical models, the information processing model assigns much greater important to consumers as participants rather than passive objects and so is more in keeping with the view of behaviour advanced in Chapter 6.

Figure 15.6 *A model of advertisement-processing behaviour*

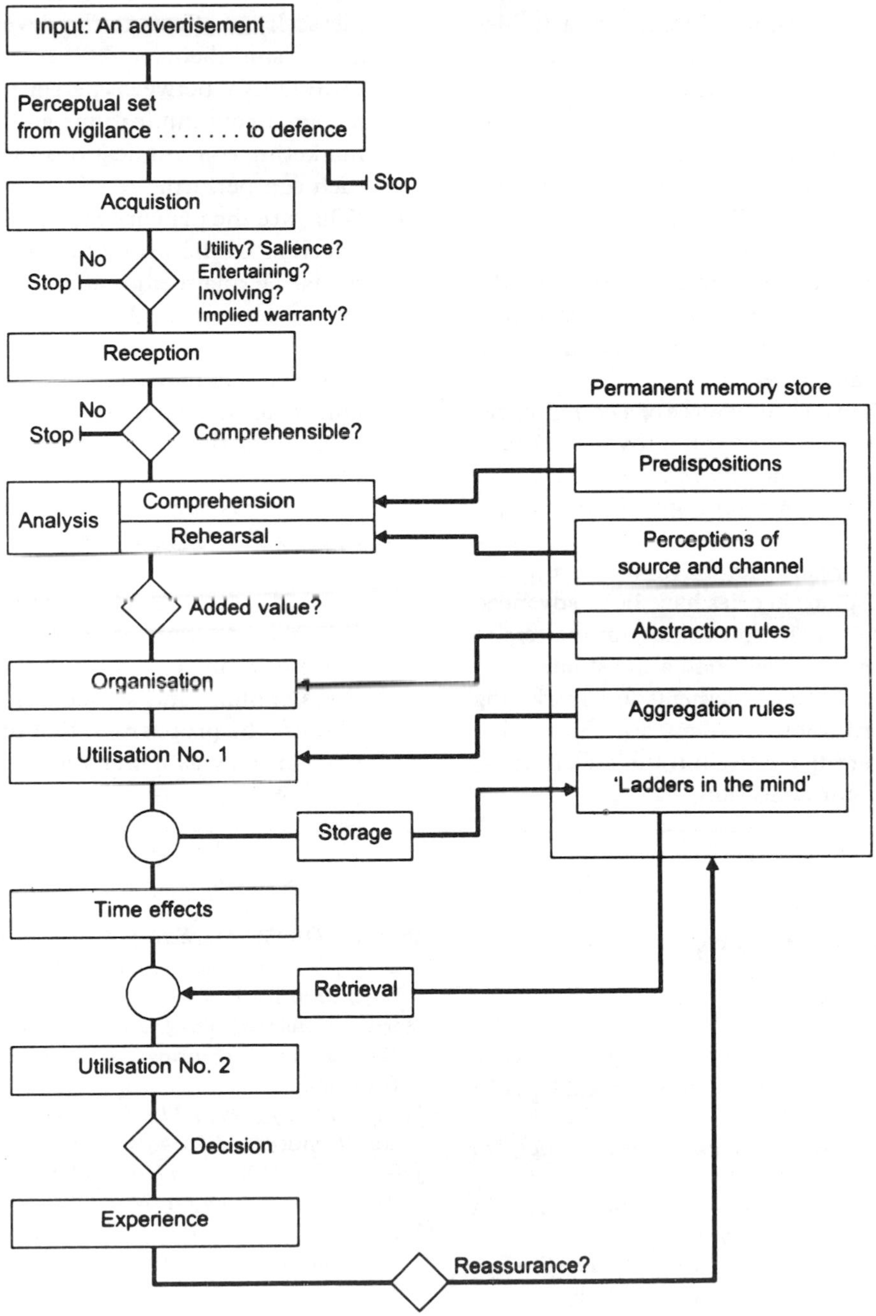

Source: Keith Crosier (1983), 'Towards a praxiology of advertising', *International Journal of Advertising*, vol. 2, no. 3 (July–Sept.).

Review questions and problems

1. It has been suggested that the major thrust of consumer protection activities should be concentrated on the provision of information. Can this be justified?
2. Sandage and Fryburger's 'model' of how advertising is thought to work is based on four stages: exposure/perception/integration/action. Describe what takes place at the *integration* stage.
3. How might the characteristics of the 'message' itself affect the success or failure of an advertisement? Discuss with specific examples.
4. With regard to the source of a communication, what factors can provoke attitude change in the recipient? What alternatives to attitude change are open to the recipient?
5. Do we really know how advertising works? What theories have been advanced that might help you to explain matters to a person who asks such a question?
6. Identify the main elements in a marketing communication system and say what factors are likely to limit the effectiveness of the communication.
7. Discuss the contribution of models of the hierarchy of effects to the development of advertising theory.
8. Distinguish between personal and non-personal communications and outline the marketing communications functions that each can perform.
9. What are the primary factors affecting the selection of the promotional mix components? Explain the effect each of the factors has on the final promotional mix adopted.
10. What factors may explain the widespread failure to set objectives for a marketing communications campaign before it begins?
11. The famous sage, Dr Johnson, remarked in 1759 that 'advertisements are by now so numerous that they are but negligently perused, and it is therefore become necessary to gain attention by magnificence of promise and by eloquence sometimes sublime and sometimes ridiculous.' Discuss the proposition that his view is as relevant now as it was then.

Supplementary reading list

Aaker, David A. and Myers, John G. (1990) *Advertising Management*, 3rd edn (Englewood Cliffs, N.J.: Prentice-Hall).

Baker, M. J. (1995) *Marketing Theory and Practice*, 3rd edn (London: Macmillan).

Baker, M. J. (1994) *The Marketing Book*, 3rd edn (Oxford: Heinemann), Chapter 21.

DeLoizier, M. Wayne (1976) *The Marketing Communication Process* (New York: McGraw-Hill).

Dyer, Gillian (1982) *Advertising as Communication* (London: Methuen).

Fill, C. (1995) *Marketing Communications: Frameworks, Theories and Applications* (Englewood Cliffs, N.J.: Prentice-Hall).

Harris, Richard, J. (ed.) (1983) *Information Processing Research in Advertising* (Hillsdale, N.J.: Lawrence Erlbaum).

Hart, N. (ed.) (1995) *The Practice of Advertising*, 4th edn (London: Butterworth-Heinemann).

Jefkins, F. (1985) *Public Relations in Marketing Management* (London: Macmillan).

Van Riel, C. B. M. (1995) *The Principles of Corporate Communications* (Englewood Cliffs, N.J.: Prentice-Hall).

Advertising

Contents

Learning goals

The issues to be addressed in this chapter include:

1. The nature and objectives of advertising.
2. The evolution of advertising.
3. The structure of advertising in the marketing mix.
4. The role of advertising in the marketing mix.
5. The organisation of advertising in terms of both advertisers and agencies.
6. Agency selection and remuneration.
7. The characteristics of the major advertising media.
8. Campaign planning and setting the advertising appropriation.
9. The measurement of advertising effectiveness.
10. The economic and ethical aspects of advertising.

After reading this chapter you will be able to:

1. Define advertising.
2. List specific objectives which advertising may be used to achieve.

3. Describe the historical development and evolution of advertising.
4. Cite some vital statistics to help describe the size and nature of the advertising industry.
5. Outline the structure of the advertising industry and distinguish the roles of the three main parties involved in the advertising process – advertisers, agents and media owners.
6. Discuss the role of advertising in the marketing mix.
7. Suggest how a firm might organise for advertising.
8. Review the role and function of advertising agencies.
9. Explain the basis of agency remuneration.
10. Give advice on agency selection.
11. Indicate how to evaluate different advertising media.
12. Summarise some of the key features of the national press, regional press, Sunday newspapers, magazines, television, commercial radio, outdoor advertising, the cinema and direct mail.

13. Outline the procedure to follow when planning an advertising campaign.
14. Review alternative methods for setting advertising appropriations.
15. Describe methods for assessing advertising effectiveness.
16. Indicate some of the economic and ethical issues associated with advertising.

■ Definitions and objectives

Essentially advertising is a means of spreading information. This is too broad a description, however, to be useful as a definition, or to distinguish it from other forms of communication. The American Marketing Association has adopted the following as a definition: Any paid form of non-personal presentation and promotion of ideas, goods or services by an identified sponsor. This is certainly a very succinct statement and merits some elaboration. Firstly, advertising is paid for, it is a commercial transaction, and it is this which distinguishes it from publicity. It is non-personal in the sense that advertising messages, visual, spoken or written, are directed at a mass audience, and not directly at the individual as is the case in personal selling. Direct mail is, of course, targeted at individuals but is still regarded as an impersonal source in the terms of this definition. Finally, advertisements are identifiable with their sponsor or originator, which is not always the case with publicity or propaganda.

The nature and role of sales promotion are dealt with in the next chapter, but it will be useful at this point to give the AMA's definition to avoid confusion with advertising *per se* in the meantime. Sales promotion: those marketing activities, other than personal selling, advertising and publicity, that stimulate consumer purchasing and dealer effectiveness, such as displays, shows and exhibitions, demonstrations, and various non-recurrent selling efforts not in the ordinary routine.

□ *Objectives*

The ultimate purpose underlying all advertising is increased awareness. Many authors would also ally this with some form of statement concerning an increase in profit, but this is anticipating an end result applicable only to trading organisations, which is also attributable to a host of other factors (clearly, advertisements sponsored by government departments concerning road safety, or the health hazards of smoking, are not designed to increase profits).

Despite the problems inherent in measuring the effectiveness of advertising, which are the subject of a subsequent section of this chapter, it is only realistic to state that firms invest in advertising expenditures in the expectation of an improvement in profitability. If one examines the specific objectives which may motivate a particular advertising campaign, it is clear that an improvement in profit varies from a primary, to a very subsidiary, motive. An examination of the specific objectives listed by Matthews, Buzzell, Levitt and Frank (1964) in *Marketing: An Introductory Analysis* makes this clear:

1. To build primary demand;
2. To introduce a price deal;
3. To inform about a product's availability;
4. To build brand recognition or brand preference or brand insistence;
5. To inform about a new product's availability or features or price;
6. To help salesmen by building an awareness of a product among retailers;
7. To create a reputation for service, reliability or research strength;
8. To increase market share;
9. To modify existing product appeals and buying motives;
10. To increase frequency of use of a product;
11. To inform about new uses of a product;
12. To increase the number or quality of retail outlets;

13. To build the overall company image;
14. To effect immediate buying action;
15. To reach new areas or new segments of population within existing areas;
16. To develop overseas markets.

The above list is by no means exhaustive, but it does indicate that the aim underlying a campaign may be directed at a short-term increase in sales volume (price deals and other promotional offers), the development of a new market, an increased share of an existing market, or the building of a favourable attitude to the company as a whole (corporate advertising). The latter, like an increase in retail distribution, is a long-term objective for which it would be difficult to assess the actual return on the advertising investment.

Whatever the specific objective or purpose, it is generally agreed that its statement in explicit terms is an essential prerequisite of a successful campaign. Similarly, it is also agreed that certain conditions are more favourable to successful advertising than others, for example an expanding market, or possession of a feature which differentiates the product from its competitors. This point will be returned to when discussing advertising strategy.

The evolution of advertising

It is often erroneously assumed that the advertising function is of recent origin, a point commented on by Henry Sampson (1874) in his *History of Advertising*, 'It is generally assumed – though the assumption has no ground for existence beyond that so common among us, that nothing exists of which we are ignorant – that advertisements are of comparatively modern origin.'

There is some evidence to suggest that the Romans practised advertising, but the earliest indication of its use in this country dates from the Middle Ages with the adoption of surnames indicative of a man's occupation, as opposed to some other distinguishing designation (Harrison = Harry's son). The producer's name is of equal importance today as a means of identifying the source of goods and services.

Signs represented the next stage in the evolution of advertising, acting as a visual expression of the tradesman's function as well as a means of locating the source of goods at a time when the numbering of houses was unknown. One can still see vestiges of the practice in the barber's pole, or the symbolic boot or glove.

The craft guilds of the Middle Ages disapproved of competition among their members, but were not averse to competition with one another in the adoption of distinctive liveries, or the sponsoring of mystery plays – an early form of institutional advertising! At the same time many guilds adopted trade marks as a means of identifying the producer, and as a guarantee of quality – the adoption of corporate symbols, as a more immediate means of recognising the firm's identity than the written word, is an interesting reversion to this practice.

Although Caxton had invented the hand press by the end of the fifteenth century, the use of the written word in advertising was limited by the low level of literacy, so confining written advertisements to the clergy. By Shakespeare's time posters had made their appearance, and the few remaining examples make it clear that advertising had assumed the function of fostering demand for new products as well as increasing demand for existing products.

Another important development at this time was the emergence of the pamphlet as an advertising medium, early examples of which disclose their sponsorship by companies bent on generating goodwill for their activities. (Later examples are more veiled as to their origin and, properly, should be considered as propaganda.) However, the seventeenth century was a period of unrest in England, resulting in government censorship which was to hinder the development of regular publications. From 1620 onwards a number of Mercuries, Gazettes, etc., made their appearance, but were mainly short-lived, and carried few advertisements.

The high cost of posters and handbills encouraged a number of publishers to experiment with the issue of free papers comprised solely of advertisements. Their success was limited, however, and posters and handbills continued as the main media until the early eighteenth century. An examination of the periodicals of the early 1700s, such as the *Tatler* and *Spectator*, reveals an increasing number of advertisements, but this growth was abruptly curtailed in 1712 by the imposition of a tax on both papers and advertisements. The first Stamp Act levied a tax of $\frac{1}{2}d$ per copy on publications and $12d$ per advertisement, supposedly to raise revenue but in fact intended to curtail a libellous and seditious press.

The effect of the tax was virtually immediate – the majority of unsubsidised papers ceased publication, and the legitimate businessman severely curtailed his use of advertising. On the other hand, the quacks and charlatans, with their enormous profit margins to fall back on, continued to advertise, and it is worth noting that the generally unsavoury nature of the advertising of this time was a direct consequence of government censorship and heavy taxation. Under the circumstances neither government control nor taxation would appear to be as effective as modern critics of advertising would have one believe.

The tax on advertisements was abolished in 1853, at a time ripe for the development of mass advertising as we know it today. Mass production was a reality, and channels of distribution were being developed to cope with the physical movement of goods, creating a need for mass communication to inform consumers of the choice available to them. This need was soon recognised by the forerunner of today's advertising agent – the space salesman. Initially space salesmen located customers for the media owners, receiving commission on the space they sold. Gradually the position changed, and the agent became a space-broker, or middleman, buying space wholesale from the media owner and reselling it retail, often at a profit of 25 per cent. The profits to be earned attracted competition and the agents found it necessary to offer incentives to advertisers to purchase space from them, in preference to their competitors. Thus the practice evolved of giving the advertiser free assistance in preparing his copy and later, as the number of publications increased,

of selecting the media which would prove most effective in reaching the advertiser's potential customers. In essence this is the system which still obtains today, with the agent looking upon the advertiser as his client, while deriving most of his income from commissions paid by the media owner. (Many advertising agents now charge a service fee on smaller accounts, or where additional work is undertaken on-behalf of the advertiser.)

Towards the end of the last century increased competition between advertising agencies led to the practice of 'commission rebates' in both Britain and the USA whereby the agencies offered the client a discount or rebate from the commission received by him from the media owner. The practice was frowned upon by the more professional agencies, on the grounds that it could only lead to lower standards of service, but after a few years the issue ceased to be contentious, presumably because the practice was limited. Recently, however, competitive pressures have seen a revival of rebating in the UK with strong attacks on the system headed by Allen Brady and Marsh (ABM) who argue that a 15 per cent commission only yields 2 per cent net profit after tax for the typical full service agency. ABM stated publicly that they would refuse to work for a client seeking a rebate, and in 1983 resigned the £3.5 million B & Q account on just those grounds. While a negotiated fee system would seem to be the safest way of ensuring that both client and agency receive what they expect, there is no indication that the commission system will be changed in the foreseeable future.

Reference to ABM's campaign to discourage rebating underlines an important facet of the practice of advertising: namely, that while it is subject to a certain amount of statutory regulation it has been particularly successful in retaining responsibility for its own *self-regulation*. Thus while the Television Acts and the 1973 Sound Broadcasting Act which superseded them imposed a duty to establish an obligatory pre-clearance of commercials, press advertising is subject to the Advertising Standards Authority Code of Advertising Practice which is a logical evolution of earlier codes of practice devised by the profession in response to criticism of certain kinds of advertisement. Full details of the ASA's code and *modus operandi* are contained in leaflets published by them and additional information may be obtained from both the Advertising Association (AA) and the Institute of Practitioners in Advertising (IPA).

■ Industry statistics

Before looking at the present-day practice of advertising and the salient characteristics of the major media it will be helpful to review some of the industry's vital statistics.

In 1994 total advertising expenditure by UK advertisers amounted to £7979 million while the institute of Sales Promotion estimates total expenditure for 1987 at £1500 million. The break-

down of this expenditure and some comparisons with other budget headings are contained in Tables 16.1 to 16.7 inclusive. While accurate at the time of writing the sources cited should be consulted regularly for up-to-date statistics.

■ The structure of advertising

The above description outlining the evolution of advertising makes it clear that at least three separate parties are involved in the advertising process:

- The advertiser;
- The advertising agent;
- The media owner.

Table 16.1 *Total advertising expenditure and its relation to consumers' expenditure and gross national product*

			Total expenditure as a percentage of:	
Year	Total expenditure at 1990 Prices[1] £m	Total expenditure at current prices £m	Consumers' expenditure[2] at market prices	Gross National Product[2] at factor cost
1981	4862	2884	1.87	1.31
1982	4987	3211	1.90	1.34
1983	5477	3689	1.99	1.40
1984	5924	4188	2.11	1.47
1985	6144	4608	2.12	1.49
1986	6869	5328	2.21	1.60
1987	7532	6084	2.29	1.67
1988	8361	7085	2.37	1.75
1989	8630	7883	2.41	1.77
1990	7946	7946	2.29	1.66
1991	7215	7637	2.09	1.54
1992	7208	7915	2.07	1.52
1993	7383	8233	2.03	1.50
1994	7979	9119	2.13	1.55

Notes: [1] Data are the current price figures deflated buy the Retail Price Index (1990 = 100)

[2] Due to revisions made by the Central Statistical Office to GNP and consumers' expenditure data – often going back many years – the ratios given in this table may differ slightly from ratios given in previous years

Source: The Advertising Association's *Advertising Statistics Yearbook 1995*, tables 2.1, 3.1.1, 3.1.2. Please see this source for definitions.

Table 16.2 *Total advertising expenditure by medium and by type*

	£ million						Percentage of total					
	1989	1990	1991	1992	1993	1994	1989	1990	1991	1992	1993	1994
By medium												
National newspapers, incl col. suppl.	1222	1187	1121	1155	1220	1336	15.5	14.9	14.7	14.6	14.8	14.6
Regional newspapers, incl. free sheets	1707	1715	1628	1640	1715	1871	21.7	21.6	21.3	20.7	20.8	20.5
Consumer magazines	536	541	506	466	448	499	6.8	6.8	6.6	5.9	5.4	5.5
Business & profesional magazines	838	790	708	746	741	828	10.6	9.9	9.3	9.4	8.7	9.1
Directories	439	492	504	523	551	589	5.6	6.2	6.6	6.6	6.7	6.5
Press productions costs	389	412	417	427	438	478	4.9	5.2	5.5	5.4	5.3	5.2
Total press	**5131**	**5137**	**4884**	**4957**	**5085**	**5600**	**65.1**	**64.7**	**64.0**	**62.6**	**61.8**	**61.4**
Television, incl. prod. costs	2288	2325	2295	2472	2605	2873	29.0	29.3	30.1	31.2	31.6	31.5
Outdoor & transport, incl. prod. costs	271	282	267	284	300	350	3.4	3.5	3.5	3.6	3.6	3.8
Cinema, incl. prod. costs	35	39	42	45	49	53	0.4	0.5	0.5	0.6	0.6	0.6
Radio, incl. prod. costs	159	163	149	157	194	243	2.0	2.1	2.0	2.0	2.4	2.7
Total	7883	7946	7637	7915	8233	9119	100.0	100.0	100.0	100.0	100.0	100.0
By type												
Display advertising												
Press[1]	2987	2961	2875	2951	3008	3281	37.9	37.3	37.6	37.3	36.5	36.0
Television	2288	2235	2295	2472	2605	2873	29.0	29.3	30.1	31.2	31.6	31.5
Other media[2]	465	483	458	485	543	646	5.8	6.1	6.0	6.2	6.6	7.1
Total display	**5740**	**5769**	**5628**	**5908**	**6156**	**6800**	**72.8**	**72.6**	**73.7**	**74.7**	**74.8**	**74.6**
Classified advertising[3]	**2143**	**2176**	**2009**	**2006**	**2078**	**2319**	**27.2**	**27.4**	**26.3**	**25.3**	**25.2**	**25.4**
Total	**7883**	**7946**	**7637**	**7915**	**8233**	**9119**	**100.0**	**100.0**	**100.0**	**100.0**	**100.0**	**100.0**

Notes: [1] Including financial notices and display advertising in business and professional journals, but not advertising in directories
[2] Outdoor and transport, cinema and radio
[3] Including all directory advertising
For expenditure on Direct Mail (£1050m in 1994) see page 81

Source: The Advertising Association's *Advertising Statistics Yearbook 1995*, tables 3.1.1, 3.1.3, 4.1.1 and 4.1.2. Please see this source for definitions.

In market terms, advertisers constitute buyers and media owners sellers, and consequently they take considerable direct interest in each other's activities. In many instances advertiser and media owner will negotiate direct with one another, but beyond a certain point the intervention of a third party becomes desirable, which accounts for the existence of advertising agents.

From the advertiser's point of view the agency constitutes a reservoir of skills which it would be difficult to duplicate in even the largest company at an economic cost – for the smaller company it would be impossible. Further, the discount on the purchase of time and/or space in the various media is usually restricted to established and recognised advertising agencies, which enables

Table 16.3 *Trends in UK advertising expenditure (excluding direct mail)*

	Advertising expenditure (£m)	GDP at market prices £m	Adv as %	Consumers' expenditure £m	Adv as %
1975	957	105 852	0.92	65 590	1.49
1976	1207	125 247	0.96	76 225	1.58
1977	1524	145 983	1.04	87 165	1.75
1978	1869	168 526	1.11	100 524	1.86
1979	2187	198 221	1.10	119 212	1.83
1980	2604	231 772	1.12	136 564	1.88
1981	2884	254 927	1.13	154 274	1.87
1982	3211	279 041	1.15	169 393	1.90
1983	3689	304 456	1.21	185 611	1.99
1984	4188	325 852	1.29	198 820	2.11
1985	4608	357 344	1.29	217 485	2.12
1986	5328	384 843	1.38	241 554	2.21
1987	6084	423 381	1.44	265 290	2.29
1988	7085	471 430	1.50	299 449	2.37
1989	7883	515 957	1.53	327 363	2.41
1990	7946	551 118	1.44	347 527	2.29
1991	7637	573 641	1.33	365 057	2.09
1992	7995	595 258	1.33	382 362	2.07
1993	8257	627 149	1.32	405 647	2.03
1994	7555	508 859	1.48	324 348	2.33

Source: Advertising Association, *Advertising Statistics Yearbook*, 1994.

the agency to offer its services free of charge to the advertiser under normal circumstances. From the media owner's point of view, agencies act as wholesalers, bulking together a host of orders from a variety of sources, thus reducing the area of contact between buyer and seller to manageable proportions. In addition the agent is familiar with the media owner's language and method of operation, and, in a sense, acts as an interpreter between the parties. Both these factors create economies which the media owner considers justification for the payment of commission.

In addition to these three major participants at least two others have emerged in recent years – the *creative* specialist and the *media* specialist. Advertising agencies of the kind referred to above had traditionally handled all aspects of their clients advertising business and so were known as *full service* agencies. However, their ability to provide the depth and quality of service across

the board was questioned by some and led to the establishment of 'boutiques' or 'hot shops' specialising solely in the creative aspects of campaign planning. Not being eligible for commission on media buying, creative specialists

Table 16.4 *Annual expenditure by product category, 1993*

	£m
Government	60.8
Food	559.4
Motors	405.2
Toiletries and cosmetics	230.9
Leisure equipment	149.3
Household appliances	76.2
Tobacco	24.1

Source: Advertising Association, *Advertising Statistics Yearbook*, 1994.

Table 16.5   *Key holding companies'*
advertising expenditure

	Total 1993 £000	Total 1992 £000	Change %
Unilever	211 043	192 636	9.6
Procter and Gamble	140 786	140 718	0.0
HM Government	79 739	59 938	33.0
Nestlé Holdings (UK)	76 974	85 263	−9.7
Kingfisher	74 224	61 613	20.5
Mars (GB)	70 702	65 779	7.5
Kellogg	61 641	61 494	0.2
British Telecom	61 056	48 499	25.9
Ford	60 818	53 655	13.4
General Motors	56 880	41 567	36.8

Source: *Marketing Week* Magazine, 13 May 1994.

work on a fee basis. By contrast media specialists are eligible for media commission and, because they have lower overheads, often rebate part of this as an inducement to advertisers.

Before examining the interaction of the parties in the development of an advertising campaign it will be useful to look at the role of the three major parties – advertiser, agents, and media owners – in somewhat greater detail.

The role of advertising in the marketing mix – the advertiser's viewpoint

As was noted earlier, the justification for advertising from the advertiser's point of view is that it increases profitability, even though it is difficult to quantify precisely to what extent. (Mail order is the only case where a sale can be directly credited to the publication of an advertisement.) Advertising is but one variable in the marketing mix, albeit an important one, and it is difficult to separate its contribution from that of the other mix elements. As was implied in the list of advertising goals in the section on 'Objectives', there are a number of ways in which advertising

may increase the profitability of the firm. R. H. Colley (1961) lists 52 specific goals in *Defining Advertising Goals*, and these are stated more explicitly below:

1. To increase demand to the point where economies of scale are achieved. The larger the fixed costs of production, the greater the unit contribution once the break-even point has been reached – 'leverage'. The advertiser may wish initially to build primary demand for the product group as a whole, anticipating that he will benefit proportionally from the overall growth of the market. Once product acceptance has been achieved, advertisers usually concentrate on building brand recognition and loyalty. Colour television is a good example of this in that early advertisements for sets tended to emphasise the benefits of colour as compared with black and white, that is selling colour rather than brand A, B or C. As the market becomes more competitive, advertisers concentrate on extolling the features of their product which differentiate it from that of other producers.

2. The building of a 'brand image' in a competitive, mature market has other benefits in addition to maintaining or improving the firm's competitive position. Brand recognition and brand loyalty relieve the producer of their dependence on the distributive channels. This is particularly true of convenience goods, but is also applicable to shopping goods where the manufacturer can place little reliance on either the ability or interest of the retailer to sell their specific product. Only where a retailer is a sole distributor can the producer rely on an equal and corresponding interest in the sale of their product.

3. Information gathering invariably precedes the purchase of a product to some degree and, clearly, the ready availability of such information in the form of advertisements reduces the prospective purchaser's dependence on personal selling. Personal selling is a cost to the producer, both directly, in the payment of his sales force, and indirectly, through the margin he has to offer middlemen

Table 16.6 *The top 25 advertisers, 1994*
(compiled by Register-MEAL)

| | | | Advertising expenditure | | |
Rank	Advertiser	Total £'000s	TV %	Radio %	Press %
1	Proctor & Gamble	117 444	94.3	0.2	5.5
2	British Telecom	94 682	55.9	2.1	42.1
3	Ford Motor Company	69 338	70.5	0.5	29.0
4	Lever Brothers (Unilever)	66 827	86.3	2.0	11.6
5	Kellogg Company	66 224	94.2	—	5.8
6	Proctor & Gamble (Health & Beauty)	55 312	94.5	1.0	4.6
7	Vauxhall Motors	52 022	44.3	1.1	54.6
8	Dixon's Stores	48 829	6.3	2.9	90.8
9	Birds Eye Wall's (Unilever)	43 666	80.3	0.1	19.5
10	Peugeot Talbot	39 010	38.8	0.6	60.6
11	Renault (UK)	38 870	57.4	3.6	39.1
12	Elida Gibbs (Unilever)	35 883	84.0	0.4	15.6
13	Rover Group	34 932	45.9	1.2	52.9
14	Citroën (UK)	33 900	42.9	1.2	55.9
15	Mars Confectionery	32 514	94.6	0.5	4.9
16	Nissan (GB)	32 380	42.4	1.8	55.8
17	VAG (UK)	32 136	46.3	0.6	53.1
18	Tesco	32 035	37.3	0.5	62.2
19	Gallaher Tobacco	31 845	—	1.1	98.9
20	Boots The Chemists	29 554	33.1	0.1	66.9
21	Pedigree Petfoods	29 047	96.0	—	4.0
22	McDonalds Restaurants	29 000	77.0	12.8	10.2
23	Nestlé Rowntree	28 163	93.6	2.0	4.4
24	Abbey National	26 930	18.0	1.3	80.6
25	Van den Bergh Foods (Unilever)	26 772	67.3	1.8	30.9

Outdoor, cinema, industrial and overseas publications are excluded. TV expenditure reflects an average discount of 1.3%. Comparison with previous years should be made with caution.
Source: Advertising Association, *Advertising Statistics Yearbook*, 1995.

to perform the service on his behalf. The physical separation of producer and prospective buyer, coupled with competition, make advertising a more economic means of communication than personal contact in both the industrial and consumer selling field. Further, a good advertisement can go a long way to achieve the first two stages of the sales process – the creation of awareness and interest.

4. Most firms are subject to a fluctuating demand for their output, be it seasonal, cyclical or secular, and advertising can do much to minimise such fluctuations though its impact is greatest in the case of seasonal variations. Ice cream and soup are classic examples of building year-round demand for products formerly consumed during a particular season, through informing consumers of alternative uses by means of advertising.

5. Finally, it is maintained that advertising improves profitability in a less tangible way by creating goodwill for the firm as a whole and by improving the morale of its employees; everyone likes to work for a well-known firm.

Table 16.7 *The top 15 UK advertising agency groups in 1993*

Rank 1993	1992	Group	Billings in £m
1	1	WPP Group – UK capitalised	2155
2	2	Interpublic	955
3	3	Saatchi & Saatchi – UK capitalised	896
4	4	Omnicom UK	816
5	5	Euro RSCG	550
6	6	Grey Communications	404
7	7	DMB + B Holdings	385
8	9	Abbot Mead Vickers	342
9	8	MMS	327
10	11	Young and Rubican	295
11	12	Gold Greenlees Trott	201
12	13	BDDP	130
13	14	WMGO	108
14	—	DFSD Bolell	98
15	—	Arc Group	95

Source: Advertising Association, *Advertising Statistics Yearbook*, 1994.

Organisation for advertising within the firm

Recognising the enormous disparity in the size and nature of firms, it is clear that the formulation of generalisations about the nature of the advertising function within the firm is fraught with danger. At the same time, some description of the mythical 'average' firm is useful in that it provides a starting-point for an examination of actual practice in a company with which one is familiar by association, or through reading the practitioners' journals. This caveat should be continually borne in mind, however, in reading this section.

Whatever the specific objective behind the mounting of an advertising campaign, the maximum return on expenditure will only be achieved if the right information is conveyed to the right people in the right way. This is unlikely to be the case unless those responsible for the firm's advertising have a thorough understanding of:

Figure 16.1 *Working relationships in the advertising business*

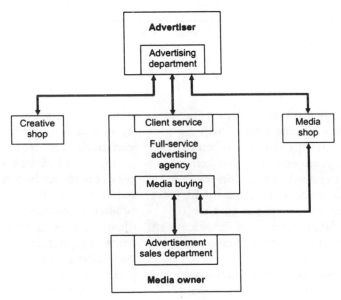

Source: K. C. Crosier (1989), Strathclyde University, MBA Marketing, Distance Learning Module.

Figure 16.2 *Organisation chart for the advertising department of a large, diversified company*

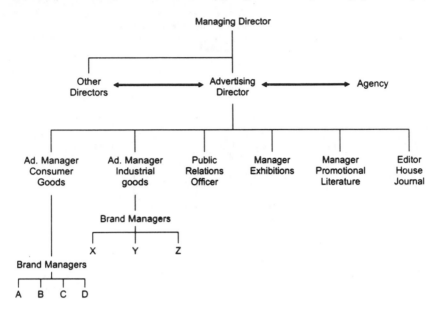

- The nature of the market;
- The nature of the product;
- The nature of the channels of distribution;
- The nature of the channels of communication – the media available, and their characteristics.

From the discussion of the structure of advertising earlier it is clear that advertisers have four options open to them. First, they can do it for themselves 'in-house'; second, they can hand over the responsibility entirely to a full service agency; third, they can buy in creative services but handle the remainder themselves; and, fourth, they can develop their own campaigns but devolve media buying to a specialist. In fact any combination of options could be used and this so-called 'à la carte' approach is proving increasingly popular, so that working relationships in the advertising business can be represented as in Figure 16.1.

In so far as the services of the full service agency and media specialist are 'free' it makes sense for the advertiser to use those wherever possible and avoid duplication within the firm. The critical factor is ability to communicate to the agency what the firm wishes to achieve, and what it has to offer the consumer which differentiates it from its competitors. Essentially, therefore, the advertising manager's role is one of liaison and interpretation (i.e. explaining management's objective to the agency and vice versa).

In the large firm the percentage of revenue allocated to advertising may constitute a very large sum in absolute terms and necessitate the employment of a number of persons to manage it effectively. The organisation chart in Figure 16.2 indicates the appointments that might typically be found in such a company – the actual number of staff employed in each section depending on the importance of advertising and promotion to the firm's marketing effort, and the financial resources allocated to it.

■ The advertising agency

The modern advertising agency of today has advanced a long way from the space salesman of a century ago, to the extent that some feel it would be more appropriate to call it a marketing agency.

Figure 16.3   *Organisation chart for a large advertising agency*

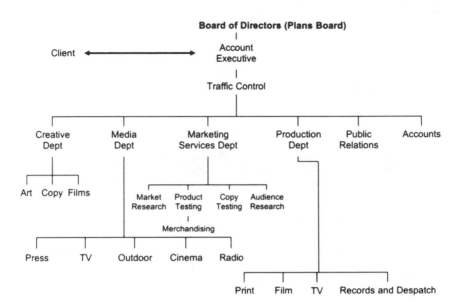

With increasing competition, advertising agents have extended the range of services available to clients, the scope of which is indicated in the organisation chart for a large agency in Figure 16.3. Figure 16.4 indicates more clearly the functions and relationships within a full-service agency. Despite the apparent extent of the agency's expertise implied, it would be incorrect to assume that the agency could substitute for the firm's own marketing department. As was suggested in the preceding section, the advertiser might regard the agency as an extension of their own business, in that it would be uneconomical to duplicate its skills in terms of the creative aspects of advertising, but, at the same time, it would be foolish to delegate the whole marketing function to a third party specialising in only one aspect of it. It is a rule of agencies not to hold competing accounts, and for this reason alone it is unlikely that one could secure the services of an agency with the necessary experience to handle the total marketing of a specific product. It is also true that accounts change hands, so that one might be able to engage an agency with experience in the relevant product field, but this experience will invariably be limited to the advertising problems involved.

If one accepts that the agency is expert in the advertising function, it follows that it will only be able to perform effectively if it is given the full support and confidence of the advertiser. Much of the conflict which arises between advertiser and agent is the direct result of the former only giving the latter part of the information necessary to devise a successful campaign; it is the advertiser's responsibility to feed in the marketing inputs and data around which to build the campaign. While on the subject of the advertiser/agency relationship, it is appropriate to comment that there seems little evidence to suggest that agencies 'wear out', in the sense of losing their creative touch, a belief which prompts some advertisers regularly to change agencies to avoid such an occurrence. Most of the firms which are well known for the quality of their advertising have enjoyed a long and unbroken association with their agency, which suggests that mutual confidence improves over time, as does the expertise of the agent in advertising a particular product.

Figure 16.4 *Functions and relationships in a conventional full-service advertising agency*

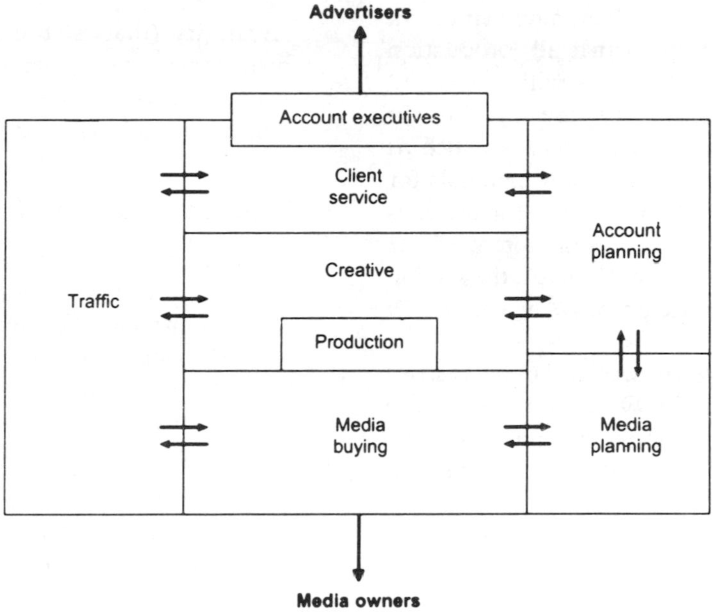

Source: K. C. Crosier, Strathclyde University, MBA Marketing Distance Learning Module.

☐ *Agency remuneration*

Passing reference has already been made to the fact that most, if not all, of the full-service agency's income is derived from commission paid by media owners, but a fuller explanation of this practice will be helpful here.

First, media commission is payable only to *recognised agencies* which have been approved by a consortium of trade associations acting on behalf of the media owners. Two criteria are of particular importance – competence and liquidity – and evidence of both must be provided.

Second, while the arithmetic of commission payments is simple enough it is widely misunderstood, as Crosier makes clear (Strathclyde University, MBA Distance Learning materials):

Suppose that the total *rate-card cost* of media bookings, as published in the media owners' rate cards and in *British Rate and Data* ('BRAD'), is £234 567. A recognised agency is actually charged 15

per cent less than that figure by the media owners concerned. This figure has been the norm since Volney B. Palmer invented the system in 1841, though it took some time to standardise in Britain thereafter. Having said that, it is important to note that smaller-circulation newspapers and magazines give only $12\frac{1}{2}$ or 10 per cent, and that only the five major media (press, television, posters, radio, cinema) offer commission at all; in the business, they are therefore sometimes designated 'above the line', all other vehicles being 'below the line'.

Assuming a straightforward fifteen per cent transaction in this case:

Rate card cost	£234 567
Less 15%	£35 185
Charge to agency	£199 382

The agency invoices its client £234 567, the full cost which the latter can readily check in *BRAD*, and thereby earns £35 185 on the transaction – from the media owners not from the client who has ostensibly 'employed' them.

However, it is widely accepted that 15 per cent media commission is insufficient to cover all the costs involved in a major advertising campaign, and it has become accepted that all 'production charges' and some creative costs will be charged direct to the advertiser by the agency. In addition, if the agency buys in services such as market research or sales promotion materials for its client it will add 17.65 per cent to the price, as this will be equivalent to a commission of 15 per cent on the new 'total' price. (Consult the section on Marketing Arithmetic on p. 474 if you're still not clear!)

The commission system was declared a restrictive trade practice by the OFT in 1978 but the ruling has had little apparent effect so far. However, it seems likely that EU rulings will require a change to either negotiated commissions with the media owners or a service fee between agency and advertiser.

☐ *Agency selection*

From the above comments it is clear that the selection of an advertising agent is not to be undertaken lightly, and the following is suggested as a structured approach to the problem. (This is based on the method adopted by Gateway when selecting an agency.)

1. Prepare a short-list of agencies that you think might be suitable. Details of agencies and their existing accounts can be obtained from the *Advertiser's Annual*. There is nothing to prevent you approaching an agency currently handling a competitor's account, but if they are prepared to drop the existing account to bid for yours, it is unlikely that you will achieve lasting success in this direction. Subjective information on agencies may be obtained from business acquaintances, or by asking media owners to identify the agency responsible for advertisements which you admire.

2. Construct a check-list of the factors on which you intend to base your decision and assign each a weight commensurate with the importance which you attach to each; for example:

   Creativity (that is, the ability to develop a distinctive/novel approach) – 10
   Previous experience in the product field – 8
   Ability to undertake *ad hoc* research – 6, and so on . . .

3. Draw up a questionnaire to:

   (a) Elicit the agency's grasp of the problems inherent in marketing your product, and its approach for dealing with them.
   (b) Provide a basis around which to build a 'Presentation' – that is, an outline for a campaign.

4. Approach the agencies on the short-list and ask them if they are interested in competing for the account. (Some indication should be given of the annual appropriation to be allocated to advertising.) Once the news gets around that you are looking for an agency it is quite likely that several agencies not on the short-list will ask if they may make a presentation. One should resist the temptation to expand the field, if the initial selection was undertaken thoroughly, as it will only serve to confuse the issue, unless there is some very valid reason, for example an agency thought to be unavailable having severed its connection with a competitor.

5. Rate the completed questionnaires in line with the previously determined weights.

6. Convene a selection board from the company's executives, that is Managing Director, Marketing Director, Advertising Manager, and rate the presentations made as for the questionnaires. (To avoid difficulty in resolving the final outcome it is recommended that both the weights and rating scale be given a large spread, thus instead of rating from 1 to 5 use an interval of 5; Worst 5 . . . Best 25.)

In a survey conducted for *Marketing* (15 November 1990) with marketers in 120 companies to find out what clients really think of their agencies the most important factors in choosing an agency were reported as:

Understanding of client needs	8.9*
Creativity	8.6
Media buying	8.0
Brand strategy and planning	7.8
Accessibility of senior management	7.4
Willingness to negotiate on fees	7.0

* Mean score based on clients scoring different aspects of agency performance on a scale of one to ten.

A survey undertaken almost simultaneously by *Marketing Week* provided slightly different results as can be seen from Table 16.8.

Even if one follows a methodical selection procedure such as the one advocated above there is ample evidence that the result may not be satisfactory and a change of agency will be called for. Ken Gofton (1984) examined the agency–client relationship in an article entitled 'What moves the client', and points to J. Walter Thompson's loss of the Guinness account as a classic example of the break-up of an apparently perfect partnership. To throw light on the question, *Marketing* undertook a survey of 100 companies that had changed agencies recently, and concluded that, 'The ability of an agency to understand the client's marketing problem and to

get the staff of both organisations pulling in the same direction emerged as one of the crucial issues.' The findings of the survey are reproduced on the following pages as Tables 16.9 and 16.10.

The findings of the *Marketing* survey correspond quite closely to those reported by Grahame Dowling (1994) based on a survey of 95 Australian companies which had recently changed their agency and 61 which thought they might change in the near future. Table 16.11 reports the 'Reasons for changing advertising agencies' while Table 16.12 summarises the 'Variables important in the final selection of a new advertising agency'.

Of course the success of an agency in meeting its clients' objectives will depend very heavily upon the quality of the briefing it receives. As to what constitutes an ideal brief, Crosier suggests 'First, there should be *general* broad guidelines on creative and media strategies ... Thereafter, the following *specific* ingredients should preferably be included:

1. Unequivocal, measurable objectives;
2. Product profile – technical specifications *and* satisfactions deliverable;
3. Company image/style/atmosphere;
4. Market analysis;
5. Production capacity;
6. Price structure;

Table 16.8 *Criteria ranked in order of importance for overall assessment of agency performance*

Rank 1989	Rank 1990		On 10 point scale Percentage rating 9 or 10 'very important'	Change in % rating very important 1989 to 1990	Average rating
1	1	Creativity	61%	−3%	8.7
2	2	Value for money in results achieved	55%	+9%	8.3
3	3	Media buying and placement	42%	−9%	7.7
5	4	Attentiveness and adaptability to client companies	32%	+4%	8.0
4	5	Quality of account managers	31%	−5%	8.0
6	6	Marketing strategy and analysis	23%	−4%	7.1
7	7	Coverage of major markets outside the UK	3%	−2%	3.3

Source: *Marketing Week*, 16 November 1990.

Table 16.9 *Why clients sack their agencies (% mentioning)*

In a rut – needed new ideas	41%
The results fell short of our expectations	36%
They didn't understand our problems	32%
Couldn't develop the right chemistry with the staff	30%
We weren't getting value for money	25%
Needed to rationalise the agencies used	20%
Product launch or relaunch coming up	14%
Changes of personnel in the agency	11%
Not sufficiently competitive on media buying	11%
Conflict of interests between accounts	9%
Not sufficiently international	9%
Expected more marketing support	7%
We weren't big enough for them	7%
Competitors' activities meant we needed to take a fresh look	5%
Needed to spread our work between more agencies	5%
Offices too distant for easy communication	5%
We'd outgrown the agency	5%
Agency wouldn't negotiate on fees/commission	2%
Security	—

Source: K. Gofton (1984), 'What moves the client', *Marketing*, 27 Sept.

Table 16.10 *What clients look for when choosing an agency (% mentioning)*

Creative record	77%
Evidence that the agency understands my marketing problem	64%
Good personal chemistry with staff	61%
Good media buying record	34%
Marketing skills to supplement those of in-house departments	20%
The agency made the best pitch	16%
A range of services other than marketing	7%
Specialised knowledge of my industry	7%
Appropriate size – our wish to be big fish in the agency pool	5%
A recommendation from people I trust	2%
Location	—
Security	—
Willingness to negotiate on commission fees	—

Note: Respondents were asked to choose three factors from the list.
100 companies were polled, of which 44 replied. Of these, 13 were in food and drink, ten in other FMCG areas, eight in consumer durables, five in services, five in business-to-business or industrial marketing and three in retail

Source: K. Gofton (1984), 'What moves the client', *Marketing*, 27 Sept.

7. Distribution;
8. Media and creative allocations;
9. Criteria for evaluation of effectiveness.

Clearly, given such a brief the potential for misunderstanding is greatly reduced and the likelihood of a harmonious working relationship much improved.

■ The media

The third party to the advertising process is the media owners, and the aim of the following section is to review briefly the salient characteristics of the media available. Before proceeding to this review it will be helpful to outline a checklist as a basis for assessing the value of the various media. In common with most other similar lists appearing elsewhere, the outline given below is based on Hobson's (1956) *Selection of Advertising Media*, published by Business Publications on behalf of the IPA.

An evaluation of an advertising medium requires consideration of four major factors:

1. The character of the medium;
2. The atmosphere of the medium;
3. The coverage of the medium;
4. The cost of the medium.

Two further factors which should be taken into account are the size and position of the advertisement.

Character
The character of a medium may be largely determined on an objective and factual basis through consideration of the following:

Table 16.11 *Reasons for changing advertising agencies*

Rank	Reason	Average score
1	Need for new creative ideas	5.2
2	Need for a new marketing approach	4.8
3	Poor account service	3.9
4	Senior staff no longer giving sufficient attention	3.7
5	It was just time for a change	3.6
6	Advertisements not generating sales	3.6
7	Did not like agency's advertisements	3.5
8	Agency had frequent cost over-runs	3.3
9	Key people moved from the agency	3.2
10	Disagreement over campaign objective	3.1
11	Could not tell if advertisements were working	2.9
12	Agency's media buying was poor	2.5

Note: Number of 'important' reasons, i.e. rated 6 or 7 on the 7-point scale:
- average 2.4
- mode 0

Source: Dowling, Grahame (1994), 'Searching for a New Advertising Agency: A Client Perspective', *International Journal of Advertising*, 13, pp. 229–42.

Table 16.12 *Variables important in the final selection of a new advertising agency*

Rank	Factor	Average score[1]
1	Understands our product/service	6.1
2	Rapport with agency staff	6.0
3	Professional agency's formal presentations	5.7
4	Agency's advertisements display a creative flair	5.6
5	Direct contact with agency principals	5.6
6	Displays strong cost awareness	5.5
7	Extensive resources and experience	5.4
8	General reputation of agency	5.3
9	Agency fits with current marketing strategy	5.1
10	Agency offers media buying	5.0
11	Proven track record in our market	4.9
12	Agency suggests new marketing strategy	4.7
13	Size of agency	4.6
14	Agency suggests research to test advertisements	4.4
15	Agency offers design services	4.0
16	Prior experience with agency	3.9
17	Prior experience with an individual employee	3.5
18	Agency offers direct marketing	3.4
19	Part of an international group	3.3
20	Good track record in creative awards	3.3
21	Small, specialized agency	3.2
22	Convenient location of agency	3.1
23	Agency offers sales promotion	3.0
24	Age of agency	2.7
25	Agency offers public relations	2.6[2]

[1] 1 = not important, 7 = highly important
[2] Significant difference between 'have change' and 'may change' groups
Source: Dowling (1994), *op. cit.*

(a) The geographical coverage of the medium; for example national, regional, local.

(b) The socioeconomic composition of the audience.

(c) Composition of the audience by age and sex groupings.

(d) The medium's physical characteristics – visual, oral, standard of reproduction, availability of colour, possibility of movement, and so forth

(e) Frequency of publication. Allied to this is the duration of interest in the medium – most daily papers are thrown away the same day, while magazines may be kept for several weeks and read by a number of people. The frequency of publication also has a direct effect on the booking of time or space, i.e. the timing of the appearance of an advertisement.

(f)   The power to reach special groups – this is closely related to (b) and (c) above; for example the *Economist* or the *Financial Times*, *Vogue*, etc., preselect a particular type of audience and so are especially suited to selling to this segment of the population. Further, the association of a product with a medium may give that product favourable connotations by transferring confidence in the publication to items advertised therein, for example *Good Housekeeping*.

Atmosphere

The atmosphere of a medium is difficult to define in that it is based on a subjective evaluation of its content, presentation, and so on. A broad distinction may be drawn between acceptable and intrusive media, in that the latter create impact through intrusion and irrelevance to context, for example television commercials, whereas many magazines are purchased as much for their advertisements as their other content. The concept will become clearer when related to individual media.

Coverage

The essential criterion on which coverage is judged is the actual number of persons exposed to the medium, in the sense of being made aware of its content. For example, the number of people who actually see a poster is considerably less than the number that have the opportunity to see it; on the other hand, the readership of a magazine may well exceed ten times its actual circulation.

Cost

For purposes of comparison the cost of publishing an advertisement is usually expressed in terms of 'cost per thousand', which is arrived at by dividing the cost of publication by the audience in thousands. The difficulty in ensuring comparability in the measurement of audience size in terms of coverage, as defined above, makes this a rough measure at best, and media planners are actively seeking more sophisticated measures of cost effectiveness.

Advertising expenditure by media for the years 1988 to 1993 is indicated in Table 16.2.

Size

The effect of increased size or duration of an advertisement is to increase effective coverage, but on a progressively diminishing scale. Larger advertisements enable the advertiser to make more selling points, or to create greater impact when properly used. It is also contended that 'bigness', of itself, creates confidence and prestige.

Position

Detailed studies of the positioning of advertisements within a medium have shown that certain 'slots' consistently achieve greater coverage than other positions. Further, certain positions can be very useful in isolating a particular segment of the general audience. (Timing has the same effect for broadcast messages on radio and television.)

In the following pages are given synopses of the various media available to the advertiser. While correct at the time of writing this type of information is subject to constant change and very quickly becomes dated. For detailed and up-to-date information the reader should consult *British Rate and Data* (*BRAD*). Contact with The Advertising Association (Abford House, 15 Wilton Road, London SW1V 1NJ, Telephone: 071 828 2771, Fax: 071 931 0376) is also strongly recommended as they publish an excellent range of material including a set of 'Student Briefs' covering various aspects of advertising. Chapter 19 in *The Marketing Book* (M. J. Baker, 1994) also contains an excellent survey of media characteristics by Keith Crosier.

☐ *The national press*

Since the publication of the previous edition there have been radical changes in the national press. Writing in 1985 the erosion of advertising revenues due to competition with commercial television was seen as a major threat to several of the national dailies following the collapse of the *News Chronicle*. In a report from the Economist Intelligence Unit it was argued that publishers needed to charge economic selling prices which are estimated to be twice the then cover cost. A conservative attitude to change on the editorial side and the absence of marketing were also cited as threats to the national dailies existence. In the period since then not only have we seen significant changes in ownership and editorial attitudes, the introduction of a successful new 'quality' paper (*The Independent*) and the widespread adoption of modern marketing techniques but we have also witnessed a radical change in working practices and the conversion to modern information technology in place of the antiquated methods of yesteryear.

During the 1990s competition has intensified and, at the time of writing (1995), a major price war is in process as publishers seek to increase market share in what is essentially a saturated market (the circulation of National newspapers has declined by approximately 11 per cent over the past six years). The outcome is still uncertain but it seems likely that one or more papers will be forced out of business with the *Independent* now looking like a potential casualty.

Following Hobson's 'check-list', the salient characteristics of the national press may be summarised as:

Character

Newspapers are bought largely for their news value and so are singularly appropriate for announcing new products and new developments of existing products. Because of their frequency of publication they are also well suited to 'opportunity' markets; for example advertising anti-freeze during a sudden cold spell, such-and-such a race was won on X tyres, Y petrol, Z oil, and so on. Despite their short life, newspapers have a high attention value and it is estimated that an 11×3 advertisement (that is 11 inches long by 3 columns wide) is seen by one-third of the readers. Further, the advertisements in the national press are more likely to be seen by the retailer (also true of TV commercials) than are those appearing in magazines, and so have an indirect effect on the distributive channels.

In addition to their news content newspapers are also bought for the regular features they carry, and certain days have been developed to cater to specific reader interests, for example Thursday and Friday for grocery products, as the majority of grocery purchases are made on Friday and Saturday; mail order advertisements on Saturday and Sunday, to coincide with the weekend letter-writing peak, and so forth.

As their name implies, the national papers have national coverage. Their regional strength varies, however, and up-to-date data should be sought from *BRAD* or JICNARS (Joint Industry Committee for National Readership Surveys).

Atmosphere

In general terms this may be summarised as a sense of urgency and importance coupled, to a varying degree, with a certain authority. Most people read a newspaper which confirms their own view of the word and so is regarded as a high credibility source (that is the content is accepted at face value). To a certain extent, the authority of the factual content is transferred to the advertisements and may be regarded as 'assistance to selling' under the heading of 'Character'.

Quantity/Coverage

Table 16.13 gives recent circulation figures for the best-known national newspapers. Clearly, an evaluation based solely on the number of copies bought would be an inadequate guide to the suitability of a particular paper for a particular advertisement, and these 'raw' data must be related to the demographic composition of the audience *vis-à-vis* the consumer profile of the product or service in question. (This is a useful rule-of-thumb guide to media selection – that is define the demographic characteristics of the target consumers, and then select the medium which offers the closest match to this profile.)

Cost

Most newspaper advertising rates are based on a charge per standard column centimetre (SCC) – that is one column wide by one centimetre deep. The actual column width varies, as does the cost, from paper to paper. In general, the cost per thousand tends to be roughly equivalent, but once again reference should be made to *BRAD* for exact and up-to-date information. Charges also vary within each paper depending on the actual position of the advertisement – see 'Position' below.

Table 16.13 *National newspaper circulation trends, 1988–94*

	1988 '000s	1989 '000s	1990 '000s	1991 '000s	1992 '000s	1993 '000s	1994 '000s	+ or − '88/94
The Sun	4 183	4 095	3 896	3 679	3 566	3 640	4 078	
Daily Mirror	3 120	3 146	3 106	2 919	2 815	2 631	2 495	
Daily Mail	1 776	1 737	1 689	1 702	1 713	1 743	1 774	
Daily Express	1 658	1 582	1 574	1 542	1 525	1 460	1 338	
Daily Record	770	773	778	761	755	751	751	
Daily Star	991	902	916	858	803	768	743	
Today	478	589	560	475	520	548	597	
Popular Dailies	**12 976**	**12 824**	**12 519**	**11 936**	**11 697**	**11 541**	**11 776**	**−9.2%**
The Daily Telegraph	1 134	1 108	1 081	1 066	1 040	1 021	1 042	
The Times	444	435	426	396	385	390	544	
The Guardian	454	435	427	421	415	407	401	
The Independent	381	408	412	383	372	335	281	
Financial Times (UK)	206	202	195	183	177	173	170	
Quality Dailies	**2 619**	**2 588**	**2 541**	**2 449**	**2 389**	**2 326**	**2 433**	**−6.9%**
All National Dailies	**15 595**	**15 412**	**15 060**	**14 385**	**14 086**	**13 867**	**14 214**	**−8.9%**
News of the World	5 287	5 240	5 046	4 812	4 710	4 639	4 790	
Sunday Mirror	2 866	2 969	2 902	2 811	2 719	2 637	2 563	
The People	2 746	2 651	2 577	2 277	2 096	2 012	2 029	
The Mail on Sunday	1 926	1 927	1 896	1 949	1 988	1 979	1 960	
Sunday Express	2 088	1 899	1 695	1 638	1 727	1 691	1 510	
Sunday Sport	482	500	426	367	306	251	290	
Popular Sundays	**15 395**	**15 186**	**14 542**	**13 854**	**13 546**	**13 209**	**13 142**	**−14.6%**
Sunday Times	1 339	1 283	1 176	1 163	1 190	1 128	1 237	
Sunday Telegraph	705	645	590	571	568	591	650	
The Observer	736	667	559	564	538	502	493	
Independent on Sunday	—	—	327	379	396	374	324	
Quality Sundays	**2 780**	**2 595**	**2 652**	**2 677**	**2 692**	**2 595**	**2 704**	**−2.7%**
All National Sundays	**18 175**	**17 781**	**17 194**	**16 531**	**16 238**	**15 804**	**15 846**	**−12.8%**

Source: A.B.C. (January–December).

Size

As a general rule, readership does not increase with the size of the advertisement in a directly proportional manner. Despite diminishing returns, the consensus of opinion favours larger advertisements because of the greater impact which they achieve and because readers 'select' advertisements to a certain extent; that is, there is a tendency to notice those of direct interest to the reader. This means that a series of small advertisements, costing the same as a single large advertisement, may be seen many times by the same people, but pass unnoticed by those with a latent demand – it is unlikely that a full-page advertisement will pass unnoted by these potential customers in the same way.

Position

The location of advertisements within the medium is at the discretion of the advertising manager, who, naturally, attempts to satisfy as many clients as possible. Owing to the demand for certain positions, however, it has been found both simpler and more lucrative to charge special rates for these favoured positions. It is clear that certain pages preselect a particular segment of the readership owing to the nature of the features on that page, for example the women's and sports pages. It follows that if one is advertising a product which has a particular appeal to a segment of the readership, there is a greater probability of it coming to their attention if it is located on a page that caters to that interest.

The actual position within the printed media may be defined by one of the following, largely self-explanatory, terms:

- *Top, centre, bottom*.
- *Inside*, that is towards the fold, or outside.
- *Next matter*, that is next to editorial content.
- *Under matter*, next and under matter.
- *Island position*, that is matter on at least three sides.
- *Solus*, on its own, no other advertisements appearing on the same page.
- *Semi solus*, only one other advertisement on the same page.

Research evidence on the value of such positions is inconclusive, but media planners contend that better results are obtained from some positions than others. For example it is contended that as the eye is accustomed to starting at the top of a piece of printed matter there is a greater possibility of catching the reader's attention if the advertisement is on the upper half of the page. Intuitively one is inclined to agree with observations of this type until adequate research either confirms, or infirms the hypothesis.

☐ *The regional press*

At the time of writing there were 1715 regional newspapers published on a regional basis in the United Kingdom. In many respects the characteristics of the regional press are similar to those of the national dailies already described, and this summary will be confined to noting certain differences, and the major advantages and disadvantages of local papers as an advertising medium.

First, local papers have the advantage that they achieve concentrated coverage of a limited area, and so are likely to achieve a greater density of readership than a national paper. Because of the 'local' content they also tend to receive closer scrutiny, but against this must be set the greater authority of the national paper.

Second, regional papers are ideally suited to developing regional markets based on local preferences – an examination of consumption patterns on a regional basis soon indicates that the British population is far from homogeneous in this respect.

Third, the limited circulation of the regional and local papers makes them a good medium for copy testing (that is, running different versions of an advertisement in order to measure their relative effectiveness as a basis for final selection). The lower circulations of these papers also makes them more economical, although the CPT rate may be comparable to, or even greater than, those of the nationals.

Fourth, and this also applies to the national papers to a lesser degree, the frequency of publication permits the development of a theme by instalments, or early repetition if desired to 'stiffen up' a campaign.

Finally, evening and weekly papers have the advantage over morning daily papers that they are taken *into* the home, and so are likely to be seen by more members of the household at greater leisure.

The major disadvantages associated with both regional and national papers are:

1. The poor quality newsprint does not permit a very high standard of reproduction – this may be improved by colour printing 'Inserts' on a glazed paper that will accept a smaller screen size than ordinary news-print, for example the *Daily Express*.
2. News dates rapidly, so most papers are scanned rapidly on the day of issue and discarded; that is, a newspaper advertisement is virtually a 'one-shot' attempt at attracting

the public's attention, and so will usually require a number of repetitions if it is to be seen by the majority of the paper's readers.

☐ *Sunday newspapers*

J. D. Hughes of Hobson, Bates and Partners wrote of this group: 'The British Sunday press is a unique phenomenon. No other country possesses anything remotely like it. It is, moreover, a phenomenon rooted deeply in the habits and behaviour of the people it serves' (*Advertiser's Weekly*, 21 Oct. 1966). When one considers that the *News of the World* alone has a readership of 27 per cent of the United Kingdom *adult population*, one begins to appreciate how deeply ingrained is the Sunday newspaper habit.

Unlike daily papers, which tend to be scanned, the Sunday paper is perused at leisure and so achieves greater attention value. The readership figures are given in Table 16.15; however, the actual composition of the readership varies from paper to paper, and the serious student should consult the JICNARS for a detailed breakdown on both a national and regional basis.

A second feature of the 'quality' Sunday papers (*Sunday Times*, *Sunday Telegraph* and *Observer*) which used to differentiate them from most of the dailies is the colour magazine, which largely overcomes the criticism of low standards of reproduction associated with newspapers in general (the 'popular' press has now entered the Sunday newspaper magazine market, for example the *News of the World* and the *Sunday Express*).

☐ *Magazines*

The major factor which differentiates a magazine from a newspaper is that the former preselects its readership through the nature of its content. A second distinguishing feature is that it is read at leisure.

Magazines, as a group, may be further subdivided into categories, and media planners have adopted the following classification:

1. General magazines – so designated because of their general appeal, as contrasted with:
2. Specialist magazines, which cater for the readership with clearly defined and specific interest – for example doctors, philatelists.
3. The retail trade press. This subdivision is justified because of the medium's importance in 'selling-in' a product prior to the start of a campaign aimed at the consumer.

General magazines

This category may be further subdivided into those which have a predominantly male or female readership, as compared with those which appeal to both sexes. For example *Woman* has a predominantly female readership, *Autocar* male, *Radio Times* male and female. Overall, the characteristics of the general magazine are so diverse that one should properly attempt to rate each separately by reference to the check-list. At the same time there are a number of points which justify generalisation, namely:

Character
- Read at leisure.
- Preselect their audience by the content; for example *Practical Gardening*, *Homemaker*, *Yachting Monthly*.
- Better standards of reproduction than newspapers.
- Longer duration of interest – for example of the ultimate readership of a woman's weekly, 60 per cent see it within two weeks of publication, 30 per cent in the next two weeks, and the remaining 10 per cent over a period of six months or longer.
- Readership may be ten to fifteen times circulation.
- The lower frequency of publication necessitates booking of space well in advance; that is, magazines are less flexible in this respect than newspapers.

Atmosphere
- More stable than that of the newspaper, which is affected by the news it carries.

- Higher standards of reproduction convey a greater sense of luxury than is possible with a newspaper, particularly where colour is used.

Coverage/Cost

- Difficult to estimate on a comparative basis owing to the variation in page size, on which rates are based, and of readership. Overall, the CPT is higher than that for the national or regional press, and ranges from about £1.00 – in the mass circulation broadcasting publications, to around £5.00 – in the glossy fashion magazines. This higher cost is offset by the greater intrinsic worth of the advertisements to the reader, which ensures a higher 'page traffic', that is number of readers per page expressed as a proportion of the total readership.

Specialist magazines

Detailed information on specialist magazines is more limited than in the case of the general magazine, largely because so few of them are included in the National Readership Survey. In addition to the above generalised comments, one may add that the magazines in this category are even more selective in their readership appeal. Further, the advertising content is often of equal interest to the editorial content, for example collectors' magazines listing objects for sale, technical magazines detailing new products and product improvements. With the exception of direct mail, the specialist magazine offers the greatest opportunity of reaching a highly specific audience.

Retail trade magazines

The need to ensure adequate distribution and availability of a product prior to the opening of a campaign directed at the ultimate consumer is advanced as the main reason for using this medium. Some media planners are sceptical as to its value, owing to the generally low level of readership – around 25 per cent – which is compounded by the sheer volume of advertisements, thus making the actual possibility of any particular advertisement being seen correspondingly small. It is also argued that the smaller retailer, at whom much of the effort is directed in the anticipation that it will reduce the amount of direct selling required, is an ordinary mortal who reads newspapers, watches TV and so on, and that advertisements in these media are more likely to be seen and carry popular authority. In the light of these arguments it is clear that each case should be considered on its merits, and that particular attention should be given to position within the medium.

Controlled circulation media

A review of print media would not be complete without some reference to controlled circulation papers and annuals and directories.

There has been a considerable growth in controlled circulation papers in recent years, particularly in the trade, technical and professional fields. Papers or magazines with a controlled circulation are not sold but are distributed free of charge to persons with a known interest in the magazine's editorial content. As with all other media, space is sold on the basis of the medium's ability to reach an audience which in this instance is closely defined. Many of these publications claim virtually total coverage of the predefined audience. This assertion should be treated with circumspection, but it is indisputable that some achieve spectacular results.

Annuals and directories may be subdivided into four categories:

1. Annual special numbers – these are published by the parent publication, usually a magazine or newspaper, as a completely separate entity; that is, they are not a 'special issue'. Example: *Country Life Annual*.
2. Annual consumer reference books. Examples: *Whitakers Almanack*, *Daily Mail Year Book*, *Pears Cyclopaedia*.
3. Trade, technical and professional diaries, buyer's guides, year books. These usually contain a mass of information which the practitioner may require at a moment's notice. Example: *Electrical Trade Directory*.

4. Annual street directories and shopper's guides. (Telephone directories might be considered to come within this category, especially the classified directories or 'Yellow Pages'.)

Obviously the greatest disadvantage associated with this medium is the low flexibility that is a concomitant of annual publication. Against this may be set low cost – *AdWeekly* published a 'case history' of Automat some years ago which demonstrated how this company had concentrated its limited advertising appropriation in trade directories and, through careful positioning and repetition, achieved excellent results (25 Aug. 1967).

☐ *Television*

Television advertising is a relatively recent development in the field of advertising media and, as inferred when reviewing the national press, its impact has been enormous. In terms of expenditures, TV is second only to the press as a whole, and its growth in recent years has consistently exceeded that of all other media. The importance of the medium is reflected in the publication of books devoted solely to the subject of commercial television, and the serious student should refer to these sources for a detailed description. Limitations of time and space dictate that the barest outline can be developed in this context.

Character

Above all, commercial television is a mass medium: it can be received in over 99 per cent of all British homes. On an average evening over 50 per cent of these homes will be tuned in to a commercial television station and, in the course of a day, an average of 2.9 hours of commercial transmissions will be received by the households capable of tuning in. Although, in theory, it would be possible to reach all these households simultaneously with a single advertisement, few advertisers would in fact attempt this as coverage is subdivided among sixteen contractors, who cover thirteen geographical regions, namely:

Carlton, London and London Weekend Television }	London
Central Ind. TV	Midlands
Granada TV	North West
Yorkshire TV (Link)	Yorkshire
Scottish TV	Central Scotland
HTV	Wales and West
Meridian	South and S. East
Tyne Tees TV (Link)	North East
Anglia TV	East
West Country TV	South West
Ulster TV	N. Ireland
Border TV	Border
Grampian TV	N. Scotland
GMTV	Network

Thus, while national coverage is possible, most advertisers tend to advertise selectively on a regional basis. This trend is encouraged by the contractors, who on the one hand stress the purchasing behaviour which differentiates the consumers within their area from those in other areas, thus making a case for regional marketing, while on the other hand they publish statistics that demonstrate that their audience is an accurate reflection of the national audience and so suitable for a national campaign. If a note of scepticism is detected, the reader should consult some of the commercial television contractors' own publicity material to see how it is possible to substantiate essentially opposing claims from the same basic data. (This tendency is most marked in the case of those companies offering test marketing facilities, where a representative sample is a desirable prerequisite – it is difficult to accept that the inhabitants of central Scotland are identical with those of Kent and Sussex, or vice versa!)

With such a large potential audience, it follows that commercial television reaches all socio-economic groups. As might be expected, there is a slight bias towards the lower social groups, to larger families and to housewives, but as these constitute the mass market for consumer goods, this has clear advantages for the marketers of such products.

The great advantage of television over all other media, with the exception of the cinema, is its ability to combine sound, vision and movement. This combination permits the use of advertisements that demonstrate the product and its advantages, which, most would agree, is far more effective than a written or static visual representation.

Commercial television channels operate seven days a week, frequently around the clock, with the result that the composition of the audience varies according to the time segment selected: for example programmes for housewives in the afternoon, children's programmes from 4 to 6 p.m., 'family programmes' 6 to 9 p.m., adult programmes from 9 p.m. onwards. The composition of the audience also varies from day to day, and once again the student is referred to *BRAD* or the publications of the Joint Industry Committee for Television Advertising Research (JICTAR) for a detailed breakdown.

Television commercials themselves vary from 7-second 'spots' through multiples of 15 seconds to a normal maximum of 2 minutes. In practice, few advertisements exceed 60 seconds and most are in the 15, 30 and 60-second bracket. A readily observed feature of television commercials which is infrequently commented on is the fact that the advertisements are concentrated into a series of 'natural breaks'. Research on the effect that this has on the viewer suggests relatively few 'viewers' attend actively to commercials and the practice of 'zapping', or switching channels during breaks, is widespread. Some media planners have also commented adversely, however, to the effect that viewers must find it difficult to assimilate a fairly large number of advertisements within a short space of time. (An examination of peak loadings, in terms of water and electricity consumption, might lead one to believe that in fact the majority of viewers avoid the problem by attending to their toilet and making cups of tea during such breaks!)

Atmosphere
It is often claimed that a major advantage of television is that it is viewed in the home, in a relaxed atmosphere, when the audience is more receptive than is normally the case when exposed to advertising messages. Against this one must set the disadvantage that the injection of advertising into a programme is both intrusive and irrelevant. While attention may be concentrated on the programme itself, the popularity of the first and last 'spots' in the break would seem to indicate that media planners recognise that attention may wander once it is realised that a break has started, and only returns in anticipation of the commencement of the programme. With the introduction of infra-red remote controls a new phenomenon known as 'zapping' has emerged. Simply put, zapping consists of switching channels during commercial breaks just to see what is going on on other channels and so reduces exposure to the advertisements being screened. No satisfactory data to quantify the possible effect of this behaviour was available in 1995.

The more successful television advertisers, judged on the basis of their sales results, appear to have recognised both the intrusive and irrelevant aspects of commercials, and to have made a virtue out of necessity by issuing advertisements that superficially appear to have both these characteristics. Judging by the adverse comments directed at a margarine that gave one delusions of grandeur, one should be surprised to learn that at a time when margarine sales were in a decline the only brand showing an absolute increase in sales happened to be the one with the 'stupid' commercial.

Coverage/cost
With fourteen contractors, each with its own rate structure that varies both in terms of the time of day and the day of the week, little of general use can be said.

Position
In terms of television commercials, this refers both to the time segment and the position within the segment.

Size
This is measured in terms of the duration of the commercial.

Current developments in television

Since the appearance of the 5th edition, major developments have occurred in the fields of Cable Television and Direct Broadcasting by Satellite (DBS). The 1996 *Marketing Pocket Book* summarises these as follows:

CURRENT DEVELOPMENTS IN TELEVISION

ITC

Since 1st January 1991 the Independent Television Commission has been responsible for controlling all aspects of independent commercial TV in the UK, taking over the previous responsibilities of the IBA and the Cable Authority. The ITC is located at 33, Foley Street, London W1P 7LB (0171 255 3000).

TERRESTRIAL TELEVISION

Channel 3 (ITV): Channel 3 is split into 14 regions, in each of which one contractor has the sole right to broadcast TV programmes, and sell advertising between 9.25 am and 5.59 am the following day. The sole exception to this is London, which is shared between the two contractors one of which has the weekday (Monday–Friday) contract and the other the weekend (Friday evening–Sunday).

Each contractor holds his licence for around 10 years. The last re-allocation was in 1991, when licences were awarded on a tender basis to the highest bidder, subject to a quality threshold. 12 licences remained with their existing contractors, and 4 changed hands: those for the South and South-East (from TVS to Meridian), the South-West (from TSW to Westcountry TV), the London weekday service (from Thames to Carlton), and the national breakfast service (from TV-am to GMTV).

During the last few years there has been considerable consolidation of advertising sales within ITV mainly as a result of changes in ownership of the ITV franchises. In a fifteen month period (November 1993–February 1995) Yorkshire and Tyne Tees merged, Carlton successfully bid for Central, Granada bought LWT and MAI (owning 61% of meridian) bought Anglia. Since autumn 1994 three sales houses (Carlton, Laser and TSMS) have been responsible for selling the various regions.

Programme schedules on Channel 3 stations are broadly similar at present, with about 70% of programming being the same for all stations at the same time, particularly in peak-time. From January 1993 this situation has been consolidated, with the appointment of a network scheduler.

Most areas broadcast for the full 20.5 hours a day to which they are entitled. Advertising minutage is an average of seven minutes an hour, with a maximum of seven-and-a-half minutes at peak time.

Channel 4: Channel 4 is a statutory corporation operating under licence from the ITC with a remit to be complementary to (and different from) Channel 3. It is responsible for commissioning its own programming (it has no production fecilities of its own) and (from January 1993) for selling its own advertising. If its advertising revenue falls below 14% of total terrestrial advertising, Channel 3 is responsible for contributing up to 2% more, and if it rises above 14%, Channel 4 has to pay 50% of the surplus to Channel 3. In 1994 Channel 4 took almost 20% of total ITC qualifying revenues, and the channel continues to actively campaign for an early review of the funding formula provisions in the 1990 Broadcasting Act.

Although Channel 4 is a national channel it does offer macro-region airtime opportunities for advertisers. These advertising areas are generally larger than those available to Channel 3.

S4C: The Welsh language channel, S4C is broadcast on the Channel 4 frequency in Wales (part of the Wales and West area). It started off at the same time as Channel 4, and differs from that channel, in that it carries a high proportion of Welsh language programming. Programmes carried by both Channel 4 and S4C are often broadcast at different times.

Breakfast TV: The licence for the national breakfast TV service on Channel 3 was awarded to GMTV in 1991 and started in January 1993. From this date, Channel 4 has also been responsible for its own breakfast-time service and advertising sales. Again, the channel can be bought nationally or on a regional basis.

Channel 5: The ITC is expected to announce the winner of the Channel 5 licence (the last remaining analogue TV frequency to be auctioned) by the end of November 1995. The ITC received four applications (from Channel 5 Broadcasting, New Century Television, UKTV and Virgin), with bids ranging from £2m to £36m.

Teletext: Teletext UK Ltd was awarded the franchise for teletext services on ITV in 1991. The service took over from Oracle Teletext on 1st January 1993.

CABLE TELEVISION

Cable penetration in the UK is still relatively low. In July 1995, 5.0% of all homes were connected to cable systems (21% of homes passed) of which the majority (4.4% of all homes) were connected to new broadband systems. Of the operating franchises, over 73 had more than 2,5000 subscribers in July 1995. Licences covering over two-thirds of the UK population have been issued. The largest operators are:

Operator	Homes Passed	Connected	Penetration %
Telewest	965,252	203,518	21.1
Comcast	587,100	155,259	26.4
NYNEX	780,275	146,575	18.8
SBC CableComms	574,268	116,787	20.3
Videotron	469,095	100,983	21.5

After the launch of the Channel One cable channel in London during November 1994, two more *national* cable exclusive channels – Live TV and Selec TV – have been launched.

Advertising and Sponsorship: Advertising and sponsorship on all TV channels in the UK are controlled by the ITC, under codes of Advertising Standards, Programme Sponsorship, and Rules on Advertising Breaks published in January 1991. These codes apply to both ITV and satellite broadcasters, and incorporate elements of previous rules established by the IBA and the Cable Authority, as well as the European Directive on Television Broadcasting. Sponsorship income has grown rapidly but remains very small. It amounted to £23m in 1994, a 34% increase on 1993.

DIRECT BROADCASTING BY SATELLITE

DBS is the name which is given to television transmissions via medium-to-high-powered satellites which can be received on dishes of less than 1 metre diameter, suitable for private homes. It has been available in the UK since February 1989, when SKY TV started broadcasting on the Astra satellite. During autumn 1995 a further five channels were launched as part of the Sky multi-channels package including The Disney Channel and Paramount TV. At November 1995 the ITC had over 100 non-domestic satellite licences in existence. The vast majority of 'English language' channels broadcast via the Astra satellites 1a, 1b, 1c and 1d with an increasing number of the channels sharing transponders.

Astra 1e is due to launch in late 1995 – the first satellite in the fleet entirely dedicated to digital broadcasts.

English Language Channels on Astra

Autumn 1995

Premium channels	Sky multi-channels	Others
Sky Movies	Sky One	QVC
The Movie Channel	Sky News	NBC
Sky Movies Gold	Sky Travel	Superchannel
The Disney Channel	Sky Soap	Eurosport
Sky Sports	Discovery	CNN
Sky Sports 2	Bravo	TNT/Cartoons
Sky Sports Gold	CMT Europe	Adult Channel
	TCC	Playboy TV
	UK Gold	Television X
	UK Living	
	Family Channel	
	MTV Europe	
	VH-1	
	Learning Channel	
	Nickelodeon	
	Paramount	
	History Channel	
	EBN	
	Sci-Fi	

Subscription income, both from individual subscribers and cable operators (who pay programme licencees for the right to broadcast their programme services), is the main source of income for non-terrestrial licences. It amounted to £542m in 1994 (circa 80% of total subscriptions/advertising revenues).

AUDIENCE MEASUREMENT – BARB

Introduction: The Broadcasters' Audience Research Board Ltd was set up in August 1980 by the BBC & ITCA (now the ITV Association) and started operating in August 1981 to provide a single system for TV audience research in the UK. The BARB television audience measurement contract is held jointly by AGB and RSMB and was updated in 1991 to cope with the changes in the market. RSMB have responsibility for the establishment survey and for panel recruitment, AGB have the data supply and data processing contracts. The measurement of Audience Appreciation of television programmes is carried out for the BBC, the ITV companies and Channel 4 by RSL (Research Services Ltd) under contract to BARB.

☐ *Commercial radio*

Until the autumn of 1973 the only commercial radio transmissions which could be received in this country were those of Radio Luxemburg. However in October 1973 Capital Radio came on the air as the first of approximately sixty local commercial radio stations authorised for the country as a whole. A second London station, London Broadcasting, came on the air shortly afterwards, while the third, Radio Clyde, started transmissions on New Year's Day 1974. There are at the present 65 local radio stations and the whole ILR network has an average weekly reach of 59 per cent of the total adult population. Stations are allowed to include up to nine minutes of advertising in each hour of broadcasting. Time is sold on a 'spot' basis (like TV) but peak periods are different being highest in the morning and evening rush-hours (especially in-car reception).

☐ *Outdoor advertising*

(The 'check-list' approach will not be used for the remaining media – the student may like to formulate his/her own.) Outdoor advertising is often thought of as consisting solely of the poster medium. This ignores transportation advertising, illuminated signs and several lesser media which properly fall into this category.

As with the press and the cinema, the advent of commercial television resulted in outdoor advertising having to reappraise its role as an advertising medium. It was realised that television had become the prime medium for the advertising of a wide range of mass consumption goods which had formerly depended far more on press, poster and cinema. There are still instances in which outdoor advertising may be used as the prime medium, but in the majority of cases outdoor advertising is sold as a complement to a television campaign on the grounds that it serves as a reminder at, or near, the actual point of sale. This fact is supplemented by a gradual increase in audience size due to increased personal mobility.

The main outdoor medium is the poster, which suffers from three main disadvantages. First, to ensure that its message is conveyed quickly and concisely it can only accommodate a short copy story. Second, posters are not seen in the context of other matter of editorial or entertainment value. Finally, production costs are relatively high, as are maintenance costs. Offsetting this are a number of advantages.

It has been estimated that over 90 per cent of the population goes out of doors in the course of a week and thus has an 'opportunity to see' a poster. Actual poster sighting will obviously be considerably less than this but, unlike most other media, an accurate predictive model has been developed which enables the prospective advertiser to determine in advance the type of campaign he will have to mount to reach an audience of a given size. (See Mills and Rockley's Studies and the IPA Audience Measurement Study, 1964.) Current information on the poster audience can be obtained from OSCAR (Outside Site Classification and Audience Research) which is controlled by JICPAR and funded by the poster contractors. Second, poster advertising offers greater geographic flexibility than virtually any other medium; one may use a single site in a specific locality, cover all or part of a town, or all or part of the country. Third, the cost of poster advertising is relatively low, so that an advertiser with a limited appropriation can mount both an extensive and prolonged campaign for an amount that would make little impact on television when ranged against the large budgets of the major television advertisers. (This is not to say that posters will have more impact than a television commercial as such, but rather that impact is relative such that a limited television campaign would tend to be completely dominated by that of a major advertiser on the medium.) Fourth, posters can make full use of colour and achieve high standards of reproduction. Posters are increasingly being used with great dramatic effect and more thought is going into the use of the medium. The advertisements for 'Araldite' adhesive are a good example of this. In this poster campaign an actual motor car was attached to the poster seemingly by Araldite to show the great adhesive qualities of the glue.

Table 16.14 Posters (selected packages)

Contractor	Site type	Size	Panels	Areas	Periods	Cover (all adults)	Frequency	Package cost
Adrall	4 Classic	4 sheets	600	London GLC	Monthly	—	—	£30k p.m.
	4 Termini	4 sheets	110	Central London	Monthly	—	—	£11k p.m.
	4 City	4 sheets	55	City of London	Monthly	—	—	£6k p.m.
	4 Women	4 sheets	200	London ITV	Monthly	—	—	£14k p.m.
Adshel	Adshel	4 sheets	6000	National	14/28 days	79%	25	£180k 14 days
	Adshel Superlites	4 sheets	5000	National	14 days	79%	25	£395k
		1.8m × 1.2m	700	Midlands	14 days	78%	24	65k
		1.8m × 1.2m	1271	N. England	14 days	77%	23	120k
		1.8m × 1.2m	473	Scotland	14 days	82%	28	50k
		1.8m × 1.2m	476	Wales & West	14 days	76%	21	43k
BTA	Citipak	96 sheets	50	Gt London	15/30 days	42%	14	£110k p.m.
	Corpak National	48 sheets	300	National	15/30 days	27%	10	£120k p.m.
CP Posters	Premium	48 sheets	50	TVS	15/30 days	23%	10	£29k p.m.
Dolphin	View	96 sheets	50	GLC	Mthly (2 × 2 wks)	40%	13	£115k p.m.
	300-2 (×4)	48 sheets	300	National	Mthly (2 × 2 wks)	23%	10	£130k p.m.
Force 4	Gateway	4 sheets	450	National	Monthly	—	—	£32k p.m.
	Asda (×3) A/B/C	4 sheets	100	National	Monthly	—	—	£7.5k p.m.
LTA	Underground	48 sheets	25	London	Monthly	See TRAC on p. 118		£18k p.m.
		16 sheets	50	London	Monthly			£5k p.m.
	Tube car panels		4000	London	Monthly			£18k p.m.
	Excalator panels		200	London	Monthly			£6k p.m.
	Bus T sides		350	London	Monthly			£58k p.m.
Arthur Maiden	Capital 96 (×2)	96 sheets	50	GLC	Half month	32%	8	£67k p.h.m.
	Maiden 800 Rot'g	48 sheets	1600	National	½ mthly rotate	54%	12	£380k p.m.
	Motorpak	48 sheets	41	Motorway Areas	Monthly	5.7m visitors		£17k p.m.
	Motorpak	48 sheets	38	Motorway Areas	Monthly	5m visitors		£15k p.m.
	Scotpak 80	48 sheets	80	Scottish National	Half month	39%	9	£20k p.h.m.
	Spectacolor	30' × 15'	1	Piccadilly	1 week	3m per week		£20k
Mills & Allen	Magnum 1 & 2	96 sheets	140 (2 × 70)	GLC	14 day min	56%	12	£190k 14 days
	Maincity 1 & 2	96 sheets	400 (2 × 200)	National	14 day min	43%	9	£350k 14 days
	Master 1 & 2	48 sheets	1900 (2 × 950)	National	14 day min	54%	11	£515k 14 days
	Urban 600	48 sheets	1200 (2 × 600)	National	14 day min	59%	13	£355k 14 days
More O'Ferrall	National 270	64 sheets	250 × 2	National	14/28 days	60%	13	£300k p.m.
	London 96	96 sheets	50	Within M25	Monthly	41%	14	£100k p.m.
NSS	Classic Yellow	48 sheets	350	National	15/30 days	25%	11	£99k 15 days
	Classic Blue	48 sheets	350	National	15/30 days	25%	11	£99k 15 days
	Nat'nal Super 16	16 sheets	1200	National/Regional	15/30 days	52%	17	£56k 15 days
	Nat'nal Super 32	32 sheets	650	National	15/30 days	37%	13	£78k 15 days
Primesight	Citibus 1250	Bus T sides	1250	National excl. London	—	—	—	£175k p.m.

Source: Poster Marketing.

Poster sites come in a range of sizes: 4-sheet, 60″ × 40″; 12-sheet, 60″ × 60″; 16-sheet, 120″ × 60″; 48-sheet, 120″ × 240″; supersite, 10 feet high by a range of widths from 27 feet upwards. The cost of a poster site depends on its location, and it is therefore difficult to generalise. The poster industry offers advertisers various ways of mounting a poster campaign. From 'line by line' where the contractor offers individual sites to build up a specific display to suit particular marketing objectives, and 'key plans' which are specially built displays offered by Independent Poster Sales Ltd. Details are given in Table 16.14 and further information can be obtained from *BRAD*.

Transportation advertising is a familiar aspect of our everyday lives which should not be overlooked when considering media selection. The general points made with regard to posters apply equally to transportation advertising, so that further description will be confined to a review of the sites available and the approximate costs associated with them. Some details are contained in Table 16.14

☐ *The cinema*

The impact of television on the cinema is readily apparent in any major town where former sites have been converted into bingo halls, warehouses or simply pulled down to make way for redevelopment. Although many may regret the passing of the local cinema and retain nostalgic memories of a 9d seat in the stalls, there can be no doubt that the competition of television has forced the cinema industry to undertake a massive face-lift. Cinema operators have realised that if they are to persuade customers to leave the comfort of their own fireside, and the hypnotic attraction of the 'box', they must make cinema-going an event. Despite the closure of many cinemas, many of which were themselves a mute reminder of the days of music-hall, there can he no doubt that the improvement and rebuilding programmes have greatly improved the standards of comfort offered to patrons. At the same time the film producers have concentrated on the competitive advantages which they possess, and which cannot be duplicated on the small screen – size and colour. The box office success of the James Bond films, and films like *Star Wars* and *Indiana Jones and the Temple of Doom* testify that the formula is a good one.

An examination of the composition of the cinema audience provides an interesting insight for the media planner.

Clearly, the Screen Advertisers Association's claim that it is the medium for reaching 'young adults' is justified by these statistics. This audience is of particular interest to the manufacturers of both semi-luxury goods, such as cosmetics, and consumer durables, appealing to single persons with high discretionary spending power, engaged couples and young marrieds.

Television can still offer a lower cost per thousand for the same audience but lacks the high attention value of a captive audience, viewing under ideal conditions over which the advertiser, not the viewer, has control, for example sound volume, quality of picture.

An indication of the cost of using the cinema for an advertising campaign may be judged from Table 16.15.

Advertisements are normally of 15, 30, 60 and 120 seconds in length. Actual rates vary by cinema and may be obtained from the Screen Advertising Association's master list of cinemas.

Although the cost per 1000 of using the cinemas is greater than for television, the Screen Advertisers Association justifies this on the grounds that the cinema possesses undeniable qualitative advantages, particularly the combined impact of colour, sound, and the big-screen presentation upon a captive audience.

☐ *Direct mail*

Direct mail is 'printed material mailed direct to customers' addressed to entice prospective customers or donors' (Dibb, Simpkin, Pride and Ferrel, 1994). The 1990s has seen direct mail grow rapidly as a media form and it looks set to

Table 16.15   *Cinema advertising costs (July 1996)*

ISBA area	Admission share, %	Number of screens	Weekly cost all screens, £ 30 secs	Weekly cost all screens, £ 60 secs
London	27.2	436	25 650	51 300
Southern	7.6	168	7 167	14 334
East of England	5.4	125	3 540	7 080
Midlands	14.6	302	9 570	19 140
Yorkshire	8.4	170	5 506	11 012
North East	5.0	84	3 278	6 556
Lancashire	13.1	226	8 587	17 174
Wales & West	5.9	149	3 867	7 734
South West	1.5	60	983	1 966
Border	0.5	22	328	656
Central Scotland	6.5	109	4 261	8 522
North Scotland	1.3	31	852	1 704
Northern Ireland	3.0	88	1 967	3 934
Total	**100**	**1 970**	**75 556**	**151 112**

Buying routes available[1]

- **Audience discount package** — *Based on a fixed cost per thousand admissions*
  £ per 30 seconds — *Industry*

London/Southern	41.00
All other Isba regions	28.50
National average	33.50

- **Screen by screen:** *Screens may be bought on an individual basis*
  £ per 30 seconds — *Average rate per week*

  Greater London: 139.00;   Rest of UK: 85.00;   National average: 85.00

- **Film packages:** Individual titles can be followed. School holiday (Disney) and art screen packages also available

Adult audience composition (Jan.–Dec. 1995)*   *Percentage population profile*

	Average audience	UK population		Average audience	UK population
Men	51	48	Class AB	32	22
Women	49	52	Class C1	35	27
Age 15–24	44	15	Class C2	16	23
Age 25–34	30	20	Class DE	17	28
Age 35+	26	65			

Coverage and frequency (using all screens), Jan–Dec 1995*

Target audience	8 weeks duration % cover	8 weeks duration Av. OTS	16 weeks duration % cover	16 weeks duration Av. OTS
15–24 Adults	42.3	2.27	56.3	3.42
15–24 Men	40.1	2.34	53.6	3.49
15–24 Women	44.4	2.24	58.5	3.40
15–24 ABC[1]	51.5	2.33	66.4	3.61
15–34 Adults	33.9	2.10	46.7	3.05
15–34 Men	33.6	2.19	46.1	3.05
15–34 Women	34.0	2.02	46.9	2.94
15–34 ABC[1]	42.8	2.18	57.4	3.25
All Adults 15+	**17.7**	**1.92**	**25.6**	**2.66**

Notes: 1 Rate increase due January 1997
* CAA/NRS.
Sources: CAA (other data available on request).

continue to grow in importance. It has become more prominent as advertisers have realised their markets are less homogeneous and can no longer be simply classified into arbitary groups like ABCD social classes.

Faced with a growing tide of 'individualism' there is a need to use an advertising vehicle that can account for a decline in market homogeneity. *Marketing Business Magazine* (October 1992) quotes the example of the 15–24 year old age group. In the 1960s this was seen as a complete market segment but now it is made up of a variety of different individualistic segments. In Europe these problems are accentuated by the advent of cross-border marketing where it will be harder to establish stereotypical consumers to target with advertising. Some clear trends can be identified transnationally such as the increasing role of working women. But the complexities outweigh these trends. *Marketing Business Magazine* describes the case of Tetley tea which is a standard commodity product in the UK but is more exclusive in other European countries like France.

The use of direct mail allows advertisers to get directly in touch with its consumers and potential consumers. It is much easier to monitor in terms of responses, usage and effectiveness than other advertising medias. The use of such techniques will become increasingly simple as technological advances improve databases. Data can be found by questionnaires, transactional/point-of-sale information or by telephone. The legislation that governs how such information can be collected and used will be crucial in the development of future databases.

In the 1980s and early 1990s the number of pieces of direct mail increased from over 1 billion to over 2 billion pieces. This is still not as dramatic as other European countries, for example Switzerland whose population receive 120 pieces of direct mail per capita each year compared to only 40 in the UK. Small fragmented markets like Switzerland that are diverse and multilingual provide the perfect environment for direct mail to show its value in reaching a fragmented market. (*Source*: T. Coad, *Marketing Business Magazine*, October 1993. p. 12.)

The great advantage of direct mail, by comparison with all other media, is its selectivity. Postal delivery is possible in every part of the country – a potential which enables the advertiser to reach a small, closely identified audience with a precision that could not possibly be duplicated by any other medium.

In the author's opinion direct mail is grossly underrated as an advertising medium, probably because of the dangers inherent in generalising from the particular. The common belief that the recipients of a direct mailing 'shot' immediately consign it to the waste-paper basket without a glance is not borne out by a recent American survey, which showed that approximately two-thirds do read the advertisement, and that more than 30 per cent subsequently make a purchase of the item advertised. Similar findings are reported by the British Market Research Bureau in its *Direct Mail Summary of Research*.

Direct mailing lists may be compiled by the advertiser himself from customer records, or from the same basic sources used by the direct mail house – classified telephone directories, trade directories, and so forth. Where it is intended to mount a campaign designed to increase one's market or to enter a new market, the cost would be disproportionate by comparison with the cost of

Table 16.16 *Marketing expenditure by sector (% value), 1994*

	Direct mail	Tele-marketing direct	Marketing services
Mail Order	12.5	3.7	12.5
Financial Services	20.4	22.7	19.5
Retailers	5.8	3.7	5.7
Media	1.7	3.6	4.8
Charities	5.1	11.4	6.3
Manufacturers	4.3	10.8	3.9
Other	22.3	18.9	21.3
Total Consumer	72.1	74.8	74.0
Total Business-to-Business	27.9	25.2	26.0

Source: *Marketing Week*, 26 January 1995.

'buying' a list from a specialist direct mail house. (Lists are rarely sold as such – the rate quoted is for a mailing using the direct mail company's list.) The price of a direct mail shot depends upon the production costs of the items to be mailed and the size, volume, folding, inserting and labelling requirements of the mailing. In addition to the production charges, the postage must be paid and the Post Office offers discounts and incentives for direct mailers. Some statistics on direct mail advertising are given in Table 16.16 and a guide to planning a direct mail campaign suggested by the Royal Mail is given in Figure 16.5 (The Royal Mail is an excellent source of advice on the whole topic.)

As with other aspects of advertising, the employment of an agency is to be recommended owing to the specialisation which they can bring to bear on the advertiser's problem. Those direct mail shots which do finish up in the waste bin most frequently do so because of either incorrect identification of a 'prospect' or poor copy and layout. A good agency will not be guilty of either of these faults.

On average a direct mailing will cost £250–£300 per thousand, which, when it is considered that three mailings is considered a desirable target to aim at, makes a campaign of any size an expensive undertaking. Against this must be set the precision with which potential customers may be reached by comparison with the lower costs of the 'buck shot' approach of the other media. A further advantage of direct mail is that its effectiveness can be measured directly, which, as a later section will show, is not the easiest of things to achieve. A summary of key areas to look for is provided by the Royal Mail's 'Planning a Direct Mail Campaign' shown in Figure 16.5.

An off-shoot of direct mail is door-to-door distribution of advertising material. Several

Figure 16.5 *How to plan a direct mail campaign*

Analysis of results can be more or less sophisticated, depending on your resources and the complexity of your campaign. The important thing is to use your defined objectives as the benchmark for measuring your success. Key areas to look at are as follows . . .

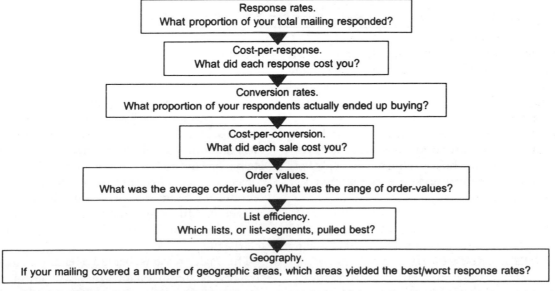

Collate all this information and you will have not only an accurate analysis of the success of your campaign but also a set of valuable planning data to apply to your next campaign.

Figure 16.5   *(continued)*

Planning a Direct Mail campaign is a logical step-by-step process. Whether you are using a direct mail agency or mailing house, or doing it yourself, it is important to make sure you have built these steps into your plan . . .

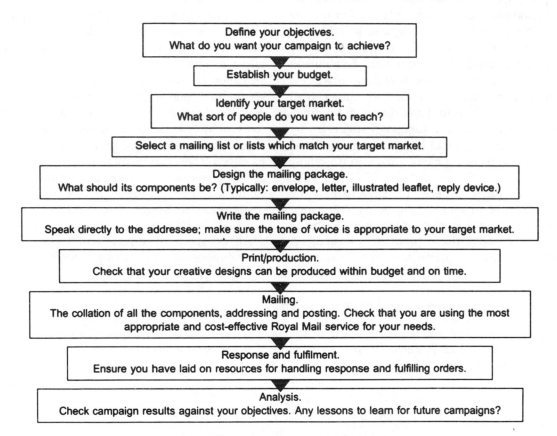

Define your objectives.
What do you want your campaign to achieve?

Establish your budget.

Identify your target market.
What sort of people do you want to reach?

Select a mailing list or lists which match your target market.

Design the mailing package.
What should its components be? (Typically: envelope, letter, illustrated leaflet, reply device.)

Write the mailing package.
Speak directly to the addressee; make sure the tone of voice is appropriate to your target market.

Print/production.
Check that your creative designs can be produced within budget and on time.

Mailing.
The collation of all the components, addressing and posting. Check that you are using the most appropriate and cost-effective Royal Mail service for your needs.

Response and fulfilment.
Ensure you have laid on resources for handling response and fulfilling orders.

Analysis.
Check campaign results against your objectives. Any lessons to learn for future campaigns?

companies offer this service for the distribution of samples, coupons and leaflets, utilising the services of part-time employees under the control and supervision of a full-time area supervisor, for example Vernon's Distributors. Rates vary, depending upon the nature of the material to be distributed, and the frequency, that is every house, every tenth house, and so on. The Post Office will also deliver unaddressed mail to all 21 million UK homes.

☐ *Direct marketing*

More and more major brand manufacturers are placing a greater emphasis on the use of direct marketing techniques. Kotler and Armstrong (1993) describe such techniques as 'marketing through various advertising media that interact directly with consumers, generally calling for the consumer to make a direct response' (Glossary). Such techniques include direct mail, catalogues, telemarketing and electronic marketing. In 1994 Heinz, one of the UK's leading fmcg (fast moving consumer goods) manufacturers, decided to concentrate the bulk of their £12m UK advertising budget on direct marketing techniques backed up by an umbrella branding campaign run on television.

The main reasons behind Heinz's change in strategy relate to factors that will effect most fmcg companies in the modern marketplace. Firstly, people's attitudes towards brands are changing and brands are becoming more and more threatened by the retailers' own label brands/products which in the grocery market have a growing market share (33 per cent in 1993). These retailers also have a greater contact with their consumers through the point of sale and so are better equipped to fill gaps in the market. Secondly, there are more and more products on the shelves for consumers to choose from and so it is less easy for a brand to dominate a sector and distinguish itself. Thirdly, there is expected to be an explosion in the number of television channels for advertisers to use and so such advertising will become increasingly diluted and the right message may not be reaching the right person – the target consumer.

Because of this market fragmentation Heinz have called upon their successful direct marketing experience in the US to develop a more direct relationship with their customers and thereby aim to induce brand loyalty. Modern technology makes direct marketing techniques far more practical as huge databases exist and can be accessed. This allows marketers to identify their customers and directly contact them. IBM predicts that the cost of processing such information will decrease 99 per cent over the next decade. Other brands that have adopted these direct marketing techniques include Nestlé's Buitoni, Brooke Bond tea bags and Rothman's Raffles. By producing consumer clubs for brand users, newsletters and money-off coupons it is hoped that companies can stay in touch with their heavy brand users and stay a step ahead of the competition.

☐ *Television Sponsorship*

Television sponsorship is becoming increasingly prominent as a means of advertising. For example, between 1993 and 1995 the value of sponsorship more than doubled from £15m to £30m. The UK has seen many high-profile television programmes entering into sponsorship with various brands.

Two examples are the sponsorship of Channel 4's 'The Word' by Swatch Watches, and Yorkshire Television's 'The Darling Buds of May' by Tetley Tea. Using this form of advertising affords advertisers certain advantages. For example, Swatch watches knows that viewers of 'The Word' will have similar psychographic profiles and fashions. Or, in the case of Tetley Tea, the product is being associated with a programme that may have similar perceived values or attributes such as homeliness and warmth. Therefore, sponsorship allows products to automatically target certain segments and allows a product's attributes and image to be reinforced by the nature of the programme it sponsors.

The logistics of sponsorship also make sense. Sponsorship highlights products at a time when the viewers' attention is most intense – at the beginning and end of interesting programmes. If sponsorship can work effectively with particular programmes then it allows products to reinforce its image that has already been established by other methods of advertising. (*Source*: R. Millar, *Marketing Business Magazine*, June 1993, p. 39.)

Changes adopted by the patent office have also encouraged the use of sponsorship. Since 1994 legislation has permitted slogans to be incorporated in to TV sponsorship credits. So long as the slogan is registered as part of the trade mark it may be incorporated into the credits. Now many companies are producing a much higher profile of sponsorship that interacts more closely with the relevant programme. For example, Kellogg's Frosties' sponsorship of 'The Gladiators', Diet Coke's sponsorship of 'Movie Premiers' and the Sun's sponsorship of 'The Wheel of Fortune'. (*Source*: 'Media Speak', *Marketing Week* 26 January 1995, p. 9.)

☐ *Some other advertising media*

The following list in Table 16.17 gives examples of other types of advertising media, and typical rates in 1994.

Table 16.17 *Some other advertising media*

Media	Typical rates
Aerial advertising (aircraft-towed banners)	£250–£400 per hour
Book marks	£47 per 10 000
Local authority advertising	£15–30 per 1 000 with rate demand etc.
Matchboxes	From £54 per 1000
Playing cards	£220 per 100 packs with single colour printed
Parking meter advertising	£140–£350 per 100 displays
Teleguide (telephone recordings)	Recruitment ads: £200–£400 per week Product ads: £190 per week
Travel wallets	£23 995 for 1m wallet advertisements
Hot air balloons (8 man)	£750 per day
Electronic outdoor advertising display	From £200 per 10 sec transmission per week
Lorry-side posters	£75 per side per month
Ships' advertising	£44 per site per month (summer rates, Sealink I.o.W. service, double crown size)
Litter bins	£25 per panel per month (minimum 4 panels)
Advertee golf signs	£1 per week per tee (minimum of 6 tees)
Video tape publications	£1852–£21 000 per minute
Video in Post Offices	£10 950 for 30 sec spot every 15 min over 5 weeks
Taxicabs	Tip up seats from £3.50 per month, exteriors from £25 per month

Note: Other advertising media listed in *BRAD* include calendars, year planners, business cards, car blinds, milk bottles, sporting events, town maps, exhibition centres, air-ships, airports
Source: Advertising Assocation.

■ Campaign planning

An excellent treatment of this subject used to be available in Olaf Ellefsen's *Campaign Planning* published by Business Publications on behalf of the IPA but, sadly, this is now out of print. No suitable substitute has been identified and the following notes will have to suffice until a fuller treatment becomes available.

Earlier in the chapter a number of advertising objectives were stated, and it was noted that the determination of such an objective was an essential prerequisite to the formulation of a campaign plan. Assuming that management has given its advertising agency a clear statement of what it wishes to achieve, it then becomes the agency's responsibility to devise a campaign that will maximise the return on the appropriation allocated. As was inferred when discussing the agency–client relationship, the preparation of a campaign plan will require close cooperation between the parties. This will become clear if one considers the stages leading up to the introduction of a new product.

The first stage in the process is the recognition of a business opportunity. Once this has been identified, the marketer will undertake marketing research as a basis for quantifying the nature and extent of this opportunity. As a result of such research a consumer profile will be drawn up stating the demographic characteristics of the potential consumer, the geographical location of the market, the frequency and method of purchase, and so on.

Armed with this 'blueprint' of the intended consumer, the next stage in the process is the development of a product to satisfy the demand represented by recognition of the original opportunity. Once developed, the product will be tested. It is at this stage that the agency should be brought in. Given the consumer profile, the nature of the product and a statement of the features which differentiate it from competitors' offerings, the proposed channels of distribution and intended price bracket, the agency will be in a position to suggest an appropriate name and package. The continued growth of self-service retailing, described in Chapter 9, demands that very careful attention be paid to the latter two factors (name and package), as recognition at the point of sale is a vital stimulus to purchase. For these reasons alone the advertiser will want to feature both the brand name and pack in his advertising. If concept and product testing have been carried out the comments of the respondents should also be made available to the agency, as they invariably provide leads as to the copy platform to be adopted. A good example of this was Johnson's Wax in the United States. When housewives were asked to list the most important properties of a floor polish, the majority gave considerable weight to the polish's ability to resist scuffing. Although 'scuffing' was not a word in common currency, the panel housewives had independently selected it as the most descriptive. When Johnson introduced their new brand it was advertised as the 'non-scuff' polish and achieved immediate success – it was just what housewives were looking for!

A further reason for bringing in the agency at this time is to discuss the method of launching the product – test market, regional or national launch – and the timing, from selling in to the channels of distribution to the product's appearance in the retail outlet. On the basis of all this information, the agency will draw up a plan for submission to the advertiser comprising two major elements – the copy platform and the media schedule.

The copy platform is the theme around which the campaign is based, for example 'It's the real thing. Coke', while the media schedule lists the media in which the advertisements are to be published with details of size, timing, frequency and cost. The advertising literature is full of advice on the selection of USPs (unique selling points), EBTs (emotional buying triggers) and the like, but for an insight into the preparation and execution of advertising campaigns the student is strongly recommended to read one, or all, of the following books: David Ogilvy, (1965) *Confessions of an Advertising Man*, a highly readable and somewhat unconventional description of how Ogilvy became one of America's top advertising men, packed with information and advice for the aspiring advertising agent; and his

more recent book (1983) *Ogilvy on Advertising*; Rosser Reeves (1970) 'Reality in Advertising', a short but highly concentrated coverage of do's and don't's in advertising, full of actual examples of advertising campaigns; Martin Mayer (1958) *Madison Avenue*, a colourful and interesting description of what goes on at the heart of the US agency business, rather dated now but still worth reading.

Setting the advertising appropriation

The decision of how much to spend on advertising and other promotional activities is one of the more difficult budgeting problems that management is called upon to make. As will become clear in the next part of this chapter, the measurement of advertising effectiveness is, to say the least, difficult. In the absence of a directly measurable relationship between the volume of advertising and the overall profitability of the firm, the majority of managements have adopted one, or a combination, of the following 'rule-of-thumb' approaches.

Fixed percentage of sales

Under this method management allocates a percentage of either past or anticipated sales to advertising. A BIM *Survey of Manufacturers' Marketing Costs* (Information Summary No. 111) published in 1964 indicated that there is a considerable variation in the percentage allocated to advertising, even within an industry, which, in turn, is a reflection of the different competitive strategies adopted by marketers. Although dated, this observation is equally true in 1995 as it was in 1964. In this context it is noteworthy that total expenditures on advertising have remained a virtually constant percentage of the GNP in most advanced economies during this century.

Adoption of this policy may be justified on the grounds that it is rational to allocate a fixed proportion of sales revenue to advertising in the absence of a model which permits a prediction of variation in sales volume in response to variations in the volume of advertising. On the other hand, it ignores the fact that a decline in sales volume will result in a contraction of the advertising appropriation at the very time when increased advertising may be the stimulus necessary to halt the decline or reverse the trend.

In the case of companies operating in markets with an inelastic demand, the policy helps stabilise the competitive situation, always providing that it is a commonly accepted practice. Certain oligopolistic industries appear to exhibit this characteristic – the knowledge that increased advertising will not result in an increase in primary demand dissuades individual firms from attempting to improve their market share through increased advertising owing to the strong competitive response which it is bound to provoke. (This tendency was also noted with regard to the use of price reductions as a competitive weapon, unless the instigator had a clear cost advantage over his competitors.)

The 'me-too' approach

The adoption of this 'policy' was implied above, and constitutes the adoption of a level of advertising which corresponds to that of one's competitors. This is a purely defensive and negative reaction. Clearly, the firm is interested in what its competitors are doing as a guide to the policies it should adopt, but it also follows that if the firm is to improve its competitive position it must pursue policies that will enable the consumer to distinguish it from the competition and perceive it as superior.

What we can afford

This method tends to relegate expenditures on advertising to the bottom rung of the corporate budget ladder. It implies that whatever remains after meeting operating costs, dividend payments and so on, will be spent on advertising. As with the fixed percentage of sales method, the most likely outcome is that as sales fall the unit contribution will decline to the point where no

advertising can be afforded at all. Conversely, as sales rise an increasing amount will become available and the possibility of wasteful expenditures will become a reality.

The 'task' approach

In the absence of a normative model of the relationship between various levels of advertising and profitability, this method is to be preferred to any of the above practices. The first step in this method is the definition of a clear objective. Given the objective, one can prepare a campaign plan that would achieve this goal. An examination of the costs of mounting such a campaign may indicate that it is beyond the company's available resources. Within this constraint, the plan may be modified by closely evaluating each of its component parts and dispensing with the least essential. Obviously the end result will be a lesser objective than originally laid down, but it will be a realistic statement of what the firm can hope to accomplish related to current resources.

The BIM *Survey of Marketing Organisation in British Industry* (Information Summary 148) indicated that the respondents used the following basis for determining their advertising appropriations.

	%
Proportion of expected future sales	39
Analysis of needs or objectives	19
Proportion of past sales	11
Proportion of profit	7
Historical expenditure	2
As much as can be afforded	1

Table 16.18 reports the findings of the survey undertaken by Hooley, West and Lynch (1983) on behalf of the Institute of Marketing into methods of setting the advertising appropriation. More recently (*The Marketing Book*, 1991), Crosier has reported that analysis of a number of surveys in the UK and USA between 1970 and 1985 indicates that on average 44 per cent of companies based their spend on actual or projected sales, 21 per cent used judgement ('all you can afford', 'notional sum', 'arbitrary method', 'affordable approach'

Table 16.18 *Method used to set advertising budget's frequency*

Method used	Regularly (%)	Tried it (%)	Heard of but not used (%)	Never heard of or no reply (%)
1. Percentage of expected sales	38.4	15.7	21.2	24.8
2. Match competition	8.3	15.5	39.8	36.4
3. What we can afford	48.5	16.6	10.8	24.2
4. Desired share of voice	11.4	12.0	27.8	48.7
5. Objective and task	39.8	13.4	15.0	31.9
6. Accept agency proposal	4.2	19.9	35.4	40.5
7. Experimentation and testing	13.6	20.9	28.5	37.1

Source: G. J. Hooley, C. J. West and J. E. Lynch (1983), *Marketing in the UK: A Survey of Current Practice and Performance* (Institute of Marketing).

and so on), 18 per cent used a task approach, with all other methods accounting for the remaining 17 per cent.

A more extended set of descriptions for setting the advertising appropriation is set out in Table 16.19.

The measurement of advertising effectiveness

When discussing media selection, frequent reference was made to *BRAD* and the IPA Readership Surveys as a source of information on audience composition. Head counting is a long-established practice that yields sound demographic data. A measure of audience size is of interest to the advertiser but, ultimately, the advertiser is much more concerned with the effectiveness of the advertising; that is, to find he wants a measure of the results of exposure to advertising. Five basic methods have been evolved to measure advertising effectiveness and these are reviewed below.

The measurement of awareness

Awareness is defined as 'knowledge about a company or its product without reference to the source of knowledge'. As, by definition, awareness tests do not relate knowledge to source they

provide only a rough and ready guide to advertising effectiveness, and are usually undertaken as a preliminary to further tests. In the case of a new product it may be possible to isolate the source of awareness, but this is virtually impossible in the case of an established brand.

Actual measurement is obtained by asking respondents:

(a) Straight dichotomous questions, e.g. Have you ever heard of the XYZ company?'

Yes... No...

(b) An open-ended question; for example, 'Do you know of any companies that make a detergent with a blue whitener?'

(c) Check-list questions with rating scales; for example, 'How familiar are you with the XYZ company?'

Very familiar...
Know something about...
Know very little about them...
Never heard of...

Low cost and speed are cited as the major advantages of this method.

The measurement of recall

Recall – what people can remember about advertising messages – is the most frequently used measure of advertising effectiveness, on the basis that if the message has left a memorable

Table 16.19 *Methods of determining the promotional appropriation*

Category 1: Executive judgement
  AYCA: All you can afford
  Notional sum
  Arbitrary method
  Affordable approach

Category 2: Internal ratios
  Historical parity
  Same as last year
  Inertia
  Fixed amount
  A/S ratio: advertising-to-sales
  A/M ratio: advertising-to-margin
  Per-unit allowance
  Case rate

Category 3: External ratios
  Competitive parity
  Share of voice
  Share of market
  Dynamic difference

Category 4: Computer modelling
  What-if models
  Prescriptive models
  Simulation
  Econometric analysis

Category 5: Experimentation
  Experiments
  AMTES (Area Marketing Test
    Evaluation System)

Category 6: Objective-and-task
  Task method

Source: Michael J. Baker (ed.) (1994), *The Marketing Book*, 3rd edn (London: Butterworth-Heinemann), p.520.

impression it has fulfilled its communicative function. If the advertising objective is to communicate information then the method is appropriate, but in many instances the objective is to promote action, for example mail-order advertisements. Recall is also a useful measure when copy testing.

Recall studies are capable of measuring several dimensions of advertising effectiveness. At the lowest level they consist of the respondent's describing the basic theme of an advertisement, and progress through association of the correct theme with the product advertised, measures of comprehension, credibility and conviction, to significance.

Essentially, the method employed is to ask the respondent to reconstruct what he or she can remember having seen or heard advertised, either unaided – unaided recall – or with a varying degree of assistance to direct the respondent's thinking along particular lines – aided recall. Aided recall is generally preferred, as few people will spontaneously recall past events without some stimulus, in which case the researcher must guard against bias arising from too much assistance, or false answers resulting from guessing. Gallup and Robinson conduct regular surveys of recall, and attempt to minimise bias by first establishing that the respondent has read the issue being tested by showing them the cover, and then asking them to establish knowledge of its content. Once the respondent has demonstrated familiarity with the test issue, they are then asked to reconstruct their memory of the advertisements without opening the magazine. The final stage is to show the respondent brand names, advertisement logotypes, and so on, and after telling them that some did not appear in the issue in question, ask them to identify those they remember. A sample of 400 is used, the interviews are recorded verbatim and, after editing, are compiled into an index of recall – the 'proved name registration'. A PNR is calculated for the medium as a whole, for the product group and for the specific brand. Although it is difficult to assign an absolute value to a PNR, it provides a useful guide to the advertiser in that they can measure their advertisement's performance against that of all other advertisers in the magazine and that of their immediate competitors. Further, over a period of time they can determine whether the impact of their advertising is increasing, declining or static.

A hybrid test which incorporates both aided and unaided recall is 'working along the time line'. For example you ask a respondent to describe what he did yesterday evening, anticipating that he will recall an event which involved consumption of a product in which you are interested. If the product group is mentioned, for example 'I washed, cleaned my teeth and went to bed', you might ask the name of the brand of soap or toothpaste and lead into further questions related to these products. If the product group is not mentioned then the interviewer will ask directly 'Did you clean your teeth?', and so on.

Three problems are inherent in all recall studies:

1. Respondent confusion, due to either confusing the advertisement and its sponsor – Kellogg's Puffed Wheat – or identifying advertisements correctly from recollections of previous campaigns.
2. Recall of advertising messages in the interview situation is not the same as recall at the point of sale (a strong argument for both poster advertising and POS display), nor does it indicate an intention to buy.
3. The ever-present danger of misinterpretation of the results.

For the two latter reasons recall investigations are often combined with:

Attitude surveys

A favourable attitude towards a company or its product nearly always precedes a decision to buy, even if this favourable predisposition is at the preconscious level, that is a consumer picks up a product on impulse without consciously identifying the motivation to purchase.

Attitude measurement may consist of a general assessment or be restricted to various dimensions of a specific brand – acceptance, preference or insistence – of either one's own or one's competitor's product. Unfortunately, it is difficult to construct a true measure of a person's attitudes, and several techniques are frequently used in combination to permit cross-checking. The more common methods are:

(a) Direct questions of the 'Do you like X?' type, followed by a request to explain why you do, or do not, like X. Direct questions suffer from their inability to distinguish between varying degrees of intensity of feeling. Rating scales provide a partial solution and are amenable to rapid analysis, but suffer from the disadvantage that the choice of phrases which are precise, yet universally understood, is extremely difficult; that, however large, the scale may still not permit a truly accurate expression of intensity of feeling; that intermediate positions are capable of varying interpretation, for example 'What is your attitude to Widgets?'

> Favourable ...
> Mixed ...
> Indifferent ...
> Unfavourable ...

Alternatively, one might use the scale: Excellent, 4, 3, 2, Poor, or even a seven or ten-point scale.

(b) A second method is to ask the respondent to complete a checklist by indicating the most appropriate answer/description of those assigned to each question. By undertaking a preliminary survey it is usually possible to design questions that will cover the attributes which consumers, as opposed to advertisers, think important.
(c) A semantic differential test, in which a respondent indicates where a brand or company stands on a scale of paired opposites, either descriptive adjectives or phrases, for example reliable–unreliable.
(d) Partially structured interviews, in which the interviewer memorises the points to be covered and 'discusses' the subject with the respondent, rather than posing formal questions from a questionnaire. The lack of trained interviewers, the length of the interview and difficulties of interpretation severely limit the use of this method.

Attitude related to usage is usually considered a more significant measure of advertising effectiveness than attitude on its own, and it is usual to obtain a measure of usage as a basis for a comparison of attitudes.

Psychological measurement

The three techniques described above are designed to measure a respondent's reaction to advertising at the conscious or preconscious level. Psychological techniques are designed to probe deeper and reach to the subconscious mind. At this level the respondent is unaware of the reasons which result in certain expressed patterns of behaviour, although if asked, they will usually advance an acceptable and rational reason. As most advertising messages are directed at large audiences, the peculiarities of the individual are of little or no consequence unless they are common to a large number of individuals. It is to determine basic motivation that advertising researchers, among others, use psychological methods where direct questioning might lead to rationalisation or evasion.

Psychological techniques have limitations which require great care in their execution and interpretation, and it must be recognised that the results will be qualitative not quantitative. As noted above in regard to partially structured depth interviews, the lack of suitably qualified interviewers usually restricts the use of these techniques to small samples from which it is difficult to make acceptable projections of consumer behaviour.

The most frequently used method is the unstructured depth interview of from one to three hours, in which interviewer and respondent talk about a specific subject in the belief that if the respondent is kept talking about the same thing long enough some of their unconscious attitudes will begin to emerge.

A popular variation of the depth interview is the focused or directed group interview, in which a skilled interviewer leads a group of six to twelve people in an unstructured discussion that relates to the product and/or its advertising.

Other projective techniques used include thematic apperception tests, picture probes, narrative probes, sentence completion tests and word association tests.

Sort and count

Many advertisements contain an invitation to interested parties to write in to the advertiser for further information, free samples, and so forth. By sorting and counting the requests generated by such advertisements the advertiser can obtain much useful information at low cost.

Despite the potential bias due to respondent self-selection, this method does give valuable information in relative terms of the pulling power of different media, of different copy platforms and advertisement make-up, and of different sizes and positions within the media. The advertisements are usually keyed, that is given a coding to assist identification, either by including the code in the address, for example Dept DM7 for an edition of the *Daily Mail*, or by requiring the respondent to clip the coupon on which the information is similarly recorded.

As mentioned by Ogilvy (1965) in *Confessions of an Advertising Man*, direct mail advertisers have a continuous feedback of the pulling power of their advertisements, which supports his suggestion that those selling though more conventional channels might do well to adopt some of the former's advertising practices, for example use of long copy.

Others

Under this heading are a number of techniques which attempt to measure a causal relationship between advertising and measurable indicators of the firm's performance such as increased distribution (on the premise that if retailers are asked for goods not in stock they will seek supplies) or sales volume. The 'dealer playback' technique also deserves mention, and has been used by Black & Decker in a competition designed to increase sales push at the retail level. (Company representatives visit stores selling the goods in question, express an interest in them, and note the number of selling points suggested in their recent advertising that the salesman advances as a reason for purchase.)

In May 1990, AGB announced a new development in measuring advertising effectiveness and claims that it can demonstrate not only whether a particular TV campaign has worked, but which viewers bought more products as a result of the advertising and how the budget should be deployed to bring the best sales results (*Marketing Week*, 1 June 1990). AGB's claim is based on the use of a technique called *data fusion* which involves the integration of two existing data sources. Ideally the answer to many research questions is to use single source data in which a representative sample of consumers can be surveyed in terms of their purchasing behaviour related to their reading, viewing and listening habits. However, attempts by Central Adlab and Neilsen and HTV's Statscan to set up sufficiently large panels to provide such data proved to be prohibitively expensive and had to be abandoned.

To overcome this problem, BMRB launched its Target Group Ratings service in April 1990 which is based on the fusion of TGI which measures product usage, and BARB which measures viewing. The aim of Target Group Ratings is to enable advertising agencies to plan campaigns more accurately by selecting programmes watched by the users of their products rather than more broadly defined demographic groups. However, the AGB service differs in that its primary purpose is to aid campaign evaluation by quantifying the effect of advertising on sales. The AGB method also uses BARB data but fuses it with information from its own TCA panel which measures product purchases in 6500 homes. *Marketing Week* reported:

> By developing a computer model of TV viewing behaviour, based on the individual viewing patterns of housewives on the BARB panel, AGB can now predict when an individual housewife on the TCA panel is likely to be watching ITV or Channel 4. From this it can work out the number of times she is likely to have seen a particular commercial.
>
> The model depends on certain key demographic characteristics and viewing claims, such as the fact that non-working women are much more likely to watch TV during the day than those who are out at work.

In a test on a new fast moving consumer good, the fusion model showed that among heavy viewers who saw a commercial an average of 8.6 times, their purchases increased by 44 per cent compared with an increase of only 29 per cent by light viewers who saw the commercial on average 2.7 times during the campaign. The analysis also showed that advertising primarily increased trial of the brand and sales to occasional buyers rather than increasing the purchase rate of regular buyers demonstrating that the ads were much more effective with some demographic groups than others.

Clearly such results are very promising but, as *Marketing Week* cautions, they also depend heavily on the judgement and integrity of the researcher. Only when sufficient case histories are available will we be able to assess fully the potential of data fusion as a means of both campaign planning and measuring advertising effectiveness by merging existing databases.

Laboratory techniques for pre-testing advertisements

A number of techniques have been developed to try and obtain an objective measure of people's response to advertisements, which interviewing methods are unable to elicit owing to an inability to verbalise or a tendency to rationalise. The use of the instruments listed below is based on the knowledge that emotional arousal in a human being results in various responses which are under the control of the autonomic nervous system and thus largely independent of conscious control. These responses include increases in pulse and respiration rates, erection of hair follicles, changes in pupil size and electrical brain pulses, perspiration rates and so on. As each person reacts to different stimuli to a varying degree, ideally one should measure all responses simultaneously, but this is clearly impossible under normal conditions. As such it is necessary to select the method(s) which provide the most reliable results in monitoring reactions to the specific variable under test with the minimum disturbance to the subject. The most frequently used are:

1. *The psycho-galvanometer*. This instrument measures changes in the activity of the sweat glands via electrodes attached by suction to the subject's hands. Prior to exposing the subject to the test advertisements the basal level must be established for control purposes and care taken to maintain a constant temperature throughout the test. The highest reading recorded indicates maximum arousal.

2. *The eye observation camera* is used to measure pupil dilation. As light also affects the pupil, care must be taken to ensure that both control and test material are of the same luminosity. The material to be tested is back-projected into a closed box while the camera records the pupil dilation over a period of time. The greatest change occurs with the highest level of arousal. The camera may also he used to measure the subject's blink rate – the higher the rate the greater the arousal. Blinking is partly under conscious control, and is also affected by humidity, irritation and fatigue, all of which must be controlled if an accurate measure is to be obtained.

3. *The tachistoscope* is an instrument used for exposing material for controlled periods of time ranging from 1/100 of a second to several seconds. Its main use is in measuring the impact of an advertisement by determining either the point at which its features are registered (noting and legibility studies) or its visual impact (what is communicated) when exposed for only a brief period. As individual 'thresholds' vary, a norm must first be established for each subject.

4. *The eye-movement camera* tracks the movement of the eye over an advertisement by filming a point of light projected on to the eyeball. The track indicates the order and degree of attention given to the features of the advertisement.

All the above methods are subject to criticism on the grounds that they are unrealistic as a result of the laboratory situation; that only a limited number of respondents may be tested (owing to the high cost of the test and data processing equipment required), and these may not be representative; that no indication of the direction of the response is given, so that respondents have to be questioned as to their feelings, which reintroduces subjectivity into the test; that is, a marked reaction may be due to either repulsion or attraction.

In mitigation, any test is better than no test if it helps in establishing whether or not advertisements are communicating their basic point to the subject. Further, it is only through experimentation that satisfactory techniques for measuring advertising effectiveness will be evolved.

■ Advertising case histories

An excellent series of case histories of different advertising campaigns is available from ITCA (Independent Television Companies Association), 56 Mortimer Street, London W1, and two of these are reproduced below with their kind permission. (*Campaign*, *Ad Weekly* and *Marketing* also publish such case histories on a regular basis.)

An increasing number of retail advertisers are now putting greater emphasis on the strategic use of television advertising to achieve corporate long-term objectives compared to those using the medium to communicate short-term tactical price promotions. Argos successfully combined the two as this case study demonstrates.

□ *Argos*

Argos is a wholly owned subsidiary of BAT Industries and is managed by the BAT Stores division which also takes in International Supermarkets and Jewellers Guild. BAT acquired Argos, which was part of the Green Shield operation, in 1979. At that time the chain comprised just 17 showrooms; today, and expanding at an annual rate of 15–20 units, there are over 140, with an annual turnover in excess of £300 million at retail selling prices (rsp). The Argos concept of catalogue/showroom retailing is unique in the

UK and originates from North America where it has operated successfully for many years. It comprises catalogue browsing in the showroom and/or home, merchandise display in the high street, filling in a purchase selection form and then payment/collection in the showroom.

The market

The total value of retail sales in the 25-plus markets in which Argos currently operates is worth around £1000 million rsp (source: AGB). These markets include electricals excluding white goods (Argos has significant penetration of kitchen, domestic and personal electrical appliances) ; also toys where Argos with around 5 per cent of the market shares leadership with Woolworths; garden equipment and furniture; and jewellery where, in a fragmented market, Argos has 3 per cent penetration and is thought to be one of the most important named retailers.

Penetration by Argos varies, according to AGB between 1 per cent and 13 per cent sterling in the 25 markets covered, with around 2 per cent in total of all the markets in which it competes; the showrooms stock around 2800 individual lines in all.

Competing with a wide diversity of other retailers due to the broad range of products stocked, Argos offers a distinctive means of shopping and a very competitive price proposition. Bulk buying in branded goods and efficient modern systems of retailing produce resources that give prices comparable with if not lower than the specialist chains as well as the department and superstores. The Argos system means minimum shop assistants, optimum merchandise display and computerised stock control, the economics of which are passed back to the consumer in the form of lower prices. The prime vehicle for communicating the broad choice of products available is the catalogue backed up by showroom displays.

Developing a long-term strategy

In just over 10 years Argos grew from virtually nothing to a massive multiple chain and an enormous amount of research has gone into evaluating and improving the showrooms, the catalogue, the shop locations (via Acorn data in particular) and in communication. The chain has become mass market but in consumer perception is perceived to be more down market and discount than is in fact the case. Consumer research confirmed that this was an inhibiting factor in what otherwise would have given Argos even greater market penetration and in the longer term, with continuing competitive improvements, was a problem which needed to be resolved to ensure long-term prosperity.

At the same time the company needed to, each year, re-launch the catalogue to ensure that it reached the maximum number of potential customers and also to ensure maximum awareness and current use. In this form of retailing, catalogue awareness and usage are the keys to offtake; passing traffic and window shopping following Argos research confirmed that 80 per cent of Argos purchases were decided before the consumer entered the showroom, but that only just under half of the people in possession of a catalogue were actually persuaded to buy.

Over the last five years, the company's activity has tended to be promotional rather than strategic, comprising press advertising of the catalogue linked with price promotion and accurately targeted catalogue door-to-door distribution involving around 21 million households. Whilst tactically delivering short-term results, this promotion was not providing any longer-term benefits in terms of attitude shifts; furthermore the mechanics of printing and distributing the extra millions of catalogues were becoming cumbersome to the degree that it was seriously inhibiting marketing, pricing, product buying and stock control since the time pressure at lead times were considerable. The increasing size of the chain compounded the problem.

The company decided that it simply needed to improve attitudes as fast as it possibly could to take advantage of the rapidly growing markets in which it operated and also to combat an increasingly competitive number of high street retailers which were also beginning to diversify and specialise. To do this it needed to increase familiarity of the Argos shopping concept through advertising and first-hand experience. The key was to increase awareness and usage of the catalogue but at the same time to promote more positively the concept of catalogue shopping. The decision was made in 1983 to use television in a big way to achieve both a tactical and immediate offtake of catalogues as well as a strategic change of attitudes.

Why television

Television was chosen by Argos and their agency Chetwynd Haddons because creatively it provided the opportunity to humanise through gentle humour the rather clinical and unusual nature of the store, but at the same time had a proven track record in delivering immediate sales offtake (in this case the object was catalogue uptake). The other reasons for choosing television were as follows:

- The facility to test and to weight the advertising according to areas of sales strength;
- The opportunity to, in effect, place the catalogue in the actual home of the potential customer;
- The greater prestige that using television imparts, which was important to Argos in combating the second division high street retailer image that they had among many people;
- And last but not least, television could counter criticism of inertia selling often levelled at door to door distribution.

Advertising objectives

1. To maximise offtake of the new Argos catalogue.
2. To improve attitudes and imagery towards the Argos system of high street shopping.
3. To penetrate the wide non-user and aware visitor to Argos.

The commercials

Four 20-second commercials were developed by Chetwynd Haddons and as a result of

pre-testing, three were finally chosen to run. Announcing the catalogue in a humorous, slightly anti-establishment way, the commercials succeeded also in communicating the two key customer benefits of convenience and economy. Through situations in a courtroom, a government department and a hospital outpatients, the commercials invited people to get their catalogue from Argos showrooms; the whole campaign was summed up in the line: 'You can't put a good book down'.

The campaign was tested in Central and Anglia from August 15 to September 11 1983; in Central the campaign achieved 81 per cent housewife coverage and 5.9 opportunities to see (OTS); in Anglia the comparable figures were 86 per cent and 7.5 OTS. In Spring 1984 the test was extended to London, all three areas accounting for around 50 per cent of Argos sales. The ratecard spend in Spring 1984 was over £250 000.

Campaign results

- In strictly controlled measurement conditions, there was a 33 per cent increase in catalogue uptake in the areas carrying television advertising compared to those not receiving TV. This success was achieved in Autumn 1983 and repeated in Spring 1984.
- £ sales in the television areas were up between 20 to 30 per cent on the previous year compared to a 10–15 per cent increase in the areas without television support.
- Well after the television advertising had finished, the plateau of sales was significantly up on the preceding year and higher than in those areas without television advertising. These extra sales were achieved profitably since no additional price promotion was used in the TV areas.
- Pre- and post-awareness and attitude research showed a sharp increase in awareness and a significant increase in the numbers of catalogue-aware potential customers intending to purchase.

The future

In the light of these results, Argos have extended the campaign to all areas in Autumn 1984 with a ratecard spend in excess of £1 million. According to Stuart Colley, marketing manager, Argos:

> Television has provided a better opportunity in return on investment than alternative promotional activity and as a result we are looking to expand our investment in the medium into 1985. We are particularly pleased with the strategic possibilities of the medium which the campaign has proved can be achieved at the same time as meeting immediate tactical objectives. Its intrusiveness and ability to convert inertia into energy has been aptly demonstrated for us at Argos!

The success of this strategy is confirmed by its continuing use into the 1990s.

☐ *Swatch Quartz*

Characterised by falling unit prices, the UK watch market remained almost static in volume during the late 1970s and early 1980s, declining in real value by between 20 and 30 per cent. During this period Japanese brands dominated the market. It is all the more remarkable, therefore, that a unique concept of a watch from Switzerland has achieved sales in excess of £12 million at retail selling prices (rsp) in just 18 months. Branded 'Swatch', the product was launched solely on ITV and Channel 4, opening up, as this case study demonstrates, an entirely new sector of the market.

Louis Newmark

Louis Newmark Limited was founded in the 1880s as an importer of quality Swiss watches and clocks, and soon established a strong position in the UK market. It has always enjoyed a strong working relationship with the Swiss watch industry and, in 1981, it acquired the rights to the Avia name, a brand which it had marketed since the 1920s. The decision to appoint Louis Newmark to market Swatch was therefore to be expected.

Today, Louis Newmark has diversified into a wide range of technological fields, encompassing the Aircraft division, which manufactures the flight control systems for the Sea King Helicopters and Hawk fighter aircraft; and the subsidiary company McMurdo which manufactures the safety lights used by all the world's major airlines. The combined turnover of the company is now 30 million per annum.

The UK watch market

According to Louis Newmark, around 11 million watches were sold in the UK in 1983, worth in excess of £200 million rsp. This excludes very cheap watches selling below £5 which are estimated to account for a further 2 or 3 million units. (This market is notoriously difficult to quantify because of variations in trade mark up; all figures are therefore approximate.) Unit growth has been healthy but due to dramatic falls in the average price following the introduction of new technology, the value of the market has remained almost static. By price, the market segments are as follows: £5–25 (65 per cent); £25–60 (30 per cent); and over £60 (5 per cent) – source: Louis Newmark.

Traditional buying patterns have been upset by both the frequency of product innovation, although in recent years the market has returned to the traditional analogue style pioneered by the Swiss, and changes in the nature of distribution.

Worldwide, the Swiss watch industry has witnessed a decline in volume, with its retention of the traditional movement in the face of intense Japanese competition; only in the premium sector did the traditional qualities of the Swiss industry ensure a dominant hold on the world market.

The watch market has also undergone a dramatic change in the nature of retail distribution. The strength of the long-established traditional jeweller has been progressively eroded by the opening up of non-traditional stockists, including departmental stores, W H Smiths, Boots, Underwoods, Dixons and others which have taken a substantial slice of the market, particularly at the cheaper end. This has been paralleled by the growth of the mail order business and outlets such as Argos and the other discount operators, who have similarly established large shares at the cheaper end of the market.

Swatch – creating a new market sector

Swatch is the direct result of intense research and development carried out by ETA, the Swiss watch industry group, and represents a major product breakthrough. Although retailing at less than £20, it provides the consumer with similar technology found in the very expensive Swatch 'Delerium' which sells at over £3000.

In essence, Swatch is based on a solid case into which the movement is built and sealed with the dial and glass, providing the consumer with a totally shock- and water-resistant product. The combination of high technology, durability and fashionable appearance at a low unit cost positions Swatch uniquely in the watch market.

Louis Newmark and their agency Shackle Hanmer commissioned a series of research studies to establish the most effective UK launch strategy in terms of positioning, targeting and communication. Initially available only in a man's version, the product benefits highlighted by research indicated a major opportunity for Swatch amongst the younger (aged under 35) watch purchasers, both male and female who pursued an active lifestyle, or at least believed that they did.

In this respect, one important feature emerged. It was not essential for the target group to actually have participated in any of the activities featured, but rather that they 'felt' they participated. The term vicarious participation might he most properly applied because many potential consumers felt they were actually involved in a sport by virtue of following it on television or elsewhere.

The product was seen as being particularly appropriate for sporting and other outdoor pursuits, yet was equally suited for wearing on fashionable occasions. Research also indicated

that Swatch would have a particular appeal during the summer months, which was significant, since some 60 per cent of watch sales occur in the last week before Christmas.

Television – an essential element of the launch

Television was seen as essential to the successful launch of Swatch for the following reasons:

- Research amongst both 'traditional' and 'new' watch retailers showed that the trade felt television was essential to generate the immediacy of awareness and high speed offtake that they required from a watch priced at under £20;
- The trade referred to the success of Japanese watches launched on television as well as many consumer durables with which they were familiar;
- Television provided the benefit of colour – vital to a product range which was differentiated essentially in terms of colour and features;
- And, most important of all, television provided the facility for movement, vital to ensure the effective demonstration of the key product benefits.

The decision was made to test market in one area and then progressively roll out across the country. No other advertising medium was used.

Advertising objective

To create awareness of Swatch amongst the prime target audience of all adults aged 25 or over as a unique form of watch combining fashion and durability.

The commercial

The 30-second launch commercial utilised a quick-cut still treatment to demonstrate the watch being used in a series of energetic sporting situations by young people with whom consumers could identify. Although shot on location in the USA, the treatment proved very economical as well as effective, the high beat music track helping to pull the fast-changing frames together into one communication.

This unusual execution compared to other advertising in the watch market aided recall and impact. A 10-second version supplemented the initial 30-second launch commercial; in year two the treatment was extended to include women (for the launch of the ladies version of Swatch) which demanded a greater emphasis on fashion, and to suggest a change of season. Again the music, lifestyle and situations featured were chosen only after a considerable amount of qualitative research.

Summer campaign

The launch campaign in the Summer of 1983 commenced on Central TV in June and rolled out to include Granada and London (LWT and Thames) during the latter part of the month, and July. The agency took full advantage of the available discounts to purchase an effective £723 000 rate card expenditure.

The initial campaign on four ITV stations achieved 241 adult ratings producing 79 per cent coverage and 5.3 opportunities to see (OTS); Channel 4 was used to help build coverage and frequency of the under 35s in particular.

The campaign was extended pre-Christmas, using the same commercials in 30- and 10-second time lengths, and with the addition of STV, Tyne Tees and additional spots on TV-am. In 1984, advertising for Swatch was totally national running throughout June and July and planned for pre-Christmas.

Campaign results

- In 18 months Swatch achieved sales of £12 million rsp, exceeding all sales targets by a considerable margin. Thus in 1983 150 000 units were sold against a target of 50 000; in 1984 the target is 500 000 units and already Swatch looks set to exceed this. In 1983 sales in areas with television were 300 per cent up on those without.

- Distribution targets have been vastly exceeded and the brand is generally recognised to have received unparalleled trade support in such a short period of time. Every major multiple jeweller, the majority of independents, most department stores, W H Smiths, Dixons, Underwoods, Duty Free shops, even some airlines, are currently stocking Swatch.
- These results have been achieved profitably and without recourse to price cutting. Furthermore, sales have maintained their high volume long after television advertising was halted, each new burst of TV moving the sales growth even higher.

The future

Ted Day, managing director of Louis Newmark Limited Watch Division, states

Swatch is the most significant development in the UK watch industry for 5 years and we confidently predict the brand will sell three quarters of a million units worth £15 million rsp next year. Television has been the major factor in this success and 90 per cent of an increased budget will be deployed in the medium in 1985.

In 1991 Swatch is firmly established as a major and distinctive brand in the watch market.

Economic and ethical aspects of advertising

The above review of advertising has concentrated on the practical aspects of the subject in so far as they affect the marketer. At the same time one must be aware that advertising is frequently the subject of criticism, and the aim of this section is to summarise the arguments both for and against. In view of the author's interest in marketing it follows that he has a favourable attitude towards advertising, and the reader is warned that this treatment is bound to be somewhat subjective.

☐ *The economic argument*

Essentially the question is 'Is advertising productive in the economic sense, that is does it maximise satisfaction through the utilisation of scarce resources?' The cliché, 'It pays to advertise', is tacit recognition of the fact that advertising improves the profitability of the advertiser, but this is nót to say that it necessarily makes any real contribution to the welfare of the community as a whole.

From the economist's point of view, the acid test of any economic activity is the utility of the output of that activity, which is measured by the extent to which it satisfies wants. For the economist the difficulty of accepting that advertising creates utility in this sense is both semantic and conceptual. The economist would argue that rather than satisfy existing wants the advertiser seeks to create wants for something that is already available. Advertisers would probably argue that you cannot create wants – you can only create better ways of satisfying existing wants, and that consumers derive satisfaction from advertised goods is undeniable. Similarly, to argue that advertising persuades people to consume things they do not want is to deny one of the basic assumptions of the economist – that, by and large, people are rational in their purchasing behaviour.

Many economists draw a distinction between 'informative' and 'combative' advertising, following the definition of Alfred Marshall (1919) in his book *Industry and Trade*. The distinction was further elaborated by Braithwaite (1928) in the *Economic Journal*, where it was claimed that advertising which contains information may be regarded as a true selling expense, whereas advertising designed to stimulate demand is non-essential and largely unproductive. In the April 1962 issue of the same journal, Samuel Courtauld was to assert 'most competitive advertising is a costly national extravagance'.

It would seem, therefore, that the critics concede the value of informative advertising as a means of making the consumer aware of the existence of goods and services and their basic properties, but that they consider combative or persuasive advertising to be a wasteful use of resources. It is difficult to see how the distinction can be maintained, since an advertisement for a new product may be justified as informative in that it makes consumers aware of the existence and characteristics of this product, but combative in that it seeks to persuade consumers to buy the new product in preference to a previously available substitute.

All advertisements contain some information, and it is a fruitless exercise to try and evaluate their individual utility in any precise manner as the informative/persuasive distinction will depend entirely on the existing state of knowledge of each individual member of the audience.

Partial recognition of this fact has diverted many economists, and other critics of advertising, to accept that 'persuasive' advertising can be beneficial, providing that it results in lower prices. Unfortunately, this distinction ignores the fact that price stability is the same as a price reduction under conditions of inflation, and that a consistent improvement in quality may represent the equivalent of a price reduction in that it increases consumer satisfaction for the same nominal money outlay.

To summarise, the case against advertising may be stated as:

1. Advertising leads to higher prices by conditioning demand and so leads to distortion of the productive machine, for example maize may cost only £0.01 per pound, but when converted into branded cornflakes it retails at about £0.80 per pound.
2. Advertising leads to non-price competition; for example, the use of promotions. This creates diseconomies due to difficulties associated with the accurate measurement of demand, and results in a high proportion of product failures.
3. It is an unreliable guide as to value and satisfaction.
4. It leads to oligopoly and monopoly.
5. It is a waste of national resources.

Proponents of advertising would argue that:

1. Advertised goods are cheaper because:

   (a) Advertising brings about economies in 'true' selling costs, for example by reducing the need for direct selling, encouraging the development of self-service, and so forth.

   (b) It raises the scale of production, helps to stabilise output and promotes standardisation.

   (c) Competition ensures that the benefits of these economies will be passed on to the consumer.

2. Advertised goods are better goods because:

   (a) The identification of the product with the manufacturer through branding constitutes a guarantee of quality which must be maintained if the manufacturer is to secure repeat purchases from users.

   (b) To maintain market share manufacturers must constantly strive to improve their product to meet, or exceed, the claims of competing products.

3. Branded and advertised goods create a freedom of consumer choice that was unknown when the same articles were sold from bulk.

4. Advertising improves the standard of living by making new developments quickly available to the public and, by stimulating demand, creates investment, production and employment opportunities.

☐ *The ethical argument*

Advertising is indicted on ethical grounds on the basis that it encourages the development of materialism. F. P. Bishop (1952), in his book *The Ethics of Advertising*, defines materialism as '...an acquisitive ideology in which the satisfaction of material desires is held up as the sole or principal end for the individual or group'.

In the creation of a materialistic society advertising is charged with deliberately concentrating on those motives that are least desirable in man and of the least value to society. One can be shown innumerable advertisements that appeal to one or more of the 'seven deadly sins', or that play on the emotion most easily stimulated in the human animal – fear. Fear of being left out, of being socially unacceptable, or of being considered socially inferior in some way or other, for example dull, lifeless hair; B.O.; halitosis; X washes whiter – and it shows.

Advertising is further indicted in that it sets out to eliminate nonconformity and discourage originality in thought, word and deed. Admass leaves no room for reason, and cultivates the herd instinct.

Finally, in the words of A. S. J. Baster (1935) in *Advertising Reconsidered*, 'The major part of informative advertising is and always has been a campaign of exaggeration, half-truths, intended ambiguities, direct lies, and general deception' (quoted by Bishop, 1952).

Most marketers would readily agree that the acquisition of material things is a means to an end and not an end in itself, but would also argue that man has free will and therefore the right to decide for himself what level of material consumption he will seek to attain. Religion and philosophy offer us a wide range of alternatives from which to choose a set of principles that will constitute a 'good life'. Whereas mere possessions are unlikely to result in satisfaction in the total sense, it is also true that a certain level of material goods is essential to the maintenance of life. Over and above these essentials, the desired level of material possessions will depend on the society of which we are a member, our education and income.

It is also appropriate to point out that it is only in this century that the possibility of a reasonable standard of living for all members of society has been achieved, and this, as yet, only in advanced economies. Earlier civilisations were largely based on the sweated labour of the masses and only the aristocracy could afford the luxury of philosophising about the 'good life' – only in the next world was it conceivable that all might share in the material comforts enjoyed by the few. (It is an interesting reflection on middle-class morality that the demand for labour-saving kitchen equipment only really got off the ground in this country with the passing of personal servants following the creation of alternative opportunities for female employment in the Second World War.)

Present-day 'welfare economics', designed to remove 'poverty in the midst of plenty', have grown out of the belief that we are now capable of producing sufficient to permit an adequate standard of living for all, and that the major problem is a more equitable distribution of output. At the same time, experience of a full employment policy in the post-war period has taught us that in the absence of adequate demand, production is frustrated and both human and physical resources lie idle. Many would argue that restriction of demand in recent years has mainly resulted from government policies designed to curb inflation, rather than from the inability of the productive machine to create goods in demand. It is my opinion that the inflationary trend is largely the result of a lack of demand.

In the case of the average consumer, the material possessions which constitute the good life are limited to a relatively small number of goods and services. There is a latent demand for many other goods and services, but their utility is less than the effort necessary to earn sufficient to pay for them owing to the disincentive of increasingly punitive levels of taxation. Consequently there is no incentive to work more effectively and improve productivity, an attitude which is compounded by the Government's provision of a range of social services that caters for virtually all of life's emergencies.

Even after ten years of Thatcherism, both government and management have been singularly ineffective in explaining the real benefits that will accrue from increased productivity, and the working man resists measures to achieve this in the belief that he may be making himself redundant. The possibility of redeploying labour into new industries creating new products to satisfy existing wants is overlooked. On the other hand if the consumer could be made to want dishwashing machines, VCRs, DSB, electric

toothbrushes or any other similar but 'non-essential' item, this might provide sufficient incentive to call forth the increase in productivity that is so urgently required.

In a sense, therefore, materialism and an acquisitive society are necessary if we are to maintain and improve the quality of life for both ourselves and those less fortunate in the developing economies. The more wealth we create domestically, the greater will be our ability to help others.

The other argument for the retention of advertising is that it helps preserve freedom of speech and freedom of choice. Modern media are dependent upon advertising revenues for their continued existence. On their existence largely rests the continued freedom of speech for, as noted when discussing the evolution of advertising, one of the first acts of a dictatorship is to secure control of the means of mass communication. (See Crosier 1994, *The Marketing Book* for an extended discussion of these issues.)

■ Public relations

According to Haywood (1995) public relations barely existed as a management function, outside some Western governments and their military forces, before the 1950s. Today it is a widely established professional practice with its own professional bodies and qualifications. As a subject Public Relations is also widely taught at the undergraduate and postgraduate level in business schools around the world.

In common with other business disciplines numerous definitions are to be found. According to the UK Institute of Public Relations (1994) it is 'the planned and sustained effort to establish and maintain goodwill and mutual understanding between an organisation and its publics'. Haywood (*op. cit.*) suggests that a useful working definition is 'those efforts used by management to identify and close any gap between how the organisation is seen by its key publics and how it would like to be seen' (p. 723). He also emphasises that public relations is about corporate personality – what the organisation is, believes in and is seeking to achieve – rather than simply its 'image', albeit that image is an intrinsic and essential element of the corporate personality.

It is also important to emphasise that public relations involves much more than publicity. Publicity is vital in projecting an organisation's personality but is simply the visible expression of corporate policy and strategic intent. Professional public relations has an important role and contribution to make to the formulation and implementation of both policy and strategy which goes far beyond a marketing communications activity. (Corporate PR covers an organisation's relationships with all of its publics, not just its customers.) That said, PR must work closely with other marketing communications such as advertising, selling and sales promotion, and be integrated with them to achieve an efficient and effective communication strategy.

As noted, public relations seeks to project the organisation's personality and thereby establish and develop its corporate reputation with all those audiences or publics on whom it depends for its commercial success. While customers usually come first in importance there are many other constituencies – employees, shareholders, government/politicians, the media, the general public, and so on – whose support, explicit or implicit, is vital to successful performance. Shell's handling of the Brent Spar incident in 1995 was a vivid example of how public opinion forced a major multinational corporation to revise a decision, endorsed by the British Government, with considerable loss of face for both parties. Originally, Shell proposed to sink an obsolete oil storage 'rig' in the deep Atlantic. Public concern for the possible impact of this on the environment, orchestrated by Greenpeace and other environmental organisations, resulted in a boycott of Shell products in Europe which forced the company to abandon its plans and promise to dismantle the rig onshore. In this case Greenpeace's positive PR achieved a desired outcome while Shell's ineffective PR caused considerable damage to its reputation.

In the same sense that marketing is the primary responsibility of the Chief Executive, so too is public relations. Indeed, many senior executives see acting as spokesman for their organisation as one of their major functions. By the same token the personality and image of an organisation is often inextricably linked with that of its Chairman and/ or Chief Executive. For example, the flamboyant John Harvey-Jones transformed ICI's image from that of a staid, conservative industrial company into one of a thrusting and dynamic modern corporation, undoubtedly paving the way for the re-organisation of the firm into two distinct organisations (Zeneca and ICI). At the corporate level public relations is inextricably linked with the mission and objectives of the organisation and it is through public relations that the values and aspirations which these represent are communicated to its various publics.

In a seminal article 'The Company is the Brand', Stephen King (1989) argued cogently that as it becomes increasingly difficult to distinguish between the products and services offered by firms, so customers use their corporate reputation or 'brand' to distinguish between them. Loyalty or goodwill towards a company is a major determinant of its asset value, as the frequently cited case of Nestlé's acquisition of Rowntree Macintosh makes clear. At the time of the acquisition (1988), Rowntree Macintosh's physical asset value was under £500 million but Nestlé paid £2.5 billion to secure ownership of international brands such as Kit Kat, Smarties and so on. While marketing will usually assume responsibility for individual brands such as Kit Kat, it is public relations which is responsible for promoting the corporate brand. Thus, when an organisation adopts a *monolithic* branding approach (all activities are transacted under a single, corporate name), or an *endorsed* branding strategy (all distinctive activities or 'brands' are promoted jointly with the corporate name) public relations will have a major role to play. Haywood (*op. cit*) suggests ten pointers to help ensure that advertising and public relations work together.

1. Involve both disciplines in the marketing planning;
2. Define complementary public relations and advertising objectives;

3. Allocate separate and firm budgets to each;
4. Agree responsibilities and planned activities;
5. Establish practical routines for coordination;
6. Have regular joint liaison sessions;
7. Get public relations/advertising to present their campaign to each other;
8. Arrange for them to make a joint presentation to the organisation's management;
9. Ensure regular exchange of all documents/information;
10. Insist that all parties work together this year – or they might not get the chance next.   (p. 735)

Summary

This rather long chapter has attempted to provide an overview of a large and complex subject – advertising. Inevitably, it has only been able to scratch the surface and the reader is strongly encouraged to refer to some of the sources cited.

Beginning with some definitions we looked next at the objectives which advertising may be used to help achieve. A discussion of the evolution of advertising followed which suggests that, while evidence of it dates back to Roman times, it is only since the abolition of taxes on advertisements in 1853 that the modern advertising industry has developed.

Several tables of statistics provided some 'feel' for the size and structure of the UK advertising industry. These data were accompanied by a warning that they rapidly become dated and that one should consult the latest edition of the various sources for an accurate and up-to-date position. The *Marketing Pocket Book* is particularly useful in this context as it summarises so many other data sources.

The next section examined the structure of advertising and, specifically, the roles of advertiser, the advertising agency and media owners. This led to a discussion of agency remuneration and selection.

An overview of the major media followed. This opened with suggestions as to how one might evaluate the available media in terms of character, atmosphere coverage and cost. Some features of and data on the major media followed – the national and regional press, magazines, television, commercial radio, outdoor advertising, the cinema and direct mail.

A short section on campaign planning reviewed some of the considerations the advertiser should take into account when planning a campaign. This was supported by advice on setting the appropriation or budget and measuring advertising effectiveness. Two case histories of successful advertising campaigns rounded out this part of the chapter.

Finally, we looked at some of the economic and ethical issues which are frequently raised about advertising but concluded that, in a free country, advertising is strongly associated with the democracy of the market place.

Review questions and problems

1. Your company is considering changing its advertising agency. How would you undertake the selection of a replacement?

2. Analyse the following publications, using the 'check-list' described in the text: *TV Times, Vogue, Financial Times,*

3. Discuss the merits of the cinema as an advertising medium.

4. Develop an outline campaign plan for either frozen concentrated orange juice or off-peak travel on British Rail, assuming an annual budget of £500 000.

5. What are the economic arguments for and against advertising? Which do you find more convincing? Why?

6. How would you determine the advertising budget for a new household detergent with an expected sales volume of 5 million, a recommended retail price of £1.50, and a gross margin of 25 per cent? Distinguish between above- and below-the-line expenditures.

7. What problems do you associate with the derivation of a measure of advertising effectiveness?

8. What are the objectives of sales promotion? What type of promotion would you use:

   (a) When launching a new consumer product?
   (b) During the growth phase?
   (c) When the product has reached maturity?

9. Evaluate each of the following statements:

   (a) Advertising costs the consumer millions of pounds every year. If advertising were eliminated, prices could be reduced and everybody would benefit.
   (b) Most advertising is a social waste because it merely diverts demand from one firm to another.
   (c) Advertising is of no value to the consumer because it consists of doubtful claims of small differences between similar products.

10. 'We believe in advertising; it is an essential factor in the economics of modern industry.' Discuss.

11. State your views on the purpose and value of sales promotion and merchandising schemes, ranging from contests to premium offers, as additions or alternatives to conventional advertising. What effect are they likely to have on brand loyalty?

12. 'People in advertising are parasites. They contribute nothing to the real wealth of the community.' These sentences occur in a letter in your local newspaper. Write a reply, putting the case for advertising and advertising agencies.

13. Summarise and evaluate any five different methods by which a national advertiser can determine the annual advertising appropriation.

14. 'It is not possible to make a realistic test of the effectiveness of a (television) commercial in a laboratory situation in advance of real-life exposure' (Alan Hedges). Explain.

15. What are the main print media? What are the main electronic media? List each. Take one media group from each category and describe its advantages and limitations.

16. Repetition is the key to advertising success. Evaluate the values and limitations of a repetitive campaign.

17. The Stimulus–Response Theory, as applied to advertising, stresses the importance of frequency and recency of exposure to advertisements by target audiences. Explain why this theory cannot by itself offer a satisfactory explanation of the influence of advertising on consumer buying behaviour.

18. What social benefits, if any, do the community derive from creative/display advertising? Explain your opinion with examples.

19. 'Personal influence is seven times more effective than magazine or newspaper advertising in the persuasion of women to switch brands of household products' (Katz and Lazarsfeld). How can this factor be employed in media planning?

20. Explain the advantages and disadvantages of exhibitions and trade fairs for the industrial advertiser.

21. Write a headline and 50–60 words of copy for a quarter-page ad for a teenage magazine selling a two-week desert tour of Morocco by minibus. Describe or draw the illustration if you want to use one.

22. The economist Alfred Marshall (1922) drew a distinction between 'constructive' advertising and 'combative' advertising. Can such a distinction usefully be made? Discuss with examples.

23. Describe the main functions of a full-service advertising agency. Explain how advertising agencies are remunerated. Discuss the viability of alternatives to the advertising agency system.

24. Discuss three methods used in setting an advertising budget for a particular product, discussing their advantages and disadvantages.

25. Summarise the arguments for and against the proposition that advertising has a beneficial economic effect.

26. 'Advertising tends to encourage gross materialism and dissatisfaction.' (Labour Party Green Paper 1972.) Discuss.

27. The Direct Mail Sales Bureau was set up to promote the medium to both advertising agencies and advertisers. Explain what you know about the Direct Mail medium and consider situations where Direct Mail could become an integral part of the total media plan.

28. Explain the importance of campaign planning and indicate the elements which you would expect to be included in a campaign plan for the launch of a new toothpaste.

29. It is likely that before long the availability of cable and satellite TV will give a television viewer as many as 50 channels from which to select, thus offering to the advertiser a range of specialised audiences. What are the implications for the marketer of this fragmentation of TV audiences?

30. Following on from the VCR revolution in terms of viewing, what are your opinions on the future of cable television within the UK? What are the likely problems and/or solutions in the following areas: (1) measuring the growth of cable homes, (2) research measurement of audiences, (3) mechanics of wiring up homes, (4) the interface of satellite and cable viewing.

31. 'In the end a client gets the advertising he deserves, from an advertising agency.' What does this mean, and do you agree?

32. What type of promotional mix is a company likely to use when a product is in the mature stage of the product life cycle and why?

33. Define 'major media', give their respective shares of total UK advertising expenditure in 1995, and explain (with reasons) what significant changes in those figures you expect by the year 2005, if any.

34. Explain why you agree or disagree that direct mail still deserves the description 'junk mail'.

35. Setting objectives is often considered a key stage in advertising decision-making. What objectives might an advertiser usefully set and what contribution can research play in guiding decision-making in this area?

▌ Supplementary reading list

Broadbent, S. (ed.) (1980) *Market Researchers Look at Advertising* (London: Sigma-text).

Broadbent, Simon and Jacobs, Brian (1984) *Spending Advertising Money*, 4th edn (London: Business Books).

Davis, M. (1981) *The Effective Use of Advertising Media* (London: Business Books).

Glover, D. (1984) *The Sociology of the Mass Media* (Ormskirk: Causeway Press).

Hart, Norman (1984) *Business to Business Advertising*, 3rd edn (London: Associated Business Press).

Hart, Norman (ed.) (1995) *The Practice of Advertising*, 4th edn (London: Butterworth-Heinemann).

ISBA (1990) *Choosing the Advertising Agency* (London: ISBA).

McDonald, Colin (1992) *How Advertising Works* (Henley: The Advertising Agency).

Nevett, T. R. (1982) *Advertising in Britain: A History* (London: Heinemann).

Turner, E. S. (1952) *The Shocking History of Advertising* (Harmondsworth: Penguin).

White, Roderick (1988) *Advertising*, 2nd edn (New York: McGraw-Hill).

■ *Chapter 17* ■

Sales Promotion

Contents

Learning goals

The issues to be addressed in this chapter include:

1. The nature and objectives of sales promotion.
2. Determining the sales promotion appropriation.
3. The types of promotion in current usage.
4. The selection and use of a given promotion.

After reading this chapter you will be able to:

1. Distinguish between 'above and below the line' promotional activities.
2. Set out the objectives which may be achieved through the use of sales promotion.
3. Explain how to determine the size of the appropriation for expenditure on sales promotion.
4. List and describe the major types of sales promotion in current use – sampling, off-price labels, banded offers, premium offers, competitions and personality promotions.
5. Review the issues to be considered in deciding whether to run a promotion.
6. Evaluate the factors to be taken into account when choosing a particular type of promotion.
7. Describe the legislation related to the use of sales promotion.
8. Relate in detail the use of sampling as a major promotional activity.
9. Summarise typical sales promotion problems and their solutions.

■ Introduction

The previous chapter was concerned solely with media, or 'above the line', advertising. The balance of promotional expenditure 'below the line' is accounted for by a wide variety of sales promotion activities which, collectively, now account for around 60 per cent of the total promotional spend. However, despite the magnitude and importance of sales promotion, comparatively little attention is given to it in most textbooks and journals, a fact which no doubt prompted the title of an article in the 1 November 1984 issue of *Marketing* by Christian Petersen – 'Cinderella in the Limelight'.

Petersen points out that it was not until 1977 that sales promotion expenditure exceeded advertising expenditure but, as noted, it now accounts for 60 per cent of the average UK marketing budget, which is approximately equal to the proportion in the USA and other European markets. For 1988 the Institute of Sales Promotion estimates expenditure at £5.5 billion, of which approximately £3 billion will be on price-related promotions.

In a book of this type it is impossible to do justice to all aspects of marketing and this is very much the case with a subject like sales promotion. However, *Marketing Week* magazine runs regular features and special reports on the subject and is a mine of up-to-date information, while Ogilvy, Benson & Mather have published an excellent handbook on the subject. Ogilvy, Benson & Mather have kindly consented to the reproduction of extracts from this handbook (*A Guide to Consumer Promotions*, A. Morgan, 2nd edn, 1976) which, although somewhat dated now, provides an excellent overview of when and how to use sales promotion.

In addition to the above sources several of the major market research agencies publish reports on the subject and the current revision has benefited greatly from reference to Key Note Publications Ltd 1989 analysis *Sales Promotion*.

■ Definition and objectives

The Institute of Sales Promotion defines sales promotion as follows:

Sales promotion is a facet of marketing which is adding value, usually of a temporary nature, to a product or service in order to persuade the end user to purchase that particular brand.

Much advertising also satisfies this definition which accounts for the difficulties of distinguishing the precise division between above and below the line expenditure, a problem which is further compounded by the distinction between consumer and trade promotions. Thus the ISP's estimate of total spend, which remains at around £5.5 bn per annum, is reckoned to include 60 per cent on trade promotions leaving between £2 bn and £2.5 bn for promotions targeted directly at the end user. This expenditure is claimed to be increasing by about 20 per cent per annum, but data published by MS Surveys and Promotional Services suggests that the *number* of promotions declined steadily from 16 964 in 1980 to 12 886 in 1988 – a fall of 24 per cent. Clearly, readers need to consult the sources listed for up-to-date information.

The basic objective underlying all promotions is an increase in sales. This aim may be further subdivided, in terms of the time dimension, by devising strategies designed at achieving either short or long-term gains. Hopefully, both aims will be achieved, but the immediate objective will condition the strategy and the promotional tools employed.

Although display advertising can be very effective in making consumers aware of the existence of a product, inertia frequently prevents consumer sampling and some additional incentive is required to persuade non-users to try it. Promotions are designed to provide this incentive. Consumers invariably view trial of a new product as containing a risk element – perceived risk – yet without trial there is no possibility of repeat purchases. A product may be totally new, in the sense that it has never previously been offered for sale, or new in the sense that the individual has no previous experience of it. A different strategy will apply to each of these situations.

In the case of a totally new product the initial campaign will seek to obtain the widest possible trial and will employ a combination of methods, for example coupons, free samples, in-store trial, banded offers, and so forth. Where the brand is already established and has a known brand share, the promoter will adopt a more selective approach and concentrate on those segments of the market with the lowest usage rates. A totally new offering will also merit a more prolonged campaign to encourage repurchase; this would not be justified for an established brand because of the cost of 'subsidising' users who would have bought the product without a promotion. Against this element of subsidy must be set the fact that a 'bonus' helps maintain brand loyalty in the face of one's competitors' promotions.

In highly competitive markets, where product differentiation is difficult, if not impossible, such as detergents, breakfast cereals, petrol and so on, promotions are frequently employed to secure short-term increases in sales in the knowledge that once the promotion is finished the new buyers will revert to their former brand, or a competitive brand which is running a promotion. Clearly, promotions of this type are subject to criticism on the grounds that they are combative and do nothing to increase primary demand, and it is argued that the consumer would be better served by a permanent price reduction. From an industry viewpoint there is some truth in the argument, but from the position of the individual firm there is little incentive in adopting such a policy. Faced with an inelastic demand all firms would follow suit and reduce price, but would still be faced with the need to continue promotional activity to protect their individual brand shares. If it is assumed that the manufacturer would protect his profit margin, one is drawn to the inescapable conclusion that such a price reduction would eventually lead to an overall decline in product quality.

In the case of a product like petrol, which has to conform with a technical specification, a reduction in quality of this kind is not permissible. It follows that unless a price cut or promotion can be offset against lower raw material prices then the only justification for either tactic must be the hope that the resulting increase in market share will offset the costs involved. But as the upsurge of promotional activity by the major British petrol companies in recent years has showed, petrol is essentially a commodity with convenience and price the major choice determinant. The result is that gains in market share tend to be short-lived as the suppliers to an oligopolistic market react in the way theory predicts they will. None the less, the 1984 promotional wars sparked off by Shell's revival of its Make Money campaign, after ten years of almost no promotional activity and an emphasis on price cutting, did demonstrate the benefits of modifying the marketing mix and making a significant short-term gain. Thus for an outlay of around £2 million, Shell picked up 2 per cent market share in a virtually stagnant market. (See *Marketing Week*, 11 May 1984, for a full analysis.) Some data concerning consumer attitudes to sales promotion are set out in Table 17.1.

To sum up, sales promotion can be used to achieve a number of marketing objectives which were summarised by C. D. Moss, P. Thorne and P. Fasey (1963) in 'The Distribution of Coupons', as follows:

1. To gain customers and convert them to regular users – particularly for new or improved products;
2. To widen the distribution of a product;
3. To influence stock levels which may be too high or too low;
4. To reduce sales peaks and troughs and maintain economic production levels;
5. To cushion the effect of a price increase;
6. To create new interest in an established product and improve results from in-store displays.

Finally, in the *Companion Encyclopedia of Marketing* Ken Peattie (1995) summarises the growth in promotions as follows:

1. Growing doubts about the cost effectiveness of advertising, in the face of rising prices and increased advertising 'clutter': a lack of conclusive evidence to link advertising directly to consumer preference and buying behaviour, and apparent consumer hostility towards advertising has fuelled these doubts.

Table 17.1 *Consumer attitudes to sales promotion*

	Agree a lot (%)	Disagree a lot (%)	Percentage variation
Promotions save you money	15	13	+2
Promotions make shopping fun	9	30	−21
Promotions encourage you to try new products and brands	10	21	−11
Competitions are fixed	18	21	−3
I prefer no frills	47	4	+43
I welcome the return of trading stamps	13	33	−20
Manufacturers try to put one over on ordinary people	28	7	+21
Saving packet tops is not worth it	39	11	+28

Source: *Marketing Week*/Harris International/Key Note 1989.

The advent of videos and television remote controls which allow adverts to be 'zapped' has also eroded television advertisers' confidence in their ability to reach their target audience.

2. Sales promotions have acquired new found 'respectability' through greater use by market leaders and increasing professionalism among sales promotion agencies.

3. Increased impulse purchasing, particularly for FMCG products: according to the American Point of Purchase Institute, some 80 per cent of all purchase decisions are now made in-store, and can therefore be influenced by in-store promotions.

4. Planning time horizons have been shortened, reflecting increasing market volatility and rivalry, and accelerating product life cycles. The development of advertising campaigns which build and nurture the desired image for a brand is a slow and painstaking process. The more immediate boost offered by promotions is attractive to marketers under pressure to improve market share and sales volume in the short term.

5. Micro-marketing approaches: in response to fragmenting markets, promotions can provide more tailored and targeted communication than mass media.

6. Declining brand loyalty: caused by widening choice, narrowing perceived differences between brands and, in fmcg markets, retailers' own brands becoming increasingly credible.

7. A 'snowball' effect in some markets, with companies feeling obliged to match rivals' sales promotion activity, or risk losing market share and competitive position.

8. Affordability: national mass media have become prohibitively expensive for many companies, particularly during recessionary squeezes on marketing budgets. Promotions allow national coverage at a lower cost, cost sharing with co-promoters and can even be self-funding.

Determination of the appropriation

A distinct advantage of promotions as compared with display advertising is that the former is capable of reasonably accurate costing in terms of a desired result whereas the latter is speculative.

In setting the appropriation a two-stage approach is possible. The first stage requires the quantification of only two variables, which are reasonably accessible to the company – sampling cost and the additional contribution arising from the sale of a marginal unit. The second stage requires the determination of three further, and less accessible, facts – the conversion rate from sampling to regular usage, frequency of purchase among regular users, number of purchases by those sampled who do not adopt the product and become regular users.

The sampling cost can usually be calculated in advance and comprises two elements – the distribution cost and the value of the sample or coupon. Where the promotion consists of a coupon redeemable on purchase of the item being promoted, the value of the unit discount must be adjusted in line with the anticipated redemption rate to arrive at a total cost – previous experience usually provides a reliable estimate of this rate.

The growth of the promotions business has resulted in the setting up of firms which specialise in all its aspects, several of which are wholly owned subsidiaries of agencies like Young & Rubicam, J. Walter Thompson and LPE. These companies are well qualified to advise on all aspects of promotions, and will provide estimates of redemption rates with a reasonable degree of accuracy.

Once the sampling area has been defined and the nature of the offer decided, it is a relatively simple matter to calculate the redemption rate/sales volume which will ensure break-even in the short term. In order to allow for the long-term potential of a promotion an estimate must be made of the three second-stage variables referred to above. Conversion rates, like redemption rates, may be estimated with reasonable accuracy on the basis of past experience. The same is true of the percentage of those who will 'make subsequent purchases without becoming 'brand adopters'. (Many large companies undertake continuous market research which enables them to predict at an early stage in the life of a promotion exactly how repurchase patterns will develop.) Product usage is also quite well documented, both by independent firms like Nielsen and by the larger agencies and manufacturers. Armed with this data it is possible, with a little educated guess-work to formulate an acceptable forecast of the long-term benefits.

In the article by Moss *et al.* (1963) on 'The Distribution of Coupons' referred to earlier there is a very useful example of the methods of distribution available, the comparative costs and the likely redemption rates. For example, in 1961, 73 per cent of all coupons (7614 million) were distributed through the national press and accounted for 16 per cent of the 324 million redemptions at an average media and distribution cost of 12.4p per redemption (of which 6p was the coupon value). This is equivalent to a redemption rate of 0.93 per cent of coupons distributed while other methods showed the following returns:

Method	*Redemption rate*
In/on pack	37.70%
Door to door	5.25%
Magazine	2.16%

Table 17.2 provides the most recent data available in 1995. More up-to-date information is, of course, available directly from Nielsen.

Promotions in current usage

As every consumer is aware there is a bewildering array of promotional offers available. A short review of these is given below.

Free samples

Of all the promotions this method offers the greatest chance of getting a consumer to actually try the product. At the same time it is the most expensive, and its usage is invariably restricted to brands with potential annual sales of several million pounds. A number of companies seek to reduce sampling cost by cooperating in a joint promotion of non-competing products on similar lines to the gift pack given to mothers of first babies.

Off-price labels

In terms of consumer acceptability the label featuring *X*p off the regular price is the most

Table 17.2   *Coupons – volume and expenditure*

Data included under 'Sales Promotions'	1989	1990	1991	1992	1993	1994
Number of coupons distributed (millions)	4865	5074	8109	5402	2984	4286
Number of coupons redeemed (millions)	311	376	451	365	278	194
Total value of coupons redeemed (£m)	70.0	92.0	113.0	105.1	91.2	65.6
Coupon's average face value	22.5	24.4	25.0	28.8	32.8	34.0
Manufacturers' average handling allowance*						
to retailers (pence per 100 coupons)	178	186	260	230	251	251
Distribution medium of coupons redeemed* (%)						
Newspaper	4	7	6	5.5	7.5	4.9
Magazine	4	3	4	3.5	5.7	6.0
Door-to-door	31	26	22	22.7	18.2	13.1
In/on pack	28	25	35	37.0	31.6	39.1
In store	18	28	23	27.8	15.2	18.3
Direct mail	—	—	—	—	—	13.4
Others	15	11	10	4.1	21.9	5.2
Average redemption rates by media (%)						
Newspaper	1.3	1.7	1.1	1.6	3.5	1.2
Magazine	1.2	1.2	1.5	1.6	3.0	1.2
Door-to-door	7.6	12.8	6.8	8.6	10.3	4.5
In/on pack	11.9	15.4	13.9	16.7	29.7	20.3
In store	—	—	—	—	—	3.7
Direct mail	—	—	—	—	—	16.0

Note: * Excl. retailer-made promotions (1994 figure is the recommended retailer handling allowance)
Source: NCH Promotional Services.

popular promotion. It is also popular with retailers as it involves none of the diseconomies associated with coupon redemption and also provides the opportunity to feature a price reduction in their local advertising.

The actual extent of the price reduction is an important determinant of the level of sampling, and careful thought, and preferably testing, must be given to the selection of a discount. As discussed in the chapter on pricing, some prices have the apparent effect of being perceived as less than they really are, and it is these which have the greatest impact on impulse purchases. Obviously, if sales volume can be increased sufficiently the firm may be able to both even out seasonal fluctuations and make a profit.

A price reduction is a short-term strategy, however, and the simplest for one's competitors to duplicate. For these reasons it is avoided by companies that are sensitive to a price war

wherever possible. That said, in 1996 the oil majors made significant price reductions to combat the loss of market share to retailers' (e.g. Sainsbury) inroads into their market using discounts to build volume.

Banded offers

This type of promotion takes two forms:

1. The use of an existing and well-known brand to 'carry' a free sample of another non-competing product. Both products may be produced by the same firm, for example soap and toothpaste, which has the dual advantage of increasing sales of the carrying brand while securing trial of the carried brand, or complementary products of different producers, for example instant coffee and sugar.

2. Two-for-the-price-of-one.

Premium offers

There are three main varieties of premium offer:

1. *The free gift.* This may be contained in the package – plastic animals in breakfast cereals; attached to it – a plastic rose, tea-towels and so forth; given out at the checkout to those purchasing the item carrying the offer – bowls, china, waste-paper baskets, and so on. In some instances the offer will be the pack itself, as is the case with instant coffee packed in storage jars. A common feature of these promotions is that they encourage a collecting habit and so achieve extended trial as the consumer builds up the collection.
2. *The free, sendaway premium.* This type of promotion offers a free gift in exchange for proof of purchase of the product. This approach has greater appeal to the retailer than those promotions which require him to stock 'giveaways', especially as the promotion usually involves point of sale material that builds store traffic and stimulates impulse purchases. From the promoter's angle an added advantage is that many people buy the product intending to send off for the premium but in fact never do.
3. *Self-liquidating premiums.* These differ from the other type of premium in that the consumer has to send both money and proof of purchase to obtain the offer. The advantage to the consumer is that he secures merchandise, often carrying a leading brand name, at a significant discount on its normal retail price. The promoter benefits in that, as the name suggests, the offer pays for itself. If combined with a collecting habit, offers of this kind may run for years ensuring long-term usage, for example Kellogg's silverware offer.

Competitions

Like all other promotions these are no newcomers to the marketing scene (Lever Brothers were spending £1 million a year on promotions at the turn of the century), but they have attracted more than their usual share of attention of late as a result of tangling with the betting and gaming laws. Interest in competitions is considerable owing to the attraction of a very large prize, together with a sufficient number of consolation prizes on an area basis to encourage people to continue to try their luck. National newspapers frequently offer prizes of £1 million in their bingo games and even *The Times* entered the fray with its Portfolio game.

Personality promotions

As with the door-to-door distribution of samples, this type of promotion is limited to the big brands with large advertising appropriations. The method employed is to offer a prize if the housewife has the advertised product in her

Table 17.3   *Types of promotion (percentage share of total promotions), 1984–8*

	1984	1985	1986	1987	1988
Premium	41	42	44	44	44.5
Special offer	23	21	17	9	7
Multi-pack	16	13	14	17	19
Coupon	11	11	11	11	11
Reduced price offer	9	9	10	14	14
Other	—	4	4	5	3.5
Total	100	100	100	100	100

Source: MS Surveys & Promotional Services Ltd.

Table 17.4 *Major forms of consumer promotions*

Type	Key users	Notes	Example
Discount pricing and sales	FMCG firms Retailers	Additional volume must compensate for lost revenue. Can spark price wars. Generally a defensive move	January sales. Retailer campaigns, e.g. Tesco's 'Checkout' and 'Asda Price'
Money-off coupons	FMCG Grocery retailers	Redemption rates determine costs. Require retailer cooperation. Allows some differential pricing	Mattel Inc.'s 1988 toy marketing campaign involved 582 million coupons
Payment terms	Consumer durables Retailers	Reduces real cost rather than price. Useful for seasonal demand smoothing	Curry's 'Buy in May, pay in November' offer. Interest free credit offers
Refunds	FMCG Consumer durables	Avoids problems of reference price changes. Non-redemptions reduce costs compared to discounts	The 'More money with Sony' direct-mail cashback offer. Trade-in allowances
Samples	Foods Toiletries	Expensive. Encourages trial. Effectiveness hard to measure. Can generate market research	Agree shampoo became No.1 in the US market in 6 months by using 31 million samples
Multipacks and multibuys	Packaged goods Retailers	Best for small, high purchase frequency items	Boots '3 for the price of 2' campaign
Special features	Consumer durables	Often packaged as a 'special' or 'limited' edition	Audi's giveaway of a free catalytic converter
Quantity increases	Packaged foods, canned and bottled drinks	Relies on ability to customize packaging processes	Canned beers feature regular 500 ml for the price of 440 ml offers
Valued packaging	Packaged goods	Packaging can be useful in itself, or can provide a game, activity, recipe or other information	Persil's EcoBox offer. Sony's tape ten pack in a free cassette case offer
In-pack premiums	Packaged goods	Items placed in foodstuffs need care regarding food safety	Ovaltine's 'Treasure Hunt' coin-in-every-tin promotion
In-mail premiums	Packaged goods	Usually relies on handling houses for redemption	'Collections' from Kodak and Carlsberg's Special Brew
Piggybank premiums	Packaged goods	Usually joint promotions. Can generate complementary sales and encourage product trial	'Free Gillette GII with Kleenex for men' gained Gillette 100 000 trials and KFM 13% extra sales
Gift coupons	Petrol retailers Draught beers	Useful for non-packaged goods. Helps encourage repeat purchases	Gift collections from BP, Esso Shell and Texaco. Air miles

Table 17.4   *(continued)*

Type	Key users	Notes	Example
Information	Industrial firms Consumer durables Services	Important for reducing perceived risk. Provides consumer benefits of convenience and saved time	Product catalogues. Holiday brochures. Investment prospectuses.
Competitions	Packaged foods Retailers	Good for creating interest and reinforcing ad campaigns Needs care with legalities.	McDonald's $40 million 'Treasure Hunt'. Heinz's 'Win a Car a Day for 100 Days' offer
Product trial	Consumer durables	Often twinned with a competition. Needs close sales support	200 000 Apple Macs were 'home tested', 40% led to sales
Guarantees	Consumer durables Retailers	'Pricebeat' promises often back up sales to reduce perceived risk	Ski Yoghurt's 'Best ever taste: or your money back' offer
Buybacks	Consumer durables	Costs depend upon redemption rates. Over-redemption can be insured against	Sanyo's 1988 ten-year buyback pledge boosted TV sales by 62%
Clubs	Airlines and hotels Childrens products	Useful for generating customer loyalty	Marriott Hotels' 'Honoured guest' scheme

Source: *The Marketing Book*, 1994.

home when the personality (Egg-chick, Ajar Superman, etc.) calls, provided that she can answer a simple question. Including in-store displays, leaflet distribution and so on, but excluding display advertising, this type of promotion can cost in excess of £400 000.

From the above description of the major types of promotions, it is clear that there is a wide choice of alternatives. Ogilvy, Benson & Mather offer both general and specific advice on how to evaluate these, and the following sections are reprinted from their handbook. It should be stressed that the section on sampling has been chosen for illustrative purposes only and all the other major alternatives are given the same detailed treatment. Table 17.3 summarises the share of different types of promotions for the period 1984 to 1988. Table 17.4 taken from *The Marketing Book* (1994) provides a comprehensive review of the major forms of sales promotions.

How to decide whether to run a promotion and which promotion to choose*

☐ *Introduction*

Consumer promotions are not a panacea. They have, unfortunately, become fashionable. A belief has developed that they are *the* modern marketing technique. This is nonsense. Consumer promotions are just one part of the marketing mix, not a substitute for it. If a promotion is run it will

*The extract quoted (pp. 423–31) is reproduced by kind permission of Messrs Ogilvy, Benson & Mather. As noted it is now dated on points of detail but the issues and approaches discussed are still valid.

normally work better as a part of the whole, fitting in with the advertising, product development, packaging, trade incentives and salesmen's incentives as a logical development of the marketing strategy.

In particular, it must be made clear that 'promotions' and 'advertising' are complementary techniques, not substitutes for each other. There is a growing body of evidence that companies who switch their marketing expenditure exclusively 'below-the-line' make temporary gains in volume at the expense of permanently undermining their brand-image and the loyalty of their most regular buyers.

A well-designed promotion can help solve certain specific marketing problems, and together with the rest of the marketing mix help to achieve a marketing objective. Therefore, before discussing whether to mount a promotion at all, and certainly before selecting the type of promotion, the *marketing objectives* of the brand must have been agreed, specific *marketing targets* set, and the problems to be overcome identified.

This assumes that the following information is available:

(a) Who is the target market for the brand?
(b) Why they use the product and how?
(c) How frequently it is bought and where?
(d) Who are its main competitors?
(e) How the consumer rates the brand compared with its competitors?

If these facts are not known, then what is needed is not a promotion but basic research into the brand to determine its problems and marketing positioning.

How to decide whether to run a promotion

(a) Determine, in order of priority, the problems facing the brand.
(b) Determine the money available to solve the problems.

(c) List and cost all the possible alternative solutions to the problems: e.g. more advertising, consumer promotions, pricing strategy, product change, etc.
(d) Estimate (or guesstimate) the effectiveness of each solution.
(e) If the answers to (c) and (d) suggest that a promotion is the most efficient answer to the brand's problem and if the answer to (b) shows there is enough money for a successful promotion then a promotion is indicated.
(f) It does not make sense to run a promotion simply because a competitor is running one unless this has caused problems for your brand which a promotion would solve. If the problems confronting your brand, at that time, would not be solved by a promotion, then it would be a costly mistake to allow your competitor's action to stampede you into panic action. His problems or his perception of his problems may be quite different from those confronting your brand.

Which promotion to choose?

(a) The one most likely to solve the brand's problem successfully, within the available budget.
(b) You can help to decide this by looking up your problems in the chart (in the next section).
(c) Then for each promotion listed as likely to help, look up the separate section on that type of promotion.
(d) Look initially at the sub-sections on

　(i)　Advantages
　(ii)　Disadvantages
　(iii)　Essentials for success
　(iv)　Points to look out for
　(v)　How much will it cost?

(e) Does the promotion offer an incentive to the market target, from their point of view?
(f) Consider the impact of the promotion on the image of the product. An expensive, high-quality product, should have an expensive, high-quality promotion.

(g) Consider whether the consumer has any problems which the promotion could solve: e.g. if a product is messy to use, it may be worth considering a free spreader or spatula.

(h) Promotions are tactical tools. There is no formula for picking the correct one. They will usually be better if they are designed in the context of the individual brand's consumers, its market and its trade practices.

(i) Because of this need for bespoke designing it is usually better not to copy other companies' promotions but to think ideas out from scratch.

Problems and an indication of the consumer promotions most likely to help in solving them

These are suggestions, not hard and fast rules. Altering the design of a promotion may make it a suitable solution for other problems. The nature of the product, the company and the trade will also affect the best solution to any problem.

		Promotions which may help
(a)	To get consumer trial of new or existing product	Free with-, in- or on-pack premium Money-off voucher Money-off offer Sampling Proprietary promotions
(b)	To obtain repeat purchasing	Any premium offer of a collectable item (free or 'self-liquidating promotion') Competition Free mail-in Free continuous mail-in (coupons) 'Money-off voucher promotion' 'Self-liquidating promotion'
(c)	To obtain long-term consumer loyalty	Continuous 'self-liquidating promotion' (coupons) Trading stamps
(d)	To increase frequency or quantity of consumer purchase in the short run	Competition Free on-, with-pack premium Free mail-in Household stock reward scheme (personality promotion) In-store self-liquidator Money-off offer (including banded packs) Shop-floor promotions Tailor-made promotions
(e)	To move high stocks out of stores	Competition Free with-pack Free mail-in Shop-floor promotions Tailor-made promotions
(f)	To get consumers to visit your premises	Free gifts Money-off voucher Shop-floor promotions Tailor-made promotions Trading stamps Proprietary promotions

(g) *To get increased distribution.* This will call for trade and salesmen's incentives primarily although a consumer promotion may be necessary to 'pull the product through'. However the choice of consumer promotion will really depend on other problems facing the brand at the time.

(h) *To obtain increased stock levels/stocking in depth.* As with the increased distribution this calls for trade and salesmen's incentives. The choice of a consumer promotion to 'pull the product through' will depend on other problems facing the brand at the time.

(i)   *To obtain information on consumer product usage.* This is a research, not a promotional problem.

Points which may arise in connection with any promotion

☐ *Legal clearance*

The number of UK Statutes with which marketing activity has to comply has proliferated in the last decade. Key Acts are quoted throughout this document.

The EEC is developing a body of Directives towards harmonisation of the laws of member countries, which include 'misleading advertising', 'premium offers' and 'informative labelling' among other market topics. These could affect planning for the long-term, or a continuing promotion.

In addition there are several voluntary codes of practice. Most important is the British Code of Sales Promotion Practice (CAP Committee 1977). Compliance with this code reduces but does not eliminate the risk of illegality.

For multinational operations, also consult the series of Codes by the International Chamber of Commerce.

It is important to check for copyright. Similarity to a previous promotion by another company might give rise to a claim of 'passing off' or breach of copyright (apart from causing confusion among consumers and retailers!). If an outside agency is involved it should be made quite clear whether or not any work done by the agency is their copyright.

☐ *Claimed value of premium items or gifts or prizes*

These must comply with the provisions of the Trade Descriptions Act 1966. It is also wise to check whether a prize or premium is on public sale and at what price. It is advisable to be aware of the practices deemed acceptable and unacceptable by the Office of Fair Trading in their Consultative Document on 'Bargain Offer Claims' (1975). While no legislation is in prospect, it offers guidelines for any promotion in which the price of the product is modified temporarily or where some other product is offered in connection with it.

The EEC is developing legislation on 'unit pricing' whereby both the price of the pack and of the relevant unit (pound, kilogram, litre, etc.) must be quoted. This will also apply to price modifications.

☐ *The printing of any promotional offer on the pack*

The following problems arise:

(a)   Ensuring adequate supplies have reached direct and indirect outlets by the time advertising breaks (IPA regulations).

(b)   The Advertising Standards Authority requires that details of the closing date and of any limitations on an offer (e.g. 'while stocks last') must appear on the outside of the pack or label.

(c)   While the special pack is on offer, the retailer may put away 'Normal' merchandise which may have deteriorated when it is returned to the shelves.

The sending of items or literature by post:

(a)   There are restrictions of overall size, weight and nature of items that can be sent by post.

(b)   The GPO will not pay compensation for the loss of items with a monetary value, unless sent by registered mail. (Postal regulations concerning paper money introduced 3/10/66.)

(c)   Substantial discounts are available for bulk postage if some regional pre-sorting is done.

(d)   Care should be taken that goods sent by mail to adults should not fall into the hands of children.

☐ *Promotions advertised on TV*

There are ITCA rulings:

(a)   That such promotions must be available to all consumers whether viewers or not.
(b)   That if a promotion is limited to certain sizes or packs, this must be made clear in the advertisement.

☐ *Promotions aimed at offering prizes to children*

Promoters should take extra care that the promotion accords with the letter and spirit of the laws and guidelines. There are specific and stringent ITCA rulings related to:

(a)   Exaggerated claims and trade puffery, such as the use of the word 'free' or 'free with'.
(b)   Promotions on a product whose brand choice cannot normally be considered to be a child's prerogative, e.g. floor polish, soap.
(c)   Promotions where the premium, gift or reward is dependent upon collecting a number of items.
(d)   In the case of children under 16, entry forms should require the consent of a parent or guardian (particularly where a prize or gift is a holiday, a pet, or goods to the value of £50 or more).

☐ *Company administration*

Check that there is provision in salesmen's order forms, accounting procedure, etc., for special packs sold alongside normal packs.

Check that any liabilities incurred by the promotion are adequately covered by your insurance or that of the promotion company concerned.

Check that all advertising and promotional material include closure dates and adequate descriptions of the rules of the promotion.

Check that all liabilities to *tax* are included when budgeting the costs of a promotion. Even when an item is given away 'free', the promoter may be liable to VAT on its value. Consult the VAT General Guide, or the Customs and Excise.

■ Sampling

☐ *Definition*

The consumer is either:

(a)   given some of the product free; or
(b)   allowed to use the product freely during a given period.

The size of the product give-away may vary from a taste or spray to a full-sized pack.

The samples can be distributed in a number of ways:

(a)   Given by a demonstrator in a store. These are usually used instantly, e.g. a tasting of food or drink, a spray of perfume, a cigarette to smoke.
(b)   Given away with another product.
(c)   Distributed in some medium, e.g. a shampoo sachet in a magazine.
(d)   Delivered door-to-door.
(e)   Sent on application from the consumer.
(f)   Given to visitors to some specific location, e.g. hotels, exhibitions, showrooms, race tracks, etc.
(g)   Where the consumer is invited to use the product freely, e.g. a car or television set, then the 'sample' is delivered, by arrangement, to the home or place of business.

☐ *Advantages*

The advantage to the consumer is immediate and obvious (this does not apply if the consumer has to apply for the sample).

The consumer has to make no effort, is involved in no expense (again except in the case where he has to apply for it).

Mass sampling is by far the quickest way of obtaining widespread consumer trial.

Demonstrates to the consumer the product's qualities, and the manufacturer's faith in his product.

Creates excitement.

☐ *Disadvantages*

This is very expensive.

Considerable administration is involved in distributing the samples.

The special costs of trial sized packs can be as expensive as a normal pack.

The product needs to have an advantage, or difference, that the consumer can perceive.

It will not increase usage by existing consumers.

☐ *Essentials for success*

A good product.

Efficient distribution, especially in:

(a) getting the samples to the potential market
(b) preventing samples going astray.

Where the sample is left with the consumer, it should be of sufficient size for the consumer both to appreciate the product's qualities and to form the habit of using the product. Consumers show disproportionately more gratitude for a 'full-size' sample.

Trade co-operation. This is very important. If the nature of the product makes a large sample necessary it may be necessary to persuade the trade that you are not depriving them of the profit they could have made selling the product.

A product that regular users are likely to buy frequently.

Advertising support.

Good distribution for the product so that consumers who are persuaded by the sample have the maximum opportunity to buy.

That consumers are informed where they can obtain further supplies of the product.

While not essential the conversion rate to product usage will be increased, if the consumer is given a money incentive to make the first purchase. Thus if the sample is distributed in a store the consumer's attention can be drawn to a money-off offer. If the sample is distributed away from the store or shop the sample should be accompanied by a money-off coupon or voucher.

☐ *Decisions that have to be taken*

What size sample to distribute? This will depend on:

(a) The nature and value of the product.
(b) Consumer usage, e.g. do not give consumers a year's supply, preferably sample the size you most want them to buy.
(c) How apparent is the difference or advantage, e.g. can it be discerned on the first try or bite of the product?
(d) The method of distribution to be used, e.g. you cannot put a pound pack inside a magazine; retailers prefer in-store samples to be small.
(e) The cost of special sample packaging.
(f) The promotional budget.

How to distribute the sample. This will depend on:

(a) The size of the sample.
(b) The nature of the product, e.g. is it breakable?

(c)   The market target. If it's not a mass market product there is no point in distributing door-to-door.

(d)   The possibilities for sample misuse.

(e)   The promotional budget.

(f)   The promotional objects.

☐ *How research can help*

It could help to determine the most efficient sample size, e.g. how little of the product is needed to convert the consumer to the product (but see also (third para.) under Disadvantages). There could, however, be a security problem here with a new product.

Subsequently, in measuring conversion rate to the product and in planning further operations.

☐ *Points to watch/problems which may arise*

In connection with any form of sampling operation. That there is adequate check on samples at all stages of distribution.

That the packaging of the sample will stand up to its method of distribution. It is advisable to check this in action. The standard pack may encounter much rougher treatment in a

Table 17.5   *Typical problems and possible promotional solutions*

Problem	*Solution*
1. To increase consumer awareness:	In-store raffle/display; phone-ins; sweepstakes; free draws; competitions
2. To increase penetration of new or existing products:	Free offers (with in or on-pack) ; money off coupons or offers; sampling; refund offers; multibrand schemes; banded packs, reduced price offers
3. To improve repeat purchase:	Competitions; free offers; on-pack money-off coupons; reduced price offers; refund/buy-back offers; giveaways; self-liquidating premiums; re-usable container premiums
4. To increase consumer loyalty:	Premium offers; money-off offers; personality promotions; coupons; buy one, get one free offers; twin packs; refund offers; re-usable container premiums
5. To increase purchase frequency or amount bought:	Competitions; share-outs/giveaways; free offers; personality promotions; tailor-made promotions; multibrand schemes; in-store promotions; banded packs; reduced price offers
6. To move high stocks out of stores:	In-store raffles/competitions; free offers; tailor-made promotions; in-store merchandising
7. To attract consumers to premises:	Free gifts/trials; tailor-made promotions; money-off coupons
8. Trading up to larger sizes:	Consumer choice coupons; refund offers; multibrand schemes
9. To increase distribution:	Tailor-made promotions; multibrand schemes; trade competitions; salesman's incentives; sample distribution
10. To encourage display:	On-pack premiums; banded packs; premium offers; heavy price cuts

Source: John Williams (1984), 'Picking the winners', *Marketing*, 26 April.

distributor's sack than in a standard outer moved by a forklift truck.

That any quotation received for distribution has been made with knowledge of both the weight and dimensions of the sample.

That there is no chance of the sample tainting other products or of being tainted by them.

See also 'Points which may arise in connection with any promotion'.

Sampling in stores and shops. That all details are fully discussed and agreed with the store in advance, e.g.
(a) Dates.
(b) Amount of space.
(c) Location of space.
(d) Hours the demonstrator will work. It can cause conflict if these are markedly different from store staff.
(e) Any necessary equipment, e.g. electrical socket.

That demonstrators are subject to adequate supervision and spot checks.

That adequate provisions are made for demonstrators to have clean overalls, etc under all circumstances.

That if food is being sampled to eat, all food hygiene rules are strictly observed.

Samples given away with another product. That the market target for the two products is similar.

That the products are non-competitive.

Samples distributed in a Press medium. That there are no disputes between media owners and their distributors that will interfere with sample distribution.

Samples distributed door-to-door. Medicinal samples may not be distributed door-to-door.

Both the Board of Trade and CAP require manufacturers to exercise care in putting samples through letter boxes. Complaints have been made of products dangerous to children or dogs and where there is any danger of this CAP recommend personal handing over of the sample instead of distribution through the letter box.

That a sample intended to go through a letter box can go through the average letter box and that instructions cover premises with no letter boxes.

That a household sample is sufficient for a household. If it is something desired and there is not enough to go round you may cause ill-will and the market target may never even see the sample.

Table 17.6 *The promotional brief*

Brand(s) or service(s)	Other comments/constraints in particular, space available for on-pack promotions
Pack size(s) involved	Legal
Area(s) involved	Cautionary information to be included
Outlets involved (if appropriate)	Printing restrictions – number of colours permitted, print area, use of drawings /photographs, etc.
Timing	Other support activity planned
Budget	Other relevant information – e.g. logo references, pack dimensions
Target group	Confidentiality
Promotional objectives	Standard of response required – concepts, roughs, presentation layouts
Restrictions as to type of promotion (if applicable)	Response from consultancy
Promotion communications e.g. if on-pack the number of packs involved, leaflet circulation, etc.	
Proofs of purchase required	

Source: John Williams (1984), 'Picking the winners', *Marketing*, 26 April.

Table 17.7   *Criteria for efficient and effective promotions*

1. The promotional objectives, budget and success criteria have been specified.
2. It does not attempt to do what other items in the mix can do better.
3. It is the best promotion for achieving the objectives.
4. It has maximum effect for the least cost.
5. It is consistent with the behaviour pattern of those to whom it is addressed.
6. It is consistent with brand image.
7. It gets attention and has urgency and action built into it.
8. It does not use complicated or confusing copy and is simple, clear and easy to act on and understand.
9. It uses emotional as well as rational appeals to self-interest.
10. It is legal and decent and evidently honest.
11. It sufficiently rewards all on whom its success depends.

Source: John Williams (1984), 'Picking the winners', *Marketing*, 26 April.

☐ *How much will it cost?*

The following list includes some of the main costs likely to be incurred:

(a) Cost of sample contents.
(b) Sample packaging.
(c) Distribution.
(d) Advertising.
(e) Display material.
(f) Merchandising force.
(g) Supporting trade and salesmen incentives.

■ Picking a promotion

The foregoing extract from OBM's Hand-book relates specifically to sampling, which is but one of many methods available. While the others are discussed in similar detail it will be helpful here to provide a summary of typical sales promotion problems and possible solutions. Table 17.5 is taken from 'Picking the Winners' by John Williams (1984) who is also the author of *The Manual of Sales Promotion*.

Table 17.8   *Sales Promotion Code*

PRINCIPLES

- All promotions should be legal, decent, honest and truthful.
- All sales promotions should be prepared with a sense of responsibility to consumers and to society; they should be conducted equitably, promptly and efficiently and should be seen to deal fairly and honourably with consumers. Promoters should avoid causing unnecessary disappointment.
- All sales promotions should respect the principles of fair competition generally accepted in business.
- No promoter or intermediary should bring sales promotion into disrepute.
- Sales promotions must conform with the Codes. Primary responsibility for observing the Codes falls on promoters. Intermediaries and agents also accept an obligation to abide by the Codes.
- Any unreasonable delay in responding to the ASA's enquiries may be considered a breach of the Codes.
- The ASA will on request treat in confidence any private or secret material supplied unless the Courts or officials acting within their statutory powers compel its disclosure.
- The Codes are applied in the spirit as well as in the letter.

John Williams also offers a very useful outline of the factors to be included in a promotional brief, and this is reproduced as Table 17.6, together with a check list of criteria for effective promotions – Table 17.7.

In selecting a promotion the OBM Handbook emphasises the need to conform with both statutory requirements and the various codes of practice. Of the latter the most important is the British Code of Sales Promotion Practice, the sixth edition of which was launched in February. The eight principles are reproduced in Table 17.8.

Summary

This chapter has been concerned with sales promotion which now accounts for the largest proportion of all promotional expenditure and is usually referred to as 'below the line'. Having defined sales promotion we then looked at its objectives and some of the reasons underlying its growth in recent years.

Next followed a discussion of some of the factors to be taken into account in determining a budget for sales promotion and an overview of the main promotions in current usage. This was supported by a discussion of when to consider running a promotion and which promotions to use. An extended analysis of sampling was then given as an example of the issues involved in deciding upon any of the major promotions.

Review questions and

1. 'Unlike Advertising, there are no accurate national expenditure figures available for Sales Promotion, because many companies are undertaking such promotion without realising that they are doing so.' Explain this statement and outline some of the major uses of Sales Promotion.

2. From some situation in your experience, illustrate the role of 'below-the-line' sales promotion as part of the overall promotional campaign. Show how the 'below-the-line' component may be integrated with and contribute to the success of the total.

3. Define 'selling-out' and 'selling-in'. Show how a well-designed promotional campaign keeps the two elements in balance.

4. It is often suggested that the main role of 'below-the-line' expenditures for sales promotion is to encourage the marketer's and dealer's sales people. Give examples of such promotional activities, some of which would tend to support and others to refute this view.

5. In deciding on the promotional mix for a particular range of products, what circumstances would tend to favour special emphasis on:

   (a) dealer incentives;
   (b) sales force activity;
   (c) sampling.

6. There are a wide variety of types of sales promotions – coupons, competitions, price-off etc. – from which a brand manager may choose in writing annual product promotional plans. What factors should be considered in the selection/rejection process?

7. Define sales promotion and give FOUR examples of the kind of marketing objective that can be achieved by the use of sales promotion. Say which techniques you would use to achieve the objective in each case.

8. Name the four major components of the promotional mix. What function does each perform and how does the marketing manager determine the amount of money to be allocated to each element in order to achieve a given communication objective?

9. Account for the boom in sports sponsorship in the last ten years.

Supplementary reading list

ISBA (1988) *Guide to Sales Promotion* (London: ISBA).

Piper, J. (ed.) (1980) *Managing Sales Promotion* (London: Gower).

Quelch, John (1989) *Sales Promotion Management* (Englewood Cliffs, N.J.: Prentice-Hall.

Spillard, Peter (1977) *Sales Promotion: Its Place in Marketing Strategy*, 2nd edn (London: Business Publications).

Ward, J. (1969) *A Guide to Sales Promotion* (London: IPA), The Thomson Medals and Awards for Advertising Research, Thomson Organisation.

Chapter 18

Personal Selling and Merchandising*

Contents

Learning goals

The issues to be discussed in this chapter include:

1. The role of personal selling.
2. The economics of personal selling.
3. The deployment of the sales force.
4. The employment, training and compensation of salesmen.
5. The nature and role of merchandising.

After reading this chapter you will be familiar with:

1. The complementary nature of personal selling and impersonal methods employing advertising and promotion.
2. The various roles performed by salesmen and the distinction between 'order-takers' and 'order-makers'.

3. The costs and benefits associated with personal selling.
4. Factors governing the deployment of the field sales force.
5. Newton's four-way classification of selling styles – trade selling, missionary selling, technical selling, new-business selling.
6. Factors which influence the selection and training of salesmen.
7. Methods of salesmen's compensation together with their various advantages and disadvantages.
8. Criteria for evaluating salesman performance.
9. Factors underlying the increased importance of merchandising and its influence on in-store behaviour.
10. Merchandising services available from TV contractors.

*Throughout this chapter references to the 'salesman' should be taken to apply equally to women.

■ Introduction

Despite the importance of advertising and sales promotion in disseminating information and stimulating interest in products and services, there are many circumstances where personal contact is necessary to effect a sale. Of necessity most advertising is generalised, and so cannot answer all the consumer's information needs; it cannot elaborate upon specific points perceived as significant by the individual, nor can it resolve doubts as to suitability in a particular context. Further, there can be no guarantee that the potential user's media habits will expose him to advertisements for a given product, or that if he does see the advertisement he will perceive it as relevant.

The function of personal selling is to provide the specific inputs which advertising, or non-personal selling, cannot offer at the individual level. It should be remembered that advertising and personal selling are complementary activities, and that their relative importance will vary depending upon the nature of the product and the buying behaviour associated with it.

Many theorists stress the nature of the product as a determinant of the appropriate promotional mix and are collectively identified as the 'Characteristics of Goods School'. Members of this school would argue that advertising will be dominant in the case of small, simple and frequently purchased items of low unit value, while personal selling is appropriate to high-priced, technically complex products which are bought infrequently.

Figure 18.1   *Selecting the promotional mix*

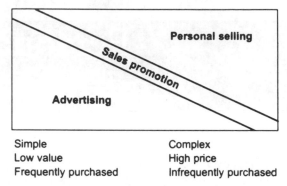

Simple	Complex
Low value	High price
Frequently purchased	Infrequently purchased

Source: Based on R. J. Robinson and Bent Stidsen (1967), *Selling in a Modern Perspective* (Boston: Allyn & Bacon).

According to this view the appropriate promotional mix might be represented diagrammatically as in Figure 18.1, while the relative importance is suggested in Table 18.1.

Although useful this approach is oversimplified, for the user's perception of any given product defies classification into convenient categories, such that a 'convenience' good may be perceived as a 'shopping' good and vice versa depending upon the individual's frame of reference. The importance of allowing for the behavioural dimensions of perception is implicit in the different promotional strategies adopted by firms selling near-perfect substitutes in the economic sense, for example; Avon sells cosmetics door-to-door, Estée Lauder products are available in less than 150 outlets, Yardley and Coty are available in some 7000 department stores and chemists'

Table 18.1   *The relative importance of elements of marketing communications*

Type of marketing activity	Industrial goods	Consumer durables	Consumer non-durables
Sales management and personal selling	Very high	High	High
Media advertising	Very low	Moderate	High
Special promotions	Low	Moderate	Moderate
Pack, brand, other	Low	Low	Moderate

Note: 5-point scale: Very low, low, moderate, high, very high.
Source: Bill Donaldson (1990), *Sales Management* (London: Macmillan).

shops, while Miner's brands are sold through variety chains and supermarkets. There are no hard-and-fast rules which dictate the adoption of a given promotional strategy for a product.

The evolution of the salesman

Although our stereotype of a salesman probably owes more to the music-hall comedian than to reality, there can be no doubt that selling has long occupied a relatively low position in our social and economic hierarchy. Fortunately, there are signs that this state of affairs is slowly changing and that selling is increasingly regarded as a profession rather than a trade. Several factors may be distinguished as contributing to this change and the resultant increase in the flow of better qualified recruits, namely:

1. 'Salesman' applies equally to all persons engaged at all levels of selling, from the retail sales clerk to the negotiator of multi-million-pound contracts. In that the former greatly outnumber the latter, selling tends to be identified with the functions performed by retailers rather than with manufacturer's salesman. However, increased labour costs have led to wide-scale reduction in personal selling at the retail level and have thus brought more sophisticated sales functions into sharper focus; that is, an emphasis on creative selling as opposed to mere order-taking.
2. Growing awareness of the need for personal selling in the service sector – for example banks, insurance and other professional services – has resulted in a significant improvement in both the visibility and credibility of the function.
3. The concentration of retail buying power has resulted in a clear distinction between the negotiating skills demanded in organisational buying situations and the merchandising effort called for at the point of sale with a consequent increase in the salesman's status and importance.

4. The pressures of international competition have made it clear that the manufacturer can no longer leave his product to 'speak for itself' – effective selling and promotion are essential.
5. Increased product complexity, and more sophisticated buyers demand high-calibre salesmen. The scarcity of such personnel has boosted salary levels above those offered in many other occupations, improving selling's economic status and attracting in better-qualified recruits.

Collectively, these factors have made a career in sales more respectable, and resulted in a better understanding of the sales function.

☐ *The salesman's role*

In view of the possible variations in product and market characteristics it is virtually impossible to formulate a single definition of the saleman's role.

Where a user/consumer has previous experience of a product the salesman is often a passive 'order-taker' whose function is to price the product specified, take payment and effect delivery; for example 2 kg of potatoes, a packet of Whizzo, 50 tons of cold-reduced mild steel sheet. Such a situation is very different from the case where the potential buyer has no previous experience of the product and is actively seeking information; and different again from the situation where the consumer has only an ill-defined or latent demand for a product to fill a given need. In the latter situations the salesman becomes an 'order-maker' and plays an active role in the purchasing decision.

Although there is more than an element of truth in the generalisation that retailers are order-takers, whereas manufacturers' salesmen are order-makers, no such clear-cut distinction exists in reality. Many manufacturers have become sensitive to the important influence which the retail sales assistant can have on the purchasing decision, and have installed their own employees in leased departments or provided training for their customers' staff. Similarly, the high cost of personal selling has persuaded many manufacturers to adopt standardised reorder procedures and to eliminate unnecessary or uneconomic sales calls. Alternatively, less experienced personnel are assigned to perform routine functions, leaving the salesman free to devote more time to missionary and developmental selling.

Although emotional factors undoubtedly influence both industrial and consumer purchasing decisions at all levels, it is felt that there is a tendency to overemphasise these and, consequently, to overstress the salesman's role as a 'persuader'. In everyday speech, 'persuasion' is often used to suggest that a person has been, or can be, induced to act against his better judgement – this is certainly the context in which Vance Packard views 'The Hidden Persuaders' of advertising. In reality it is doubted if consumers are persuaded by spurious arguments as frequently as Packard suggests, and the salesman's role might be more usefully viewed as a problem-solving activity in which facts and arguments are used to justify the selection of a given product to satisfy a specific want. The salesman's skill lies in his ability to perceive the attributes which the 'prospect' considers important, and to structure his presentation so that his product's suitability along those dimensions is adequately conveyed to the potential customer. Thus, the car salesman will emphasise performance to his male customers, and finish and trim to his female customers – if he is a good car

salesman he will also realise that the middle-aged bank clerk's concept of performance is rather different from that of the junior account executive and so on. (There is more than a grain of truth in the old adage 'Let the customer tell you what he wants and then sell it to him'; that is, given the wealth of detail which you could give the customer, concentrate on the points in which they express interest.)

The economics of personal selling

A recurring theme of this book is that the well-managed firm will seek to develop strategies that will enable it to achieve certain predetermined objectives. Fundamental to the firm's ability to achieve its stated aims is the need to earn profits, so that the adoption of policies, and the strategies by which they will be implemented, will revolve largely around cost/revenue considerations. This point has already been stressed at some length elsewhere but it is particularly relevant in the context of personal selling.

In absolute terms personal selling is the most expensive method whereby the producer can establish contact with the potential consumer. A guide to the cost of employing a salesman in

Table 18.2 *Guide to the cost of employing a salesman*

	Overall* annual cost	*Daily cost based on 200 working days*	*Total no. of selling calls per day*	*Cost per call*
Manufacturer's salesman selling to retail trade	£27 000	£135	10–12	£13.50–£11.25
Pharmaceuticals salesman selling to doctors and hospitals	£38 000	£190	6–8	£31.66–£23.75
Industrial salesman selling to OEMs	£38 000	£190	4–6	£47.50–£31.66
Capital goods salesman selling to end users	£45 000	£225	3–5	£75–45

Note: * In 1993 the *Financial Times* estimated the average cost of a salesman as 36 000 p.a.
Source: John Lidstone (1983), 'Putting Force Back into Sales', *Marketing*, 22 September.

four industry sectors is provided in Table 18.2. In 1993 the *Financial Times* estimated the average cost of a salesman as £36 000 p.a. Relatively, however, it is often the least expensive method owing to the higher conversion factor achieved by direct selling *vis-à-vis* the use of middlemen or other promotional efforts. Whether the manufacturer should employ his own sales force, how big it should be, and how he should deploy it to maximum effect are questions which may only be resolved through a full evaluation of the alternatives. Although it is possible to quantify many of the parameters no single prescriptive formula is available, but a number of steps can be offered as the basis for structuring such an evaluation:

1. The company should state its sales target for the coming year and for the next five years or so.
2. The promotional budget should be reviewed in the light of the sales target to ascertain whether the proposed expenditures will be sufficient to generate the desired sales volume – see 'The task approach' in Chapter 16.
3. Personal and non-personal selling are complementary activities and should not be segregated when determining the size of the promotional budget; that is, management should decide how much it is willing to spend on all promotion, before attempting to allocate it to specific promotional efforts.
4. The optimum mix of personal and non-personal promotional efforts will vary by product, firm, industry and market, and is subject to change over time, therefore the total budget should be allocated roughly in accordance with the relative importance attached to each.
5. The adequacy of the sales budget may be evaluated by reference to past sales data or, if the firm has no previous experience of direct selling, by reference to the industry/product data published by trade associations, the BIM, the trade press, and so forth. A rough and ready guide is to substitute such data into the formula:

$$\text{Sales} = \frac{\text{Sales budget}}{\text{Average cost per call}}$$

$$\times \text{Average sales per call}$$

In the absence of hard data, the firm would have to rely upon its own subjective estimates of likely events, and could easily test a large number of alternatives by running a simulation on a computer.

Once a field sales force is in existence, a continual process of adjustment is necessary to maximise its productivity. Ideally, salesmen should be used to the point where the marginal cost of making a sales call is equivalent to the marginal revenue which it generates. In practice, adoption of this principle is rarely feasible because of the high fixed costs associated with the addition of an 'incremental' salesman, unless payment is on a straight commission basis.

☐ *Deploying the field sales force*

Optimum deployment of the sales force is an ever-present problem for the sales manager. Essentially this problem has three dimensions:

1. The geographical dispersion of potential customers.
2. The nature of the company's product mix.
3. The buying needs of customers.

The geographical dispersion of customers imposes a major constraint on sales force productivity in that time spent travelling between customers is largely wasted. The amount of travelling time will vary considerably depending upon a number of factors but, on average, it is estimated that salesmen only spend 40 per cent of their time actually in contact with customers. Clearly a major objective must be to minimise the spatial distribution of accounts, which suggests that the sales force should be organised on a territorial basis.

However, such an organisational structure may conflict with the essential requirement that a salesman know his product. For the single product company, or the company with a limited range of closely related products, this may not create any problems, but as product line diversity and/or complexity increase, so product specialisation becomes progressively more essential. In the steel industry it would be impossible for any individual to be completely familiar with all products, and specialists are required for the sale of tinplate, mild steel sheet and plate, electrical steels, billets and bars, and so on.

In turn, product knowledge must be backed by an understanding of the buying needs and practices of different customer groupings. Thus the detergent manufacturer's salesman will find it necessary to adopt a very different approach when selling to a major grocery chain as opposed the small independent outlet. Similarly, it will be necessary to use a very different strategy when selling to industrial users.

There is no simple rule which dictates that the manufacturer should organise his sales force on a territory, product or market basis and, in fact, many companies have adopted a composite structure. Many of the arguments examined when discussing product and market management in Chapter 19 are equally applicable in this context, but it is important to recognise that the internal organisation of the marketing department on either product or market lines does not automatically require that the sales force be organised in the same way. For obvious reasons of economy most sales forces are organised on a territorial basis, but within these boundaries salesmen may specialise on either a product or customer needs basis. The role of the product or market manager is to supply the salesman with detailed information of the most appropriate marketing inputs, such that several product managers may brief a single salesman on the 'best' tactics to be used in respect of each of their different products. Similarly, the market manager will lay down the nature of the selling approach most suited to the particular customer grouping for which he is responsible.

At the territory level a number of techniques have been evolved in recent years to improve sales efficiency. The sales call pattern is in the nature of a 'transportation problem' in the language of

operations research or management science, and is capable of at least partial solution through the use of linear programming techniques. In order to permit analysis it is necessary to adopt a number of simplifying assumptions, for example the relationship between time spent with buyer and size of order, the value of new account development or 'prospecting' and so on, and it is clear that no true optimum solution is possible. None the less, the discipline of developing empirically valid generalisations is in itself worth while as it can lead to valuable insights into the more effective deployment of the field sales force.

 # Selling situations classified

One of the central themes of this chapter is that selling situations vary across a number of dimensions and that one must be careful to distinguish between them. At the same time there are sufficient similarities to permit the identification of a number of situations in which a particular kind or type of selling will be appropriate. It will be useful, therefore, to outline the basis characteristics of each as a first step towards identifying the sales situation facing the company and the necessary sales inputs to cope with it effectively.

In an investigation into sales management practice undertaken by Dr Derek Newton (1969) of the Harvard Business School, a secondary finding was that '...one can effectively isolate four basic styles of selling that cut across industry boundaries to a large degree...'

These four styles are characterised as:

1. Trade selling;
2. Missionary selling;
3. Technical selling;
4. New business selling.

Although there is nothing new in identifying selling styles and attaching labels to them, this classification is preferred by the author in that it offers the broadest level of categorisation consistent with utility. In summary the characteristics of the four styles are:

Trade selling

- Major aim to build sales volume by providing customers with promotional assistance, that is selling *through*; for example food, textiles and wholesaling.
- Personal selling subsidiary to non-personal activities.
- Low-pressure selling, with an emphasis on continuity and a thorough understanding of customer practice.

Missionary selling

- Primary aim is to build sales volume by providing direct customers with personal selling assistance; that is, to persuade ultimate users and/or consumers to buy from the company's immediate customers.
- Most typical of firms selling to distributors for resale.
- Low pressure but requires energetic, articulate persons capable of making a large number of calls in order to cover all the potential users; for example medical representatives.

Technical selling

- Primary responsibility is to increase sales to present customers through the provision of technical advice and assistance.
- Requires an ability to identify, analyse and solve customer problems, and so places a premium on technical and product knowledge.
- Continuity is an important factor in building up buyer confidence and goodwill.

New business selling

- Primary aim is to secure new customers.
- The high level of rejection of new product propositions favours the employment of mature, experienced salesmen who can take an objective view of 'failure' and have a wider range of techniques to deal with buying objections.

The recruitment, selection and training of salesmen

Attributes of the successful salesman

Given the possible variations in the role which salesmen are called upon to play in different selling situations, it would be surprising to find that potentially successful salesmen may be identified by the presence, or absence, of a stereotyped set of personality variables. On the other hand, the high costs of selection and training make it essential that wastage through salesmen turnover be minimised, and have prompted the construction of innumerable check-lists which purport to identify the attributes of a successful salesman. The majority of such lists emphasise factors such as 'intelligent, extrovert, energetic, self-confident' and so on, and a number of selection tests have been devised to measure such characteristics.

Collectively these lists, and the associated tests, presume the existence of a stereotype the validity of which is doubted by the author. This doubt would appear to be supported by the findings of Samuel N. Stevens (1958), in 'The Application of Social Science Findings to Selling and the Salesman', who has summarised 'the major conclusions which social scientists have reached in regard to social and psychological characteristics of salesmen...' as follows:

1. There is no significant relationship between intelligence test scores and sales success.
2. No significant relationship has been found between independent measures of personality traits and sales success.
3. No correlation exists between age and sales success.

4. There is no correlation between measurable character traits and sales success.

5. There is no significant correlation between level of education and sales success.

6. No significant correlation exists between level of sales activity and sales success among individual salesmen.

7. Each of the above factors has significance when studied in relation to all of the others in individual salesmen.

8. Such a study as that indicated in point 7 above can provide a useful tool for selection and development.

9. Salesmen are more likely to succeed when chosen with regard to the kinds of customers they will deal with than in terms of the types of products sold.

10. Salesmen differ from non-salesmen in four important ways:

   - Salesmen are persuasive rather than critical;
   - Salesmen are intuitive rather than analytical;
   - Salesmen have higher average energy levels (expressed in activity);
   - Salesmen are more strongly motivated by the desire for prestige, power, and material gain than by a service ideal or the need for security.

11. Salesmen's interests cluster around a dominantly persuasive common core.

(pp. 85–94)

☐ *Recruitment*

As noted in point 7, factors 1–6 have no individual significance and their collective importance will vary depending upon the selling task to be performed – point 9. If this is so, then it follows that firms should develop their own selection procedures based on a job specification appropriate to their own sales policies and objectives. Such a job specification is vital to efficient recruitment and selection.

Most sales positions are advertised in the classified columns of the major newspapers and trade journals, and media representatives frequently quote the number of applications received by advertisers as an indication of their publication's 'pulling power'. Such statements would seem to confuse volume with quality, and usually indicate that the advertisement has failed in its function as a screening device. On occasion a loosely worded advertisement is a useful guide to the calibre of people who are actively seeking new jobs – as a means of securing applicants for a specific post it is both a wasteful and 'sloppy' approach. (A leading firm of management consultants once informed the author that they had received over 800 applications for a sales manager's post requiring previous experience with a highly specialised product. As there could not have been more than fifty people with such experience, either the consultant was 'fishing' for applicants to fill other vacancies, or he didn't know his job. In either case he was wasting his client's time and money.)

Most job advertisements require applicants to submit details of their previous experience and other evidence to indicate their potential suitability for the post. Where the job specification is fairly loose or the employer intends to give recruits extensive training, standardised application forms greatly assist the preparation of a short-list as they ensure that all applicants supply information considered important by the prospective employer.

☐ *Selection*

Once a short-list has been prepared, the final selection of candidates usually involves some combination of tests and interviews. If a job specification has been prepared the purpose of the selection procedure will be to identify the applicant who most closely matches the job profile. In the absence of a job specification selection is likely to be overly subjective.

Although many factors will be common to all sales positions, and permit the use of structured interviews, the relative importance of these factors will vary depending upon the precise nature of the selling job to be performed. To deal with this problem and permit the development of standardised selection procedures, it is recommended that some form of factor rating be employed, similar to that described in connection with the screening of new product ideas.

In recent years an increasing number of firms have adopted some form of psychological testing in addition to the traditional personal interview. Such tests are seen as a cross-check on both interviewer bias and respondent consistency, and fall into four main categories:

- Aptitude
- Interest
- Mental ability
- Personality

Tests of this kind conform more with the American than with the British ethic and are most frequently used in companies with strong links with the United States; for example Esso, Procter & Gamble, Mars.

Criticism of psychological tests is not based solely on cultural differences, however, and a number of American marketers are equally as sceptical as their more conservative British counterparts. For example, David Mayer and Herbert Greenberg (1964) in 'What Makes a Good Salesman?', discern four reasons which appear to account for the failure of aptitude tests:

1. Tests confuse interest with ability;
2. It is possible to fake answers and give the response the interviewer is looking for;
3. Tests favour conformity not individual creativity;
4. Tests concentrate on personality traits in isolation and fail to measure the person as a whole.

In the companion volume *Sales Management: Theory and Practice*, Bill Donaldson (1990) reports that an increasing number of firms are now using assessment centres which employ a variety of techniques and may appraise six to eight candidates over one to three days using a team of selection specialists.

However, psychological testing techniques are becoming increasingly sophisticated and it is anticipated that they will come into wider use in the future.

☐ *Training*

The function of the selection procedures described above is to recruit candidates who are potentially suited to the company's selling tasks. Often the firm will use previous experience as a selection criterion, although a BIM survey (1966) indicated that only 40 of the 75 respondents stipulated that this was essential. (This survey, *Methods of Selecting and Training Salesmen*, Information Summary 87, provides useful background data but is based on too small a sample to permit valid generalisation.) Even where the new recruit has previous experience it is unlikely that this is directly relevant to the products, markets and administrative procedures particular to his new employer, and some training will be necessary.

The objective of training is to make the salesman more effective *as judged by the firm's criteria*. As is evident from the distinction drawn earlier between trade, missionary, technical and new-business selling, sales volume is only one criterion, and may be totally inappropriate in some circumstances. Although the need for training is clearly greatest in the case of new, inexperienced recruits it should be looked upon as a continuing process. Over time products, channels and markets change, and the well-managed firm will adjust its policies accordingly – continuation training is fundamental to the effective implementation of such changes in policy.

The length, content and cost of the sales training programme varies enormously between companies, but all seek to cover two main areas – knowledge and skills. Knowledge is concerned with the acquisition of facts and will normally include coverage of:

- The company – its history, structure, policies and procedures.

- The product(s) – composition, manufacture, performance and usage.
- The market – size, structure, composition, buying behaviour, and so on.

Skills may be subdivided into two categories – technical and behavioural. Technical skills cover training in techniques appropriate to various stages of the buying process such as securing interviews, opening the interview, overcoming objections and the 'close'. If the product can be demonstrated this would also be considered a technical skill.

Behavioural skills are concerned with the development of empathy between buyer and seller. They are difficult both to define and to acquire, and are usually described in texts on salesmanship under titles such as 'How to be a good listener', 'How to excite curiosity', and so forth.

According to John Lidstone (1983) in 'Putting Force Back into Sales', the modern salesman must develop his knowledge and skill in three key areas:

- First, he must have a fluent confidence in the financial facts upon which buying and selling are based, and in the impact of his product on his buyer's business and on his own company's costs, profits and cash flow. In a world of constantly changing costs and prices, the salesman must be capable of ensuring not only that an order is obtained, but also that it is a profitable one.
- Second, he must know how to prepare, in far more detail than before, strategies for each major customer. He must know how to ensure that all the company's resources are harnessed to achieve both short and longer-term customer satisfaction, at a profit. Such strategies, skilfully and imaginatively implemented, will do much to eliminate the 'pyrrhic sale' produced by a salesman under pressure from management, which too often has resulted in short-term gains but the long-term loss of an account.
- Third, he must know how to negotiate a mutually satisfactory order and long-term business, rather than just using persuasive techniques to conjure up the 'your turn next' type of order. Many of the larger buyers have no option but to purchase from the major suppliers. But the key to success is the terms on which the contract to trade is agreed.
- Negotiation skills of the highest order must be developed to deal on equal terms with these major customers, many of whom have been trained to buy. So far, little more than lip service has been paid to this fact. Indeed, an uncomfortably large number of sales managers, let alone salesmen, still think that negotiation is just a smart word for selling. It is nothing of the sort.

☐ *Salesman compensation*

Selling is a function which lends itself to some kind of payment by results in the majority of cases. If it is borne in mind that every incentive has a corresponding disincentive, then it follows that one must determine which incentive is most appropriate to a given selling situation.

Surveys into the remuneration of salesmen by the TACK organisation and the BIM indicate that about 18 per cent of salesmen are paid a straight salary, with no bonus or incentive, while the remaining 82 per cent all receive some form of financial incentive. Every method has its advantages and disadvantages and these may be summarised as:

Salary only

- The salesman's income is based on his overall performance and not subject to fluctuations beyond his control, for example the impact of a credit squeeze or marked seasonality of demand.
- The method is fairest where the salesman is engaged in missionary selling or required to spend much of his time providing technical services.
- Where there are variations in territory potential it prevents friction between salesmen, and gives flexibility in sales and journey planning.

- It simplifies payment and avoids complications in the salary structure of the company as a whole.

As suggested, each of these advantages has a built-in disincentive:

- Sales effort will not be maximised when most needed.
- The quality of the services rendered will affect sales volume and so should be measured in just the same way.
- Territories should be designed so that they have the same potential to encourage salesmen to compete with one another.
- If incentives are properly designed they will ensure that all members of the company receive a reward proportionate to their contribution.

Salary and commission

This is the most frequently used method on the grounds that:

- The salary provides a basic income while the commission provides the incentive to extra effort to achieve a better standard of living.
- Variable commissions on different products ensure that salesmen give them the degree of attention desired.

Commission only

In practice this method is found very infrequently – TACK reports 5.5 per cent, BIM nil – as it has little attraction to any but the most confident of salesmen. From the employer's point of view it has the great attraction that payment is directly related to the results achieved, but it can also create considerable friction among other employees owing to the very high earnings which can be achieved by a good salesman.

Bonus schemes

Bonuses may be paid in addition to commission, either as an individual or group incentive, as a reward for sustained effort or the achievement of a pre-designated target, or where a purely quantitative assessment would not adequately reflect performance; for example reduced sales on a falling market when such sales still represent an increase in market share.

A survey by C. K. Manolis (1990), a postgraduate student at Strathclyde University, reported by Donaldson (1990), in *Sales Management*, revealed that 30 per cent of UK salespeople were on straight salary, 35 per cent on salary + commission, 17 per cent on salary + commission + bonus and 5 per cent on commission only.

☐ *Evaluation of salesmen*

In the preceding section little reference was made to the methods used in evaluating salesmen's performance, on which most remuneration schemes are based. Once again it is necessary to reiterate that the relevant criteria will depend upon the company's own sales policies and objectives but, in general, performance will be measured in both quantitative and qualitative terms. Quantitative criteria include:

- Sales volume;
- Number of orders secured;
- Number of sales calls made;
- Number of service calls made;
- Expenses incurred;
- Territory contribution to profit.

Among the qualitative criteria in common use are:

- Degree of product knowledge;
- Quality of sales presentation;
- Rating on personality traits such as initiative, judgement and so on;
- Self-organisation, that is use of time, handling of correspondence, reports and so forth;
- Customer relationships.

Once the relevant criteria have been selected, some basis for evaluation must be chosen.

Methods based on past performance, or involving a comparison of salesmen, suffer from the disadvantage that present conditions may differ markedly from those obtaining in the past, and that sales territories, and hence salesmen, are rarely, if ever directly comparable. To overcome these difficulties many companies prefer to measure performance against prescribed standards; for example actual sales versus forecast, number of new accounts secured versus target, expenses incurred versus budgeted expense, and so on.

■ Merchandising

In the chapter on patterns of distribution reference was made to the transference of some of the 'traditional' retailing functions to the manufacturer intent upon securing greater control over the marketing of his output. Subsequently, the role of packaging, advertising and sales promotion were examined in the context of generating demand for particular goods and services. It now remains to consider merchandising as an extension of the selling process whereby the manufacturer seeks to ensure that the retailer sells his products as quickly and as profitably as possible.

From the manufacturer's point of view the retail outlet provides the ready availability and convenience which are so expensive to achieve by direct selling methods. Once the retailer has taken delivery of goods from the manufacturer they become his property until he can effect their resale to ultimate consumers, and it follows that until he is able to achieve this he will have neither space nor capital with which to purchase further supplies from the producer. Clearly any assistance which the manufacturer can give the retailer to stimulate demand and encourage purchase will be to their mutual advantage – this is the role of merchandising.

To maximise sales volume the sales force must ensure that its products are in the right place at the right time, in order to translate potential demand for them into effective demand. The right place means not only the outlets with the highest turnover or largest clientele but also the right place within the outlet to achieve the maximum impact on the prospective purchaser. Given the cost of a salesman's time, plus the cost of point-of-sale display material, it is obvious that merchandising efforts must be concentrated on the larger outlets which promise the greatest potential return. Within outlets, research has shown that certain locations are to be preferred. Thus in self-service outlets the best positions have been found to be:

1. At the end of gondolas facing the main traffic flow. (A gondola is a shelving unit on the main floor area which subdivides this area into a series of aisles.)
2. At eye level on the shelves around the sides of the shop. Impact can be further improved by siting the product immediately prior to the area normally set aside for display of the product group.
3. In dump displays in the main traffic aisles as these tend to cause congestion and focus attention on them.
4. Immediately next to the checkout – here again congestion creates a captive audience.

In shops which still retain counter service the preferred positions are:

1. On the counter itself. If this is extensive, then next to the till or scales.
2. At eye level behind the counter.
3. In a dispenser placed in front of the counter.
4. Next to a complementary product, for example cream next to tins of fruit.

Timing is also an important factor underlying successful merchandising. Research indicates that the majority of purchases are made at the weekend and so emphasises the need to ensure adequate display at this time. Similarly, seasonal products such as mincemeat, Easter eggs and the like must be put on display in plenty of time, as must goods which are to be the subject of heavy promotion.

The major pitfall to be avoided by the salesman is that of becoming a merchandiser first and a salesman second. The salesman's role is to instruct retailers in the use of proven techniques to stimulate demand at the point of sale, and it is undesirable that he should become involved in routine activities associated with stocking shelves and putting goods on display. The salesman's job is to ensure that his products are given sound merchandising and a fair share of the favoured sites, and the normal call frequency precludes his devoting much time to in-store promotion.

In view of the heavy demands on the salesman's time, many firms now employ personnel whose sole function is to assist the retailer with the creation of effective store displays. Much merchandising is purely mechanical and so can be performed by part-time or less highly paid employees than is the case when salesman are required to do their own merchandising. In view of the desirability of achieving maximum impact simultaneously over a wide area at the commencement of an advertising campaign, several independent television companies now offer additional sales and merchandising support to supplement the advertiser's own efforts.

Tyne Tees, Border, Granada and HTV all have their own retail sales force. The remainder, less LWT and Ulster, offer this service through a contracted company. London and South & S. East England are the exceptions with Thames TV and TVS not offering this service. Some indicative costs using the Television South West retail force are set out in Table 18.3.

The foregoing discussion of merchandising has tended to emphasise the manufacturer's involvement. It is important to stress, therefore, that increasingly retailers are adopting much more sophisticated approaches to extract the fullest possible return from their space and so are likely to have strong views on in-store promotions and point of sale material. Some clues to their attitudes are to be found in two articles published in successive weeks in *Marketing* – 'Centres of Attraction' by Brian Seymour (6 September 1984) and 'Supermarket Scientists' by Maureen Johnson (13 September 1984). In the first article Seymour points to the growing difficulty experienced by FMCG manufacturers in getting in-store display space to influence customers near the point of purchase and advocates that such manufacturers should follow the US pattern and seek to get display in shopping centres.

Table 18.3 *Costs of TSW's contract sales force*

Cost per salesperson day inclusive of fee and expenses		
(TSW – £59)		£65.00
Briefing per operative, inclusive of fee and expenses		
(TSW – £65)		£70.00
Supervision and administration (covering production of		
all documentation plus reporting)	2 weeks	£500.00
	3 weeks	£600.00
Agency representative travel to attend briefing in Plymouth		£150.00
Sales bonus – allowance per person	2 weeks	£30.00
	3 weeks	£50.00
Total costs		
2 weeks (800 call) Grocery/CTN campaign		
(TSW – £3845)		£4145
3 weeks (1200 call) Grocery/CTN campaign		
(TSW – £5420)		£5970
2 weeks (500 call) Licensed grocer campaign		
(TSW – £3255)		£3495

Source: TSW Brochure.

Johnson's article provides a number of insights and findings based on studies by Research Bureaux which illuminate the dynamics of point-of-sale activity. For example, 20 per cent of purchases are decided in-store (worth £1 billion plus); but are estimated at 89 per cent in the USA. For 2 per cent of purchases the brand is undecided before the shopper enters the outlet, and 9 per cent of purchases involve switching from intended purchase on entering the store, while 9 per cent are impulse or reminder buys. Clearly, the ability to influence such decisions with effective point-of-sale displays and in-store promotion is considerable.

■ Telemarketing

The 22 June issue of *Marketing Week* in 1990 contained a review of telemarketing in which it reported the findings of the British Direct Marketing Association that half of companies already use the phone to win business and currently spend about £5 billion on telemarketing. Currently, the main use is to fix sales appointments or to take enquiries for brochures but with the radical changes in technology which have occurred in recent years *Marketing Week* predicts that increasingly the telephone will come to be seen as a strategic sales medium.

A recent Key Note Report shows that use of the telephone as a major marketing technique grew 126 per cent between 1987 and 1990 as compared with a 63 per cent growth in the use of direct mail over the same period. Currently 93 per cent of all households own a telephone which approaches levels in the USA and the day is not far off when access to both households and organisational customers will be almost 100 per cent. Perhaps equally important to the growth of telemarketing is the change in attitude to the telephone as an information and communication medium greatly encouraged by the break-up of the old Post Office monopoly and the introduction of competition between British Telecom and other suppliers such as Mercury; that is, the telephone companies are marketing their services too.

In addition to establishing initial contact with potential new customers (cold calling) for example double glazing, time shares, financial services and so forth – the telephone is seen as providing an increasingly important role in improving service levels and maintaining customer loyalty. *Marketing Week* cites the General Electric Answer Center in Louisville, Kentucky as a prime example of how to use the telephone to add value. GE products promote a toll-free number for consumers to call if they have any questions or problems. Staff have access to 750 000 items of information about GE products to help callers when washing machines go wrong, recommend a type of refrigerator, and so on. GE found that such a service encouraged consumers to buy more from the company, and then to recommend it to others. Similarly, research by the Technical Assistance Research Program for Coca-Cola established that complaints and queries could be answered more effectively by telephone than by letter. Given that Nielsen studies show that only one out of 50 unhappy customers complain – the rest simply switch brands – any service which can keep customers in contact with suppliers must add value and help retain customer loyalty.

Increasingly sophisticated technology such as automated call distributed (ACD) systems and predictive dialling will undoubtedly accelerate the growth of telemarketing. In the case of ACD, calls are routed to available operators automatically with full details of the caller being displayed on a computer terminal while, with predictive dialling, the computer will estimate pick-up rates and average call length to determine how many calls can be handled at any one time. However, the UK has banned the use of equipment which dials an endless list of telephone numbers linked to a computer which then makes the sales call.

By 1993 direct expenditure on Telemarketing stood at £75 million, a 250 per cent increase on 1988. In the *Marketing Pocket Book* (1995) the following summary data appears:

Telemarketing may be defined as 'the systematic use of the telephone as a communications channel between a company and its customers'.

Services to build the relationships associated with telemarketing activity:

- Inbound (live, automated, combination)
- Outbound
- Consultancy
- Fulfilment
- Database Management
- Associated services e.g. fulfilment, direct marketing, customer service, etc.

Service split is estimated at 66% inbound, 34% outbound, in volume terms in the UK.
Developments are towards call-centre management of customers, linking people through the telephone network, telephone switches, automatic call distributors, integrated computers and supporting applications software.

Range of telemarketing network services available:

- Free*fone* 0800 – free to caller
- Lo-call 0345 – charged at local rate to caller

- 0891 charged at premium rate to caller; service provider takes a proportion of the revenue. Other network providers carry their own range of numbers.

UK volume 1993/94; 540 million Free*fone 0800* and Lo-call *0345* calls made. Prompted awareness of Free*fone 0800* 86% and Lo-call 0345 24%.

Agencies & Bureaux:

Telemarketing agencies are well established in the UK (offering live, automated or a combination of services). The top 10 agencies command about 90% of the market. Approximately 50% of agencies offer 24 hour activity.
Costs vary widely but consist of: set-up fee; ongoing management fee; variable charge (cost per minute/per hour/per call etc.).

Sources: BT, Henley Centre Telebusiness Survey 1994. For further information call Free*fone 0800 660099*.

Summary

This chapter has focused mainly on the role of personal selling. To begin with it was emphasised that personal selling is complementary to impersonal selling using other promotional methods – the precise mix depending very much upon the type of product and markets served.

Next we looked at the role of the salesman and the economics of personal selling concluding that some form of 'task' approach was best suited to determining where salespersons could be used to greatest effect. This and the deployment of the sales force were both seen as being amenable to simulation and quantification using management science techniques.

Several different selling tasks were then distinguished – Trade, Missionary, Technical and New Business – which led to a review of the factors to be taken into account in the recruitment, selection and training of salespersons. Methods of compensating salespersons and evaluation of performance followed.

The chapter then looked briefly at merchandising and telemarketing as aspects of personal selling now largely the responsibility of a new kind of salesperson.

Review questions and problems

1. Direct selling is the most expensive method of establishing contact with the potential customer. Under what circumstances is this expense justified?

2. Distinguish the essential differences between trade, missionary, technical and new-business selling. What 'type' of salesman do you consider to be best suited to each?

3. Compare and contrast the various methods of compensation discussed in the text. Which would you select in each of the following situations? Why?

    (a) Sale of capital equipment.
    (b) Sale of industrial lubricants.
    (c) Door-to-door selling of cosmetics, 'encyclopaedias, etc.
    (d) Sale of packaged goods to independent retail outlets.

4. Account for the recent emphasis given to merchandising.
5. What is systems selling? What advantages does it have over the traditional product specialisation approach?
6. Critically examine the alternative methods of compensating salesmen.
7. 'There is something of the salesman in every good buyer. However, very few salesmen would ever make good buyers.' Discuss this view.
8. How should a sales manager determine the size of the sales force?
9. What do you think is the ideal way in which to recruit and select salesmen?

10. Show how a knowledge of interaction and influence processes in personal selling can contribute to an enhancement of salesforce productivity.
11. To what extent are psychological tests of value in the selection of salesmen?
12. What are the main factors which sales managers should bear in mind when evaluating the performance of their sales forces? Give your views on the extent to which remuneration of salesmen should be related to their performance.
13. Outline the value of a retail audit operation in helping to control the efficiency of a sales force.
14. What are the most important things a salesman can do to improve his sales performance? How can management help him to do these things?
15. How would you decide to divide available resources between direct sales representatives and other promotional activities?
16. What factors should be taken into account when designing sales territories?
17. Write a job description for a salesman in a company manufacturing electronic components.

Supplementary reading list

Cundiff, E. W. and Leonard, E. W. (1981) *Readings in Sales Management* (American Marketing Association).

Donaldson, W. G. (1990) *Sales Management: Theory and Practice* (London: Macmillan).

Furlong, C. (1993) *Marketing for Keeps* (New York: John Wiley).

Harvard Reprint Series (1988) *How to Improve Sales Management*

Lancaster, G. and Jobber, D. (1990) *Sales Technique and Management*, 3rd edn (London: Pitman).

Still, R. R., Cundiff, G. W. and Govoni, N. A. P. (1987) *Sales Management: Decisions, Strategies and Cases* (Englewood Cliffs, N.J.: Prentice-Hall).

Wilson, M. (1983) *Managing a Sales Force*, 2nd edn (London: Gower).

Part IV
MARKETING IN PRACTICE

■ *Chapter 19* ■

The Company: Organising for Marketing

Contents

Learning goals

The issues to be addressed in this chapter include:

1. Basic organisational structures.
2. The organisation of the marketing department.
3. The nature of product and market management.
4. The impact of marketing on organisational structure.
5. The nature of corporate resources.

After reading this chapter you will be able to:

1. Recognise different forms of organisational structure.

2. Explain the need for both *differentiation* and *integration* in the effective organisation.
3. List and describe seven basic methods of organising a marketing department.
4. Describe the origin, evolution and application of the product manager concept.
5. Describe the market manager concept and compare and contrast it with the product manager concept.
6. Discuss the relationship between the marketing concept, marketing orientation and organisational structure.
7. List some of the influences on the structure of an organisation and particularly the various corporate resources it may have at its disposal.

■ Introduction

The change from a seller's to a buyer's market in the 1950s precipitated a rash of literature promising managerial salvation through adoption of the marketing concept. With the desperation of a drowning man, corporations in every field of activity seized the straw, and marketing staff appointments proliferated. As anticipated profits failed to materialise, disillusionment set in and marketing became the scapegoat. Supporters of marketing responded by pointing out that adoption of the marketing concept requires a complete reorientation of the firm's activities which renaming the sales function was unlikely to bring about.

Superficial as this description is, it serves to underline that the firm's organisational structure is critical to marketing success. In the era of excess demand, top management attention was rightly focused on increasing output, and a production orientation was both necessary and understandable. However, a firm is more than a collection of individuals, it is a social system with its own norms, status structure and system of rewards and punishments. It is unrealistic to assume that these can be changed overnight, yet many firms which have rejected the marketing concept have done so because they failed to appreciate the inherent organisational implications, or else instituted extensive changes without full consideration of the possible ramifications. Fortunately, the unhappy experiences of the disillusioned have served to concentrate attention on the organisational implications associated with a marketing orientation.

In this chapter we look first at some of the factors which influence organisational structures in general and marketing departments in particular. A discussion of the product manager concept follows which is compared and contrasted with the idea of market managers. This leads to a consideration of the impact of marketing on organisational structure supported by a short review of corporate resources and the importance of corporate culture as a factor closely associated with corporate performance.

Basic organisational structures

Given the possible variations in the extent of corporate resources, the products they manufacture and the markets they serve, it is clear that there can be no single organisational structure of universal applicability. Despite the infinite variations in degree, the fundamental organisational choice revolves around grouping activities by product or function. This dilemma was the subject of an article by two well-known authorities on organisation behaviour, Arthur H. Walker and Jay W. Lorsch (1968), 'Organizational choice: product vs. function', on which the following discussion draws heavily.

Traditionally, organisational theorists have suggested that the appropriate structure should be decided on the basis of three criteria:

1. Which approach permits the maximum use of special technical knowledge?
2. Which provides the most efficient utilisation of machinery and equipment?
3. Which provides the best hope of obtaining the required control and coordination?

Walker and Lorsch feel that these traditional criteria ignore the trade-off between functional specialisation and difficulties of coordination, and product specialisation which promotes collaboration between specialists but tends to lose identification with functional goals. To make good this omission the authors propose that three findings from the behavioural sciences should also be taken into account, namely:

1. Functional specialists tend to develop patterns of behaviour and thought that are in tune with the demands of their jobs and their prior training, and as a result these specialists (for example industrial engineers and production supervisors) have different ideas and orientation about what is important in getting the job done. This is called *differentiation* and is necessary for functional specialists to perform their jobs effectively.
2. Differentiation is closely related to achievement of coordination, or what behavioural scientists call *integration*. This means collaboration between specialised units or individuals. Recent studies have demonstrated that there is an inverse relationship between differentiation and integration: the more two functional specialists (or their units) differ in their patterns of behaviour and

thought, the more difficult it is to bring about integration between them.

3. While achievement of both differentiation and integration is possible, it can only occur when well-developed means of communication among specialists exist in the organisation and when the specialists are effective in resolving the inevitable cross-functional conflicts.

It is suggested that these findings raise three basic questions which must be answered when choosing between a product, or functional basis of organisation:

(a) Does it permit sufficient differentiation for the effective performance of specialist tasks?
(b) Is the degree of differentiation consistent with the desired level of integration?
(c) How will the structure affect intra-firm channels of communication?

Although the appropriate structure will depend upon external factors, Walker and Lorsch suggest two useful generalisations:

1. The functional type of structure is appropriate where the firm is faced with a routine and repetitive task. Under these circumstances integration can be achieved through plans, and conflict resolved by the hierarchy.
2. Where the task involves problem-solving, that is dealing with new situations, then the product organisation is more appropriate.

However, as the authors note, most firms are faced with a combination of both routine tasks and problem-solving, e.g. the marketing of established products and new product development. As a result most firms find it necessary to adopt some form of compromise as is evident from current organisation charts. The question of the most appropriate structure for the firm as a whole will be returned to following a consideration of the organisation of the marketing department *per se*.

Organisation of the marketing department

In practice it appears that the marketing department may be organised in one of seven basic ways:

1. Functionally oriented.
2. Product oriented.
3. Market/customer oriented.
4. Regionally oriented.
5. Functional/product orientation.
6. Functional/market orientation.
7. Functional/regional orientation.

A marketing department organised on functional lines is illustrated in Figure 19.1. Under this structure, personnel are grouped by functional specialisation and their activities are

Figure 19.1 *Marketing department organised on a functional basis*

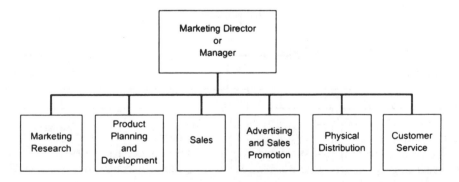

Figure 19.2 *Product-oriented organisation*

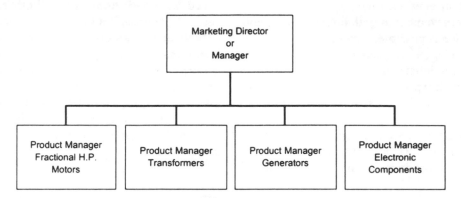

coordinated by the marketing director or manager. Such a system enjoys the advantages of
simplicity and clearly designated areas of responsibility. On the other hand such advantages are
often negated by the restricted outlook which
such compartmentalisation inevitably breeds.
There is a tendency for each department to
plough its own furrow, and efforts to coordinate
the diverse interests of specialists imbued in a
specific functional practice can be exceedingly
wasteful of managerial time and effort. The larger
the company the worse the problem becomes.

Firms with broadly differentiated product lines
frequently organise their marketing functions of a
product or product group basis. This form of
structure, depicted in Figure 19.2, is only viable
where each product or product group generates
sufficient sales volume to justify the inevitable

duplication of effort. Consequently, this form of
structure is usually found in large, decentralised
companies, where each division is concerned with
the manufacture of a specialised product and may
be regarded as a strategic business unit or SBU.

As an alternative to a product orientation, the
hypothetical firm illustrated in Figure 19.2 might
prefer to organise on a market or customer basis,
when its organisation chart would appear as
shown in Figure 19.3.

A regional marketing organisation is most
frequently found in the case of a large, decentralised company with extensive markets capable of
subdivision into distinct geographical units. It is
particularly appropriate to multinational firms
but, in common with the product and market
structure, it suffers from duplication of effort, and
problems of communication and coordination.

Figure 19.3 *Market-oriented organisation*

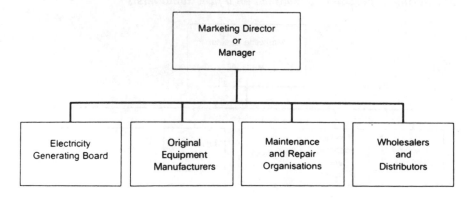

In an attempt to overcome these defects, many firms have adopted a line and staff structure which seeks to combine the benefits of functional specialisation with the varying demands of different products and markets. Currently there is considerable debate about the relative merits of organising on a product or market basis and some discussion is appropriate here.

The product manager concept

It is often implied that the product manager concept is of recent origin but there is evidence to suggest that General Electric had adopted such a title in the United States as early as 1894, while Libby, McNeil & Libby claim to have appointed product managers in 1919. Generally, however, the introduction of the concept is credited to its leading exponent, Procter & Gamble, who appointed a brand manager for Lava soap in 1928. (Product manager and brand manager are interchangeable terms for the same basic function.)

Essentially, the product manager's function is to coordinate all activities associated with the marketing of a given product – a function which became critical with the adoption of a product differentiation as a major dimension of competitive strategy. Opinions differ as to the precise responsibilities and authority of the product manager but, in general, it is possible to discern four major activities:

1. *Planning.* At the tactical level the product manager is usually responsible for the preparation of detailed plans for the marketing of his product, for example the preparation of budgets and determination of the precise mix of marketing inputs. At the strategic level he is responsible for anticipating change and the preparation of plans to deal effectively with this change, for example new product development.
2. *Information seeking and evaluation.* In order to anticipate change it is necessary continually to scan the environment and monitor the strength and direction of relevant trends. Specifically, this involves keeping track of competitors' activities in the widest sense; that is, one must not only keep informed about directly competing substitutes but also attempt to identify the less immediate threat implicit in new products and processes. Equally, one must be sensitive to marketing innovations such as the development of automatic vending machines, systems selling, and so on.
3. *Coordination.* As the product 'expert', it is the product manager's responsibility to coordinate all those company functions which impinge upon the successful marketing of that product. Of all the functions, this presents the greatest challenge to the product manager as it inevitably requires him to be all things to all men. On the other hand these are the same skills required of top managers, and the product manager position can prove a valuable training and proving ground for senior appointments.
4. *Control.* This function not only incorporates the familiar price/cost and budgetary dimensions but also includes the introduction of new products and the phasing out of old products.

No valid generalisation can be offered as to the relative importance attached to these four activities in practice as, of necessity, this will vary from firm to firm.

In an article 'Product Management versus Market Management', Michael J. Thomas (1982) looked at the role of the product manager and commented:

A long-time complaint of most product managers is that they are given responsibility without commensurate authority. But companies who have been filling product manager positions with younger, less experienced people have had to question how much responsibility should be delegated to their product managers. Responsibility often has been assigned for achievement of sales volume, market share, and sometimes profit goals but the product manager has no line authority over the functional departments that execute his plans.

Yet, we know that product management works to the satisfaction of many companies. The key to understanding why is found in the expertise of the product manager. He knows more about his product and the marketing plan that supports it than anyone else, and this expert power is the source of his being able to enlist the support of others. Thus the product manager is 'a recommender, a coordinator, and a watchdog who keeps an eye on his product and market place and sounds the alert when danger or opportunity arises' (Richard M. Clewett and Stanley F. Stasch, 1975, in 'Shifting Role of the Product Manager').

■ Market managers

As with any organisational innovation, the product manager system has not enjoyed unqualified success and many firms that adopted such a system during the first flush of enthusiasm in the late 1950s have since discarded it. In those instances where the product manager system has 'failed', examination usually reveals that the company was fundamentally unsuited to such an organisational structure. In a company like Procter & Gamble which is producing a group of nearly identical products from the same manufacturing facility, all of which are to be sold through the same distributive outlets, the product manager system ensures that each brand is given the individual attention it needs. On the other hand, where a company is selling the same product into a number of different end-use markets, emphasis on the product will be inappropriate. As noted earlier, the concept of market segmentation rests on the proposition that there are differences in the needs, and buying behaviour, of subgroups which collectively comprise the aggregate demand for a product. From this it follows that a different marketing strategy will be appropriate to each segment, which, in turn, predicates the appointment of market managers.

In the author's opinion the appointment of a market manager represents the purest implementation of the marketing concept, for it is implicit that consumer requirements will take precedence over all other activities. It is an overt recognition that different market segments represent distinct, and often dissimilar, needs, not only in terms of precise product specification but also in terms of service requirements and buying behaviour. Further, in the case of industrial goods, it recognises that many buyers have a need for a series of related products which may usefully be combined into a 'system'; for example, National Cash Registers do not just sell business machines, they sell accounting 'systems' tailor-made to the end-user's specific requirements. Emphasis on the product may well result in the employment of salesmen specialising in given products and thus miss out on such opportunities.

As a broad generalisation it would seem that where customer buying habits are conditioned by the nature of the product and are similar across industry or user categories, then the responsibility for marketing should be vested in a product manager. Conversely, if it is possible to distinguish marked differences in the needs or buying behaviour of separate customer groups, then these should be regarded as different markets and market managers appointed.

However, as Michael Thomas (1982) points out in the article cited earlier, it would be a mistake to assume that the product-manager and market-manager approaches are mutually exclusive options. Thus:

> When companies have a variety of products channelling to a variety of markets, neither the product manager approach not the market manager approach alone is appropriate. This is a situation when a dual management approach could be utilised. If the product manager is used alone, it is very unlikely that he will be able to collect data and utilise market information for the entire market. On the other hand, if the market manager is used, he well most likely be concerned with the welfare of his own market and not care about anyone else's. He may want all the products and attention for his own market which can have a damaging effect on other markets and, in turn, on the overall effectiveness of the company.

Clearly, running product managers and market managers in tandem is a potential source of conflict, but Thomas and others regard this as a positive force which can be beneficial if managed correctly. Thomas cites B. Charles Ames (1971) who offers six rules for achieving this:

1. Determine the need for dual management;
2. Define each manager's role;
3. Change the information and planning systems;
4. Select the right candidates;
5. Explain the concept to key functional managers;
6. Monitor the activities of both product and market managers.   (pp. 66–74)

Provided one can achieve and control the kind of matrix organisation which is required for such a dual management system, then 'The benefits of increased market opportunities, stronger competitive position, and, in the long run, greater profits far outweigh the added costs and conflict that will arise with its use' (Thomas, 1982). Table 19.1 taken from Nigel Piercy's (1985) book *Marketing Organisation* summarises well the advantages and disadvantages of various kinds of marketing structures.

Table 19.1 *Comparison of marketing structures*

Form	Advantages	Disadvantages	Situational indicators
Functional	Specialisation in task activities to develop skills. Marketing tasks and responsibilities clearly defined	Excess levels of hierarchy may reduce unity control. Direct lines of communication may be ignored. Conflicts may emerge. Integration problem for CME	Simple marketing operations. Single primary product/ market
Product/brand	Specialisation in products/ brands. More management attention to marketing requirements of different products/brands. Fast reaction to product-related change	Dual reporting. Too much product emphasis. More management levels and cost. Conflict	Wide product lines sold to homogeneous groups of customers, but sharing production/ marketing systems – i.e. proliferation of brands and diversified products requiring different skills/activities
Market/customer/ geographical	Specialisation in a market entity – focus on customer needs. Fast reaction to market-related changes	Duplication of functions. Co-ordination problems. More management levels	Limited, standardised homogeneous product line sold to customers in different industries – i.e. proliferation of markets each meriting separate efforts
Product/market overlay	Advantages of functional product and market specialisation and integration	Allocation of responsibilities is difficult. Duplication inefficiencies	Multiple products and multiple markets

Source: Nigel Piercy (1985), *Marketing Organisation* (London: George Allen & Unwin).

The impact of marketing on organisational structure

In the organisational context, marketing may be viewed as both a function and a philosophy. All firms have marketing function, even if it only involves selecting an intermediary to sell their output, but not all firms have a marketing philosophy as embodied in the marketing concept and described in Chapter 1. Unfortunately, the distinction between the function and the philosophy is rarely stated explicitly, and has resulted in considerable misunderstanding and even acrimony.

As a function, marketing is no more, nor less, important than finance, legal, personnel, production, purchasing, research and development, or any other conceivable area of specialisation. In a given context it is only natural that more emphasis will be accorded to a specific function, which will tend to predominate over the others, but there is nothing to predicate that it will, or should, be marketing. The widely held misconception that marketers are seeking to take over other functional areas is a myth, albeit one fostered by the profession, which largely owes its existence to the high 'visibility' of marketing in the consumer goods field. Even so, firms manufacturing private brands will probably place far greater emphasis on production economies and quality control than on marketing. In the industrial goods field this tendency will be even more pronounced.

As a business philosophy, marketing requires the firm to do what it has always set out to do – combine the resources at its disposal in the manner which will best enable it to achieve its long-run profit goals. What distinguishes it from other business philosophies is that marketing perceives consumption as a democratic process in which consumers have the right to select preferred candidates and elect them by casting their money votes. As the political critics of marketing, and advertising in particular, should appreciate, you may delude the electorate once with spurious campaign promises but you had better not seek re-election. Further, unless you propose policies of which they approve you will have to give way to the candidate who does.

In the democratic environment of a free enterprise economy, success comes to the firm which sets out to discover the nature of human wants and develops products to satisfy such wants in highly specific ways. Satisfying customers can only be achieved through the concerted efforts of all members of the organisation recognising this as a common goal and working towards it. Thus, the production manager who insists on maximising productivity, in the conventional sense of maximum volume at lowest cost, by excluding non-standard items from his production schedule lacks a marketing orientation. He fails to see that the non-standard item might develop into a market leader, or that the fact that his salesman cannot offer it will predispose the firm's largest customer to switch to the company that can. Conversely, the production manager who balances the conventional criteria against such considerations is marketing oriented, despite his function and job title.

Acceptance of the marketing concept by individuals is insufficient in itself to make the firm marketing oriented – it must also develop an organisational structure that will permit it to translate thought into action. In today's increasingly competitive environment this demands that the firm be more creative and flexible than in the past; specifically, it requires:

- That the firm continually scan the business environment; that is, the firm must develop its own early warning system so that it is in a position not only to meet change but also to initiate it.
- That the firm utilise incoming data to formulate creative plans stating not only what it wishes to achieve, but also how and in what sequence.
- That these plans be communicated effectively to those charged with the responsibility for their implementation, and that such responsibility be backed with the necessary resources and authority.

- That the firm make full use of new managerial techniques developed to assist the decision-maker in arriving at an informed decision, for example management science and Bayesian decision theory.

At a given point in time, however, the firm's immediate success depends on its existing product line. If previous planning has been effective the production and sale of these products should be routine and demand a functional organisation. As noted, however, planning and new product development are problem-solving activities for which a functional structure is unsuited and some form of compromise structure is called for.

One solution is the setting up of project teams comprised of representatives from each of the functional departments (sometimes referred to as a 'matrix' organisation). Such a team may be formed on an *ad hoc* basis to suggest solutions to a particular problem, or to review suggestions from functional departments. Alternatively, the team may be established on a permanent basis and function as a separate department; for example, some companies have set up Long-range Planning Departments, New Product Development Departments and so on.

Another solution is evident in the trend to what has been termed 'recentralised decentralisation'. During the 1950s concepts such as the 'span of control' predisposed the management of large, diversified companies to decentralise authority on a divisional basis. Under this system each division operates virtually as a separate company, and sets up its own production and marketing

organisations. In many instances, however, the benefits of specialisation were negated by diseconomies arising from duplication of effort and poor coordination, and prompted top management to recentralise certain functions at corporate headquarters. Foremost among these are purchasing and marketing. Centralised purchasing offers clear benefits due to the economics of bulk buying, while centralised marketing services permit greater specialisation and the development of a consistent marketing approach across the whole field of the firm's activities.

Some indication of the preferred form of marketing organisation is to be found in the findings of a survey undertaken by Hooley *et al.* (1984) as shown in Table 19.2.

The extent to which a firm can improve its competitive standing through organisational change is, in the final analysis, conditioned by the resources at its disposal and some reference to this dimension is called for.

The protracted recession of the late 1980s and early 1990s has had a considerable impact on organisational structure. As technological innovation and information technology have had their impact upon the production and manufacturing function, the numbers employed have declined significantly with a consequential increase of the numbers employed in service industries. In parallel with this switch in emphasis there has been a much wider acceptance of the marketing concept and recognition that this requires the organisation to develop relationships with its customers. To develop effective relationships firms must meet the expectations of their

Table 19.2 *How is your marketing organised?*

	Total sample (1298)	Better performers (160)	Others (1138)	Better performer variation from others
All products under one manager	40.7%	30.0%	42.2%	−21%
Separate product managers	15.9%	17.5%	15.7%	+11%
Separate market managers	12.6%	16.9%	12.0%	+41%
A combination of the above	30.8%	35.6%	30.1%	+18%

Source: G. J. Hooley, C. J. West and J. E. Lynch (1984), *Marketing in the UK: A Survey of Current Practices and Performance*, The Institute of Marketing.

customers and this requires them to devote much greater effort to establishing their needs (marketing research), to add value by building quality into the product or service (total quality management) and to providing additional services to add value in consumption (after sales service and customer care).

The establishment and maintenance of mutually satisfying exchange relationships (our preferred definition of marketing) calls for a new approach to organisational structure. Two important aspects of this have been delayering and empowerment. By delayering is meant the reduction in the number of hierarchical levels to achieve flatter structures with less psychological distance between senior management and other employees. By empowerment is meant the willingness to devolve responsibility to the individual employee who, ultimately, is responsible for the quality of the firm's products and actions/relationships.

In turn these changes have led to a reduction, or even elimination, of specialist service departments such as strategic planning. There is also evidence that some firms are greatly reducing their functional marketing departments, based on the belief that marketing is everybody's business, and giving increased attention to what has been termed 'internal marketing' in the belief that every employee is another's 'customer' and should behave accordingly.

The extent to which a firm can improve its competitive standing through organisational change is, in the final analysis, conditioned by the resources at its disposal and some reference to this dimension is called for.

Corporate culture and resources

In this chapter it has only been possible to look at the organisation of the marketing function in a superficial way when, as many readers will know, the topics of organisation design and development are the subject of books and courses in their own right. Before leaving the issue, however, it is vital to stress that, while organisational forms and structures may have an important part to play in determining a firm's efficiency and performance, as we saw in Chapter 3, it is the corporate culture which most often determines whether a firm will succeed or fail in the market place.

Although the concepts of climate and corporate culture have been around for several decades (indeed I used them myself in the 1960s and 1970s when researching innovativeness (see *Marketing New Industrial Products*, 1975) it is only in the 1980s and 1990s that they have moved to centre stage with the recognition that it is the 'people factor' which ultimately determines the quality of a firm's performance. Given the accelerating pace of technological change and the growth in telecommunications it is now estimated that even radical innovations will be diffused world-wide within 18 months of their first appearance. Maintaining a differential advantage in terms of the actual product or service has become increasingly difficult even in multinational corporations firmly committed to a policy of continuous new product development. Indeed, it is this very commitment which results in the rapid erosion of tangible product advantages and leads to shorter and shorter life-cycles. Under these circumstances it is the relationship between a supplier and user which is critical to user patronage and loyalty. In turn, the maintenance of the relationship depends upon the commitment and quality of the implementation by the supplier.

The validity of this claim has been borne out by the findings of numerous management books published in the 1980s based upon both anecdotal and rigourous survey based research (see, for example Peters and Waterman, 1982, *In Search of Excellence*; McBurnie and Clutterbuck, 1987, *The Marketing Edge*; and Baker and Hart, 1989, *Marketing and Competitive Success*). It is also the central theme in Stephen King's (1991) article 'Brand Building in the 1990s', in which he argues that the absence of objective differences will make consumers increasingly dependent upon the company 'brand'. He argues:

It's arguable that in a competitive situation getting the company brand right is the most important job for the management. Equally, it's clear that not many companies have organised their management structures with that in mind.

The companies behind the classic brands are not by any means a good model (indeed they may be increasingly wrong for their own purposes). They tend to rely too much on the traditional 'family tree' type hierarchy. That means they are too split by function to lead naturally to the innovation and imagination that any brand constantly needs. Decisions tend to be made too tactically, too low down in the organisation, with too little guidance from the top.

The right organisation for a company brand implies that brand management should reside right at the top. And since inventive organisations tend to be based on small, flexible, interactive, multidisciplinary working groups, I think that our model (at a symbolic, rather than organisation chart, level) should be something like the figure on the following page (Figure 19.4).

The skills needed for this management working group would be those of *production* (the organisation and efficient running of the company's products/ services); *personnel* (recruitment/training/inspiring of the people who make up the corporate brand);

communications (all aspects of communications, marketing and consumer/customer research); and possibly as a separate skill that of *brand designer* a new type of animal, concerned with design in its broadest sense (Lorenz, 1986), from R&D to adding services to products and vice versa, with a passion for the totality of the brand). The whole group to be led by the *CEO* – he's the real brand *manager*.

However, such a model is translated into reality, it seems to me that many companies need to take a new look at their organisation charts, with brand-building in mind. Most authorities (e.g. Pascale and Athos, 1981; Doyle, Saunders and Wong, 1990) seem to agree what there will have to be a more flexible and less hierarchical approach, with more informal networking, in order to get the rapid response and to attract the rare skills that a successful company brand needs.

It clearly goes a lot further than organisation. What the best company brands represent is a common culture – common aims, standards, language, approaches and style. A common personality, rather than a book of rules. This may sound a little abstract and qualitative, but it is what consumers value in company brands (IBM, ICI or Marks & Spencer, for

Figure 19.4 *New brand management*

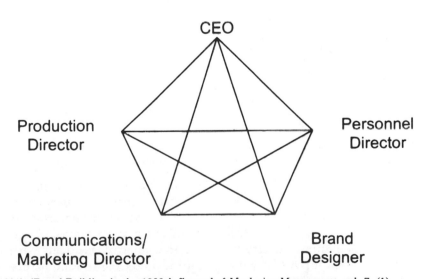

Source: S. King (1991), 'Brand Building in the 1990s', *Journal of Marketing Management*, vol. 7, (1).

instance). That puts an enormous premium on sheer leadership from the top (Hamel and Prahalad, 1989). A company brand cannot succeed if the individuals doing the detailed work are zombies who aren't allowed to take any initiatives. Equally, it will not be a brand at all if there are no common links or if they don't know how they're expected to behave.

Implicit in all of this is the belief that it is the truly marketing oriented company which is most likely to have the kind of corporate culture which will ensure that its objectives match precisely those of its intended customers.

☐ *Corporate resources*

The resources which a company has at its disposal are of two main types – human and physical. Such resources may be internal to the organisation, or they may be external to it in the sense that the firm can gain or exercise control over them, for example the distributive channel.

Within the firm, resources, both human and physical, tend to be specific, and so limit the possible range of production and marketing activities which the firm can undertake. In the long run, however, the firm can change its 'resource mix', and the aim of planning is to determine:

- What activities will maximise the productivity of existing resources?
- What markets offer the greatest potential in future?
- What changes need to be made in the present resource mix to enable the firm to exploit these future opportunities?

Clearly, the answers to these questions must be based on an analysis of existing resources, which will be facilitated by the use of a check-list on the following lines:

1. *Physical resources*
   - Land
     - as a source of raw materials.
     - as a location for manufacturing and distributive activities.
   - Buildings – general purpose or specific, i.e. designed for light engineering, assembly, storage, etc., or for heavy manufacturing requiring special foundations, services, etc.
   - Availability of and access to
     - power supplies, drainage and waste disposal
     - transportation: road, rail, canal, port facilities, etc.
   - Plant equipment
     - general purpose, e.g. lathe, press
     - specific, e.g. steel rolling mill, foundry, etc.

2. *Technical resources.* Essentially these reside in the technical expertise of the firm's employees, together with the possession of patents, licences or highly specialised equipment.
3. *Financial resources.* These are comprised of the liquid assets in the firm's balance sheet, the ability to secure loans against fixed assets and the ability to raise capital in the market on the basis of past and anticipated future performance. They also comprise the skill of the firm's financial management.
4. *Purchasing resources.* Managerial expertise backed by any special advantage enjoyed by the firm by virtue of its size or connection; for example reciprocal trading agreements.
5. *Labour resources.* The skills, experience and adaptability of the work force.
6. *Marketing resources.* The degree of consumer/user acceptance or 'franchise' developed through past performance. Access to and degree of control over distribution, the specialised skills and experiences of its personnel.

The above list is by no means exhaustive but serves to indicate the factors the firm must take into account when appraising its own ability to undertake a given course of action. Clearly, the importance attached to any particular factor will depend upon the unique nature of the problem under consideration.

Summary

In this chapter we have looked at some of the more important factors which influence the role and positioning of marketing within an organisation. In doing so we have returned to the distinction developed initially in Chapter 1 that marketing is both a philosophy of business and a business function. Ironically, as more organisations accept the former proposition so the importance of the marketing function becomes more widely diffused through the organisation. This leads, in turn, to a lesser emphasis upon the formal marketing department. Indeed, the new organisational structures of the 1990s place emphasis upon organisations as networks rather than hierarchies.

An authoritative and up-to-date discussion of these changes and trends is to be found in the *Companion Encyclopedia of Marketing* (Piercy and Cravens, 1995) in which the authors (Piercy and Cravens) summarise some of the most significant organisational implications of environmental and strategic change in marketing as follows:

1. Breaking hierarchies – speed and flexibility come from reducing organizational levels and numbers of employees, creating smaller business units, and empowering line manage-ment to manage key business processes (Quinn, 1992; Doyle, 1994).
2. Self-managing teams – critical changes will be managed by groups with complementary skills (see Katzenbach and Smith, 1993), in the form of high-performance multi-functional teams to achieve fast precise and flexible execution of programmes (Quinn, 1992), possibly organized around market segments (Schultz, 1993), and possibly temporary (Doyle, 1994) – perhaps in the form of the 'collateral' or 'supplemental' organization like the task force for the major innovation (Huber, 1984).
3. Reengineering – critical organizational processes will be radically restructured to reduce cost and increase speed and flexibility (see Hamner and Champney, 1993) and to improve responsiveness to customers (Quinn, 1992).
4. Transnational organizations – competing globally requires more complex structures and new skills (see Barlett and Ghoshal, 1989).
5. Learning organizations – organizations will require the continual upgrading of skills and the corporate knowledge-base (Doyle, 1994), leading to the adding of value for customers through knowledge feedback to create competitive advantage (Quinn, 1992).
6. Account management – customer focus may be achieved by structural mechanisms (Schultz, 1993; Doyle, 1994).

Source: *Companion Encyclopedia of Marketing*, ed. Michael J. Baker (1995), p. 263.

Readers seeking further information should consult this source and the further readings suggested in it.

Review questions and problems

1. Distinguish the salient differences between the functional and product forms of organisational structure. Under what circumstances is each to be preferred?
2. What is the 'product manager concept'? Name five firms which have adopted this concept. (See the classified ads for clues!)

3. How does the concept of market management differ from product management? When is the former organisational structure to be preferred?

4. What distinguishes the marketing oriented firm from those which have not adopted the marketing concept?

5. Using published data, e.g. annual reports, articles in the trade press, etc., and/or personal knowledge/experience, summarise the corporate resources of a major manufacturing company. Based on your summary, what recommendations would you make to the firm's top management concerning its future strategy, i.e. on what markets/products should it concentrate its efforts?

6. Discuss the proposition that the position of the marketing department in the total organisation is particularly difficult because of the types of conflicts which tend to occur between the logic of customer satisfaction and the cost minimisation logic pursued by other departments.

7. The system of organising marketing divisions around the job of the brand manager, or product manager, has recently been widely criticised. What criticisms of this system would you expect to be valid in practice, and what opportunities does this system offer for more effective marketing management?

8. The marketing function is so central to the company's continued success that it requires to be carefully controlled by those in charge of the company. Outline a comprehensive system of such controls on marketing to ensure top management retain the responsibility with which they are charged.

9. Indicate the types of conflict which might arise in a firm employing sales, marketing and product managers and the ways in which these might be organisationally resolved.

10. Write a job description for a product manager in either:

    (a) A typical company making products for industry;

    (b) A typical consumer goods company.

11. In what ways would the Marketing Manager of a large company be able to do a more effective job if they were appointed to the Board as Marketing Director? How would their responsibilities change?

12. It should be possible to assess the extent of a company's commitment to marketing by looking at its organisation chart. Discuss.

13. Companies differ greatly in the organisation of their marketing functions. Discuss these differences and explain the reasons for them.

14. How does a production/sales based business organisation differ from a marketing-based one?

15. Discuss the organisational implications of a company progressing from being sales oriented to being marketing oriented.

16. Consider the scope and duties of the product manager in his/her relationship with one of the following organisational functions:

    (a) Research & Development;

    (b) Sales Force;

    (c) Manufacturing.

17. Review some of the characteristics of new organisational designs and assess their implications for marketing strategy.

■ Supplementary reading list

Peircy, Nigel (1985) *Marketing Organisation* (London: George Allen & Unwin).

Piercy, Nigel (1992) *Market Led Strategic Change* (Oxford: Butterworth-Heinemann).

■ *Chapter 20* ■

Planning for Marketing

Contents

Learning goals

The issues to be discussed in this chapter include:

1. The concept of corporate strategy.
2. The nature of the marketing audit.
3. The preparation of marketing plans.
4. Financial measures for marketing analysis and control.

After reading this chapter you will be familiar with:

1. The nature of corporate strategy and the key phases in the strategic process – appreciation, plan and implementation.

2. The design and execution of marketing audits.
3. The design, layout and content of a formal marketing plan.
4. The calculation of mark-ups, discounts and stock turn.
5. The application of standard costing and budgetary control to marketing planning.
6. Ratio analysis and its use in competitive analysis.

■ Introduction

Planning is a pervasive human activity by which we seek to exercise some degree of control over the future. As a process it will vary enormously depending upon a number of variables, foremost among which will be the complexity of the activity and the degree of uncertainty concerning the future situation in which the activity will take place. Fundamentally, however, all planning seeks to arrive at a present decision concerning future action – the more complex the activity and the more uncertain the future, the greater the need for formal, systematic planning procedures. The purpose of this chapter is to provide a brief synthesis of the separate treatment given the marketing environment and the various mix elements, and to indicate how the marketer can integrate all these considerations into a marketing plan. It must be stressed that this is the briefest of introductions to a large and complex subject, which is dealt with at length in *Marketing Strategy and Management* (Baker, 1991) which was written specifically for those students who have completed an introductory course of the kind provided for by this text. Marketing planning does not figure in such introductory courses and the brief discussion provided here is intended solely to emphasise the point that the various marketing functions described earlier need to be seen as part of a coherent and integrated action plan if they are to be used effectively.

The concept of corporate strategy

Some reference has already been made to the concept of corporate strategy, as, for example, when discussing new product development, but some elaboration is necessary here. Like marketing, corporate strategy is an old concept in a new and revitalised form. Probably the most important distinction between strategy as practised by earlier generations of entrepreneurs and today's professional managers is that the latter consciously and explicitly state their aims and objectives and develop plans designed to achieve them.

In his book *Strategy and Structure*, Alfred D. Chandler (1962) defines corporate strategy as 'The determination of the basic long-term goals and objectives of an enterprise, and the adoption of courses of action and the allocation of resources necessary for carrying out these goals'.

This definition suggests three distinct phases in the strategic process:

- Appreciation;
- Plan;
- Implementation.

Each of these stages is capable of further subdivision, and Kotler (1988) in *Marketing Management*, 6th edn offers the following progression:

- Diagnosis: where is the company now, and why?
- Prognosis: where is the company headed?
- Objectives: where should the company be headed?
- Strategy: what is the best way to get there?
- Tactics: what specific actions should be undertaken, by whom, and when?
- Control: what measures should be watched to indicate whether the company is succeeding?

Similarly, the Marketing Science Institute (see Patrick J. Robinson and David J. Luck, 1964) has developed a model called APACS (Adaptive Planning and Control Sequence) which recognises the following stages which were first discussed in Chapter 7, namely:

- Step 1.   Define problem and set objectives.
- Step 2.   Appraise overall situation.
- Step 3.   Determine the tasks to be accomplished and identify the means to achieving these aims.
- Step 4.   Identify alternative plans and mixes.
- Step 5.   Estimate the expected results arising from implementation of the alternative plans.
- Step 6.   Managerial review and decision.
- Step 7.   Feedback of results and post audit.
- Step 8.   Adapt programme if required.

In turn, each of these models is capable of further subdivision, but the basic three-stage model will serve our purposes here.

Appreciation: the marketing audit

This section builds on the ideas first introduced in Chapter 3. In 1959 the American Marketing Association published an extensive management report entitled 'Analysing and Improving Marketing Performance: Marketing Audits in Theory & Practice'. While much has been written since, this still remains the most comprehensive treatment of the subject and provides the framework for this section.

According to Edward B. Reynolds (1959):

The term 'audit' is generally understood in business usage to mean a review or appraisal of some business function or activity. As a management tool, it is traditionally used to determine the accuracy and adequacy of accounting and financial operations ... In the field of marketing, however, the application of the audit technique as a device for evaluating not only the operational aspects of marketing but also the philosophy and policies upon which marketing operations are based is still a far from common practice.

This is certainly not the case today in marketing where auditing is also used as a device for evaluating possible future courses of action in addition to its traditional role as a means of assessing past performance. Thus, while audits first came into use as a diagnostic device for sick and ailing companies they are now used by many organisations for a regular 'check-up'.

In his Introduction, Reynolds discerns a wide range of views on the nature and practice of the audit but identifies general agreement on four basic points:

1. A planned review is an essential requirement not only for the company in difficulty but also for the company enjoying an apparently sound marketing operation.
2. The evaluation of the marketing operation must be all inclusive, involving not only every marketing activity and every marketing practice but also the underlying marketing philosophy and policies upon which these activities and practices are based.
3. The most significant requirement for successful appraisal is the establishment of valid and realistic standards of performance.
4. The evaluation process must not confine itself to the marketing operation as it exists today but must range into the future to explore untapped marketing possibilities.

Subsequently, Abe Schuchman (1959) argued that it is important to distinguish the marketing audit from the continuous evaluations which executives make of the various marketing mix functions, on the grounds that such appraisals are far too limited in scope and are not undertaken in a planned and coherent fashion. 'They do not, within a specified interval, examine each and every facet of the *total* operation. There is no integrated, co-ordinated, comprehensive appraisal encompassing all marketing activities and executed systematically in accord with a planned program and schedule.' Thus he defines a marketing audit as:

a systematic, critical, and impartial review and appraisal of the total marketing operation: of the basic objectives and policies of the operation and the assumptions which underlie them as well as of the methods, procedures, personnel, and organisation employed to implement the policies and achieve the objectives.

Schuchman also emphasises that the marketing audit is a prognostic as well as a diagnostic tool:

The audit is, in addition, concerned with identifying the particular strengths of the marketing operation. It is a search for opportunities, existing and potential ...

Continued success requires continual adaptation to a constantly changing environment. It requires, therefore, continual scrutiny of the environment and of the firm's relationship to the environment, with the aim of spotting the ones which indicate both a need for modifying the firm's marketing program and the direction such modification should take. It requires an unremitting search for emerging opportunities that can and must be exploited if the marketing operation is to remain highly successful.

The need to implement a formal programme of market auditing is that otherwise marginal adjustments to facets of the mix may well result, collectively, in the operation getting out of synchronisation with its environment; that is, there is a difference between 'fine tuning' and 'tinkering'. Similarly, auditing needs to be continuous: 'in marketing as in home maintenance the time to fix the roof is when the sun is shining'.

Schuchman (1959) also identifies several problems associated with auditing:

1. Defining appropriate criteria or measures for assessing the effectiveness of the mix elements and marketing activity.
2. Selection of auditors.
3. Scheduling the audit.
4. The impact of the audit.

Alfred R. Oxenfeld in 'The Marketing Audit as a Total Evaluation Program' (1975) argues that in the absence of a formal plan of evaluation some aspects will be appraised frequently and possibly at excessive costs while some phases of the business go unappraised for very long periods – often until the company is experiencing serious difficulties. Accordingly, a marketing audit must comprise the review of objectives, policies, organisation, methods, procedures and personnel in a total evaluation programme. He then proposes five broad approaches:

1. Audits classified by major marketing functions;
2. Audits classified by managerial aspects;
3. Audits classified by standards of appraisal;
4. Audits classified by frequency of evaluation;
5. Audits classified by sources of evaluation.

In auditing the marketing mix it is essential to do this in an integrated way so that the contribution of the individual elements may be related to each other and not just looked at in isolation. In the latter case it is quite likely that optimising on one dimension will lead to sub-optimisation on others and it is the maximum overall effect which is being looked for. In other words, one is seeking to achieve the optimum 'balance' between the various mix elements while, at the same time, one is monitoring them for incipient problems.

Auditing in terms of the major managerial aspects of the marketing function(s) is complementary to the auditing of the actual functions themselves, and should be executed in terms of the six dimensions (objectives and so forth) identified previously.

When auditing the objectives of a given activity one should ask the manager responsible to give you an explicit statement. Frequently such statements reveal important differences in emphasis and approach and it is essential to ensure that such differences do not render specific objectives incompatible with each other or with the overall purpose of the organisation. In a recent consultancy assignment for a national non-profit organisation, it was found that Headquarter's concern with the level of subsidy required by its operational units which had led to exhortations to these units to increase their revenue generation activities, was diametrically opposed to the objective that the units give priority access to designated users at nominal charges – that is, the direct opposite of normal commercial practice whereby priority is given to those able and willing to pay the highest price, and surplus capacity is sold off at marginal rates. Clearly, until one resolves such a contradiction of scrambled objectives, operating managers will be unable to determine the appropriate policies and tactics for the management of the function or operation for which they are responsible.

As Oxenfeld notes, it is sometimes difficult to distinguish sharply between objectives and policies in practice, but in principle the difference is clear. 'Objectives represent goals and targets; policies represent broad principles which indicate how management believes these goals can best be achieved, and therefore are guides for decision and action.' Such a distinction underlines the desirability of seeking to specify objectives and policies with the greatest possible clarity in order to avoid confusion between ends and the means of achieving them.

Once the objectives and means of achieving them are clear the auditor must seek to determine whether the remaining four elements of organisation, methods, procedures and personnel are appropriate to each sub-function, such as advertising and sales, as well as to the marketing function overall.

The third approach to classifying marketing audits suggested by Oxenfeldt is in terms of the standards of appraisal used. By definition auditing is a process of making comparisons, usually between current and past achievement, so that one can assess the rate and direction of change in the parameters being evaluated. In turn such an analysis is an essential prerequisite to the formulation of future objectives against which performance can be evaluated.

In making a comparative analysis one may use both quantitative and qualitative methods and there is a fairly vigorous debate about which is most appropriate in what circumstances. The nature of the argument is well exemplified by the comparisons which many academics and managers make between leading business schools, such that Harvard is seen as being concerned with a qualitative emphasis upon judgemental decision-making while Chicago stresses precise measurement and quantitative analysis. In turn this leads commentators to classify Harvard as a school for general (line) managers and Chicago as a school for specialist (staff) managers. Of course, what the example points out is that you can make comparisons by emphasising differences while, at the same time or for other purposes, one could easily have stressed similarities and argued that Harvard and Chicago are identical in that they are first-rate business schools. As in most things the truth lies somewhere in between and an effective marketing audit will call for a judicious blend of both quantitative measurement and qualitative judgements. That said, there is much to be said for seeking to quantify subjective and judgemental appraisals through the use of Bayesian analysis as described in Chapter 10.

A further factor which has to be taken into account when devising marketing audits is the frequency of evaluation. The basic guide here must surely be the cost effectiveness of the auditing procedure, and one must beware of dissipating managerial time upon the collection of data for its own sake. Similarly one must not gravitate to the other extreme of assuming that managers are paid to make judgements and so need not dwell upon facts.

Finally, Oxenfeldt addresses the question of who should carry out the auditing function (source of evaluation). Five basic alternatives suggest themselves.

First, auditing may be considered the responsibility of the person in overall charge of an activity – 'auditing from above'. Second, one may invite a person from another functional area but at the same level in the organisation. Third, one can commission a 'task force' of individuals from various other areas in the organisation. Fourth, one can adopt a scheme of self-appraisal. And finally, one can bring in outside consultants to carry out the task. Each of these alternatives has its merits and demerits but as a general principle an audit is only likely to enjoy the confidence of a management group if it is actually involved in the auditing process itself to some degree. That said, most authors prefer a task force approach where this is feasible (usually restricted to large companies) followed by the use of external consultants. Where a company is attempting a marketing audit for the first time and needs to establish both a base line (where we are today) and a procedure for implementing auditing on a continuous basis, then it is unlikely to possess the necessary expertise from within its own ranks and so will prefer to commission an experienced consultant to perform the task.

In the same manner that an overall management audit is an essential prerequisite of corporate planning, so the marketing audit is an essential prerequisite of marketing planning. In making this implied distinction, that corporate and marketing planning are different, one must be sensitive to the issue raised in Chapter 1 concerning the difference between the marketing concept and the marketing function. Following this distinction, all marketers and the great majority of successful managers would argue that in setting its corporate objectives the organisation should give priority to the needs of the market – in other words the corporate plan should be marketing orientated. However, this does not make it a marketing plan for, to be strictly accurate, such a plan is concerned with the management of the marketing function per se and its interface with the other functional areas of the business. These other functional areas will have management plans of their own (R&D, Purchasing, Production, Finance), each of which will be designed to implement the overall corporate plan. By the same token a corporate management audit will involve an evaluation of all the functional areas and go far beyond the scope of a marketing audit internally. Externally, however, the position is very different and it is this which sometimes leads people to perceive corporate and marketing audits and plans as being the same thing.

Because it is through the market that the organisation seeks to realise its objectives, much of its external evaluation of threats and opportunities is highly consonant with the primary concerns of the marketing function. Such distinction as one would make would tend to emphasise the corporate analysis of its environment as being conducted at a macro level while the external marketing audit is largely concerned with micro aspects. However, to conduct a micro analysis of, say, brand shares it is necessary to have some feeling of the status of the market itself and whether it is expanding, contracting or stationary *vis-à-vis* other competitive markets – namely, the macro position. For these reasons corporate and marketing audits of the external environment will possess a high degree of overlap although their emphasis will differ substantially. In the Appendix 'The Written Analysis of Cases' we return to some of the specific factors which might be looked at in both an internal and external audit.

■ Planning

At this stage in the process it is important to distinguish clearly between the environmental constraints within which the firm must operate and those activities over which it can exercise control. It is also important to recognise that in the long run all fixed constraints are variable in some degree – thus in the short term management must accept the existing distributive network, in the long term it can modify it through its own action, just as it can develop new markets and shape the nature of competition. However, in time the environment will change too, owing to

technological innovation and competitive activity, and the firm must seek to develop objectives which are sufficiently well defined to require commitment, yet flexible enough to permit a change in emphasis and direction as the situation evolves. 'Servicing the travelling public' is a good example of an overall long-term objective which meets these criteria. In the short term, the skill lies in developing strategies which make the best use of available resources in moving the firm from where it is to where it wants to be.

The statement in the preceding paragraph reflects the reality that most planning is undertaken by existing organisations which comprise a mix of assets, resources and skills which are being deployed to service an existing market and customer base. By contrast most textbooks tend to follow the opposite assumption that the planner is in a green field or new start-up situation and so can follow the best theoretical advice of first establishing a need and then organising resources and skills to satisfy it. This latter approach has the advantage that it allows one to spell out best practice (what is sometimes called the 'normative theory') and recommends what needs to be done in what sequence if the circumstances allow. Usually, however, this is a counsel of perfection and most managers spend their time seeking to identify opportunities which will enable them to make optimum use of existing strengths and resources while, at the same time, seeking to adjust the future direction of the firm to ensure that it will have the necessary resources and skills to avoid future threats and exploit future opportunities.

The normative theory of strategic marketing planning is a subject in its own right and the student should consult one of the specialised texts recommended in the Supplementary Reading List for further information and advice.

■ Implementation

In essence a strategy is a broad statement of the means to be employed in achieving a given objective, while the actual methods used constitute the tactics. Thus, a firm's strategy might be based on skimming the cream off the market, which suggests that the appropriate tactics would be:

- High product quality;
- Distinctive design and packaging;
- High price;
- Selective distribution;
- Direct sale;
- Extensive after-sales service;
- Low pressure advertising, etc.

At the risk of overstating the obvious, the success of a given strategy depends upon the coordination of the tactics into an integrated, complementary and cohesive whole. There is a finite number of alternative strategies open to the firm and, in a given market, it is usual to find several competing firms pursuing the same basic strategy simultaneously. If this is so, then observed variations in performance must arise out of the quality of the plan, or statement of tactics, and its execution. Factors such as motivation and morale have an important bearing on the execution of a plan, but also tend to be a function of the plan's quality and credibility.

The preparation of a marketing plan

If the author has segmented the textbook market correctly, many readers will be preparing for examinations, such as those set by the Chartered Institute of Marketing, which require the student to analyse a case study and prepare a written marketing plan. Hopefully, the following outline will help the student in preparing such an analysis.

Analysis of the situation: appreciation

There is little point in restating the descriptive content of a case as the objective of an appreciation is to define the central issue. This is probably best achieved by a systematic analysis of the available material in terms of:

1. What business is the company in and what are the salient features of this business?
2. What is the firm's goal, explicit or implied?
3. What resources has the company
   - Productive?
   - Technical?
   - Financial?
   - Marketing?
4. What policies, explicit or otherwise, has it adopted in respect of these resources?
5. Is there a single strategic variable which dominates all others – if so, what is it?
6. Has the firm any special skill or distinctive competence?

In analysing the case (or problem, in real life), one should seek to isolate those areas which bear directly upon both the immediate problem and the more general problem of which it is symptomatic. Once these areas have been defined they should be ranked in some rough order of importance and analysed in detail. For example, if a major issue is the nature of the product itself, one should list all the advantages and disadvantages which one can think of to permit an overall conclusion to be drawn. Similarly with all other issues. The conclusions drawn from the separate analysis of the relevant issues should then be summarized and stated as the basis upon which the plan has been based. This statement should also make explicit any assumptions which have been made, together with the reasons which support their adoption.

The marketing plan

This must be realistic in the light of the analysis described in the appreciation, and should commence by stating the overall objective or aim. If a student feels that the company's stated aims are incapable of attainment they must be able to present a very convincing argument as to why, and how, they should be changed. Thus the statement of the long-term aim must be supported by an exposition of all those factors which will affect the company's ability to achieve its objective, paying particular attention to environmental changes and changing consumer needs.

Following the statement of the long-term aim, the plan should state the short-term objective and the specific policies to be adopted to achieve it. In the interests of both clarity and coverage of all salient factors, some form of outline should be used similar to that given below:

1. Short-term aim, for example to increase market share by 5 per cent;
2. Forecast of market conditions for the period of the plan;
3. Statement of further marketing research to be undertaken to provide feedback on performance and to be used in the preparation of future marketing plans;
4. Statement of product policy;
5. Statement of pricing policy;
6. Statement of packaging policy;
7. Statement of distribution policy;
8. Statement of advertising and sales promotion policy;
9. Statement of sales policy;
10. Budget statement with explanation of how it is to be used for control purposes;
11. Outline of how plan is to be financed;
12. Timing for implementation of various policies;
13. Feedback and control procedures.

Clearly, the amount of detail will vary considerably depending upon the central issue identified in the appreciation, and the data available. It should be remembered, however, that the overall marketing plan cannot be expected to go into the same detail as would be expected of, say, the media plan, but it should provide the skeleton around which such plans can be prepared by the various functional specialists. In an examination context, the main intention is to discover whether the candidate has acquired a sufficient understanding of theoretical principles, and these should always be outlined, even though case data is not available for purposes of exemplification. For example, if the case concerns a convenience good the student may consider

sales promotion relevant, even though it is not specifically referred to, and so might suggest the use of a banded offer designed to increase consumer sampling, achieve increased consumer and retail inventories, and so on.

Finally, the impact of a marketing plan will be lost if it lacks clarity of expression, no matter how logical the sequence or how sophisticated the analysis. To this end, students must practise expressing themselves clearly and concisely in order to convey the maximum information in the least number of words.

■ Marketing arithmetic

On first acquaintance one of the more confusing aspects of marketing is the basic financial data associated with selling – mark-up, discounts, and stock-turn – and that necessary to monitor the financial health of the marketing function – standard costing, budgetary control and ratio analysis. While these factors, and the latter particularly, are more properly the province of a financial text, a brief overview is essential to underline their relevance to marketing and encourage more detailed study. (It is appreciated that many students will be pursuing a broadly-based course which includes a study of accounting and finance. Such students should regard the next few pages as basic revision material.) Each of the topics identified is the subject of separate treatment in the following pages.

□ *Mark-up*

This is the amount which a firm adds to its cost of goods in order to arrive at its selling price, i.e.

$$SP = C + M$$

where SP = selling price; C = cost of goods; and M = mark-up or margin.

The mark-up, or margin as it is sometimes termed, is intended to cover *selling*, *general* and *administrative* expenses ('SGA' in some accounting texts and case studies) as well as a percentage for profit. The convention which frequently causes confusion is that mark-up is usually expressed as a percentage of selling price rather than cost, probably due to sellers working backwards from a going market price, as would be essential under conditions of perfect competition. That is, one accepts the market price, deducts the desired profit, assesses the SGA associated with the anticipated volume of sales and deducts this, and is left with the amount for which the product will have to be made. If this amount is less than the actual cost, one will have to accept a lower profit, or even a loss, or decide not to produce, while if it is greater an above-average profit becomes possible.

Four basic calculations are frequently called for in connection with margins and mark-ups and these are as follows:

1. Determination of selling price when costs and percentage mark-ups are given. Since the selling price always equals 100 per cent we can substitute the data given into a simple formula to arrive at the retail price; that is:

$$C + M = SP$$

Thus if cost $= £100$ and the mark-up $= 25$ per cent, then:

$$£100 = SP - 25\%$$
$$= 100\% - 25\%$$
$$= 75\%$$

$$\therefore \quad £SP = \frac{£C}{100\% - M}$$
$$= \frac{£100}{75\%}$$
$$= £133.33$$

2. To find the margin, given cost and selling price, using the same figures as above, we have:

$$C + M = SP$$
$$M = SP - C$$
$$M = £133.33 - £100$$
$$M = £33.33$$

This may be expressed as a percentage of the selling price:

$$M = \frac{£33.3}{£100}$$
$$= 33.3\%$$

3. To convert a margin based on selling price to one based on cost. Here the formula is:

% margin on cost
$$= \frac{\% \text{ margin on selling price}}{100\% - \% \text{ margin on selling price}}$$
$$= \frac{33.3}{100 \quad 33.3}$$
$$= 50\%$$

4. To convert a margin based on cost to one based on selling price:

% margin on selling price
$$= \frac{\% \text{ margin on cost}}{100\% + \% \text{ margin on cost}}$$
$$= \frac{50}{100 + 50}$$
$$= 33.3\%$$

Discounts

The calculation of discounts is a constant source of confusion due to the fact that a discount is always expressed as a percentage of the *reduced* price and not the original retail selling price. For example, a 25 per cent discount on £100 is in fact £20 and not £25; that is:

$$\text{discount} = \frac{\text{amount of discount}}{\text{original price} - \text{discount}}$$

$$= \frac{20}{80} \text{ (i.e. } 100 - 20)$$

$$= 25\%$$

(Note: in American texts/case studies, discounts are often termed 'mark-downs'.)

☐ *Stock-turn*

As the term suggests, the stock-turn is the number of times the stock 'turns over' during a given period and gives a useful indicator of how a particular type of outlet is performing. Clearly the rate of stock-turn will vary enormously according to the nature of the goods sold, being fastest in fresh foods and slowest in durables such as furniture or luxuries such as jewellery, cameras and so on. There is usually a direct relationship between the margins which manufacturers anticipate in recommending a retail selling price and the stock-turn of the average outlet. It follows that more efficient outlets (that is, those with lower operating costs) will earn higher net profits if they maintain margins and achieve average stock-turn. However, in recent years many retailers have pursued a more aggressive strategy designed to increase market share, and thereby long-term profitability, by offering discounts and increasing stock-turn.

To compute stock-turn one must divide net sales for the period by the average inventory (at selling price) for the same period. Average inventory is simply:

$$\frac{\text{opening stock} + \text{closing stock}}{2}$$

while net sales is total sales less any returns or allowances.

☐ *Standard costing and budgetary control*

Traditionally, the accounting function concerned itself solely with recording the historical performance of an organization. It is for this reason that many people seek to differentiate between the major business functions by characterizing accounting as an orientation to the past. By the same token production is seen as being preoccupied with the present – a 'present orientation' – and marketing is conceived of as a 'future orientation', with an emphasis upon the planning and control of future activities. Nowadays such a simplistic distinction would be very far from the truth, for all business functions are conscious of the need for forward planning and the need to control operations so as to achieve the desired outcome. Standard costing and budgetary control have been developed for just this purpose.

In his excellent introduction to the subject, *Costing: A Management Approach*, A. H. Taylor (1974) expresses the view that defining standard costs as predetermined costs or yardsticks fails adequately to 'convey the fundamental change in viewpoint of costing which occurs when a standard costing system is instituted in place of an historical costing system'. Taylor goes on to say:

> The standard cost is what the cost of an operation or service ought to be under given conditions and subject to given conventions of costing. It is thus a notional amount which depends entirely on the conditions predicted. It is this notional amount which is treated as the value of the stock and the cost of the goods sold.
>
> The conditions associated with a standard cost are essentially a standard of efficiency and a level of activity. Using material as an example, the standard material cost of a product implies the purchase of the required quantity of material at an economic price and in economic lots. This in turn implies the existence of a production plan and a storing policy. All the standards inherent in the elements of cost which comprise a product cost or the cost of an operation are interdependent. To carry the argument to the extreme, it could be said that the standard costs derive from the corporate plan.

Put another way, using standard costs is very similar in principle to the economist's use of *ceteris paribus*: it enables one to predict outcomes due to the interaction between factors under consideration given no change in all the other factors which might influence that interaction. In this sense standard costs do act as yardsticks, for they enable management to ascertain whether the business is performing as planned according to the predetermined conditions necessary for that achievement – conditions which it is management's responsibility to create. Any departure or variance from the standard will immediately warn management of a difference between planned and actual which will enable it to analyze the nature of the variance and the possibility of rectifying it. Of course, all variances are not negative, though this is most often the case in periods of inflation when costs are often rising in an unpredictable manner which cannot be accommodated when setting the standard cost. However, when positive variances do occur it is equally important that management be aware of the fact so that they may capitalize on an opportunity if such exists, for example a seasonal fall in raw material prices.

It must also be emphasised that conformity with the standard should not be accepted at face value, for it may well conceal countervailing trends – for example, a fall in cost due to greater machine efficiency counterbalanced by increased labour or material costs. Thus to use a standard costing system as one of management by exception could be dangerous. Its major benefits lie in its requirement that one should plan future operations; that is, prepare a budget, identify the conditions necessary for the successful execution of the plan, the creation of such conditions and the comparison of actual and planned performance as the basis for controlling activities (hence 'budgetary control').

To cite Taylor again:

The merits of a standard costing system may be summarized as follows:

1. Information is provided for managerial control through the comparison of actual expenditure against standard expenditure.

2. The analysis of variances between actual expenditure and standard expenditure saves managerial time, because the managers need only give their attention to those operations where substantial variances occur.
3. Stable and presumably, sound figures of cost are provided to assist price determination.
4. Stable values are assigned to stock and work in progress, thus eliminating...anomalies...and assisting in the production of a true and fair view of profit and a reliable trend of profitability.

For a discussion of the anomalies mentioned, of costing principles and their managerial use the reader should refer to the original source or consult one of the texts in the Supplementary Reading List.

☐ Ratio analysis

In most countries, trading organizations are required to publish an annual statement of their financial affairs – most usually a balance-sheet, which summarizes the financial position, and a profit-and-loss account, which is a statement of income and expenditure. The manner in which companies choose to publish these financial statements varies enormously, from the elaborate and extensive documents put out by large public companies to the minimum required by law characteristic of most private firms. However, even this minimal information can provide an analyst with a great deal of insight into the strengths and weaknesses of an organization and the purpose of this section is to indicate a small number of ratios which can enable such an evaluation to be made. (Such analysis is particularly important for students preparing for formal examinations using the 'case method' (see Appendix), as most cases contain financial statements. Only if you are able to interpret these can you decide whether or not they are relevant to the marketing problem you have been asked to solve.)

In *The Meaning of Company Accounts*, Walter Reid and D. R. Myddelton (1971) group the more common ratios under three headings:

Investment measures

(a) Return on equity

$$= \frac{\text{Profit after tax}}{\text{Shareholders' funds}}$$

(b) Earnings per share

$$= \frac{\text{Profit after tax}}{\text{Number of shares issued}}$$

(c) Price/earnings ratio

$$= \frac{\text{Market price per share}}{\text{Earnings per share}}$$

(d) Dividend yield

$$= \frac{\text{Dividend per share}}{\text{Market price per share}}$$

(e) Dividend cover

$$= \frac{\text{Earnings per share}}{\text{Dividend per share}}$$

Measures of performance

(f) Return on net assets

$$= \frac{\text{Earnings before interest and tax}}{\text{Net assets}}$$

(g) Profit margin

$$= \frac{\text{Earnings before interest and tax}}{\text{Sales}}$$

(h) Asset turnover

$$= \frac{\text{Sales}}{\text{Net assets}}$$

Measures of financial status solvency

(i) Debt ratio

$$= \frac{\text{Long-term debt}}{\text{Capital employed}}$$

(j) Interest cover

$$= \frac{\text{Earnings before interest and tax}}{\text{Interest}}$$

Liquidity

(k) Current ratio

$$= \frac{\text{Current assets}}{\text{Current liabilities}}$$

(l) Acid test

$$= \frac{\text{Liquid assets}}{\text{Current liabilities}}$$

The purpose of all the foregoing ratios is to enable an analyst to conduct a spot check on the financial health of an organisation in much the same way that a doctor takes one's pulse, temperature, blood pressure, and so forth. Diagnostically, ratios are used in combination so that a satisfactory outcome for one test is not sufficient to guarantee that all the others will yield the same result. Accordingly it is necessary to work systematically through a series of tests before a clean bill of health can be issued. Which series of tests is most appropriate will vary according to one's viewpoint, but in general all analysts will wish to consider *liquidity*, *solvency* and *performance*, with less importance attached to investment measures *per se*. (For a discussion of how to interpret ratios one should consult Reid and Myddelton (1971), *The Meaning of Company Accounts*; or B. K. R. Watts (1978), *Business and Financial Management*. Another excellent source is Chapter 6, 'Profitability – Measurement and Analysis', in John Sizer's (1989), *An Insight into Management Accounting*.

Review questions and problems

1. 'Management's sensitivity to strategy should be proportionate to the instability of the environment of the firm.' Explain this statement and emphasise in your answer the major characteristics of strategic change, and the problems to be encountered by the firm committing itself to such change.

2. What would be the main headings in an annual marketing plan? Select one of these headings and show the detail with which it would be concerned, explaining how the content of your detailed section of the plan would be related to the whole.

3. 'While the marketing planner is the central figure in drawing up the annual product plan, other departments in the company will make important contributions to the final plan.' Discuss.

4. Describe how a marketing audit might be conducted in a firm, and evaluate the contribution of such auditing to overall marketing control.

5. Assess the impact on marketing tactics and strategies of changes in roles within the family during the last 20 years.

6. Leading businessmen have been quoted as relying to a large extent on the regular submission and analysis of financial ratios from the trading companies under their control. Why do you think they regard such measures of control as so important?

7. What is the function of a Marketing Plan and how does it relate to the Corporate Long-Range Plan of an organisation?

8. Explain the purpose and application of any six of the commonly used financial ratios relating to the operation of a business.

9. 'Every major industry was once a growth industry' (Theodore Levitt). Discuss.

10. 'Every major business enterprise requires a clear long-term marketing strategy in order to enable it to fulfil its obligations to its employees, shareholders and society.' Discuss.

11. Marketing planning begins with an analysis of a variety of factors including an internal audit of the firm's capabilities. What are the major factors to take into account in such an internal audit?

12. What arguments might you use to persuade a business organisation of the need to develop strategic marketing plans?

13. For what reasons might you require a marketing audit to be carried out and what types of information would you expect to achieve from it?

14. Discuss the importance to a company of adequately defining what business it is in.

▌ Supplementary reading list

Abell, Derek F. and Hammon, John S. (1980) *Strategic Marketing Planning* (Englewood Cliffs, N.J.: Prentice-Hall).

Ackoff, R. (1969) *The Concept of Corporate Planning* (New York: Wiley).

Ansoff, H. I. (1969) *Corporate Strategy* (Harmondsworth: Penguin-Pelican).

Bureau, J. R. (1981) *Brand Management: Planning and Control* (London: Macmillan).

Kotler, P. (1988) *Marketing Management: Analysis, Planning and Control*, 6th edn (Englewood Cliffs, N.J.: Prentice-Hall).

Luck, D. *et al.* (1980) *Marketing Strategy and Plans* (Englewood Cliffs, N.J.: Prentice-Hall).

Sizer, J. (1989) *An Insight into Management Accounting*, 2nd edn (Harmondsworth: Penguin).

Vause, R. and Woodward, N. (1981) *Finance for Managers*, 2nd edn (London: Macmillan).

Chapter 21

Marketing in Foreign Environments

Contents

Learning goals

The issues to be discussed in this chapter include:

1. The stages of development through which economies pass in order to become advanced industrialised economies with a strong marketing function.
2. The contribution of marketing to economic growth.
3. The nature of comparative advantage and theories of international trade.
4. The identification of market opportunities.
5. Globalisation versus differentiation as international marketing strategies.
6. Marketing in a foreign environment.
7. The challenge of the EU and regional trading blocs.
8. The effects of a changing global environment.

After reading this chapter you will be familiar with:

1. Rostow's concept of the stages of economic growth and development.
2. The reasons why the marketing function adds value and improves productivity even in countries with endemic supply deficiencies.
3. Ricardo's Theory of Comparative Advantage and benefits which flow from specialisation and international trade.
4. The factors which encourage firms to enter foreign markets.
5. Sources of information and methods for establishing the existence of foreign market opportunities.
6. The differences between a globalised or undifferentiated marketing strategy compared with the use of a segmentation (differentiated or concentrated) approach.
7. The alternative approaches to marketing in foreign environments.
8. The implications of regional trading blocs for international competition.
9. The effects of environmental change on international marketing practices.

Introduction

As with earlier editions this chapter seeks to provide a synoptic and greatly simplified introduction to three questions.

1. To what extent are the principles and practices discussed in this book relevant to other countries at different stages of economic development?
2. For what reasons might countries wish to engage in international trade?
3. What alternatives are open to firms wishing to sell in another country?

Thus the intention of this chapter is to provide the reader with an introduction to some of the issues associated with marketing in foreign environments. It cannot and does not pretend to be an exposition of the important subfield of marketing known as International Marketing which is the subject of text books and courses in its own right.

Stages of economic development

In Chapter 1 we introduced the reader to Walt Rostow's model (1962) of 'The Stages of Economic Growth'. It will be recalled that Rostow proposes that in achieving the status of an advanced, modern economy all economies must pass through a series of evolutionary phases identified as:

1. The traditional society.
2. The pre-conditions for take-off.
3. The take-off.
4. The drive to maturity.
5. The age of high mass consumption.
6. Beyond the age of high mass consumption – the search for quality.

Elsewhere (*The Marketing Book*, Baker, 1994), we have pointed out that Rostow's stages of economic development correspond quite closely to Maslow's need hierarchy such that traditional societies are concerned very much with survival while the modern, advanced and affluent economies are moving from the esteem/high mass consumption phase into one dominated by self-actualisation and the search for quality.

The evolutionary and sequential nature of Rostow's 'stages' demonstrates close parallels with our now familiar concept of the product life-cycle (PLC), albeit that it is not clear whether stage 5 represents a decline into decadence and senility and stage 6 a new PLC or a rejuvenation of the existing life-cycle/progression. Nonetheless, the concept does possess the advantages which have led us to advocate the PLC – it describes a process and it distinguishes a number of discrete phases which can be used both as a basis for classification and for prognosis. Thus as our discussion of 'The Evolution of an Economic Theory of Consumption' in Chapter 1 shows, we can both diagnose the stage of development which an economy has reached and propose strategies and policies for reaping the maximum advantage from its existing status as well as suggesting how it might best move to a more advanced stage if this is desired and possible.

The question as to whether economic growth and development are desirable objectives may seem a naive one, but it is important to recognise that much of the criticism levelled against marketing arises from its close association with the stage of high mass consumption. Indeed marketing is often seen as both the agent and engine of mass high consumption which is criticised for its emphasis on excessive materialism (Galbraith, 1957), its wasteful use of resources (q.v. *The Waste Makers* by Vance Packard, 1961, or *Limits to Growth*, Meadows *et al.*, 1972) and its destruction of our environment. If these things are bad, and most would agree that they are, then it is all too easy to see marketing as guilty by association. At least two points deserve to be made in this context.

First, while marketing as we know it *appears* to be a consequence of an ability to create an excess supply of particular goods and services, which only exists to a significant degree in mature high consumption economies, this is not the same as proving that its concept and practice are only relevant to this phase of economic development. Second, the most vocal adversaries of economic growth are those who directly and indirectly are enjoying its benefits to the full and so have both the leisure and the means to proselytize their views. Things doubtless look different to a subsistence farmer with an annual income measured in hundreds rather than thousands of dollars.

In a book called *In Defence of Economic Growth*, Wilfred Beckerman (1974) sums up the basic issue succinctly when he observes that:

> The growth problem is a problem of how resources should be allocated over time. Economists, and we hope politicians too, are concerned primarily with maximising welfare, which may be seen as comprising two elements – the level of consumption and the equality of its distribution. In addressing the problem of how to maximise welfare it is of the utmost importance that we consider the time dimension, for it is apparent that future consumption is highly dependent upon present *consumption*, in the sense that investment in new plant and equipment, in research and development, in education, etc. requires us to accept a lower level of current consumption in order to reap greater benefits (or welfare) in the future.

It follows, as Beckerman pointed out, that 'the essential point is that it is *consumption over* some relevant time period which should be maximised, not the growth rate'.

To be correct we should recognise that what we are seeking is *optimum* growth, which we can define as the growth rate at which the sacrifice of present consumption necessary to promote future growth is just balanced by the extra future consumption this will generate.

In assessing what is an optimum growth rate we are again faced with the intractable problem identified earlier – namely, that 'optimum' is a subjective concept and will be perceived differently by different pressure groups. Thus, influential critics like Galbraith have suggested that mankind keeps on raising the definition of optimum instead of being satisfied with what it

has got. If we regard the United States as the pacemaker, in that its citizens enjoy the highest standard of living in the world, we can see immediately that standards there have increased significantly in the past decade – for the rest of us trying to catch up we are faced with an ever-receding frontier. And so we come to the crux of the controversy, for it is marketing which is cast in the role of villain in the piece. In *The Affluent Society*, Galbraith (1974) comments:

> As a society becomes increasingly affluent, wants are increasingly created by the process by which they are satisfied. This may operate passively. Increases in consumption, the counterpart of increases in production, act by suggestion or emulation to create wants. Or producers may proceed actively to create wants through advertising and salesmanship. Wants then come to depend on output.

In the same vein Professor Harry Johnson (1961) of Chicago made the following observation in his *Money, Trade and Economic Growth*: 'The fact that wants are created and not original with the individual, raises a fundamental philosophical problem, whether the satisfaction of wants created by those who satisfy them can be regarded as social gain.' It would appear, then, that while growth is essential to ensure an improved standard of living, for most of us the marketing function is in some way responsible for exaggerating consumption needs to the point where the level of growth necessary to sustain such consumption is beyond the optimum and becomes wasteful.

▌ Marketing and economic growth

From the foregoing discussion it seems reasonable to conclude that while one may have some reservations about both the nature and extent of consumption in affluent and mature economies, the achievement of such a state is desirable and one to be pursued by economies at lower levels of development. That said it seems reasonable to inquire into the relevance which marketing has both in advanced economies, where it has been accused of creating conspicuous consumption, and in developing countries, which by definition are foreign environments when compared with the UK and where many point to the scarcity of basic commodities as evidence that it is production not marketing which is needed.

Let me deal first with the advanced economies. While marketing is often identified with materialism it is important to recognise that this is not the same as proving that marketing is a materialistic business philosophy. It is probably nearer the truth to assert that, as a business philosophy, marketing is neutral and that overtones of materialism merely mirror society's preoccupation with improving the standard of living. In turn, this laudable objective became embroiled with a perceived need to maintain a high level of employment; and employment results in increased production of goods. Obviously, if such increased supplies are not consumed, the process becomes sterile so we get into a vicious circle of stimulating consumption to increase demand and maintain employment opportunities. If we are not careful we lose sight of our real objective of improving human welfare and begin to confuse the means (growth) with the end (a better standard of living). The standard of living is concerned primarily with the quality of life and, while an increase in the quantity of goods and services may be an essential part of that quality, the two are not synonymous. In fact in advanced countries it would seem that beyond a certain point the consumption of physical goods is subject to diminishing returns and may reduce the quality of life due to environmental pollution, creation of stress, loss of leisure and recreational opportunities, and so on.

It seems to me both ironical and paradoxical, assuming that marketing is so powerful in persuading people to consume more against their own interests, that few suggest that these same skills and techniques cannot be used in the interest of conservation and moderation. In fact they can, and I predict that this will increasingly be the case. Thus in post-industrial society marketing will have a crucial role to play in identifying the satisfactions which people are seeking, for, as we have seen, the central economic problem is that of maximising satisfaction from the consumption of scarce resources. Where marketers tend to differ from economists is in the emphasis they give to measuring individual consumer preferences as the basis for resource allocation – in other words they give greater attention to the subjective and qualitative dimensions of demand than is common with economists.

As has been pointed out to me on numerous occasions on visits to developing economies, their problem is seen very differently. Supply deficiency or scarcity is seen as the fundamental problem and marketing is regarded as superfluous when there is such an obvious imbalance between supply and demand. Such a viewpoint is perfectly valid if you think marketing is a sort of sophisticated selling and concerned solely with demand stimulation by means of advertising, promotion and packaging.

To recapitulate, economies are concerned with maximising the satisfaction gained from the consumption of scarce resources. It is the satisfaction of individual consumers we are concerned with, and it would be paternalistic, not to say presumptuous, to assume that any single person is able to specify just what gives people the greatest satisfaction without asking them. To point to the fact that the available supply is consumed is not to prove that we are maximising satisfaction – it only goes to prove that something is better than nothing. My need for shoes is stronger than my need for brown shoes. If you only produce black shoes which I do not particularly like, they are still preferable to no shoes at all, but you are not maximising my satisfaction. Certainly you are not going to motivate me to work harder to own two pairs of shoes I do not like. (In passing it should be mentioned that one of the reasons why marketing is now practised in what used to be Soviet countries is that they had an awful lot of black shoes no one would buy!)

In a thoughtful analysis of the relevance of marketing to developing countries, Fred Austen (1978) discusses the following ten areas which he considers to be characteristic features of developing countries:

1. *Segmented.* In Western countries considerable skill and ingenuity is displayed in dividing homogeneous groups by social purchasing-power grouping, consumer attitudes, and so forth. In developing countries no such ingenuity is necessary. Peasants and townsmen, rich and poor, are clearly separated. Even a medium-sized country like Nigeria has not merely three main religious groups but 200 different tribes, each with its own tradition and language.

2. *Fast-changing.* The cries of woe from the beggars for foreign aid disguise the fact that growth in national income is commonly as fast as in England during the heyday of the industrial revolution and the change in balance between town and country is taking place at a staggering rate. Places like Kathmandu, Dar-es-Salaam and Jakarta are not only now enormous by any standard but are growing at an alarming rate.

3. *Badly administered.* Fast growth, plus major, often frequent, political changes, combined with little administrative tradition and ambitious concepts of state control, have almost universally overstretched the administration. The prevailing tribal and family loyalties are a further important cause which lead administrators and executives to have priorities out of line with good practice or optimum effectiveness.

4. *Low general purchasing power.* Not only are the countries poor, with general money incomes usually well under £250 p.a. per head, and in many countries well under £100 p.a. per head, but much of the work is absorbed in subsistence farming, or food purchase. The well-off, who have purchasing power high even by our standards, contribute comparatively little to the move towards Western styles of market economy. The rich in developing countries, like Adam Smith's feudal barons, spend a disparately high proportion of income on servants, imported luxuries or purpose-made articles,

none of which are generators of low-cost, mass-market structures.

5. *High military expenditure.* A reflection of insecurity – and the influence of military leaders – is shown by the staggering expenditure on defence. George Dalton (1974), in *Economic Systems and Society*, looked at developing countries, defined somewhat more broadly than we have, and quotes 1970 figures of 200 billion dollars, compared with 168 billion dollars for education and half that for public health, with rates of growth (1961–70) of 8 per cent, nearly four times the growth rate in developed countries, and often well over 10 per cent of GNP. Looked at slightly differently, according to figures quoted by Dalton, developing countries spent twenty times on armaments of what they received in aid.

6. *State dominated.* Almost regardless of political complexion the state plays a greater role in the economy than in developed nations. Partly this is due to balance-of-payments problems, partly due to ideology, partly to the absence of an existing management and commercial infrastructure. Normally the economy is geared to a five-year plan, handsomely printed but indifferently executed. Restriction of imports is particularly common. Foreign capital aid normally operates through state channels.

7. *Monopolistic.* In most products monopoly or oligopoly is the rule and competition the exception. This largely follows from the common import restrictions, small fragmented markets and the associated problem complex.

8. *Poor infrastructure.* Both social items, such as roads, hospitals, schools, sewers, postal and telephone services, and also private networks in the transport, finance and media fields are deficient, causing a completely different pattern of requirements and opportunities.

9. *Vulnerable exports.* In general developing countries are dependent on a few products. Characteristically one primary product will be 55–85 per cent of total exports (see

Industrialisation of Developing Countries, Moscow, Progress Publishers, 1973), and apart from the recent rises in commodity prices (petrol, cocoa, coffee and tea especially) the long-range terms of trade appear to be moving against developing nations (see *Terms of Trade Policy for Primary Commodities*, Commonwealth Secretariat, 1975). This can largely be attributed to the fact that the goods produced by developing countries stayed the same, while the markets changed and the more sophisticated countries changed products and product mixes in line with market valuations. It also reflects the fact that the sharpest discrimination was by developing countries against other developing states. Tyagunenko quotes revealing figures which show that from 1955 to 1971, trade with the developed Western countries and Soviet bloc countries rose by 2–3 per cent for each bloc (as a percentage of the total), which was balanced by a 5 per cent drop in the already small trade (about a quarter of the trade) with other developing countries. Incidentally the same figures show how insignificant the proportion of trade with the Eastern bloc is when compared with the massive (about three-quarters) proportion of commerce with capitalist countries. If anything this situation is worsening in the 1990s rather than improving.

10. *Inadequately documented*. British marketers envy the information commonly available in the United States, while industrial marketers similarly respect the published consumer data, but differences between our fields are as nothing when compared with most developing countries. Even where there is a superficial veneer of sophistication in the presentation of figures, they are nearly always out of date, generally ineffectively collected and frequently deliberately tailored. It must be appreciated that with the differences in culture it is often almost impossible to get urban, numerate patriates who can still communicate with the predominantly rural peasant population. Beyond this, in a subsistence economy with a population which is largely illiterate, worried about tax implications and with no general traditions as to the integrity of information and the importance of figures, one cannot expect good primary statistics, or find gathering secondary statistics easy.

To overcome the barriers to economic growth implicit in these features of developing countries, Austen argues that 'It is clearly vital, therefore, that the management process at organisation level, as opposed to governmental planning level, which optimises and predicts the relationship of inputs to outputs over time, i.e. Marketing, should play an increasingly significant role' an assertion which echoes the sentiments of such well-known authors as Galbraith, Drucker and McCarthy.

Consider what Drucker had to say as far back as 1958 in 'Marketing and Economic Development':

> My thesis is very briefly as follows, Marketing occupies a critical role in respect to the development of such 'growth' [i.e. underdeveloped] areas. Indeed, marketing is the most important 'multiplier' of such development. It is in itself in every one of these areas the least developed, the most backward part of the economic system. Its development, above all others, makes possible economic integration and the fullest utilisation of whatever assets and productive capacity an economy already possesses. It mobilises latent economic energy. (pp. 252–9)

In the first instance most would agree with Kindleberger (1958) in *Economic Development*, that whether markets stimulate development or vice versa, distribution systems tend to be neglected and are the source of considerable inefficiency. It follows that improvements in physical distribution are likely to have a high pay-off and help break the vicious circle so typical of the developing economy, where surpluses are small or non-existent, leaving little or nothing for investment to provide the necessary stimulus to growth. Allied with developments in physical distribution it is also clear that efficient retail practice has a significant contribution to make in optimising the satisfaction derived from the available supply. Austen cites a study by Slater which showed that ten years after supermarkets were introduced into Puerto Rico they accounted for 40 per cent of all food sales in San Juan and offered lower prices than traditional small outlets. In a similar vein several studies in Latin America have claimed that mass retailing methods used by Sears, Roebuck have been an important contributor to economic growth.

However, marketing can perhaps make the greatest impact by ensuring that scarce resources are channelled into those products which offer the greatest consumer satisfaction. Unfortunately in economies where scarcity is endemic it is often difficult to persuade managers that an ability to sell everything they can make is not necessarily the same as maximising satisfaction. A simple case history will help make the point.

In Nigeria soft drinks such as coke, lemonade and orangeade are extremely popular and often difficult to obtain. A survey by marketing students at the University of Nigeria in Enugu showed that although the major bottling company was able to sell all its output, customers were not entirely satisfied with the product mix, which emphasised coke and contained relatively small proportions of orange and lemon flavours. It appeared that consumers had a very strong preference for orange and deliveries were consumed immediately; lemon ranked second, but it was only after both orange and lemon were sold out that coke became acceptable as third best, but still preferable to no soft drink at all. Because demand exceeded supply, the manager assumed that all was well and paid little attention to new firms being set up concentrating mainly on orange and lemon flavours. In ignoring this potential competition he clearly had forgotten that some years previously coke had built up its sales in preference to beer, which had now lost its dominant place in the beverage market.

The moral is as clear in developing economies as it is in developed ones – an understanding of consumer needs is fundamental to long-run business success, and therefore to optimising the allocation of scarce resources. In turn it is clear that the scarcer resources are, the greater the need to optimise the return from them, so that even

where growth is restrained voluntarily marketing practices and techniques have a major role to play in ensuring the greatest possible return in terms of consumer satisfaction.

By improving the efficiency of the marketing function we improve profitability, and increased profitability means a larger surplus to invest in expanding production facilities. In other words marketing productivity is an essential contributor to reducing and solving the scarcity problem.

To conclude, it seems to me that the marketing concept is universal to all stages of economic development and to ignore it is to slow down the optimum rate of growth as I have defined it – put another way, neglect of the marketing concept wastes scarce resources. When it comes to application of the concept then it is clear that different marketing functions are more relevant in some situations than in others. In developing countries one needs market research as an essential input to planning future development; one needs greatly improved distribution to ensure that the limited goods available are put into consumption in the most efficient manner possible; one needs greater control over distribution to eliminate distortion of the price mechanism through diversion into a black-market operation. One has proportionately a much lesser need for promotional and selling activities than is the case in advanced economies, where supply and demand are much closer to equilibrium. However, these differences do not deny the relevance of marketing, merely a better understanding of its application.

It follows, therefore, that in principle the concepts and practices discussed in this book are of relevance to all countries whatever their stage of economic development. However, in seeking to apply the ideas in this book one should be mindful of Robert Bartels' (1968) conclusions when addressing the question 'Are Domestic and International Marketing Dissimilar?', namely:

1. Marketing is a process of twofold character: technical and social.
2. Marketing technology, i.e. '. . . the application of principles, rules, or knowledge relating to

the non-human elements of marketing', has universal validity and potentially universal applicability.

3. 'The applicability of marketing technology is dependent upon circumstances of the environments in which it is applied'; that is, cultural and societal factors condition the technical factors.

4. There are wide differences in cultural and societal factors between countries and, therefore, in marketing practice. Despite these differences the *relationships* between marketing practice and environment are susceptible to generalisations in analysis termed 'comparative marketing'. Thus, although the marketer may expect both differences and similarities between foreign and domestic markets, 'both are embraced within a consistent body of marketing theory'.

Having read this section you may well be struck by the fact that many (indeed most) of the references are 20 or more years old. Unfortunately, this does not reflect inadequate revision by the author. It reflects the sad fact that comparatively little has occurred to improve the lot of the under-developed economies in the second half of this century. The rich continue to get richer and the poor, poorer. While it is true that a number of less developed economies have achieved take-off (the South East Asian 'Tigers'), their numbers are depressingly small and Austen's 1978 analysis remains essentially true today. Perhaps the most hopeful development since the publication of the previous edition in 1991 has been the collapse of the old-style Soviet command economy and the recognition that free markets hold the greatest promise for improving human welfare through effective marketing.

So much for marketing within countries at different stages of economic development. What about trade between them?

■ International trade

While trade between nations is of almost equal antiquity as exchange between individuals, the theoretical explanation for it had to await the statement of David Ricardo's 'Theory of Comparative Advantage' in the early nineteenth century. To demonstrate the application of his theory and the benefits which would flow from specialisation by nations, Ricardo used the following example (see *Dictionary of Modern Economics*, ed. David W. Pearce, Macmillan, 1981):

| | Labour hours required to produce ||
	1 gallon wine	1 yard cloth
Portugal	80	90
England	120	100

Portugal has an absolute advantage in the production of both commodities since the input requirements are less than those for England. Portugal's comparative cost advantage for wine is 80:120 which is less than the rate of 90:100 for cloth. If Portugal specialises in accordance with her comparative cost advantage then for every yard of cloth she ceases to produce she can have $1\frac{1}{8}$ gallons of wine, for each embodies 90 labour hours. If, as Ricardo postulates, the exchange rate after trade between cloth and wine is 1:1, then Portugal can exchange her $1\frac{1}{8}$ gallon of wine to obtain $1\frac{1}{8}$ yards of cloth. In other words, Portugal can obtain $1\frac{1}{8}$ yards of cloth for the 90 labour hours which would only have yielded 1 yard of cloth produced domestically. However, England gains too, for despite her absolute inferiority she can translate the 120 hours required to produce a gallon of wine into the production of $1\frac{1}{5}$ yards of cloth which by international exchange can be converted into $1\frac{1}{5}$ gallons of wine.

Nowadays, modern theory has established that the only necessary condition for the possibility of gains from trade is that price ratios should differ between countries but the essential concept remains the same – that by specialisation and through trade countries improve their overall standard of living. The strict application of this doctrine was challenged by Bruce Scott (1984) in an article 'National Strategy for Stronger US Competitiveness'.

According to Scott one must reject the static theory of comparative advantage in favour of a dynamic approach founded on a national strategy towards long-run competitiveness. Thus:

> Japan's remarkable post-war economic growth is based, in considerable measure, on the Japanese government's rejection of static, conventional economic theories. Japanese leaders recognised that Japan could create competitive advantages by mobilising technology, capital, and skilled labour to attack problems or identify opportunities in selected sectors. They created a strategy of dynamic comparative advantage at the national level that parallels the strategy of a diversified company as it shifts resources from less to more promising areas. As a high level MITI official explained in a 1970 OECD publication:
>
> > 'Should Japan have entrusted its future, according to the theory of comparative advantage, to these industries characterised by intensive use of labour? [With a population of 100 million] had [Japan] chosen to specialise in this kind of industry, it would almost permanently have been unable to break away from the Asian pattern of stagnation and poverty...'

The Ministry of International Trade and Industry decided to establish industries which require intensive employment of capital and technology, such as steel, oil refining, petrochemicals, automobiles, aircraft, industrial machinery of all sorts, and later electronics, including electronic computers. From a short-run, static viewpoint, encouragement of such industries would seem to conflict with economic rationalism. But, from a long-range point of view, these are precisely the industries where income elasticity of demand is high, technological progress is rapid, and labour productivity rises fast. It was clear that without these industries it would be difficult to raise [our] standard of living to that of Europe and America; whether right or wrong, Japan had to have these heavy and chemical industries.

As Scott points out, Portugal should have chosen to specialise in the growth industry of the day (cloth) and forsaken the production of port wine! (In *The Comparative Advantages of Nations*, Michael Porter, 1990, dismisses Ricardo's theory as inadequate and incomplete and proposes that the only lasting, sustainable advantage is a country's people. This book is essential reading for those seeking a modern and detailed analysis.)

However, Japan's success in penetrating world markets with its modern products confirms the necessity for international trade, for without imports it would be impossible to produce these and exports are essential to pay for them.

Of necessity, Britain has long been involved in foreign trade in order to make good her limited endowment of land and raw materials. During the middle of the last century we had a virtual monopoly of international trade, but since that time our share has declined continuously. In large degree this decline has been due to the enormous expansion in international trade, for in absolute terms our total trade today is many times greater than it was during the last century. Several factors may be distinguished as having contributed to this growth, including:

- Nationalistic policies, emphasising self-sufficiency, have yielded to the logic of the theory of comparative advantage; that is, that countries will maximise their growth by specialising in those activities with the greatest marginal product, and exchanging excess supplies for the surplus output of other specialised economies. The creation of international trading communities is an implicit recognition of this, for example EU, EFTA, LAFTA (Latin America Free Trade Association), NAFTA, and so on.
- Politically, it has been realised that the removal of trade barriers will not only stimulate the growth of economies but will also lead to cultural exchange and the easing of international tension.
- The 'population explosion' has created new mass markets and expanded the demand for all types of goods and services.
- Developments in communications and transportation have opened up hitherto inaccessible markets.

- The removal of trade barriers has intensified competition in formerly protected markets, and encouraged domestic manufacturers to develop new products and to look farther afield for markets in which to sell them.

Factors which predispose the firm to enter international markets

Fundamentally, entry into any new market, domestic or foreign, is undertaken to increase overall profitability. In turn, the decision to enter the international market may arise from any combination of a number of factors, among which may be distinguished:

1. Loss of domestic market share due to increased competition. Whereas a price reduction in the home market might be suicidal, the firm using a contribution approach may be able to increase total profits by selling at a lower price in foreign markets. (This strategy is often precluded by the existence of anti-dumping agreements.)
2. Loss of domestic market share due to product obsolescence. In many cases products made obsolete by the introduction of more sophisticated substitutes are still appropriate to less advanced countries, for example oil lamps.
3. Saturation of the domestic markets precluding the attainment of scale economies. Unlike the previous points, which presume the existence of excess capacity, this situation suggests that an increase in market size will permit the firm to expand its production and reduce average cost. In turn, this will permit the firm to expand its domestic market, as well as compete more effectively overseas.
4. The provision of incentives. Incentives to enter international markets are of both the 'push' and 'pull' variety, and invariably originate at government level. International agreements such as GATT (General Agreement on Tariffs and Trade) frequently exclude the provision of direct subsidies to exporters, but there are a number of ways in which a government can provide indirect support.

In addition to the information and promotional support represented by these expenditures, the exporter can also call upon other departments such as those of the DTI (Department of Trade and Industry) for specialised help, can insure against loss through the Export Credits Guarantee Department, and receive preferential tax treatment for expenses incurred.

'Pull' incentives are those offered by foreign governments to encourage entry into their national market. Originally, such incentives included import licences and tax relief on profits, but these are less common now. Most developing economies wish to develop domestic industry, in order to create employment opportunities, as well as wishing to conserve foreign exchange. Consequently, pull incentives are now largely designed to attract foreign firms to establish subsidiaries, rather than to attract the importation of finished goods. Probably the strongest incentive of all, however, is the existence of potential demand backed by purchasing power. Essentially, such market opportunities are of three types:

- Type 1: One can offer an equivalent product at a lower price.
- Type 2: One can offer a better product at a competitive price.
- Type 3: One can offer a product which is not available in the foreign market.

In view of the high labour costs/low productivity of many of our industries, few type 1 markets are open to British exporters and attention is largely concentrated on type 2 and type 3 situations.

Over the years many traditional British exports have built up a reputation for quality, soundly based on product superiority, for example woollens, speciality cotton textiles, china, machine tools, and so forth. Unfortunately, complacency and poor marketing have allowed competitors to pre-empt many type 2 markets, although personal experience of the American consumer goods markets suggests that these markets are not irretrievably lost, as many British products of unrivalled quality could be sold at twice their domestic price and still undercut the Japanese imports which predominate.

Type 3 markets offer the greatest profit opportunity of all, but are the least common. Further, the small size of the domestic market, and insular thinking, frequently delay the development of technological innovations, allowing other countries to overtake us, for example the Hovercraft.

The location of market opportunity

In general, the identification of foreign market opportunities will result from systematic marketing research of the type described in Chapter 10. In the particular, however, it is usually necessary to modify this approach for a number of reasons:

1. Most companies are seeking a market for an existing product with which they have had considerable domestic experience; that is, one is seeking to match needs with a product, rather than develop a product to satisfy identified but unfilled needs.
2. Few companies or executives have any 'feel' for foreign markets, which tend to be totally unknown quantities in a way which the home market can never be. Some might argue that this is an advantage in that it demands a fuller and more scientific analysis, with less dependence on subjective, judgemental opinions.
3. Few countries possess the wealth of published data available for use in domestic desk research, making precise quantification difficult.
4. Field research using survey methods is frequently precluded because of language difficulties, the non-availability of trained personnel, cost, and so on.
5. There are literally dozens of countries which might represent a potential market, and some form of screening procedure is essential to reduce the list to manageable proportions.

In the latter context the development of comparative marketing as an area of study offers considerable hope in that it is concerned with 'The identification and analysis of common factors and differences in marketing concepts, systems and techniques among various societies, including nations' (David Carson, 1967, in 'Comparative Marketing – A New-Old Aid'). As the title of Carson's article suggests, comparative analysis is a long-established technique, but it is only in the 1970s that it became the subject of formal study in the marketing context. As a result of these studies a number of formal classificatory systems have been, or are in the course of being, developed which take into account economic, geographic and human factors. Although none of these systems has yet been accepted as definitive, reference to any or all of them should permit early elimination of countries which are clearly unsuited as potential markets for a given product or service. Similarly, a study of the differences and common factors between countries should sensitise the marketer to their relative importance when formulating a marketing strategy.

Sources of information

In the nature of things, the classificatory systems being developed by comparative marketing theorists are based largely on generalisations, and should be regarded as a screening device. Once a short-list of potential markets has been decided upon, the researcher must seek out more detailed data. A number of sources are available to assist him in this task, some of which have already been quoted in Chapter 10. These may be supplemented by reference to:

*   The Department of Trade and Industry;
*   Chambers of Commerce;
*   Commercial Officers of the Diplomatic Service;
*   Export Councils;
*   Federation of British Industries;
*   Institute of Directors;
*   Chartered Institute of Marketing;

- National Association of British Manufacturers;
- Trade Associations;
- The Foreign Departments of the major banks, and so on.

(The DTI publishes a wide selection of free publications which are available on request and contain full details of sources of information, export services available, etc.)

Many of the sources quoted can provide first-hand information on specific opportunities, as well as advising on the procedure to be followed, and the pitfalls to be avoided, when entering specific markets.

☐ *Field research*

Although it is generally true that few countries have market research organisations capable of undertaking field research, this certainly does not apply to the advanced, affluent economies which represent the best potential markets for British goods. On the other hand few companies are prepared to make a large-scale entry into a foreign market, and so baulk at the expenditure that an extensive survey would involve. Consequently, many would-be exporters confine their field research to a 'fact-finding' tour in which they solicit the opinions of informed sources, the quality of which varies enormously. Owing to the uncertainties associated with entry into a foreign market, as opposed to risks which are quantifiable, many marketers prefer to enlist the support of a third party in the country concerned, that is an indirect approach, which is usually regarded as a substitute for field research.

Globalisation versus segmentation

Since the publication of 'Marketing Myopia' in 1960 Ted Levitt has been recognised as one of the foremost marketing thinkers of our time with the added advantage that he can and does communicate his ideas clearly and vigorously. This is certainly the case with his article which appeared in the May–June 1983 issue of the *Harvard Business Review* – 'The Globalisation of Markets' – which opens with the following sentences:

> A powerful force now drives the world toward a single converging commonality, and that force is technology. It has proletarianised communication, transport, and travel, making them easily and cheaply accessible to the world's most isolated places and impoverished multitudes. Suddenly no place and nobody is insulated from the alluring attractions of modernity. Almost everybody everywhere wants all the things they have heard about, seen or experienced via the new technological facilitators that drive their wants and wishes. And it drives these increasingly into global commonality, thus homogenising markets everywhere.
>
> The result is a new commercial reality – the explosive emergence of global markets for globally standardised products, gigantic world scale markets of previously unimagined magnitudes.

The article, which is reprinted in his book *The Marketing Imagination*, 1983, develops this theme at some length, and argues that countries (Japan) and firms (Coca Cola) which have appreciated this trend enjoy enormous economies of scale in production, distribution and marketing, and by using price as a competitive weapon are able to devastate the competition. This trend is accelerated by the newly industrialising countries' (NICs') desire for modernity, as a result of which they have run up enormous external debts, and made the old patterns of international trade obsolete. As a consequence the multinational corporations which have dominated the scene for so long are giving way to the global corporation, and:

> The multinational and the global corporation are not the same. The multinational corporation operates in a number of countries, where in each case it adjusts with accommodating care and therefore high relative costs to the presumptive special conditions of the particular country. In contrast, the global corporation operates with resolute constancy and therefore at low relative costs as if the entire world (or major regions of it) were

a single, largely identical entity; it does and sells the same things in the same single way everywhere.

My own view is that in the not-too-distant future this thesis will be seen as being as overstated as 'Marketing Myopia' was. The weakness in Levitt's argument is that he is overlooking a basic concept of marketing, which is that one can pursue three quite different strategies, distinguishable as undifferentiated, differentiated and concentrated. Global corporations pursue an undifferentiated strategy, while multinationals follow a differentiated and sometimes concentrated approach; that is, they adjust the product or service to what they perceive as the particular needs of different groups of customers or 'market segments'. Of course Levitt has to recognise the existence of such segments which, if nothing else, will continue to exist because of the unequal distribution of income, and has to admit that the global corporation will appeal only to those who don't mind an undifferentiated product.

Now under certain circumstances an undifferentiated product will be preferable to no product at all, as we saw in the example of coke in Nigeria cited earlier, but, as I have pointed out elsewhere ('Maxims for Marketing in the Eighties', Baker, 1980–81), one of the marketing's maxims is that 'The act of consumption changes the consumer.' In other words, the Model T at $500 was much preferable to no car at all, but once you had come to appreciate its basic benefits you also became aware of its basic faults, including that 'you can have any colour you like so long as it's black', and so come to want a product which is differentiated in some way or other. General Motors recognised this fact when Ford would not accept it and displaced him as market leader.

Experience suggests that while one can pursue an undifferentiated (global?) strategy successfully for some of the time, ultimately you will have to change it – at least to a different undifferentiated strategy, but probably to a differentiated or concentrated strategy. As such this argument is inconsistent and contradictory – a fact which is emphasised with some irony by Chapter 4 of Levitt's *Marketing Imagination*.

This view would certainly seem to be shared by Alvin Toffler (1984) in his book *Previews and Promises*, when he observes:

> Take mass production. Nothing was more characteristic of the industrial era. Yet we're already moving from a mass production, mass consumption economy to what I've called a 'de-massified' economy.
>
> In traditional mass manufacturing, factories pour out a stream of identical objects, by the million. In the Third Wave sector, mass production is replaced by its opposite: de-massified production – short runs, even customized, one-by-one production, based on computers and numerical controls. Even where we turn out millions of identical components, they are frequently configured into more and more customized end products.
>
> The significance of this can't be overestimated. It's not simply that products are now more varied. The processes of production are themselves transformed. The smokestack – that symbol of the industrial, assembly-line society – is becoming a relic.
>
> We still think of ourselves as a mass production society, yet in the advanced sectors of the economy, mass production is already an outmoded technique. And the idea that we can keep our old mass manufacturing industries competitive indefinitely is based on ignorance of what is actually happening on the factory floor.
>
> The new technologies make diversity as cheap as uniformity. In fact, in many industries, it's customize or die. This is exactly the opposite of what was required in the Second Wave economy.
>
> In fact, it is almost a dialectical return to pre-industrial, one-of-a-kind production, but now on a high technology basis.
>
> And exactly the same trends are visible in the distribution system, too, where we see more and more market segmentation, direct mail targeting, specialty stores, and even individualized delivery systems based on home computers and teleshopping. People are increasingly diverse, and, as a result, the mass market is breaking into small, continually changing sectors.

Perhaps the most telling indictment against the globalisation argument is that it is production-orientated in the sense that it seeks to 'drive' the wants and wishes of potential users toward commonality rather than modify the supply to match a varying demand. As we shall see in the next sections, which look at different approaches to marketing in foreign environments, such an approach is reasonable when one is entering foreign markets for the first time or has only a limited interest in selling to such markets and wishes to minimise the risk. Otherwise, given the diversity of behaviour discussed in Chapters 6, 7 and 8 (Consumer Behaviour, Organisational Buyer Behaviour and Market Segmentation), it would be surprising, to say the least, if extending the geographical scope of one's marketing did not increase this diversity.

Notwithstanding the above comments, more and more products are being perceived and launched as global brands. National borders are becoming less significant to many major corporations in the promotion of their key products. Companies like Coca-Cola, Mars and Ford are trying to have a more homogeneous strategy and product that promotes their products to a large market. According to *Marketing Week* marketing research has shown that the variations in consumers' attitudes and tastes may not be as great as would be expected. These trends are often attributed to cheaper travel and the globalisation of the media. The convergence of consumers' tastes and attitudes means it is becoming easier to globalise brands, especially commodities like soft drinks, cosmetics and confectionery.

A key date in the globalisation of brands was the change that one of the leading confectionery brands underwent in 1990 when Mars' Marathon bar attempted globalisation of the product. When globalising brands there is a need to search out common factors to name and position the product effectively in a cross-section of markets. This can lead to a watering-down effect. In order to avoid this problem local variations will often be needed, for example in terms of naming or packaging. Different cultures will have sensitivities to certain colours, names or advertising campaigns for example, and it may be necessary to account for these. Only when a brand develops a stereotype that can transcend cultures do these problems diminish, as is the case with products like Coca-Cola and Marlboro cigarettes.

Two recent product launches show how large corporations are striving to launch global products. Ford launched the Mondeo as a 'global' car. The name Mondeo could be used in Europe and has obvious 'world' connotations whilst other markets have different names, for example Contour and Mercury Mystique in the US. Advertising also varied in different countries and was handled by three different agencies. The benefits of this global brand relate mainly to the fact that costs will be lowered with the centralisation of design and development and the use of worldwide technological link ups. Similarly, Gillette launched its Sensor brand globally, a scheme that took ten years to plan and was completed in ten months. This meant the launch gained worldwide momentum and benefited from more generic campaigns that promoted Gillette – 'the best a man can get'. Again, local differences could be compensated for, for example with advertising. However, homogeneity in terms of design, development, production and advertising led to reduced launch costs and a far greater potential market. (*Source*: *Marketing Week Magazine*, 10 June 1994.)

▌ Approaches to marketing in foreign environments

As we have seen, there are numerous threats and opportunities which might predispose the firm to consider selling in foreign markets – the question is, 'How does one set about it?' In ascending order of commitment the alternatives available may be summarised as:

- Exporting;
- Licensing;
- Contract manufacturing;
- Management contracting;
- Joint Venture;
- Establishment of subsidiaries.

Direct exporting is essentially direct selling in a foreign market, and thus requires the firm to take full responsibility for establishing contact with potential customers. Indirect exporting occurs when the exporter employs the services of middlemen to look after the distribution, and often the complete marketing, of the product.

Channel policy is a technical aspect of marketing, and the general principles discussed in Chapter 4 and elsewhere are equally applicable to foreign and domestic markets. Thus, the same considerations of cost versus control should be evaluated in the context of direct versus indirect exporting. The decision to export direct will almost always necessitate the establishment of sales offices and the appointment of full-time employees to staff them, although other functions, such as physical distribution and advertising, may be delegated to agents. Supporters of the direct approach argue that the setting up of branch offices and the employment of salesmen are reassuring to potential buyers as they represent a definite commitment to the market, as well as giving the marketer direct control over elements such as price, credit policy, after-sales service, and so forth.

In the case of technically complex industrial goods, with a small, clearly defined potential market, the direct approach is probably to be preferred. However, where the product is simple, largely undifferentiated and aimed at a mass market, most manufacturers prefer to use middlemen and test the market before committing themselves to an extensive sales and distribution network. As in the home market, middlemen fall into two main categories – merchants or wholesalers who purchase goods outright for resale, and agents who act on the manufacturer's behalf in return for a fee or commission on sales. The same problems of control discussed earlier have to be discounted against the economics of using middlemen, although it is probably true to say that the middleman's contacts in a foreign country are more valuable to the manufacturer than they are in a domestic market.

In a recent survey, 'Strategy and Performance in British Exporters', Rick Brown and David Cook (1990) provide an excellent overview of current practice. Some key tables are reproduced below (Tables 21.1–21.6).

Table 21.1   *Reasons for exporting*

	%	Respondents	Ranking
	1–3*	4–6*	2–6*
Gain more sales	73.4	3.7	77.1
Long-term survival	52.9	16.7	69.6
Achieve market leadership	36.5	24.3	60.8
Lack of UK opportunities	32.7	27.6	60.3
Exporting more profitable	21.4	28.5	49.9
Absorb overheads	12.6	34.5	47.1

* where 1 = most important;   (N = 214)
6 = least important

Source: Rick Brown and David Cook (1990), 'Strategy and Performance in British Exporters', *Quarterly Review of Marketing*, vol. 15, no. 3 (April).

■ Other alternatives

Broadly speaking, three other alternatives are open to the firm which wishes to operate on an international scale:

1. It can license a foreign company to manufacture to its specification, for example Pilkington has licensed Corning Glass to manufacture float glass in the United States.

Table 21.2   *Methods of overseas market research*

Rank	Number of companies using	Weighted mean
Exploratory trips by management	173	5.96
Distributors/agents	143	5.64
Salesmen	134	5.82
Government agencies	111	4.44
Banks/Chambers of Commerce	65	3.34
Consultancies	58	4.55
In-House researcher	54	5.31

Source: Brown and Cook (1990).

Table 21.3 *Export product policy*

	Number	%
Standard UK product	31	15
Standard UK product with limited customisation	80	40
Substantially different from UK product	20	10
Custom designed for each customer	71	35
Total	202	100

Source: Brown and Cook (1990).

Table 21.4 *Export pricing*

	Number	%
Different for each market related to local circumstances	98	47
Based on assessment of customer value	33	16
Based on UK price list	39	19
Based on total costs	30	15
Based on marginal costs	8	3
Total	208	100

Source: Brown and Cook (1990).

Table 21.5 *Success factors*

	Number of companies ranking	Weighted mean
Quality	173	3.88
Effective selling	122	2.80
Delivery	114	2.75
Design specification	112	3.50
Agents/distributors excellence	97	2.95
Service	95	2.43
Ability to tailor products	86	2.60
Low price	59	3.03
Market research	48	3.08
Agent/distributor relationship	48	2.85
Advertising/promotion	36	2.19

The top and bottom 3 factors are:

	By number of companies ranking	By weighted means
Top three	– quality – effective selling – delivery	– quality – design specification – market research
Bottom three	– market research – agency/distributor excellence – advertising/promotion	– ability tailor products – service – advertising/promotion

Source: Brown and Cook (1990).

Table 21.6 *Failure factors*

	Number of companies ranking	Weighted mean
Price	114	4.43
Specification problems	68	3.16
Delivery	58	3.21
Finance	58	3.24
Quality	49	3.76
Adaptation problems	35	2.63
Company image/reputation	31	2.65
UK image/reputation	24	2.89
After sales requirements	22	2.32

The top and bottom 3 factors are:

	By number of companies ranking	By weighted means
Top three	– price – specification problems – delivery/finance	– price – quality – finance
Bottom three	– company image/reputation – UK image/reputations – after sales requirements	– UK image/reputation – adaptation problems – after sales requirements

Source: Brown and Cook (1990).

2. It can undertake a joint venture with another company; for example Gerber's alliance with Corn Products.
3. It can set up a subsidiary company.

Licensing has several factors to recommend it:

*   It avoids the risk of expropriation of assets by the 'host' country, already familiar to many British companies with subsidiaries overseas.
*   It avoids direct competition with the licensee on his home ground. (Obviously, the licensee must have the same skills and resources as the licensor or there would be no point in taking up the license.)
*   It allows the capital resources that would be tied up in increased capacity, at home or abroad, to be deployed in other profitable opportunities. In the absence of the necessary capital resources, it permits the earning of increased profits which would otherwise be unattainable.
*   It enables the product to be produced at a competitive price, which might not be possible if it were to be exported as a finished good; for example float glass is both bulky and fragile and transportation costs would probably price it out of every foreign market where it is currently produced under licence.
*   Licensing avoids import tariffs and restrictions, and minimises the possibility of loss due to a change in trade policy.
*   It avoids the risks of product failure.

The major disadvantage to licensing is that the royalties are invariably less than the normal profits which would be earned if the product were manufactured and sold by the licensor.

Joint ventures require a greater commitment by the firm than is necessary in the case of licensing but, if successful, offer greater rewards for the risks assumed. An alliance with a well-established foreign distributor or manufacturer smoothes the exporter's entry into the market, but can lead to bitter conflict over policy and practice (for example, Concorde).

The establishment of a foreign subsidiary exposes one to all the risks which licensing minimises. Tax incentives are often offset by requirements that nationals of the foreign country hold a majority of the shares in the subsidiary, in which case it becomes a joint venture. It is also probably true to say that such incentives are directly proportionate to the risks.

In politically stable countries, however, the wholly owned subsidiary frequently offers the greatest potential – a factor which tends to be overlooked by restrictions on overseas investment. Economies of local production can be reinforced by the parent's technical, financial and marketing expertise and resources. Past experience would seem to suggest that the parent should avoid keeping too tight a rein on its subsidiary, and should be prepared to appoint foreign managers and delegate authority for all but major policy decisions to them. Long established European companies active in international markets would appear to have accepted this principle, but American firms have only lately begun to come round to this point of view, after some fairly costly attempts to retain full control at 'head office'.

Space limitations preclude fuller analysis of international marketing, for which the reader must refer to specialised texts on the subject. It is worth reiterating, however, that such texts rest on the same marketing principles as have been discussed in this book, so that their major contribution lies in the descriptive content rather than in their treatment of marketing technology.

The marketing challenge of the EU

John A. Quelch, Robert D. Buzzell and Eric R. Salama (1990) in *The Marketing Challenge of 1992*, consider that while effective marketing will be especially critical to competitive success in Europe post-1992, the economic studies prepared for the Commission largely ignore or take for granted the marketing processes by which many of the benefits must be achieved. More specifically they identify new product development for a 'Euromarket', the rationalisation of distribution systems and the development of new advertising and promotion programmes as calling for particular attention.

The need for an initiative which would release the latent potential of the EEC as an economic grouping able to compete effectively with the United States and Japan is readily apparent from an analysis of the EC's performance from its inception in 1957 to the publication of the White Paper in 1985. Over this period Europe steadily lost ground against the other members of the Triad. However, as Quelch *et al.* point out, what was particularly worrying was that following the recession triggered by the oil crisis of 1979, Europe recovered more slowly than either Japan or the USA despite an effective reduction in exchange rates of 35 per cent which should have significantly improved it competitiveness. Worse still, Europe was losing share in the technology based industries of the future while recording gains in sunset industries such as leather and footwear goods, wood and furniture, and textiles and clothing. Thus 'Europe's performance was best in those areas where research and development was relatively unimportant and where economies of scale could often be realised (at least in production terms) at the national market level (for example, food, drink, tobacco, textiles, clothing, and building materials).'

Recognition of the threat to Europe's competitiveness was not new and had been the subject of constant comment and criticism since the 1960s (see for example J. J. Servan-Schreiber, 1967, *The American Challenge*). What was different in the early 1980s was the identification of non-tariff barriers to trade and the fragmentation of European markets as a major contributory factor underlying a lacklustre competitive performance. The detailed analysis of academics, which documented specific cases of diseconomies due to conflicting national standards and to wasted R&D due to unnecessary duplication, were reinforced by industry's calls for European-wide standards and the elimination of discrimination between national governments within the community. Clearly the community was falling to achieve the vision of its architects as spelled out in the original 1958 Treaty of Rome which, *inter alia*, called for:

- The removal of customs duties and quotas, and any other regulatory measures which would impede the free flow of import, and exports.
- The establishment of a common commercial policy and customs tariff toward non-member countries.
- A common competition policy to prevent distortions between members.
- Common transport policies and the free movement of people, services and capital between member states.
- The coordination of member states' economic policies and procedures to achieve equilibrium in international competition.

This failure to realise the potential of a united Europe was even more depressing when one considers the basic advantages which an effective coalition could build upon. As James Dudley (1992) points out:

Half the world's trade is conducted in the European Community. The combined gross domestic product (GDP) of all its members make it the second largest economic bloc in the world, behind North America. The EC has an approximate population of 323 million people, making it the second largest populated market in the free world behind India.

It has 228 of the top 1000 companies in the world – behind Japan with 310 and the US with 345. Europe has 115 companies with profits exceeding $200 million compared with Japan with 58 and the US with 205. Even so the EC has a technology deficit of $10.6 billion with its competitors mainly Japan and North America.

However, and despite the successive failures of the Fouchet plan (Foreign Policy), the Werner plan (economic and monetary union) and Tindeman's proposals for a European Union, which foundered on the protectionist policies of natio-nalistic governments, in 1985 the European heads of state agreed to a programme of legislation which would lead to a single unified market by 1992. The benefits which such unification would confer were summarised in the Cecchini Report to the European Commission and are set out in Tables 21.7 and 21.8.

What was different about the 1985 Single European Act was that while its primary objec-tive was as in 1958 to create 'an area without internal frontiers in which the free movement of goods, persons, services and capital is ensured', this time 300 separate pieces of enabling legisla-tion were spelled out and the Act provided for decisions to be made by a majority of 54 votes of a possible 76. Prior to this decisions required the unanimous agreement of all members with the inevitable result that progress was at best slow and often non-existent.

Quelch *et al.*, Dudley and others provide extended discussion of the particular provisions for the programme of legislation to be com-pleted by 1992 and these will not be repeated here. What is often overlooked, as Quelch *et al.* point out, is that while the legislation changes the rules of the game they will not by themselves confer gains or losses on individual companies. As in any other competitive situa-tion such changes represent both threats and opportunities and it will be the response of competing firms which will determine whether they benefit or lose out as the result of a changed environment.

In general there is a wide measure of agreement that the creation of a unified single market will be beneficial to firms, to industries and member nations. That said, it is also clear that many of these perceptions are founded on the belief that such firms, industries and nations will be winners

Table 21.7 *Potential gains in economic welfare for the EC resulting from completion of the internal market*

	Billions Ecu	Per cent of GDP
Step 1		
Gains from removal of barriers affecting trade	8–9	0.2–0.3
Step 2		
Gains from removal of barriers affecting overall production	57–71	2.0–2.4
Gains from removing barriers (sub-total)	65–80	2.2–2.7
Step 3		
Gains from exploiting economies of scale more fully	61	2.1
Step 4		
Gains from intensified competition reducing business inefficiencies and monopoly profits	46	1.6
Gains from market integration (sub-total)	62*–107	2.1*–3.7
Total		
• for 7 Member States at 1985 prices	127–187	4.3–6.4
• for 12 Member States at 1988 prices	174–258	4.3–6.4
• mid-point of above	216	5.3

Note: * This alternative estimate for the sum of steps 3 and 4 cannot be broken down between the two steps
Source: *Commission of EC*, study of Directorate-General for Economic and Financial Affairs.

Table 21.8 *Macroeconomic consequences of EC market integration for the Community in the medium term*

	Customs formalities	Public procurement	Financial services effects	Supply side	Average value	Total Spread
Relative changes (%)						
GDP	0.4	0.5	1.5	2.1	4.5	(3.2–5.7)
Consumer prices	−1.0	−1.4	−1.4	−2.3	−6.1	(−4.5– −7.7)
Absolute changes						
Employment (millions)	200	350	400	850	1800	(1300–2300)
Budgetary balance (percentage of GDP)	0.2	0.3	1.1	0.6	2.2	(1.5–3.0)
External balance (percentage of GDP)	0.2	0.1	0.3	0.4	1.0	(0.7–1.3)

Source: HERMES (EC Commission and national teams) and INTERLINK (OECD).

rather than possible losers (see, for example, Chapter 2 in Quelch *et al.*).

As of 1995, Quelch *et al*'s diagnosis would appear best to summarise the creation of the EU – while legislation may have changed the rules of the game it does not confer any particular benefits or disbenefits on specific companies. Such gains or losses flow from the firm's ability to respond to the environmental change by deploying and redeploying its skills, assets and resources to optimum effect. To do so it needs to understand and apply the general principles for effective marketing practice described in this book.

The changing global environment

In their introduction to the *International Marketing Reader*, Stanley Paliwoda and John K Ryans Jr (1995) provide an excellent summary of 'the primary change agents that have altered the gloval environment of business' (p. 2), as well as eight new directions in international marketing which have resulted from this changing environment.

To begin with, Paliwoda and Ryans cite three major changes which have and are impacting on international business:

1. Regional integration and global organisation;
2. Industry concentration;
3. Technology developement.

The establishment of the European Union touched on in the preceding section is but one example of a wave of regional integration that has created new economic alliances. Thus Canada, Mexico and the US formed the North American Free Trade Association (NAFTA) which continues to attract new members while similar alliances have developed around the Pacific Rim building upon ASEAN (the Association of South East Asian Nations), and the Indian Ocean Rim (IOR). Concurrently with these new regional alliances the world has seen the disintegration of the old Soviet Bloc with the USSR becoming a group of quasi-independent republics while countries such as Poland, Hungary, Czechoslovakia (now two countries) have

Table 21.9 *Eight new directions in international marketing*

1. The full impact of the EU (and its partners), NAFTA, and economic integration in general are just beginning to be recognized by marketers. For example, Eurobrands are just beginning to gain importance
2. The increased number of strategic alliances, especially marketing alliances, have dramatically altered new product strategy and development, especially in high technology firms
3. More and more firms are testing the use or moving directly to standardized (or global) marketing, particularly promotion. This has increased dramatically the segmentation and pre-testing work in overseas markets
4. Time-to-market and product differentiation (physical and psychological) are becoming even more significant in the second half of the 1990s
5. The importance to the firm of getting immediate awareness, image and preference data from the EU, etc., has led to new types of marketing research, suich as the use of omnibus tracking studies
6. Regulation is becoming an increasingly important factor in marketing planning; the developments in GATT and the new World Trade Organization highlight this importance
7. Greater concentration in retailing and the total channel for consumer products is underway, as is the growth of the international retailer. Business-to-business markets are finding it increasingly difficult to identify exclusive agents and reps, as concentration is becoming stronger in most European middlemen categories
8. Cconsumers in virtually all markets have shown more price sensitivity, as evidenced by the success of private brands. To date, market concentration in most industries has failed to lead to price increases

Source: Paliwoda, Stanley and Ryans, John K. Jr (1995) *International Marketing Reader* (London: Routledge).

become fully independent. Apartheid has ended in South Africa and countries such as China, India and Vietnam have increasingly encouraged foreign investment. To cope with these changes firms need to reappraise radically how they organise their operations in order to compete effectively.

The second major trend identified is the continuing move to larger and larger global corporations through a process of merger, acquisition and strategic alliance. A major factor driving this increased concentration is the pursuit of global economies in *marketing*, particularly in leveraging brand values and economies of scope and scale in promotion and distribution.

In terms of technology development the major impact on marketing has undoubtedly come from communications and the strategic use of information technology. The fax, satellite television, video-conferencing, the internet, E-mail and so on, have all made instantaneoeus, real-time contact possible 24 hours a day, every day. 'Time' has assumed a whole new significance in both the planning and execution of marketing operations.

As a consequence of these and other trends Paliwoda and Ryans propose eight new directions in international marketing. These are essentially self-explanatory and are reproduced as Table 21.9.

Summary

In this chapter we have attempted a broadly based and wide-ranging review of the scope and nature of marketing in a Foreign environment. We have deliberately avoided using the more commonplace term 'International Marketing' for two reasons. First, this is an introductory text book concerned with general principles. In our view the general principles of marketing are universally applicable so that the material contained in earlier chapters is just as relevant to foreign markets as domestic ones. Despite this, our second reason for not using the more usual and more fashionable 'international marketing' is because this constitutes a distinctive sub-field of the subject which deserves specialised treatment and it is not possible to achieve this in an introductory text.

For these reasons we have chosen to emphasise how marketing is a vital element in economic growth wherever it occurs. Given that economies are associated with nation states, then the advantages and disadvantages of competition and exchange between them is

an issue of major importance and the theory of comparative advantage provides important insights into the benefits of international trade. It also prompts the question as to whether a single global market will eventually emerge or whether we will see the continued existence of differentiated national markets. Some consideration of these issues prompted a review of alternative approaches to marketing in foreign environments. Next we examined the marketing challenge of the EU as a specific example of the creation and development of regional trading blocs which led naturally to a review of the implications of global trends on international marketing practice.

Review questions and problems

1. Planning for international market entry and development involves a process of matching company capabilities and objectives with the requirements and characteristics of selected country markets. Discuss with reference to company and country examples.

2. Using company examples to illustrate your answer, evaluate the major trends currently taking place in the global competitive strategies of MNEs.

3. Do you agree with the view of Bartlett and Ghoshal (1989) that the concept of globalisation has become dated, being superseded by the need for transnationality?

4. 'Global marketing is not just standardisation of the marketing mix.' Evaluate this statement with particular reference to the product and promotion elements of the mix.

▌ Supplementary reading list

Bennett, R. (1995) *International Marketing: Strategy, Planning, Market Entry and Implementation* (London: Kogan Page).

Bradley, E. (1995) *International Marketing Strategy*, 2nd edn (New York: Prentice-Hall).

Czinkota, M. and Ronkainen, I. K. (1995) *International Marketing*, 4th edn (London: Dryden Press).

Douglas, Susan P. and Craig, C. Samuel (1995) *Global Marketing Strategies* (New York: McGraw-Hill).

Jain, S. C. (1993) *International Marketing Management*, 4th edn (Wadsworth).

Jeannet, J. P. and Hennessey, H. D. (1995) *Global Marketing Strategies*, 3rd edn (Boston: Houghton Mifflin).

Paliwoda, S. J. (1995) *International Marketing*, 2nd edn (London: Heinemann).

Piercy, N. (1982) *Export Strategy: Markets and Competition* (London: George Allen & Unwin).

Segal-Horn, S. (1994) *The Challenge of International Business* (London: Kogan Page).

Usunier, J. C. (1993) *International Marketing: A Cultural Approach* (Englewood Cliffs, N.J.: Prentice-Hall).

Yip, G. S. (1992) *Total Global Strategy: Managing for Worldwide Competitive Advantage* (Englewood Cliffs, N.J.: Prentice-Hall).

Young, S., Hamill, J. and Wheeler, C. (1989) *International Market Entry and Development: Strategy and Management* (Brighton: Wheatsheaf).

■ *Chapter 22* ■

The Marketing of Services

Contents

Learning Goals

The issues to be addressed in this chapter include:

1. The nature of factors which underlie the growth of services in the economy.
2. The types of services available.
3. The characteristics which distinguish services from physical products.
4. Specific issues involved in the marketing of services.

After reading this chapter you will be able to:

1. Identify and describe three basic factors which account for the growth of the service sector.

2. List the principal types of services available.
3. Specify and describe the four characteristics – intangibility, inseparability, heterogeneity and perishability and fluctuating demand – which are used to distinguish services from physical products.
4. Compare and contrast the view that service marketing is the same as the marketing of goods with the opposing view that it is significantly different and calls for a distinctive approach.
5. Define and describe the seven Ps of the service marketing mix – product, process, price, place, promotion, physical evidence and people.

■ Introduction

One of the most striking features of the last three decades has been the enormous growth in the service sector within the world's advanced industrial economies. In part this growth has been due to the relentless acceleration in the pace of technological change which has resulted in significant improvements in productivity. In part it is due to the fact that the slowing down of population growth in these countries has reduced the expansion of demand for physical goods. Taken together these trends have seen a marked shift in employment from the secondary or manufacturing sector to the tertiary, services sector accompanied by a similar shift in expenditure patterns from goods to services. In this chapter we will first review the nature and extent of this growth in services before examining the factors or characteristics which are seen as differentiating services from physical products – intangibility, inseparability, heterogeneity, and perishability and fluctuating demand.

Examination of these distinguishing characteristics leads naturally into a discussion of whether the marketing of services is similar to or different from the marketing of physical goods. As one might expect two schools of thought exist – those who claim they are the same and those who claim they are different! Our analysis will suggest a compromise and argue that, while the basic principles are equally applicable to both, the distinctive nature of services calls for an extended marketing mix comprising seven elements with process, physical evidence and people being added to McCarthy's familiar four Ps of product, place, price and promotion. Each of these is explored in some detail and points to the potential for applying marketing principles and ideas to the whole range of economic activity, including the service sector.

However, in the same manner that it is necessary to adjust the nature of the marketing mix to suit the nature of the product and the market which it serves, so it is with services. In the case of services this need is emphasised because as Shostack (1982) has observed:

> the difference between products and services is more than semantic. Products are tangible objects that exist in both time and space; services consist solely of acts or process(es), and exist in time only.

She believes that:

> the basic distinction between 'things' and 'processes' is the starting point for a focused investigation of services. Services are rendered; products are possessed. Services cannot be possessed; they can only be experienced, created or participated in.

Table 22.1 summarises some typical differences between manufacturing and service industries.

Table 22.1　*Some typical differences between manufacturing industry and service industry*

Manufacturing	Service
The product is generally concrete	The service is immaterial
Ownership is transferred when a purchase is made	Ownership is not generally transferred
The product can be resold	The service cannot be resold
The product can be demonstrated before purchase	The service cannot usually be effectively demonstrated (it does not exist before purchase)
The product can be stored by sellers and buyers	The product cannot be stored
Consumption is preceded by production	Production and consumption generally coincide
Production, selling and consumption are locally differentiated	Production, consumption and often even selling are spatially united
The product can be transported	The service cannot be transported (though 'producers' often can)
The seller produces	The buyer/client takes part directly in the production
Indirect contact is possible between company and client	In most cases direct contact is necessary
Can be exported	The service cannot normally be exported, but the service delivery system can

■ Growth of services

The growth in service can be seen by the increase in employment in the service sector and the growth of services' contribution to GDP. In 1971, services accounted for 48 per cent of GDP whilst in 1993, the share of employment in the service sector was 68 per cent. The reasons for the growth in services can be attributed to the following:

1. *Impact of technology* – The major technological breakthroughs achieved in recent years have been one reason for the growth in services. Technology has had a significant impact on the volume and quality of products now available, and it has been suggested by Markin (1982) that more goods or products often lead indirectly to an increased demand for services (the 'knock on' or 'multiplier' effect).
2. *Deregulation and increased competition* – In certain industries there have been changes governing the market entry requirements for firms which has resulted in greater opportunities for service companies to offer more services to customers more easily. For example, this has been a prominent feature of the financial sector in the UK, where building societies can now offer cheque accounts, and created a competitive advantage over the bank by offering interest on these accounts which the banks have had to match. Likewise, banks now offer mortgages to customers and estate agents can now provide complete legal services as part of a house sale and purchase for clients.
3. *Customer sophistication* – As society becomes wealthier and people have more time available compared with 30 to 40 years ago, the basic needs in life such as housing and food are more easily satisfied, and people begin to spend more of their income on wants, rather than needs. In this respect, they do not need more cars, refrigerators or clothing, but increasingly use their income to follow other, more leisure-based activities, such as holidays, eating out or taking up new hobbies.

☐ *Types of services*

Services may be mainly professional or consumer oriented. Professional service firms may serve the business-to-business market, the private individual or may serve both market segments. Professional services are often characterised by the following: advisory and problem solving; provided by a qualified professional known for their speciality; include an assignment requested by the client; provided by a professional who is independent and not connected with other suppliers; supervised by professional associations which attempt to define the nature of the profession, to lay down requirements of competence, to control the practice of the profession and to enforce a code of ethics (Gardner, 1986). These would include services like financial advice, advertising, business and management consultancy, engineering, architectural and interior design, legal, and medical (Gardner, 1986) to which may be added other agencies and brokers, such as estate agents, stock and insurance brokers and market research agencies (Yorke, 1990). Those firms which tend to be non-professional again may either be in the business-to-business market, or be consumer oriented. Those services which may be included in the former category can include office catering services, cleaning services or offer cash transference services such as Securicor. Those service firms which may be in the latter category are the ones which the consumer is more acquainted with, such as holiday tour companies (for example Thomsons, Lunn Poly), fast food outlets (for example Burger King, MacDonald's) or entertainment companies (for example Mecca, Canon).

▮ The nature and characteristics of services

The characteristics of services have been classified under four main headings, namely intangibility, inseparability, heterogeneity, perishability and fluctuating demand (Stanton, 1981).

☐ *Intangibility*

Intangibility is probably the single most important factor in distinguishing services from goods.

While it is possible to describe the nature and performance of physical products using objective criteria, this is only possible to a limited extent in the case of services. Intangibility has two dimensions (Bateson, 1977) – the physical inability to touch an item and the mental difficulty in accepting an idea. Whilst it may be possible to elicit opinions or attitudes from friends or colleagues about a service before purchase is made, these characteristics have important implications for marketing planning. The evaluation of competitive is more difficult *vis-à-vis* goods purchasing since the customer can touch most products to evaluate them, whereas the customer has to search for tangible clues of the service in order to evaluate it.

Another important aspect of the intangibility factor is the ease with which services can be imitated and the lack of formal patent protection –

which leaves the service organisation the problem of distinguishing themselves from their competitors. Shostack (1982) states that, 'while "that which is marketed" may still be a simple product or unadorned service, it is often a more complex combination of products and services'. She illustrates her point in Figure 22.1.

However, some marketers regard the physical nature of a product as secondary in the sense that buyers are primarily concerned with the 'bundle of satisfactions' which flow from the product, rather than the product itself – for example the technical specification of a television set is rarely considered by the user, who will probably judge it on the basis of picture and sound quality as they appear to them. Further, as it has been pointed out (Wickham *et al.*, 1975), for many products tangibility does not permit physical evaluation in

Figure 22.1   *Scale of elemental dominance*

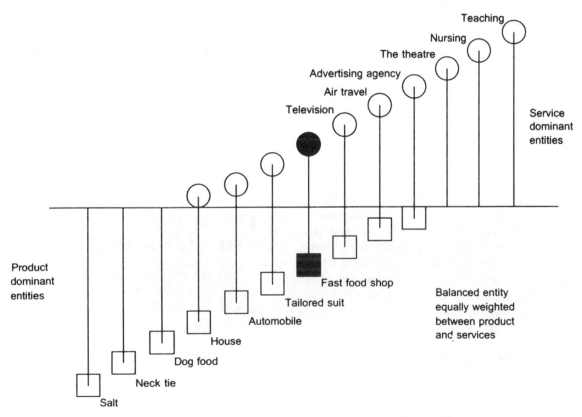

Source: G. L. Shostack (1982), 'How to Design a Service', *European Journal of Marketing*, vol. 16(1).

any meaningful way, so that such products tend to be selected on the basis of reputation, advice and experience rather than on the basis of physical examination. If this is the case, a consideration of ascertaining the *benefits* that consumers want or expect would be a more powerful means of developing effective marketing strategies.

☐ *Inseparability*

The second differentiating factor of services is inseparability – that is to say, there is no distinction between *delivery* and *use* due to many services being produced and consumed simultaneously. Unlike manufacturing firms, the sale of the service must be made before production and consumption occurs and the customer receives the 'product' they are buying at the same time as it is being supplied. For example, you must be physically present at the dentist to receive dental treatment or at the hairdressers to have your hair cut. In this way therefore, a retail outlet may encounter problems with unobliging staff, a restaurant may have a poor chef, or a businessman may be unhappy with the bank teller's attitude on a Monday morning. Alternatively, the service company also must realise the significance of customer participation in the process. For example, customers may not have the ideal knowledge of filling out an application form for a mortgage or bank loan, or know how a self-service petrol pump works. This then breaks down the production/consumption interface because the customer is behaving in a difficult way for the firm. Therefore, service firms need to control the production side of the service as much as possible through the use of internal marketing as customers' perceptions of the service can be badly affected by the quality of the input as well as making the service easier to use for customers. The company must remember that some customers may not complain to the service firm directly about the poor quality service they received, but would rather show their dissatisfaction by taking their custom elsewhere or spreading the news around their friends or colleagues about the poor treatment they received.

☐ *Heterogeneity*

The third characteristic which distinguishes services from goods is the ability to be uniform or standard. Services are heterogeneous, that is, variable, while goods are usually uniform. One would usually know what to expect when one buys a car, but it is difficult to predict whether a rock band will give the same quality of performance at a concert on the opening night of their tour versus the final night performance, or for that matter, whether the same performance would be appropriate for their fans anyway. This problem of expecting people to perform in an identical way each time is hampered due to the high level of contact between 'producer' and consumer – for example, how would you feel if a customer is aggressive towards you or if a sales assistant is too impatient to answer your queries? Therefore it is difficult to forecast and ensure provision of the same quality of a service over time when the quality itself can be affected by both the performance of the provider of the service, at the time at which it is provided, as well as the behaviour of the consumer. Due to this inseparability it therefore is difficult, if not impossible for the service organisation to standardise output and gain economies of scale in much the same way as a manufacturing organisation.

☐ *Perishability and fluctuating demand*

The fourth major dimension which distinguishes between services and goods is that services cannot be stored or inventoried in the same way as physical goods. This inability to store services means that unused service capacity and revenue is lost forever. For example, empty seats in theatres, unsold air tickets, and unbooked rooms in hotels illustrate the risk inherent in service perishability. This problem is overcome, usually, in certain service industries such as tourism and communications where service firms encourage the ordinary consumer to take a weekend break at a quiet time of year or to use the telephone at off-peak times, in order to encourage people to use these services thereby ensuring the service organisation will not suffer from too great a fluctuation in demand. Demand management in services is far more subtle than it is for products, and it would be much more constructive to think in terms of capacity availability; that is, one can only consume what is available, yet this point is frequently ignored in developing marketing strategies for services.

Managing services marketing – the seven Ps

Many marketing scholars have been preoccupied with discussing whether the marketing of services is similar to or different from the marketing of physical goods. There are two different schools of thought with regard to the applicability of product marketing concepts and techniques to services marketing – that is product-based versus service-based approaches. One school of thought believes that services are not different from physical goods, and that therefore the same concepts and techniques used in goods marketing can be directly translated to services marketing. Most of the arguments suggested by the adapters of this view centre round the following two points:

1. The claimed differences between goods and services are exaggerated and provide little insight to understanding either of them. In addition the preoccupation with such a simple service–product classification is myopic and likely to be unsuitable. Instead more multidimensional classifications are needed in which the marketing strategy of the firm is a function of offer characteristics, market characteristics and characteristics of the exchange process (Wickham *et al.*, 1975; Goodfellow, 1983).

2. The most important criterion to be considered when marketing any product (including physical goods, services, ideas and so forth) is the buyer's expectations. Many commentators argue that consumers are not buying goods or services, but the value satisfaction of the offering. So it is suggested that the process of marketing strategy formulation should start with a product concept which recognises the bundle of benefits, often including both tangible and intangible aspects as it is perceived by the potential buyer (Levitt, 1974; Donnelly and George, 1981).

Dissatisfaction with this approach leads many authors to take their thinking to the other extreme and call for a theory for marketing services. According to the service-based approach, it is argued that services possess certain distinguishing features which make them fundamentally different from physical goods. Therefore the suggestion advanced is that service marketers must develop a unique process of marketing strategy formulation for services which differs from the traditional one.

The development of a service marketing theory as a frame of reference which guides the marketer's thinking deals with either the service area (that is, its organisational aspects (Blois, 1982), consumer behaviour (Blois, 1982), marketing mix activities (Shostack, 1984; Donnelly, 1976)) or a specific aspect of it, for example, professional services (Gummesson, 1979).

According to this approach, it is argued that the marketing of services is much more complex than the marketing of goods due to fundamental difference in the end products and the simultaneous production and consumption processes. As such it is suggested that service marketers need new tools, strategies and organisation structures to carry out the process of marketing services effectively.

Drawing on the concept of McCarthy's four Ps for product marketing, the services marketing mix has been extended to seven Ps (Cowell, 1984, adapted from Booms and Bitner, 1982). These have been described as product, process, price, place, promotion, physical evidence and people.

☐ *Product*

From Chapter 11 it can be clearly seen that the marketer of physical goods has a variety of strategic options open to them when determining their product range. In the same way, the service marketer is faced with similar decisions in developing their product mix. The product mix should take into account that services are made up of two parts – the 'core service' and the 'auxiliary service' (Gronroos, 1980). The core service is similar to what Kotler (1988) termed the 'core product'; that is, it is the basic service which is offered, for example, dry cleaning. The 'auxiliary' service is similar to Kotler's (1988) 'augmented product'; that is to say, the added benefits which differentiate the service from competitors. In the case of dry cleaning, this could be same day delivery service to your home or office so that you do not have the hassle of picking the garment up at the end of the day. The quality of the service can be divided into two types – technical quality, that is the actual cleaning of the garment, and the functional quality, that is how the service is actually presented or delivered (Gronroos, 1982). This aspect of the service is important with respect to 'physical evidence', as the customer will evaluate anything which is tangible about the service, such as the care with which the garment is packed or the uniform of the delivery boy, so it is therefore necessary to ensure all aspect of the service, be it core or auxiliary, are of a high standard.

☐ *Process*

The process element of the service marketing mix is concerned with the way in which the service is delivered to the customer. This has two points of interest to the service marketer. First, the inseparability characteristic of services has an important implication for how the service company's personnel deliver the service to the customer and how the customer participates in the service delivery process. Secondly, the 'auxiliary' aspect of the service, that is the added value of the service, becomes an important competitive weapon in differentiating the service from competitors when the service is experienced by customers. One example of how process can be used to competitive advantage is through the marketing of financial services. The basic need for a bank is to store money in a safe place until we need access to it. This access has been improved considerably over the last few years by banks when they introduced services such as ATMs (Automated Teller Machines), charge cards, and through a variety of cheque book accounts on offer. However, when ATMs were first introduced, although advances in technology did increase the availability of the service, customers did not know how to use them, and they were then left to work it out for themselves. Therefore, the overall effectiveness of the service process fundamentally depends on how the customers use the service. Lowe (1988) reinforces this point that services have been defined as 'acts rather than things' and this casts some light on the concept of 'process'. Many benefits from services occur not so much as a result of what is offered, as in the way in which it is offered.

☐ *Price*

Pricing a service is generally believed to be more difficult than the pricing of manufactured goods as discussed in Chapter 13. Cowell (1984) has produced a useful table highlighting the variety of prices for selected services.

From Table 22.2, it is clear that services range from those supplied by the private company, to public utilities and professional service groups. It is also fair to assume that there are many different factors which influence price, one of which can be the service's role in society. For example, the pricing for public transport such as buses or trains will often be determined by public regulation in order to make the service attractive, and within reach of the majority of people. Pricing in professional services such as solicitors' and stockbrokers' fees are largely governed by professional

Table 22.2 *Price terminology for selected services*

Terminology	Typical service
Admission	Theatre entry
Charge	Hairdressing
Commission	Stockbroking service
Dues	Union membership
Fare	Transport
Fee	Legal service
Honorarium	Guest speaker
Interest	Use of money
Premium	Insurance
Rate	Municipal services
Rent	Property usage
Retainer	Consultant's services
Salary	Employee services
Subscription	Membership
Tariff	Utilities
Toll	Road use
Tuition	Education
Wage	Employee services

Source: D. Cowell (1984), *The Marketing of Services* (Oxford: Heinemann).

bodies, whereas services such as hairdressing or car hire charges are largely governed by market demand. This classification by Rathmell (1974) has proved useful in clarifying how prices in the service sector can be set, but it leaves a great deal to be desired when setting price at the tactical level and using price as a marketing weapon.

Wilson (1972) believes 'Outside the areas of fixed, standard or customary prices, the use of pricing in the marketing mix remains primitive and awaits only intelligent application for substantial rewards to be reaped'. This is echoed by Cowell (1984) who believes 'pricing has not yet received the attention it deserves' with regards to service marketing, and that 'As with other marketing mix elements, the price of a service should be related to the achievement of marketing and organisational goals and should be appropriate for the service organisation's marketing programme'. The difficulty, it is said, lies in the diverse nature and characteristics of services which leads to sweeping generalisations.

Cowell (1984) discusses how the characteristics of services can influence the service price, although he emphasises that these should be considered *in addition to* the traditional forces which influence price, these being costs, competition and demand. There are five categories which he considers:

1. Service perishability – since services cannot be inventoried like manufactured goods, service companies have to be prepared for fluctuations in demand at certain times of the year. Cowell (1984) cites the example of the holiday tour market, where price discounts can be made at the last minute, in order to sell unused holidays. However, he warns against increasing 'customer sophistication' where buyers almost expect these bargains to be made available at certain times of the year, and therefore hold back until the cheaper holidays are advertised, since they know the tour operator will he more keen to sell at a cheaper price then to have unsold holidays. However, in order to offset this trend and encourage potential customers, some companies have offered discounts of up to £100 off summer holidays to those customers who book early.

2. Competition between service companies increases in certain industries when customers can afford the luxury of postponing the use of the service and be able to 'shop around' for the best deal by telling the interested parties how little other companies have offered, for example van removals.

3. Intangibility – since customers using the service for the first time may not know how to evaluate what they are receiving for their money exactly, they may evaluate the service on the basis of the tangible features of the service that they receive. Taking you back to Shostack's (1977) tangibility/intangibility continuum (Figure 22.1), most goods have a degree of the service element attached to them, and likewise, most services have a degree of tangibility as well. 'The higher the material content, the more will prices set tend to be based on costs and the greater the tendency towards more standard prices. The

smaller the material content the more customer orientated and the less standard will prices be' (Cowell, 1984).

Service companies can use this to their advantage when, if a customer negotiates a lower price for the use of the service, the company has at its disposal the ability to vary the quality of the service according to what it perceives the customer is getting for their money.

4. When services are more or less standardised with regards to their use (for example laundrettes), prices are usually very competitive. Alternatively, companies may be subject to regulations regarding the minimum price they may charge, or they may have the freedom to sell at whatever price the market will bear.

5. Inseparability – The degree of price competition in the market will to a large extent be influenced by the number of competing firms within that area. Customers may be limited to a small geographic area in order to experience the service or only be able to use the service at particular times, which will influence the price service companies can charge.

The price of services is influenced by a number of factors, namely: the planned market position for the service product; the stage of the life-cycle of the service product; elasticity of demand; the competitive situation; and the strategic role of price (Christopher *et al.*, 1980). Gabor (1980) identified two methods for pricing services:

1. *Cost-based pricing* – either a profit-oriented method, where price setting is done by professional associations, or government controlled.

2. *Market-oriented pricing* – the company is either setting prices for competitive reasons or because the firm is customer oriented.

Cowell (1984) feels that 'many of the tactical price techniques used to sell tangibles can be used to sell intangibles', citing such tactics (as identified by McDonald and Stromberger, 1969) as differential or flexible pricing; discrete pricing; discount pricing; diversionary pricing;

guarantee pricing; high price maintenance pricing; loss leader pricing; offset pricing; and price lining which can be suitable for setting prices in services. He also outlines three additional aspects of service pricing which are inherent to services:

1. *Price negotiation* – many services' prices can be negotiated before the client receives the service, such as interest payments on loans or advertising agency fees.

2. *Competitive bidding* – this is more prominent in organisational markets when the client can shop around for the best deal.

3. *Price awareness* – similar to the pricing of goods, this is when the service company can set its pricing strategy according to how the market perceives the nature of pricing in that particular service industry. When the customer is relatively unsure of the price, the service company can use this to its advantage, as they tend to perceive price as an indicator of quality, due to the lack of evidence available (Eiglier and Langeard, 1977).

However, in summary, Cowell (1984) believes that the pricing of services 'still remains largely a combination of good management, experience, trial and error, intuition and good luck'.

☐ *Place*

This is the environment in which the service is assembled and where the firm and customer interact, and any tangible commodities which facilitate performance or communication of the service.

Place has a number of aspects of concern to the service marketer – the actual location of the premises, the look of the premises, and the channels of distribution used. All of these aspects vary in importance of course, depending on the service offered, and the preferred channel(s) of distribution of the service marketer.

First, the inseparability characteristic of services means that the distribution channels are far shorter than for a goods manufacturer – the customer almost always has to visit the 'manufacturer' in order to receive the service. Therefore the location of the premises is an important factor. The location of a dentist will vary according to whether he would like to be based in a local community where the customers' main requirements would be to visit somewhere nearby for treatment, or whether he should set his surgery in the middle of a large town, where it would be convenient for commuters to visit him during the day without too much disruption to their working day, and thereby saving them the inconvenience of taking a day off work to visit the dentist. This means that in order to expand, service firms have to either build more outlets (unlike goods manufacturers who expand production facilities or make them more efficient). This has an important drawback in that it is a very capital intensive process. Alternatives for service firms may be to franchise the operation or to use agents to promote the service. However, although this may solve the expansion problem, the service company is faced with losing control over the quality of the service since it will not be their own staff they are training and who will be providing the service.

As far as the look of the premises is concerned, the client will be searching for physical clues in assessing the success of the company. For example, the client would not have a great deal of confidence in a solicitor if the solicitor's office was poorly furnished. This would imply that the solicitor either did not care about his job, and therefore the client's problems, or that they were not successful enough even to afford to pay a few hundred pounds to have the office decorated, in which case, there may be something wrong with the solicitor's services or reputation.

The channels of distribution available to a number of service marketers have improved considerably over recent years due to improvements in telecommunications. This is especially the case in banking, where transactions can be made using either electronic systems or ATMs.

☐ *Promotion*

From Chapters 16 and 17 the uses and benefits of promotional techniques such as advertising, sales promotion, and public relations became clear for physical products, but how appropriate are these same techniques for the promotion of services?

Service firms are very rarely national or international in size and scope, but tend to be local firms servicing the local community. There are of course exceptions to this, especially with regards to franchise operations such as the Body Shop and Tie Rack and the international professional service firms, such as advertising agencies, management consultancies and accountancy firms. However, by and large, most service firms are based locally. By implication, therefore, this would mean that most service firms undertake promotion only at the local level. However, the effectiveness of promotional campaigns has been disputed regarding the advertising of services.

Rathmell (1974) has stated that the intangibility feature of services means that the service cannot be viewed physically, and it therefore cannot be advertised or shown in the same way as physical goods, but needs to be presented as an idea. The difficulty is made even more acute in trying to use sales promotion techniques such as demonstrations, money off coupons, and posting samples of the service around the areas you would like to target because of the intangibility feature. Unwin (1975) echoed this difficulty in saying:

> service advertising is difficult. It offers no tangible rewards, no immediate sensations. The service advertiser has to deal in abstractions like prudence, safety and peace of mind. He is often left with describing the invisible, articulating the imaginary and defining the indistinct. It is difficult to know what to highlight and where to draw the line. And how many service customers really know what they want, or even if they want it?

In order to minimise the problems associated with advertising a service, Shostack (1977) recommended neutralising the intangibility of the service by associating some form of tangible evidence to the service in the promotional material. Berry

(1980) also feels that this would make the service more 'palpable' (that is, understandable) for the consumer. Other strategies could be through seeking professional endorsements by trade associations or using popular personalities in order to create or improve customer confidence. Lowe (1988) has found that word-of-mouth promotion is perhaps the best for service companies:

> The intangible nature of services means that people find it difficult to make a judgement on relatively objective grounds, so they rely on the experience of those who actually used the service to a greater degree than might be the case if a tangible product were involved.

☐ *Physical evidence*

Since a service is inherently intangible, it is important for the client to search for tangible or physical clues which enable them to evaluate the service. 'Service firms must be aware that every aspect of the company with which the consumer comes into contact will be used as a measure of the level of service that he can expect from the organisation' (Lowe, 1988). Physical evidence are those tangible clues which the consumer may receive during the process of receiving the service, which 'verify either the existence or the completion of a service' (Shostack, 1982). She further classifies physical evidence into two categories – peripheral evidence and essential evidence.

- *Peripheral evidence* – is usually 'possessed as part of the purchase of a service, but it has little or no independent value'. She cites the example of a cheque book which is not of any use without the funds transfer and storage service that it represents.
- *Essential evidence* – is 'unlike peripheral evidence . . . [as it] cannot be possessed by the consumer'. However, Shostack believes that essential evidence may be 'so dominant in its impact on service purchase and use that it must be considered virtually an element in its own right'. She cites the example of a consumer who purchases transportation in the form of an airline ticket (peripheral evidence) who will probably have been influenced by the type of aircraft that 'facilitates' the service since it will have a strong impact on service perceptions and even purchase.

However, one important point should be made about the management of physical evidence. Research should be conducted in order to assess the expectations of the target market's perceptions of the service environment – what may represent the standard of physical evidence expected from a particular service organisation, may seem like an expensive luxury which will be passed on to the client in the form of higher prices or fees. An example of this would be having a doorman in splendid livery outside a restaurant.

☐ *People*

Of all the controllable variables marketing executives have at their disposal, the people factor in the services marketing mix is perhaps the least they can rely on in getting their marketing mix 'right', and the most important one they *have* to get right. The problem lies in inseparability of the production/consumption interface, and therefore, the satisfaction of not only the recipient of the service, that is the customer, but also the providers of the service, that is the company's own personnel become extremely important.

Service personnel are present at two levels within the organisation – contact personnel and support personnel. Contact personnel are those individuals whom the customers see – such as waiters or receptionists – and whom the customers judge the service upon when they search for tangible clues as to the quality of the service. The value they attribute to the service relies a great deal on the conduct of the contact personnel.

It is very rare for customers to meet the chefs who prepare the meals or the cleaning staff who prepare guests' bedrooms. Imagine being served by a waiter who has an unkempt appearance when you are visiting a restaurant or being told by a member of the cabin crew that the only difference between paying for a first class air ticket and club class is that you have spent £200 more than the other passengers. This type of behaviour is hardly conducive to developing customer loyalty in the medium-to-long term, and yet both are real examples of the behaviour of service personnel. Had the individuals been happy with their jobs, this type of ill-mannered and off-putting behaviour could have been avoided and customer satisfaction maintained. How can a company ensure that its personnel at both levels will provide a quality service leaving a favourable impression on customers?

The answer lies in 'internal marketing' (Gronroos, 1982), the purpose of which is to have 'motivated and customer-conscious employees'. Employees are seen as internal customers, and jobs as internal products, who work in an organisation that should 'create an internal environment which supports customer consciousness and sales-mindedness among their personnel' (Gronroos, 1982). Employees need to become 'ambassadors for the organisation' (Lewis, 1989) as the 'quality of the service and the quality of the service providers are inseparable' (Chase, 1978). The more competent the customer contact personnel, the better the service–business–client relationship will be, which will culminate in the service organisation receiving a positive reference. This relationship has been termed 'positive circles' (Normann, 1985).

So how should the service company attract and maintain the type of desirable personnel who will leave a positive impression on customers? Lowe (1988) proposes the use of good communications within the organisation since 'customer contact personnel cannot be expected to perform well if they are not fully informed about what the company is doing, and why'. In addition, it has been recommended (Berry, 1980) that a service employer apply traditional marketing tools such as market research and market segmentation in order that '(1) the best possible people can be employed and retained and, (2) they will do the best possible work' by identifying and satisfying employees needs, wants and aspirations.

Considerations an employer needs to make regarding the company guidelines and practices would be working conditions, shift work, flexible working hours, day-to-day benefits, either financial or in-kind (for example tips, taxi fares home or free meals at the end of the shift), holiday entitlement, training, career development opportunities, promotion prospects, career evaluations, pensions and life assurance. By identifying what one is able to afford to give personnel, and the minimum standard of benefits personnel are prepared to take, one is partially on the way to satisfying the personnel one would like to hire. The marketing executive can also apply market segmentation techniques when it comes to identifying the ideal personnel to hire. 'Market segmentation is relevant as people are as different as employees as they are as consumers' (Lewis, 1989). The aim of internal marketing is to 'increase job satisfaction, increase productivity and decrease absenteeism . . . and to train personnel to enhance their skills and to encourage a customer orientation; and to supervise and evaluate their performance' (Lewis, 1989).

However, internal marketing has been viewed as insufficient, and it is believed that internal marketing should be viewed as a managerial philosophy that has strategic as well as tactical implications throughout the company and its various business functions. In other words, it should permeate the whole of the service company.

If service organisations care about both employees and customers, the pay-off will be in terms of increased motivations and satisfaction; a high level of service quality as compared to the quality expected by customers, and therefore customer satisfaction; and in turn, hopefully, customer loyalty and increased level of business activity.　　　　(Lewis, 1989)

In the same manner, two other functions to be performed in a service firm have been suggested (Gronroos, 1989), namely the interactive marketing function in order to manage all the resources involved in the buyer-seller interface (that is, the physical/technical environment, the contact personnel, and the customers), and the internal marketing function which is concerned with satisfying the employees as the first market of the service firm.

The proposition is of a 'relationship definition of marketing' which states 'marketing is to establish, maintain, enhance and commercialise customer relationships (often, but not necessarily long-term relationships) so that the objectives of the parties involved are met. This is done by a mutual exchange and fulfilment of promises' (Gronroos, 1989). The relationship and the transaction definitions of marketing would be enhanced by developing a service culture amongst most if not all employees, and treating each customer as an individual, rather than a one-off single financial transaction. Relationship-building skills have been classified into such categories as joint problem definition, and to 'listen, be patient and modest' (Kubr, 1976), but these have been taken further (McGivern, 1983) with the need for high levels of interaction between parties, the need for trust, and the contingency of the methods used being advocated.

However, this basic marketing mix has been criticised (Gronroos, 1989) with the emphasis being put on continuously adapting the supplier's operations to meet customer's needs and more particularly to match customers' expected and perceived needs. This continuous adaptation (Yorke, 1990) will involve many people at different levels within the organisation, but the overall objective would still be to protect the existing customer base resulting in continuing exchanges and lower marketing costs per customer.

It is concluded (Yorke, 1990) that at least in professional service firms:

> organisations should adopt a more client-centred or market-oriented approach to their planned growth. The organisation should not focus entirely on production efficiency, current service offerings or sales, but on meeting the needs of particular clients, recognising, in addition, that client needs are rarely static but continue to evolve as the nature of their business changes.

This would suggest that this 'strategy demands new thinking on the part of professional organisations, not only in continually appraising client needs, but also in developing a flexibility of operation involving changes in organisation structure and the continuing education of partners and employees in dealing with client problems'.

Summary

The importance of services to the British economy has been growing both in terms of employment and in relation to GDP. This growth can be attributed to the impact of technology, deregulation and increased competition and increasing customer sophistication. Services may be professional or consumer oriented, and there is a great deal of crossover between the two categories. Services also have characteristics which differentiate them from goods and which make marketing planning more difficult – namely, intangibility, inseparability, heterogeneity, and perishability and fluctuating demand. The service marketing mix has since been extended to seven Ps, which may be product, price, process, promotion, place, physical evidence and people, although some now consider that the emphasis should be placed on continuously adapting the supplier's operations to meet customers' expected and perceived needs.

Review questions and problems

1. Describe and evaluate the marketing techniques used to match supply and demand in one of the following:

   (a) The package holiday industry;
   (b) Fast-food restaurants.

2. Why are product positioning and differentiation such difficult concepts to operationalise in many service industries?

3. 'In most cases the everyday contact with customers is a more important part of marketing activities than advertising and mass communication' (Gronroos, 1984, p. 42). Provide a reasoned explanation of why 94.1 per cent of a randomly selected group of 219 service companies agreed with the above contention.

4. Describe why marketing activities in service companies are different from those carried out in manufacturing companies.

5. Evaluate the use of information technology (IT) in improving the service provision in ONE of the following services:

   (a) A major high-street retailer of up-market clothing and interior design;
   (b) A national distribution company;
   (c) An international airline.

6. 'Managing supply and demand is the key task of the service manager' (Sasser, 1976). Discuss this statement, and explain ways in which a marketing specialist could help service managers achieve this objective.

7. Describe and evaluate the marketing channels and delivery systems used by ONE of the following organisations:

   (a) A trans-Atlantic charter airline business;
   (b) An international firm of chartered accountants;
   (c) A UK-based package holiday company catering to the needs of young people.

8. 'Could marketing itself be "myopic" in having failed to create relevant paradigms for the service sector?' (Shostack, 1977). Discuss this contention.

9. 'The internal marketing concept is the key to service marketing' (Gronroos, 1981). Evaluate this concept and choose a service which might especially benefit from this approach, and indicate why.

10. How, and why, does the need to manage demand affect the marketing of services? Illustrate your answer as extensively as possible.

11. 'Deregulation and increased competition is changing the marketing environment of financial services.' Discuss this contention.

12. Evaluate the usefulness of having a different approach to marketing personal services from that used in marketing manufactured goods.

13. Describe how either a national clearing bank or large firm of management consultants could benefit from an awareness of service marketing theory.

14. In the last few years, customer care has been receiving increased attention from both academics and practitioners. Is this a passing fad or a real, substantive change in the way a business operates? Discuss.

Supplementary reading list

Bateson, J. E. G. (1992) *Managing Services Marketing*, 2nd edn (London: Dryden Press).

Cowell, D. (1995) *The Marketing of Services*, 2nd edn (London: Heinemann).

Davidson, M. (1992) *The Consumerist Manifesto: Advertising in Postmodern Times* (London: Routledge).

Gronroos, C. (1985) *Strategic Marketing: Marketing in Service Industries* (Oxford: Chartwell-Bratt).

Chapter 23

Current Issues and Future Trends

Contents

Learning goals

The issues to be addressed in this chapter include:

1. An evaluation of marketing as a new philosophy of management.
2. Consumerism.
3. Marketing as a social process.
4. Marketing for non-profit organisations.
5. Green marketing.
6. Ethics in marketing.
7. Adaptable marketing systems.
8. The company as a brand.
9. Total quality management.
10. Customer care.
11. Future trends.

After reading this chapter you will be able to:

1. Explain how and why environmental change has resulted in the need for a revised approach to exchange relationships and the 'rediscovery' of marketing.

2. Suggest why marketing and a marketing orientation appear to offer the best chance for corporate success in an increasingly competitive environment.

3. Describe the origins of consumerism and indicate why marketing should be regarded as a response to these concerns rather than the cause of them.

4. Propose why consumer concern should be regarded as a marketing opportunity.

5. Review the arguments which suggest that marketing is a pervasive activity or social process which is relevant to all kinds of exchanges, both for profit and not-for-profit.

6. Discuss the view that consumer choice will increasingly be determined by subjective perceptions as the objective differences between goods and services are increasingly eroded by competitive imitation.

7. Explain the implications of environmental concern and the 'Green Movement' for the practice of marketing.

8. Discuss the relevance of ethical considerations in marketing.
9. Account for the success of Japan over the past 40 years through the development of adaptable marketing systems.
10. Understand why the company as a 'brand' will be of critical importance in determining competitive success in the future.
11. Define the nature of Total Quality Management (TQM) and illustrate its relevance for marketing.
12. Describe the nature of customer care and its role in successful marketing.

■ Introduction

As in previous editions the purpose of this chapter is to identify and evaluate significant trends in the development of marketing thinking and practice and to speculate on where they might be taking us.

In retrospect it is gratifying to find that the major trends identified in earlier editions are still of both relevance and importance, although it is surprising that progress has been slower than anticipated in some areas concerned with the application of technology, and particularly information technology. In the earlier editions considerable importance was attached to the development of consumerism and to the evolution of marketing from a commercial practice to a social process. Both trends are still with us and reflect the continuing transition from an era of mass consumption into a post-industrial society. Accordingly they will figure prominently in this chapter and, to a considerable degree, subsume our 1979 prognostication that in the 1980s perhaps the most important developments would occur in four main areas:

1. The interface between marketing and public policy, with the choice between self-regulation from within and imposed regulation from without becoming more acute.
2. The growing importance of services in advanced economics and the transfer of product marketing techniques and practices into the service sector accompanied by 'demarketing' of physical consumption goods.
3. An increased emphasis upon the transferability of the marketing concept and marketing practice into the not-for-profit sector.
4. A growing recognition of the benefits of marketing in centrally planned and developing economies.

Writing in 1995 it is clear that these 4 'megatrends' are still with us. The recognition of the Germanic-Alpine model of capitalism and the ascendancy of relationship marketing over the marketing management model is implicit in Areas 1 and 4. Indeed we have seen the collapse of the centrally planned command economies of Eastern Europe and are currently involved in strenuous attempts to establish free market economies there. Similarly, the growth of the service economy continues apace and marketing is now generally accepted as the key philosophy in the not-for-profit sector too.

In this chapter we will look first at the proposition that marketing has become the core managerial philosophy. Next we examine the nature of consumerism which many would regard as a key indicator of how well organisations are interpreting and implementing the marketing concept. This discussion leads naturally to a consideration of the application of marketing principles and practices in not-for-profit organisations. The social implications of marketing are then developed further in an examination of the impact of mass consumption on the environment – a topic generally designated 'green marketing'. Finally, to complete this section of the chapter we provide an overview of some of the ethical issues which have emerged in recent years associated with the practice of marketing.

The second major section of this chapter is concerned with current issues and recent developments in the practice of marketing. The first topic discussed is the evolution of adaptable marketing systems which has been a distinctive feature of Japanese success in international markets. Next, we provide a short overview of total quality management which has been central to enhanced competitiveness throughout the world and conclude the section with a discussion of customer care. As it becomes increasingly difficult to differentiate between the objective benefits conferred by products and services so customer care has emerged as a distinctive source of competitive advantage.

To conclude the chapter we look briefly at some future trends and speculate where marketing is going as we approach the millennium.

▌ Marketing – the core managerial philosophy

In recent years it has become increasingly fashion able to talk of accelerating technological change, increased international competition and environmental turbulence. Taken together these trends are seen as calling for a radically different approach to business and management than that which has prevailed for the better part of this century. In response to this call for a radical change in business attitudes and practices, 'marketing' has emerged as both a philosophy of business and a business discipline best suited to survival and success as we move into the twenty-first century. To assess the validity of this claim it seems to me that we must first establish the nature and implications of the changes in our environment. Next, we must attempt to define just what marketing is, or is claimed to be. And, finally, we must examine whether marketing, as defined, does seem to offer the best prospects for increased consumer satisfaction in the years ahead and, if so, what is needed to promote its full acceptance.

☐ *Environmental turbulence*

It has become increasingly fashionable in recent years to speak of environmental turbulence as if it were a new phenomenon discovered by later twentieth-century man. Given that the origins of the word are to be found in the Latin *turba* meaning 'confusion or uproar', from which 'disturb' is also derived, this is a typical case of modern arrogance. That said, the increased incidence of flying has made many of us aware of the uncomfortable unease engendered by physical turbulence in our environment and endowed the term with an immediacy and impact which it may previously have lacked.

Fortunately most turbulence is predictable in that it originates with a discontinuity such as those between pressure systems in the atmosphere or when approaching the sound 'barrier'. Normally we can measure and plot these discontinuities and, while we are occasionally taken by surprise by clear air turbulence, in the majority of cases we can take actions to minimise or avoid interruptions to a smooth progression from where we are to where we want to be. It follows that environmental forecasting is as important to the corporate strategist and marketer as meteorological forecasting is to the airline pilot. Unfortunately, and to pursue the analogy, the further in advance that we try to predict specific events the less accurate our specific predictions become and the less willing many people become to make the effort. A major consequence of this managerial myopia has been the emphasis upon short-term financial milking and paper entrepreneurialism which dulled the competitive edge of the UK and USA and allowed the Japanese, West Germans and others with a long-term vision of the future to penetrate our domestic markets and steal our foreign markets.

Despite the fact that the history – and progress – of man is one of continuous change people prefer to act and behave as if the future will be like the present and so ignore, avoid or resist change. But, not only is change continuous – it is accelerating. It follows that if management is to fulfil its primary roles of analysis, anticipation, planning and control then it must give particular attention to the nature and direction of change. In doing so it is clear that, as Martel has argued, change as a process exhibits distinct regularities or patterns 'with dimensions of direction, magnitude, pace and duration that can be seen and measured'.

Martel argues that failure to recognise and use change leads to three common errors:

1. Believing yesterday's solutions will solve today's problems;
2. Assuming present trends will continue;
3. Neglecting the opportunities of future change.

He cites the American automobile industry as an example of Error 1 in that until the late 1980s it was still pursuing Alfred Sloan's manufacturing and marketing strategy enunciated in the early 1920s. Basically this strategy is founded on the concept of trading-up or 'upsizing' and is facilitated by trade-ins and instalment buying. The economies of scale for a full line of cars exist in using many of the sub-assemblies and components of cheaper models in the more expensive models enabling, in Sloan's words, 'the mass production of automobiles to be reconciled with variety of product'. But, the strategy does not work in reverse so that when the market wants small, high quality, low cost cars 'downsizing' is not a feasible route to continued profitability. As a result foreign competitors, who had anticipated the change, were able to penetrate the US market and establish a foothold from which it has proved extremely difficult to dislodge them.

Martel points to 'a variant of this error' in the so-called 'sailing ship' phenomenon' whereby the introduction of steam ships stimulated conventional shipbuilders to build better sailing ships rather than switch to the new technology. Numerous examples of the phenomenon are to be found, not only in product development but also in systems and procedures, especially as a result of recent advances in IT.

Error 2 assumes present trends will continue – an assumption of linearity totally belied by the cyclical behaviour of most phenomena. Thus, while one may be able to project a theoretical trend or smooth past oscillations to represent past change as a continuous process, the reality is that attempts at achieving equilibrium invariably result in over-correction around the central trend and give rise to bursts of acceleration and deceleration, of stop and go clearly apparent in the business and related economic cycles.

The energy crisis of the 1970s provides clear evidence of the impracticality of the inevitable logic of extrapolation *if one assumes no reaction to restore equilibrium*. If one assumes that consumption of any finite resource will continue to grow in accordance with past trends then, inevitably, the finite resource will become exhausted. But, such projections precipitate actions which themselves initiate counter-reactions.

Thus projections of future oil scarcity encourage supply restriction and price rises; but price rises encourage the exploitation of previously marginal resources (which increases supply), conservation and energy saving practices (which decreases demand) and innovation to find alternative energy sources (which may make the previously scarce resource obsolete). As Martel points out, oil demand declined by over 15 per cent between 1979 and 1984, prices plummeted and the oil producers, both countries and companies, moved from growth to recession.

Error 3 is the neglect of the opportunities offered by change and is usually illustrated by reference to the small number of radical innovations which have subsequently revolutionised an industry/market. In reality such examples are the exception rather than the rule and, while they will always enjoy the attention given to exceptions, the managerial requirement to plan and control require that innovation and change should be managed in such a way as to try and dampen the violent oscillations which discontinuous or radical change can precipitate. Clearly, the need is to recognise that change is inevitable and so welcome it as an opportunity rather than regarding it as a threat to the comfortable familiarity of the status quo.

Once we accept that change is inevitable then clearly we will be more prepared to meet and even modify it. It is for this reason that in successful companies so much effort has been devoted to environmental analysis in an attempt to define broad underlying trends and assess their implications in terms of future scenarios. Thus a survey of top European CEOs in the 1980s identified eight factors which characterise the environment facing top management, namely:

1. A demand for quality and advice;
2. A move towards a service culture;
3. An emphasis upon the specialist;
4. Shortening strategic time horizons;
5. Scenario planning is replacing forecasting;
6. A reduction in head office functions;
7. A wider international outlook;
8. Tighter legislation.

These trends correspond closely to those identified by Naisbitt (1984) in his best-selling book *Megatrends*. According to Naisbitt we are changing from an industrial to an information society, from a national to a world economy in which decentralisation and diversity are replacing centralisation and homogeneity and in which participation and self-help are replacing representative democracy and institutional help. This shift from an industrial society founded on high mass consumption to a post-industrial information era reflects a change in emphasis from quantity to quality, from standardisation to customisation, from centralisation to decentralisation, from dependence to self-help, from autocracy to participation, from hierarchy to network, from transportation to communication and from information scarcity to information overload.

Clearly these are massive changes and call for equally massive changes in the way we think about and do business. In fact the conditions which precipitated what I have always referred to as the *rediscovery* of the marketing concept.

☐ *The rediscovery of marketing*

As we all know there are almost as many definitions of marketing as there are persons willing to formulate one. Despite this variety most contain the common elements that start with and concentrate upon the consumer as the catalyst for an exchange relationship which gives satisfaction to both buyer and seller. In recent times, and in my own opinion, there has been a tendency to overemphasise the interests of the consumer and my own preferred definition of marketing is that it is concerned with *mutually* satisfying exchange relationships. If this is the case then it is ironic that marketing as both a philosophy of business and business function should be perceived as new. In reality marketing came into existence with the first exchange of goods and services and has been the catalyst for economic growth through its encouragement of task specialisation and the division of labour which, in turn, have led to the emphasis upon the pursuit of comparative advantage and involvement in international trade.

Given the existence of unsatisfied basic needs it is unsurprising that society perceives its main priority as increasing the volume of output of such basic goods. The pursuit of efficiency in the application of technology to production results in it becoming concentrated and requires the creation of channels of distribution to enable mass production to be converted into mass consumption. The consequence of this, of course, is that the producer loses direct contact with his customer and tends to perceive demand as the homogeneous entity beloved of economists rather than representing the differentiated needs of a heterogeneous collection of individuals who comprise the 'market'.

It is unsurprising, therefore, that as our ability to increase supply accelerates and the natural growth of markets decelerates through a slowing down of population growth there begins to develop a mismatch between the producer's perception of consumer needs and the reality. One consequence of this misperception which became apparent in the 1950s and early 1960s was the rise of consumerism and environmentalism. Many marketing scholars claim that consumerism is the shame of marketing. My own view is that it is exactly the opposite – consumerism is in fact a protest against the absence of marketing.

The origins of the consumerist movement were prompted by the scholarly writings of persons like John Kenneth Galbraith, who pointed to the excesses of materialism, and the populist works of people like Vance Packard in books such as *The Waste Makers* (1963) and *The Hidden Persuaders* (1957). In turn, particular focus was given by Ralph Nader's indictment of the quality of American motor cars in his 'Unsafe at any Speed'. Sued unsuccessfully by General Motors, Nader became the giantkiller and numerous others sprang to his cause. While this groundswell of complaint against the lack of perceived quality and value for money in many goods and services was undoubtedly justified one must remember that this was and is a relative perception that requires a high level of material well-being before it is likely to find expression.

Beggars can't be choosers and, as Maslow's well-known hierarchy reminds us, we progress upwards from satisfying basic physiological needs through higher-order needs for safety, love and esteem before we arrive at the point where we have a sufficient level of material satisfaction that we can become concerned with the more abstract and spiritual 'better' things of life. Elsewhere I have suggested that Maslow's esteem stage corresponds to Walt Rostow's age of high mass consumption in his model of economic growth. In Rostow's model the final stage of economic development was originally but unoriginally labelled the 'age beyond high mass consumption'. In a revised version which reflected the changes in American society during the 1950s and 1960s Rostow relabelled the ultimate stage of economic development as 'the search for quality'. Clearly, a search for quality implies that the individual will want to define quality more precisely in terms of their own particular needs and wants. It follows that if producers are to succeed then they, too, must spend more time and energy in defining individual needs and aggregating them into worthwhile market segments.

In essence, then, marketing is a very simple philosophy which requires producers to start with the identification and specification of consumer needs and then mobilise their companies' assets and resources to achieve a mutually satisfying exchange relationship from which both parties derive the benefits they are seeking. While this is a simple and appealing proposition there is no doubt that producers have been very slow to change. Levitt articulated the need in 1960 in his seminal article entitled 'Marketing Myopia' but despite his emphasis upon the inevitability of change in the ways in which basic human needs like transportation and entertainment may be satisfied comparatively few managers and companies fully appreciated the implications. As is so often the case it took a crisis to precipitate a change but in the process there were many casualties. Thus, the energy crises of 1974 and 1978 and the recessions which followed in their wake resulted in a widescale reappraisal by producers as to the changes in organisation and activity which are called for by the new environment in which they find themselves.

☐ *What now?*

The past decade has witnessed a flood of managerial bestsellers purporting to contain the secrets of competitive success. Few would argue that something called a marketing orientation has a major part to play in achieving this goal. The problem rests in converting managers to a true belief in consumer sovereignty, which constitutes the substance of marketing, rather than allowing them to drift into the acquisition of the trappings of a marketing function. Such a change will require a fundamental shift in attitude of a kind which may only be accomplished by effective education and communication.

Given that human beings exercise control over the other factors of production, it seems reasonable to claim that output or performance is a function of the interaction between the knowledge, skills and attitudes of those people. The reason why people speak of knowledge, skills and attitude in that sequence is because it reflects the sequence of personal development. Knowledge is distilled experience of the way things are and the way in which they work. Equipped with knowledge we can attempt particular tasks and acquire skills in the practice and application of that knowledge. In the process we will develop attitudes which will tend to reinforce the importance of the knowledge and skills acquired. It is unsurprising, therefore, that people will resist change which challenges their knowledge base or seeks to make obsolete the skills they have acquired. To accomplish change one must first change attitudes for only if this is accomplished will people be willing to acquire new knowledge and skills.

As I have indicated the changes in the balance between demand and supply have been apparent for decades and, with the benefit of hindsight, it is not difficult to understand the social and economic turbulence which exist at the interface between a society concerned with increasing quantity to one which is able to pursue an enhanced quality of life.

I believe that attitudes have changed, that quality will now take precedence over quantity and that, ultimately, this depends upon the quality of management and implementation. Thus, as we move towards the millenium, we have rediscovered the importance of defining quality from the consumer's point of view and have recognised that its achievement depends upon the supplier's understanding of that need and his skill in matching it. This, in my view, it the very essence of marketing. But, if marketing starts and ends with the consumer, why is it that significant numbers of well-educated consumers have found it necessary to band together in order to challenge the complacency of an establishment which at best seems unaware or indifferent to this precept? To answer this question it is necessary to review the origins and evolution of consumerism.

■ Consumerism

In the first chapter of this book we examined the nature of the marketing concept and suggested that a somewhat simple statement of it might be:

> If economies are comprised of people, and we are endeavouring to allocate scarce resources in order to maximise satisfaction, then it is the satisfaction of people which we are aiming at. This being so it is essential that we determine first what people want and then allocate our resources accordingly. In other words, we must determine the nature and strength of demand and create supplies of goods and services to satisfy these demands.

Further, we suggested that free market economics largely permit the evolution of consumer sovereignty by allowing consumers to express their preferences as between goods and services through the daily casting of their money 'votes'.

It would be naive to suggest that any such system is or ever could be perfect. None-the-less, market economics and the marketing philosophy rest upon the same fundamental proposition that consumer preferences will determine the allocation of available inputs to the creation of the most desired outputs.

So much for marketing. What is consumerism?

The term 'consumerism' first came into currency in the 1970s when it was applied to a number of issues which had first attracted serious concern in the 1950s. Vance Packard (1957) was one of the first to use the expression in relation to these concerns foremost among which were planned obsolescence (see *The Waste Makers*), declining quality and the absence of satisfactory after-sales service, particularly in saturated mass consumption markets for convenience goods. This connotation was gradually extended as the 1960s progressed. In 1962 Rachel Carson's *Silent Spring* drew attention to the impact which pollution of the environment was having upon plant and animal life. In 1962 President Kennedy addressed his first consumer message to Congress in which he stated four basic consumer rights:

1. *The Right to Safety* – to be protected against the marketing of goods which are hazardous to health or life.
2. *The Right to be Informed* – to be protected against fraudulent, deceitful or grossly misleading information, advertising, labelling or other practices, and to be given the facts needed to make an informed choice.
3. *The Right to Choose* – to be assured, wherever possible, access to a variety of products and services at competitive prices and in those industries in which Government regulations are substituted, an assurance of satisfactory quality and service at fair prices.
4. *The Right to be Heard* – to be assured that consumer interests will receive full and sympathetic consideration in the formulation of Government policy and fair expeditious treatment in its administrative tribunals.

(Quoted by Senator Warren G. Magnuson (1972) in 'Consumerism and the Emerging Goals of a New Society'.)

Still later in the decade Ralph Nader (1966) was to publish *Unsafe at Any Speed*, a book which might well have gone unremarked had it not been for General Motors' attempts to discredit Nader which resulted in their losing a lawsuit brought by him. The publicity given the trial focused intense attention upon the standard of car manufacture and resulted in Nader himself being cast in the role of consumer champion.

The consumerism-marketing interface

Oversimplified as they may be, the foregoing statements on the nature of marketing and consumerism reflect a fundamental paradox for while they are invariably seen as being in conflict both activities possess the same basic objective – consumer satisfaction. A still more fundamental paradox is that while everybody is in favour of consumer protection there is still a need for it.

At various points in the text, reference has been made to particular issues where consumerists and marketers appear to be at cross-purposes with each other.

Among those which the reader may wish to explore in greater depth are the following:

1. *Product Policy* – Issues of Quality/Brand proliferation;
   Planned obsolescence;
   After-sales service.
2. *Pricing Practices* – Recommended prices and Price-off promotions;
   Unit pricing.
3. *'Truth in Advertising'* – By category of product;
   By media.
4. *Pollution* – By product, for example motor-cars, enzyme detergents;
   By packaging – non-returnable containers;
   non biodegradable materials.
5. *'Truth in Lending'* – Statement of true costs of borrowing.

In considering these and similar salient issues it would be unreasonable to follow the practice favoured in certain quarters of ascribing all the blame to private industry. We must accept that existing institutions have succeeded very well in terms of their aims and objectives as originally stated. Because society now questions the desirability of continued and rapid economic growth due to excesses derived from its past pursuit, society is not entitled to belabour those organisations which previously enacted its collective will. A more constructive attitude recognises that the emergence of the marketing concept reflects an awareness of the side-effects of mass production and mass consumption, and that enlightened self-interest will predispose business to vary its response to consumer needs as these change. In a far from perfect world we cannot expect all firms to be equally responsive to these changed needs, and so will have to resort to legislation to ensure compliance with certain minimum standards. In the long run, however, we see no reason to believe that the greatest success will not continue to accrue to the firms most sensitive to their markets' needs.

Consumerism – threat or opportunity?

Because of the manner in which many consumer concerns were expressed, many firms tended to react defensively. In consequence of this defensive reaction there was a tendency in certain quarters to regard the consumerist movement as a threat to business. More farsighted firms considered it as an opportunity.

One particularly salient feature of consumerism is that it is both overt and vocal, which is a marked contrast with most market situations where considerable time, effort and money has to be expended upon eliciting consumer attitudes and opinions. In other words, expressions of consumer concern clearly indicate the wishes of at least a sizeable segment of particular markets and reduce the need for research activity. More astute companies have already perceived this opportunity. Consider the following examples.

Increased concern over pollution and the quality of the environment has enabled many firms to cash in on devices for monitoring, reducing, alleviating, or avoiding pollution. Thus firms have developed instruments to measure the nature and extent of pollutants discharged into the air and water and clearly this market will grow as states seek to enforce laws against pollution and firms try to ensure that they comply with such laws. Having detected the existence of pollutants then a need arises to remove or mitigate their effect resulting in a demand for sewage and effluent treatment, water purification, air filtration plants and so on. Similarly, alternative solutions are required as in the case of the internal combustion engine, or fossil fuel sources of energy.

At a lesser level, firms can cash in on explicit anxieties such as the need for more informative labelling by providing it, of non-returnable containers by making them returnable, of packaging waste by making it capable of re-use through recycling. Similarly the express demand for after-sales service represents considerable scope for creative marketing – if leasing television sets is possible why not other household consumer durables?

Marketing as a social process

Probably the first influential statement of a need to re-examine the scope of marketing was contained in a seminal article by Philip Kotler and Sidney Levy (1969), 'Broadening the Concept of Marketing'. In the opening paragraphs the authors review briefly the traditional emphasis on the marketing of products in a business context and go on to assert: 'It is the authors' contention that marketing is a pervasive societal activity that goes considerably beyond the selling of toothpaste, soap and steel.'

In essence, the argument that marketing is a pervasive societal activity is predicated on the observation that as man's productive capability has grown, so he has been able to devote more of his energies to social activities and that in order to do so he has had to develop organisations other than business firms. In reality, many non-business organisations have a longer history than the now dominant business firms; for example, the Church, universities, government departments, hospitals, and so forth. However, the very forces which were to lead to an emphasis on marketing, namely the ability to create supplies in excess of basic consumption needs, were also necessary to permit such non-business organisations to realise their potential. Thus, only when we can release human and physical resources from the treadmill of satisfying the basic needs of food and shelter can we turn our attention to the satisfaction of higher needs such as education, the Arts, health, and social welfare. Further, we require new forms of social organisation to cope with enfranchisement of the whole population, that is political societies, the need for organised labour to be able to express its view, that is the trade unions, and so on.

As Kotler and Levy (1969) point out, all these social organisations perform the classic business functions. Finance is necessary to pay for the organisation's operations and a personnel function is necessary to ensure that people are available to discharge such operations. A production function is necessary to organise the most economic use of inputs to achieve the desired level of outputs. Purchasing is necessary to acquire these inputs and presumably marketing is required to dispose of them. If the marketing function has not been particularly conspicuous, however, we should not be surprised for, as we have seen in earlier chapters, the need for such a function has only just become apparent in the case of physical goods.

But, given the exponential acceleration which has characterised all spheres of human endeavour throughout history we may anticipate a rapid diffusion of the marketing concept through non-business organisations within the next few years. To determine how the marketing concept may be applied we must first identify those ideas which have appeared generally useful in marketing other goods and services. In our opinion, in marketing industrial goods there is no fundamental difference in principle as compared with the marketing of consumer goods. This I believe is equally true of the marketing of services whether they emanate from profit or non-profit organisations.

In the same spirit, Kotler and Levy suggest that a useful basic approach is to think in terms of three fundamental constructs or ideas – products, consumers, and tools.

Products

All organisations produce a product although in the interests of definitional clarity we frequently prefer to differentiate as between categories of products. Thus in Chapter 5 we offer specific definitions for categories of consumer and industrial goods. To these may be added services which are intangible, such as insurance and banking, although they may confer a tangible benefit such as health and welfare services. Such services may be offered by private or public organisations which may or may not have a profit motive. Evidence of the marketing of such services is most marked in the case of those private firms such as banks which are profit-orientated and least evident in the case of public sector welfare services. To these easily recognised categories, Kotler and Levy add persons, organisations and ideas, while in a more elaborate statement (1969) in 'Beyond Marketing: The Furthering Concept', they add 'places'. In the case of these latter categories a limited marketing activity may be noted in the past but it has largely concentrated on public relations type activity supported by a limited amount of paid promotion. Clearly, there is considerable scope for the use of other elements of the marketing mix, especially in the field of marketing research, to better define consumer needs. This observation leads naturally to consideration of the second basic construct.

Consumers

In a limited sense consumers are viewed solely as those persons or organisations which consume the output of another organisation. In the wider concept 'consumers' includes at least three other groups with a *direct* interest in any given organisation. First, there are persons responsible for the control of the organisation. These may be shareholders in a company or those nominated by them (directors), they may be the trustees of a private foundation, or the elected ministers who control our government departments and so on. The second category is comprised of persons or organisations which take a direct interest, and the third of those with a passive or *indirect* interest. Examples of the former are, say, consumer organisations or government departments in the case of business firms, former students and local and central government in the case of a university; while the latter category conveniently encompasses all those who might be influenced by or wish to influence the organisation at some future time.

Tools

The third construct is that of the tools of marketing. Among these we may distinguish the four 'p's of product, price, place (distribution) and promotional policy, each of which has an important role in marketing the output of any type of organisation. We have already stressed that change is symptomatic of the world in which we live – accordingly all organisations must continually reappraise and update their 'product' in order to best satisfy changing needs. Pricing has an important role to play although it frequently seems to be ignored in the provision of many public services. It is difficult for the individual citizen to decide whether the collective taxes we pay are being allocated to the ends we most desire except in a very gross way. Certainly it is impossible in the particular to determine whether we are getting value for money and the suppliers often seem insensitive to the concept of cost-benefit. Indications of changing attitudes in the latter area are to be seen in the concept of contract research in which the researcher is required to produce results in line with a prearranged budget and the suggestion that individuals be given 'tickets' which they can exchange for, say, education. In the present social climate it seems unlikely that the latter idea will gain support but its currency does imply that the consumers of such services would like a more effective way of demonstrating their wishes other than at general elections. Equally some of the dangers of monopoly power which we monitor so closely in the private sector merit more attention for they appear to exist in the pricing and quality decisions of many public services. The publication of the Citizens' Charter and the intervention of Regulators in industries like electricity and water in the mid 1990s indicate that Government is aware of these concerns.

In the case of distribution and promotion there is also scope for the application of marketing techniques, although perhaps somewhat less than in the product and price areas. Distribution still merits attention, however, in that in many cases it appears to be dictated by the convenience of the supplier rather than the consumer. Similarly, some of the promotional techniques already in use would no doubt benefit from comparison with the sophistication typical of the promotion of consumer goods.

Essentially, therefore, we are arguing that the philosophy and techniques which have apparently worked so much to the advantage of private profit-oriented organisations are equally relevant and meaningful to all other forms of organisation. Three things must be appreciated, however. First, one must not strain the analogy between business and non-business organisations too far and so try to force the latter to fit patterns which have proved successful in the former context but which may be wholly inappropriate to non-business organisations. Second, success in marketing depends upon commitment – mere lip-service to the concept and changing the sales function's title is insufficient. (See, for example, B. Charles Ames, 1970, 'Trappings vs. Substance in Industrial Marketing'.) Finally, success depends upon matching skills with opportunities.

Collectively, these three caveats indicate that the greatest benefit is likely to accrue where one attempts a transfer of basic ideas from the traditional content of marketing physical products rather than promote the wholesale adoption of particular marketing techniques. This is particularly apparent in the case of marketing for non-profit organisations.

 # Marketing for non-profit organisations

Throughout this book the primary emphasis has been upon the application of marketing principles to enhance the performance of commercial organisations. While it is now generally accepted that 'profit' is not the sole objective of commercial organisations, it is also recognised that it is an essential one if the firm is to survive. However, there are many other organisations, particularly in the public sector such as health, education, defence, which do not have a profit motivation at all albeit that they are accountable for the resources entrusted to them. Similarly, there are numerous charitable and social organisations which have other objectives than profit making. The question to be addressed briefly here is: 'What contribution, if any, does marketing have to offer to non-profit organisations (NPOs)?' As noted earlier, Philip Kotler and Sidney Levy (1969) were among the first to consider the implications of this question when they wrote a seminal article entitled 'Broadening the Concept of Marketing'. In this article it was proposed that the marketing concept or philosophy was equally relevant to NPOs as to organisations with a profit motivation – a proposal which immediately stimulated a flow of other articles both supporting and denouncing this view. But, while many opposed the transferral of marketing thinking and practices to NPOs, the debate is now over. It is widely accepted that both the marketing concept and marketing practices have widespread application to NPOs and this has given rise to a whole new sub-field of marketing including activities designated as 'Social Marketing' (see below).

According to Kotler and Andreasen (1991), *Strategic Marketing for Non-profit Organisations*, the application of marketing to NPOs involves five key activities:

1. Developing a customer orientation;
2. Strategic planning and organisation;
3. Developing and organising resources;
4. Designing the marketing mix;
5. Controlling marketing strategies.

As we approach the millenium few would challenge the relevance of marketing to the management of public and non-profit organisations. At the time of the first publication of this book in 1971 the situation was quite different. Indeed, for most people marketing was seen as 'selling with knobs on' or advertising and public relations. The thought that these practices might be appropriate to anything other than the manufacturers of fast moving consumer goods (fmcg) was entirely alien. However, as we have seen, particularly in Chapter 1, it is now generally accepted that marketing is all about mutually satisfying exchange relationships, the creation and maintenance of which depends upon developing a customer orientation. We have also seen that this involves more than the operation of free markets, if for no other reason than that organisations possess more market power than individuals so that some social intervention is necessary to maintain a balance. (the Germanic-Alpine version of capitalism, qv. p.25/6). The creation of a market economy for public sector services was fundamental to Thatcherism in the 1980s while John Major's Citizens' Charter was an affirmation of the importance of a customer orientation. Similarly, the privatisation of many public services in the UK and elsewhere has forced managers to consider carefully the nature of their relationship with their customer.

At the same time the encouragement of customer sovereignty and individual independence has also had a significant impact upon many voluntary organisations. With increasing numbers of women remaining in or returning to employment the 'pool' of volunteers who have provided the backbone of many charities or organisations like the Red Cross, has shrunk dramatically. Accordingly, such organisations need to become much more professional in their practices if they are to survive, particularly in competition with other NPOs who are seeking to exploit the same reservoirs of public goodwill. Faced with such environmental and competitive change it is clear that a marketing orientation and professional marketing practice are key to the survival of many NPOs. The creation of a customer orientation is the first, and probably most important step in the process.

Once an organisation has become customer orientated then it needs to develop a strategic marketing plan which involves four basic steps:

1. Articulation of the organisation's culture and its implications for the mission, objectives and goals of the organisation.
2. A SWOT analysis to identify the organisation's strengths and weaknesses in relation to the opportunities and threats facing it.
3. Identification of its key publics and competitors.
4. Development of specific objectives and goals which will enable the organisation to maximise its potential.

Central to this process is the development of a clear understanding of the motivations, attitudes, interests and opinions of the target public(s) with whom the organisation wishes to interact. It is here that the insights developed through the study of consumer behaviour and market research have a major contribution to make. Similarly, the concepts of segmentation, targeting and positioning will be vital in creating an effective strategy.

Once a strategy has been developed following the principles set out in Chapter 3 then the next step is to develop a marketing plan which identifies which elements of the marketing mix are to be used; what resources are required and when; and what procedures are to be established to ensure implementation, feedback and control.

Given that complete text books, such as the one by Kotler and Andreasen cited earlier, have been devoted to the subject of marketing for non-profit organisations it is not proposed to dwell on the topic here. (An excellent summary of Kotler and Andreasen's book is to be found as Chapter 53 in the *Companion Encyclopedia of Marketing*, p. 930ff.) As with other sub-fields of marketing such as industrial or business-to-business marketing, international marketing and so on, it is our belief that the principles and practices are the same. That said, as with any marketing issues the difference between success and failure invariably boils down to 3 key issues which comprise what may be called the 3 I's of successful management:

- Information;
- Interpretation;
- Implementation.

Success depends upon the assembly of information relevant to the problem to be solved, its correct interpretation to provide a workable solution to the problem and then effective implementation. In other words effective marketing solutions tend to be situation specific which means that specialised knowledge and experience related to a *context* (such as NPOs, international, and so on) is invaluable in developing successful marketing strategies. More specialised textbooks dealing with other sub-fields provide the necessary contextual information.

Earlier, passing reference was made to Social Marketing and a brief comment on this is called for. As yet no commonly agreed definition has emerged. In the *Companion Encyclopedia* (*op. cit.*) social marketing is defined as 'the application of generic marketing to a specific class of problems where the object of the marketer is to change social behaviour primarily to benefit the target audience and the general society' (p. 942). A classic example which fits this definition is health education such as anti-smoking campaigns, information on AIDS, healthy eating, and so forth. In these applications there can be no doubt that marketing has had a major impact upon attitudes and opinions but perhaps less success in changing behaviour. For example, almost everyone knows of the association between smoking and lung cancer but many refuse to stop, and large numbers of young people become smokers every year. On the other hand, awareness of the dangers of passive smoking has led many organisations to declare themselves 'smoke-free zones' to protect non-smokers from smokers. Thus, while marketing practices may influence attitudes and opinions it is clear that behavioural change requires the consent of the individual. In other words, marketing cannot make people do what they don't want to do, even when it is in a good cause – a fact which should do much to counter the criticisms of those who claim marketing is manipulative.

Finally, it should be noted that some authors and practitioners accord social marketing a wider role, which includes the whole field of marketing for non-profit organisations as well as taking in a number of other issues which have received increased attention in recent years. Two of these – Green Marketing and Ethics – are reviewed below.

■ Green marketing

In recent years the terms 'green' or eco-marketing have come to prominence and reflect a growing concern at all levels of the impact of increased consumption on our physical environment. This concern was central to the consumerist movement of the 1950s, 1960s and 1970s but, in many cases, it was subordinated to the more pressing and immediate problems associated with consumer protection. As we have seen, in the 1950s John Kenneth Galbraith questioned the values of a materialistic, throw-away society, while in *The Waste Makers* Vance Packard challenged business practices which destroyed scarce resources without thought of their conservation or replacement. In the 1960s Rachel Carson's *Silent Spring* predicted that excessive use of pesticides in farming would destroy the bird population, and the Club of Rome's *Report* forecast the exhaustion of many irreplaceable raw materials.

As noted, however, these concerns tended to be subordinated by the much more obvious issue of consumer rights of the kind summarised at p. 523. By the mid-1970s and early 1980s consumer legislation, self regulation and recognition that looking after consumers is good business had greatly reduced the need for action on these issues. At the same time the implications of the destruction of forests, the appearance of 'holes' in the ozone layer and the potential consequences of global warming were widely publicised and engendered a wave of concern about the destruction of our natural environment. This concern was fuelled by the phenomenon of acid rain caused by airborne pollutants and was exacerbated by the Chernobyl disaster which gave rise to a major escape of radio-active particles. As a result of these and similar incidents the green movement has gathered tremendous momentum and has had a major impact on marketing practice and the application of marketing techniques. In their contribution to *The Marketing Book* (Baker, 1994), Peattie and Charter summarise the evolution of environmental concern in a table reproduced here as Table 23.1.

Paradoxically, marketing is seen as a major contributor to the creation of conspicuous consumption while, at the same time, it is also seen as a potential saviour. As long ago as 1968, Philip Kotler coined the term 'demarketing' to describe the use of marketing techniques to *dissuade* people from doing certain things. For example, smoking, drinking and driving, using aerosol products, using CFC which destroys ozone in the atmosphere, and so on. Clearly, the logic is that if marketing techniques can be used to influence attitudes and behaviour, then they can be used to promote sustainable consumption as opposed to conspicuous and unsustainable consumption.

In their contribution to the *Companion Encyclopedia of Marketing* (1995, pp. 979), Meffert and Kirchgeog report a 1992 survey of 4600 respondents in 16 countries, 86 per cent of whom agreed with the statement 'I am very worried about the state of the environment'. The survey covered both advanced and newly industrialising countries and reveals widespread concern for the issue. As Meffert and Kirchgeog point out this represents both a threat and an opportunity. It is a threat to those organisations which are seen to be harming the environment. It is an opportunity for organisations which are seen to be environmentally friendly. In the final analysis, however, organisations and individuals are motivated by self-interest and will adopt these practices and patterns of behaviour which maximise their satisfaction. For

Table 23.1 *The evolution of environmental concern*

Factor	1970s environmentalism	1990s green
Emphasis	On 'environmental' problems	On the underlying problems with our social, economic, technical or legal systems
Geographic focus	On local problems (e.g. pollution)	On global issues (e.g. global warming)
Identity	Closely linked to other anti-establishment causes	A separate movement embraced by many elements of 'the establishment'
Source of support	An intellectual elite, and those at the fringes of society	A broad base
Basis of campaigns	Used forecasts of exponential growth to predict future environmental problems (e.g. Limits to Growth)	Uses evidence of current environmental degradation (e.g. the hole in the ozone layer)
Attitude to businesses	Business is the problem. Generally adversarial	Businesses seen as part of the solution. More partnerships formed
Attitude to growth	Desire for zero growth	Desire for sustainable growth
View of environment/ business interaction	Focused on negative effects of business activity on the environment	Focuses on the dynamic inter-relationship between business society and the environment

example, a survey by the Australian Bureau of Statistics of 16 000 people indicated 75 per cent were concerned about environmental problems, environmentally-friendly products were still overlooked for reasons of brand loyalty (26 per cent), perceptions of inferior quality (25 per cent), and higher prices (24 per cent).

As we have seen, perceptions of satisfaction vary considerably so that some individuals who are particularly conscious of environmental issues will go out of their way to acquire and use environmentally friendly products. Indeed, they may even be prepared to pay a premium for them. For them green products and eco-friendly consumption behaviour are of high perceived value and may be regarded as speciality products (qv. p. 103). However, expressing concern about the state of the environment is not the same as being willing to change one's behaviour personally in order to improve it. It is likely that the great majority of consumers are in favour of environmentally friendly products and, other things being equal, will favour them. But this is not the same thing as being willing to make a special effort to acquire such products, and certainly not the same thing as being willing to pay more for them.

In much the same way that it was consumer activists who had to raise public awareness about consumer rights, and to lobby government and business to act in a more socially responsible way so it is with green issues. Even then individuals may not be willing to change their personal behaviour while overtly expressing support for an issue. At the time this was written (August 1995) the author was based at James Cook University in Far North Queensland, Australia. A major issue at this time was the French decision to carry out nuclear tests in the South Pacific – a decision which had attracted strong protests throughout the region. In Australia trade unions boycotted the handling of French goods, demonstrations were held in many cities, the French Ambassador was recalled to Paris, and government relations between the two countries were strained. Given strong international pressure of this kind the question at the level of international relations was whether France would change its decision. But,

at the level of the individual consumer, comparatively few were willing to stop drinking French wine or using French perfume to express their disapproval.

The point we are seeking to make is that there is an important difference between social and individual benefits. In the summer of 1995 many German motorists boycotted Shell petrol because of the company's decision to sink the Brent Spar oil platform in the Atlantic with the result that Shell changed its mind. The real question is, however, would these German motorists have stopped buying Shell petrol if it was the only source of supply? Past evidence suggests that only the highly committed would have gone quite that far. While public opinion may encourage firms to act in a socially responsible way, their self-interest and commitment to their stakeholders may prevent them from doing so if it will have a negative effect on their profitability. Shell was under no illusions about the opposition to its proposed sinking of the Brent Spar but it was only when its sales/profits were directly affected that it changed its mind.

Meffert and Kirchgeog (1995, pp. 983–4) see this distinction between individual and social benefit giving rise to tension between push and pull effects. Ecology push comes from public opinion as reflected in legislation and pressure groups, lobbying and so on, while ecology pull is the result of the perception of a market opportunity. This tension is summarised clearly in Figure 23.1 reproduced below.

The distinction between push and pull, social and individual benefit is mirrored by wide differences in attitudes and opinions and actual behaviour in those countries where research has been undertaken. This research also reveals wide variations between countries in terms of their sensitivity and response to environmental issues (see Meffert and Kirchgeog for details). Because of these variations, each firm must give careful attention to the environmental and competitive conditions which prevail in the markets it seeks to serve, when developing its own strategies and plans. What our discussion has indicated is that, like virtually every other market, an attribute like 'green' or 'eco-friendly' may have a special

Figure 23.1   *Environmental marketing in the tension between 'ecology push' and 'ecology pull'*

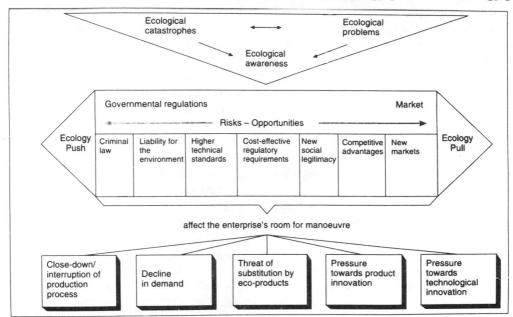

significance for a segment and constitute a niche market for which a focused strategy can be developed. For the majority these attributes will have varying levels of importance and could have an influence upon people's decision behaviour as suggested by our model of buyer behaviour (p. 186). In other words, green attributes may influence both one's perception and behavioural response. It is unlikely, however, that they would override the more objective cost–benefit analysis which lies at the heart of the decision process. For example, many recycled paper products are less attractive, less effective and more expensive than 'original' products made from raw materials. Unsurprisingly, only a highly committed minority will choose the less satisfactory, recycled substitute. Given such a scenario a more effective and eco-friendly strategy for a paper products manufacturer would be to guarantee that it had taken active steps through its sourcing policy to ensure that for every tree used another was planted.

Eco or green concerns focus on 4 main issues:

1. The excessive or wasteful use of non-renewable resources such as oil, minerals, and so on.

2. Pollution of the air, land and water.
3. Increasing and wasteful use of energy leading to excessive consumption of resources and global warming.
4. Processes which harm other people's, and animals', quality of life.

Addressing these problems calls for innovative solutions in the areas of product design and development, manufacturing and packaging.

In terms of product development numerous possibilities present themselves. For consumer durables which use energy they can be designed to use less. Engines which burn oil and gasoline can be designed to be more fuel efficient and emit fewer pollutants into the atmosphere. Durable products can be constructed using resources which are renewable or recyclable, as can the great majority of packaging material. Structures and machines can be designed to use less energy, to be easier to service and maintain, and to dispose of at the end of their useful life.

Where legislation exists, as for example is the case for car emissions, firms have no option but to comply and compliance confers no competitive advantage. Otherwise, however, many manufacturers have recognised environmental concerns as a source of competitive advantage and have developed products with a green image. Thus Macdonald's have stopped packaging their hamburgers etc. in polystyrene containers and now use cardboard which comes from a renewable resource and is biodegradable and/or recyclable. Similarly, many soap and detergent manufacturers have reformulated their products for use in cold water, to save energy, and have reduced the phosphates and other chemicals which pollute water supplies. Bodyshop have used the fact that their products are not tested for safety on animals and so on. As noted earlier, such moves constitute both a socially responsible attitude and good business. That said one might be forgiven if, occasionally, one is somewhat cynical about producers' claims of environmental concern.

Cynical or Concerned?

Help us help our environment

Dear Guest,

We here at Castaways Beachfront Resort welcome all suggestions, ways and methods to help preserve our fragile environment and eco system. So much so that we actively recycle all our glassware, cardboard and plastic products.

It is with this in mind that we invite you to assist us in a small but significant way . . .

How? Just by holding onto your towels for that extra day! That's it!!

If you wish to assist us – so that we are not using quite so much detergent, chlorine, sodium hydroxide, ammonia, dichlorocyanuric acid etc. and thus polluting this special area . . . then please hang your towels up for another day. On the other hand should you require fresh towels please leave them on your W.C. seat and we will collect and renew them.

We thank you for helping to preserve our environment.

Is this a genuine appeal?

Do you need to use all these chemicals to wash towels? Would you feel they really meant it if they offered $1 for every towel you used twice to go to a worthy cause?

In the longer term, however, it is clear that we will all have to take care of our environment if we are not to destroy it. But as Peattie and Charter (1994, p. 693) observe in *The Marketing Book*

> Green marketing's central concepts of sustainability and holism are both apparently simple but can be extremely difficult to translate into action. This is largely because they go against the accepted management wisdom, which depends upon reductionalism and specialism, and which is founded on economic theories that mistakenly treat environmental forces as limitless, free (beyond the cost of extraction) or, for marketless commodities like stratospheric ozone, worthless.

Clearly, this must be a case where consumer attitudes and behaviour must be mobilised to achieve the desired result.

■ Ethics in marketing

While ethical issues have always existed in the domain of marketing, it is only in recent years that they have begun to attract explicit attention in mainstream marketing text books. Indeed the contemporary interest in ethics would seem to be closely related to the emergence of relationship marketing as the dominant paradigm in place of the marketing management model with its focus on the transaction which preceded it. Under the latter representation the transaction has often been seen as an adversarial model in which business seeks to 'win' at the expense of the consumer. It was this perception which gave rise to the consumerist movement of the 1950s and 1960s, epitomised by books such as Vance Packard's *Hidden Persuaders*.

Nowadays, it is widely accepted that marketing is all about mutually satisfying exchange relationships in which both parties gain the satisfaction and benefits they are seeking. It is also accepted that 'relationship' implies a long-term and continuing association whereas 'transaction' refers to a one-off, or single exchange, albeit that a sequence of transactions may lead to a relationship. For a relationship to succeed there is an assumption that certain principles of behaviour will be accepted and observed and it is these which constitute the ethical dimension of the association.

According to N. Craig Smith (1995, p. 905):

> Marketing ethics can be defined as both the study of the moral evaluation of marketing and the standards applied in the judgement of marketing decisions, behaviours and institutions as morally right or wrong. It refers to a discipline and the subject matter of that discipline, the 'rules' governing the appropriateness of marketing conduct. It is a subset of business ethics, which in turn is a subset of ethics or moral philosophy. More simply, marketing ethics is about the moral problems of marketing managers. It includes, for example, the ethical considerations concerned with product safety, truth in advertising, and fairness in pricing. It is an integral part of marketing decision-making.

As noted earlier, questions of what is right and wrong in business relationships have been discussed and debated for centuries, and Smith cites the Roman philosopher Cicero who examined the moral duets of merchants in his *De Officiis* as an early example. These questions found expression in the concept of social responsibility as an issue for corporate decision makers, and in classes with titles such as 'Business and Society', during the 1960s and 1970s. Within the subject of marketing, ethical issues were most often identified with specific topics, with truth in advertising being one of the earliest and widely discussed themes. Product safety also attracted considerable attention, particularly after Ralph Nader's *Unsafe at any speed* drew widespread attention to product

defects in GM cars during the mid-1960s. Similarly, an increasing concern for the environment and the birth of the 'Green' movement focused concern on products and processes damaging to the environment such as the use of CFC as a propellant in aerosol products.

The latter is an excellent example of the need for both improved consumer education and regulation of business practice. Traditionally buyers and sellers have been regarded as being on an equal footing with the onus resting on the buyer to ensure that they received what they bargained for. Thus the Common Law concept of *caveat emptor* (let the buyer beware) assumes that if goods are openly available for sale then it is the buyer's responsibility to decide whether or not they wish to buy. With the increased availability of manufactured goods following the Industrial Revolution, and the insertion of intermediaries in channels of distribution between producer and consumer, legislation (the Sale of Goods Act 1892) was enacted to give greater protection to consumers and ensure that goods were fit for the purpose for which they were sold.

During this century the growing complexity of goods and services has required a significant expansion in legislation to provide consumers with protection in terms of their basic rights as spelled out by President Kennedy in his first consumer address to Congress in 1962 namely:

1. The right to safety;
2. The right to be informed;
3. The right to choose;
4. The right to be heard.

While the emergence of consumerism, and the need for legislation to protect consumers, has been designated 'the shame of marketing' on the grounds that a business discipline founded on the concept of mutual satisfaction should have no need for imposed regulations – most reasonable people would agree that in the real world of rapid technological innovation and change the market is too imperfect a mechanism to ensure producers will always act ethically to protect their long-term interests. Equally, in a competitive marketplace the formulation of rules and regulations, through legislation and industry codes of practice, provides a base line for minimum standards of performance common to all.

Clearly, if legislation exists breaches are illegal and can be dealt with by legal processes. That said, there will always be controversy about marginal cases and grey areas where interpretation will differ according to the individual's point of view. The nature and extent of these grey areas will become even more difficult where clear guidelines don't exist as is often the case with legislation. In a survey of marketing practitioners to determine what constitutes the most difficult ethical problem, Chonko and Hunt (1985) identified the following ten issues in rank order of frequency of citation:

1. Bribery (most frequently cited; includes gifts from outside vendors, 'money under the table', payment of questionable commissions).
2. Fairness (manipulation of others, corporate interests in conflict with family interests, inducing customers to use services not needed).
3. Honesty (misrepresenting services and capabilities, lying to customers to obtain orders).
4. Price (differential pricing, meeting competitive prices, charging higher prices than firms with similar products while claiming superiority).
5. Product (products that do not benefit consumers, product and brand copyright infringements, product safety, exaggerated performance claims).
6. Personnel (hiring, firing, employee evaluation).
7. Confidentiality (temptation to use or obtain classified, secret or competitive information).
8. Advertising (misleading customers, crossing the line between puffery and misleading).
9. Manipulation of data (distortion, falsifying figures or misusing statistics or information).
10. Purchasing (reciprocity in supplier selection).

As Smith (*op. cit.*) observes, many of these issues are not unique to marketing and apply to all managers. That said, as issues in the domain of business generally, they all impinge and impact upon the marketing function itself. In his chapter in the *Companion Encyclopedia of Marketing*, however, Smith concentrates on those issues which he considers specific to marketing, namely:

- Marketing Research;
- Target Marketing;
- Product Policy;
- Pricing;
- Distribution;
- Personal Selling and Salesforce Management;
- Advertising and Sales Promotion.

Some of the key topics and issues which he identifies are as follows:

Marketing Research: Research integrity – the potential conflict between scientific/professional objectivity and business/commercial obligations. The rights of respondents – to choose, to safety and privacy (anonymity), to be informed (lack of deception) and to respect.

Target Marketing: As this involves the selection of particular individuals this can give rise to problems of inclusion – intrusion of privacy, stereotyping, exploitation of vulnerable persons – and exclusion such as the withholding of products or services from disadvantaged subgroups.

Product Policy: 'The major ethical issues in product policy are:

- Product safety;
- 'Questionable' products, that are harmful, in bad taste, or not considered socially beneficial;
- 'Me-too' products and product counterfeiting;
- Environmental impacts of products and packaging;
- Deceptive practices in packaging or product quality specifications;
- Planned obsolescence;
- Arbitrary product elimination;
- Service product delivery.

(Smith, pp. 912–30)

Pricing: Like product issues, pricing is subject to extensive regulation on issues such as price fixing, price discrimination, predatory pricing and deceptive pricing.

Distribution: Most issues in distribution relate to the exercise of channel power whereby the larger and more powerful members in a channel use this power to exact an unfair advantage from their suppliers and/or customers. A particular topic of concern here is the power of multiple retailers. Franchising has also been cited as an area subject to abuse.

Personal Selling: Smith (p. 917) suggests that conflicts can arise in three distinct areas or interfaces: between salesperson and customer, salesperson and company, and competitors. These are summarised as:

Salesperson – customers
1.   The use of gifts and entertainment;
2.   Questionable/psychological sales techniques;
3.   Over-selling;
4.   Misrepresentation;
5.   Account discrimination/favouritism;
6.   Conflicts of interest.

Salesperson – company
1.   Equity in evaluation and compensation;
2.   Use of company assets;
3.   Falsifying expense accounts and sales reports;
4.   Salesperson compliance with company policy.

Salesperson – competitor
1.   Disparagement;
2.   Tampering with a competitor's product;
3.   Spying;
4.   Exclusionary behaviour;
5.   Discussing prices.
(These activities are generally illegal.)

Advertising and Sales Promotion: The basic issue here is truth in advertising. This may involve a deliberate intention to deceive (deception) or be unintentional (misleading). In most countries the advertising profession has sought to retain responsibility for self-regulation preferring this to excessive regulation through legislation. To this end regulating bodies such as the Advertising Standards Authority in the UK publish detailed codes of practice and have formal procedures for receiving and dealing with complaints.

The above summary clearly identifies specific areas of particular concern to marketers. The key problem in handling ethical issues is that there are often no hard and fast rules concerning individual or corporate behaviour. Where society has a clear view on what is acceptable/unacceptable these views are enshrined in legislation which is enforceable through the process of law. Where the interpretation of moral values, such as those contained in various religions, is left to the individual then it is unsurprising if the boundaries between right and wrong become blurred or fuzzy. Offering a client a cup of tea would hardly be regarded as bribery, or occasionally using office stationery as theft. On the other hand a weekend in the Ritz, or hiring out your company car to someone else would probably be regarded as wrong. As the concern for ethical behaviour in marketing grows it may be expected that philosophical issues such as these will receive more formal attention. As to whether this increased attention will permeate the treatment of the various sub-fields as identified above or become focused in specific courses on Marketing Ethics remains to be seen. To conclude, however, Smith (p. 924) proposed the following maxims for determining whether or not your marketing is ethical:

● The Golden Rule: Do unto others as you would have them do unto you.
● The Media Test: Would I be embarrassed in front of colleagues/family/friends, if my decision was publicised in the media?
● The Invoice Test: Are payments being requested that could not be fully disclosed within company accounts?
● Good Ethics is Good Business: The belief that good ethics is in the long-term best interests of the firm.

- The Professional Ethic: Would the action be viewed as proper by an objective panel of professional colleagues?
- 'When in doubt, don't.'

Adaptable marketing systems

One of the major success stories of the second half of the twentieth century has been the emergence of Japan as a world-class economy. From a situation where 'Made in Japan' was seen as synonomous with 'cheap and nasty', Japan is now regarded as a leading-edge competitor in international markets with a reputation for quality, innovativeness and high value added. So, how was this transformation accomplished?

Without a doubt the period of post World War II reconstruction based upon American aid and technology was a major catalyst. But, the sustained growth and development achieved by Japan calls for a much more sophisticated explanation which goes much beyond the scope of an introductory marketing text book. However, some insight into modern Japanese practice is to be found in a chapter (11) by Ken'ich Yasumuro (1993) in a book entitled *The Rise and Fall of Mass Marketing*.

Yasumuro's chapter is concerned with analysing 'the forces in the market environment which have stimulated Japanese manufacturing enterprises to develop an adaptable marketing system (AMS)'. The focus of this analysis is the replacement of mass marketing and 'the recent move in business from mass production to the flexible manufacturing system (FMS), also known as "lean production"' (p. 205).

In studying AM & FM systems many scholars have used Toyota as a classic example. Because of the automobile industry's scale it has been argued that lean production may involve complicated methods that will be difficult to apply outside Japan or in other industries. Yasumuro dismisses this belief and argues that 'simple, effective applications can be found almost everywhere, especially in the production of electrical appliances and electronics' (p. 205). His own examples

are mainly drawn from the refrigerator and washing machine industries.

'Contrary to received wisdom, Japanese manufacturing firms in the 1960s and early 1970s were awkward mass producers, at least in relation to their domestic market' (p. 206). For a whole host of factors – evolution of traditional markets from feudal days, sharp changes in the climate between seasons, differences in regional markets, neurotic quality-conscious consumers, and the operations of the Keiretsu – 'the Japanese market is one of the most dynamic and confusing markets in the world and difficult to approach' (p. 206).

The creation of a standardised mass market in the post World War II era resulted from the cultural influence of the Americans and supply shortages which led to the acceptance of standardised goods. In the 1970s as disposable incomes rose Japanese consumers reverted to 'their inherent natural "diversity"' (p. 207), and 'the market for mass products began to be eroded by degrees'.

Because of fierce internal competition many newcomers were forced to abandon the domestic market and pursued export markets for standardised products in the West and especially the USA. 'Typical examples include Sony in consumer electronics, Honda in motor cycles, Sanyo in colour televisions, Akai in tape recorders, and JVC in audio systems, etc.' (p. 207). Yasumuro continues, 'However, their major competitive advantages depended on such country-specific factors as cheap labour costs, government support for exports, and an under-valued element of vulnerability.'

Many large firms were attracted by the success of the small export oriented firms and established mass production facilities alongside the small-batch diversified systems developed to serve the domestic market. One consequence of this was a lesser degree of diversity and standardisation than found in Western markets – a factor which prevented the entrance of foreign firms into the Japanese market.

However, the 'hotchpotch' of mass production alongside small-batch systems revealed a marked disparity in the two systems in terms of productivity and efficiency which could only be sustained through the profligate use of energy and other natural resources. Despite double digit growth in the 1960s, by the early 1970s the Japanese economy was on the verge of collapse. As a result of the international monetary crisis in 1971 a floating currency saw the Yen re-valued against the US dollar and Japanese export firms began to lose their price competitiveness. This problem was further compounded by labour shortages and soaring wages to which was added the impact of the first oil crisis in 1973. Inflation raged and Japan experienced its deepest and most prolonged recession in post-war history.

Having lost their competitiveness in export markets Japanese firms turned to their domestic market and had to develop a more flexible and adaptable approach to manufacturing and marketing to meet its needs. This need was emphasised by the post-war generation of baby boomers who, like their contemporaries in the USA and Europe, had grown up in a period of increasing affluence and a predilection for differentiated as opposed to standardised products.

'To adapt to market uncertainty, the product life cycle needs to be shortened to minimise product exposure in the risky conditions, (volatile and unpredictable consumer demand) and lot size (production volume of each item) should be minimised to adjust to elastic demand. In short, there is a well-known law of cybernetics, the law of requisite variety – that if the market environment becomes diverse, production must be more flexible, and products must be more diversified (Ashby, 1956; Pascale, 1990)' (p. 210).

As a consequence of these environmental changes, Yasumuro identifies the emergence of a new paradigm of marketing strategy comprising five steps:

1. An incremental approach to the flexible manufacturing system;
2. The concept of 'the compound assembly line';
3. Selection of a market share strategy and the application of FMS;
4. The logic of adaptable marketing;
5. The emergence of a new business paradigm.

The salient features of these steps were as follows.

First, the deterioration in economic conditions required Japanese industry to attempt every possible means of saving energy, materials and labour. As a result of its conservation efforts Japanese management came to see mass production as both uneconomical and wasteful in energy and materials. By investing in labour-saving machines and energy-saving equipment costs and product defect ratios could be reduced drastically. Through careful design and maintenance automation helped eliminate operator error and improved both productivity and quality.

However, more sophisticated production systems call for more sophisticated operators and Japanese firms invested heavily in training. 'For this purpose, the "self management by team" concept was necessary, and group activities such as "quality circles" arrived in the workshops' (p. 211).

Although the problem was clear the solution was difficult. Yasumuro comments: 'The core of the problem was how to achieve product diversification without losing the merits of "scale economies"?' (p. 211).

The solution – a lean production system using a compound assembly line – was developed by Toyota in the 1960s and 1970s. Toyota's initial flexible production system was developed without the benefits of information technology and so relied heavily on appropriate and professional management. Its achievement was the ability to produce more than 2000 different types of car one after the other on the same assembly line. As information technology developed so it became possible to substantially improve the 'Toyota system' and adapt it to different products and industries. In the late 1970s many such flexible manufacturing systems (FMS) emerged.

While the adoption of FMS enabled Japanese firms to resolve the traditional conflict between scale and scope economies, it could only lead to competitive success if reinforced by appropriate marketing. The third step, therefore, was to pursue an aggressive market share strategy and invest in both production and marketing in pursuit of the longer-term strategic goals. 'As a result, the world-wide market share of Japanese manufacturing firms consistently increased in the

1980s, but their average ROI ratio began to decrease' (p. 213).

In pursuit of market share, however, it was clear that individual markets were becoming increasingly fragmented through finer and finer market segmentation strategies. 'The logical consequence of a growth strategy through full-line policy in the segmented market is FMS, which is characterised by the "compound assembly line" and "just-in-time". In short, when markets become diverse, production systems also become diverse to adapt to market conditions – the law of requisite variety – *and then adaptable marketing has a strategic importance*' (p. 213, my emphasis).

Adaptable marketing is the obverse of mass marketing. For mass marketing to be successful, precise demand forecasting is called for and considerable effort is devoted to monitoring and seeking to predict consumer behaviour. Still more effort is devoted to seeking to influence consumers to make them want the products which the system makes available. In adaptable marketing the seller offers the intending buyer a wide variety of products from which he can select the one most suited to his particular needs. Adaptable marketers don't push products at customers, they appeal to their intelligence and ask them to choose what they would prefer. The emphasis is on quality and supplier reputation rather than the product or service itself. To succeed, however, the adaptable marketer must also offer greater value and so cannot ignore the price competitiveness of mass produced products.

It is this combination of Flexible Manufacturing (FM) and Adaptable Marketing (AM) systems which constitutes the new business paradigm and underpinned Japan's startling performance in world markets through the 1980s. As Maslow's need hierarchy makes clear it is the inevitable consequence of growing affluence and increased disposable incomes. Wider choice and greater diversity now represent demand and supply and production has become the servant rather than dictator of consumption.

[Yasumuro continues with a detailed explanation of how Sharp developed FMS for refrigerator and washing machine manufacture. This description also highlights the need for integration of manufacturing and marketing in NPD].

But adaptable marketing is not without its pitfalls. Carried to its illogical conclusion it leads to what Yasumuro terms 'market share absoluism'. As with most things the pursuit of market share leads inevitably to diminishing marginal returns. Yasumuro notes:

> When marketing managers began to insist that low-turnover products also had to be produced to ensure maximum market share they began to erode corporate revenues. Every executive worried about an unlimited proliferation of products damaging profitability and it was hard to prevent because of the overwhelming priority of market share in more Japanese companies. Thus ineffective product diversification was disseminated. (p. 230)

And a little later: 'There is no exception to the iron rule that if product diversification increases beyond a certain limit, as a logical outcome, productivity goes down and costs go up at an acute angle' (p. 230).

Three cases of consumer packaged goods companies in Japan underline the point. In 1989 Ajinomoto, one of the largest packaged and frozen foods companies in Japan, reviewed its product lines. It discovered that the marginal 800 products in its line only accounted for 0.4 per cent of market share, the marginal 1200 only 4 per cent. The Kewpie Corporation, a large processed food maker, discovered that if 2700 items representing 30 per cent of its products were eliminated, the loss of market share would be less than 1 per cent. Similarly, the Lion Corporation, the second largest toiletries maker in Japan, discovered that while its products had increased from 150 in 1980 to 580 in 1989 its sales had decreased by 6 per cent and profits by 47 per cent over the same period.

Yasumuro concludes: 'It is paradoxical to say that the key factor for success in flexible manufacturing and adaptable marketing systems lies not in product diversification itself, but in skill in preventing unlimited proliferation of product diversity' (p. 231).

But then real marketers have always known that it is profits not volume or share which is the key performance indicator!

▪ The company as a brand

In 'Brand Building in the 1990s' Stephen King (1991) identifies six areas of change which are exerting pressure on companies and which are likely to intensify over the next few years, namely:

- More confident consumers;
- New concepts of quality;
- Shortage of skills;
- Tightening of the competitive screw;
- The side-effects of new technology;
- Restructuring.

In respect of consumers King points out that they have become more confident, readier to experiment and trust their own judgement, have more disposable income and are more worldly wise. They have a greater understanding of 'marketing' in all its activities and this understanding will help ensure customers in business-to-business marketing become more demanding too. Consumers have strong views on what gives them satisfaction and are less tolerant of goods and services that do not live up to their expectations. Finally, and probably as a consequence of the preceding changes, they have become more independent and closer to the highest level of Maslow's need hierarchy – self-actualisation. The World may be a global market but its tribes and their members still have a need to distinguish themselves from one another to express their growing individualism. Nowhere is this more the case than in consumers' increasing demand for quality and a quality founded on real values which go together to make up 'the good life' such as green products rather than products which consume non-replaceable resources, pollute the atmosphere or cause pain or suffering to other species.

Satisfying the needs of these 'new' consumers will call for radical changes on the supply side but here skills shortages, due to declining birth rates, and insufficient education and training pose a threat to our ability to make these changes. However, international competition looks certain to intensify and will become even more acute as the leading players seek to secure the necessary labour inputs.

While it has become a cliché to talk of accelerating technological change, the trend persists. As King observes, 'Constant innovation will be a necessary part of normal commercial life, but few companies will be able to rely on having any *demonstrable* product or service advantage for more than a few months'. In the absence of objective criteria to guide the choice decisions then the *relationship* between seller and buyer will assume even greater importance. In consumer markets King believes this will reinforce the retailer's position as the consumer's friend at the expense of the manufacturer.

Faced with changes of the kind discussed above, producers will continue to restructure in an effort to secure economies of scale in manufacturing and marketing. In many cases this will involve mergers and takeovers, in others the striking of strategic alliances. Inevitably it will result in still greater concentration of market power in the hands of a small number of global players in the majority of industries.

In order to survive, King, amongst others, is of the opinion that success will depend critically on *brand-building* which he defines as:

> using all the company's particular assets to create unique entities that certain consumers really want; entities which have a lasting personality, based on a special combination of physical, functional and psychological values; and which have competitive advantage in at least one area of marketing (raw materials/sourcing, product/design/patents, production systems, supply/sales/service networks, depth of understanding of consumers, style/fashion, and so on).

Only through brand building will it be possible to:

- Build stable, long-term demand;
- Add values looked for by customers;
- Develop a sound base for future growth and expansion;
- Resist the growing power of intermediaries;
- Become recognised as a company with a reputation and going places that people will want to work with and for.

However, King believes that brand building in the 1990s will be quite different from that of the past which led to the emergence and dominance of classic single-line brands like Coke, Pepsi, Marlboro, Persil, Oxo, Kit-Kat and Andrex. As King points out, in 1969 19 of the 25 top spending brands in the UK were repeat purchase packaged goods; in 1989 it was just one. Now the trend is to the *company brand* in which it is the subjective, difficult-to-define aspects of service and reputation associated with a company which will position it in the consumer's mind and the market place:

> In essence, brand-building in the 1990s will involve designing and controlling all aspects of a company, leading people and activities well beyond the traditional skill of the marketing department and the agencies that it employs. It will be a lot closer to the marketing of services (such as airlines, hotels, retailers, building societies) than to the brand-building of the classic brands. (King, 1991)

But such brand-building will have to be very different from most managers' current perception of 'brands' as fmcg or possibly the company's logo and corporate identity programme. In future the company 'brand' will have to encapsulate and communicate what an organisation is and what it stands for – its mission, culture and aspirations. In doing so it will be as important for the internal marketing of the firm as it is for its efforts to win a distinguished and distinctive place in the perception of its actual and prospective customers. To achieve this will require organisations to be market orientated and customer driven in a manner which embraces all members and functions of the organisation.

▌Total Quality Management (TQM)

At numerous places throughout this book we have made explicit and/or implicit reference to the importance of 'quality' as a determinant factor influencing customer buying decisions. From these references it should have become clear that 'quality', like 'satisfaction', possesses both objec-

tive/tangible elements as well as subjective/intangible elements. In the composite model of buyer behaviour (p. 132) it was argued that the objective, performance characteristics determine whether a product or service can satisfy the customer's felt need. However, this ability is a basic requirement for any seller seeking to serve any given end-use market. Due to the relative ease with which such objective performance characteristics can be measured and copied, they provide buyers with only a limited basis for discriminating between competing suppliers with the result that buyers have to make judgements of the subjective benefits on offer. These include after-sales service and customer care (see p. 761) and it will be the buyer's perception of the quality and value of these which will inform their final decision. In this section we examine what constitutes 'quality' and how this may be managed to enhance competitiveness and build long-term buyer–seller relationships.

John Oakland (1995) in the *Companion Encyclopedia of Marketing*, Chapter 54, believes that, quite simply, quality means 'meeting the customer requirements'. However, this simple definition has been expressed in numerous ways by different authorities and Oakland (p. 954) cites the following:

> 'Fitness for purpose or use' (Juran, 1988).
>
> 'The totality of features and characteristics of a product or service that bear on its ability to satisfy stated or implied needs' (BS4778: 1987).
>
> 'Quality should be aimed at the needs of the consumer, present and future' (Deming, 1982).
>
> 'The total composite product and service characteristics of marketing, engineering, manufacture and maintenance through which the product and service in use will meet the expectation by the customer' (Feigenbaum, 1991).
>
> 'Conformance to requirements' (Crosby, 1979).

Clearly, these definitions, proposed by four of the world's leading authorities on TQM, together with the British Standards definition, fall within Oakland's idea of 'meeting the customer's requirements'. However, they also help to make this more specific by introducing and reinforcing the notion that quality is largely a subjective concept which is judged against the customer's expectations. As we have explained elsewhere, expectations are strongly influenced by the claims made by sellers, reinforced by the asking price, and it is this which leads to the ideas of conformance to requirements, fitness for purpose and similar meanings.

In a study undertaken by Baker and Hart (1989) we identified 16 different properties or attributes which various authors have claimed to be 'critical success factors' in determining product performance. Respondents from a cross-section of both successful and less successful firms in a sample of six industries (electronics, medical equipment, pharmaceuticals, paper and board, agricultural machinery, and toys) were asked to rank order these in terms of their perceived importance. The results are reproduced below:

Critical success factors – product factors influencing competitiveness (in rank order)

1. Performance in operation
2. Reliability
3. Sale price
4. Efficient delivery
5. Technical sophistication
6. Quality of after-sales service
7. Durabiltity
8. Ease of use
9. Safety in use
10. Ease of maintenance
11. Parts availability and cost
12. Attractive appearance/shape
13. Flexibility and adaptability in use
14. Advertising and promotion
15. Operator comfort
16. Design
      (Baker and Hart, 1989, Table 3.1, p. 49)

It must be stressed that these results *only* reflect the views of the managers in our sample. For example, when the management of a carpet manufacturing firm were asked to rank order these factors there was unanimous agreement that the most important was 'Design', a factor ranked last by the survey respondents. The reason for this is that, when faced with a vast array of carpet products, it is the surface appearance and design which first attracts the customer's attention. If you don't get this you will have no further opportunity to make a sale.

Similarly, if you were to ask colleagues to rank order these attributes in terms of their importance to them when considering an important purchase like a car you might be surprised at the wide variations in perceptions which would emerge. It is this *diversity* which underpins the need for suppliers to constantly consult with prospective customers to establish their precise needs. In turn, this enables sellers to *segment* markets in terms of clusters of similar needs, to *target* those of most interest, and then *position* their product or service to appeal to particular individuals.

It is this ability to match the product to the exact needs of a customer that leads to the establishment of customer loyalty and a mutually satisfying exchange relationship that is the very essence of the marketing philosophy. But, apart from one-to-one personal services, such as a haircut, medical consultation, purchase of a bespoke suit and so on, most products and services are created by organisations comprising anything from a few up to tens of thousands of employees. The need for, and interest in TQM has grown with the recognition that each and every one of these employees can have an influence on the relationship between the organisation and its customers. It follows that if one is to ensure the customer receives the expected and desired quality then *all* employees must be trained and involved in total quality concepts. For example, at the present time British universities are undergoing assessment of their teaching quality. Narrowly defined, one would expect this to constitute an evaluation of the teachers' performance using a combination of direct and indirect measures – do they give clear, well structured, interesting and informative lectures, do the students achieve good results and get good jobs; what do the students think? However, the evaluations go much beyond this and take into account the documentation and administrative procedures used; the accessibility and attitudes of academic support staff; access to library and computing facilities; the quality of teaching accommodation, and so forth. In other words, the *total* quality of the teaching and learning experience.

To achieve the levels of quality desired it is necessary to think of all the employees in an organisation as links in a quality *chain* the strength of which will only be as good as its weakest link. Obviously, the first requirement will be to establish the nature of both the internal and external interfaces, or linkages, in the quality chain. Once these have been identified it will become possible to define what is required to make the linkages both effective and efficient and to establish appropriate performance indicators so that one can measure and control the inputs and outputs involved. Oakland (1995, pp. 957–8) takes the view that at each interface or linkage a transformation process occurs. The nature of this transformation process is summarised in Figure 23.2.

The importance of this conceptualisation is that in defining the desired output – a consistently satisfied customer – it forces one to consider and define what inputs and processes are necessary to achieve this end result. Through this kind of analysis one is able to build quality into the process from the beginning rather than having to take corrective action to rectify faults later on. The objective must always be to get it right first time. This view also underlines that TQM starts with and is a major responsibility of the marketing function. Marketing has the responsibility to identifying those customers with whom it believes the organisation can establish a fruitful exchange relationship. It then has the responsibility to identify the precise needs and wants of these prospective customers and to communicate these clearly to everyone else in the firm so that they understand exactly what is required to achieve the desired end result. Our earlier discussions of buyer behaviour (Chapters 6 and 7), environmental analysis (Chapter 2) and marketing research (Chapter 10) have all looked at issues to be considered in defining customer requirements, while all the other chapters have been concerned with how the firm should use this information to craft effective marketing strategy.

Plainly, marketing has a central interest in and responsibility for quality. However, in the same sense that marketing – the creation of satisfied customers – is the responsibility of all, so is quality. By the same token, quality management,

Figure 23.2 *The systematic approach to process management*

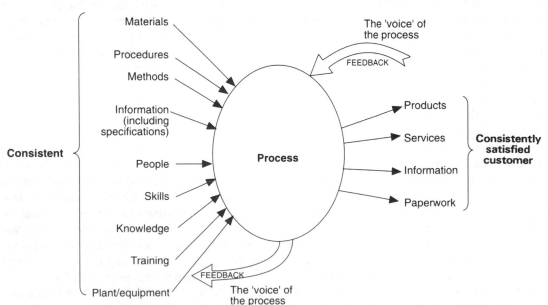

Source: Oakland, John (1995) *Companion Encyclopedia of Marketing*, Chapter 54 (London: Routledge).

like marketing management, calls for specialist knowledge and practices and this requires the employment of qualified practitioners to facilitate the development and implementation of total quality procedures. An introductory marketing text book is not an appropriate place to examine these. Readers wishing to explore this topic further should consult the recommended readings starting with the chapter by John Oakland (1995), already referred to, which provides an excellent overview of the topic

■ Customer care

Ideologically, marketing is all about customer/consumer orientation and the organisation of the seller/supplier's activities to meet the customer's needs efficiently and effectively. As such the idea of customer care ought to be central to the practice of marketing. It would seem, therefore, that the highly specific interest now shown for the topic, which has merited a separate section on it in this book, implies that customer care has not received the attention it deserves, a view endorsed by Donaldson (1995, p. 330). In this section we consider this proposition through a discussion of the origins and nature of customer care and the marketing activities designed to create and deliver it.

In David Carson's (1995) view (*Companion Encyclopedia*: p. 751), 'The origins of customer care and satisfaction stem from attempts by marketers to enhance the dimensions of after-sales service.' Such after-sales service was traditionally associated with industrial goods and consumer durables where advice on use or application, maintenance or repair were essential elements of the life-cycle cost and the total package bought by the customer. In many cases, after-sales service was (and is) the only effective means of differentiating between the offerings of competing suppliers. For example, in the late 1950s and early 1960s, when the author was a steel salesman, both the price and specification were fixed so that the only means buyers had of differentiating between competing

sellers was on the basis of the quality of the service offered. In addition to obvious dimensions such as quality, reliability, delivery and so forth, this extended to offering extensive technical advice to users to ensure they obtained the maximum value from their purchase. It is this 'added value' which is now seen as the major benefit offered by customer care programmes.

Originally, and as the phrase implies, added value was seen as something additional to the basic product offering. It was this distinction which prompted Levitt and others to distinguish between the core product – the object which would meet the consumer's basic *need* – and the augmented product which was designed to meet the specific *want* of particular customers through the addition of benefits and values looked for by them. Under this concept the added values were bundled in with the core product or service as opposed to being offered separately in the form of service contracts, provision of spare parts, and so forth.

Customer care is a natural consequence of increased competition and the search for a sustainable competitive advantage through segmentation, targeting and positioning. It is also inextricably linked with the concept of relationship marketing through which the seller seeks to establish a long-term, mutually satisfying exchange relationship with the buyer as opposed to regarding each contact with the customer as a one-off transaction (see Chapter 1). Such a perspective is one of commercial common sense, for it has been estimated that it costs five times as much to create or win a customer as it does to keep one through the continuing supply of a quality product or service backed-up by appropriate customer care. If each sale is regarded as a one-off transaction then it is likely the seller will seek to make a profit on the initial sales which requires him to recover all of the 'capital' costs incurred in identifying, prospecting for and selling to that customer. If these costs are five times as great as those incurred in maintaining an on-going relationship then it is not difficult to see how and why the transactional approach will lead to a higher price and a perception of lower added value.

By contrast, if the seller takes a long-term view then he will seek to spread the costs of his initial capital investment, incurred in creating the customer, over a series of transactions for frequently purchased consumer goods and through a life-cycle approach for durable products which are purchased infrequently but require upkeep and servicing through their useful lives. However, the economics of relationship marketing make it clear that there will always be an initial capital cost involved in entering or creating a new market and that it will require customer loyalty and repeat purchase to recover or amortise these costs. It is for this reason that the established seller always has an advantage over the newcomer. Only if a new entrant is offering additional benefits or values, perceived as important by the buyer, will the seller be able to get the buyer to change his or her behaviour and, possibly, pay a premium price for the added value. It is for this reason that innovation and new product development has assumed such importance as a competitive strategy.

☐ *What is customer care?*

In its widest sense, customer care embraces everything an organisation does to establish and sustain a relationship with its customers. In its narrow sense it is any activity or action which adds value to the relationship so that an organisation's customer care programme may consist of a listing of a series of highly specific activities. This is particularly so when a firm publishes an explicit statement of its customer care programme. In a sense this distinction between the concept of customer care, embracing all aspects of the customer relationship, and its implementation through a series of specific functions, is very similar to the distinction between the marketing concept and the marketing function. At one level customer care is a state of mind which permeates the thinking of the selling organisation. At another level it is a highly focused and closely defined set of activities designed to add values and satisfactions important to specific customers.

Donaldson (1995, p. 331) makes an important distinction between the concepts of customer loyalty, customer satisfaction and customer care.

As he points out, a customer may be loyal due to the absence of competitive alternatives. However, this does not automatically mean they are satisfied, such that if a new competitor enters the market with an improved or better product or service then customers are likely to switch to them. Loyalty is always fragile in buyer–seller relationships if for no other reason than that, ultimately, the customer's loyalty is first to him or herself, then to their family and then to their employer. As Donaldson observes, 'Customer loyalty can be measured but it is earned and cannot be delivered.'

Similarly, as we discuss later, customer satisfaction may be measured and delivered but it is essentially a subjective concept and so specific to each individual. Accordingly, satisfaction is 'a measure of customer responsiveness to marketing stimuli in a given competitive environment' (Donaldson, 1995, p. 331). It is a consequence or result of all aspects of the seller's interaction with the customer including the service and care elements of the exchange. While some authors distinguish between customer service and customer care, Donaldson considers them to be the same and defines them '*as all those activities provided by the seller which have value for the buyer thus increasing customer satisfaction and encouraging patronage and loyalty between the parties*' (original emphasis, p. 332).

As an activity, Carson (1995, pp. 753–4) sees customer care as a concept which encompasses at least four kinds of distinct activity which he explains as follows:

1. *Customer service*: Generally includes advice and information for customers regarding the technical specifications of a product or service and after-sales back-up arrangements and procedures. To emphasise this point, Christopher (1986) writes that 'ultimately customer service is determined by the interaction of all those factors that affect the process of making products and services available to the buyer.'
2. *Product quality*: Relates to standards and measures set to ensure a product conforms to specifications and is therefore fit for its purpose and safe to use.

3. *Service quality*: Refers to the company–customer interface and relationship, focusing on the customer's experience during the process of the transaction.
4. *After-sales service*: Covers after-sales enquiries and complaints, together with repair and maintenance procedures.

Clearly, the current scope of customer care goes much beyond the original idea of after-sales service, which is only one of several elements in the above taxonomy. As conceived here, customer care includes all activities from anticipation and identification of the intended customer's need, through initial contact, to negotiation, sale and consumption. The organisational implications of this concept are important. Like marketing, as a whole it requires people within an organisation, with specific organisational responsibilities, to take a holistic view and see how their contribution fits into the overall interface with the customer. Workers on a production line are just as involved and concerned, possibly more so, in ensuring customer satisfaction, through building quality into the product, as is the salesperson or service engineer in ensuring that the customer gets what they want. Indeed the concept of Total Quality Management (TQM – see p. 541) underlines the importance of designing and building satisfaction into a product or service in the first place.

Customer satisfaction is very much a subjective concept and its achievement is difficult because it is particular to every individual customer. At one level it is not too difficult to specify what the customer wants in terms of performance factors and what price/value they will place upon different performance levels (cost/benefit). But, as we saw in Chapter 6 (p. 132) the composite model of buying behaviour makes it clear that prior learning and experience leads to the formation of attitudes and the phenomenon of selective perception. Thus, the same objective 'facts' are likely to be interpreted differently by different individuals. One consequence of this is that we develop different expectations, and satisfaction is essentially a measure of the degree to which performance matches or exceeds expectations.

For example, you book into a 5-star luxury hotel at a cost of £200 per night. The environment is superior and elegant, the service is discreet and attractive, the food is excellent. But, for £200 per night that's the least you would expect so the overall experience is probably 'satisfactory' or 'very satisfactory' on the customer questionnaire you are asked to complete on departure. If you're used to this type of hotel it is very rarely that you will tick 'excellent' or 'superior'. You only do this if performance exceeds expectations. Contrast this with spending a night in a Two-crowns, Bed and Breakfast establishment in the Outer Hebrides for £25 including dinner. You have a very comfortable room with a wonderful view and en-suite bathroom with lashings of hot water. Your wet walking gear disappears on arrival but is clean and dry by the time you leave in the morning. You have lobster and fresh raspberries and cream for dinner and a breakfast in the morning that will keep you going all day. There is no questionnaire to complete but the experience so exceeds your expectations that you write and thank the landlady, you write to the Scottish Tourist Board saying what a wonderful place it is, and you, foolishly, tell everyone the same thing so next time you want to make a reservation it's fully booked. Satisfaction is complete!

The implications are obvious – the higher the expectation the more difficult it becomes to exceed them and the harder the supplier will have to work to ensure they meet the required standard. In doing so, it quickly becomes apparent that one must distinguish clearly between the tangible/objective aspects of an object and the intangible/subjective elements associated with it. Carson and Gilmore (1989–90, p. 52) provide a very helpful diagram which summarises these two dimensions of customer care and this is reproduced as Figure 23.3.

The implications are clear. Even though individuals may interpret tangible elements somewhat differently from one another, they are still comparatively easy to measure. A 1.6 litre, 4 cylinder petrol engine is likely to be common to most mid-range family saloon cars while features like overhead cams and number of valves are also

Figure 23.3 *Dimensions of customer care*

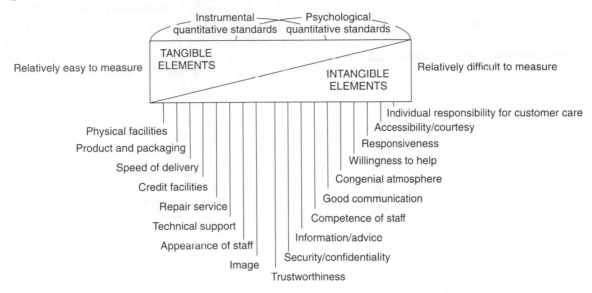

Source: Carson D. and Gilmore A. (1989) 'Customer Care: the neglected domain', *Irish Marketing Review* 4(3): 49–61.

easy to compare between one model and another. But, in selecting a motor car we are likely to take into account the whole range of tangible and intangible elements listed in the figure. Further, as the model of buyer behaviour (p. 132) makes clear, when products appear objectively the same then we will have to resort to less tangible, subjective elements to enable us to discriminate between competing products. It follows that the objective and tangible elements which are amenable to specification and, therefore, to rules and procedures are the necessary conditions for being considered as a supplier. But it is the subjective and intangible elements, which are less easy to define and/or standardise, which are most likely to influence the intending buyer's perception and so determine their final decision. It is recognition of this, combined with the difficulty of maintaining objective performance superiority for long, which has thrown into sharp relief the importance of customer care.

It is clear from Figure 23.3 that the less tangible elements of an exchange relationship are largely services, the performance of which will depend very largely on the individual

supplying them. As Levitt (1976) demonstrated in his 'Industrialisation of Service' paper, it is possible to reduce the human element on many service activities through specific techniques and practices; for example, standardised portion control in fast food outlets, or the development of formal procedures for the service supplier to follow, such as the preparation of quotations, billing and guarantee provision in Kwik Fit establishments. It is also possible to train people to achieve and sustain a high level of service delivery, and it was the implementation of such a programme in British Airways which has enabled it to claim to be 'The World's Favourite Airline'. In the final analysis, however, it all comes down to the individual performance of the service provider and it is their behaviour which will usually determine whether or not one's satisfaction meets or exceeds expectations. It follows that the training, motivation and supervision of service delivery personnel is central to any customer care programme.

In addition to training and motivating service personnel it is also very important to pay careful attention to what, otherwise, might be considered 'trappings'; that is, elements of the service delivery package which, in and of themselves, are complementary to the service but not of its essence. Service organisations are often judged by their appearances. The huge banking hall of the past, intended to communicate the security and probity of the bank, has now come to be seen as intimidating to many private customers who prefer the more friendly atmosphere of the local building society office. Many parents might be concerned about their children's predilection for 'junk food' but can have no qualms whatsoever about the spotless hygiene of McDonald's or similar outlets. Clean delivery and service vehicles, smart livery and uniforms all provide tangible evidence of the supplier's professionalism and tangible concern for their customers.

The creation of the kind of 'esprit de corps' which motivates every individual in the organisation to give of their best has come to be seen as the responsibility of '*internal marketing*'. As the phrase suggests, internal marketing consists of regarding employees as 'customers' and configuring the organisation to ensure that the needs of individual employees are understood and satisfied. This requires considerable management attention and effort if it is to be achieved. Otherwise there can develop a tendency for an 'us and them' mentality to develop where the front-line contact personnel come to be seen as somehow more important, better or superior to the back-room personnel who support them. Total quality management has a major role to play in this internal marketing activity.

Summary

In this section we have looked briefly at some of the factors which have resulted in customer care receiving much more explicit attention than in the past. Essentially, this interest is a direct consequence of three major environmental trends:

1. Increased competition;
2. The rapid elimination of objective differences between competing suppliers;
3. The growing importance of services, which now account for two thirds or more of all consumption in advanced economies.

As a result of these trends, sellers have had to pay much more attention to the less tangible elements of the exchange relationship, and add value to the core product or service through the provision of additional benefits.

In order to provide and deliver superior customer care the organisation must motivate and train *all* its employees to understand the importance of creating and delivering satisfaction. In doing so, however, it is important to bear in mind that satisfaction is the extent to which a product or service meets or exceeds one's expectation. Accordingly, one needs to offer sufficient satisfaction to encourage people to buy, but not so much that the reality cannot possible live up to the expectation (see, for example, D. Carson and A. Gilmore (1993–4), 'Enhancing Service Quality: A Case Study').

Review questions and problems

1. 'As the general rate of change in society accelerates, the economics of permanence are being replaced by the economics of impermanence' (Toffler). Is there any evidence to suggest that the above statement is an accurate description of the way in which UK society is developing? What effects would such a change have upon marketing and, in particular, upon the marketing of consumer goods?

2. Write a critique of the concept of meta-marketing, showing the extent to which you believe marketing ideals can legitimately be extended beyond business products and services.

3. It has been argued that a continued expansion of output will create intolerable ecological problems. Do market-oriented firms therefore perform a social disservice by encouraging more purchases? Give reasons for your answer.

4. A recent government publication described the main trends in the United Kingdom during the last decade. Identify these trends and comment on those of particular significance in marketing.

5. A major problem in the development of a consumer-oriented economy is defining the relative roles of government and business in ensuring consumer satisfaction. Evaluate the response of business to the consumerist challenge.

6. Advertising is often used to add subjective value to products (e.g. cosmetics, soft drinks). This practice is widely regarded as socially undesirable. Discuss this proposition.

7. Consumerism has arisen because management has been guilty of one-way communication with the buyer; it is not listening to what is being said in reply. Discuss.

8. Has consumerism become a casualty to inflation?

9. Consumer sovereignty is the myth of the contemporary market-place. Discuss the role of this concept in the development of a realistic consumerist philosophy.

10. What do you understand by the term 'social marketing'? What is the relationship between social marketing and consumerism?

11. Describe the factors leading to the growth of consumerism in the 1960s and 1970s and consider how adequately the present UK consumerist structure and philosophy meets the demands that arise from these factors.

12. Waste – in excess production of undesirable goods, in unnecessary packaging, in squandering precious resources – is an inevitable outcome of marketing freedom. Discuss, suggesting constraints and controls if you feel they are necessary.

13. Does the growing power of consumer groups mean that marketers have failed in their aim of meeting consumer needs?

14. How are marketing principles and techniques applied to non-profit-making activities in the public sector? Give examples.

15. You have just become promotions manager of a national charity concerned with disabled children. Up to now the charity's fund-raising has been very low key, involving a discreet level of promotion on a relatively modest budget. On your appointment you have decided upon a radical change of policy, involving a full-blooded marketing approach to the problem of raising money. The attitude of the charity's committee is hostile, their view being that the application of product marketing techniques is wholly inappropriate to a charity. Write a report to your board justifying your viewpoint.

Supplementary reading list

Adamson, C. (1982) *Consumers in Business* (London: National Consumer Council).

Baker, M. J. (ed.) (1991, 1992, 1993, 1994) *Perspectives in Marketing*, Vols 1–4 (New York: John Wiley).

Baker, M. J. (ed.) (1994) *The Marketing Book*, 3rd edn (Oxford: Butterworth–Heinemann).

Baker, M. J. (ed.) (1995) *Companion Encyclopedia of Marketing* (London: Routledge).

Baker, M. J. (ed.) (1995) *Marketing: Theory and Practice*, 3rd edn (Basingstoke: Macmillan).

■ *Appendix* ■

The Written Analysis of Cases

Learning goals

The issue to be discussed in this Appendix is the preparation of a formal, written analysis of a marketing problem particularly of the kind used in examination case studies.

After reading this Appendix you will be familiar with:

1. The purpose of using case studies as a basis for classroom discussion and formal examination.

2. Approaches to defining problems and developing a formalised approach to problem solving.
3. The objectives of problem analysis.
4. The conduct of internal and external audits (see also Chapters 3 and 20).
5. Problems associated with the quantity and quality of information.
6. The structure and presentation of formal reports.

■ Introduction

While case studies are usually employed as the focus for a classroom discussion, they are being used increasingly as the basis for a written assignment. This is particularly so where the case method of instruction is followed in a formal course of study when the written analysis of a case is frequently adopted as the appropriate means of examination. Similarly, case studies often provide excellent material for examining students who have pursued a more conventional programme of instruction by means of lectures and tutorials. For these reasons it will be useful to consider the objectives of a written analysis and suggest some approaches to the execution of such an exercise. (It goes without saying that the following observations apply equally to case analysis, where a formal, written analysis is not required.)

■ Objectives

Despite the fact that most European teachers tend to spend more time upon the discussion of an individual case study than their North American counterparts, it is still rare for such an extended consideration to cover all the issues contained in a given situation. Certainly, if the case study is used as a catalyst for encouraging an exchange of ideas between students, it is unlikely that spontaneous contributions will occur in the logical or ordered manner one would expect in a formal lecture. Indeed, one suspects that if the case leader succeeds in eliciting a structured analysis, then it can only be at the expense of ruthlessly discouraging digressions and diversions, some of which inevitably would prove both stimulating and illuminating. Clearly the latter approach would eliminate much of the interest and involvement engendered by a lively debate in open forum, which is one of the strengths of the case method.

However, it is generally recognised that while case discussion has a vital role to play in management education, it possesses deficiencies which can best be remedied by alternative teaching methods. As implied above, case discussions frequently lack the cogency and impact which can be achieved by marshalling one's thoughts in a logical sequence, as well as neglecting issues of possible relevance and importance. Further, at the individual level discussion can result in a superficial treatment as students soon learn that their fellows have often not undertaken a rigorous analysis, and so will not challenge apparently complex analyses of data, while the case leader may not have opportunity. A similar danger exists in that the student can struggle through by 'debating' the points made by others, or simply by preparing a detailed analysis of one issue which is regarded as their 'contribution'.

The basic objective of the written analysis is to eliminate these deficiencies while developing skills in:

- problem definition;
- analysis;
- presentation.

We consider each of these in turn.

■ Problem definition

There is wide support for the view that problem definition is the most critical and most difficult step in problem-solving. This view is generally predicated on the grounds that while problem definition is invariably cited as the first stage in problem analysis, in fact it only becomes possible after an extensive consideration of a wide range of other issues. Consider two popular statements of the normative approach to problem-solving.

First, there is the Adaptive Planning and Control Sequence (APACS) proposed by Robinson and Luck which we introduced in the previous chapter and which comprises eight steps:

- Step 1 Define problem and set objectives;
- Step 2 Appraise overall situation;
- Step 3 Determine the tasks to be accomplished and identify the means to achieve these aims;
- Step 4 Identify alternative plans and mixes;
- Step 5 Estimate the expected results arising from implementation of the alternative plans;
- Step 6 Managerial review and decision;
- Step 7 Feedback of results and post audit;
- Step 8 Adapt programme if required.

Second, there is the operational approach to research suggested by Ferber and Verdoorn (1962) in *Research Methods in Economics and Business*, with six stages:

1. Formulating the problem;
2. Development of working hypotheses;
3. Planning the study;
4. Collecting and processing the data;
5. Analysis and interpretation;
6. Presentation of results.

While the second model may appear rather different from the first, in fact they both cover the same basic elements. Similarly, both convey the impression of an orderly sequence stemming from the identification and statement of a problem, though steps 7 and 8 in the APACS model suggest that feedback and revision of the initial problem definition are omitted by the second model.

In reality we feel that feedback and adjustment of the original problem statement will be a major feature of the whole problem-solving process. This is not to suggest that no problem is ever solved, but rather than the depth analysis of one issue will inevitably raise questions concerning related but previously unconsidered issues. Given the dynamic nature of the business environment it would be surprising if this were not the case. However, we make this point solely to reinforce the fact that the steps in the problem-analysis model are neither discrete nor necessarily sequential and, having given this warning, we will immediately find it simpler to treat them as if they were both.

In simple terms we can distinguish two alternative scenarios for the case analyst:

1. They are given a case study and a problem statement; or
2. They are given a case study with no indication of the specific problem to be addressed.

The first alternative is typical of the examination situation and also encompasses certain cases in which the opening or closing paragraphs contain a statement of the problem as perceived by the case writer or a character in the case itself. Such a situation corresponds well with the circumstance where an organisation has identified the existence of a problem and wishes to brief a consultant (internal or external) to analyse and solve it. The second alternative is much more open-ended and usually adopted by teachers where they wish their students to decide whether in fact a problem exists at all. A real-world parallel of this approach might be the study of an industry, market or company by a financial analyst. Fundamentally the case analyst is well advised to treat both situations in the same way.

If given a brief, then it is necessary to establish that it does reflect the real issue to be investigated rather than a symptom or effect of the real problem. Similarly, it is essential to eliminate any possible ambiguities in the problem statement or brief and to define any terms capable of differing interpretations. Equally it is of vital importance to establish the precise parameters of the topic. How long is 'the short term', 'the long term', 'the future'?; what firms are to be taken as comprising 'the textile industry'?; what is understood by 'competition' – immediate and direct competition from firms producing similar products or services, or is it intended to include competition from substitute products? Clearly exactly the same points need to be taken into account when preparing a brief of one's own.

Naturally the above is a counsel of perfection. If, for example, one knew that declining sales were directly and solely attributable to a specific cause, then, as claimed earlier, the problem is largely resolved, for one can focus all one's efforts upon eliminating or avoiding that cause. While pedants will argue that such elimination or avoidance is itself a problem requiring resolution, it is believed that it will usually be a relatively trivial one. If, for example, one is certain that declining sales are the result of product inferiority due to the absence of an ingredient or feature present in a competing product, it would seem that all that needs to be decided is:

(a) Do we wish to increase our sales to their former level?
(b) If yes, can we improve our product at a cost which will enable us to sell them at a price and volume which will earn us a satisfactory profit (including issues of complementarity, goodwill and so forth)?
(c) If the answer to (b) is 'no', then clearly we must revise our original position.

On the other hand, if the problem has been incorrectly identified and the decline in demand has resulted from other causes, then treating the wrong symptoms (product composition) is unlikely to have much effect. Of course, if one could survive long enough it might permit problem-solving by elimination!

Essentially we are arguing that it would probably be more accurate to define the first stage in problem analysis as 'setting up a working problem definition' in much the same way as the scientist sets up a null hypothesis. In this way we acknowledge that problems exist because of imperfect information and uncertainty – it would be surprising if the acquisition of more information did not help to reduce uncertainty and so permit more exact problem formulation. How, then, should we set about acquiring more and better information?

■ Analysis

Armed with a working problem definition and a declared objective the analyst is well placed to commence formal investigation. At this juncture it is well to accept that while one may be embarking upon a voyage of discovery many other explorers have done the same and much can be learned from their experience. In other words there is a body of knowledge and experience concerning problem-solving which is relevant to the solution of any particular problem. While several different approaches have been proposed (and we will only discuss our own preferred method), all are agreed on the fundamental point that a structured procedure is to be preferred. This claim does not deny the utility of unstructured methods such as brainstorming, lateral thinking or the like but would suggest that these are techniques to be used in particular circumstances and especially where a structured analysis has revealed deficiencies which cannot be remedied by more formal methods. Further, the more complex the problem, the more necessary is a detailed and structured approach to its solution. Thus where the nature of the problem is very well understood, as, for example, launching a space probe or landing an aircraft, it is usual to develop a checklist of all the steps to be taken in the sequence in which they are to be taken, and to follow this unswervingly unless there are indications to the contrary. Even in the latter case, for example a pilot observes an obstruction on the runway just prior to touchdown, alternative procedures are also likely to be highly specific.

Of course, business problems are far less amenable to the highly structured analytic method characteristic of the sciences, and appropriate to science-based activities, for example flying and aerodynamics, largely because business is an activity arising from the interaction of people who are far less predictable in their behavioural patterns than are materials. However, experience would seem to suggest that human behaviour patterns are perhaps more open to observation and prediction than has generally been appreciated. If this is so, then an ability to predict how a person or organisation would react under a specified set of circumstances must help reduce the uncertainty faced by decision-makers and so reduce the need to exercise judgement. Unfortunately it often appears that many decision-maker's confuse the amount of judgement they exercise with the quality of the decisions made. While it is true that the true exercise of judgement is the function and responsibility of the decision-maker, none but a fool would seek to substitute uncertain judgement for fact or known risk where the alternatives can be completely specified and probabilities attached to their occurrence (as in life insurance). Nonetheless it seems that this is just the error to which so many would-be decision-makers fall prey they cannot be bothered with the labour, much of it boring, repetitive and trivial, necessary for a rigorous analysis and so flee into the exercise of 'judgement'.

From the above comments it is clear that I am proposing at least two steps to formal analysis, namely:

1. The identification and measurement of all facts which impinge upon the problems.
2. The application of judgement to the uncertain areas which are the residual remaining following the factual analysis.

The first step is frequently described as a 'management audit' and is usually sub-divided into two parts – internal and external.

■ The internal audit

The purpose of the internal audit is to develop a comprehensive list of the organisation's resources, together with an assessment of their relative importance *vis-à-vis* each other. As suggested in Chapter 20 this audit should encompass all of the following:

1. *Physical resources*
   Land – as a source of raw materials;
       – as a location for manufacturing and distributive activities.

   Buildings – general purpose or specific; that is, designed for light engineering, assembly, storage and so on, or for heavy manufacturing requiring special foundations, services, and so forth.

   Availability of and access to – power supplies, drainage and waste disposal – and to transportation: road, rail, canal, port facilities, and so on.

Plant and equipment
– general purpose, for example lathe, press;
– specific, for example steel rolling mill, foundry, and so on.

2. *Technical resources*:   Essentially those which reside in the technical expertise of the firm's employees, together with the possession of patents, licences or highly specialised equipment.

3. *Financial resources*: These comprise the liquid assets in the firm's balance-sheet, the ability to secure loans against fixed assets and the ability to raise capital in the market on the basis of past and anticipated future performance. They also comprise the skill of the firm's financial management.

4. *Purchasing resources*: Managerial expertise backed by any special advantage enjoyed by the firm by virtue of its size or connections; for example reciprocal trading agreements.

5. *Labour resources*:   The skills, experience and adaptability of the workforce.

6. *Marketing resources*:   The degree of consumer/user acceptance or 'franchise' developed through past performance. Access to and degree of control over distribution; the specialised skills and experiences of personnel.

While such an audit should provide a good summary of the nature and extent of the company's assets, together with an indication of the relative importance of the major business functions, its value can only he realised by comparison with similar data for companies with which it is competing. To obtain this one must carry out an external audit.

■ The external audit

An assessment of the environment in which the company has to operate should be carried out at two levels. First, one should appraise the overall economic climate and seek to establish whether it is growing, static or declining and for what apparent reasons. Second, within this broad framework one should evaluate the industry or market in which the company is competing. Our own preferred approach to this stage of the analysis is to use the framework developed by the well-known management consultants McKinsey & Co. and built on by Michael Porter in his 'value chain analysis'.

The basis of the McKinsey approach is to subdivide the business system into a series of subsystems, as indicated in Figure A1. Starting with raw material extraction, the analysis proceeds by examining each major sub-system in turn in order to establish the interrelationship and interdependence between them in terms of:

1. The degree of *competition* within and between each sub-system; for example raw material extraction might be in the hands of only one or a few producers so that conditions are oligopolistic while retail distribution could be characterised by thousands of small sellers none of whom could influence the market. Clearly the latter circumstances describe perfect competition, and both sets of conditions apply in the oil industry. Thus in establishing the nature of competition one should measure:

   • The number of competitors;
   • Their profitability;
   • Their degree of integration;
   • Their cost structure;
   • The existence and nature of any barriers to entry; for example technological, size of investment in production and/or marketing.

2. Where, in the total system, *value* is *added* by the activities of members of the production, distribution, or servicing sub-systems. For example, a significant proportion of turnover in many consumer-durable industries is accounted for by after-sales servicing and the efficiency of this sector may have a radical influence upon the market shares of individual suppliers, as well as on industry profitability.

3. The location of *economic leverage* in the system. Does this arise from being a fully integrated producer, or can one exercise

Figure A1 *The business system*

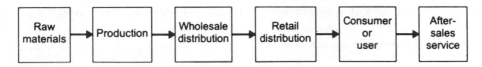

| Raw materials | → | Production | → | Wholesale distribution | → | Retail distribution | → | Consumer or user | → | After-sales service |

leverage by avoiding the extensive fixed investment implicit in vertical integration and concentrating on only one sub-system?
4. Where is the system's *marketing leverage*? Usually this is associated with control of a scarce resource which might be an essential raw material, a patent on a process, control of a distribution channel, a brand name ('Hoover', 'Elastoplast') or some other type of consumer franchise.

Once the analyst has established the major characteristics of the production, distribution and servicing sub-systems, their next task must be a thorough documentation of the consumer or user. Such documentation requires one to supply answers to the five basic questions which underlie all market research – who, what, where, when and how.

1. *Who* buys in terms of demographic and socio-economic criteria such as age, sex, income, education, occupation, marital status and so on (for consumers), or status, authority, functional specialisation and so on (for users)? Who *consumes*? (Compare consumption and purchase of breakfast cereals; of hand tools in a factory; and so forth.)
2. *What* do people buy in terms of variety, design, quality, performance and price characteristics?
3. *Where* do people buy? In specialist outlets, in general purpose outlets, by mail or telephone from a catalogue, in the home or on their premises; that is, how important is direct selling through representatives versus indirect selling via the media?
4. *When* do people buy? Are purchases seasonal, regular, irregular, associated with another activity, and so on?

5. *How* do people buy? Impulsively, after considerable deliberation, in large quantities, small quantities, from multiple sources or a single source, and so forth?

A sixth and equally important question is 'Why?' Unlike our other five questions one cannot usually supply a definitive and factual answer. However, when one considers that consumers (or users) do not buy products, as such, but rather the satisfactions yielded by the product, then even a partial understanding of the satisfactions looked for will go a long way towards explaining actual behaviour in the market-place.

At this juncture one should have developed a good understanding of both the company and the environment in which it is operating. It now remains to combine the two threads of the analysis in order to isolate the company's particular strengths and weaknesses in terms of the environmental threats and opportunities. An indication of the sort of questions appropriate to such a comparison is given in Figure A2, which is taken from McKinsey's model.

Thus far we have proceeded as if information were freely available and also as if it were of a known value. Rarely will these conditions be satisfied; in fact the most frequently voiced complaint of case students is 'lack of information'. Accordingly we turn now to consider this.

The quantity and quality of information

It is tautologous to point out that certainty exists where there is perfect information, from which it is a simple step to deduce that problems exist because of the absence of perfect information.

Figure A2 *Company's measurable strengths and weaknesses*

It is for this reason that we have stressed the methodical collection of as much information as possible as an essential prerequisite to problem-solving. However, in this task we are faced with three major difficulties – data are frequently incomplete, second, much information is presented in the form of opinion, or, third, may only be inferred from the apparent relationship between facts or events. It follows that a major job of the analyst is to screen all the available evidence for accuracy, validity and reliability as a preliminary to determining whether any relationships exist between acceptable facts that are suggestive of a solution to the problem in hand. There are many textbooks which deal with these issues at length and only a brief review is merited here.

While complete accuracy constitutes truth it would be erroneous to infer that less than complete accuracy is untruth and thereby unacceptable. In a business context it is rare that one requires the degree of precision necessary in the scientific laboratory, or even the engineering workshop, and a reasonable estimate will often suffice. What is reasonable depends upon the circumstances and may vary by several percentage points around the true value, for example an estimate of market size. Essentially the need for accuracy depends upon how sensitive the final outcome of one's analysis is to changes in the value of constituent elements – if the end-result appears to be largely insensitive, then approximation will suffice; if highly sensitive, then the more accurate the point estimate the better.

A good example of this is provided by a feasibility study of the suitability of a Scottish mountain for development as a ski-slope. While access to the slope, nature of the uplift facilities and back-up facilities (car parks, toilets, cafes and so on), price to be charged, growth trends in total demand and so forth all have a bearing upon the decision, estimates of all these parameters are relatively unimportant compared with the value of the critical or limiting factor – the prevailing weather conditions. In the event analysis revealed that when one deducted the number of days when it would not be possible to ski due to high winds or poor visibility from the total days on which snow could be guaranteed, the residue was so small as to make it quite obvious that a commercial venture was impractical almost regardless of the values one attached to any of the other parameters.

The mark of a good analyst is an ability to isolate the critical factors and then focus all available resources in eliciting the most accurate information available concerning them. When using data from published sources one must distinguish between the credibility to be attached to government statistics gathered by census and estimates extrapolated from samples by trade associations, consultants and those with a vested interest in the

interpretation of the data they convey. One must be conscious of recency and assess how delay in publishing data may affect its current validity. One must also be sensitive to changes in the collection and recording of data over time and satisfy oneself as to the comparability of such data.

Such strictures are all very well when dealing with information from published sources, but how does one deal with opinion and hearsay? Much information in case studies falls into the latter category and is often conflicting in its indication of the true state of affairs. A classic example of this is to be found in the Barnstaple case study, in which three executive managers responsible for the finance, production and sales functions each attribute the company's declining fortunes to a different cause. However, by carefully adducing factual data in the case, or inferences which may be drawn from *these data* with a very high degree of confidence, it can be clearly demonstrated that only one manager's opinion is acceptable. Herein lies a key skill of the analyst – an ability to pick out relevant pieces of information, while discarding those which only serve to confuse an issue, and link them together to demonstrate a functional relationship.

It is possible to distinguish three different levels of analysis in this sorting and synthesising process – deduction, inference and the formulation of assumptions. A deduction is made when one derives a logically necessary conclusion about a specific case from perfect information concerning the general case – for example, all retailers of cars operate on a 20 per cent gross margin; the XYZ company is a retailer of cars: *deduction* – the XYZ company operates on a 20 per cent gross margin.

The status of an inference is less clear cut than is that of a deduction. An inference may be defined as the interpretation placed upon evidence by an observer, from which it follows that the quality of an inference may range from excellent, that is a very high probability that it reflects reality, to very poor. Assuming, however, that the correct inference is drawn, then the distinction rests in the fact that there is always an element of uncertainty associated with an inference while there is none with a deduction. However, by linking logical deductions with reasonable inferences one can proceed a long way towards the solution of a problem.

The need for assumptions only arises where there is an absence of evidence necessary to link other information which seems to bear upon the problem. Assumptions may be of two kinds – working assumptions and critical assumptions. Working assumptions are those necessary to move an argument along and provide links in the chain of reasoning, but unlike critical assumptions they are not vital to the final decision. In every case an assumption should only be made as a last resort when it is obvious that other information is not available. When setting out an assumption, and especially a critical assumption, it is important to state clearly the evidence considered in deriving one's assumption, the reasons for selecting and rejecting particular points, and the precise form of the final assumption made. Only by careful attention to these factors will the analyst be able to communicate the thought processes leading to their conclusion; without them their argument will be open to criticism and lack conviction.

From the foregoing it is obvious that *both* the drawing of inferences *and* the formulation of assumptions demand the exercise of judgement, and this is the proper role for its application. In all other cases, a strictly formal and factual approach should be followed.

■ Presentation

Skill in problem definition and analysis is of little consequence if the analyst is unable to communicate their findings to others. There are several good books on report writing including, W. J. Gallagher (1969), *Report Writing for Management*, and J. Mitchell (1974), *How to Write Reports*. The student should consult these for detailed guidance on how to set about writing a report. However, in doing so it will become apparent that even the textbook writers are not in complete agreement and Gallagher and Mitchell suggest different formats for writing management reports. My own preference is for the Gallagher sequence, namely:

- Summary;
   Purpose
   Scope
   Conclusion(s)
   Recommendations

- Introduction;
- Body;
- Appendix.

However, for a Written Analysis of Cases (WAC) the Mitchell approach may be more appropriate:

- Statement of the problem;
- Factors causing the problem;
- The effects of the problem;
- Examinations of possible solutions and their implications;
- Conclusions;
- Recommendations;
- Appendices.

Whichever method is preferred two final words of warning seem appropriate. First, the student can assume that the examiner is familiar with the case and so should avoid the regurgitation of descriptive material unless it is introduced for a specific purpose. Second, facts seldom, if ever, speak for themselves.

For students seeking an extended discussion of the issues raised in this Appendix, Geoff Easton (1992), *Learning from Case Studies*, is essential reading. Based upon a seven step approach:

- Understanding the situation;
- Diagnosing problem areas;
- Generating alternative solutions;
- Predicting outcomes;
- Evaluating alternatives;
- Rounding out the analysis;
- Communicating the results.

Easton uses a series of short cases to exemplify and reinforce the key stages in a rigorous and logical analytical approach which adds greatly to the abbreviated treatment here.

Bibliography

Abbas, M. (1995) 'Relationship Marketing', unpublished working paper, University of Strathclyde.

Abbott, L. (1955) *Quality and Competition* (New York: Columbia University Press).

Aguilar, F. (1967) *Scanning the Business Environment* (New York: Macmillan).

Allen, G.C. (1970) *The Structure of Industry in Britain* (London: Longmans).

AMA (1959) *Analysing and Improving Marketing Performance: Marketing Audits*.

American Management Association (1959) 'The Marketing Audit: its nature, purposes and problems', *Analysing and Improving Market Performance, Report 32*.

Ames, B. C. (1970) 'Trappings Versus Substance in Industrial Marketing', *Harvard Business Review*, July–August.

Ames, B. C. (1971) 'Dilemma of Product/Market Management', *Harvard Business Review*, March–April.

Anderson, J. E. (1956) 'How to Price for Maximum Profits', *Management Methods*, November.

Andreasen, A. R. (1965) 'Attitudes and Customer Behaviour: A Decision Model', in Preston, L. E. (ed.) *New Research in Marketing* (Berkeley: University of California Press).

Ansoff, H. I. (1968) *Corporate Strategy* (Harmondsworth: Pelican).

Arndt, J. (1984) *The Anthropology of Marketing Systems: Symbols, Shared Meanings, and Ways of Life in Interorganizational Networks*, Paper given at the Proceedings International Research Seminar on Industrial Marketing, Stockholm School of Economics.

Austen, F. (1978) 'The Relevance of Marketing to Developing Countries', Paper to the Marketing Education Group of the United Kingdom, North Region Workshop.

Avlonitis, G. A. (1983) 'The Product-Elimination Decision and Strategies', *Industrial Marketing Management*, 12, pp. 31–43.

Baker, M. J. (1975) *Marketing New Industrial Products* (London: Macmillan).

Baker, M. J. (1980) 'Maxims for Marketing in the Eighties', *Advertising*, 66, Winter.

Baker, M. J. (1983) *Market Development* (Harmondsworth: Penguin).

Baker, M. J. (1991) *Research For Marketing* (London: Macmillan).

Baker, M. J. (1992) *Marketing Strategy and Management*, 2nd edn (Basingstoke: Macmillan).

Baker, M. J. (1994) *The Marketing Book*, 3rd edn (Oxford: Butterworth-Heinemann).

Baker, M. J. (ed.) (1995a) *Companion Encyclopedia of Marketing* (London: Routledge).

Baker, M. J. (ed.) (1995b) *Marketing: Theory and Practice*, 3rd edn (London: Macmillan).

Baker, M. J. and Hart, S. J. (1989) *Marketing and Competitive Success* (London: Philip Allan).

Bartels, R. (1968a) 'Are Domestic and International Marketing Dissimilar?', *Journal of Marketing*, July.

Bartels, R. B. (1968b) 'The General Theory of Marketing', *Journal of Marketing*, XXXII, January, pp. 29–30.

Bartels, R. B. (1988) *The History of Marketing Thought*, 3rd edn (Columbus, Ohio: Publishing Horizons Inc.).

Baster, A. J. (1935) *Advertising Reconsidered*.

Bates, J. P. and Parkinson, J. R. (1969) *Business Economics*.

Bateson, J. E. G. (1977) 'Do we need service marketing?', in Eigler, P. (ed.) *Marketing Consumer Services*, (Boston, Mass.: Marketing Science Institute).

Beckerman, W. (1974) *In Defence of Economic Growth* (London: Cape).

Bell, M. (1972) *Marketing: Concepts and Strategy*, 2nd edn (Boston, Mass.: Houghton Mifflin).

Bennett, R. C. and Cooper, R. G. 'The misuse of Marketing: An American tragedy', *McKinsey Quarterly*, Autumn.

Bennett, P. D. and Kasserjian, H. J. (1972) *Consumer Behavior* (Englewood Cliffs, N.J.: Prentice-Hall).

Bernard, K. (1995) in M. J. Baker (ed.) *Marketing: Theory and Practice*, 3rd edn (Basingstoke: Macmillan).

Berry, L. L. (1980) 'Services Marketing is Different', *Business*, May–June, pp. 24–9.

Berry, L. L. (1981) 'The Employee as Customer', *Journal of Retail Marketing*, March.

Berry, L. L. (1983) 'Relationship Marketing' in Berry, L. L., Shostack, G. Lyn and Upatis, G. D. (eds) *Emerging Perspectives on Services Marketing* (Chicago: American Marketing Association).

Berry, L. L., Zeithamil, V. A. and Parasuraman, P. (1985) 'Quality Counts in Services Too', *Business Horizons*, May–June, pp. 44–52.

BIM (1964) *Survey of Manufacturers Marketing Costs* (Information Summary no. 111).

BIM (1966) *Methods of Selecting and Training Salesmen* (Information Summary 87).

BIM (1970) *Marketing Organisation in British Industry*

Bishop, F. P. (1952) *The Ethics of Advertising*, cited in E. S. Turner (1952) *The Shocking History of Advertising* (London: Michael Joseph).

Blois, K. (1982) 'Organisational Structure and Marketing Policies in Service Firms', Paper presented at the 11th Annual Conference of the European Academy for Advanced Research in Marketing, April.

Booms, B. H. and Bitner, M. J. (1982) 'Marketing Strategies and Organisation Structures for Service Firms', in *Marketing of Services* (Chicago: American Marketing Association), pp. 47–51.

Booth, C. (1889) *The Life and Labour of People in London* (London and New York: Macmillan).

Booz-Allen and Hamilton (1982) *New Products Management for the 1980s* (New York: Booz-Allen and Hamilton).

Borden, N. (1964) 'The Concept of the Marketing Mix', *Journal of Advertising Research*, 4, June, pp. 2–7

Bowersox, D. J. (1969) 'Physical Distribution Development, Current Status and Potential', *Journal of Marketing*, XXXIII, January, pp. 63–70.

Bowersox, D. J. and Cooper, M. B. (1992) *Strategic Marketing Channel Management* (New York: McGraw-Hill).

Braithwaite, D. (1928) 'The economic effects of advertisement', *Economic Journal*, March, vol. 38, pp. 16–37.

Brand, G. T. (1972) *The Industrial Buying Decision* (London: Cassell Associated Business Programmes).

Brech, E. F. L. (1954) *Principles of Management*, 2nd edn (London: Longman).

British Rate and Data (BRAD).

Brown, S. (1995) 'Retailing', Ch. 24 in *Gower Handbook of Marketing*, 4th edn.

Brown, R. and Cook, D. (1990) 'Strategy and Performance in British Exporters', *Quarterly Review of Marketing*, Spring.

Brownlie, D. (1994) in Baker, M. J. (1994) *The Marketing Book*, 3rd edn (Oxford: Butterworth-Heinemann).

BS4778:1987 (1987).

Bucklin, L. P. (1968) 'The Locus of Channel Control', *Proceedings* of the Fall, 1968, Conference of the AMA, pp. 142–7.

Cannon, H. and Morgan, F. (1990) 'A Strategic Pricing Framework', *Journal of Consumer Marketing*, vol 17, no. 3, pp. 57–68.

Cardozo, R. (1980) 'Situational Segmentation of Industrial Markets', *European Journal of Marketing*, vol. 14, no. 516.

Carson, D. (1967) 'Comparative Marketing – A New Old Aid', *Harvard Business Review*, May–June.

Carson, D. (1995) in Baker, M. J. (ed.) *Companion Encyclopedia of Marketing* (London: Routledge), p. 751.

Carson, D. and Gilmore, A. (1989–90) 'Customer Care: the neglected domain', *Irish Marketing Review*, 4(3), pp. 49–61.

Carson, D. and Gilmore, A. (1993–4) 'Enhancing Service Quality: A Case Study', *Irish Marketing Review*, 6, pp. 64–73

Cass, T. (1968) 'Making Decisions in Marketing', *Marketing Forum*, May–June, pp. 15–24.

Caves, R. (1972) *American Industry: Structure, Conduct and Performance*, 3rd edn (Englewood Cliffs, N.J.: Prentice-Hall).

Chamberlin, E. J. (1933) *The Theory of Monopolistic Competition* (Cambridge, Mass.: Harvard University Press).

Chamberlin, E. J. (1957) *Towards a More General Theory of Value* (New York: Oxford University Press).

Chan, K. C. and McDermott, M. C. (1995) 'Beyond Relationship Marketing: Flexible and Intelligent Relationship Management Strategy (FIRMS), Ch. 21 in M. J. Baker (ed.) *Marketing: Theory and Practice*, 3rd edn (Basingstoke: Macmillan).

Chandler, A. D. (1962) *Strategy and Structure* (Cambridge, Mass.: MIT Press).

Chase, R. B. (1978) 'Where Does the Consumer Fit in a Service Operation?', *Harvard Business Review*, vol. 56, November–December, pp. 137–42.

Cherington, P. T. (1920) *The Elements of Marketing* (London: Macmillan).

Chisnall, P. M. (1992) *Marketing Research*, 4th edn (New York: McGraw-Hill).

Chonke, Laurence B. and Hunt, Shelby D. (1985) 'Ethics and Marketing Management: An Empirical Investigation', *Journal of Business Research*, 13, 339–59.

Chote, R. (1995) 'Decay of the Dismal Science', *Financial Times*, 28 March.

Christopher, M. (1992) *Logistics and Supply Chain Management* (London: Pitman).

Christopher, M. G., Kennedy, S. H., McDonald, M. M. and Wills, G. S. C. (1980) *Effective Marketing Management* (Aldershot: Gower).

Chung, E. K. and Heeler, R. M. (1995) 'The Economic Basis of Marketing', Ch. 3 in M. J. Baker (ed.) *Companion Encyclopedia of Marketing* (London: Routledge).

Churchill, G. A. Jr (1976) *Marketing Research: Methodological Foundations* (Fort Worth: Holt-Saunders/ Dryden Press), pp. 206–7.

Clark, J. M. (1961) *Competition as a Dynamic Process* (Washington D.C.: Brookings Institution).

Clarke, R. (1993) 'Trends in Concentration in UK Manufacturing, 1980–89', Ch. 7 in Casson, M. and Creedy, J. (eds) *Industrial Concentration and Economic Inequality* (Aldershot: Edward Elgar Publishing Ltd).

Clawson, J. (1950) 'Lewin's Psychology and Motives in Marketing', in Cox, R. and Alderson, W. (eds) *Theory in Marketing* (Glencoe, Ill.: Irwin).

Clewett, R. J. and Stasch, S. F. (1975) 'Shifting Role of the Product Manager', *Harvard Business Review*, January–February.

Club of Rome (1972) *Report (The Limits to Growth)*.

Coad, T. (1990) 'The Emergence of Marketing Databases and their Uses', *Direct Marketing Handbook* (Telephone Marketing Services, British Telecom).

Coad, T. (1993) *Marketing Business Magazine*, October.

Cole, H. S. D. *et al.* (1973) *Thinking About the Future* (London: Chatto & Windus for Sussex University Press).

Colley, R. H. (1961) *Defining Advertising Goals* (New York: Association of National Advertisers).

Collins, M. (1986) 'Sampling', Ch. 4 in Worcester, R. and Downham, J. *Consumer Market Research Handbook*, 3rd edn (ESOMAR).

Conference Board, The (1974). 'Why Products Fail' (October).

Converse, P. D. H., Huegy, H. W. M. and Mitchell, R. V. (1965) *Elements of Marketing*, 7th edn (Englewood Cliffs, N.J.: Prentice-Hall).

Copeland, M. T. (1923) 'Relation of Consumers' Buying Habits to Marketing Methods', *Harvard Business Review*, April.

Courtauld, S. (1962) article in the *Economic Journal*, April.

Cowell, D. (1984) *The Marketing of Services* (Oxford: Heinemann).

Cox, O. and Enis, B. (1973) *Experimentation for Marketing Decisions* (London: Intext).

Cravens, D. W. (1988) 'Gaining Strategic Marketing Advantage', *Business Horizons*, September–October, pp. 44–54.

Crosby, P. B. (1979) *Quality is Free* (New York: McGraw-Hill).

Crosier, K. (1975) 'What Exactly is Marketing?' *Quarterly Review of Marketing*, Winter.

Crosier, K. (1983) 'Towards a Praxiology of Advertising', *International Journal of Advertising*, vol. 2, no. 3, July–September.

Crosier, K. (1994) Ch. 19 in Baker, M. J. *The Marketing Book*, 3rd edn (London: Heinemann).

Crosier, K (1995a) in Baker, M. J. (ed.) *Companion Encyclopedia of Marketing* (London: Routledge).

Crosier, K. (1995b) Ch. 6 in Baker, M. J. (ed.) *Marketing: Theory and Practice*, 3rd edn (London: Macmillan).

Dalton, G. (1974) *Economic Systems and Society* (Harmondsworth: Penguin).

Davidson, H. (1981) 'How and Why Shoppers Buy', *Marketing*, 28 October.

Day, G. S. (1977) 'Diagnosing the Product Portfolio', *Journal of Marketing*, April.

Day, G. S. and Wensley, R. (1988) 'Assessing Advantage: A Framework for Diagnosing Competitive Superiority', *Journal of Marketing*, April.

de Chernatony, L. and McDonald, M. H. B. (1992) *Creating Powerful Brands* (Oxford: Butterworth-Heinemann).

Deal, T. E. and Kennedy, A. A. (1982) *Corporate Cultures* (Reading, Mass.: Addison Wesley).

Dean, J. (1951) *Managerial Economics* (New York: Prentice-Hall), p. 402.

DeLozier, M. W. (1976) *The Marketing Communications Process* (New York: McGraw-Hill).

Deming, W. E. (1982) *Out of the Crisis* (Cambridge, Mass: MIT Press).

Diamontopoulos, A. and Mathews, B. (1995) *Making Pricing Decisions* (London: Chapman and Hall).

Dibb, S., Simpkin, L., Pride, W. M. and Ferrell, O. C. (1994) *Marketing Concepts and Strategies*, 2nd European edition (London: Houghton Mifflin).

Donaldson, B. (1995) 'Customer Care', Chapter 17 in Baker, M. J. (ed.) *Marketing: Theory and Practice*, 3rd edn (London: Macmillan).

Donaldson, W. D. (1990) 'Sales Management' in M. J. Baker (ed.), *Marketing: Theory and Practice*, 3rd edn (London: Macmillan).

Donnelly, J. H. Jr (1976) 'Marketing Intermediaries in Channels of Distribution of Services', *Journal of Marketing*, vol. 40(1), January, pp. 55–7.

Donnelly, J. H. Jr and George, W. R. (eds) (1981) *Marketing of Services* (Chicago: American Marketing Association).

Dowling, G. (1994) 'Searching for a New Advertising Agency: A Client Perspective', *International Journal of Advertising*, 13, pp. 229–42.

Drakeford, J. F. and Farbridge, V. (1986) 'Interviewing and Field Control', Ch. 6 in Worcester, R. and Downham, J. *Consumer Market Research Handbook*, 3rd edn (ESOMAR).

Drucker, P. F. (1954) *The Practice of Management* (New York: Harper & Row).

Drucker, P. F. (1958) 'Marketing and Economic Development', *Journal of Marketing*, January, pp. 252–9.

Dudley, J. (1992) *1992 Strategies for the Single Market* (London: Kogan Page).

Duke, R. (1991) 'Post-Saturation Competition in UK Grocery Retailing', *Journal of Marketing Management*, vol. 7(1).

Dussart, C. (1994) in Baker, M. J., *Perspectives on Marketing Management* (Chichester: John Wiley).

Easton, G. (1992) *Learning From Case Studies*, 2nd edn (Englewood Cliffs, N.J.: Prentice-Hall).

Ehrenberg, A. S. C and Goodhardt, G. J. (1980) 'How Advertising Works', in *Understanding Buyer Behaviour* (New York: J. Walter Thompson/Market Research Corporation of America).

Eiglier, P. and Langeard, E. (1977) 'A New Approach to Service Marketing'. in *Marketing Consumer Services: New Insights Report* (Boston: Marketing Science Institute), pp. 77–115.

Elliot, D. (1974) 'Concentration in UK Manufacturing Industry', *Trade and Industry*, 1st August.

Engel, J. F., Blackwell, R. D. and Miniard, P. W. (1995) *Consumer Behaviour*, 8th edn (Fort Worth: The Dryden Press).

Engel, J. F., Kollat, D. T. and Blackwell, R. D. (1978) *Consumer Behaviour* (New York: Holt, Rinehart & Winston).

Engel, J. F. *et al.* (1972) *Marketing Segmentation* (New York: Holt, Rinehart & Winston)

Enis, B. (1980) *Marketing Principles*, 3rd edn (Goodyear Publishing Co.).

Enis, B. and Roaring, K. (1981) 'Service Marketing: Different Product, Similar Strategy', in Donnelly, J. H. Jr and George, W. R. (eds) *Marketing of Services* (Chicago: American Marketing Association).

Ennis, S. (1995) in Baker, M. J. (ed.) *Marketing: Theory and Practice*, 3rd edn (London: Macmillan).

Evans, F. B. (1959) 'Psychological and Objective Factors in the Prediction of Brand Choice: Ford vs. Chevrolet', *Journal of Business*, vol. 32, October.

Feigenbaum, A. V. (1991) *Total Quality Control*, 3rd edn (New York: McGraw-Hill).

Ferber, R. and Verdoorn, P. J. (1962) *Research Methods in Economics and Business* (New York: Collier-Macmillan).

Ferguson, P. (1988) *Industrial Economics: Issues and Perspectives* (Basingstoke: Macmillan).

Festinger, L. A. (1957) *A Theory of Cognitive Dissonance* (New York: Row and Peterson).

Financial Times/IMR (1974) 'How British Industry Buys', *Financial Times*.

Fishbein, M. and Ajzen, I. (1975) *Belief, Attitude, Intention and Behaviour* (Reading, Mass.: Addison-Wesley).

Fletcher, K. (1986) 'Social Behaviour: an analysis of information and usage during the decision process', unpublished PhD, University of Stathclyde.

Fletcher, K. (1995) *Marketing Management and Information Technology*, 2nd edn (London: Prentice-Hall).

Ford, D. (ed.) (1990) *Understanding Business Markets: Interaction of Relationships and Networks* (London: Academic Press).

Foster, P. and Davis, J. (1994) *Mastering Marketing*, 3rd edn (Basingstoke: Macmillan).

Foxall, G. R. (1983) *Consumer Choice* (London: Macmillan).

Foxall, G. R. (1987) 'Radical Behaviourism and Consumer Research: Theoretical Promise and Empirical Problems', *International Journal of Research in Marketing*, vol. 4, pp. 111–29.

Frank, R. E., Massy, W. F., Morrison, D. G. and Wind, Y. (1972) *Market Segmentation* (Englewood Cliffs, N.J.: Prentice-Hall).

Fullerton, R. A. (1988) 'How Modern is Modern Marketing?', *Journal of Marketing*, No. 1, Jan., pp. 108–25.

Gabor, A. (1980) *Pricing Principles and Practice* (London: Heinemann), Ch. 10, pp. 168–76.

Galbraith, J. K. (1958) *The Affluent Society* (Harmondsworth: Penguin).

Galbraith, J. K. (1974) *The New Industrial State* (London: Penguin).

Gallagher, W. J. (1969) *Report Writing for Management* (Reading, Mass.: Addison-Wesley).

Gardner, C. A. (1986) 'Dissertation Proposal' (Washington DC: George Washington University).

Gilbert, D. and Bailey, N. (1990) 'The Development of Marketing – A Compendium of Historical Approaches', *Quarterly Review of Marketing*, Winter.

Gofton, K. (1984) 'What Moves the Client?' *Marketing*, 27 September.

Goodfellow, J. H. (1983) 'The Marketing of Goods of Services as a Multidimensional Concept', *The Quarterly Review of Marketing*, Spring, pp. 19–27.

Gordon, W. and Langmaid, R. (1988) *Qualitative Market Research* (Aldershot: Gower).

Green, P. E. and Tull, D. S. (1978) *Research for Marketing Decisions*, 4th edn (Englewood Cliffs, N.J.: Prentice-Hall).

Green, P. E. and Carmone, F. J. (1970) *Multidimensional Scaling and Related Techniques in Marketing Analysis* (Boston: Allyn & Bacon).

Gronroos, C. (1980) 'Designing a Long Range Marketing Strategy for Services', *Long Range Planning*, vol. 13(2), pp. 36–42.

Gronroos, C. (1981) 'Internal Marketing – an Integral Part of Marketing theory', in Donnelly, J. H. Jr and George, W. R. (eds) *Marketing of Services* (Chicago: American Marketing Association), pp. 236–8.

Gronroos, C. (1982) *Strategic Management and Marketing in the Service Sector* (Helsinki: Swedish School of Economics and Business Administration).

Gronroos, C. (1984) 'A Service Quality Model', *European Journal of Marketing*, vol. 18(4).

Gronroos, C. (1989) 'A Relationship Approach to Marketing of Services: Some Implications', *Proceedings from the 18th Annual Conference of the European Marketing Academy* (Greece: Athens School of Economics and Business Science).

Gummesson, E. (1979) 'The Marketing of Professional Services: An Organisational Dilemma', *European Journal of Marketing*, vol. 13(5), pp. 308–18.

Hakansson, H. (ed) (1982) *International Marketing and Purchasing of Industrial Goods* (New York: John Wiley).

Halbert, M. (1965) *The Meaning and Sources of Marketing Theory* (New York: McGraw-Hill).

Hammond, J.S. III (1967) 'Better Decisions with Preference Theory', *Harvard Business Review*, November–December, pp. 123–41.

Hastorf, A. H. and Cantril, H. (1954) 'They Saw a Game: A Case History', *Journal of Abnormal and Social Psychology*, vol. 49, pp. 129–34.

Hawkins, E. R. (1954) 'Price Policies and Theories', *Journal of Marketing*, XVIII, January, pp. 233–40.

Haynes, W. W. (1962) *Pricing Decisions in Small Business* (Lexington: University of Kentucky Press).

Haywood, Roger (1995) Ch. 41 in Baker, M. J. (ed.) *Companion Encyclopedia of Marketing* (London: Routledge).

Hilgard, E. (1967) *Introduction to Psychology* (Harcourt Brace).

Hill, R. and Hillier, F. (1977) *Organisational Buying Behaviour* (London: Macmillan).

Hobson, J. W. (1956) *Selection of Advertising Media* (London: Business Publications Ltd).

Holmes, C. (1986) 'The Multivariate Analysis of Market Research Data', Ch. 13 in Worcester, R. and Downham, J. *Consumer Market Research Handbook*, 3rd edn (ESOMAR).

Hooley, G. J. (1980) 'The Multivariate Jungle – The Academics' Playground but the Managers' Minefield', *European Journal of Marketing*, 14(7), 379–448.

Hooley, G. J., West, C. J. and Lynch, J. E. (1984) *Marketing in the UK: A Survey of Current Practice and Performance* (Institute of Marketing).

Howard J. A. and Sheth, J. N. (1969) *Theory of Buyer Behaviour* (Wiley).

Hull, C. (1943) *Principles of Behaviour: An Introduction to Behaviour Theory* (New York: Appleton Century Crofts).

Hutchinson, P. (1970) 'The Complementary Benefit Principle of How Advertising Works in Relation to the Product', Paper given at the Market Research Society Annual Conference.

Johansson, J. K. and Nonaka, I. (1987) 'Market Research the Japanese Way', *Harvard Business Review*, vol. 65, May–June.

Johnson, H. (1961) *Money, Trade and Economic Growth*, 2nd edn (London: Allen and Unwin)

Johnson, M. (1984) 'Supermarket Scientists', *Marketing*, 13 September.

Johnson, S. C. and Jones, C. (1957) 'How to Organise for New Products', *Harvard Business Review*, vol. 35, May–June.

Juran. J. M. (ed.) (1988) *Quality Control Handbook* (New York: McGraw-Hill).

Katz, E. (1957) in Robertson, T. S., *Innovative Behaviour and Communications* (New York: Holt, Rinehart & Winston), p. 180.

Kennedy, A. (1983) in M. J. Baker (ed.) *Marketing: Theory and Practice*, 2nd edn (Basingstoke: Macmillan).

Key Note Publications Ltd (1989) *Sales Promotion*, London.

Keynotes (1992) 'Meat and Meat Products'.

Kindleberger, C. (1958) *Economic Development* (New York: McGraw-Hill).

King, S. (1989) 'The Company is the Brand', *Journal of Marketing Management*.

King, S. (1991) 'Brand Building in the 1990's', *Journal of Marketing Management*, vol. 7(1).

Klass, B. (1961) 'What Factors Affect Industrial Buying Decisions?', *Industrial Marketing*.

Kohler, W. (1925) *The Mentality of Apes* (New York: Harcourt, Brace and World).

Kotler, P. (1988) *Marketing Management: Analysis, Planning, Implementation and Control*, 6th edn (Englewood Cliffs, N.J.: Prentice-Hall) (2nd edn 1972).

Kotler, P. and Andreasen, A. R. (1991) *Strategic Marketing for Non-profit Organisations*, 4th edn (Englewood Cliffs, N.J.: Prentice-Hall).

Kotler, P. and Andreasen, A. R. (1995) 'Strategic Marketing for Non-Profit Organisations', Ch. 53 in Baker, M. J. (ed.) *Companion Encyclopedia of Marketing* (London: Routledge), p. 930ff.

Kotler, P. and Armstrong, G. (1993) *Marketing: an introduction*, 3rd edn (Englewood Cliffs, N.J.: Prentice-Hall).

Kotler, P. and Bloom, P. N. (1984) *Marketing Professional Services* (Englewood Cliffs, N.J.: Prentice-Hall).

Kotler, P., Gregor, W. and Rogers, W. (1977) 'The Marketing Audit Comes of Age', *Sloan Management Review*, Winter, vol. 18, no. 2.

Kotler, P. and Levy, S. (1969a) 'Broadening the Concept of Marketing', *Journal of Marketing*, vol. 33, January.

Kotler, P. and Levy, S. (1969b) 'Beyond Marketing: The Furthering Concept', *California Management Review*, Winter, vol. XII, no. 2.

Kotler, P. and Singh, R. (1981) 'Marketing as Warfare in the 1980's', *Journal of Business Studies*, Winter.

Krech, D., Crutchfield, R. and Ballachey, E. (1962) *Individual in Society* (New York: McGraw-Hill).

Kubr, M. (ed.) (1976) *Management Consulting: A Guide to the Profession* (Geneva: ILO).

Lanzillotti, R. (1956) 'Pricing Objectives in Large Companies', *American Economic Review*, XLVIII, December, pp. 921–40.

Lawson, R. W. (1988) 'The Family Life Cycle: A Demographic Analysis', *Journal of Marketing Mangement*, Summer.

Lazarsfeld, P. F. (1944) *The People's Choice* (Sloan and Pearce).

Lehmann, O. R. and O'Shaughnessy, G. (1974) 'Difference in Attribute Importance for Different Industrial Products', *Journal of Marketing*, April.

Levitt, T. (1960) 'Marketing Myopia', *Harvard Business Review*, July–August.

Levitt, T. (1974) *Marketing for Business Growth* (New York: McGraw-Hill).

Levitt, T. (1976) 'Industrialisation of Service', *Harvard Business Review*, September–October, pp. 63–74.

Levitt, T. (1983a) *The Marketing Imagination* (New York: Free Press).

Levitt, T. (1983b) *The Augmented Product Concept*.

Levitt, T. (1983c) 'The Globalisation of Markets', *Harvard Business Review*, May–June.

Lewis, B. R. (1989) 'Customer Care in Service Organisations', *Marketing Intelligence and Planning*, vol. 7(5/6), pp. 18–22.

Lidstone, L. (1983) 'Putting Force Back Into Sales', *Marketing*, 22 September.

Lowe, A. (1988) 'The Marketing of Services', Unit 19, University of Strathclyde MCom in Marketing for Industrialising Countries by Distance Learning (Glasgow: University of Strathclyde).

Lucey, J. (1987) *Management Information Systems*, 5th edn (Eastleigh: DP Publications).

Luck, D. J. and Ferrell, O. C. (1979) *Marketing Strategy and Plans* (Englewood Cliffs, N.J.: Prentice-Hall).

McBurnie, T. and Clutterbuck, D. (1987) *The Marketing Edge* (Harmondsworth: Pengiun).

McCarthy, E. J. (1966) *Basic Marketing* (Homewood, Ill.: Irwin).

McCarthy, E. J. and Perreault, W. D. Jnr. (1994) *Basic Marketing*, 8th edn (Homewood, Ill.: Irwin).

McClelland, W. G. (1966) *Costs and Competition in Retailing* (London: Macmillan).

McConkey, D. D. (1988) 'Planning in a Changing Environment', *Business Horizons*, September–October.

McDonald, E. H. and Stromberger, T. L. (1969) 'Cost Control for the Professional Service Firm', *Harvard Business Review*, January–February, pp. 109–21.

McFarlane-Smith, J. (1972) *Interviewing in Market and Social Research* (London: Routledge and Kegan Paul).

McGivern, C. (1983) 'Some Facets of the Relationship Between Consultants and Clients in Organisations', *Journal of Managment Studies*, vol. 20(3), pp. 367–86

McLuhan, M. (1965) *Understanding Media: the Extensions of Man* (London: McGraw-Hill).

Magnuson, W. G. (1972) 'Consumerism and the Emerging Goals of a New Society', in Gaedeke, R. M. and Etcheson, W. W. (eds) *Consumerism* (San Fransisco: Canfield Press).

Mansfield, E. (1966) *The Economics of Technological Change* (New York: W. W. Norton).

Marketing Week (1995) 'Media Speak', *Marketing Week*, 26 January, p. 90.

Markin, R. (1982) *Marketing Strategy and Management* (New York: John Wiley).

Markin, R. and Narayana (1976) 'Behaviour Control: Are Consumers Beyond Freedom and Dignity', *Advances in Consumer Research*, vol. 2, pp. 222–8.

Marshall, A. (1919) *Industry and Trade* (London).

Maslow, A. (1943) 'A Theory of Human Motivation', *Psychological Review*, vol. 50.

Matthews, J. B., Buzzell, R., Levitt, T. and Frank, N. (1964) *Marketing: An Introductory Analysis* (New York: McGraw-Hill).

Mayer, D. and Greenberg, H. (1964) 'What Makes a Good Salesman?', *Harvard Business Review*, XLII, July–August, pp. 119–25.

Mayer, Martin (1958) *Madison Avenue* (Harmondsworth: Penguin).

Meadows, D. et al. (1972) *Limits to Growth* (London: Earth Island).

Meffert, H. and Kirchgeog, M. (1995) 'Green Marketing', in Baker, M. J. (ed.) *Companion Encyclopedia of Marketing* (London: Routledge), p. 979ff.

Miles, I. (1990) 'Teleshopping: Just Around the Corner?', *RSA Journal*, February.

Millar, R. (1993) *Marketing Business Magazine*, June.

Millman, F. (1983) 'Price Wars', *Quarterly Review of Marketing*, January.

Mitchell, J. (1974) *How to Write Reports* (London: Fontana).

Moroney, M. J. (1956) *Facts From Figures* (London: Pelican).

Morrison, A. and Wensley, R. (1991) 'Boxing Up or Boxed In? A Short History of the Boston Consulting Group Share/Growth Matrix', *Journal of Marketing Management*, vol. 7(2).

Morton-Williams, J. (1986) 'Questionnaire Design', Ch. 5 in Worcester, R. and Downham, J. *Consumer Market Research Handbook*, 3rd edn (ESOMAR).

Moser, C. (1961) *British Towns: A Statistical Study of their Social and Economic Differences* (London: Oliver & Boyd).

Moser, C. and Kalton, G. (1971) *Survey Methods in Social Investigation*, 2nd edn (Oxford: Heinemann Educational Books).

Moss, C. D., Thorne, P. and Fasey, P. (1963) 'The Distribution of Coupons', *Quarterly Review of Marketing*, January.

Mueller-Heumann, G. (1992) 'Market Fragmentation and Mass Customisation', *Journal of Marketing Management*, vol. 8, pp. 303–14.

Murphy, C. (1994) 'Own Goal', *Marketing Week*, 19 August, p. 28.

Nader, R. (1965) *Unsafe at any Speed* (New York: Grossman).

Naisbitt, J. (1982) *Megatrends* (London: Pan).

Nanus, B. (1982) 'QUEST – Quick Environmental Scanning Technique', in *Long Range Planning*, vol. 15, no. 2, pp. 39–45.

National Readership Survey.

Newton, D. (1969) 'Get the Most Out of Your Field Sales Force', *Harvard Business Review*, September–October, pp. 130–43.

Nicosia, F. M. (1966) *Consumer Decision Processes* (Englewood Cliffs, N.J.: Prentice-Hall).

Normann, R (1985) *Service Management: Strategy and Leadership in Service Businesses* (London: John Wiley).

O'Brien, S. and Ford, R. (1988) 'Can We at Last Say Goodbye to Social Class', *Journal of the Market Research Society*, vol. 30, no. 3, July.

O'Reilly, D. (1995) 'Unit 3: The Buying Situation', University of Strathclyde, MSc in Procurement Management, *Organisational Buying Behaviour*.

Oakland, J. (1995) in Baker, M. J. (ed.) *Companion Encyclopedia of Marketing* (London: Routledge), pp. 957–8.

Office of Fair Trading (1985) *Competition in Retailing*, June.

Ogilvy, D. (1965) *Confessions of an Advertising Man* (New York: Dell).

Ogilvy, D. (1983) *Ogilvy on Advertising* (London: Pan).

Ogilvy, Benson, and Mather (1976) *A Guide to Consumer Promotions*, 2nd edn (A. Morgan).

Ohmae, K. (1982) *The Mind of the Strategist* (Harmondsworth: Penguin).

Oppenheim, A. N. (1967) *Questionnaire Design and Attitude Measurement* (Oxford: Heinemann).

Osgood, C. et al. (1952) *Method and Theory in Experimental Psychology* (New York: Oxford University Press).

Oxenfeld, A. R. (1975) 'The Marketing Audit as a Total Evaluation Programme', *Pricing Strategies* (New York: AMACOM).

Packard, V. (1961) *The Waste Makers* (London: Longmans Green).

Packard, V. (1957) *Hidden Persuaders* (London: Longmans Green).

Paliwoda, S. and Ryans, J. K. Jr (1993) *International Marketing Reader* (London: Routledge).

Parkinson, S. T. and Baker, M. J. (1986) *Organisational Buying Behaviour* (London: Macmillan).

Pathmarajah, A (1993) Ch. 21 in M. J. Baker (ed.) *Marketing: Theory and Practice*, 3rd edn (Basingstoke: Macmillan).

Payne, S. L. (1951) *The Art of Asking Questions* (Princeton University Press).

Pearce, D. W. (ed.) (1981) *Dictionary of Modern Economics* (London: Macmillan).

Peattie, K. and Charter, M. (1994) 'Green Marketing', in Baker, M. J. (1994) *The Marketing Book*, 3rd edn (Oxford: Butterworth-Heinemann).

Peters, T. and Waterman, R. (1982) *In Search of Excellence* (New York: Harper and Row).

Peterson, C. (1984) 'Cinderella in the Limelight', *Marketing*, November.

Piercy, N. (1985) *Marketing Organisation* (London: George Allen and Unwin).

Piercy, N. F. and Cravens, D. W. (1995) in Baker, M. J. (ed.) *Companion Encyclopedia of Marketing* (London: Routledge).

Pinxt, L. (1984) 'A Nation of Importers', *Marketing*, 4 October.

Porter, M. (1980) *Competitive Strategy: Techniques for Analyzing Industries and Competitors* (New York: Free Press).

Porter, M. (1985) *Competitive Advantage* (New York: Free Press).

Porter, M. (1990) *The Competitive Advantages of Nations* (London: Macmillan).

Quelch, J. A., Buzzell, R. D. and Salama, E. R. (1990) *The Marketing Challenge of 1992* (Reading, Mass.: Addison-Wesley).

Quinlan, F. (1981) 'The Use of Social Grading in Marketing', *Quarterly Review of Marketing*, Autumn.

Rajagopal, S. (1995) Ch. 5 in Baker, M. J. (ed.) (1995) *Marketing: Theory and Practice*, 3rd edn (London: Macmillan).

Rathmell, J. M. (1974) *Marketing in the Service Sector* (London: Winthrop).

Reeves, R. (1970) 'Reality in Advertising', in O. Klepner and I. Settell (eds) *Exploring Advertising* (Englewood Cliffs, N.J.: Prentice-Hall).

Reid, W. and Myddelton, D. R. (1971) *The Meaning of Company Accounts* (Aldershot: Gower Press).

Resnik, A. H., Turney, P. B. B. and Mason, J. B. (1979) 'Marketers Turn to Counter-Segmentation', *Harvard Business Review*, September/October.

Reynolds, E. B. (1959) *Analyzing and Improving Marketing Performance: Marketing Audits in Theory and Practice*, American Marketing Association.

Ries, A. and Trout, J. (1972) 'The Positioning Era', *Advertising Age*.

Ries, A. and Trout, J. (1986) *Positioning: The Battle For Your Mind* (New York: McGraw-Hill).

Robertson, T. S. (1970) *Consumer Behaviour* (Glenview, Ill.: Scott Foresman).

Robertson, T. S. (1971) *Innovative Behaviour and Communications* (New York: Holt, Rinehart & Winston).

Robinson, J. (1933) *The Economics of Imperfect Competition* (London: Macmillan).

Robinson, P. J. and Luck, D. J. (1964) *Promotional Decision Making Practice and Theory*, Marketing Science Institute series (New York: McGraw-Hill).

Robinson, P. J., Faris, C. W. and Wind, Y (1967) *Industrial Buying and Creative Marketing* (Boston: Allyn & Bacon)

Robinson, R. J. and Stidsen, B. (1967) *Selling in a Modern Perspective* (Boston: Allyn & Bacon).

Rodger, L. W. (1971) *Marketing in a Competitive Economy*, 3rd edn (London: Cassell).

Rodocanachi, P. (1983) 'The Sucessful Management of New Products in the 1980's', Paper given at ESOMAR seminar on New Product Development (Athens, November 1983).

Rosenbloom, B. (1995) 'Channels of Distribution', Ch. 8. in Baker, M. J. (ed.) *Companion Encyclopedia of Marketing* (London: Routledge), pp. 137–54.

Rostow, W. W. (1962) *The Process of Economic Growth*, 2nd edn (New York: McGraw-Hill).

Rothman, J. (1986) 'Experimental Designs and Models', Ch. 3 in Worcester, R. and Downham, J. *Consumer Market Research Handbook*, 3rd edn (ESOMAR).

Rothman, J. (1989) Editorial, *Journal of the Market Research Society*, vol. 31, no. 1, January.

Rothwell, R., Gardiner, P. and Schott, K (1983) *Design and the Economy* (London: The Design Council).

Said, H. (1981) 'The Relevance of Price Theory to Price Practise', unpublished PhD Dissertation, University of Strathclyde.

Sampson, P. (1967) 'Commonsense in Qualitative Research', *Commentary*, vol. 9, no. 1, January.

Sampson, H. (1874) *History of Advertising*.

Samuelson, P. (1989) *Economics: An Introductory Analysis*, 13th edn (New York: McGraw-Hill)

Sasser, W. E. (1976) 'Matching Supply and Demand in Service Industries', *Harvard Business Review*, November–December, pp. 133–40.

Schiffman, L. and Kanuk, L. (1994) *Consumer Behaviour*, 5th edn (Englewood Cliffs, N.J.: Prentice-Hall).

Schlaifer, R. (1969) *Analysis of Decisions Under Uncertainty* (New York: McGraw-Hill).

Schramm, W. (1995) *The Process and Effects of Mass Communication* (Urbana, Ill.: University of Illinois Press).

Schuchman, A. (1959) 'The Marketing Audit: Its nature, purposes and problems', *Analyzing and Improving Marketing Performance*, Report No. 32 (New York: American Management Asssociation).

Scott, B. (1984) 'National Strategy for Stronger US Competitiveness', *Harvard Business Review*, March–April.

Servan-Schreiber, J. J. (1967) *The American Challenge* (London: Hamish Hamilton).

Seymour, B (1984) 'Centres of Attraction', *Marketing*, 6 September.

Shams, H. (1989) 'Incremental Consumption and the Purchase of Experiential Products', Unpublished PhD Dissertation, University of Surrey, England.

Shannon, C. and Weaver, W. (1962) *The Mathematical Theory of Communication* (Urbana, Ill.: University of Illinois Press).

Sheth, J. N. (1983) 'A Model of Industrial Buyer Behaviour', *Journal of Marketing*, October.

Shoemaker, F. (1971) *Communications of Innovations*, 2nd edn (New York: Free Press)

Shostack, G. L. (1977) 'Breaking Free From Product Marketing', *Journal of Marketing*, vol. 41(2), pp. 73–80

Shostack, G. L. (1982) 'How to Design a Service', *European Journal of Marketing*, vol. 16(1), pp. 49–63.

Shostack, G. L. (1984) 'Designing Services that Deliver', *Harvard Business Review*, January–February, pp. 133–9.

Simon, H. (1989) *Price Management* (Amsterdam: Elsevier).

Sizer, J. (1989) *An Insight into Management Accounting*, 3rd edn (London: Penguin).

Smith, A. [1776] *The Wealth of Nations*, A. Skinner (ed.) (1970) (Harmondsworth: Pelican Books).

Smith, N. C. (1995) Ch. 52 in Baker, M. J. (ed.) *Companion Encyclopedia of Marketing* (London: Routledge).

Smith, W. (1956) 'Product Differentiation and Market Segmentation as Alternative Marketing Strategies', *Journal of Marketing*, July.

Sperling, A. D. (1967) *Psychology Made Simple* (London: W. H. Allen).

Stanton, N. J. (1981) *Fundamentals of Marketing* (New York: McGraw-Hill).

Stephenson, C. P. (1968) 'What is a Product?', *British Agents Review*, reprinted in *Marketing Forum*, March/April.

Stern, L. I. *et al.* (1989) *Management of the Marketing Channel* (Englewood Cliffs, N.J.: Prentice-Hall).

Sternthal, B. and Craig, C. S. (1982) *Consumer Behaviour: An Information Processing Perspective* (Englewood Cliffs, N.J.: Prentice-Hall).

Stevens, S. N. (1958) 'The Application of Social Science Findings to Selling and the Salesman', *Aspects of Modern Marketing*, AMA Management Report no. 15 (New York: AMA).

Strauss, G. (1962) 'Tactics of Lateral Relationships: The Purchasing Agent', *Administrative Science Quarterly*, 7 September.

Swasy, A. (1989) 'Sales lost their Vim? Try Repackaging', *Wall Street Journal*, 11 October.

Tarver, J.L. (1987) 'In Search of a Competitive Edge in Banking: A Personnel Approach', *International Bank Marketing*, vol. 5(1), pp. 61–8.

Taylor, A. H. (1974) *Costing: A Management Approach*, Pan Management Series (London: Pan).

Technology Foresight Programme (1995) *Progress Through Partnership* (Office of Science and Technology).

Tedlow, R. S. (1992) *New & Improved: The Story of Mass Marketing in America* (Oxford: Heineman).

Tedlow, R. S. and Jones, G. (eds) (1993) 'The Fourth Phase of Marketing', Ch. 2 of *The Rise and Fall of Mass Marketing* (London: Routledge).

Thomas, M. (1980) 'Market Segmentation', *Quarterly Review of Marketing*, vol. 6, no. 1.

Thomas, M. (1981) 'Customer Care: The Ultimate Marketing Tool', in Wensley, R. (ed.), *Reviewing Effective Research and Good Practise in Marketing* (Warwick: Marketing Education Group), pp. 283–94.

Thomas, M. J. (1982) 'Product Managment vs. Market Management', *Quarterly Review of Marketing*, Summer 1982, pp. 22–5.

Thomas, M. J. (1989) *The Marketing Handbook*, 3rd edn (Aldershot: Gower).

Thompson, H. U. (1962) *Product Strategy* (London: Bodley Head Business Publications).

Toffler, A. (1971) *Future Shock* (London: Pan).

Toffler, A. (1984) *Previews and Promises* (London: Pan).

Torgerson, W. (1958) *Theory and Methods of Scaling* (New York: Wiley).

Tracy, E. (1984) 'Testing Time for Test Marketing', *Fortune*, 29 October.

Treadgold, A. and Davies, R. L. (1988) *The Internationalization of Retailing* (Harlow: Longman).

Turnbull, P. and Cunningham, M. (1980) *International Marketing and Purchasing* (London: Macmillan).

Ughanwa, D. O. and Baker, M. J. (1989) *The Role of Design in International Competitiveness* (London: Routledge).

UK Institute of Public Relations (1994).

Underwood, R. (1993) Paper at the AMA Winter Educators' Conference, *Proceedings*, pp. 212–17

Unwin, S. (1975) 'Customised Communications: A Concept for Service Advertising', *Advertising Quarterly*, vol. 44, Summer, pp. 18–30.

Walker, A. H. and Lorsch, J. W. (1968) 'Organizational Choice: Product vs. Function', *Harvard Business Review*, XLIV, vi, November–December, pp. 129–38.

Warner, W. Lloyd (1960) *Social Class in America* (New York: Harper & Row).

Waterson, M. (1993) 'Are Industrial Economists Still Interested in Concentration?', in Casson, M. and Creedy, J. (eds) *Industrial Concentration and Economic Inequality* (Aldershot: Edward Elgar).

Watts, B. K. R. (1978) *Business and Financial Management*, 3rd edn (M and E Handbooks), ch. 10.

Webster, F. Jr (1965) 'Modelling the Industrial Buying Process', *Journal of Marketing Research*, November.

Webster, F. Jr (1992) 'The Changing Role of Marketing in the Corporation', *Journal of Marketing*, October.

Webster, F. Jr and Wind, Y. (1972) 'A General Model for Understanding Organisational Buying Behaviour', *Journal of Marketing*, April.

Wells, W. D. (1975) 'Psychographics: A Critical Review', *Journal of Marketing Research*, vol. XII, May, pp. 196–213.

West, C. (1995) in Baker, M. J. (ed.) *Companion Encyclopedia of Marketing* (London: Routledge), p. 350.

Wickham, R. G., Fitzroy, P. T. and Mandry, G. D. (1975) 'Marketing of Services: An Evaluation of the Theory', *European Journal of Marketing*, vol. 9(1), pp. 59–67.

Wilkie, W. K. (1994) *Consumer Behaviour*, 3rd edn (Chichester: John Wiley).

Williamson, O. E. (1975) *Markets and Hierarchies: Analysis and Antitrust Implications* (New York: Free Press).

Wilson, A. (1972) *The Marketing of Professional Services* (London: McGraw-Hill).

Wind, Y. (1976) 'Organisational Buying Centres: A Research Agenda' in Zaltman, G. and Bonoma, T. V. (eds) *Organisational Buying Behaviour* (AMA).

Wind, Y. (1978) 'Issues and Advances in Segmentation Research', *Journal of Marketing Research*, August.

Wind, Y. (1995) 'Market Segmentation', in Baker, M. J. (ed.) *Companion Encyclopedia of Marketing* (London: Routledge).

Wind, Y. and Douglas, S. (1972) 'International Market Segmentation', *European Journal of Marketing*, vol. 5, no. 1.

Winkler, J. (1991) 'Pricing', Ch. 16 in Baker, M. J. (1991) *The Marketing Book*, 2rd edn (London: Heinemann).

Yasumuro, K. (1993) 'Conceptualising and Adaptable Marketing System', Ch. 11 in Tedlow, R. S. and Jones, G. (eds) *The Rise and Fall Of Mass Marketing*, pp. 205–35.

Yorke, D. A. (1990) 'Interactive Perceptions of Suppliers and Corporate Clients in the Marketing of Professional Services: A Comparison of Accounting and Legal Services in the UK, Canada and Sweden', *Journal of Marketing Management*, vol. 5(3), pp. 307–23.

Index